RED GLOW

Davor Konjikušić

YUGOSLAV PARTISAN PHOTOGRAPHY

RED GLOW

AND SOCIAL MOVEMENT, 1941–1945

Deutscher Kunstverlag

Edited by Rosa-Luxemburg-Stiftung

ISBN 978-3-422-98640-4
e-ISBN (PDF) 978-3-422-98648-0
DOI https://doi.org/10.1515/ 9783422986480

Bibliographic information published by the Deutsche Nationalbibliothek
The Deutsche Nationalbibliothek lists this publication in the Deutsche Nationalbibliografie;
detailed bibliographic data are available on the Internet at http://dnb.dnb.de.

Cover image: Vera Hreščak and Aleša Beblerja on their wedding day, Vojna vas, Slovenia, 3 April 1945.
Photo: Stane Lenardič. National Museum of Contemporary History of Slovenia, TN728/28.

Translation: Andrew Hodges
Copyediting: Lance Anderson
Cover, Layout and typesetting: hawemannundmosch, Berlin

Printed in the European Union

www.deutscherkunstverlag.de

“They are no more because they wanted to be.”

Ivan Goran Kovačić

Contents

Photography, First and Foremost

Hrvoje Klasić

I have watched the 1972 film about the Yugoslav Partisans *Valter brani Sarajevo* (Walter Defends Sarajevo) several times. In one of my favourite scenes, Zis (played by Ljubiša Samardžić) mocks the German soldiers in her photography shop by speaking a few words in Serbian that they do not understand while they pose for their photograph. While this scene and film have little to do with Davor Konjikušić's book, what is interesting is that this scene was the first thing that sprung to mind when Davor contacted me to tell me what his book was about and ask me to write a foreword. The second image that came to mind was of Tito, injured, at Sutjeska (a key battle in the Second World War) alongside Ivan Ribar (who went on to serve in the post-war Yugoslav government). The third image was of the famous Partisan Stjepan Filipović standing on the gallows with his hands raised and fists clenched in a silent pose that best encapsulates the virtue of Bravery.

That's as far as I got with my mental associations relating to WWII war photography and the People's Liberation Struggle. I came to realise that my knowledge of this topic is thin on the ground and, to be honest, I have never considered photography – as a documentary or propaganda medium – to be a topic of any great relevance. This is also how it features in everyday life; it is somehow always there, around us – usually an object, rarely a subject. Nowadays, most people perceive photography as a medium for telling a story, rather than as a story itself. A photographer, or anyone else taking pictures, typically helps in the transmission of the story; they are rarely the author of the story too.

Consequently, and especially because of the enthusiasm and zeal with which Davor explained his intentions, I decided to make my own modest contribution to this important work.

Davor Konjikušić's book is significant for several reasons. First, he has chosen to write in an affirmative tone about the People's Liberation Struggle, the Partisan movement, antifascism and the values for which thousands of young women and men fought and died. This is of far greater importance today than the specific topics considered in the book, because in contemporary Croatian society this is not only an act of research and scholarly writing – it is also, indeed chiefly, an act of activism, a form of civic responsibility and, unfortunately, also an act of civil courage.

Second, the book's importance also lies in the themes it tackles. It shows the areas covered by research into Second World War phenomena so far, which issues it has yet to tackle, but also, sadly, its present limitations. Thousands of books have been written about the Second

World War in many languages, but their focus is mostly on military and political history. Many opinions on and interpretations of history, especially in the works of regionally based authors, have been indisputably subject to academically unfounded revisionism. Equally, there is a whole range of events that were never dealt with at all during the socialist period in Yugoslavia, such as acts of revenge and crimes committed by the victors in the immediate aftermath of the war. Bearing in mind such 'omissions' and the ideologised discourses present when speaking of the Second World War in Yugoslavia, the facts mainly remain known, at least in their political and military aspects. What is missing, and what ought to be a logical continuation of research work to date, is an examination of the social and economic history, everyday life, gender history, and so on of the period.
And while historians all over the world made this qualitative step forward a long time ago, in the former Yugoslav region, a large qualitative leap was also made – backwards. Not only are these topics rarely researched, but the prevailing scholarship now consists of typical examples of historical negationism and politically motivated revisionism. Books are being published that seek to prove the anti-fascist character of the Chetnik movement, or the criminal character of the Partisan movement. Books are also being published glorifying political and military commanders from the collaborationist forces and, conversely, demonising the military and political leaders of the People's Liberation Movement. They are relativising the crimes of the Holocaust and genocide, redefining the Jasenovac concentration camp in Croatia as a labour camp, and at the same time denying the liberating and modernising character of the Partisan struggle.

This way of dealing with the past is symptomatic of the general situation in society itself, in terms of both cause and effect. The political elites only occasionally use, but also often prompt such viewpoints on the past. The consequences of such a situation include thousands of destroyed Partisan monuments, thousands of destroyed books about the People's Liberation Struggle, the changing of street names after Partisan heroes and – most importantly – the creation of a climate of shame instead of pride regarding the Partisan past. At the same time, such a revisionist approach to the history of the collaborationist Ustashe movement and the related Independent State of Croatia (1941–45) has played a role in relativising how people view this darkest period of Croatian history. In Croatia during the wars of the 1990s, it suddenly became normal to shout Ustashe greetings in the streets and at sports stadiums, to name military units after Ustashe commanders and to rename streets after Ustashe politicians. The state provides funds for the annual commemoration of the mass killing of the Ustashe military, but not for that of the Partisan military too.

And let me thus return to my initial thought at the start of this foreword. In the current climate, each book, each contribution (however small) that fights revisionism and uses sound arguments to remind the public of the values of the People's Liberation Struggle carries with it a certain weight. If it also makes a contribution towards the aforementioned qualitative leap and shifts the focus of scholarship from military and political history to lesser-known areas, then we can claim that it also represents an outstanding contribution to historiography and indeed to society.

Which brings us to my third point. This book demonstrates the need – even the necessity – of an interdisciplinary approach to researching certain topics. While this sounds like a logical move that every academic researcher makes, in reality it is sadly often not the case. Davor Konjikušić graduated from the Academy of Dramatic Arts, ADU, Zagreb. His main area of interest is in examining photography as a medium to research various socio-political relations. At the same time, he is an established journalist whose articles explore the most diverse challenges that contemporary society faces. In both cases, he is primarily occupied with topics of contemporary relevance. Despite this focus, he has chosen to write a book about events that occurred eighty years ago. He has also chosen, as I have already touched upon, one of the most complex and controversial, yet at the same time one of the most influential events of the 20th century. Despite all the time that has passed since then, this event and its consequences continue to influence the lives of people in the 21st century.

And he has done an excellent job.

Photography has been foregrounded, as a document of the time and historical source, but also as a resource and goal of artistic expression. Davor has gone exploring in the deepest hidden corners of museum archives and private family collections. And like an experienced archaeologist, he has returned, revealing a new old world. Photography has helped him reconstruct large battles, but also the fates of everyday people. His research focus includes eminent politicians and commanders, but also everyday soldiers. He devotes an equal amount of attention to 'iconic' photographs – images that came to symbolise an era – as well as those photographs that were taken in passing, almost by chance. What makes the book especially interesting and innovative is the homage paid to the photographers, the people behind the lens. These included real professionals, true artists, as well as amateurs who perfected their photographic skills in this troubled era that was otherwise so adverse to art and culture. Little is generally known about them, their fates, and their later careers. Davor has attempted to put right this injustice, as most of the pictures transcend the photographers behind them in terms of their significance and value. And yet, that said, not one photograph would exist were it not for the people who chose to make a visual record in this way. Without these people's choice of subject, framing, perspective, or simple release of the shutter none of these past events would have been captured for posterity.

The war itself is of secondary importance in this book. In terms of the number of victims and participants, it was the biggest and worst in the history of humanity, with the Yugoslav 'theatre' of war concerning the People's Liberation Struggle on the one hand and the occupation and Axis collaboration on the other. While this book also reveals interesting details that relate to political and military history, its base motivation is much more 'grounded'. Using photographs, the author strives to evoke the atmosphere of the war and demonstrate the suffering and sacrifice, terror and solidarity, pragmatism and idealism, bravery and betrayal. The evolving relationship towards photography is used to demonstrate the evolution of the revolution. Initial floundering, scarcity and shortages, and the lack of a clear strategy grow into a well-led and well-thought-out campaign. It is as if the author almost wants to make a connection between the initial lack of photographic supplies with the lack of arms and munitions. In another vein, timeless photographs have spread the story of the struggle between David and Goliath beyond the moment of the war itself, and these photographs constitute an irreplaceable tile in the mosaic of the total (military) victory.

Davor also highlights the Partisans' interesting relationship with photography. From early distrust and even scorn, the Partisans' subsequent use of photography became highly professional and calculated. By the end of the war, pictures depicting various themes were used for ideological, propaganda and foreign-policy purposes. Victory would have been attained without these photographic materials. But the victory became more visible with them, especially immediately before it was attained.

The author himself takes a back seat in this book – Davor Konjikušić, the artist and art critic, researcher and chronicler, anti-fascist and humanist. His choice of topic and how he covers it show that all these epithets are justified – and he hints at having a talent and enthusiasm for many others too. His manuscript is clearly written, his attitudes unambiguous, and his conclusions meticulous. He defends one idea, one world view, but does not let it blind him. He values achievements, he critiques abuses. While writing about history, the author speaks of the present, and warns of the future. However much this research is underpinned by long, serious and demanding work, his enjoyment of the whole venture is more than obvious. He drops into other people's attics like an intellectual *homo ludens*, excitedly blowing the dust off old photo albums, impatiently searching for previously unseen photographs and the stories that underpin them. Despite the difficult subject matter, his observations are bursting with enthusiasm and anecdotes from the lives of the (usually unknown) people who helped shape the course of history. Davor's knowledge is backed up with facts and verified information. Irrespective of this, he does not try to persuade or convince the reader. Instead, only on some occasions, like a true activist inspired by sincere idealism, does he simply wish to show the reader the path he thinks is the correct one.

Davor Konjikušić does not use this book to place constraints on future research, neither his own, nor that of others. On the contrary, the book is an invitation, and a source of motivation and guidance to all potential historians and scholars. While making a great contribution to modern history and the history of art, it is by no means only intended for experts. The book's themes and its style convince me that it will generate broad public interest.

Davor's book offers many answers, but also poses some completely new questions. You can enjoy it just as well by reading it page by page or simply by looking at the photographs. Its basic intention is to encourage the reader to think, while its main goal is – in considering a glorious past – to imagine ourselves in the face of a very uncertain future.

'You're Taking Pictures, While We're Being Killed!'

On Materiality, Art, and the Civil Contract of the Partisan Photo Archive

Sanja Horvatinčić

Photography is much more than what is printed on photographic paper, transforming any event into a picture. The photograph bears the seal of the event itself, and reconstructing that event requires more than just identifying what is shown in the photograph. One needs to stop looking at the photograph and instead start watching it.

Ariella Azoulay, *The Civil Contract of Photography*[1]

Imagine three people. The first is a man in uniform with a rifle over his shoulder and the military insignia of his Partisan rank on his left sleeve. The second is a girl dressed in a modern, tailored, checked skirt and a low turtle-neck jumper – as if she had been walking along city streets a little while ago. Both are blindfolded. Holding them by the hand, taking bold steps forward while wearing a serene expression on his face, the third person, another uniformed man, is leading them through a dense pine forest. The scene is incredibly unusual, almost film-like. For a moment, as we imagine the scene, disquiet overwhelms us – is he leading them to be shot? (Those sentenced by fascist units to death by firing squad were blindfolded prior to execution.) Why would someone take photos of this scene in the middle of the woods during the war? Do the blindfolded pair know that their walk through the impossible was important, and that they were being captured on camera?[2]

* * *

Research into Partisan photography is not only about grasping the factual history of the Second World War in the (post-)Yugoslav region. It is also about understanding the motives, aims, and social practices of the People's Liberation Movement. For many, this is a difficult task at present: generations, systems, and ideologies have changed; and grand narratives have been trivialised, vilified, or forgotten. For those who live in, or have a connection to the former Yugoslav region, this history might be something they think they know because they sometimes feel part of the same story. It might be something they know (or think they know) because the places, people, and events recorded in photographs are familiar to them.

1 Ariella Azoulay, *The Civil Contract of Photography*, New York 2008, p. 14.
2 A description of a photograph by the Slovenian artist and Partisan Božidar Jakac, shot in 1944 at Kočevski Rog in Slovenia.

And the photos are indeed familiar to a regional audience. Yet what this same audience knows very little about are the conditions of these photographs' making, the realities of their production: how Partisan photographers mixed chemicals together in food tins, how they developed photos while under fire, why some shots were staged, and some were entirely arbitrary and almost intimate.

The photograph depicting the secret guiding of a visitor to a Partisan hospital in the woods was taken by the well-known Slovenian artist and Partisan, Božidar Jakac, somewhere on the unbeaten path to Kočevski Rog. The path leads to a Partisan heterotopia, a secret hospital commune, one of the hotspots of the resistance, the combined site of cultural events, political courses, and humanitarian care for the sick, injured, and exiled. As the author of this book reveals, Partisan photographers had already been forbidden from filming secret Partisan bases and hospitals, because of the conspiratorial atmosphere present when this picture was taken. This is thus one of the rare surviving photographs depicting a visitor being led secretly to the hospital.

These two people are not visiting because they are injured, but rather because of a sense of collective struggle and solidarity. Their eyes are not blindfolded simply to avoid seeing the path taken; the endpoint could have been seen even with their eyes closed. Perhaps, similarly, photography speaks most of all to what we, today, *cannot* see.

* * *

One of the key themes of this study is the materiality of photography and the material conditions of its production and development. Only by carefully researching and appreciating the significance of the circumstances in which Partisan photography emerged is it possible to understand the causes and long-term consequences of the radical shift in the medium's boundaries, as well as the impact of this shift on the distribution of sensory material and the dichotomy between art and politics. Indeed, what makes Partisan photography so unusually close to the contemporary observer is its social significance and political content in today's conditions, when there are almost unlimited possibilities for reproducing and distributing photographs. Perhaps it is through a desire to find 'one's own place' among the photographed faces, or it may just be the motivation to get up close to the protagonists and to a time in which progressive social thinking was accompanied by immediate action. Recording that era was not 'merely' agitational and political work – it was also a deliberate mode of communicating with future generations. For this reason, we are thankful consumers of the black-and-white impressions of the past that are gathered in this publication. If drawing and poetry are the most immediate and sincere form of expression, then photography was surely the most loyal companion to the anti-fascist struggle and socialist revolution – and not only in the case of the Yugoslav Partisans.

Contemporary interest in Partisan photography is grounded in the sharing of a related civil political space, a concept that the theoretician of photography Ariela Azoullay describes as transcending the routine understanding of the photographer's role as an 'image creator':

Over time, it became progressively clearer to me that not only is it impossible to reduce photography to its role as a producer of pictures, but that, in addition, its broad dissemination over the second half of the nineteenth century has created a space of political relations that are not mediated exclusively by the ruling power of the state and are not completely subject to the national logic that still overshadows the familiar political arena. This civil political space, which I invent theoretically in the present book, is one that the people using photography – photographers, spectators, and photographed people – imagine every day.[3]

Irrespective of whether this identification results from the political instrumentalisation of ideological conflicts from the Second World War or from a continuity of violence – the original, physical violence recorded in photographs, but also the contemporary, symbolic violence reflected in the erasing or falsifying of events and their causes – it is grounded in a kind of civil responsibility that Azoullay names 'the civil contract of photography'. She defines this as 'the civic duty toward the photographed persons who haven't stopped "being there", toward dispossessed citizens who, in turn, enable the rethinking of the concept and practice of citizenship'.[4] Azoullay uses the concept of a contract to 'shed terms such as "empathy", "shame", "pity", or "compassion" as organizers of this gaze', leading to the realisation that 'photographed persons are participant citizens, just the same as I am'.[5]

This study establishes a more complex and socially and politically aware relationship to photography, situating our civil contract with Partisan photography inside a wider spatio-temporal framework of the photographic recording of social movements. Yet it also makes a significant contribution to establishing and elaborating on a new model of archival practice. Gal Kirn uses the concept of the Partisan archive to describe a trend that has appeared in recent years as a result of the specific political conditions of Yugoslav post-socialism.[6] This trend is strongly opposed to historical revisionism on the one hand, and to the apolitical romanticisation of the past on the other. As Kirn states, 'the creation of the Partisan archive thus demands not only critical methods of reading it, but rather the revival of an emancipatory past as a mechanism for intervening in the dominant discourse, finding fragments of emancipation in our present'.[7]

Despite the contemporary trend in museum digitisation, which has included working through a substantial corpus of war-related photographic heritage from the 20th century, it seems that the farthest-reaching shifts towards reaffirming Partisan photography and making it widely available are occurring outside of institutions, through actions that we might name the activist-guerrilla emancipation of the photo archive.

3 Azoulay 2008 (see note 1), p. 12.
4 Ibid., pp. 16–17.
5 Ibid., p. 17.
6 Gal Kirn, 'Towards the Partisan Counter-Archive: Poetry, Sculpture and Film on/of the People's Liberation Struggle', in *Slavica Tergestina* (Yugoslav Partisan art issue), no. 17, 2016, p. 104.
7 Ibid.

One of the most prominent examples is the anonymous and self-financed online digital repository znaci.net, set up in 2005.[8] Not only does this project's value lie in immersing the photos in an easily relatable and searchable historical context, often missing at present in photo exhibitions in historical museums; it also lies in saving them from difficult-to-access and often poorly maintained photo archives from the former museums of the revolution of Yugoslav peoples, that is, museums built in the socialist period to document the liberation struggle of the Second World War and the socialist revolution.[9] New forms of dissemination in the digital sphere not only make the mass consumption of photographs possible; they also actualise the emancipatory potential of all signatories of the aforementioned social contract: from forgotten photographers, through to depicted subjects and contemporary viewers.

* * *

Even during the war, Partisan photography was (and later continued to be) treated as an important historical document; its political and social function during the socialist period was largely that of representing events. Partisan cultural production has not been researched as a topic in its own right, and so it has often served to illustrate chosen historical narratives and universal ideas. This has resulted in certain side-effects, such as incorrect or imprecise attributions, and it has also contributed to the mythologisation of certain historical events, a mythologisation that arose from the emphasised iconicity of certain photographs. In this sense, the structural function of Partisan photography in Yugoslav memory politics can be compared with that of monuments. Yet at the same time, we are not dealing here with familiarity as concerns the representative function of these two media, but rather with the fact that the photographic medium, through its synthesised summary of complex historical events, has partly replaced the role that public monuments had in the 20th century.[10] Iconic scenes such as the shots of Stjepan Filipović on the gallows took on the plastic quality of a monument. The design procedures themselves, such as in the work of the Slovenian sculptor Slavko Tihec, were based on examining the possibility of 'translating' photographs into the medium of sculpture and on photography serving the function of a public monument.

In this case, photography also contains a certain mnemonic function based on the material quality of original, analogue photography. However, 'without the fundamental aspect of the [material] trace that secured the temporal specificity of the photographic image, the salient position of photography in visual memory would be seriously endangered'.[11] As the materiality of photography is neglected in its translation into a digital format, the specificity of its

8 See URL: http://www.znaci.net/damjan/fotogalerija.php (accessed 4 May 2017).

9 Hundreds of titles from the historiographic literature on the Second World War and on the People's Liberation Struggle, as well as thousands of historical documents by regional and foreign sources have been digitised as part of this project over many years. A total of 4,740 photographs have been scanned, most of which previously belonged to the Museum of the Revolution (now Museum of Yugoslavia) in Belgrade.

10 Jens Ruchatz, 'The Photograph as Externalization and Trace', in: *Cultural Memory Studies: An International and Interdisciplinary Handbook*, Astrid Erll and Ansgar Nünning (eds.), Berlin/New York 2008, p. 375.

11 Vicki Goldberg, *The Power of Photography: How Photographs Changed Our Lives*, New York 1991, p. 135.

production in a given set of historical circumstances is slowly disappearing. Consequently, the focus on historical contextualisation in a book such as this takes on added significance. Taking a different view, a divergence from an artefactual approach to photography, achieved through the digital transformation of media and the unlimited distribution of images, places a greater emphasis and responsibility on content analysis and on raising an awareness of the political space of all included stakeholders. In contemporary conditions characterised by a complete disintegration in a structural reading of the historical context, or even by that context's direct falsification, the function of digitised Partisan photography nowadays lies closer to the educational and propaganda function that it had in the wartime circumstances in which it emerged, rather than the documentary and memorial function that it had during the socialist period.

* * *

In studies and theoretical debates to date on the meaning of Partisan artistic and cultural production, there has been a dominant focus on poetry, art and dramatic works.[12] This study clearly shows, however, that photography has been a neglected component of cultural production, and that some of the most radical shifts towards emancipation and the democratisation of the medium occurred within photography itself, especially if we bear in mind the class exclusivity of photography before the Second World War. One question worth posing is why – even from a Marxist position – does a certain reservedness continue to exist in placing photographs on an equal footing with other forms of Partisan cultural output as a historical phenomenon?

Drawing on Adorno's thesis regarding the impossibility of transforming the real through fiction, the Slovenian philosopher Rastko Močnik describes Partisan cultural production as:

> a transforming intervention in an aggressive and overly powerful reality. Granted, this was an intervention using representations, but representations that were produced from the perspective of another reality, one that first had to be won in a struggle – an armed struggle, but also a struggle with representations.[13]

Contemporary consumption of Partisan photography comprises the most direct or most literal gaze upon the circumstances in which such a 'second reality' was forged. These are not only shots or recordings used as historical documents in contemporary struggles 'in the field of representation' against historical revisionism and negationism, but also photo-

12 Besides the special issue of the magazine *Slavic Tergestina*, devoted to the topic of Yugoslav Partisan culture, several recent titles deal with the phenomenon of Partisan cultural production. See, for example, *Lekcije o odbrani: Prilozi za analizu kulturne delatnosti NOP-a*, Marko Miletić and Mirjana Radovanović (eds.), Belgrade 2016 (KURS & Rosa Luxemburg Stiftung Southeast Europe); and *Lekcije o odbrani: Da li je moguće stvarati umetnost revolucionarno?*, idem., Belgrade 2017 (KURS & Rosa Luxemburg Stiftung Southeast Europe).

13 Rastko Močnik, 'The Partisan Symbolic Politics', in: *Slavica Tergestina* (Yugoslav Partisan art issue), no. 17, 2016 (see note 6), p. 27.

graphs whose aesthetic quality opens up 'accidental' temporal cracks that relate to the intimate side of that same reality.

Debates over whether Partisan photography belongs to the wider field of Partisan cultural production are a kind of false dilemma originating from a limited understanding of the function of art within capitalist productive relations. If we throw out the assumption that the end goal of artistic work is to make the artistic field autonomous (the idea of 'artistic licence'), we open up a different viewpoint on the motives of individuals who had an input into the collective struggle with cameras in their hands, taking pictures, and taking the side of the unprivileged, marginalised and far weaker, all the while changing camera-related regimes and ethical norms. Bearing in mind the significance of the organisational mechanisms that led to the necessary and indispensable centralisation of photographic production in the liberation effort and the control and coordination of photographic work on the ground, is it really acceptable to bemoan a lack of a more spontaneous, individual and aesthetically competent imagery? Such as the pictures that characterised the first phase of Partisan photographic activity which, after all, was relatively weak in its political impact? The necessity of formal limits speaks volumes of the conditions in which photographic work (or any kind of artwork for that matter) can generally be reviewed and valued. How can photography develop as a craft without an adequate supply of chemicals and photographic paper, and, moreover, in an atmosphere of danger, repression and fear? The overcoming of these production constraints through invention led to the establishment of a new relationship towards the artistic medium and how it related to the portrayed subject. The hierarchical relationship between photographer and subject was eliminated, thus satisfying a basic prerequisite for the avant-garde – the fusing of art and life and the elimination of its class-privileged status.

The numerous topics and problems that Davor Konjikušić touches on in this book (each worthy of separate studies in themselves) include the ephemerality of photographic media under conditions of guerrilla struggle, the Partisan network for distributing pictures and the movement's dependency on the collective's participation (for instance, channels for sending secret packages, hiding and burying photographs). Instructional, educational insights regarding formal rules on the use of light, shot-taking and composition – insights that were earlier unknown – take on an entirely new dimension and counter aesthetic formalism. A photography handbook produced during the war and the continued immediacy and universal appeal of the pictures resulting from that time are radical examples of the demystification of art and the image-making process. Insisting on the subjective expression and aesthetic responsibility of an auteur runs contrary to the propaganda-focused and engaged practice of Partisan photography. However, as Ariela Azoullay claims, that apparent contradiction can essentially be put down to the fact that:

Photography has come into the world with the wrong users' manual. The existing common manual reduces photography to the photograph and to the gaze concentrated on it in an attempt to identify the subject. It takes part in the stabilization of what is seen, in making it distinct, accessible, readily available, easy to capture, and open to ownership and exchange. The wrong users' manual hinders the spectator's understanding that the photograph – every photograph – belongs to no one, that she can become not only its addressee, but also its addresser, one who can produce a meaning for it and disseminate this meaning further.[14]

* * *

The use of photography in the People's Liberation War, which this study highlights clearly in a well-argued manner for the first time, was not only a report-based method of documenting; rather it redefined the photographic medium itself, as well as its historical and political scope, and made it an inseparable part of the entire transformative experience of Partisan cultural production. The individuals behind the lens were participating in the same transformative socio-political process. They became its protagonists and its principal stakeholders. This makes the efforts by the author of this publication all the more significant, as these efforts reveal the personal biographies and revolutionary paths that led photographers, either professional or self-taught, to record and participate in the creation of a new social reality. They also radically reposition our own roles along the intersecting fault lines of society, politics and culture. Understanding the socio-political circumstances and material conditions that this radical turn equally enabled is therefore important, as is delving into the personal motivations of the photographer or noticing the visual talents they took with them into the forests while working undercover. As with Partisan culture and art, which Močnik warns can only be understood beyond its capitalist conceptualisation as an 'autonomous' social sphere, photography – insofar as we can understand it as an integral or synthetic part of that production – cannot be understood either as just an exclusively documentary or aesthetic medium. As with other aspects of Partisan creativity, photography 'is not a passive object, since it still affects us through its symbolic efficiency'.[15]

Within the contemporary conditions of the reception of Partisan photography mentioned earlier, which presently carries a fraught symbolic burden and political significance, the author's task here is not easy in the slightest. This makes his results and their effects even more relevant. This book is the first attempt to historicise this phenomenon, to situate it within a wider cross-section of the history of engaged war photography and the photography of social movements, precisely mapping out how it has been critically and analytically interpreted. The forgotten names of key photographers in the People's Liberation War are revealed or cited in this study all in one place for the first time. Practically unheard of topics are opened for discussion, such as women's authorship in photography, and the controversial topic of lost and destroyed photo archives. The organisational origins of the various photography units are also traced. The present publication also explores some of the key parameters for the development of the medium, such as the link between the centralisation of the People's Liberation Army and the material, formal and content-related features of the photography produced.

14 Azoullay 2008 (see note 1), p. 14.
15 Močnik 2016, p. 23.

In the complex, multidimensional story of Yugoslav Partisan photography, several key topics are outlined, while the author's approach balances between expeditiously relating to the reader the thorough archival research, and striving to raise the historical and aesthetic value of the photographs to a universal level, by analysing several exceptional case studies. These two approaches are equally important and complementary in striving to grasp the phenomenon of Partisan photography as fully as possible, and – of particular importance – making it relevant in the contemporary socio-political context. As with the recent debate surrounding the 'struggle over the past', we can turn to photography as a valuable historical source,[16] and it seems that it can be understood once again as a medium for current social and political struggles. Opening a historical perspective not only aids a better understanding of the role of the photographic medium under certain circumstances – it also opens a perspective on how it is currently mobilised in the present. The described conditions of production in which Partisan photography emerged prompt the question of the individual responsibility of the photographer towards social movements.

16 See, for example, the recently published photo monograph that partly emerged as a response to the revisionist interpretation of the post-war function of the concentration camp of Jasenovac. Đorđe Mihovilović, *Jasenovac 1945.–1947. Fotomonografija*, Jasenovac 2016.

1. Introduction

Photography dating from the Second World War in the territory of what became the Socialist Federal Republic of Yugoslavia has almost always been viewed from a documentary perspective. Its role merely consisted in filling in the gaps in particular historical sources and eye-witness accounts. The potential of the photographic medium in academic research was never fully realised because an organised approach to photography was lacking. As a result, the medium's role in Partisan photography has not been thoroughly investigated to this day. Photography has also been overlooked in left-wing political thought in general. In the first volume of Capital, Karl Marx identifies photography as one of the most important industries of the future, along with the railway, steamships, gas and telegraphy.[1]

Yet compared with other industries, photography was never systematically researched. This situation only changed in the early 20th century when Sergei Tretyakov wrote of how photography is replacing painting and becoming an active instrument in the hands of the proletariat, because 'it is able to establish the technical foundations for an active dialectical-materialist relation to the world in a way that is immeasurably simpler and more comprehensive than painting'.[2] In his essay, 'The Author as Producer', Walter Benjamin drew on Tretyakov's urgent call to turn workers into correspondents and photographers for the radical-left press. As editor of the journal Novy LEF (also known as Novyi LEF), Tretyakov insisted that in photography it is not style but rather use that is important.[3]

Photography's status as an art form was contested, even within the art world, from the moment of its invention in 1839, with painting trumping it until only recently. Yet it remains partly unexplained why historians have so far avoided the question of the role of photography in the People's Liberation Struggle and the revolutionary socialist movement that lasted from 6 April 1941 to 15 May 1945.

1 Karl Marx, Capital, vol. 1, chap. 15, sec. 1: 'The Development of Machinery', trans. Fowkes and Fernbach, London 1990.

2 Sergei Tret'iakov [Tretyakov], 'From the Photo-Series to Extended Photo-Observation' in: October, no. 118, Cambridge, Massachusetts, p. 73.

3 The journal LEF was the mouthpiece of the Leftist Art Front. It was published from 1923 to 1925. From 1927 to 1928 the journal was published under the name Novy LEF. Avant-garde artists, writers, photographers and designers with varied professional backgrounds collaborated with the journal. Its goal was to examine practices of left-wing art to date, and to favour collective over individual work. The editors of the journal Novy LEF were the poet Vladimir Mayakovsky and Sergei Tretyakov – playwright, Futurist artist and photographer. Tretyakov represented a new cultural practice named Operativism. Aided by the new media of photography and film, its main premise was that the working class should produce factographic works. Aleksandr Rodchenko oversaw the journal's graphic design.

The Partisan movement, led by the Communist Party of Yugoslavia, was one of the strongest European anti-fascist movements. It developed gradually, based on the idea that everyone should participate in the anti-fascist struggle, irrespective of whether they were communists or not. It was the only movement that actively fought – first in guerrilla and later conventional warfare – against the German and Italian occupiers and the armed units of the quisling states founded on the territory of the former Kingdom of Yugoslavia. It was the only resistance movement that created a liberated territory in occupied Europe. It drew its strength and allure from promising a new social system, more egalitarian than that of the monarchic Kingdom of Yugoslavia or of the quisling governments that had been founded through state occupation.

If we accept that Partisan art exists, and that its cultural production was an integral part of the revolutionary struggle – which aimed to bring literacy to the masses and thus also emancipate them – then Partisan *photography* surely also exists. It is worth emphasising that the main protagonists of Partisan art were cultural workers, amateurs, as well as auteurs who lacked the specific professional skills and knowledge of the craft of photography that had resulted from the democratisation of the cultural field.[4] This book focuses on the concept of Partisan photography that emerged during the People's Liberation Struggle, that is, within the Partisan movement itself.

Partisan photography's key motive was to not only win the armed struggle, but to win the struggle at the level of representation too. However, especially because of its technical and production-related limitations, Partisan photography served not merely as a propaganda resource, but also as an artistic resource for the emerging future. When the Second World War broke out, was it not Walter Benjamin, after all, who praised the mechanical reproduction of photography, and emphasised its power 'for the formulation of revolutionary demands in the politics of art'?[5] Was it not in Partisan photography that the distinction between the author and audience was lost, and the idea of the artistic avant-garde attained? Did the Partisan movement not alter the prior relationship of that same audience towards art? This book will show that this did indeed occur, because, owing to its technical properties, photography became an important revolutionary medium in the Partisan movement, just as film came to be in the post-war years. Understood as Partisan art, in a broad sense photography also includes the revolutionary intention of combining the political, social and cultural in its transformation of society. While previously reserved for the upper social classes and professional photographers, in the Partisan struggle the technical and material means of producing images reached the hands of workers and peasants. Members of the Partisan movement were trained to use cameras, and later their photographs made up the raw materials used to put together newspapers, produce falsified documents, create the Partisan archive and organise exhibitions on the liberated territories (not only in cities, but also in forests).

4 Mirjana Dragosavljević, 'Od politizacije umetničkog polja do revolucionarne umetnosti', in: Lekcije o odbrani. Prilozi za analizu kulturne delatnosti NOP-a, Marko Miletić and Mirjana Radovanović (eds.), Belgrade 2016 (KURS & Rosa Luxemburg-Stiftung Southeast Europe 31).
5 Walter Benjamin, 'The Work of Art in the Age of Mechanical Reproduction' (preface), trans. H. Zohn, New York 1930.

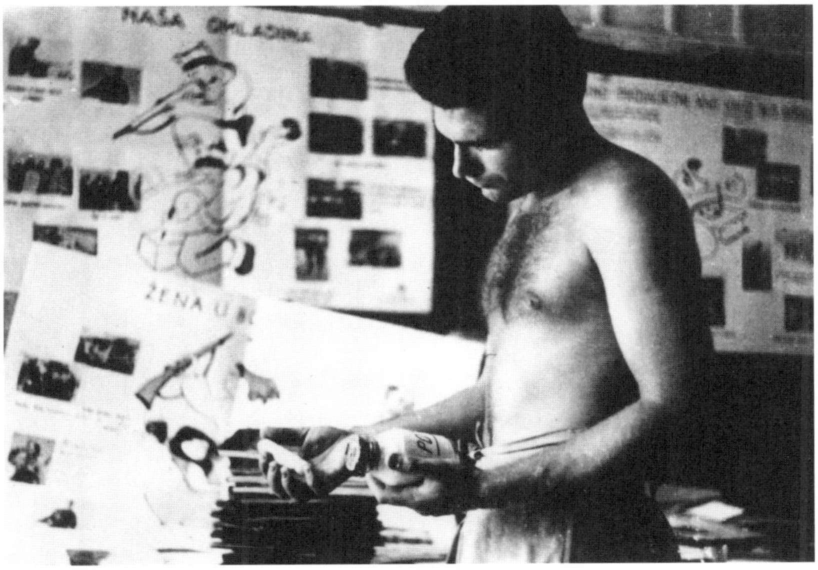

The central committee of the Communist Party of Yugoslavia's printing press, 1941. Photographer unknown. Military Museum Belgrade, 13443.

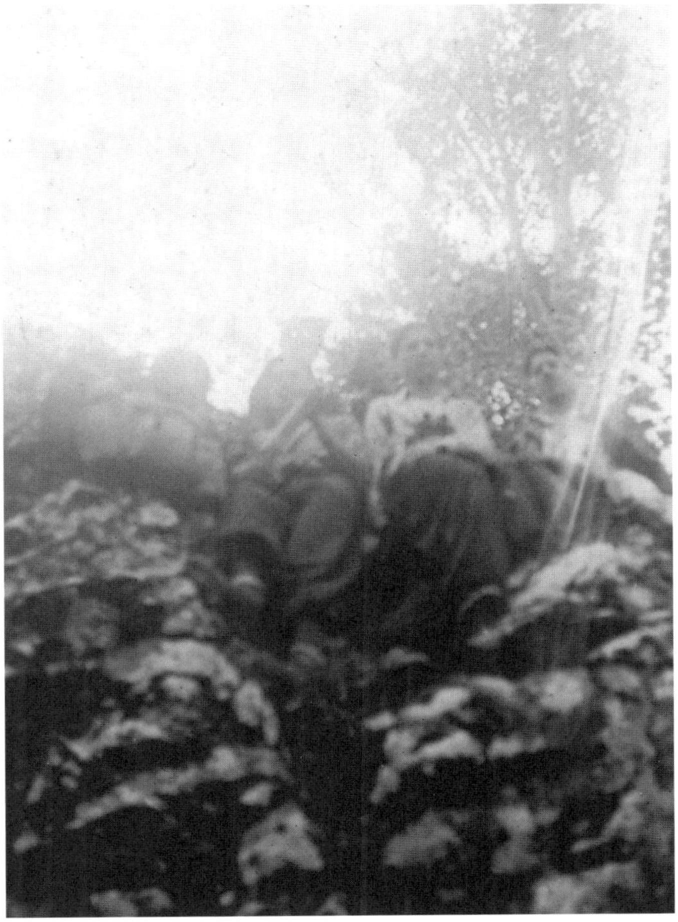

Members of the underground of the League of Communist Youth, 1941. Photographer unknown. Marko Strpić's family archive.

At its inception, Partisan photography operated outside the centralised propaganda system. It was left largely to the photographers themselves, and their work was not systematically checked before 1943, as we will see in the documents depicted in this book.

During 1944 photography units and agitprop departments organised the production of Partisan war photography. All cultural activities were carried out within their system. This brings us to the research focus of this publication, which pays special attention to analysing artistic subjectivity and freedom in choosing how and what to depict. This is also what sets Partisan photography visually apart from enemy propaganda, especially German, but also the image production of the Ustashe Photography Agency.[6] For example, Nazi propaganda photography reached its peak in 1938, during preparations for a new war, when the military propaganda units (known as Propagandakompanien der Wehrmacht) were founded, in which war reporters and photographers were mobilised in large numbers. In Germany, the idea of establishing a military propaganda unit had already emerged by the mid-1930s, because it was believed that the 1918 defeat in the First World War had largely been the consequence of inadequate propaganda, that is, to losing the war of representation. In the German propaganda units, the camera lens was understood literally as a weapon, and at their peak, these units included as many as 15,000 different trained specialists among their ranks – from those in film, education and journalism to photography and

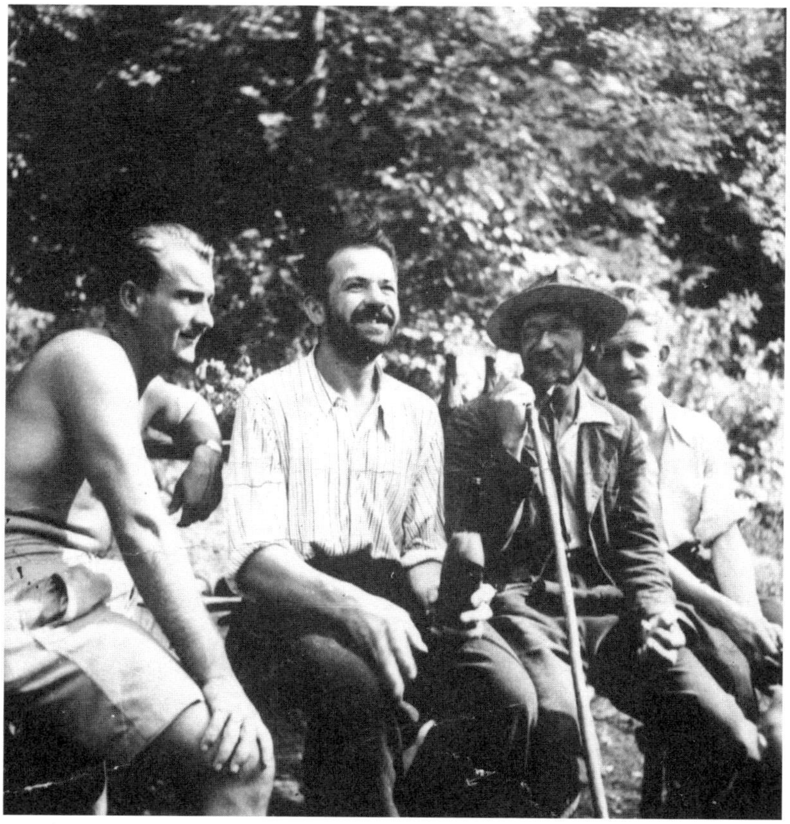

From the left: Ernest Eypper – a member of the regional committee of the Liberation Front of Trnovo, the poet Ivan Rob and an unknown Partisan at Vintgar in north-west Slovenia, July 1941. Photographer unknown. National Museum of Contemporary History (Slovenia), pl8812.

6 This was called the Svjetlopisna služba, and svjetlopis was a prescriptivist Ustashe term for photography.

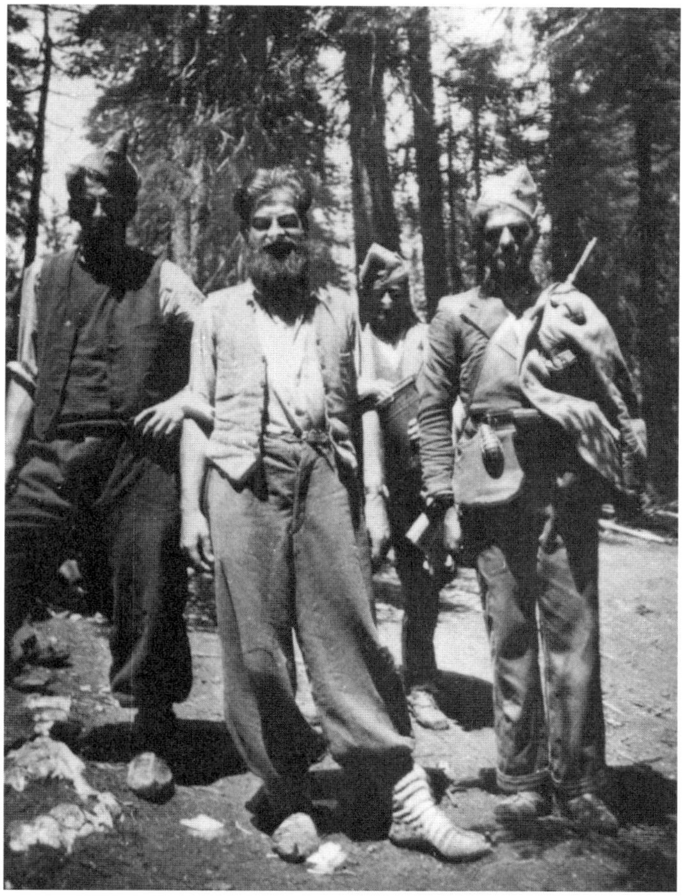

Members of the first wave of Partisan fighters at Cincar. The fighter in the middle is named Mirko Kutleša. Photographer unknown. History Museum of Bosnia and Herzegovina, FNOB 18885.

culture.[7] By comparison, Partisan photography had only just got going at the start of the war. Only a handful of technically proficient photographers had entered the Partisan movement, and they went on to lead the photography units. These Partisan photographers had limited channels of production and distribution. As their working conditions were limited in a technical sense, they mostly made reproductions of text and drawings. Nevertheless, the presence of cameras from the uprising's inception proves Walter Benjamin's thesis on the revolutionary and democratic potential of photographic media: 'What we require of the photographer is the ability to give his picture a caption that wrenches it from modish commerce and gives it a revolutionary use value'.[8] Photography, therefore, should be wrestled out of the hands of trend-following photographers and moved from a one-dimensional aesthetic field into an economic, social, technical and political context.[9] Its revolutionary path could then begin.

7 Aristotle Kallis, Nazi Propaganda and the Second World War, New York 2006, p. 57.
8 Walter Benjamin, 'The Author as Producer' in: The Work of Art in the Age of Its Technological Reproducibility, and Other Writings on Media, Michael W. Jennings, Brigid Doherty and Thomas W. Levin (eds.), Cambridge, Massachusetts/London 2008, p. 87.
9 Michael W. Jennings, 'Photography', in: ibid., p. 264.

Partisan photography is characterised by its social and propagandistic role, its production in conditions of material scarcity, and its artistic, documentary and photojournalistic value. As propaganda, photography's primary function is to transmit messages about building a new world, therein providing materials motivating the masses to build that world. From its inception there was a trade-off between the protagonists' free-wheeling approach to Partisan photography and later attempts to incorporate it within an entire information and propaganda system. Enemy offensives set Partisan photography back, as did the constant movements of units and the scarce supplies, making production almost impossible. These are all considered in more detail in chapter 4. Besides the fact that Partisan units were constantly on the move, the photo negatives themselves were also often at risk of being destroyed or lost; on many occasions they were exposed to water and fire, and many were destroyed in enemy attacks. Many negatives were also burnt by the Partisans themselves so as not to fall into enemy hands. The path to Partisan photography's emancipation was forged precisely because Partisan photography did not emerge inside a complete and well-implemented propaganda system. Under the conditions of war, this relative freedom foregrounded the photographers' imagination and pluralism in approach. One telling detail concerning Partisan photography's historical and artistic context is the fact that the TANJUG news agency[10] was founded on 5 November 1943, four years before the first international photography agency, Magnum. Many Partisan photographers matured professionally in the war environment, first as photojournalists, notably, just four years or so after the founding, in 1936, of *Life* magazine – which established modern photojournalism as a genre. Clearly then, we are dealing with an incredible period of photographic production, which became a progressive resource in the struggle to build a more just world.

All the existing archives cannot be adequately considered here in detail, owing to time constraints and the geographical distribution of the archives. However, just as with the Partisan struggle, Partisan photography has a general Yugoslav character. It is thus impossible to define a 'national' sensibility or national interest common to all the Partisan photographers featured here. Many were born in one state and continued their professional activities after the war in another state within Yugoslavia. This research is my modest attempt at approaching Partisan photography from an artistic, photographic perspective, one that reveals its internal historical mechanisms, and attempts to shed light on how Partisan photographers lived and worked. My main interest in researching Partisan photography is in this medium's nature and its revolutionary function. However, including a historiographical component here was unavoidable, due to the complete lack of any comprehensive research on this topic to date. One cannot make the first steps towards researching Partisan photography without considering that historiography was not and cannot be a photographic reconstruction of the past. I leave to future researchers the task of extending this work to include materials I was unable to access, as well as the application of different theoretical frameworks in analysing this topic.

10 TANJUG's full name is the Telegraphic Agency of the New Yugoslavia. The abbreviation is widely recognised throughout the former Yugoslav region.

During the 1960s, activists recognised the political potential of photography in social movements and used it for various purposes: from African Americans' struggle for equality in the USA, the anti-war movements, the 1968 student protests, the anti-globalisation demonstrations of the 1990s, through to present-day protests against the leaders of the richest states in the world. Partisan photography anticipates the model of activist photography in social movements that emerged in the post-war period, and it does so precisely because of the conditions in which the Partisan movement was established. Although, of course, we cannot bring them into a direct cause-and-effect relation, we can say that Partisan photography was a kind of precursor of photography within contemporary social movements. We need not observe Partisan photography, structurally speaking, as an isolated case.

The end of the war also meant the end of Partisan photography. It came under the control of the state propaganda apparatus and lost its activist potential. After the war, the careful conservation of photographic materials was neglected and forgotten, and the materials themselves were not well-looked after. This research into Partisan photography was hindered largely by there being – in most collections preserved to this day – no reliable data about the photographers, nor the place, time and conditions of their photos' creation. Even after the break-up of Yugoslavia, photographers rarely signed their work and most Partisan photography remained unsigned.

The situation did not improve following the establishing of new states on the territory of the former Yugoslavia. Interest in the People's Liberation Struggle diminished after these states were founded. Furthermore, through various revisionist narratives, the role and supranational character of the People's Liberation Struggle has been relativised, reduced and even falsified. New nationalistic state-building narratives have also emerged, based on distant myths and medieval rulers. In Croatia alone, from 1991 onwards, over 3,000 monuments dedicated to the People's Liberation Struggle have been destroyed. Some of the holdings located in certain museums have been destroyed or have disappeared. One matter of concern is the fate of the holdings previously located in the local museums of the history of the revolution, that is, the museums originally established by the socialist authorities after the Second World War. Access to the extremely valuable holdings of the Museum of the People's Revolution in Split, Croatia – now owned by the City Museum of Split – has not been possible for years, despite it being an important site for Croatian history and Croatian photography. As such, research on Yugoslav Partisan photography – as represented by the first small steps made in this book – finds itself stifled by the current climate characterised by newly forged narratives and untruths. Resolution 1481 of the Parliamentary Assembly of the Council of Europe, on the international condemnation of crimes of totalitarian communist regimes, is especially responsible for this. One example of good museological practice is the National Museum of Contemporary History of Slovenia in Ljubljana, which has adequately preserved 150,000 photographic items from the People's Liberation Struggle. This photo archive's holdings were directly inherited from the Slovenian photo section of the military headquarters of the socialist period, led by Ignac Koprivec.

One issue that proved particularly difficult was gaining access to materials in private archives. While individual owners of private collections have granted me access to information and use of their photographs – for which I especially thank them – despite great effort and good intentions, I was still unable to access certain materials. This is why this book does not include, for example, photographs by the Slovenian painter and photographer Božidar Jakac.

I believe all the above should – and must – be critically examined. However, during the archival research and later interpretation of the data, I was taken aback by the amount of intentional misuse and relativisation of documents relating to the consequences of the fascist occupation and the mass killings of communists, members of the People's Liberation Movement and civilians. Photography is often taken as proof as it is automatically assumed to be truthful, but proving the nature of the fascist occupation is not the main task of this book. Its goal is to shed light on the 'red' field of Partisan photography, to explain this field's specificities and, ultimately, to create a new archive, which is to say, a curatorial overview of photographs with new readings. These photographs arose in a period of revolutionary fervour that celebrates that which is not immanent in war: life itself.

This book's main purpose is to establish some basic points of reference for the topic of Partisan photography. The book mixes abundant photographic material and text, the latter written in such a way as to trace and contextualise the photographs. This book also responds to various important questions: the who, when, how and why behind Partisan photography. The publishing of this research as a book would not have been possible were it not for the support of the Rosa-Luxemburg-Stiftung, whose unreserved support I have had the whole time.

2. The Battleground of Representation: From the Paris Commune to Nazism

The first war documented in photographs was the Crimean War (1853–56). However, the first social revolution recorded photographically was the Paris Commune (18 March–28 May 1871). Starting as an uprising by the National Guard after Paris's surrender in the Franco–Prussian War, the Paris Commune erupted first and foremost as a reaction to the possible establishment of a monarchy. It was the first revolution in history that gathered a wide stratum of workers, and it aimed to secularise and abolish Church property, cancel workers' debts, eliminate night shifts at work, ban the fining of workers, aspire to worker self-management and establish social democracy through a territorial reorganisation of France. The death toll of Communards in the final bloody week of the Commune was around 10,000, with some estimates even citing a higher figure of 20,000. Many of the victims were killed in mass shootings and revenge attacks. Photography played a decisive role in their deaths, because the government and army used photographs taken of the Commune to identify numerous participants. This is why the photographic medium became a pressure point for the uprising – not only did it transmit representations of revolutionary struggle, but later it also featured as a basic identification technique in the police archives. While in no doubt of photography's repressive potential, the rebels readily had their photographs taken while defending the barricades, and on one occasion even received orders to be on active duty at the fortifications for the mere purpose of a photo opportunity.

Baton raised to signal his troops (or to cue the photographer), he is held against the blank whiteness, transfixed, illuminated. A defiant insurgent? A playful poseur? An angel about to ascend to heaven? I look at this man and wonder what he expected to see when he faced the camera. When the shutter closed, did he feel history's force like a storm rushing against his angel-wings?[1]

For many Communards, it was the first time they had posed for a photograph. They naively believed in the immortality that photography offered, and they wanted to be recorded. Indeed, photography in the Second French Empire, as Roland Barthes noted, was intricately linked with public identity, civic status and social belonging. It featured primarily among the bourgeoisie,[2] and then became accessible to the lower classes for a time. The tragedy of

1 Jeannene M. Przyblyski, 'Revolution at a Standstill: Photography and the Paris Commune of 1871', in: Yale French Studies 101: Fragments of a Revolution, New Haven 2001, p. 55.
2 Ibid., p. 63.

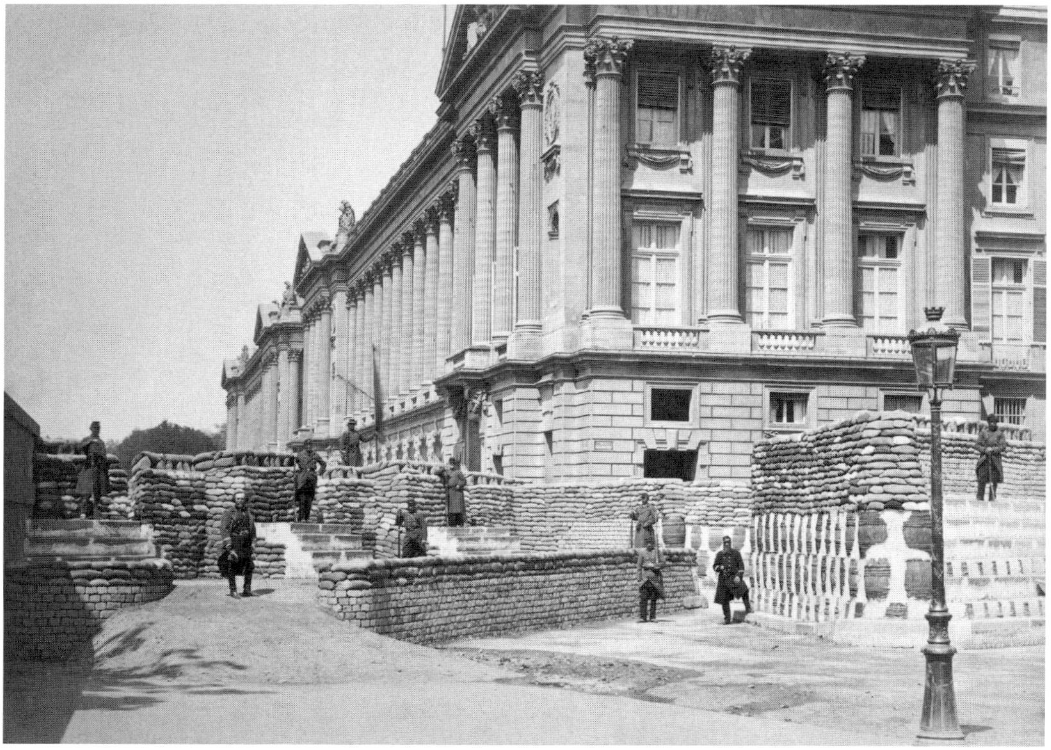

Barricades during the Paris Commune near the Hôtel de la Marine (French Navy Headquarters) and Hôtel de Crillon, 1871. Photo: Auguste Hippolyte Collard. The Metropolitan Museum of Art, 270204, The Elisha Whittelsey Collection

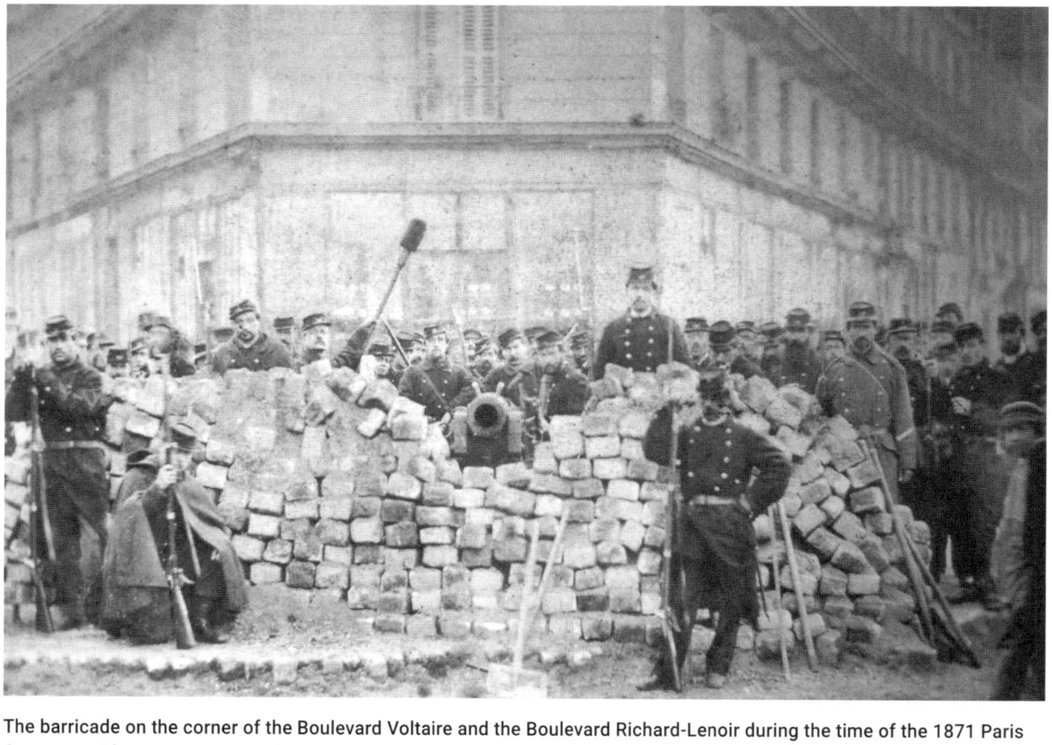

The barricade on the corner of the Boulevard Voltaire and the Boulevard Richard-Lenoir during the time of the 1871 Paris Commune. Photo: Bruno Braquehais. Bibliothèque historique de la Ville de Paris/Roger-Viollet.

this chapter of history perhaps also lies in that yearning to be immortalised in a picture. The rebels lost the battle at the level of representation because of their desire for immortality.

Bruno Braquehais was one of the most active photographers of the Paris Commune, and his photographs aided the later identification of most Communards. While better-known today, Eugène Appert, the second Parisian photographer connected with the Commune, was not as active on the ground. However, to outflank rival photographers, he devised a more deceitful way of earning money. With the government's blessing, and fulfilling their needs as well as his, he photographed members of the Commune who had been caught and locked up. In return for his efforts, he gained unlimited authorial rights for further use of the photographs. As the public's desire for these photographs grew, Appert chose to reconstruct certain events, and even engaged professional actors and actresses to do so. For the first time in history, photographs of people interacting were staged. On the one hand, this served the government's propaganda needs, while on the other, it helped the author make a profit. Thus Appert can lay claim to the dubious honour of making the first staged photographs in the history of photography. In doing so, he participated in the creation of anticommunist propaganda and contributed to the repression of captured Communards.[3] In the original photographs, the imprisoned Commune members have tired and exhausted expressions on their faces after defeat – their clothes are dirty and their humiliation obvious. The portrait of Louis Rossel, a former army colonel who switched sides at the very start of the rebellion and served as the Communards' Minister of War, was photographed by Appert in prison in September 1871, two months before his execution. Appert later superimposed Rossel's head onto the body of another person photographed in his studio,[4] and even went as far as to re-enact the scene of Rossel's execution. Little burdened by ethical questions, Eugène Appert found his way into the history of photography not because of his photographic and artistic importance, but because he was the first to use a camera manipulatively. He skilfully deceived a then naiver viewing public, which assumed photographs were a visual record of historical fact. His work marks the beginning of manipulation by photographic means.

Appert's composite portraits strike me as even more insidious, not merely because they are falsified images masquerading as real, but because they potentially expose all photographic portraits as fictions, unmasking even the fragile decorum of the Communard prisoners as little more than disguise.[5]

Although the invention of cartes de visite in 1854 made photography accessible to many, photography remained beyond the reach of the working class and the urban poor. Culture and art were intended principally for the bourgeoisie, which had time for leisure, whereas the working class did not. The inventor of the photographic carte de visite, André-Adolphe-

3 Peter Field, 'History in the Making', in: e-flux journal, 18, 2010, URL: http://worker01.e-flux.com/pdf/article_161.pdf (accessed 8 October 2016).
4 Przyblyski 2001 (see note 1), p. 67.
5 Ibid., p. 77.

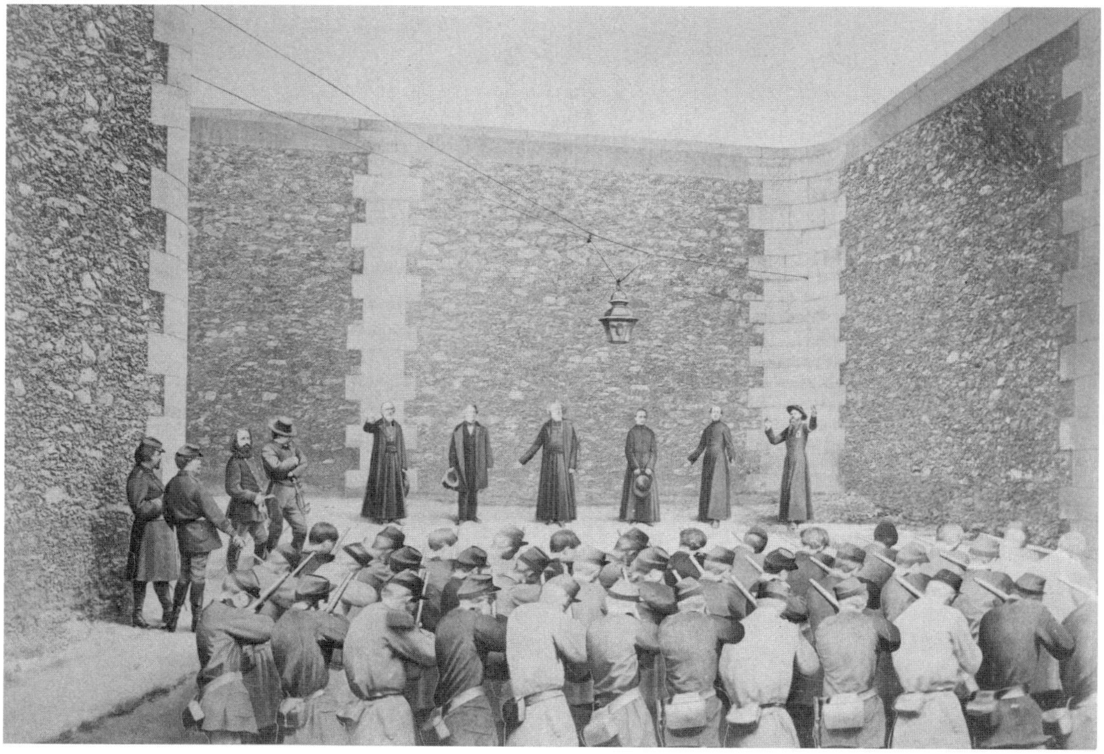

The execution of hostages by firing squad, La Roquette Prison, 24 May 1871. The Metropolitan Museum of Art, 302335, Joyce F. Menschel Photography Library Fund, 2012.

Eugène Disdéri, also photographed members of the Paris Commune on the barricades, as well as their corpses. For Versailles, Disdéri's photographs represent rebels who got the justice they deserved, while for members of the Commune, they were proof of an incredibly brutal revenge and trophy photographs of a criminal act.

During the time of the Paris Commune, photographs of the rebels were published in all newspapers, a tactic also used by the police and army to identify revolutionaries. This was because the police archive, located in the city hall, the Hôtel de Ville, had been destroyed in a blaze. The new chief of criminal identification for the Parisian police, Alphonse Bertillon, set about creating a new police archive. By 1883, he had developed an anthropometric system and statistical parameters for an archive of criminal records. Bertillon's archive was the blueprint for the modern police record and the criminal register. The method of taking one frontal and one profile shot of arrested persons ('mugshots') has remained the police standard to this day. This method has also influenced the development of contemporary biometric methods of identification and surveillance. Bertillon's system laid the groundwork for the method of record-keeping based on biological determinism and eugenics devised by his English contemporary, Francis Galton, the inventor of composite photographic portraits and of fingerprinting as a means of gaining a unique representation of a person. Galton claimed that through photography alone, the number of people sentenced to live in poverty and squalor could be reduced, with no further increase in the number of urban poor. He drew on racist theories of the superiority of the white 'race' over black Africans, as well as of the bourgeoisie over the proletariat.[6] Galton's composite portraits set the scene for the creation of an essentialist anthropology of race and the formulation of portraits of 'inferior' races and nations.

This marriage of photography and eugenics to serve theories of race roughly coincided with the birth of Nazism and partly explains why the Nazis, once in power, destroyed many of August Sander's photographs taken for his typological study Face of Our Time, which contained hundreds of portrait photographs that did not fit in with the Aryan paradigm.

Photography became a powerful and influential propaganda weapon after the Nazis came to power in 1933. It was misused to establish new theories that were primarily antisemitic. In May 1939, the exhibition Das körperliche und seelische Erscheinungsbild der Juden (The Physical and Spiritual Appearance of the Jews) went on show at Vienna's Naturhistorisches Museum. The exhibition was opened by Dr Josef Wastl, head of the museum's department of anthropology and member of the Nazi Party from 1932, long before the Anschluss. In contrast to the already well-known exhibition Der Ewige Jude (The Eternal Jew) of 1937, which presented so-called 'degenerate art' by Jewish modern artists, the later exhibition at the museum of natural history justified its pseudo-scientific approach through the abundant use of photographic material from police archives and strived to render visible the 'Judas face' supposedly common to Jews.[7] In September 1939, Wastl went one step further and carried out his racist research on 440 Jews imprisoned at a football stadium in Vienna.[8] Reporting on a subsequent Viennese exhibition on the 'battle zone in the southeast' that featured contributions by collaborationist-ruled Serbia, in its edition of 1 July 1944, the Srpski narod (Serbian People) wrote that the exhibition included 'trophies of communist-Partisan gangs' and photographs of killed Partisans, as well as images of Partisans whose detachments had been destroyed by Serbian nationalists.[9]

Bertillon's archive paved the way for eugenics. And eugenics, in turn, formed the foundation of the Nazis' race theories, which Slavs, in joining the Yugoslav Partisan movement, fought against and which were ultimately used to justify their murder. However, the Partisan movement also gave rise to its own special artistic and photographic narrative. Partisans knew from the beginning of the armed struggle that victory also demanded gains in the battleground of representation. A total of seventy years after the Paris Commune, the flag under which Communards had fought was borne aloft once again by Partisans when they set off on their struggle for freedom.[10] From the time of the Paris Commune until more recently, social movements have typically been in a weak position compared with the dominant system that controls the production and distribution channels of propaganda. The

6 Davor Konjikušić, 'Fotografija i moć', Master's thesis, Akademija dramske umjetnosti, Zagreb 2014, pp. 23–24.
7 Andras Renyi, 'Time to Gaze', in: Col Tempo. The W. Project, exh. cat. Műcsarnok Budapest 2009, URL: http://coltempo.hu/catalog/time_to_gaze.html (accessed 11 May 2021).
8 Margit Berner, 'The Nazi Period Collections of Physical Anthropology in the Museum of Natural History', in: idem, URL: http://coltempo.hu/catalog/margit_berner.html (accessed 11 May 2021).
9 Olivera Milosavljević, 'Potisnuta istina. Kolaboracija u Srbiji 1941–1944', in: Ogledi, 7, Belgrade 2006, p. 30.
10 Koča Popović, Beleške uz ratovanje, Belgrade 1988, p. 28.

members of the Paris Commune unfortunately realised this too late, and they ended up paying with their lives. Seeing is always mediated by representation and ideology,[11] which is why the Partisans soon realised that they would also have to win the war of representation.

11 Sonja Briski Uzelac, 'Mit o nevinom oku i moć reprezentacije pogleda u kulturi', in: Ars Adriatica, 5, Zadar 2015, p. 205.

3. The Social Contexts of Photography and Its Development between the Two World Wars

For decades after its invention in 1839, photography remained a hobby primarily for the male bourgeoisie. These 'gentleman scientists' had the material resources needed to purchase photographic equipment: film, chemicals for development, subscriptions to photo magazines and the means to participate in exhibitions. Yet they also met the most important prerequisite to spend time on art and photography – they were men of leisure.

Photography developed in large cities in tandem with industrialisation. The nature of the photographic medium's allegedly democratic quality and its accessibility have always been tied to technical developments and the price of photographic equipment. Only at the start of the 20th century did a real revolution in these areas occur, when the Kodak company perfected their *Brownie* camera, intended for a wide market. A second camera in this vein that granted greater artistic licence was the German-made *Leica*, whose prototype was designed by Oskar Barnack in 1913. It used the same 35 mm film we know today. However, the *Leica* did not go into production until 1924. During the Second World War it became an irreplaceable piece of equipment used by German units and a key tool for German propaganda.

As discussed in the introduction to this book, to date there has been little research into the role of photography in social movements and into how such movements relate to photography. In the 1930s, many Yugoslav communist volunteers departed to fight on the Republican side in the Spanish Civil War (1936–39), where they gained the requisite military and organisational experience for the imminent global war against fascism. However, the photographers' position in the Spanish Civil War completely differs from that of Partisan photographers just a few years later. First, there was a large amount of Western media interest in the war in Spain, and channels for media representation were agreed in advance. Consequently, this is considered to be the first conflict followed by photographers 'on the ground' in the modern sense. This war saw many photojournalists forge their careers, including two Jewish refugees from Hungary and Germany, Endre Friedmann and Gerta Pohorylle, as well as Dawid Szymin from Poland. They would later change their names to Robert Capa, Gerda Taro and David Seymour (or 'Chim') respectively, and they did so to gain more opportunities to sell their images. They ultimately succeeded at this, with their photographs being published by the media the world over.[1] Capa was the photographer

1 Sebastian Faber, *Memory Battles Of The Spanish Civil War: History, Fiction, Photography,* Nashville 2018, pp. 15–16.

behind *The Falling Soldier*, one of the most iconic photographs of all time. When considering their success, it should not be forgotten that they took a clear political position and had a measure of good feeling for their work, alongside a desire, as refugees, to stake out a decent reputation in the cultural field.[2]

To better understand the opportunities available in the field of photography between the two world wars in the Kingdom of Serbs, Croats and Slovenes (later the Kingdom of Yugoslavia), it is important to reflect first on Yugoslavia's social context. Most of the workforce was still rural, wages were below subsistence level, and the government exacted violent political penalties against oppositional thinkers. In the new political community, Croatia and Slovenia were the most developed, followed by Vojvodina and the city of Belgrade with nearby Zemun and Pančevo. After the end of the First World War, Serbia had just seventy factories, while Croatia and Slovenia had 960 factories combined. The Kingdom of Yugoslavia was the second most indebted European state, with Greece in first place.[3]

Photography's development was linked to the growth of commercial business in large urban centres, in which 17.5% of the population lived after the first Yugoslav state was founded.[4] The situation was particularly bad in relation to education and culture, and illiteracy was the most visible indicator of this lag. Of the twelve million Yugoslav citizens in 1921, 51.5% were illiterate, while illiteracy in Bosnia and Herzegovina and in Macedonia was particularly high, at over 80%.[5] In the period between the two world wars, people were occasionally photographed in studios from time to time, on special occasions. A trip to the photographer was an important event that people prepared for carefully: they polished their shoes, styled their hair and wore their best clothes.

By 1892, an amateur photography club had been set up in Zagreb. It was called the Klub fotografah amateurah and it gathered many members and was supported financially by the provincial-level government (as part of the Austro-Hungarian Empire). Despite this, it stopped operating only two years later after running into financial problems. It was later subsumed by the Društvo umjetnosti (Art Society), which founded a photography chapter that operated until the First World War.[6] Four years after that war, the Fotoklub Zagreb was founded, the successor to the Klub fotografah amateurah. This club faced operational problems into the early 1930s due to poor economic conditions. By this point in time, however, images by Croatian photographers were increasingly featuring in international exhibitions, and the club's activities also intensified. The 1929 Great Depression did not hit the Kingdom of Yugoslavia until the second half of 1931. It lasted until 1934, with peasants bearing the greatest burden of debt. At the same time, the Karađorđević dynasty's dictatorship and political repression grew stronger. The Communist Party had already been operating illegally for more than ten years, since 1921. While the price of photographic supplies and equipment became more accessible, photographers' activities continued to be linked to the

2 Ibid., p. 31.
3 Branko Petranović, *Istorija Jugoslavije 1918–1988, Kraljevina Jugoslavija 1914–1941*, vol. 1, Belgrade 1988, pp. 60–61.
4 Ibid., p. 74.
5 Ibid., p. 324.
6 Vladko Lozić, *Fotoklub Zagreb 1892-1992, prilozi za povjesnicu*, Zagreb 2000, p. 15.

higher, educated, civic classes in urban centres. In these places, photography evolved from essentially being a leisure activity for amateurs into more of a craft with professional potential and good prospects for the future. As a craft, it started to slowly attract people from outside the cities too. They began to educate themselves, initially working as apprentices in photography studios.

One of the most important exhibitions held in Zagreb in the interwar period was undoubtedly the travelling exhibition *Film und Foto* organised by the Deutscher Werkbund, which opened in April of 1930 as part of the Zagreb Spring Fair. The selection committee included Bauhaus pioneer László Moholy-Nagy, American photographer Edward Weston and Russian artist El Lissitzky.[7] Many other big names in photography also participated in the event, such as the Surrealist Man Ray and representatives of such different movements and styles in photography as Eugène Atget, Cecil Beaton and Kurt Schwitters, with films by Fritz Lang, Sergei Eisenstein and Vsevolod Pudovkin accompanying the exhibition.[8]

Contemporary critiques in the national press were conservative, making moral judgements on the celebration of 'beautiful pictures'. August Frajtić, a critic at that time and member of the Zagreb School of Photography, was disparaging of the aesthetics underpinning the New Objectivity, and instead advocated commonality over individualism[9] and the creation of a national style. In 1938 Frajtić put together a photo collection of 100 works that were displayed one year later at the Royal Photographic Society in the UK. This raised the public profile of the Zagreb School of Photography abroad but also at home. The school was active in the 1930s, with landscape and ethnographic subjects dominating.[10] Frajtić was one photographer who continued to work and organise exhibitions during the period of the Independent State of Croatia, and after the war he fled to Argentina in the wave of Ustashe emigration.

Of all the exhibitions held on Yugoslav territory in the interwar period, it is worth mentioning the *First Pan-Slavic Exhibition of Artistic Photography* organised by the Fotoklub Zagreb and held in 1935 in the Art Pavilion. A total of 150 photographers participated, with 58 from Yugoslavia, 117 from Czechoslovakia and other Slav states, and photographers from abroad with Yugoslav roots included.[11] Of the commercial photographers based in Zagreb, Franjo Mosinger and his picture *Užas* (Horror), published in 1933, deserves a special mention. This photo foreshadowed the horrors of Nazism, a movement that had by then risen to power in Germany. During the early 1930s, various art collectives formed, such as the groups Oblik (Form), Život (Life) and Zemlja (Earth). They sought to undermine traditional and conservative art institutions through their practice, and they contrasted the idea of the lone auteur with that of the collective. In the case of Zemlja, they even planned on setting up

7 Lovorka Magaš, 'Izložba Deutscher Werkbunda Film und Foto na zagrebačkoj Međunarodnoj fotografskoj izložbi i hrvatska fotografija početkom 1930-ih', in: *Radovi Instituta za povijest umjetnosti,* 34, Zagreb 2010, p. 189.

8 Ibid., p. 189.

9 Marija Tonković, 'Fotografija tridesetih godina', in: *Moderna umjetnost u Hrvatskoj 1898–1975,* Ljiljana Kolešnik and Petar Prelog (eds.), Zagreb 2012 (Institut za povijest umjetnosti), pp. 196–202.

10 Marija Tonković, *Fotograf Franjo Mosinger u kontekstu Nove objektivnosti i Bauhausa,* doctoral thesis, Sveučilište u Zagrebu, Zagreb 2011, p. 260.

11 Irina Zrinščak, *Zlatno doba hrvatske fotografije,* Master's thesis, Sveučilište u Zagrebu, Zagreb 2013, pp. 3–10.

their own photo section.[12] It was above all these photographers, Franjo Mosinger among them, who eventually went from commercial photography to emerge as protagonists of Yugoslav art photography. Mosinger was at that time owner of one of the most important Zagreb studios and editor of the magazine *Kulisa*. He went on to become a Partisan photographer. The next chapter of this book goes into more detail on his interesting yet tragic life's journey. Mosinger set up the first Photomaton (a device for taking photographs automatically) in what was then called the Edison cinema (presently the Tuškanac cinema) in 1930. The city's commercial photographers reacted in outrage and Mosinger was even barred from the Fotoklub:

Clearly discernible as the background to the dispute is a conflict between manual, part-mechanised work and full automation. The class consciousness of commercial workers was strengthened and in their discussion on the Photomaton they stated: 'And while above us stand firmly organised industry and capital, behind us stand legions of organised workers – the proletariat.'[13] This was already, at that time, a serious social warning.[14]

Croatian photographers' creative production in the interwar period was linked mainly to the photography clubs. The influence of the New Objectivity was palpable among commercial photographers such as Mosinger, and it played an especially important role in the development of photojournalism. From today's perspective, it is striking how strongly influenced Serbian photographers were by Pictorialism and Impressionism. More recent texts on the history of Serbian photography have tended to focus on aesthetic notions of media and the formal analysis of style, while neglecting the social role and importance of photography. In Belgrade, the first amateur photography exhibition was held in 1901, the same year in which Belgrade's amateur photography club was founded, although it only lasted for a year. After many years with no active photography organisation to speak of, the Beogradski Foto Klub (Belgrade Photography Club) was founded on 4 December 1928 and was intended primarily for amateur photographers – professional photojournalists were excluded. While documentary photographs did exist then, the photojournalism of the early 1930s – during the economic crisis – was not particularly politically engaged or socially attuned. Indeed, it is interesting that the magazine *Zenit*, edited by Ljubomir Micić in Zagreb, made greater use of illustrations than of photographs.[15] Only for the Surrealists – both the Serbian and French Surrealists, traditionally in regular contact with one another – did photography come to assume a position of importance within their art movement.

Here is a chance to point out a significant congruity between French and Serbian Surrealist groups, not only in relation to attitudes included in their programmes, about which much has already been written, but also as concerns their understanding of photography, about which little is known. Indeed, in 1924, the first edition of the Parisian journal *La Révolution Surréaliste*, featured six photographs by Man Ray. From that moment on, he was considered one of Breton's

12 Ivana Hanaček, Ana Kutleša and Vesna Vuković, 'Problem umjetnosti kolektiva: Slučaj udruženja umjetnika Zemlja', in: *Lekcije o odbrani: Da li je moguće stvarati umetnost revolucionarno?*, Marko Miletić and Mirjana Radovanović (eds.), Belgrade 2017 (KURS & Rosa Luxemburg Stiftung Southeast Europe), p. 73.

13 Želimir Koščević, *U fokusu: ogledi o hrvatskoj fotografiji*, Zagreb 2006, pp. 57–58.

14 Ibid.

15 Milanka Todić, *Istorija srpske fotografije (1839–1940)*, Belgrade 1993, p. 89.

circle, as a kind of official photographer of the movement. His photographs did not so much serve a strictly illustrative purpose as accompaniments to the written articles, but rather stood as free visual associations, interspersed fluidly, in keeping with the ideas of the Surrealist publication. First and foremost they had to meet the demands of the automation of thought, only to then disrupt existing habits and customs, as declared by the Parisian journal.[16]

The Belgrade Surrealists' almanac, *Nemoguće/L'impossible*, was especially important in fostering a local style of photography under the umbrella of Surrealism. Dušan Matić worked on Surrealist photo collages that coincided, in turn, with the appearance of left-wing literature,[17] and followed in the footsteps of Man Ray and Maurice Tabard by using double exposures and montages. In fact, the Surrealists saw photography as a tool through which to examine the full reality of the world in which they lived.[18] Besides Dušan Matić, it is worth mentioning Stevan Živadinović's brilliant photographic works issued under his nom de plume of Vane Bor, and Nikola Vučo, the younger brother of the Surrealist Aleksandar Vučo. Nikola Vučo was initially inspired by music and was formally outside the Surrealist circle. He composed outstanding photographs such as *Zid agnosticizma* (Wall of Agnosticism) that featured a wall put up between the Surrealists and the civic classes.[19] After the *Second Manifesto of Surrealism*, in 1929 Surrealists declared their social attitude to be revolutionary and based on the system of historical materialism,[20] and they supported liberation movements in a period characterised by the increasing repression of free and progressive ideas.
Almost a full decade later, in 1938, André Breton and Mexican painter Diego Rivera[21] would write in the *Manifesto for an Independent Revolutionary Art* that:

It goes without saying that we do not identify ourselves with the currently fashionable catchword, 'Neither fascism nor communism!' – a shibboleth which suits the temperament of the philistine, conservative and frightened, clinging to the tattered remnants of the 'democratic' past. True art, which is not content to play variations on ready-made models but rather insists on expressing the inner needs of man and of mankind in its time – true art is unable not to be revolutionary, not to aspire to a complete and radical reconstruction of society. This it must do, were it only to deliver intellectual creation from the chains which bind it, and to allow all mankind to raise itself to those heights which only isolated geniuses have achieved in the past. We recognize that only the social revolution can sweep clean the path for a new culture.[22]

This quote precisely captures the revolutionary nature of the Partisan struggle against fascism. It was a social revolution that also attempted to open a path to a new culture. Having clearly noticed the impossible conditions that emerged during wartime, the Slovenian poet and art historian, Miklavž Komelj, labelled Partisan art as 'proboj kroz nemoguće',which

16 Milanka Todić, *Nemoguće: Umetnost nadrealizma,* Belgrade 2002, p. 22.
17 Todić 1993 (see note 15), p. 95.
18 Koščević 2006 (see note 13), p. 20.
19 Todić 2002 (see note 16), p. 56.
20 Todić 1993 (see note 15), p. 93.
21 Leon Trotsky also helped write the manifesto, as available information and eye-witness accounts of their meeting in Mexico confirm.
22 André Breton and Diego Rivera (and Leon Trotsky), 'Manifesto for an Independent Revolutionary Art', in: *Manifesto: A Century of Isms,* Mary Ann Caws (ed.), Lincoln 2001, p. 473.

can be roughly translated as 'breaching the impossible'.[23] 'When we speak of the impossible, this is linked to the material conditions in which Partisan art arose; we could understand Partisan art as an art that, by breaching its own impossibility, created its own conditions.'[24] And within that space characterised by impossibility, by extreme material scarcity, the story of Partisan photography emerged.

23 Davor Konjikušić, 'Miklavž Komelj: Partizanska umjetnost je proboj kroz nemoguće', in: Novosti (2016), URL: https://www.portalnovosti.com/miklav-komelj-partizanska-umjetnost-je-proboj-kroz-nemogue (accessed 2 June 2021).
24 Miklavž Komelj, 'Partizanska umetnost iskosa', in: Umetnost kao otpor fašizmu, Marija Vasiljević (ed.), Belgrade 2015, p. 28.

4. The Red Glow of Partisan Photography

After the collapse of the Kingdom of Yugoslavia's army and the monarchy's surrender on 14 April 1941, the Communist Party of Yugoslavia fomented an uprising against the Axis forces and the quisling states in July. Professional photographers also joined them, many of whom quickly became the architects of Partisan photography. They often came from the ranks of small commercial photography businesses. Besides these there were, however, also pre-war amateurs, including those from hiking societies. Interestingly, for a time hiking groups played a large part in the spread and popularity of amateur photography.

During this period, the Partisan units did not have the conditions required to capture high-calibre shots, develop negatives, or make good-quality prints. They lacked film laboratories and equipment such as darkroom, processing chemicals, developer and fixer baths, enlarger and safelight. In periods when they were constantly on the move, changing base and living outdoors, it was extremely difficult to create an environment with the optimal temperatures required for all chemicals used in film processing. Photographers faced great challenges, and with only black-and-white film available to them, they could only record the world in tones of grey.

One problem was that they were unable to get hold of the polarising filters needed to block parts of the light spectrum, with the result, for example, that the most important symbol of the Partisan struggle – the red star – was reduced to an indistinct blur on the Partisan cap. Over time, the Partisans became accustomed to such complex conditions and they learnt how to make the most of their tools in the wartime situation, so that the five-pointed star eventually became much clearer to see. Despite the monochromy of expression available to them, Partisan photographs in fact exuded the red glow of the proletarian struggle for social change. Paradoxically, such early photographs left an indelible mark on the collective psyche, with the black-and-white five-pointed star carrying a powerful dual meaning: life in death and peace in war. This chapter presents an overview of photographic activities among the Partisans. In so doing, it draws attention to various other features of Partisan photography.

The Early Days of Partisan Photography

The first Partisan photographs emerged in 1941, when photography-related activities were still inadequately organised. In August of that year, Slavko Smolej, a member of Fotoklub Ljubljana, took pictures of the scenes following the sabotaging of an aqueduct in the Upper

Carniola (Gorenjska) region of Slovenia by a company of Partisans from Jesenje.[1] Commanders such as Mirko Bračić, Jule Sočan and Jože Kotnik photographed events in the Partisan units.[2] Underground activists in Slovenian cities, such as Sočan in Ljubljana,[3] distributed banned literature, poetry books and leaflets, and also photographed the buildings and places they lived in while under cover. Sočan soon joined Partisan ranks, taking two cameras with him that he later used to take important shots of the Tomšič Brigade. Photographs were also used to forge identity papers, which were extremely important to party members and resistance fighters when moving between cities and localities. Such movement was vital for coordinating and linking up all parts of the resistance effort, and for passing on messages.

Besides the cameras that photographers had already brought with them upon joining the Partisan movement, German *Leicas* also started landing in Partisan hands, along with other material seized in skirmishes with German troops, including weapons and supplies. There are many reports citing the importance of plundered photographic equipment and listing the precise number of seized cameras and rolls of film. One of the earliest such reports is that of the general staff of the First Šumadija Partisan Detachment, dated 14 October 1941, in which they itemise the plundered weapons, munitions, food and photographic equipment.[4]

After a successful uprising in Serbia in June 1941 and the creation (on 24 September) of the first liberated territory in occupied Europe – the Republic of Užice – the Partisans had a small quantity of photographic supplies available to them, and some photographs too. The painting studio responsible for preparations for the exhibition on the USSR (held in the small sports hall of the local chapter of the Sokol Society) chose to exhibit mainly prints, drawings, sketches and paintings,[5] with just one small section featuring photographs.[6]

After the collapse of the Republic of Užice on 29 November 1941, Partisan resistance in Serbia was thwarted. The main body of Partisan troops retreated towards Sandžak, later moving towards Bosnia and Herzegovina. Serbia came under German occupation and Milan Nedić's quisling government, subordinated to the German Military Administration that governed all aspects of civic life. The Military Administration (Militärverwaltung) issued permits for only ten photo studios and photographers permitted to work for the German Wehrmacht.[7] Aleksandar Aca Simić and Milan Roglić were both active as photographers in Serbia during the war. The latter took an iconic photograph of people riding a motorbike and sidecar during the Belgrade demonstrations against the Kingdom of Yugoslavia joining the Tripartite Pact.[8] Besides these two photographers, most noteworthy photo-

1 Franc Fabec and Dejan Vončina, *Slovenska odporniška fotografija 1941–1945*, Ljubljana 2005, p. 44.

2 Tomaž Kladnik, Katarina Jurjavčić and Jože Dežman, *Vojne fotografije 1941–1945, Partizanske jedinice*, Ljubljana 2010, p. 22.

3 Fabec/Vončina 2005 (see note 1), p. 45.

4 *Zbornik dokumenata i podataka o narodno-oslobodilačkom ratu jugoslovenskih naroda*, vol. I/20, 1965, *Borbe u Srbiji 1941–1944*, Belgrade 1965.

5 Venceslav Glišić, *Užička republika*, Belgrade 1986, pp. 174–175.

6 Stojadin Kostić, 'Kulturna i umetnička aktivnost u partizanskom Užicu 1941', in: ibid., p. 328.

7 *Novo vreme*, 22 May 1941.

8 Roglić perfected his photographic techniques in Marseille. During the Second World War he was the official photographer for Milan Nedić's government. His photographs of 27 March 1941 were later printed in post-war history textbooks.

graphic production in Serbia can be traced to the studios Miroč and Urošević, the Belgrade Photo Agency and the Photographic Department of State Propaganda. The photographer Risto Marjanović should also be mentioned in this context, best known for his photographs of the retreat of the Serbian army and Serbian people during the First World War, and later for his photographs of the liberation of Belgrade. His series of photographs depicting soldiers in peasant clothes without shoes is particularly haunting.[9]

In the Partisan movement in Serbia, the work of the amateur photographer Rade Jokić (from Valjevo in central Serbia) is especially interesting, and he ranks as one of the very first Partisan photographers. From research on this photographer recently published in Serbia,[10] we learn that for his prints Jokić used Agfa's glossy bromide paper *Brovira* (9 × 12 cm), which the Partisans most likely seized in combat or plundered from German units via some other means. Before the war, Jokić had bought a *Leica IIIb* with a *Summar* 50 mm lens.[11] He took pictures of some of the first rebels in Serbia, such as Filip Kljajić-Fićo, the painter Bora Baruh and the sculptor Vladeta Piperski. Frequent motifs of his include Partisan military columns, life in a Partisan unit and peasants. One of Jokić's photographs, taken in August 1941 near the village of Kamenica outside Valjevo, shows Stjepan Filipović with comrades leading four German spies to their death by firing squad.[12] (For more on Stjepan Filipović and his own execution, see chapter 7, 'Iconic Photographs'.) Looking at Jokić's photographs, one gets the strong sense that he was given little time to compose his shots, with many apparently taken on the run, while catching up with the column, ever at risk of being left behind:

The conditions for shooting film were exceedingly difficult. I had to quickly find a suitable corner to take pictures while the others were advancing, and afterwards we had to reach the column, keeping to the hill. It was difficult to capture on film and because of this, our comrades were not understanding enough. While I was loading the camera with a new roll of film, they would protest, demanding that the light be turned on or a candle be lit, so I had to go outside and work huddled under an overcoat beneath a canopy. They often couldn't grasp how important these documents would come to be after the war. They said: 'You're taking pictures while we're being killed.' I brought a certain amount of photo supplies with me when I left to join the Partisans, but I mostly used materials taken from captured Germans. After the fight at Stolice we seized a certain quantity of film, just as we did when we occupied Krupanj. We also seized one camera in Krupanj that I gave to Piperski to take pictures with. But he forgot it in our retreat. I managed to preserve the rolls of film by burying them in the wall of a barn at the home of the Belić family, in a village named Bogovađa. I shot a total of eleven rolls, each with thirty-six exposures, and after the war I gave them to my comrades. However, all these film rolls somehow got lost. I later received an order to search for them and managed to find only three or four in Zagreb. How they got there,

9 Milan Radanović, *Oslobođenje. Beograd, oktobar 1944*, Belgrade 2014 (Rosa Luxemburg Stiftung Southeast Europe), p. 81.

10 Branko Matić, *Valjevski partizani 1941–1942: na fotografijama Rada Jokića*, Valjevo 2015 (self-published).

11 Ibid., pp. 16–23.

12 Ibid., p. 101.

I have no idea. Today, they are in the Military Museum in Belgrade. It turns out that one of these eleven rolls had already been used by the Germans, and I used the film for a second time without realising it. Once developed, you clearly saw the German and our military columns criss-crossing each other. I shot one film in colour but that also got lost.[13]

Stolice (near Krupanj) was a site in rural Serbia of key importance in the early days of the Partisan struggle. Besides Rade Jokić stationed in the Kolubara Company (Valjevo Detachment), another Partisan photographer taking pictures was Sreten Čitaković. He managed to get his hands on a Voigtländer camera after the struggle with German units in Stolice on 1 September 1941. He seized it along with several Agfa films, and he gave his Rodenstock camera as a present to his co-fighter, Miodrag Tatović. In the early days, they mostly took photographs by using seized German film, and only later did they succeed in getting hold of photographic materials through Partisan connections in the cities.[14]

Besides taking photos to document events, a small number of Sreten Čitaković's photographs show his co-fighters' gentler side. He shot a portrait of Sofija Soja Stanišić, one of the first women to fight alongside her male counterparts in combat against German units, and Ivo 'Lola' Ribar and Aleksandar Ranković on horseback. Čitaković attempted to have

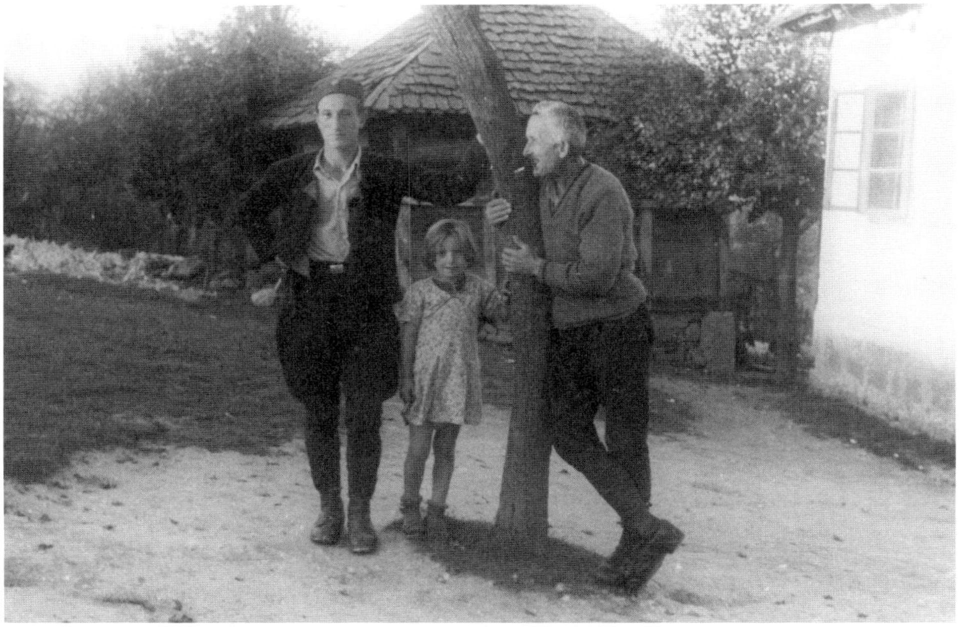

Dragoljub Dudić (right) and his son Miša Dudić, fighters in the Valjevo Detachment, Valjevska Kamenica, 1941. (The author Branko Matić claims that the photograph shows Miloš Milićević and Negosava Bojinović with Dragojlo Dudić.) Photo: Rade Jokić. Military Museum, Belgrade, 992.

13 Zdravko Ranković and Miroslav Jeremić, *Kultura u prošlosti Valjevskog kraja*, vol. 2: Slikarstvo, arhitektura, fotografija, skulptura: izbor tekstova emitovanih u emisijama Radio Valjeva, Valjevo 1979; see also Matić 2016 (see note 10), pp. 16–23.
14 Sreten Čitaković, 'Fotografije iz partizanskog života', in: *Slikarstvo arhitektura fotografija skulptura. Izbor tekstova emitovanih u emisijama Radio Valjeva*, Zoran Tripković (ed.), Valjevo 1979, p. 145.

his photos duplicated and distributed by sending them across the territory of the Republic of Užice via a young girl, Milica Pavlović, from the Liberation Committee of the Communist Party of Yugoslavia (Valjevo chapter).[15] But the rolls were irrevocably lost when German forces invaded on 29 November 1941. Čitaković also took photographs for fake identity papers:

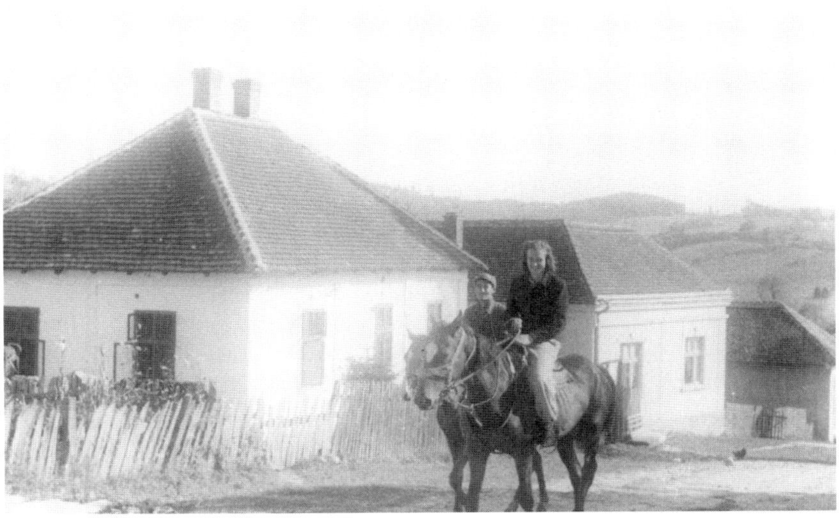

Miša Veličković and Sofija Stanišić, members of the Valjevo Detachment, Valjevska Kamenica, September 1941. Photo: Rade Jokić. Military Museum, Belgrade, 1004.

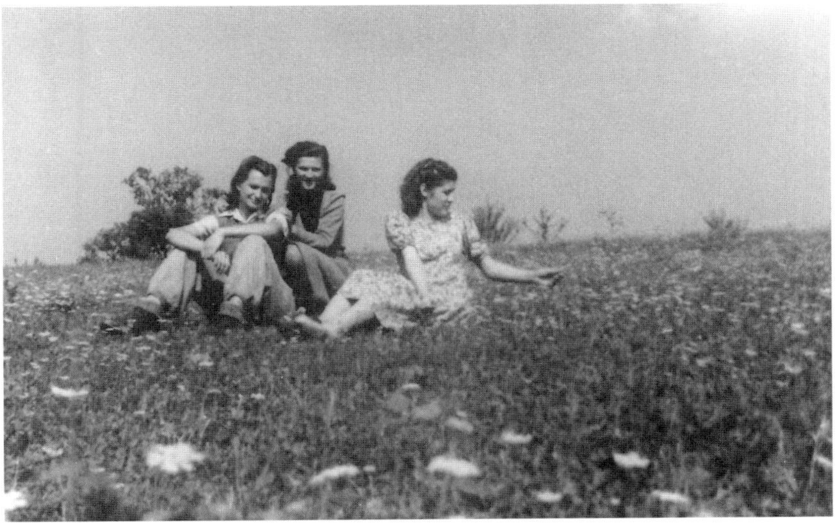

Members of the Valjevo Detachment (presumably Sofija Stanišić with two unknown friends), 1941. Photo: Rade Jokić. Military Museum, Belgrade, 1007.

15 Ibid., p. 147.

Our patrols were tasked with seizing unsigned, blank ID documents in local municipalities. When we arrived in the villages of Bukovac and Osečenica on 8 February or thereabouts, myself and one leader of the fighters went to the house of Milomir Uskoković, a photographer from Osečenica. I developed two film rolls at his house, dried them, and copied everything. I did it all myself, so Milomir didn't even see a single picture. He gave me everything I needed and was helpful throughout. We continued the journey to Brežđe, and I sent the photographs to Mirko Tomić. He delivered them to Bora Baruh who counterfeited a German stamp and turned these photographs into false identity papers.[16]

The first Partisan photographs in Croatia appeared in October 1941. Only two months after the first photographs emerged in Slovenia, an unknown photographer shot the first images of the Psunj Detachment.[17] In December of the same year, Dr Vladimir Bakarić photographed the camp at Slunj.[18] Bakarić was the General Staff of Croatia's political commissar (tasked with the staff's political education) and one of the founders of the ZAVNOH (State Anti-Fascist Council for the People's Liberation of Croatia). Later, as one of the leaders of the Partisan struggle, he had the opportunity to shoot photographs of historically important events in the People's Liberation Struggle, including images of the Partisans' Supreme Command during their stay on Vis in 1944.

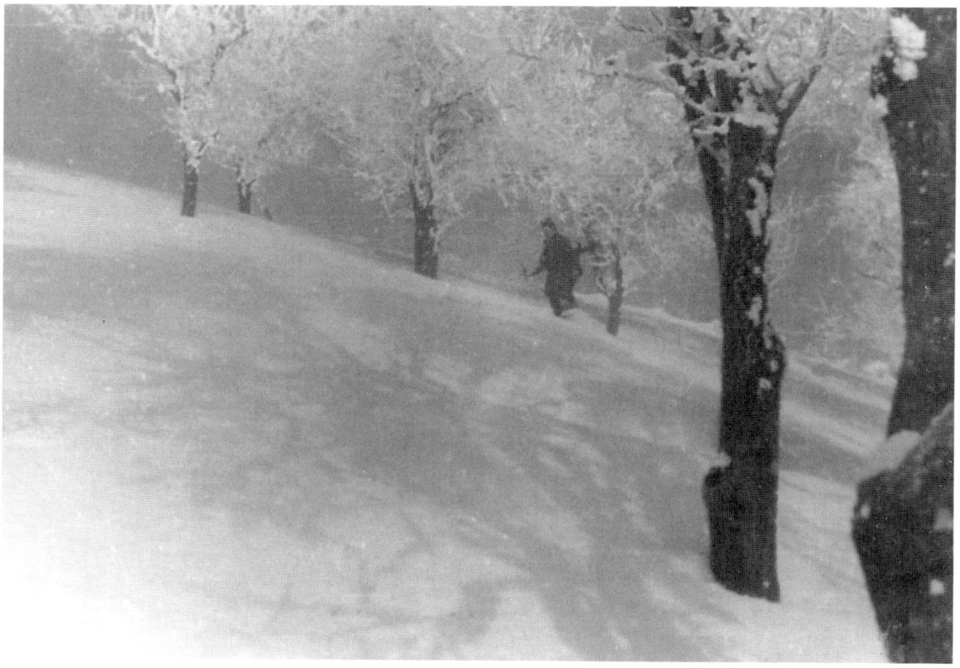

Guard patrolling in sub-zero temperatures, Leskovice, Serbia, February 1942.
Photo: Rade Jokić. Military Museum, Belgrade, 1161.

16 Ibid., p. 153.

17 Rhea Ivanuš, *Fotografski albumi u zbirci fotografija, filmova i negativa Hrvatskoga povijesnog muzeja*, Zagreb 2006, p. 23.

18 Branka Hlevnjak and Rhea Ivanuš, *Hrvatska antiratna fotografija: Prvi svjetski, Drugi svjetski i Domovinski rat*, Zagreb 2008, p. 111.

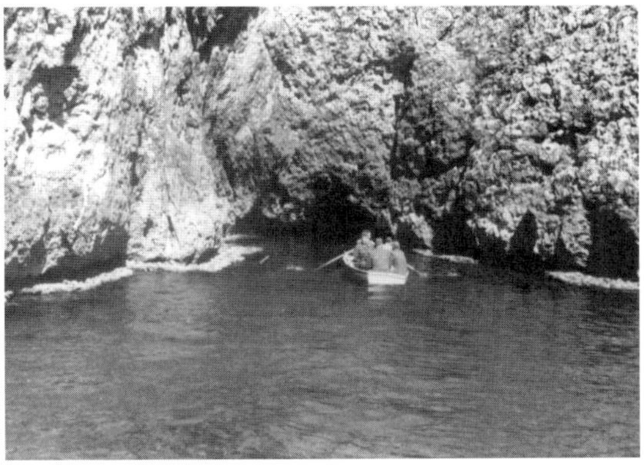

The entrance to the Blue Cave on the island of Biševo, 1944. Photo: Dr Vladimir Bakarić. Croatian History Museum, HPM/MRNH-F-5986.

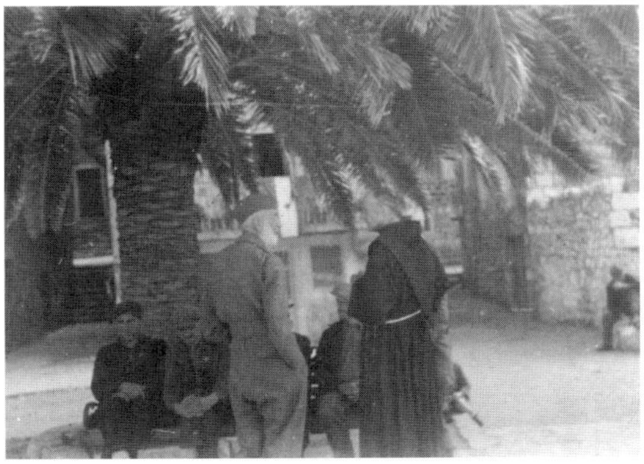

A group of delegates from the District Conference of the Unitary People's Liberation Front of Dalmatia, Hvar Island, 10 October 1944. Photo: Dr Vladimir Bakarić. Croatian History Museum, HPM/MRNH-F-5993.

The First Partisan Exhibitions

It is difficult to determine when the *first* Partisan photography exhibition was held, but it was likely the exhibition on 7 November 1942 in Bosanski Petrovac, in the second liberated territory – the Bihać Republic. Little data about the event itself has been preserved, but we do know that photographs shot by one of the first and particularly important Partisan photographers, Vili Šimunov-Barba, went on show there.[19] At that time, Bosanski Petrovac (liberated on 25 May 1942) became the administrative centre of the Bihać Republic. In this territory 'civil authorities' were organised by the People's Liberation Committees. These authorities were tasked with providing for all kinds of civilian needs. They also organised cultural and educational activities on liberated soil, such as in the Croatian coastal town of Selce in 1943.[20] This is further proof that Partisan photography had a civic, artistic character during wartime. Though short-lived like the Republic of Užice before it, the Bihać Republic was the site of the first event in the Agricultural Youth Labour campaign. The action, in the valley of Sanička, was well documented in photographs, with the number of youth volunteers estimated to between 2,000 and 3,500.[21] The Anti-Fascist Women's Front was also founded in Bosanski Petrovac on 6 December.[22]

The first Partisan photography exhibition was held on the day that the Supreme Commander, Josip Broz Tito, marshalled the First Proletarian Brigade. Its commander was the one-time Belgrade poet, Surrealist and volunteer in the Spanish Civil War, Koča Popović. Several days before the planned opening of the exhibition, on 20 October 1942, orders arrived from the chief of the Temporary Administrative Section of the Supreme Command of the

19 Pavle Jakšić, *Nad uspomenama*, vol. 1, Belgrade 1990, p. 277.

20 Vinko Antić, *Vinodolska Selca u borbi*, Selca 1975, p. 623.

21 Mile Trnjaković, 'Sjećanja na rad omladinske organizacije na području Bosanskog Petrovca do kraja 1942. godine', in: *Bosanski Petrovac u NOB. Zbornik sjećanja*, vol. 4, Vladimir Čerkez (ed.), Bosanski Petrovac 1974, p. 155.

22 For more on the Anti-Fascist Women's Front, see Andreja Dugandžić and Tijana Okić, *The Lost Revolution: Women's Antifascist Front between Myth and Forgetting*, Sarajevo 2018.

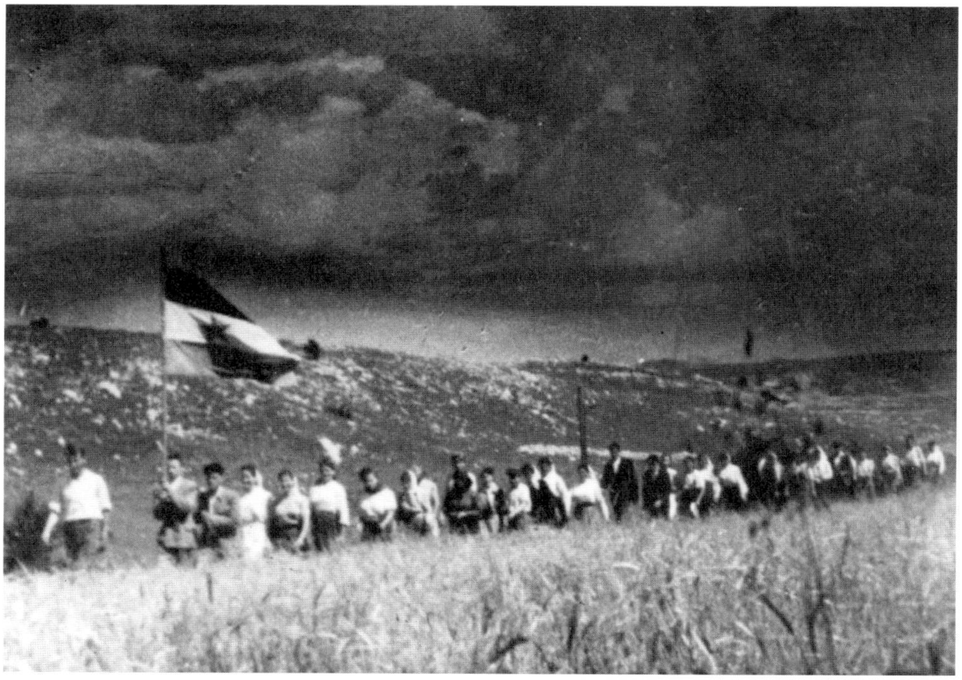

The Youth Battalion from the Bosnian town of Bosansko Grahovo, harvesting grain in the Sanička valley (Podgrmeč). Photographer unknown. History Museum of Bosnia and Herzegovina, FNOB 10737.

People's Liberation Struggle of Yugoslavia, stating that the brigade staff and the Partisan detachments should submit examples of Partisan press and documentary material on the liberation struggle and on atrocities committed by the occupiers and their lackeys. All units were asked to submit examples of their own published news-sheets, brochures, pamphlets and other printed material, as well as enemy documents. They were also asked to supply Partisan photography, the texts to folk and Partisan songs, lists of victims, data on war crimes, lists and descriptions of campaigns, but also humorous and everyday accounts of life in the units. The order was signed by Moša Pijade. He was a pre-war communist, journalist and painter with the code name 'Čiča Janko'. It is interesting that photography was the second point listed in the order. This confirms that there was an awareness of its significance in the Partisan movement at the time. The order states that the comrades should supply:

A copy of every photograph taken of our struggle, including background details to the image, as well as seized enemy photographs (especially photographs of fascist atrocities). Also, photographs of some of our fallen heroes. On the back of each photograph, or on a list that may be attached to it, write what or who is depicted, when and where the image was taken and, if possible, to whom the picture belongs. Comrades are not to bemoan submitting the only print they have, because the photographs will be reproduced, and the originals can be later returned to

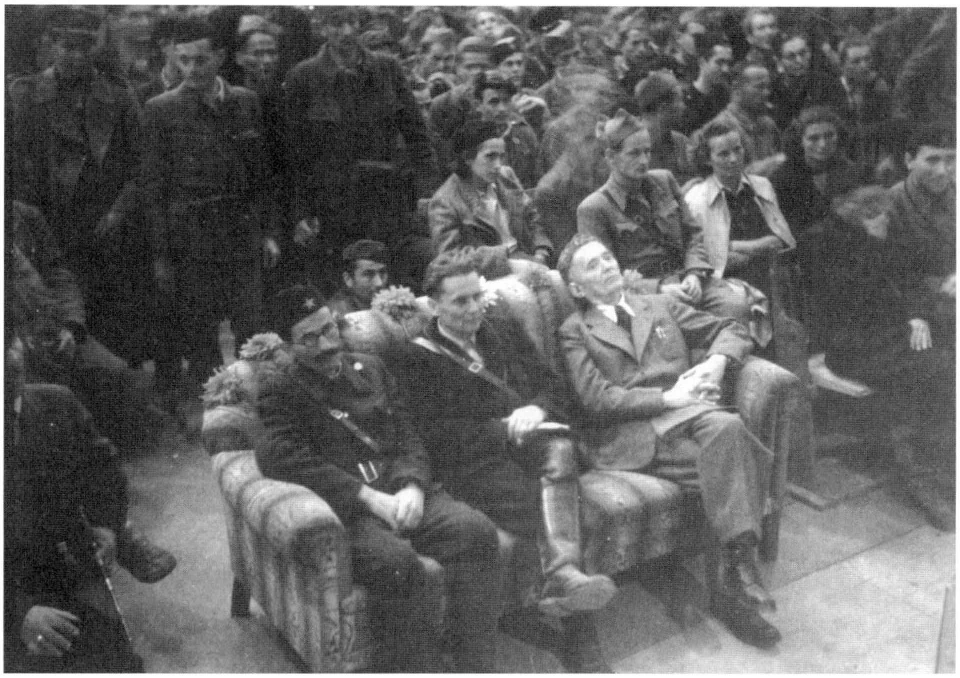

From left to right: Ivan Milutinović, Josip Broz Tito and Ivan Ribar watching a performance at the Theatre of People's Liberation, with Davorjanka Zdenka Paunović in the background, Bosanski Petrovac, 1942. Photo: Vili Šimunov-Barba. Military Museum, Belgrade, 4110.

them if they so wish. Concerning photographs that comrades think worth enlarging (if not all submitted photographic material in general), it is preferable if comrades attach the negative along with each print.[23]

One year after the exhibition in Bosanski Petrovac, on 27 November 1943, an exhibition (about which little is known) was held in the liberated town of Livno in honour of the Second Session of the AVNOJ (Anti-Fascist Council for the People's Liberation of Yugoslavia).[24] The Slovenian poet Edvard Kocbek wrote about the exhibition in his diary. He was fascinated by photography and the atmosphere of the liberated city, and began to picture film scenes in his mind, even introducing camera movements. The political scientist Gal Kirn views Kocbek's notes as an outline for the first Partisan film script.[25] The ensuing film is not so much a movie in the traditional sense, rather a series of photographs that we only envision in motion once we embrace the shortcomings of the human eye and mind.

The Republic of Užice and the Bihać Republic were the first territories where Partisan cultural activities were carried out, and where they took on a systematic, organised form. At the founding session of the AVNOJ on 26–27 November 1942 in Bihać, the Executive

23 *Zbornik dokumenata i podataka o narodno-oslobodilačkom ratu jugoslovenskih naroda*, vol. II/6: Dokumenti vrhovnog štaba Narodnooslobodilačke vojske Jugoslavije 1942, Belgrade 1957.
24 Marko Miletić and Mirjana Radovanović, 'Lekcije o odbrani: Prilozi za analizu kulturne delatnosti NOP-a', in: *Lekcije o odbrani, Prilozi za analizu kulturne delatnosti NOP-a*, ed. idem, Belgrade 2016 (KURS & Rosa Luxemburg Stiftung Southeast Europe), p. 31.
25 Gal Kirn, 'On the Specific (In)existence of the Partisan Film in Yugoslavia's People's Liberation Struggle', in: *Partisans in Yugoslavia: Literature, Film and Visual Culture*, Miranda Jakiša and Nikica Gilić (eds.), Bielefeld 2015, p. 211.

Committee passed a decree on the temporary management of the Theatre of People's Liberation. This was the new state's first cultural institution and its director the writer Ivo Frol. The head of the drama section was the actor Vjekoslav Afrić, while Nikola Popović was declared head of the acting school, with the ballet dancer Žorž Skrigin leading the ballet department. Prior to the war, Skrigin had been a performer at the Croatian National Theatre in Zagreb. He was also one of the most prominent Partisan photographers.[26] The theatre's music department was led by Nikola Hercigonja, with Oskar Danon as conductor.[27]

It is widely believed that the first Partisan exhibition of photographs in Croatia was organised in Otočac on 11 June 1943. However, I came across contrary information claiming that the first Partisan photographs to go on exhibit did so in Slunj on 23 December 1942, at an exhibition of photographs and prints[28] organised by the Agitprop District Committee of the Communist Party of Croatia and the Central Committee of the Communist Party of Croatia.[29] The exhibition held one year later at the Otočac youth centre featured Partisan brochures, news-sheets, caricatures, pictures by Vladimir Kristl, Vilim Čerić and Ivo Kušanić, and photographs by Franjo Mosinger. After Otočac, the exhibition travelled to Senj, Novi Vinodolski and Crikvenica, where it went on show in the gymnastics hall of the local branch of the Sokol Society.[30]

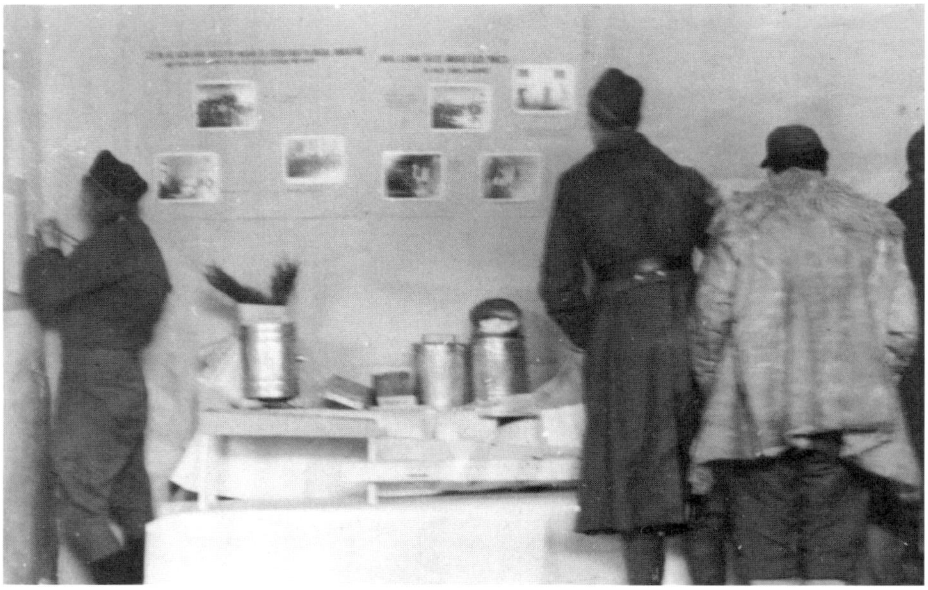

Exhibition of Partisan photography to mark the Second Session of the AVNOJ, Theatre of People's Liberation, Livno, 27 November 1943. Photographer unknown. Croatian History Museum, HPM/MRNH-F-5379.

26 Georgij Skrigin was born on 4 August 1910 in Odessa and acquired the nickname Žorž over time. I have chosen to use the moniker 'Žorž Skrigin' as he himself wrote his name like this in the post-war period.

27 Branko Petranović, *Istorija Jugoslavije 1918–1988*, vol. 3: Socijalistička Jugoslavija 1945–1988, Belgrade 1988, p. 366.

28 Mane Borcić, 'Kulturno-prosvjetna i propagandna djelatnost u kotarevima Slunj i Veljun tokom NOR-a', in: *Kotar Slunj i kotar Veljun u NOR-u i socijalističkoj izgradnji*, vol. 2, Đuro Zatezalo (ed.), Karlovac 1988, p. 758.

29 Croatian Institute of History (former Institute of the History of the Labour Movement of Croatia, AIHRPH), KP-220/4890.

30 Hlevnjak/Ivanuš 2008 (see note 18), p. 117.

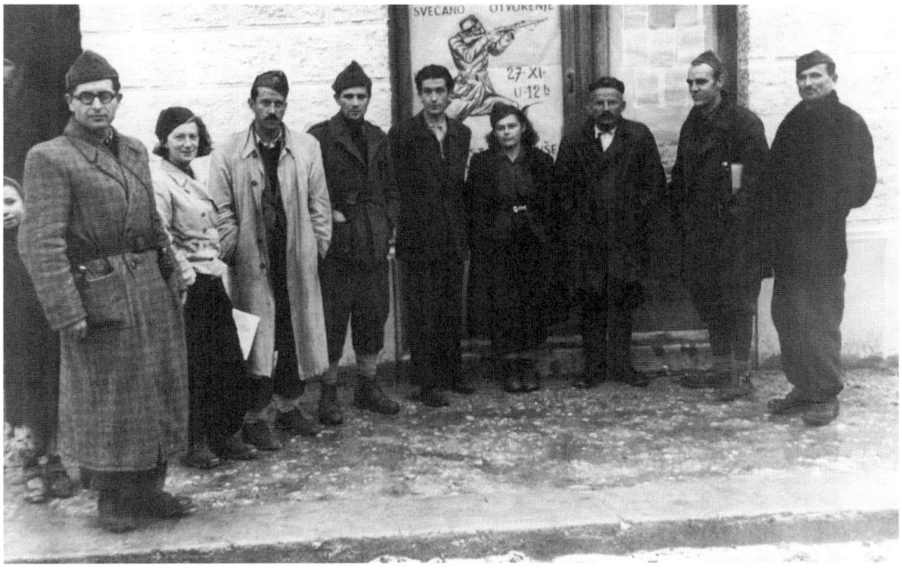

Delegates from Slovenia in Livno on their way to the Bosnian town of Jajce, standing at the entrance to the exhibition of Partisan photography dedicated to the delegates, November 1943. Photographer unknown. History Museum of Bosnia and Herzegovina, FNOB 724.

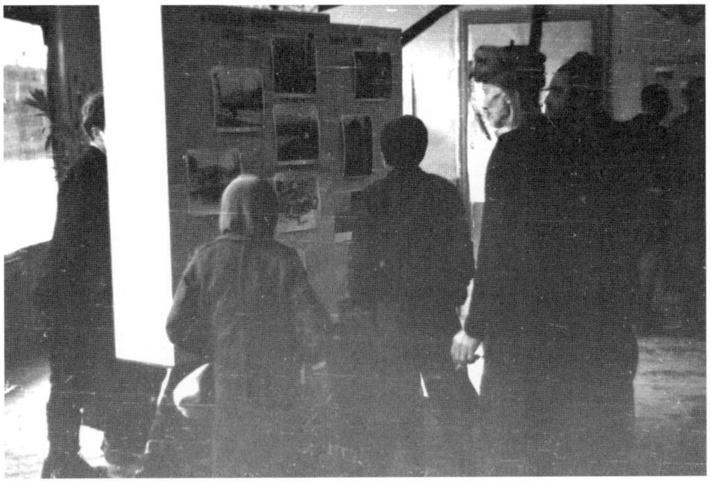

Installation view of one section of the Partisan photography exhibition, held in Livno in honour of the Second Session of the AVNOJ. Photographer unknown. Museum of Yugoslavia, MRNJ III-266.

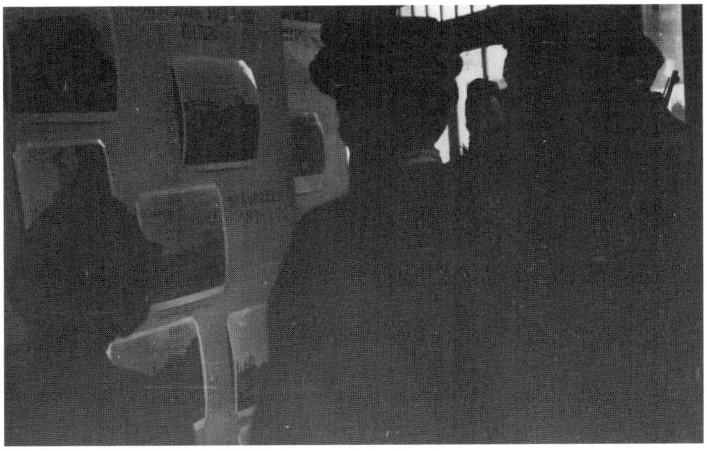

Installation view of Partisan photography exhibition, Livno 1943. Photographer unknown. Museum of Yugoslavia, CKSKJ/MRNJ III-1807.

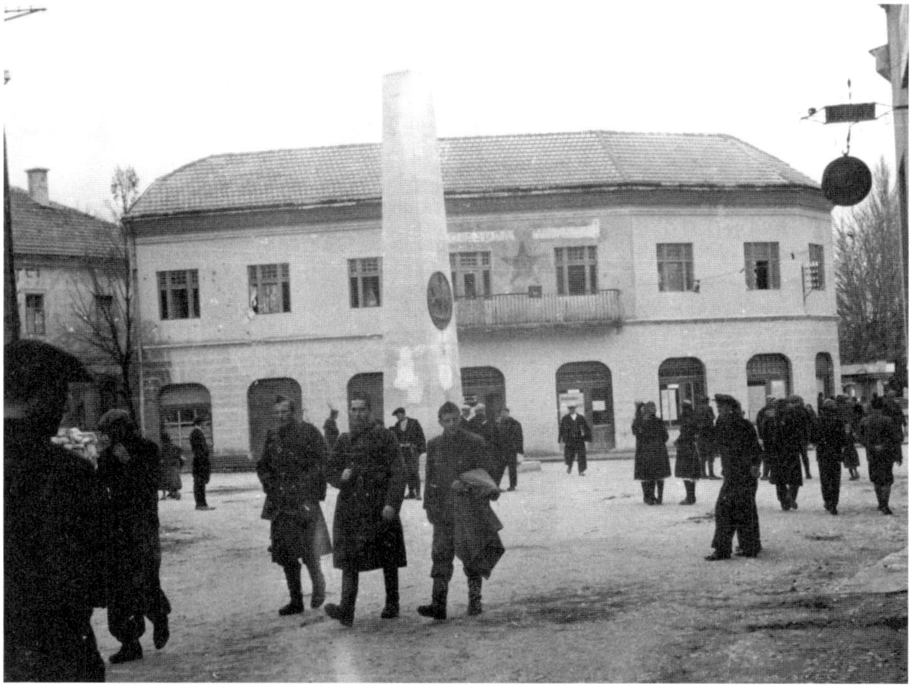

A group of Partisans on the street in Livno, 1943. Photographer unknown.
Museum of Yugoslavia, MRNJ III – 3116.

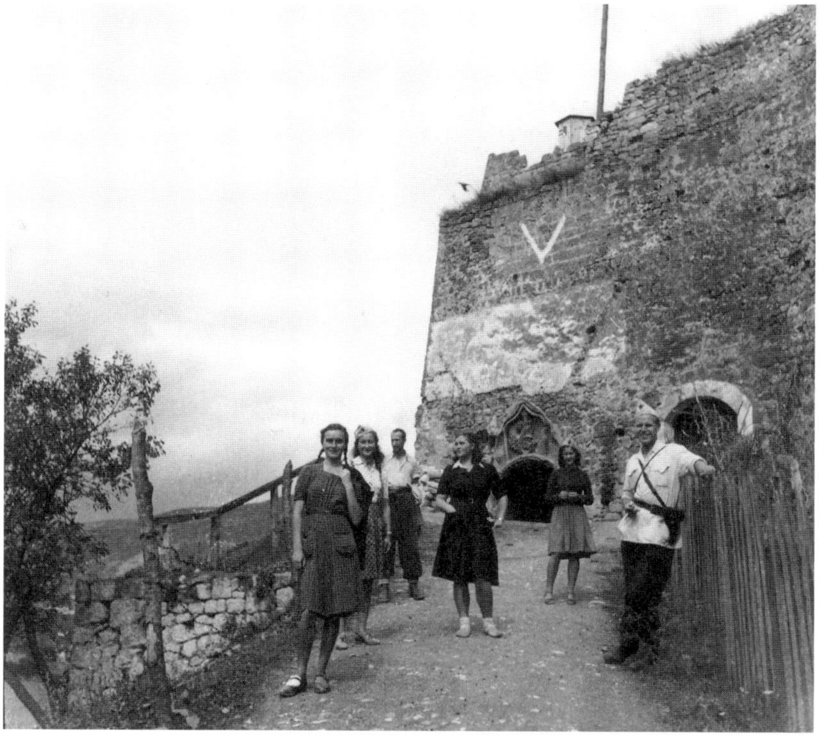

Members of the Theatre of People's Liberation of Yugoslavia in Jajce: Nada Borozan (foreground, left), Mira Afrić, Žorž Skrigin, Jože Rutić, Mira Đerić, Dara Lončar, Vjekoslav Afrić (right), September 1942. Photo: Žorž Skrigin. Museum of Yugoslavia, MRNJ- III – 3459.

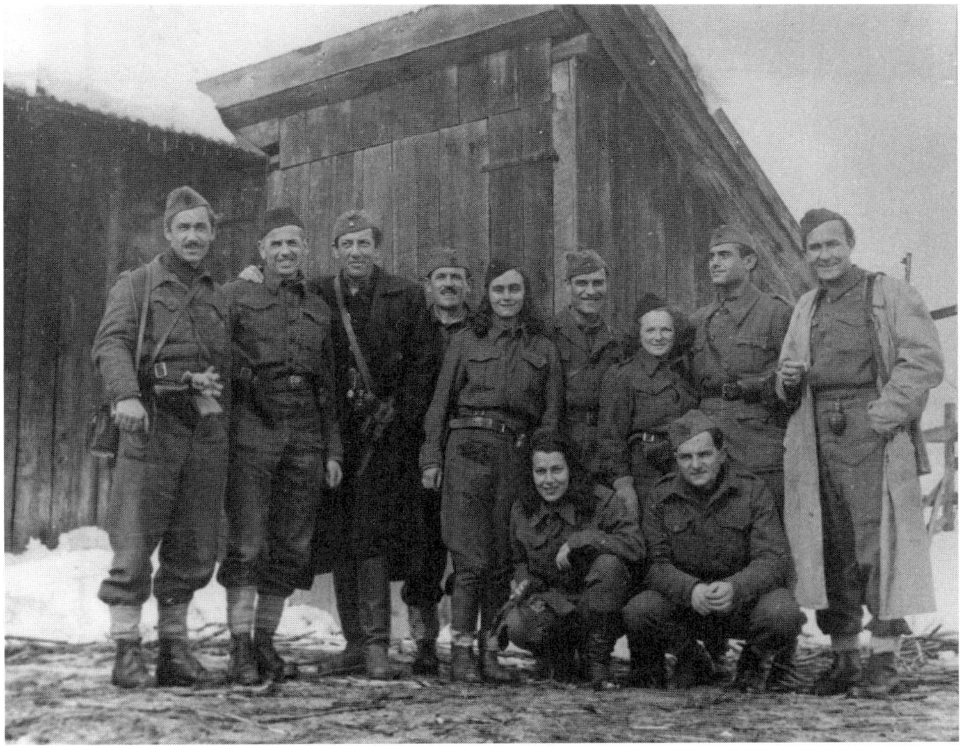

Theatre of People's Liberation at Kozara, December 1943. Photo: Žorž Skrigin (far left). History Museum of Bosnia and Herzegovina, FNOB 6485.

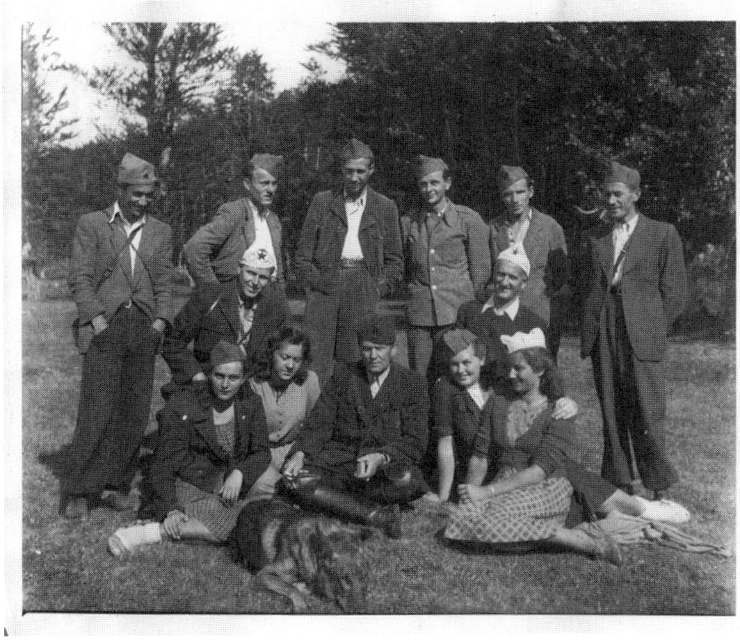

Josip Broz Tito with members of the Theatre of People's Liberation in Mlinište, September 1942. Left of Tito: Mira Đerić and Mira Afrić; right of Tito: Nada Borozan and Dara Lončar; kneeling: Vjekoslav Afrić and Milan Vujković; standing: Žorž Skrigin with unidentified theatre members. Photographer unknown. Museum of Yugoslavia, III-1249.

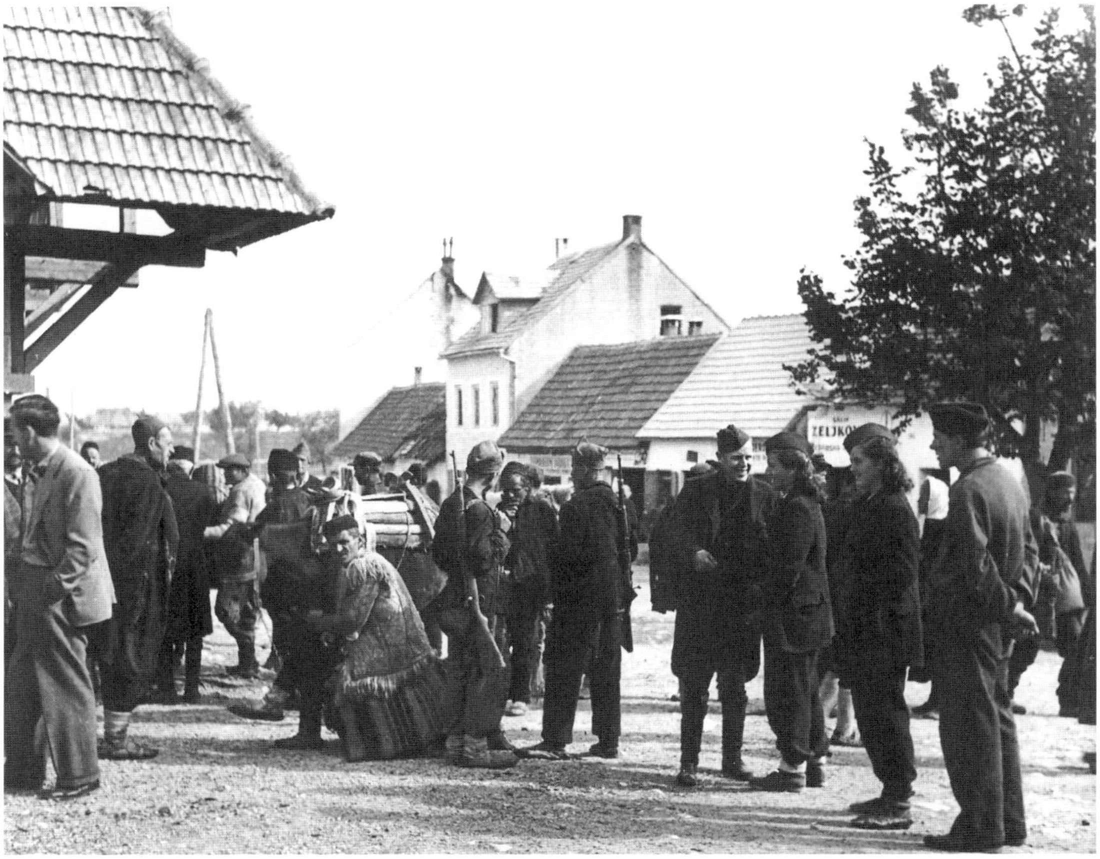

Members of the Theatre of People's Liberation of Yugoslavia, including Mira Afrić, Vjekoslav Afrić and others, in liberated Glamoč on a market day sometime in 1942. Photo: Žorž Skrigin. Museum of Yugoslavia, III-3428.

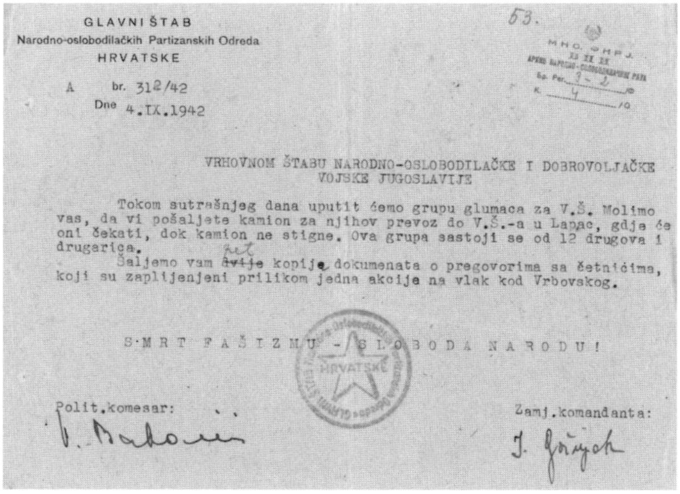

GLAVNI ŠTAB
Narodno-oslobodilačkih Partizanskih Odreda
HRVATSKE

53.

A br. 312/42
Dne 4.IX.1942

VRHOVNOM ŠTABU NARODNO-OSLOBODILAČKE I DOBROVOLJAČKE VOJSKE JUGOSLAVIJE

Tokom sutrašnjeg dana uputit ćemo grupu glumaca za V.Š. Molimo vas, da vi pošaljete kamion za njihov prevoz do V.Š.-a u Lapac, gdje će oni čekati, dok kamion ne stigne. Ova grupa sastoji se od 12 drugova i drugarica.

Šaljemo vam ~~dvije~~ pet kopija dokumenata o pregovorima sa četnicima, koji su zaplijenjeni prilikom jedne akcije na vlak kod Vrbovskog.

S·MRT FAŠIZMU - SLOBODA NARODU!

Polit.komesar: Zamj.komandanta:

General Staff of the People's Liberation Movement of Croatia requests that Supreme Command provides transportation for actors. Military Archive Belgrade, K4 F2

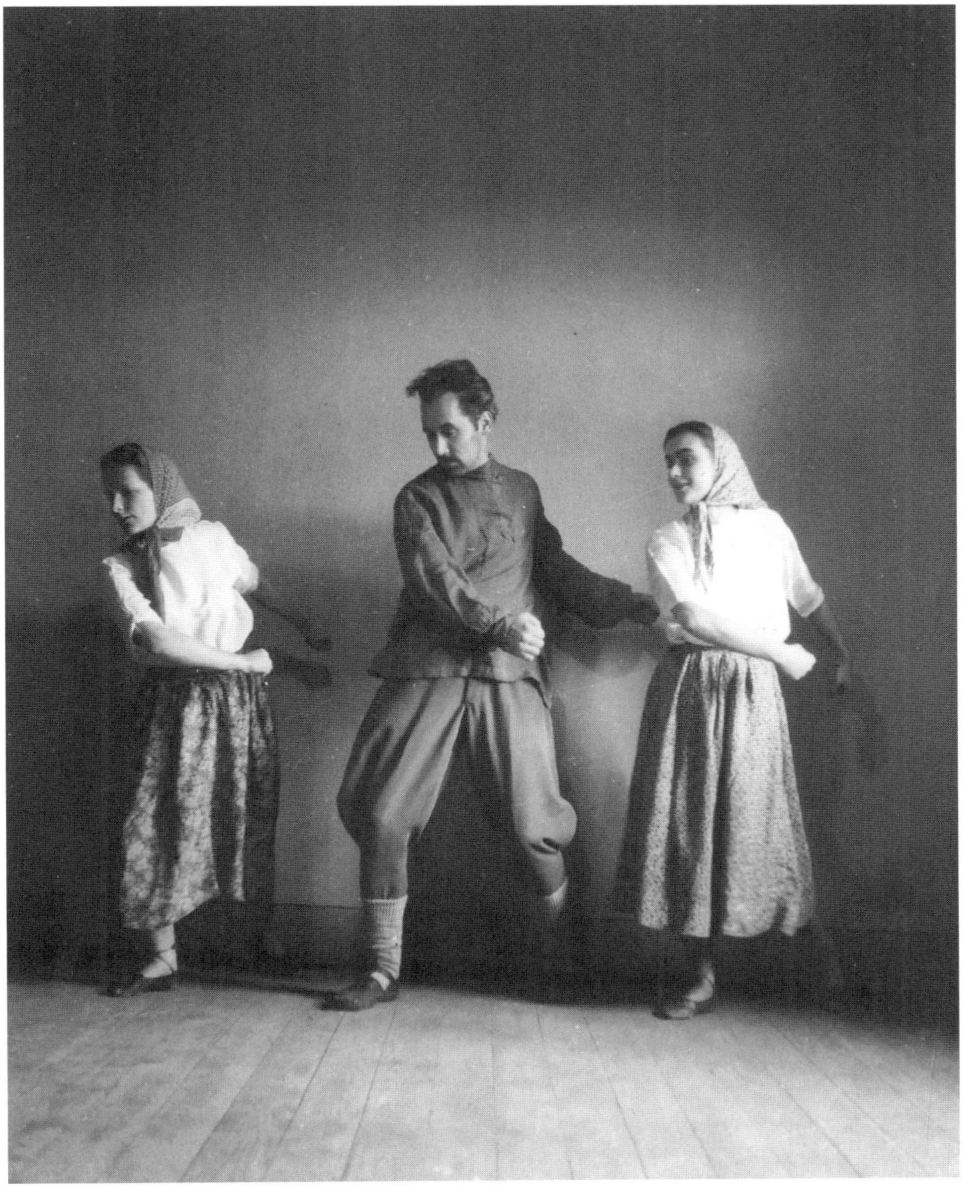

Anika Radošević, Žorž Skrigin and Nada Borozan of the Theatre of People's Liberation of Yugoslavia rehearsing for a ceremony honouring the Second Session of the AVNOJ in Jajce, 1943. Photo: Žorž Skrigin. Museum of Yugoslavia.

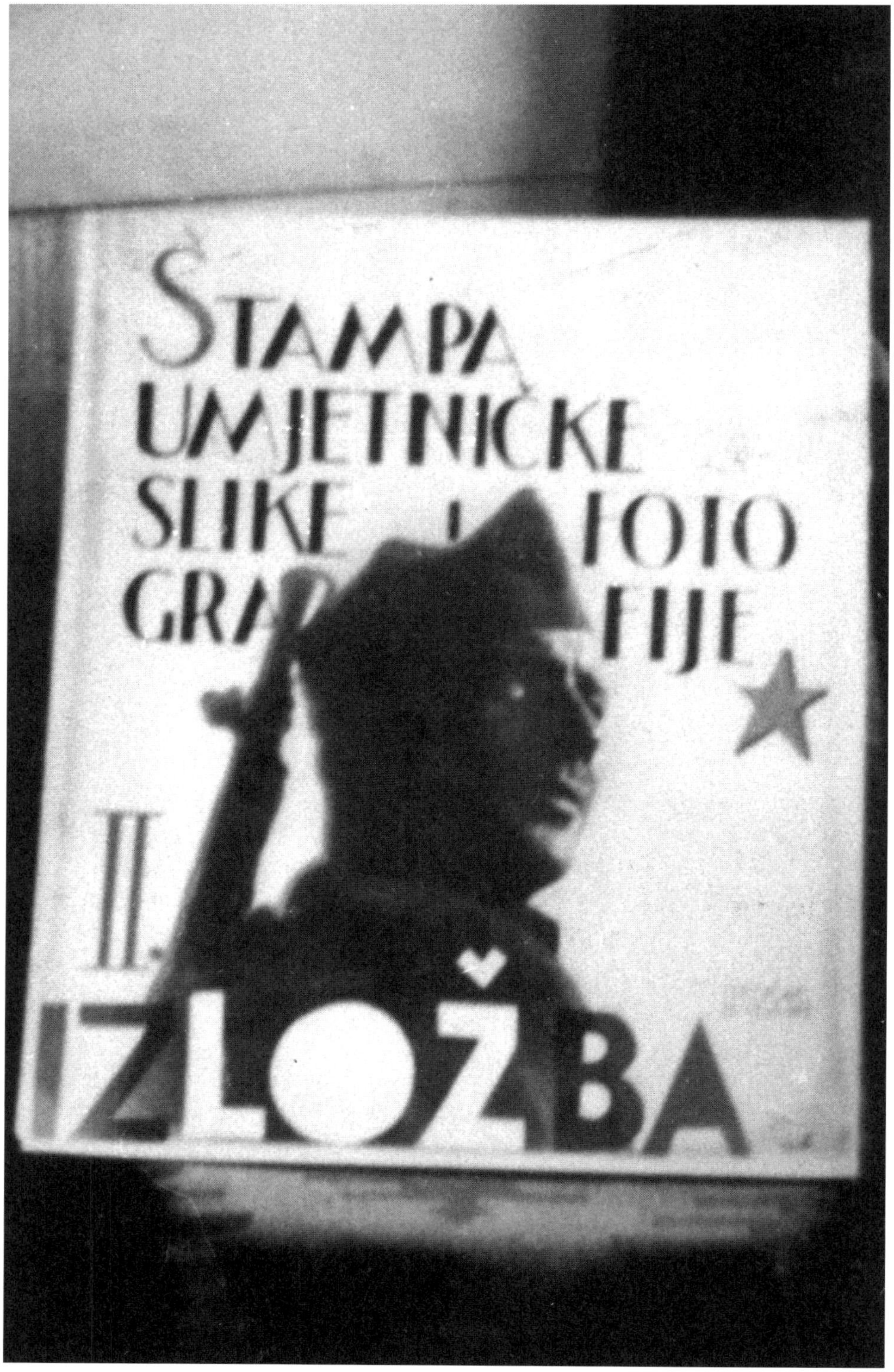

Poster for the Second Exhibition of Pictures and Photographs, Otočac, 11 June 1943.
Photo: Franjo Mosinger. Croatian History Museum, HPM/MRNH-F-3427.

Sic Transit Gloria Mundi: An Actor and a Ballet Dancer as Partisan Photographers

Vjekoslav Afrić's final role at the Croatian State Theatre was playing the eponymous hero in *Faust*. The post-war Croatian director Slobodan Šnajder used Afrić in this role as a template for his 1980s play *Hrvatski Faust* (Croatian Faust), which continues to disturb audiences to this day. The fictional figure of Afrić and the Croatian National Theatre in its present-day form (located on a square that was until recently named Trg maršala Tita: Marshal Tito Square) reveal ideologically charged memories at odds with attempts at collective forgetting. Afrić's 1942 diary entry continues to be relevant today, as it hints at the theatre's social role and speaks of the people in the audience, and of art's emancipatory action:

Liberated Partisan territory was unimaginable without an intense cultural and artistic life. Alongside the formation of the first military units, the first literacy courses, schools, libraries, news posters, print and photo exhibitions, teaching courses and newspapers were organised. Ultimately, almost every larger military unit wanted to have its own art and culture group. Every village in the liberated territory also had its own amateur art and culture group. They sang folk and Partisan songs, played folk games, organised performances, staged dramas, recitations, organised cultural and social evenings [...]. The Lika audience was extremely interested in our performances; we often performed in front of audiences of several thousand people. If news got out that we were holding an event in a certain village, even villagers from surrounding places some distance away would flock to hear the Zagreb actors. There were even audiences from Axis-occupied territory, for whom leaving the territory to attend our performances was a special feat undertaken at great risk.[31]

In the same year, Afrić and Žorž Skrigin began preparations for the theatre production of Branislav Nušić's play, *Sumnjivo lice* (A Suspicious Character). They established the first Partisan ballet, *Okupator* (Occupier), featuring, besides Skrigin himself, the wonderful Anika Radošević, along with Nada Borozan, a brilliant dancer, and Dara Tatalović, with the poet Junus Međedović appearing in an acting role. One of Afrić's diary entries written after a performance of *Sumnjivo lice* on 23 November 1942 (performed before an audience consisting of seventy captured Ustashe-controlled Croatian Home Guards) is telling of the power of Afrić's mind. It also speaks of his spiritual condition and that of his colleagues, and to his position as a cultural worker who left the comfort of the city for a life in the forests with the Partisans. In this situation, reality was much more interesting than art. At a moment in history when life and the stage had swapped places, the performers were compelled to reconsider their role and face those who, unlike them, had been prepared to collaborate:

31 Vjeko Afrić, 'Lika i teatar bez kulisa', in: Šesta proleterska divizija, Đuro Šnajder (ed.), Zagreb 1964, p. 540.

They cheered and applauded as if they were Partisans. There were also a few people from Zagreb known to us among them. After the performance they informed us in detail about the opportunities available in Zagreb, especially in Zagreb theatre. Among these familiar names was also the brother of a ballerina well known to us. He, it was understood, knew all the gossip, intrigue and inside news on the theatre scene. He updated us on every twist and turn in the situation in Zagreb theatre after we had left. Afterwards, I thought a lot about his news, and it was unbelievable how this environment that I had left had now become so alien to me, after being so familiar just a few months ago. Is it really possible that, even today in the middle of the biggest war and revolution, some people can sit peacefully in a restaurant, throw parties at home, act on a stage for an audience that includes occupiers, earn a little something on the side as the musical entertainment at soirées and cabaret performances, chat about gossip and backstage scandals, have flings, speak and recite over announcements on the radio, over the same radio that spouts the biggest lies and abominations, that shamelessly tricks and deceives the entire population, that screams the occupiers' praises and flaunts as loudly as possible their lack of humanity and brutality? Can I, dare I understand all this? If I understood, I would also have to forgive. And what am I supposed to understand? Are they really cut from a different cloth than we are and thus unable to opt for a life like ours? [...] I look at the members of the Home Guard – What? Should I pity them? Should I scorn them? Should I try and understand them? What should I think about my good and respected colleagues in Zagreb? And the more I think about them, the more I feel like this entire psychological process of mine has been turned upside down. Just like in a camera. Instead of understanding them to love them, I love them, and in so doing, I begin to understand them. When this war is over and if we're still alive, and they are too, we'll sit down together in a restaurant or at a party in someone's home and we'll talk about our experiences. They'll talk about their acting successes, affairs and gossip, and we'll talk about our war experiences and [...] draw a line under everything. We will be of interest to each other once again. '*Sic transit* – Gloria Swanson!' as my friend Dubajić would say.[32]

Sic transit gloria mundi (So passes the glory of the world) is Afrić's act of forgiveness to his colleagues, his reconciliation, the supreme gesture of an intellectual, artist and revolutionary rejecting privileges in favour of his own political being and political action, and thereby circumventing Gramscian hatred of a lack of determination in others. Afrić also emphasises his critical review of the role of art itself and the Theatre of People's Liberation, emphasising that within the Partisan movement different, often diametrically opposed attitudes towards art prevailed.[33] This reveals to us a dilemma freed from the dogmatism and moralising that characterises present-day attempts to represent the entire Partisan period in a new light. Uninterested in the limelight or in acting fame, rather than becoming a cynic Afrić serves as an engaged cultural worker who continues to examine the conditions in which he works. From the same diary, we also learn that during Afrić's time in the Partisans, he used a camera that he brought with him from Zagreb, along with several rolls of film, when he left with a group of work colleagues on 22 April 1942. The first group also included Ivka and Joža Rutić and Salko Repak. Milan Vujnović, Zvonimir Cvija and Žorž

32 Vjeko Afrić, 'Sa Kazalištem narodnog oslobođenja u Bihaću', in: *Bihaćka republika*, vol. 1, Nataša Todorović (ed.), Bihać 1965, pp. 513–514.
33 Ibid., p. 525.

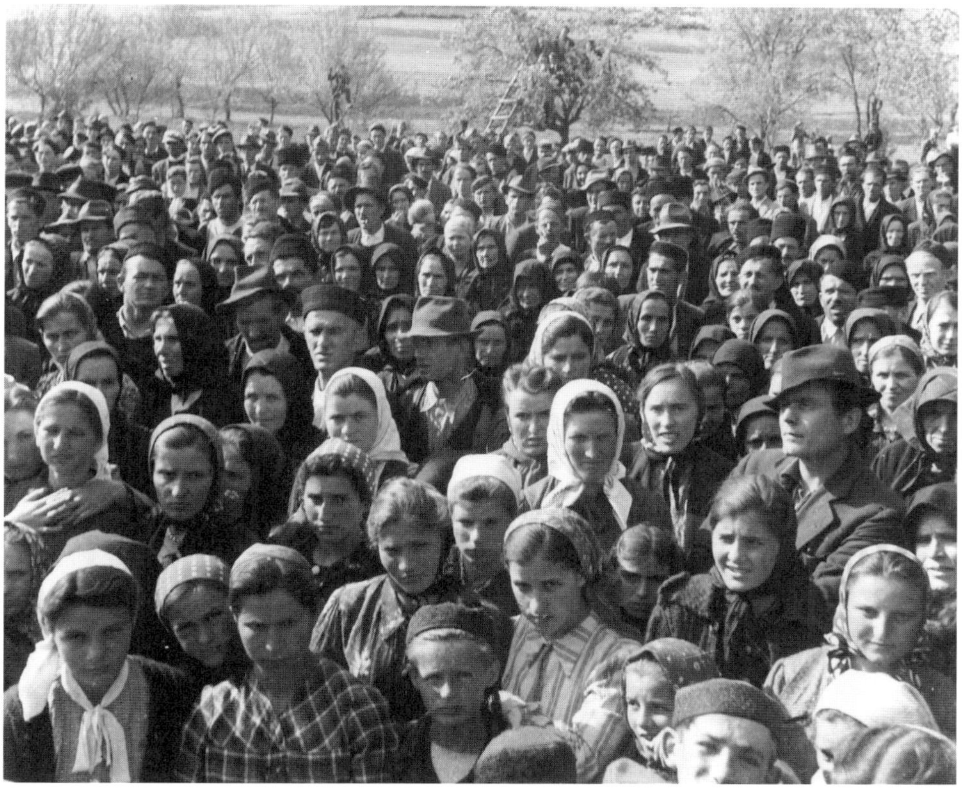

Audience of performance by the Theatre of People's Liberation of Yugoslavia, Lika 1942. Photo: Žorž Skrigin. Museum of Yugoslavia, MRNJ III – 3716.

Skrigin were in a second group that left Zagreb the same day.[34] Upon leaving his Zagreb flat, Žorž Skrigin destroyed one set of his photographs, out of fear that in the hands of the Ustashe, the images might compromise people close to him. He carried several rolls of film with him, and a Rolleiflex camera that he used during his time in the Partisans.

Before the war, Žorž Skrigin had been a prominent member of Fotoklub Zagreb and one of the top prizewinning photographers in the country and on the international stage. While in the Partisans, he was responsible for some of the movement's most important images. In following the First Croatian Proletarian Brigade on the move towards the coast, Skrigin took art photographs at Plitvice Lakes, before later taking the first photographs of combat too. On the road that linked Senj and Novi Vinodolski on the Croatian coast near the island of Krk, the Partisans prepared an ambush at the point where the road passed between the hills and the sea. The brigade's commander, Milan Žeželj, was involved in selecting the best place from which to record the action. Skrigin describes these moments thus:

34 Vjeko Afrić, 'Umjetnici u redovima boraca', in: *Zbornik sjećanja: Zagreb 1941–1945*, vol. 3, Josip Malić (ed.), Zagreb 1984, p. 237.

I set up the camera quickly and got in position so I could photograph as best as possible. The enemy was awfully close by, they were already passing the road beside me – why weren't we firing? I knew that the agreement had been that Banina would give the signal to attack by firing his revolver. Artillery was passing by, then an armoured vehicle – why weren't our forces attacking when this was the best moment to take photographs? I lay motionless so the Italian aide-de-camp couldn't see me; not a sound of human voices, and in the distance just the hum of a motor resounding. All this left me in a state of nervous tension. I was starting to fidget when I suddenly heard a revolver shot, and off the sparkling sea, calm as a mirror, rebounded its loud echo. Confusion broke out. I heard shouts: 'Proletarians advance! Strike!' At that moment I pointed my camera at the attack, when above my head our heavy machine gun shook us, having

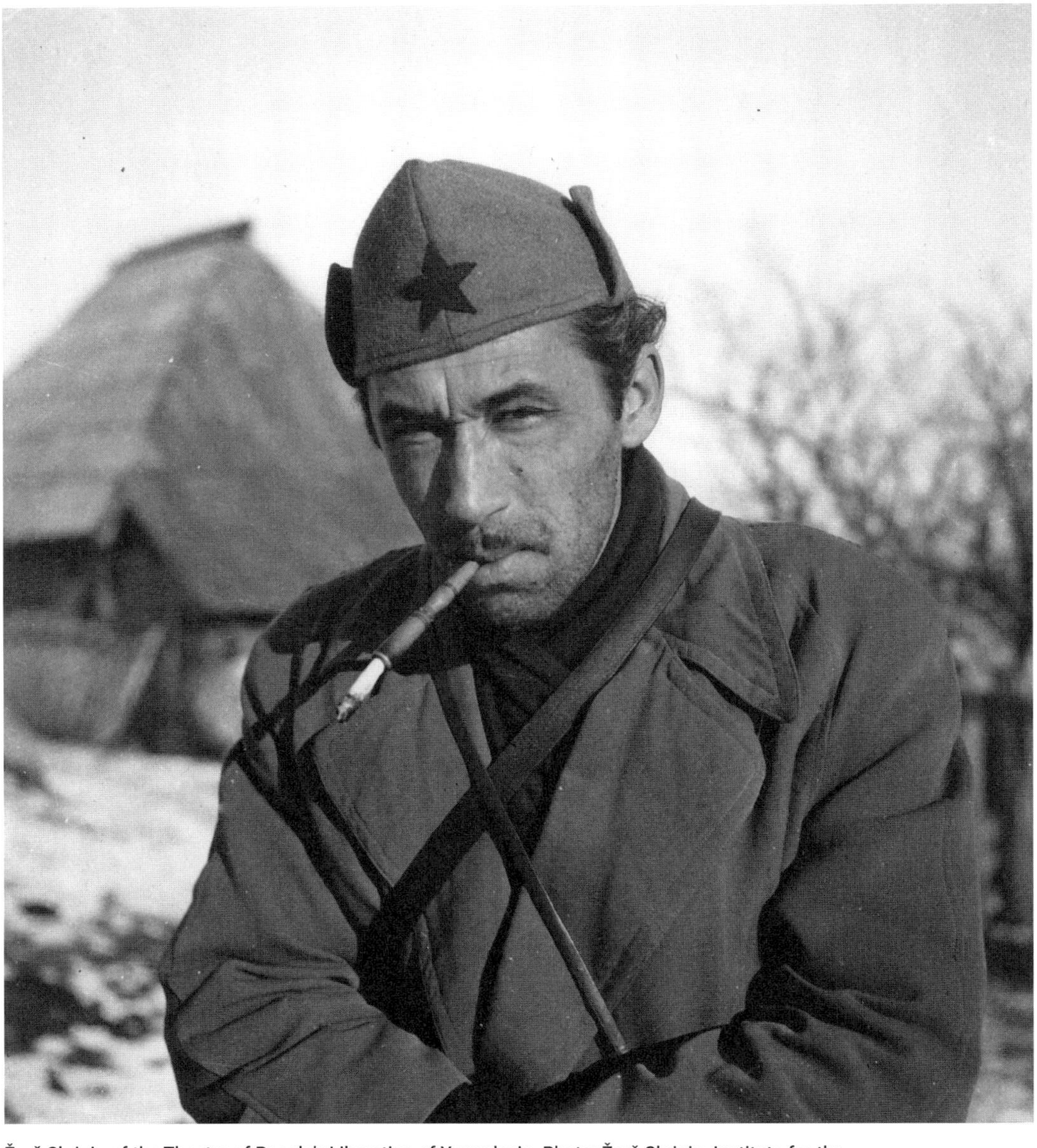

Žorž Skrigin of the Theatre of People's Liberation of Yugoslavia. Photo: Žorž Skrigin. Institute for the History of the Workers' Movement of the People of Yugoslavia, accession no. unknown.

taken up position a few metres behind me. This was my first mission. Bullets whistled above my head; it was the first time I'd heard anything like this and the first time I'd smelt the scent of gunpowder. Instinctively, I pressed my head to the ground, lower and lower, thinking: What if I'm killed on my first mission – and worse – by one of our own bullets? But then a vanity awoke in me – Am I really unable to record what's happening down there on the road? I turned the *Rolleiflex* upside down, held my arms above the top of the shelter, and observed the events on the road in the reflex mirror and thought to myself: I only hope our machine gun hits me in the hand rather than in the head![35]

The Partisan unit suffered no losses in this ambush, while on the Italian side two artillery pieces were destroyed, and three light machine guns, numerous fire arms, thousands of rounds of ammunition and one revolver were seized, with Skrigin subsequently claiming the revolver for himself.[36] As a member of the Theatre of People's Liberation, under the control of the Supreme Command of the People's Liberation Army and Partisan Detachments of Yugoslavia, Skrigin was well placed as a photographer – he was less exposed to front-line combat and well equipped with photographic supplies. In the Croatian village of Mlinište, he was one of the first to photograph Josip Broz Tito. He was constantly on the move with the main body of the People's Liberation Army and socialised with the poet Ivan Goran Kovačić, whom he photographed right before Kovačić's death in east Bosnia after the Fifth Offensive (Battle of Sutjeska).[37] His Zagreb war comrade Vjekoslav Afrić saved the text of Kovačić's poem, 'Jama' (The Pit), which he first read publicly to the injured members of the First Proletarian Brigade. In these verses, describing the weight of war and pain, the poet hinted at his own death:

Began to sob and never have ceased yet,
With throat alone, for now I have no eyes;
With heart alone, for my tears the knife
Of murderers has gorged away. I am deprived
Of eyes to see you, and that strength is gone.

But who are you, and whence? I only know
That your light warms me. All – Sing! for I can feel
At last I live; even though I'm dying now,
This in sweet Liberty, with Vengeance stolen
From death. Your singing gives my eyes back light,
Strong as our People, and our sun as bright.[38]

35 Žorž Skrigin, *Rat i pozornica*, Belgrade 1968, pp. 22–23.
36 Ibid., p. 163.
37 Ibid.
38 Ivan Goran Kovačić, *The Pit. Poem, 1943: With plates and concluding remarks by the translator Alec Brown, trans. Alec Brown, Zagreb 1961.*

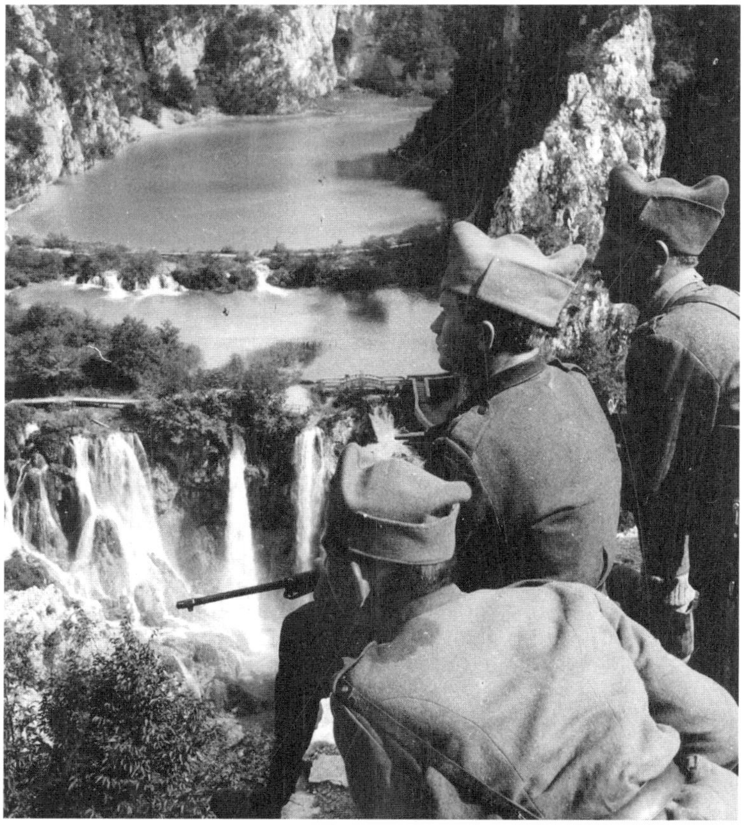

Partisans keeping watch, Plitvice Lakes, 1942. Photo: Žorž Skrigin.
Museum of Yugoslavia, accession no. unknown.

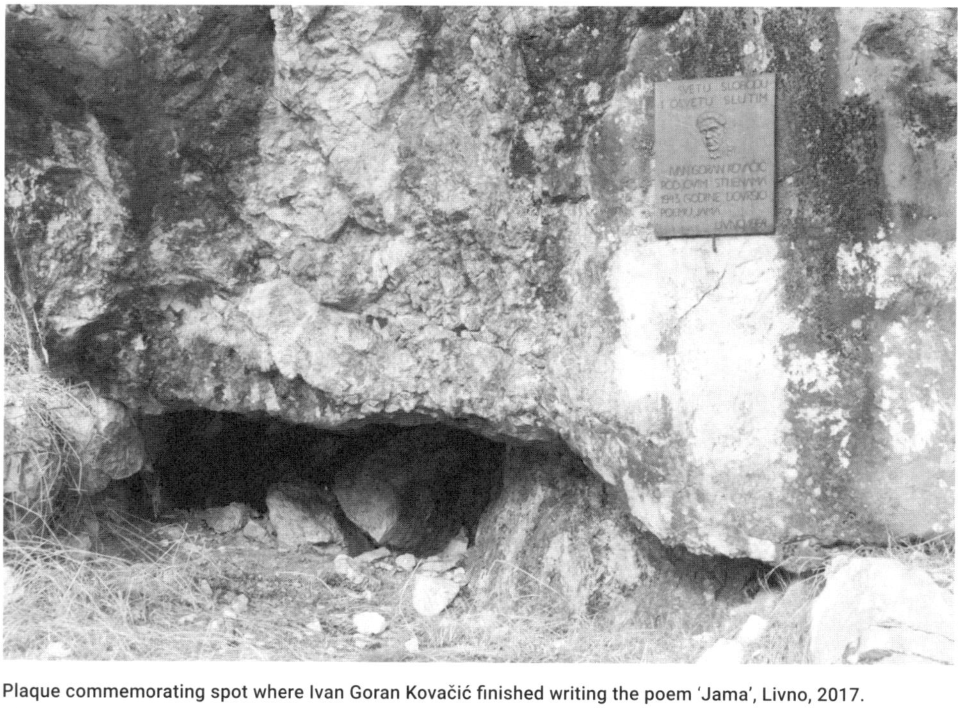

Plaque commemorating spot where Ivan Goran Kovačić finished writing the poem 'Jama', Livno, 2017.
Photo: Davor Konjikušić.

Except for Skrigin who left for the battlefield, most members of Fotoklub Zagreb remained in Zagreb. Milutin Mudrinić-Mudri, a member of the club from 1936 who worked as a teacher of Croatian, Latin and gymnastics – a polyglot who spoke eight languages – was killed together with his oldest son Veljko in Jasenovac in 1943. Just a few of his photographs have survived. He mostly taught literature at the Second Classical Grammar School of Zagreb,[39] and later at the Third Boys' Secondary School (*realna gimnazija*). He was well known for cultivating a love of socially engaged phrases among his pupils, saying to them: '"Give me your hand, worker!" – Now that's real poetry for you, children, not the dilettante kind [...].'[40]

The First Group of Cultural Workers in Occupied Europe

Although postponed a year because of an enemy offensive, the First Congress of Cultural Workers of Croatia was held in the small Croatian town of Topusko from 25–27 June 1944. This was a unique gathering in occupied Europe, of exceptional importance in the development of Partisan photography. As part of the congress, an exhibition of paintings and photographs was held on the evening of 26 June.[41]

In Otočac, the war-photography unit of the propaganda department of the ZAVNOH was formed,[42] founded by Hugo Fischer Ribarić – a photographer from Crikvenica, together with Elvira Kohn and Đurđa Koren (née Šipušić), who were among the few female Partisan photographers. Other members of the unit included the journalist and publicist Mahmud Konjhodžić, film lab technician Slavica Biluš and graphic designer Karlo Nađ.[43] Ribarić was responsible for leading the propaganda department at the ZAVNOH.

The Partisan Mladen Iveković also took photographs to document the activities of the ZAVNOH. He was a well-known lawyer and pre-war member of the Communist Party of Yugoslavia from 1934. He helped set up the newspaper *Pregled* and was a member of the editorial board of *Novi list*, *Odjek* and *Naše novine*. Early in the war, in January 1942, he was imprisoned in Jasenovac concentration camp. The Partisans managed to get him released, however, in a prisoner exchange eight months into his incarceration. As a member of the AVNOJ Executive Committee, the main editor of the daily *Vjesnik* and head of the propaganda department of the ZAVNOH, Iveković had the opportunity to take photographs all over Croatia and in Bosnia and Herzegovina. His photographs of Vladimir Nazor, Dr Ivan Ribar and Ivan Goran Kovačić deserve a special mention. The selection staff of the photo-

39 HDA (Croatian State Archives), collection 216 (MNP NDH), box. 680, no. 8693.
40 Pavle Jakšić, *Nad uspomenama*, vol. 1, Belgrade 1990, p. 49.
41 Prvi kongres kulturnih radnika Hrvatske, Topusko, 25–27 June 1944. ČSP, 8/1976. no. 2/3, 16–17; see also Drago Roksandić, 'Prvi kongres kulturnih radnika Hrvatske (Topusko, 25.–27. lipnja 1944): Iskustvo i aproprijacije', in: *Intelektualci i rat 1939–1947. Zbornik radova s Desničinih susreta 2011*, Drago Roksandić and Ivana Cvijović Javorina (eds.), Zagreb 2012, p. 112.
42 Dušan Graovac, 'Organizacija i djelatnost NOO-a u Lici između Drugog i Trećeg zasjedanja ZAVNOH-a', in: *Treća godina Narodnooslobodilačkog rata na području Karlovca, Korduna, Like, Pokuplja i Žumberka*, Đuro Zatezalo (ed.), Karlovac 1977, p. 745.
43 Branka Hlevnjak and Rhea Ivanuš, *Hrvatska antiratna fotografija: Prvi svjetski, Drugi svjetski i Domovinski rat. Zagreb: Udruga za promicanje oblikovanja i umjetnosti*, Ljubljana 2008, p. 113.

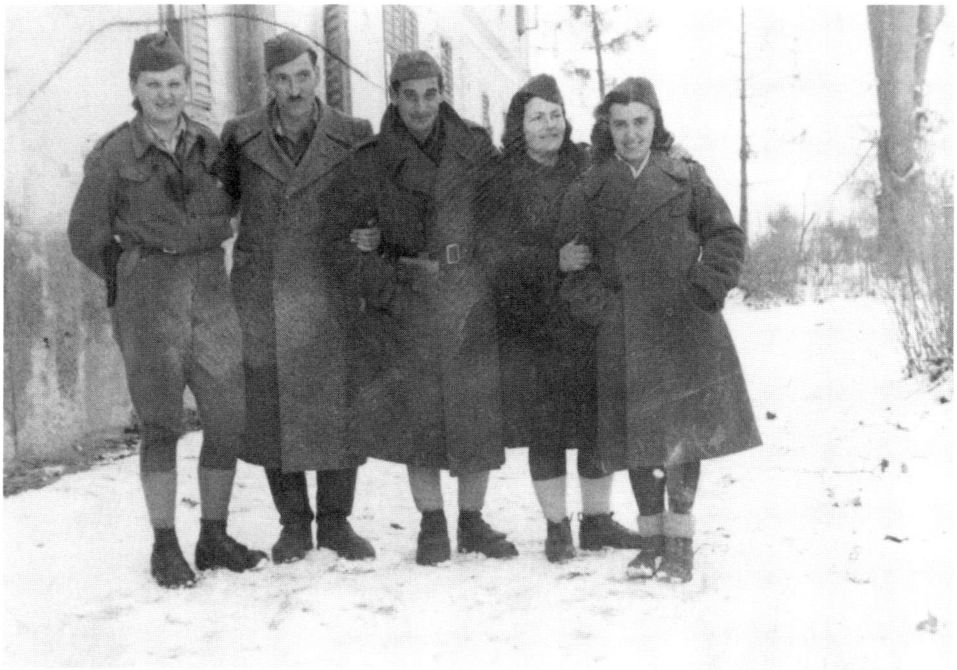

Members of the photography unit of propaganda department at ZAVNOH: Đurđa Koren (left), Karlo Nađ, Hugo Fischer Ribarić, Slavica Biluš and Elvira Kohn (right), Topusko, Autumn 1944. Croatian History Museum, HPM/MRNH-A-2602-f33-27a.

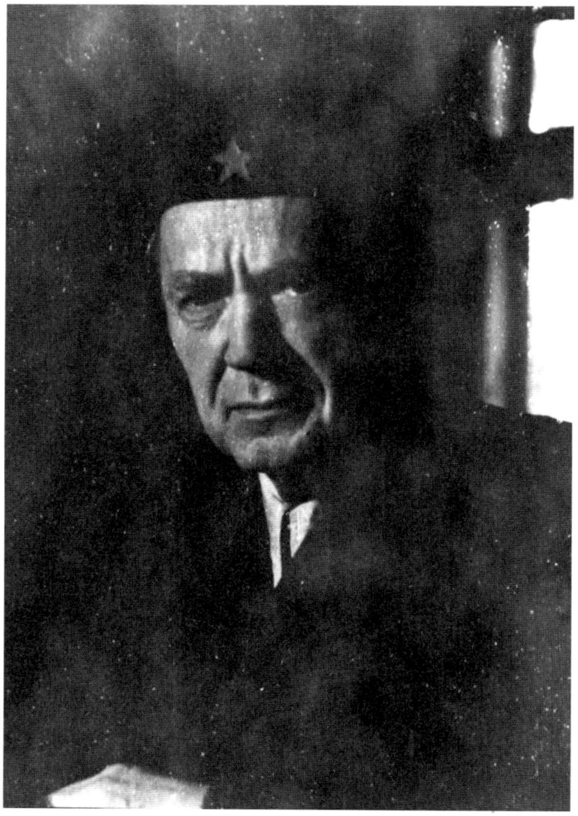

Dr Ivan Ribar, chairman of the AVNOJ. Otočac, 1943. Photo: photography unit at ZAVNOH. Croatian History Museum, HPM/MRNH-A-2601-f90-30.

graphy exhibition in Topusko faced numerous problems because the photographs were not sorted by theme and lacked captions. Recently taken images from the session of the Croatian ZAVNOH and the Unitary People's Liberation Front were missing. They lacked basic equipment and an enlarger, which Hugo Fischer Ribarić had supposedly left in a hideaway.[44]

A similar congress had been held in the town of Hvar two years before. That conference, held on 19 December 1942 for the cultural workers of Dalmatia, was organised for authors, composers, architects and artists. As the ZAVNOH developed further, at its third session it set up departments for administration and law, public health, the economy, education, social politics and propaganda – organised along the lines of the People's Liberation Committees, from the county level upwards.[45] This laid the foundations for the post-war emergence of regional Museums of the People's Liberation. On 3 September 1944, all area and district-based People's Liberation Committees received an order demanding that they gather materials for museum displays, including photographs they considered of special significance.[46] The prominent art historian and then curator of the Archaeological Museum in Split, Cvito Fisković, invited people at the newspaper *Slobodna Dalmacija* to begin gathering everything from water pipes and medical supplies to photographs.[47]

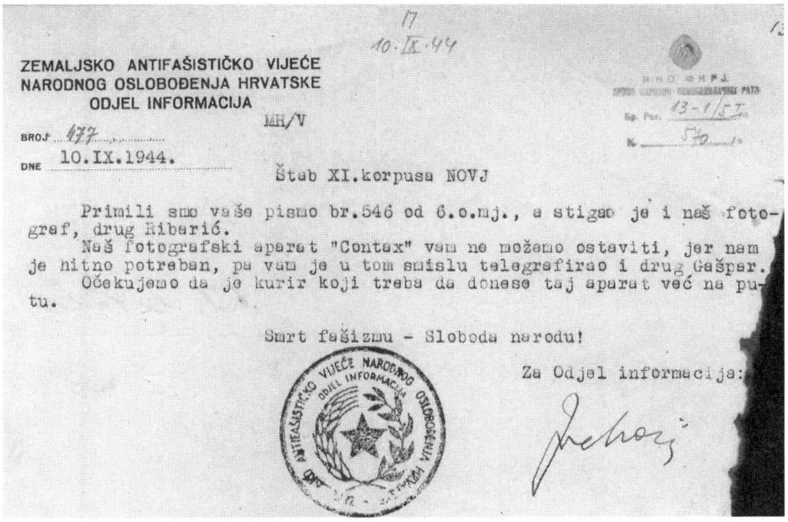
17
10.IX.44

ZEMALJSKO ANTIFAŠISTIČKO VIJEĆE
NARODNOG OSLOBOĐENJA HRVATSKE
ODJEL INFORMACIJA

MH/V

BROJ 477

DNE 10.IX.1944.

Štab XI.korpusa NOVJ

Primili smo vaše pismo br.546 od 6.o.mj., a stigao je i naš fotograf, drug Ribarić.

Naš fotografski aparat "Contex" vam ne možemo ostaviti, jer nam je hitno potreban, pa vam je u tom smislu telegrafirao i drug Gašpar.

Očekujemo da je kurir koji treba da donese taj aparat već na putu.

Smrt fašizmu – Sloboda narodu!

Za Odjel informacija:

Dispatch from ZAVNOH to the Sixth Corps of the People's Liberation Army of Yugoslavia about the lack of photographic equipment. Military Archive Belgrade, NOVJ-K570 F5i 13.

44 HDA (Croatian State Archives), ZAVNOH II/Propaganda Department (Information Section), June 1944, box. 30/206, NV-32/2905; see also Roksandić 2012 (see note 41), p. 115.

45 *Sabor u Topuskom. Treće zasjedanje Zemaljskog antifašističkog vijeća narodnog oslobođenja Hrvatske*, Zagreb 1945, p. 51.

46 *Zemaljsko antifašističko vijeće narodnog oslobođenja Hrvatske, zbornik dokumenata 1944*, Zagreb 1975.

47 Vladimir Dedijer, *Dnevnik III 1941–1944*, Rijeka 1981, p. 204.

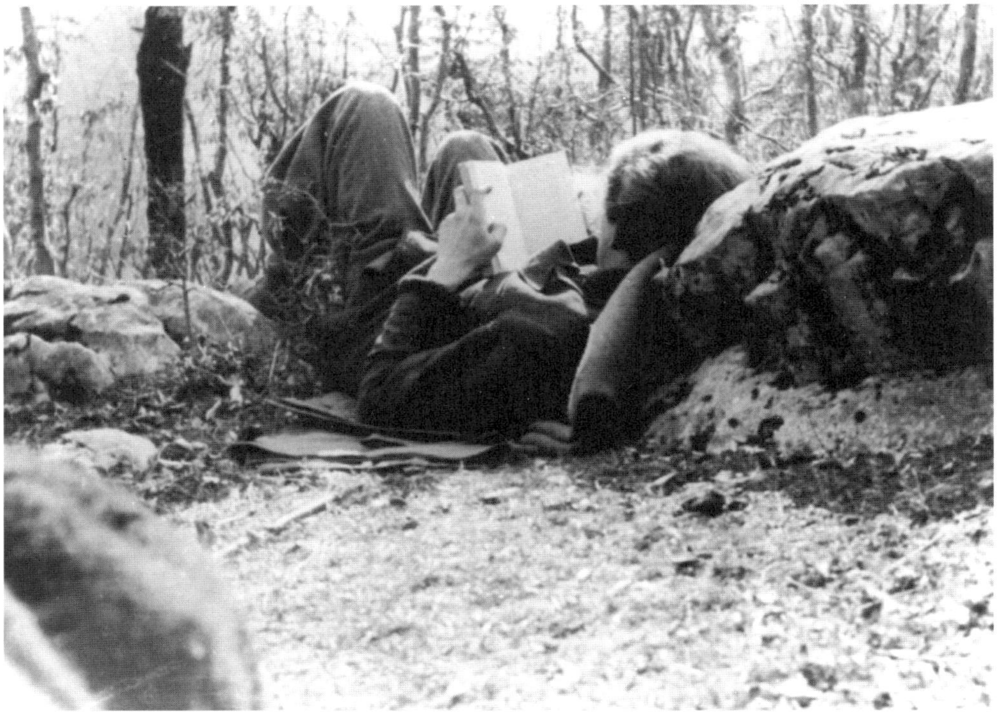

The poet Ivan Goran Kovačić reading. Photo: Mladen Iveković. History Museum of Bosnia and Herzegovina, FNOB 6440.

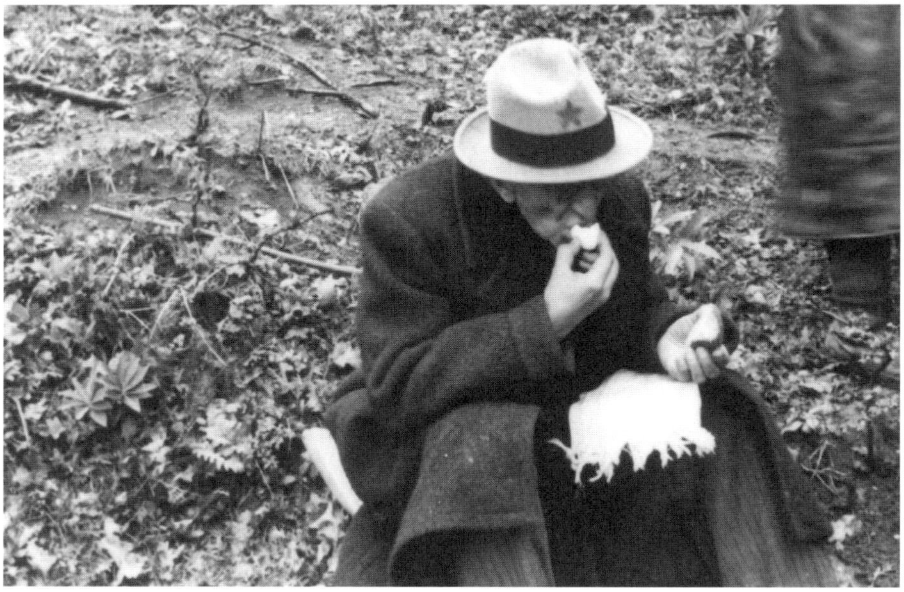

The poet Vladimir Nazor eating an apple. Photo: Mladen Iveković. Croatian History Museum, HPM/MRNH-A-6337/135.

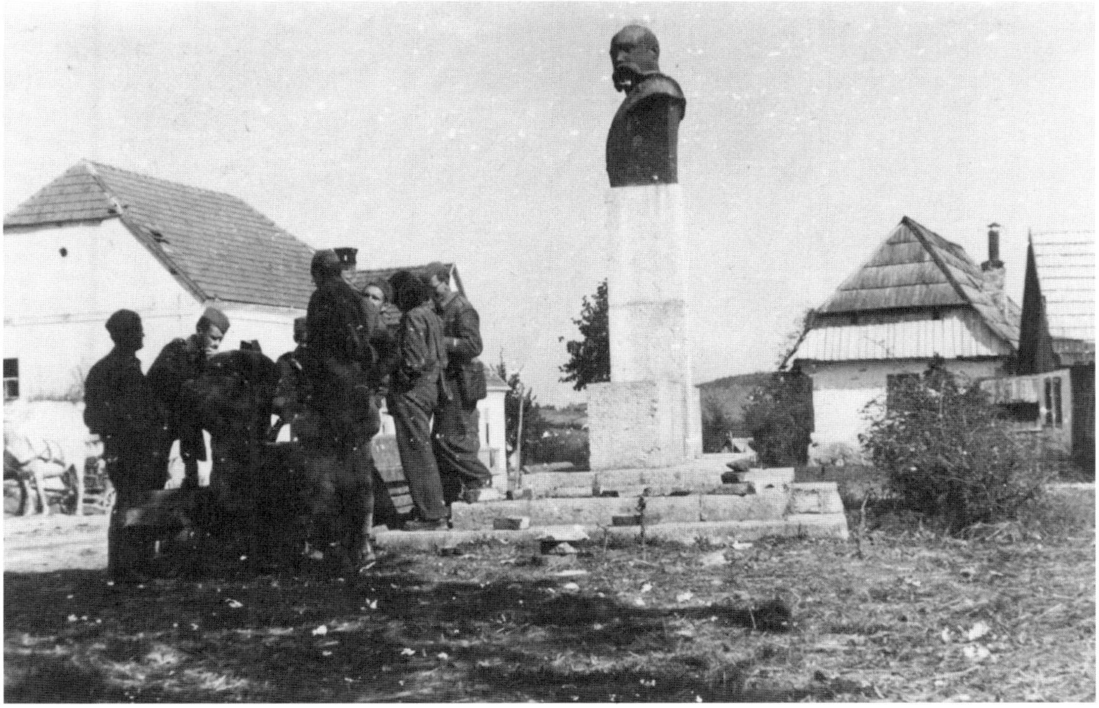

Partisans gathered beneath a statue of Eugen Kvaternik, Rakovica, summer 1944. Photo: Photography unit of ZAVNOH. Croatian History Museum, HPM/MRNH-A-2601-f129–7.

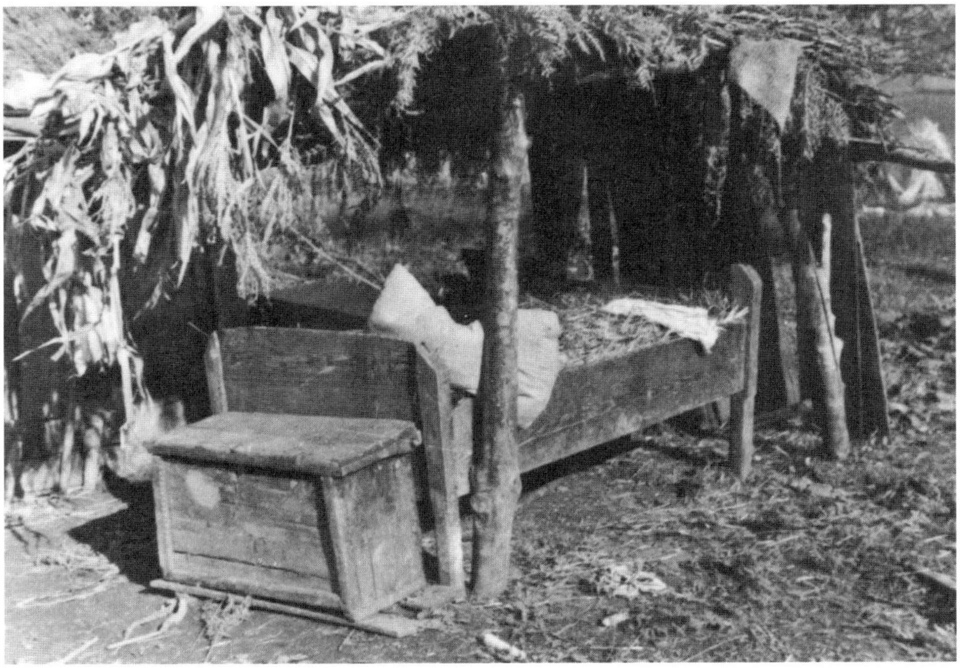

Makeshift dwelling at Kordun, 1944. Photo: Photography unit of ZAVNOH. Croatian History Museum, HPM/MRNH-2602 f88–34a.

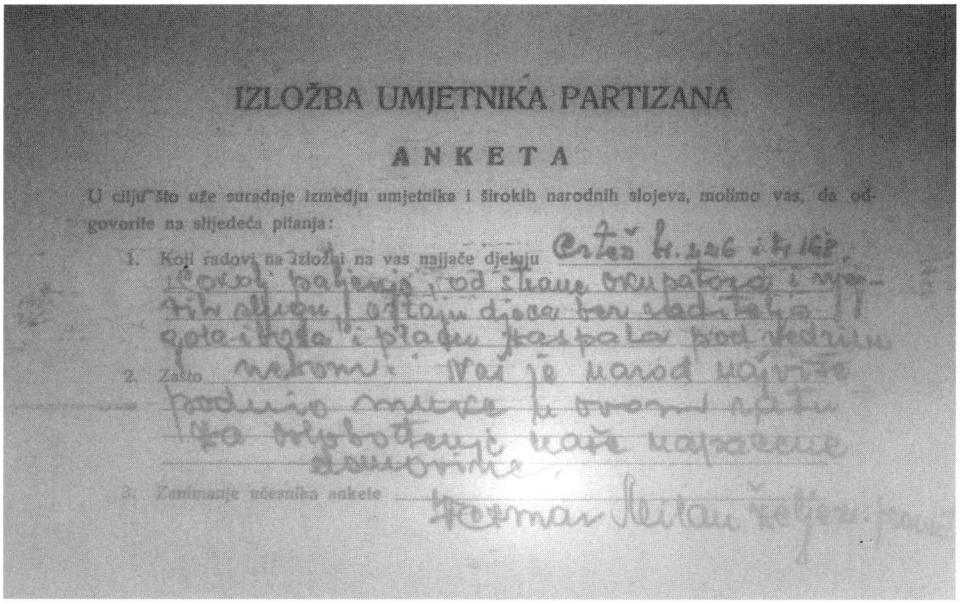

IZLOŽBA UMJETNIKA PARTIZANA

ANKETA

U cilju što uže suradnje između umjetnika i širokih narodnih slojeva, molimo vas, da odgovorite na slijedeća pitanja:

1. Koji radovi na izložbi na vas najjače djeluju Crtež br. 226 i br. 168,
[illegible] paljenja, od strane okupatora i njegovih slugu, ostaju djeca bez roditelja [illegible] i plaču [illegible] pod vedrim nebom.

2. Zašto Naš je narod najviše podnio muke u ovom ratu za oslobođenje naše napaćene domovine

3. Zanimanje učesnika ankete [illegible] seljak

Visitor survey feedback card. Croatian State Archives, ZAVNOH Archives.

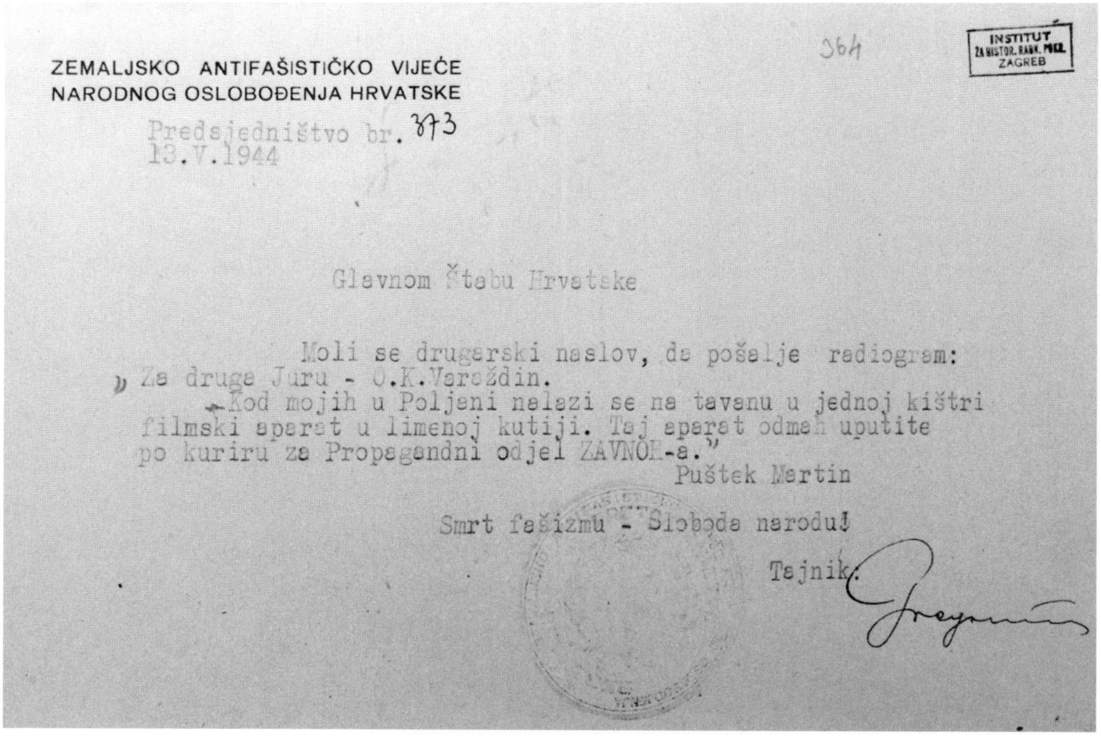

ZEMALJSKO ANTIFAŠISTIČKO VIJEĆE
NARODNOG OSLOBOĐENJA HRVATSKE

364

INSTITUT
ZA HISTOR. RADN. POKR.
ZAGREB

Predsjedništvo br. 373
13.V.1944

Glavnom Štabu Hrvatske

Moli se drugarski naslov, da pošalje radiogram:
„Za druga Juru - O.K.Varaždin.
„Kod mojih u Poljani nalazi se na tavanu u jednoj kištri filmski aparat u limenoj kutiji. Taj aparat odmah uputite po kuriru za Propagandni odjel ZAVNOH-a."
Puštek Martin

Smrt fašizmu - Sloboda narodu!

Tajnik:

Dispatch informing the General Staff of Croatia of the discovery of a camera in an attic and the order to send it directly to the ZAVNOH's Propaganda Department. Croatian State Archives, ZAVNOH Archives.

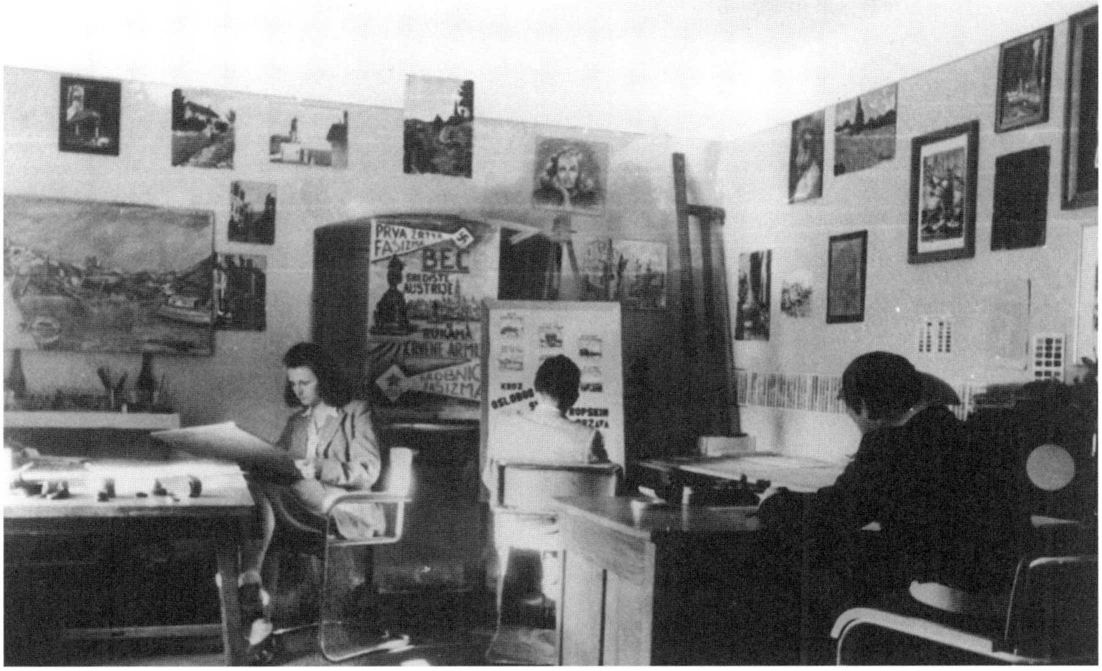

The ZAVNOH's picture archive and news desk, Dubrovnik, 1945. Photo: Nikola Rubčić.
Croatian History Museum HPM/MRNH-F-8259.

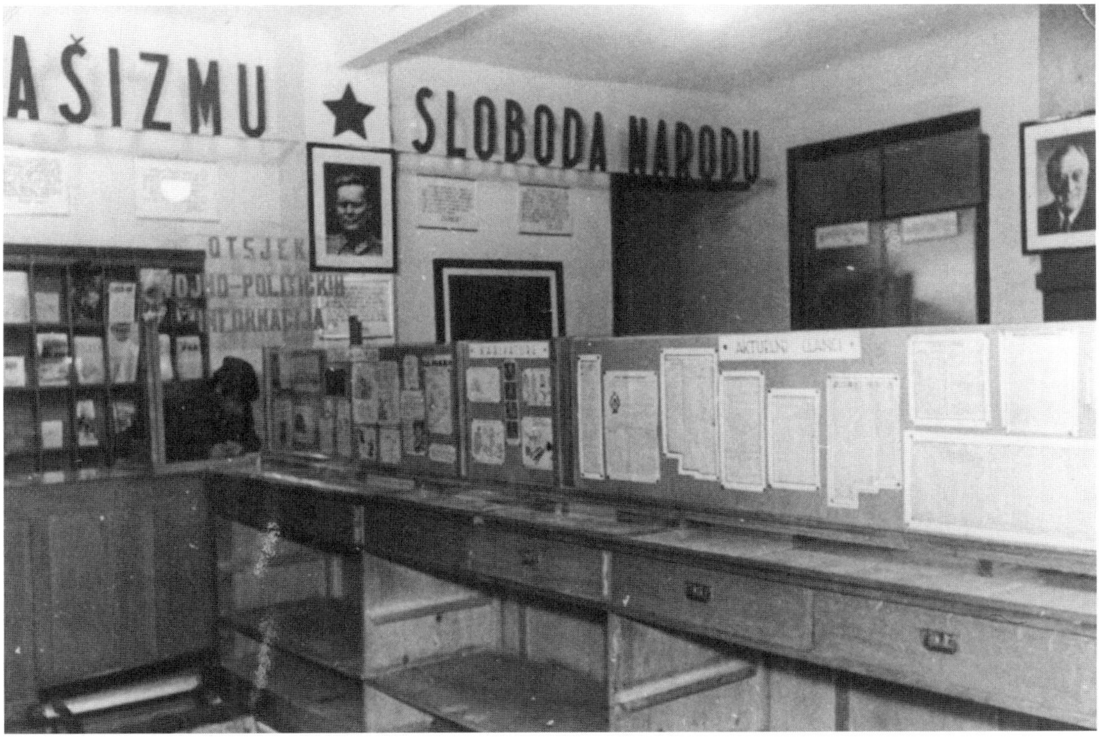

Information Office Exhibition, Dubrovnik, 1945. Photo: Nikola Rupčić. Croatian History Museum, HPM/MRNH-8247.

Franjo Mosinger's Photo Diary

After the war, many photographs were preserved in photo albums, such as Nikola Rubčić's *Rad odjela informacija u Dubrovniku* (Work of the Dubrovnik Information Department),[48] while the Zagreb photographer and Partisan Franjo Mosinger made a personal photo diary combining photography and text. This is a unique and distressing eye-witness account of his time in the Partisans, which leads us through his Partisan journey and work:

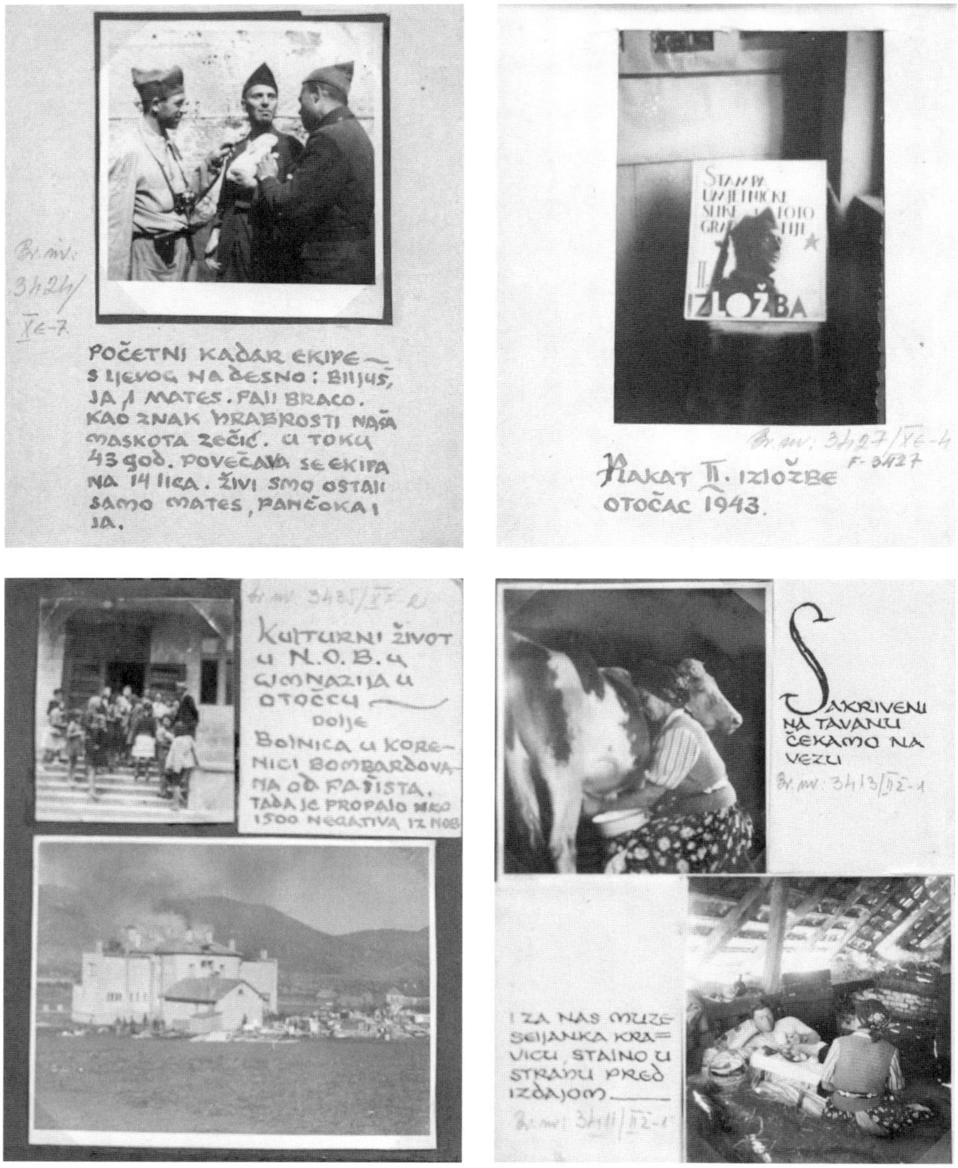

Excerpts from Franjo Mosinger's diary. Croatian History Museum.

48 Hlevnjak/Ivanuš 2008 (see note 18), p. 114.

In early spring in the fateful year of 1943, comrade Jovica Trzun led me to the Partisans. [...] From the village of Borčec outside Stenjevec, we set off beneath the Zagreb hills, passing through the village of Sesvete. We were really roughing it – I got to know the woods, its beauty and its horror. [...] At a house in Turopolje, we found a shelter on the next stretch. A villager, our loyal friend, put himself in mortal danger by helping us. [...] Hidden in the attic, we were waiting for our connection. Behind us, a village woman was milking a cow. Constantly in fear of betrayal [...]. As fate would have it, three hours after arriving in the village, an Ustashe formation showed up. It turned out their headquarters was in a neighbouring house. It was as if we were mice caught in a trap. For eight days we lived hidden in the shadows. We expected the Ustashe to enter the barn beneath us at any moment. And on the third day, they came in to requisition a cow. They didn't notice us.

From then on, the village woman barely dared enter the barn. They were all scared to death. We couldn't stay forever. [...] Day eight. [...] We dressed as villagers and went to the village wood. We passed the Ustashe guards unperturbed. Through an opening in the hayloft, I took photos of this scene right before our departure. Our host family's daughter didn't understand the danger her entire family were in, and she spent the time playing, without a care in the world. [...] At night we walked on further. Child guides led us. Every five kilometres one would take over from the other. At twilight they led us to a group in the woods. Just ten kilometres outside Zagreb, the heart of 'Independent Croatia', were dozens of Partisan 'saboteurs'.

The commander received us in high spirits. 'In two to three hours things'll get rough', he told us. 'You'll have your work cut out, you'll see!'

We camped out on the ground. Around us lay packets of paper, typewriters, pencils – all seized the day before from a nearby county. At 10 a.m. we got up and travelled two kilometres to a railway track, not far from Odra. The commander had put wires on the line. The train passed over them and with a loud crash, it flew off the tracks; the locomotive, the trailing tender and two carriages fell to the side. From one of the carriages, distraught faces ablaze with fear. [...] A month passed. Otočac became the liberated territory's main town. A team of war painters was established under my leadership.[49]

Female Photographers in the Partisan Movement

Elvira Kohn, one of the few female Partisan photographers, also worked in Croatia. She began her photography career in 1932 in the Dubrovnik studio Foto Jadran, owned by Miho Ercegović. She took commercial photographs while working for him, and her art photography was influenced by the New Objectivity. Of Jewish heritage, she was fired from the studio after Ercegović caved in to pressure from his business partner after the founding of the Independent State of Croatia. She continued to work for him in secret, however.[50] Just before her death in 2003, Elvira Kohn gave her final interview to the Vienna-based Institut für jüdische Geschichte Österreichs, in which she said:

49 Text from Franjo Mosinger's original photo diary, which is stored in the Croatian History Museum.
50 Lea Šiljak, 'Elvira Kohn', in: *centropa*, URL: http://www.centropa.org/biography/elvira-kohn#During%20the%20War (accessed 30 May 2021).

Besides wearing a badge, we were forbidden from working in the state and public services and were deprived of our freedom of movement. We could go to the beach or market only up to a certain time of day; a curfew was imposed on us. In Dubrovnik the state authorities were in Croatian, that is, Ustashe hands but the military authorities were in Italian hands. It was lucky for us that the Italians were in power. The Germans, in collaboration with the Ustashe, attempted to put us in their concentration camps, but the Italians made it clear to them that *they* were in power in Dubrovnik and that they had the right to do with us as they wished. [...] They took us to a large Italian passenger ship and many Dubrovnik residents came to see us, including my boss, Miho Ercegović. When I saw him, I walked towards him and returned the camera. But he said: 'No, you keep it, and whatever happens will be caught on film.' We were first taken to Hotel Vrek in Gruž, a few kilometres from Dubrovnik. We stayed there for a couple of months, and in early January 1943 we were taken to Kupari. There were around 1,200 Jews.[51]

In May, the Jews at Kupari were transferred to the concentration camp on the island of Rab, which was dissolved after Italy's surrender. After Elvira Kohn's liberation, she joined the Partisans with her Leica camera, which she managed to keep with her during her stay in the concentration camp. The Partisans were surprised to see a female photographer, yet they nevertheless suggested she join ZAVNOH's war photography unit, and tasked her with photographing all events. Kohn said the following in relation to this:

I was the only woman photojournalist in the ZAVNOH. There were two other photojournalists – men – who were also sometimes called up for other duties, called up for other jobs, so sometimes I was the only ZAVNOH photographer. After Supreme Command formed its own department for public relations, I started working for them and stayed there until the war ended. [...] We arrived in Zagreb on 9 May 1945 at around 5 p.m. We crossed Old Sava Bridge and arrived at the main square. The welcome was incredible. People were out on the streets all over Zagreb; they waited for us to pass, they clapped, they waved flags. The atmosphere was glorious, full of emotion, people were delighted and thrilled. Everyone knew that the war had ended, that the Ustashe and Germans had left the city, that Zagreb was liberated. After the celebrations on the main square, our group, Partisans who had been together in the war departed for Zvonimirova St., just recently home to Pavelić's headquarters. We decided to spend the night in Pavelić's headquarters and sleep there as an act of victory over the Ustashe. We were warned not to touch anything, as there was a risk that the Ustashe might have laid bombs and munitions here. We could still smell the smoke in the courtyard at the headquarters; the Ustashe must have burnt documents and papers the day before they were driven out. On my first night in Zagreb, I slept on a table in Pavelić's headquarters, in a military overcoat and with a pistol beneath me.[52]

51 Ibid.
52 Ibid.

In Serbia another female photographer also worked as part of the Partisan movement – Slavka Abramović. She learnt the craft immediately before the Second World War. Just before the war started, Hungarian fascists interned her and her family in a concentration camp in the town of Senta where they lived, and she remained there for the following three months. After her release from the concentration camp, she departed for Belgrade and Valjevo. In 1944 she joined the First Montenegrin Battalion of the First Proletarian Brigade, along with her sister, Zora. She was then transferred to the brigade's cultural and propaganda section, where she worked as a photographer until September 1945.[53]

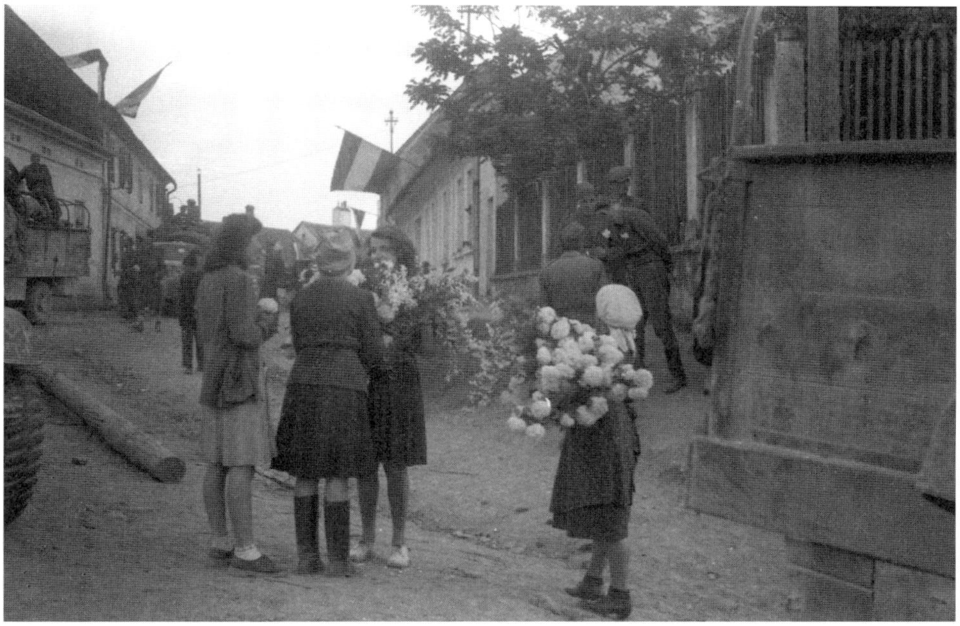

Karlovac, Croatia, after the liberation, May 1945. Photo: Elvira Kohn. Croatian History Museum, HPM/ MRNH-11474/18a.

Gattin and Bernstein: A Dalmatian Photographer and an American Journalist

In Dalmatia the Agitprop District People's Liberation Committee for Dalmatia had a photography section that was founded and led by Živko Gattin, together with the former war reporters Slavko Zalar, Jure Ruljančić and Anđelko Batinić.[54] Gattin was the only Partisan photographer in Croatia who managed to shoot film in colour. After the liberation of Split on 5 November 1944, the Dalmatian photography unit set up an exhibition in the Eden cinema in Split. The exhibition traced the development of the People's Liberation Struggle, enemy war crimes, the liberation of Split, and life in the liberated city.[55] The exhibition was

53 Milorad Čukić and Špiro Lagator, *Partizanke Prve proleterske*, Belgrade 1978, p. 161.
54 Nataša Mataušić, *Koncentracioni logor Jasenovac*, Zagreb 2008, p. 46.
55 Arhiv VII, NOB Archives, CS K16, reg. br. 34/1.

opened by Cvito Fisković (the curator at the Archaeological Museum mentioned earlier), who was then head of the education department at the District People's Liberation Committee. In his opening comments, he said:

Here you will see the occupier's crimes, the execution of our children, our burnt-out villages, our tortured but persistent fighters. You will experience once again the anxious and great days of liberation through these photographs. They show how our people were tortured, how hard they fought [...]. And isn't it strange that right here, in this old *Gabinetto di lettura* [reading room], which is really a *Gabinetto di delitto* [crime room] the truth comes to light. Under this roof, autonomists and freaks turned into fascists, they built our gallows, making a show to Europe of spreading culture among barbarians.[56]

In Gattin's records, which I received from his family while researching this topic, he writes that his love for photography stemmed from his father, Ivan, a seagoing captain, representative of the American company Standard Oil and leader of the photography section in the Croatian hiking society Mosor. As a young man, Gattin had closely read the photography magazines of the time, following his idols such as Tošo Dabac, Milan Pavić, Franjo Fuis, Žorž Skrigin and Mladen Grčević. From them he learnt photographic techniques and methods for enlarging film. In his records, he wrote:

To this day I remember the magazine's [*Foto revija's*] methods for the fine-grained and soft development of film, using brilliant negatives for great enlargements: metol 6 g, sodium sulphite 150 g, borax 6 g, distilled water 1 l; developing the film at precisely 20° C took 6 minutes. I used that excellent solution extensively throughout my life whenever developing black-and-white film [...]. When, at the end of summer 1942, I left for the Partisans, I took my *Plaubel Makina* with me and a supply of Agfa *Isopan ISS* film. At first I photographed the Partisan camp in Moseć, our hosts in Milešina below Svilaja, the Tokićs and Miletićs and their families, and the units of the emerging Third Dalmatian Brigade.[57]

Gattin's father's film lab, located in the attic of their family home, became the first Partisan lab in Klis Kosa (Solin) near the Croatian city of Split. Immediately after the Italian occupation, Gattin joined the League of Communist Youth of Yugoslavia, and then chose to join the Partisans upon coming of age:

Up until then we had written slogans around Split, distributed political literature, helped the movement in the forests. That day, after our main meal, a person came to my house and whistled in front of it. We lived in Kukuljevićeva St., which is now Tršćanska St. I got up and left the table, didn't say anything to anyone at home and set off to join the Partisans, walking a safe distance of around 50 metres behind the person who had given the signal. When we arrived in Stinice, a guy from Vranjic slowly rowed over to meet us. He also gave me some tuna, as if we

56 *Antifašistički Split, ratna kronika 1941.–1945: Listopad 1944.–svibanj 1945. Od oslobođenja grada do kraja rata. Odricanja i muke okrunjeni pobjedom*, URL: http://www.ratnakronikasplita.com/kronika/1944-2 (accessed 30 May 2021).
57 Živko Gattin's records, provided with the kind permission of Ingrid Gattin Pogutz.

were going on a fishing trip, and we rowed along shore to a place called Barbarinac. There was a third person waiting for me there; we passed through a vineyard and headed uphill along the old Klis road. Two milkmaids from Solin were waiting for me among some pine trees and they took me to Blaca on the slopes of Mali Kozjak. [...] When we arrived in Muć, I joined the Mosećki Detachment, whose commander was Duje Bašić from Solin. At that time Mirko Marasović, who was also a member of the Provincial Committee, said he was looking for someone to teach the detachment how to operate the mimeograph [a stencil duplicator] to print pamphlets. We then started printing *Naš glasnik*, whose main editor was the journalist Eli Finci, a Jew from Sarajevo. They suggested I get involved, but I wanted a gun. Marasović said to me: 'Printing pamphlets and newspapers is worth the same as four guns!' I took the *Plaubel Makina* with me and immediately started shooting photos, although there weren't any opportunities to develop them yet. I soon joined the agitprop group of the Provincial Committee for Dalmatia, which the Germans drove out of Livno. They were in Mosor, in the field, below Gornje Sitno. It was then decided that we would make a newspaper, and we called it *Slobodna Dalmacija* [Liberated Dalmatia], because it was founded on free territory.[58]

This kind of eye-witness account is extremely important, as most of the photographers and witnesses have since passed away, leaving few records about the context in which the photographs were taken. In a conversation for *Slobodna Dalmacija*, Živko Gattin revealed how he got fellow photographers Jure Ruljančić and Slavko Zalar to join him:

I requested that Maksimilijan Baće, leader of the staff, have him [Slavko Zalar], seconded to us but he didn't want to come. We argued, almost got into a fight, but then he relented. He was made number two in command. The next was Jure Ruljančić who had a well-known photo studio in Marulićeva St. He joined in Split when Italy fell. They kept him on at *Slobodna Dalmacija* as a typesetter. I almost didn't manage to get him either. It was just us six till the end of the war. One of them was the student Hrvoje Vidović from the Faculty of Electrical Engineering in Zagreb. While the photojournalists were embedded with the troops on the ground, someone had to look after the picture archive. It wasn't like today – the enemy could have launched an attack by parachute or ship at any time, wiping out everything, which is what happened with the picture archive of the Supreme Command in Drvar when the Germans attacked. [...] The first issue of *Slobodna Dalmacija* featuring our photographs was published while we were on Vis, and the copies were made on a printing machine that Jure Kaštelan and I brought from the scrubland of Blaca on Brač. The zincographs – made by transferring images to a photogravure plate of zinc or copper – were produced in the liberated Italian city of Bari. The plates with the photographs would be made there and sent back to us. [...] Under the Italians, the punishment for spreading and reading anti-fascist propaganda was prison; under the Germans, it was execution by firing squad. Yet despite this, people read and carried such propaganda far and wide.[59]

The photographers of *Slobodna Dalmacija* shot images of liberated territory in Livno, Split and on the islands of Čiovo, Hvar and Vis, where exhibitions were organised and news-

58 Damir Šarac, 'Dr Živko Gattin: Za čitanje 'Slobodne' se strijeljalo!', in: *Slobodna Dalmacija*, URL: https://slobodnadalmacija.hr/kultura/dr-zivko-gatin-za-citanje-slobodne-se-strijeljalo-204129 (accessed 30 May 2012).
59 Ibid.

papers produced. On Vis, in February of 1944, members of the photography unit also put together their first exhibition entitled *Narod Dalmacije u borbi za oslobođenje* (The People of Dalmatia in the Struggle for Liberation).[60] Afterwards, the exhibition moved to a local school on Lastovo, and then on to Drvar for the Second Congress of the United Alliance of Anti-Fascist Youth of Yugoslavia, held on 2 May 1944. According to Gattin's account, he and Slavko Zalar carried the exhibition in two bags, across Ravni kotari in northern Dalmatia to Drvar, where it was set up in one of the sheds of a timber yard named Šipad.

The exhibition then moved on to the liberated town of Hvar to coincide with the Congress of People's Liberation Committees of Dalmatia being held there. The next stop was the Eden cinema in Split, then Šibenik and then on to Belgrade, where Dalmatian war photographers were also waiting, anticipating the end of the war.

Gattin's account of his journey to Drvar also sheds light on the fantastic and thrilling tale of the American journalist Walter Bernstein, whom Gattin was ordered to accompany. Besides travelling together on foot, Gattin helped Bernstein carry the bag containing the exhibition contents. His story is especially interesting as, while serving as a lieutenant in the US Army, Bernstein managed to infiltrate the liberated territory without his superiors' knowledge and was the first Western journalist to interview Josip Broz Tito. The interview was later published in the magazine *Yank, The Army Weekly*.[61]

In 1941, as a young man aged twenty-two, Bernstein enlisted in the American army where he worked as a correspondent in the Middle East. During this time, indeed until 1944, the

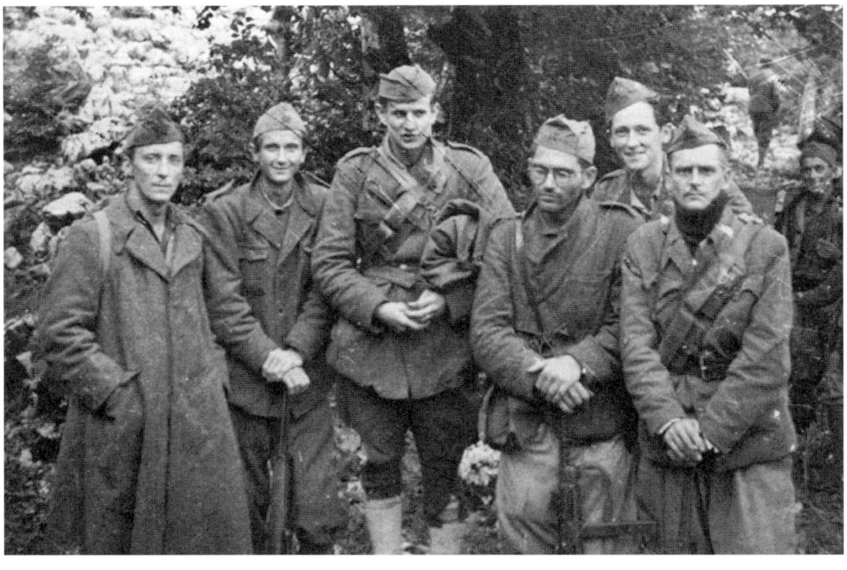

The war photography team of Slobodna Dalmacija: Ruljančić (left), Zalar, Kohn, Batinić, Gattin and Klišmanič (right), Vis 1944. Photo: Slobodna Dalmacija. Private collection of Ingrid Gattin Pogutz.

60 Hlevnjak/Ivanuš 2008 (see note 18), p. 113; Walter Bernstein, 'Interview with Tito of Yugoslavia', in: *Yank, The Army Weekly*, 16 June 1944, New York, pp. 8–9.

61 Bernstein 1944 (see note 60).

Partisan movement remained subject to Allied, particularly British, censorship, as the UK government continued its support of King Peter II, the last king of the Yugoslav government in British exile and a member of the Karađorđević dynasty. Although the People's Liberation Army did receive some Allied assistance in the form of weapons and other equipment, the Allied news blackout was pervasive. Breaking it was key, as this was the prerequisite for the Partisan movement being recognised as the only legitimate anti-fascist movement in Yugoslavia. In turn, this was a precondition for future international recognition of the new state after the war.

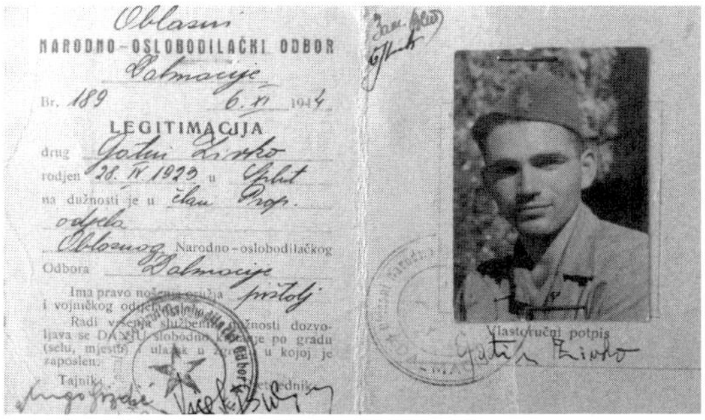
Oblasni
NARODNO-OSLOBODILAČKI ODBOR
Dalmacije
Br. 189 6.XI.1944
LEGITIMACIJA
drug Gattin Živko
rodjen 20.IV.1920 u Split
na dužnosti je u član Prop. odjela
Oblasnog Narodno-oslobodilačkog Odbora Dalmacije
Ima pravo nošenja oružja pištolj
Vlastoručni potpis Gattin Živko

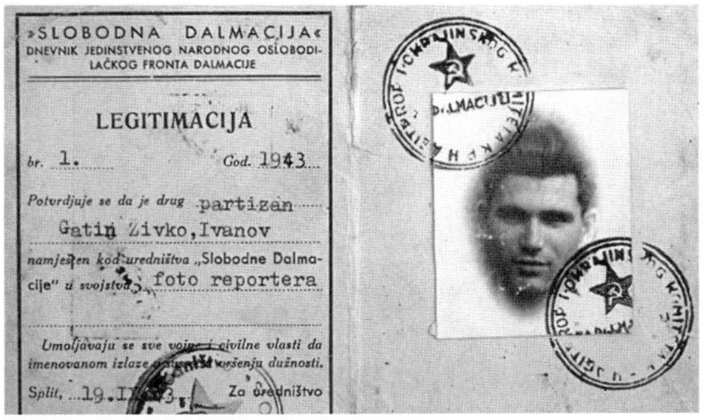
»SLOBODNA DALMACIJA«
DNEVNIK JEDINSTVENOG NARODNOG OSLOBODILAČKOG FRONTA DALMACIJE
LEGITIMACIJA
br. 1. God. 1943
Potvrdjuje se da je drug partizan Gatin Živko, Ivanov
namješten kod uredništva „Slobodne Dalmacije" u svojstvu foto reportera
Umoljavaju se sve vojne i civilne vlasti da imenovanom izlaze u susret u vršenju dužnosti.
Split, 19.I... Za uredništvo

Živko Gattin's personal documents. Private collection of Ingrid Gattin Pogutz.

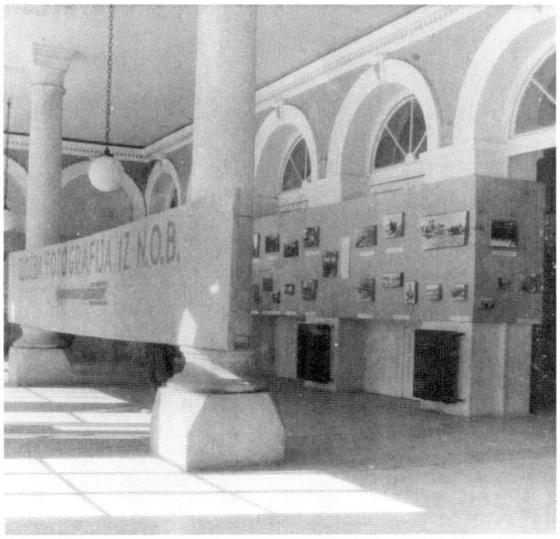

During the conference, an exhibition of photographs of the People's Liberation Struggle went on show. Installation view with banner bearing the slogan: 'Exhibition of photographs recording the People's Liberation Struggle', Hvar, 12–13 October 1944. Photo: Miloš Žanko. Croatian History Museum, HPM/MRNH-F-43.

Sadly, Walter Bernstein died in January 2021. In his later years, he lived in New York and in 2017 he agreed to a conversation for this book. During the war, he received an invitation to visit Yugoslavia from Vladimir Dedijer and Milentije Popović, whom he met in Cairo. Shortly afterwards, he travelled to Bari in Italy, a vital Allied navy base at the time, on his own initiative. His goal was to set off for Yugoslavia, which was still under Axis occupation but also under an Allied news blackout.

I came to the special Balkan section of the US Army, which supplied weapons to the Partisans. I went to speak with the American officer and told him that I wanted to travel to Yugoslavia. He laughed and said no one had been allowed to travel to the Partisans. He said: 'Stay here and

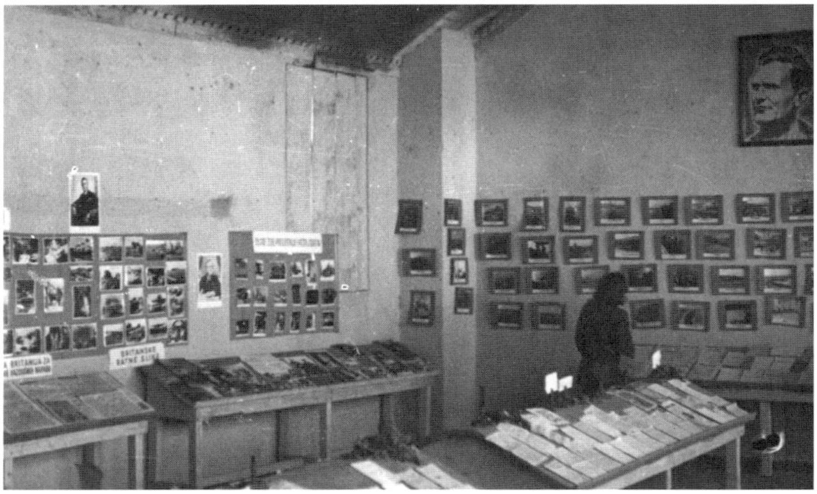

View of exhibition held at the Second Congress of the United Alliance of Anti-Fascist Youth of Yugoslavia, Drvar, May 1944. Photo: Živko Gattin. Croatian History Museum, HPM/MRNH-A-11701/52.

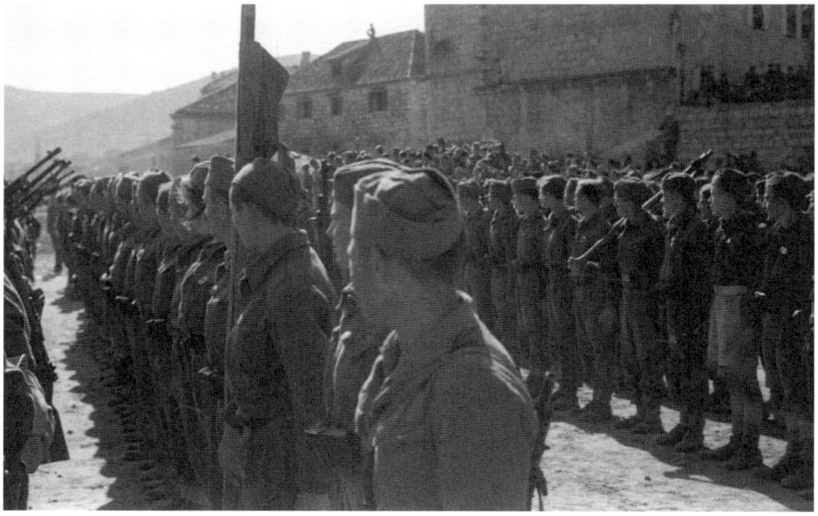

Parade of First Dalmatian Brigade on the island of Vis, September 1944. Photo: Živko Gattin. Croatian History Museum, HPM/MRNH-A-2602-f146–69.

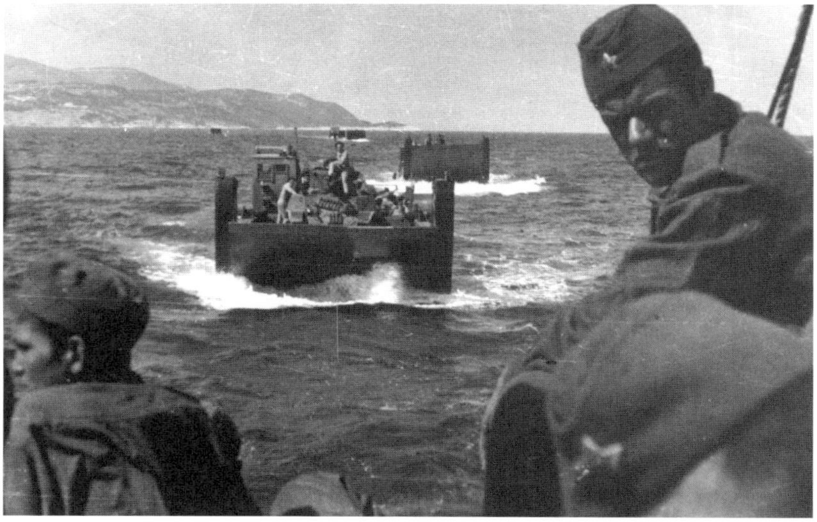

Sea convey of munitions, coast of Vis, 1944. Photo: Živko Gattin. Private collection of Ingrid Gattin Pogutz.

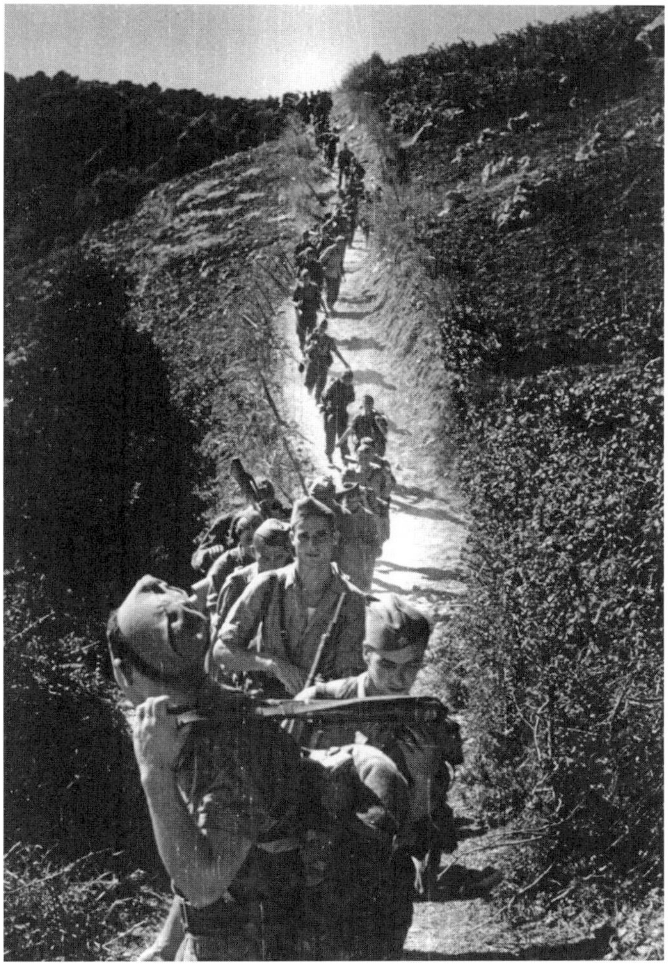

Partisans liberate Hvar, September 1944. Photo: Živko Gattin. Private collection of Ingrid Gattin Pogutz.

write articles about us.' Then I told Dedijer that I hadn't been permitted to travel to Yugoslavia, to which he replied: 'Fuck him, this is our state and if you want to come, come! We'll take you there.'[62]

On the way to Drvar, Bernstein's bag with all items and a camera was stolen in the night. After this incident, Gattin gave him his camera and all the rolls of film that he had shot on the journey from Vis, because he deemed it important that the photographs be published in the American press. After arriving in Drvar, Bernstein also organised a first meeting with Tito:

I remember him being in a big cave, a cave that protected the house he was in. I remember him having a big dog. He welcomed me from behind a big table and I just saw him briefly the first time. I believed everything I had seen in the Partisans; it grabbed me, and I wanted to be part of it all. From today's position, I think I was very young and my questions were naive. He was really impressive, his whole being. He wasn't fat as in later years. I knew that before the war, he had

62 Bernstein in conversation with the author (29 November 2017).

travelled illegally by pretending to be a rich entrepreneur. I had the feeling that he was capable of anything and everything and all that he did was tremendously important to me.[63]

The conversation between Bernstein and Tito was conducted in English, and the interpreter was a woman called Olga. The next day was supposed to include a second meeting for the young American lieutenant, but it unfortunately did not happen.

After the first preliminary conversation with Tito, another, longer, conversation had been agreed for the following day. That evening I decided to go for a walk and came across a British officer who was really surprised to see someone in Allied uniform. He was an unimportant officer on a British mission to the Supreme Command. He sized me up and asked me who I was. I explained to him what I was doing here, and then he said that I had broken all possible commands and that I had to go with him. He took me to the British mission where Randolph Churchill, the son of Winston Churchill, could be found. He thought it was funny that they'd come across me in Drvar, but he then said that I was under arrest and that they would send me back to Bari. On the plane back, I sat with him and remember him being terribly drunk. I was disappointed and somewhat afraid. I didn't know what would happen to me and I didn't believe anyone except the Partisans. I was scared then that they wouldn't publish what I had written. I wanted to stay with the Partisans for longer and write many more articles. At the same time, I knew that the British had organised a first official visit to the Partisans, with a handful of journalists and photographers. They were meant to be the ones who would tell the official story of the Partisans.[64]

Bernstein left for Bari as a military prisoner. However, outside Bosanski Petrovac on 9 May 1944, a plane did in fact land with the first official team of war correspondents to arrive with Allied command's permission. The team consisted of a reporter from *Time* magazine, Stojan Pribićević (son of the politician Svetozar Pribićević), a photographer for Reuters named John Talbot, the British photographer Gene Fowler and an American photographer named Slade. Six days later, a dinner with Tito was organised for them[65] and they are regarded to this day as the first Western press delegation to visit the Supreme Command. This is because their reports were published *before* Bernstein's interview in the issue of *Yank* released on 16 June 1944. In the interview, Bernstein wrote:

Tito's cosmopolitanism becomes more apparent the longer you are with him. He isn't a simple peasant leader, but rather a man of the world. In fact, Tito is an exceptionally sophisticated person in the best sense of the word. There are moments when he gives you the impression of being a good actor – he wears the uniform with talent.[66]

A few months later, Bernstein sent Gattin a package with his roll films and published several more articles in which he mentioned their journey together.[67] Before the war, Bernstein had not been a member of the Communist Party, but his journey to Yugoslavia was about him fulfilling his youth ideals, contributing to the struggle and breaking through the news

63 Ibid.

64 Ibid.

65 Walter E. Roberts, *Tito, Mihailović and the Allies, 1941–1945*, Durham, North Carolina 1987, p. 227.

66 Bernstein 1944 (see note 60).

67 Walter Bernstein, 'Walk Through Yugoslavia' in: *Yank, The Army Weekly*, 28 July 1944, New York, pp. 8–9.

blackout. Before Bernstein, only the Associated Press had had a conversation with Tito, in writing, through a Partisan intermediary in Bari. Allied command censored the interview, however, and only after several interventions, including by President Roosevelt himself, was the conversation published on 21 May 1944. This conversation was crucial in recognising the People's Liberation Army and key to future support from the Allies.[68] The first photographs that passed through the Allied military censors were published on 6 December 1943 in *Life*, and they were taken by the British lieutenant Lambton Burn.[69]

Just a few days after the conversation between Tito and Stojan Pribićević, on 25 May 1944 Axis forces launched their Seventh Enemy Offensive and the landing operation on Drvar. In the Germans' operation codenamed Operation Rösselsprung (Knight's Leap), the Supreme Command barely escaped with their lives, and many foreign intelligence officers and Partisans died. The Allies whisked Tito off Yugoslav territory in a Russian plane to Bari. In Drvar, Pribićević and Talbot were captured, as were the other two foreign press photographers, but Pribićević was soon freed in a Partisan counter-attack. The others were liberated in the end. The Partisan photographer Vili Šimunov-Barba, the first photographer to work for Yugoslavia's official news agency, TANJUG (Telegraphic Agency of the New Yugoslavia), did not have such luck and died in an attempt to save his negatives from fire from the road linking Drvar and Oštrelj. Born in Ogulin with the birth name Vilim Schwarz, he changed his name to Šimunov and joined the Partisan movement when the quisling Independent State of Croatia was established. He collaborated with the Communist Party of Yugoslavia before the war, too, and in Drvar he set about creating the Partisan press archive. He was also the first official photographer of the Supreme Command of the People's Liberation Army and the Partisan Detachments of Yugoslavia (NOV i POJ).

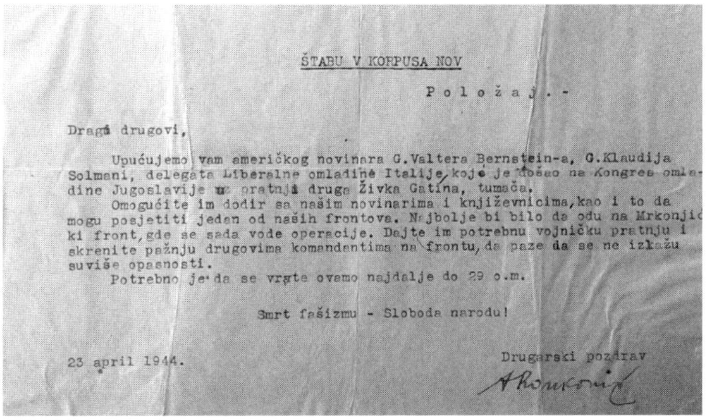

ŠTABU V KORPUSA NOV

P o l o ž a j . -

Dragi drugovi,

Upućujemo vam američkog novinara G.Valtera Bernstein-a, G.Klaudija Solmani, delegata Liberalne omladine Italije, koje je došao na Kongres omladine Jugoslavije u pratnji druga Živka Gatina, tumača.

Omogućite im dodir sa našim novinarima i književnicima, kao i to da mogu posjetiti jedan od naših frontova. Najbolje bi bilo da odu na Mrkonjićki front, gde se sada vode operacije. Dajte im potrebnu vojničku pratnju i skrenite pažnju drugovima komandantima na frontu, da paze da se ne izlažu suviše opasnosti.

Potrebno je da se vrate ovamo najdalje do 29 o.m.

Smrt fašizmu - Sloboda narodu!

23 april 1944.

Drugarski pozdrav

Aleksandar Ranković's order confirming that Walter Bernstein accompanied Živko Gattin. Private collection of Ingrid Gattin Pogutz.

68 Roberts 1987 (see note 65), pp. 227–228.

69 Nikolina Kurtović, *Communist Stardom in the Cold War: Josip Broz Tito in Western and Yugoslav Photography, 1943-1980*, doctoral thesis, Toronto: University of Toronto, 2010, p. 55.

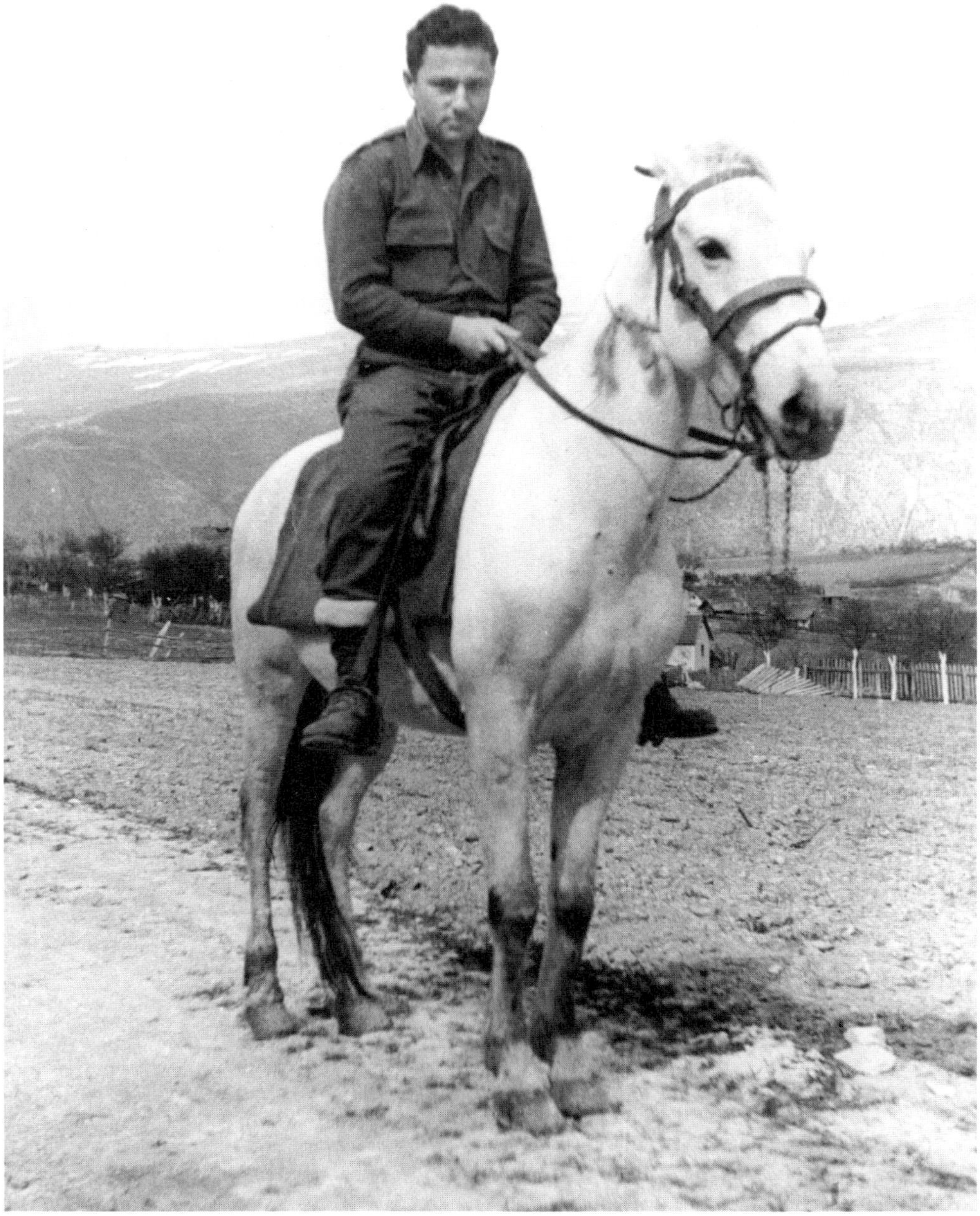

Walter Bernstein on horseback on route to Drvar. Photo: Živko Gattin.
Private collection of Ingrid Gattin Pogutz.

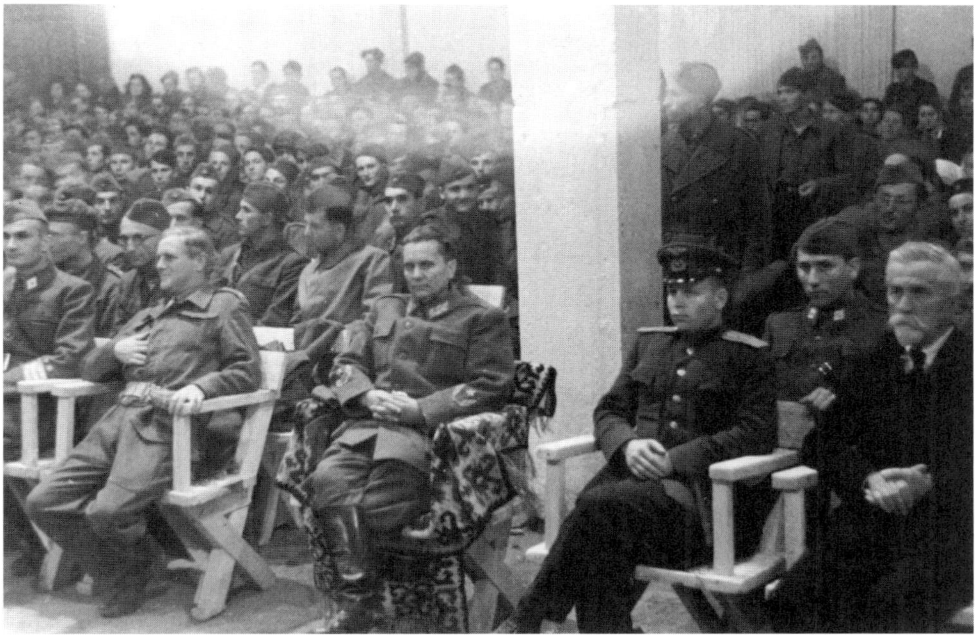

Second Congress of the United Alliance of Anti-Fascist Youth of Yugoslavia, Drvar, 1944. Randolph Churchill (left, with hand on chest) and Josip Broz Tito (centre). Photo: Živko Gattin. Private collection of Ingrid Gattin Pogutz.

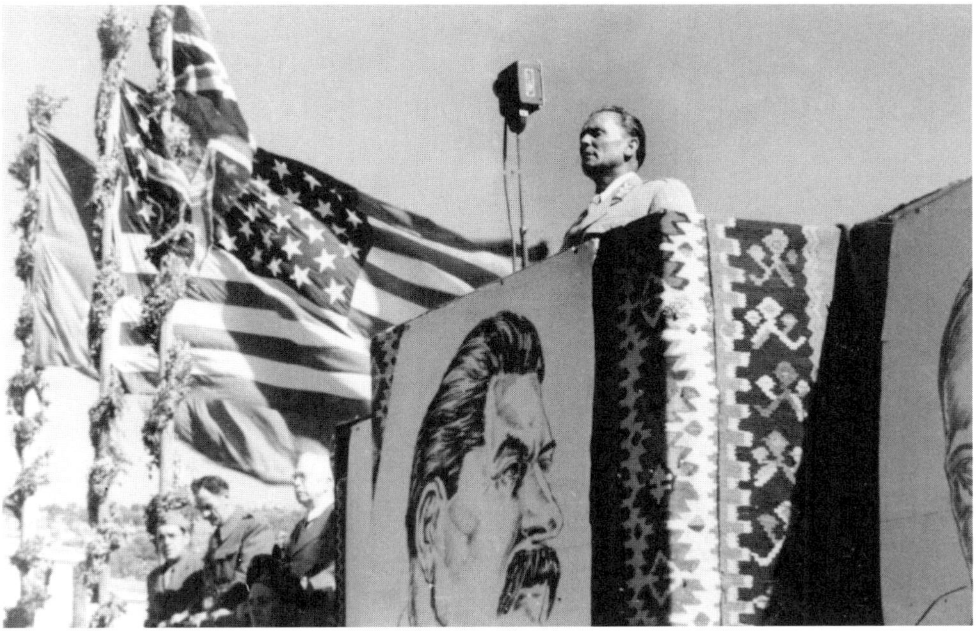

Tito's speech on Vis, 1944. Photo: Živko Gattin. Private collection of Ingrid Gattin Pogutz.

Besides the Dalmatian photographers discussed above, Ante Roca deserves a special mention. In 1943 he joined the headquarters' support unit of the North Dalmatian Division.[70] When tasked on one occasion with acquiring equipment, he fell into enemy hands and was captured by German soldiers. After interrogating him, they brought him to a prison camp in the Croatian town of Slavonski Brod. He managed to escape from there and later worked as a photographer for *Vjesnik*.[71]

A lesser-known fact to this day is that Stevan Benčić, the pre-war photographer at the daily newspaper *Politika* and parliamentarian in the Assembly of the Kingdom of Serbs, Croats and Slovenes, was also involved in the Partisan movement. Love brought him to Hvar, and over time he expanded his business down to Dubrovnik and Budva. He photographed tourist sights and made postcards. He was the Agfa representative for this part of Dalmatia. During the short-lived period of Ustashe rule on the island of Hvar he was imprisoned, but his family managed to have him freed by bribing local officials. He supported Božo Novak with equipment, and Novak later became an important Croatian journalist. In 1943, Stevan Benčić joined the ranks of the Partisans, where he later came across Vladislav Ribnikar, who helped him get involved in TANJUG. It was also during this time that he shot Tito's portrait, which was later used on postal stamps.[72]
The Zagreb small-business owner and photographer Ernest Grgić has also been overlooked in the history of Partisan photography. He was involved in the workers' movement even in the 1930s, before leaving for the Spanish Civil War as a volunteer. He collaborated with Vili Šimunov-Barba in the Partisans, and they worked together on creating the Partisan picture archive. During the war he was a radio telegrapher for the Fifth Krajina Corps,[73] and he also organised telegraphy and photography courses.

One of the especially impressive collections of photographs, now in the Croatian History Museum, was amassed by the photography section of the District People's Liberation Committee of Slavonia, in which Pero Dragila, Vlado Potočjak, Mate Tačković and Milan Crnelić worked.[74] This photography section even made photomontages for special occasions, such as to celebrate Serbian Orthodox Christmas. They successfully held photography exhibitions, such as the one held in Orahovica in 1944.

A mother with her children at the site of their burnt-down house in the village of Knezovljani in Banija, Central Croatia, April 1945. Photo: Ante Roca. Croatian History Museum, HPM-82093–2.

Besides the photographers mentioned so far in this collection, there is one photographer – unknown to this day – whose square-format photographs stand out in style and quality. After extensive research, the person behind these images is likely to be Miro Matašin, boss

70 Rhea Ivanuš, 'Ratni ciklus Ante Roce Svjetlo na pepelu i Zadar 1944', in: *Ante Roca fotograf stvarnosti*, Tončika Cukrov (ed.), Zagreb 2013, p. 71.

71 Andrija Mutnjaković, 'Ante Roce', in: ibid., p. 15.

72 According to the oral account of Stevan Benčić's daughter and the Croatian historian Zorica Stipetić (1 December 2017).

73 Metod Antunac, 'Neretva i Sutjeska', in: *Veze u NOB-u, Ratna sećanja 1941–1945*, Radomir Petković (ed.), Belgrade 1981, p. 221.

74 Hlevnjak/Ivanuš 2008 (see note 18), p. 114.

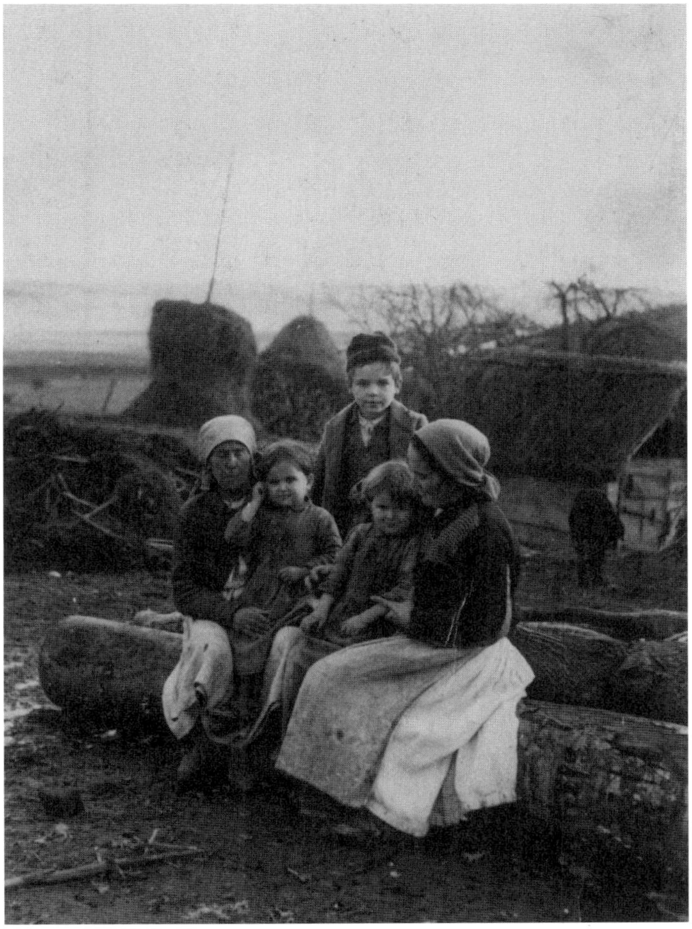

A mother with her children at the site of their burnt-down house in the village of Knezovljani in Banija, Central Croatia, April 1945. Photo: Ante Roca. Croatian History Museum, HPM-82093–2.

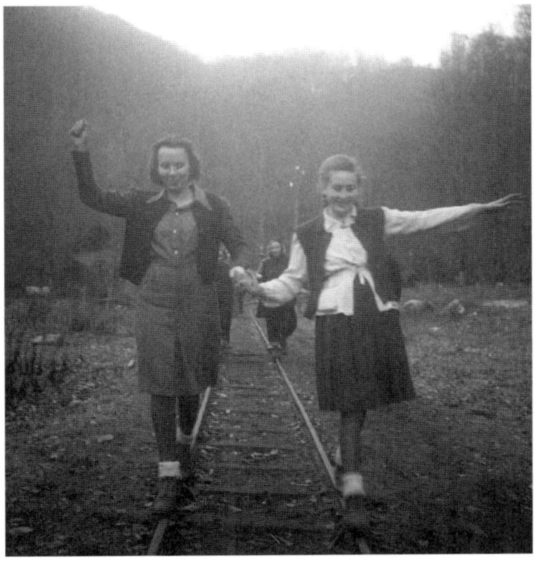

Partisan women in Slavonia, 1944. Photo: Miro Matašin. Croatian History Museum, HPM/MRNH-A-2203/1837.

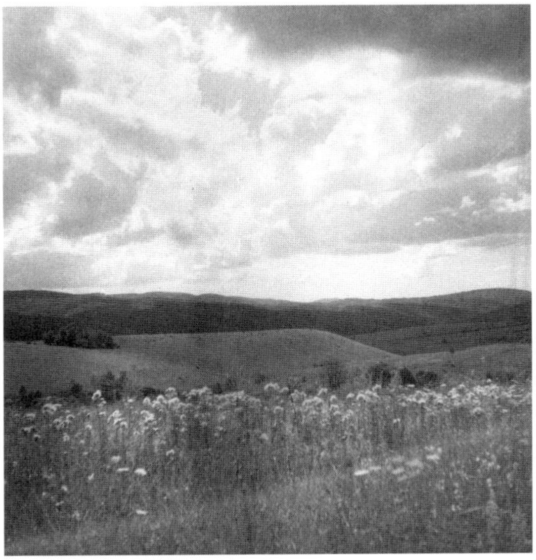

Slavonia. Photo: Miro Matašin. Croatian History Museum, HPM/MRNH-A-2203/1695.

of the photography unit of the District People's Liberation Committee of Slavonia. The photographer is named in a caption beneath the picture dated 31 May 1944, taken in Duboka River on the mountain of Papuk. According to the caption, the image shows the surgeon Jože Koporc and the scrub nurse Meri Barvinski.[75] By analysing the style, format and technical qualities, we can say that this picture is almost certainly the same camerawork as the other square-format photographs in the Croatian History Museum collection. The name stated in the caption, however, is 'Marašin'. This is most likely a mistake, however, as there is no record of a Partisan photographer with this surname. The Partisan photographer Miro Matašin was also active after the war, as the exhibition catalogue of war photography from Salon Becić in Slavonski Brod in 1981 confirms.[76] A copy is held in the Petar Preradović National Library in Bjelovar, in a local-heritage collection about people from Bjelovar. The 1981 exhibition was the first time Matašin had shown most of his photographs, which tells us that this talented photographer faded into obscurity after the war.

Who, then, was Miro Matašin? He was born in the village of Uljanik, near Garešnica in Croatia, and his father was a county clerk and trader. After finishing school, just as war was breaking out, he bought his first camera and processing equipment and took up amateur photography. At the age of twenty-two, he transported his photography equipment in a farm cart, arriving in 1943 on the outskirts of Zvečevo. At that time, he used cameras like the *Leica* and *Rolleiflex*, which was also why most of his photographs were in a square, 6 × 6 cm format. He set up a film lab on the outskirts of Zvečevo, and Nikola Popović and Drago Pavlić worked with him. He also became the photographer for the staff of the Fortieth Division, and later accompanied Kosta Nađ and the general staff of the Third Army in liberated countries up to the border between Slovenia and Austria. He was demobilised in 1946,

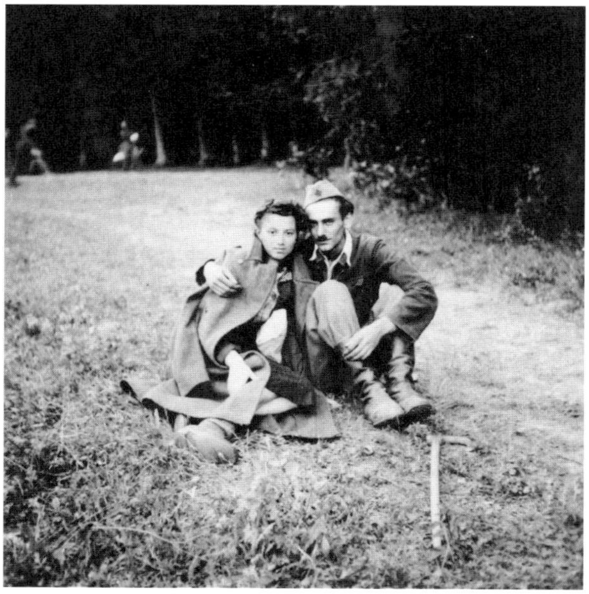

Ljutoč on Papuk mountain, convalescent home for the injured of the Sixth Corps, 1944. Photo: Miro Matašin. Croatian History Museum, HPM/ MRNH-A-2203/1718.

75 Braco Kocković, *I tamo smo samo ljudi bili (tragovima partizanskih ranjenika)*, Zagreb 1982, p. 57.

76 Miro Matašin, *Ratne fotografije: Salon Becić* (exh. cat.), Slavonski Brod 1981.

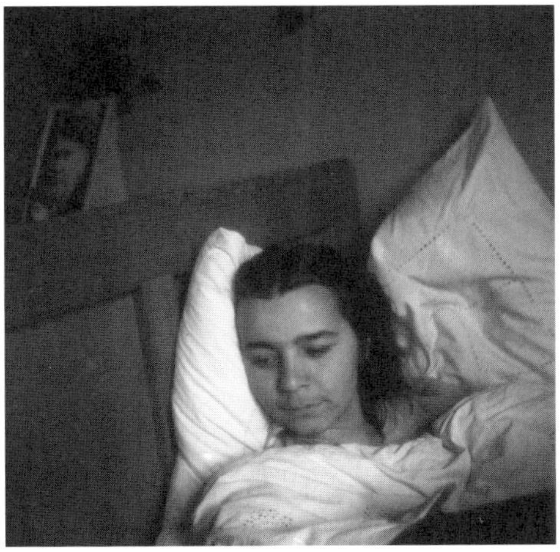

A young Partisan in hospital, Slavonia, 1944. Photo: Miro Matašin. Croatian History Museum, HPM/MRNH-A-2203/1780.

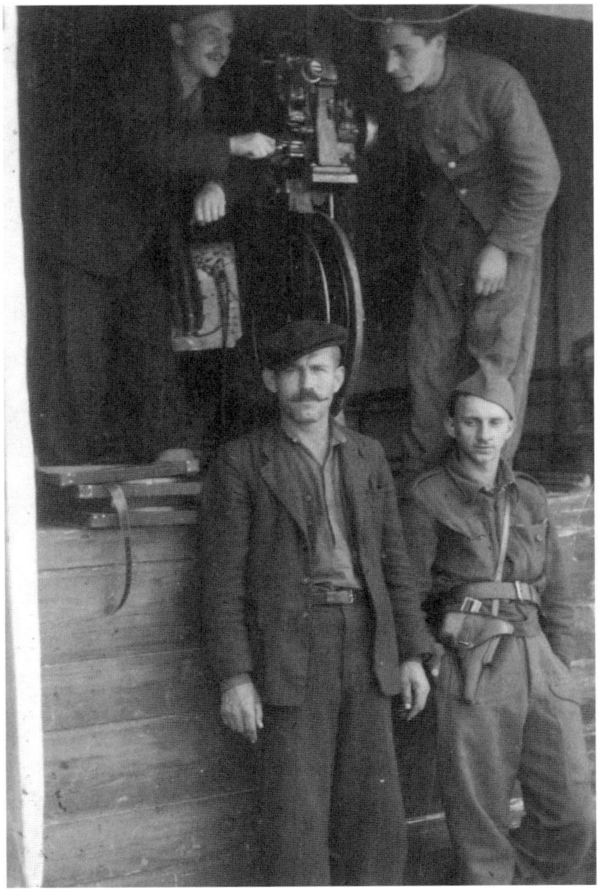

Projectionists in the first Partisan cinema team, Novo Zvečevo, Slavonia, 1943. Photo: Unknown photographer with the District People's Committee for Slavonia. Croatian History Museum, HPM/MRNH-F-4312.

and then sold photographic equipment for the company Univerzal.[77] This self-effacing photographer of great talent shot some of the most technically and artistically impressive photographs of the Partisan struggle. The people in his pictures are relaxed and often photographed from a distance, resulting in a propensity for the medium long shot, a format now customary in contemporary photography.

Jovan Ritopečki and Nikola Bibić were some of the Serbian photographers who matured as professionals during their time in the Partisan movement. During the war, Ritopečki worked as a radio technician, war correspondent and photographer for the First Vojvodina Brigade. After the war, he worked for a time as a TANJUG photographer and for the daily newspaper *Politika*. In 1966 he left for Vienna and became a photographer for the Votava news agency. Four years later he became an independent photographer, working on assignment for the Austrian public broadcaster, ORF, and for other public institutions. His photographs of the lives of so-called *Gastarbeiter* ('guest workers') in Austria were shot during this time.

77 Ibid.

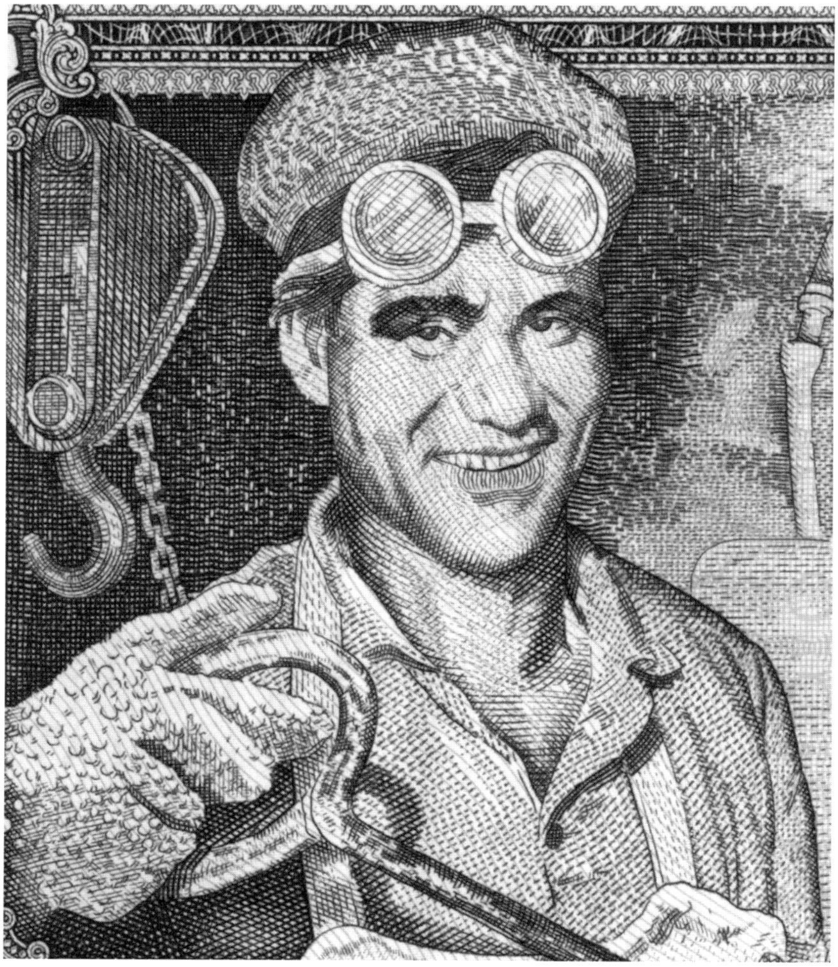

Nikola Bibić's portrait of the Zenica furnace worker Arif Heralić, taken in 1954 and subsequently featured on 1000 dinar notes.

Nikola Bibić learnt his craft from the Serbian photographer Aleksandar Aca Simić, a Belgrade resident not to be confused with Aca Simić from Čačak, who was the official photographer of the Chetnik movement[78] and a member of the Second Ravna Gora Corps, nowadays widely known as the official photographer of the Chetnik leader Draža Mihailović. During his time in the Partisans, Bibić organised amateur photography courses. His successful photography career continued after the war, and in 1957 he won a World Press Photo prize. He is the photographer behind the portrait of a smiling metal worker (Arif Heralić from Zenica, Bosnia and Herzegovina) whose face was included on 1000-dinar notes in the early 1960s. Vojdrag Berčić filmed a documentary about him in 1967 entitled *Devalvacija jednog osmijeha* (The Devaluation of a Smile).

78 Aca Simić, 'Čičin fotograf', in *Pogledi*, URL: https://www.pogledi.rs/aca-simic/ (accessed 30 May 2021).

In Bosnia and Herzegovina, the cultural worker, writer and revolutionary Drago Mažar should also be mentioned. This leader of a wartime uprising in Banja Luka was the commander of the Sixth Lika Detachment and he worked as an intelligence officer in the Operational Headquarters of Bosanska Krajina. He lost two brothers in the war – Josip Mažar-Šoša and Ivica Mažar. All three men were declared official heroes after the war. Drago Mažar shot his first photographs in 1942. Only some of his works have survived. They are now publicly archived at the Archives of the Republic of Srpska but were incompletely accessioned and remain uncatalogued. Some of these photographs were published in the (unpaginated) book *Partizanski album*, although the images are clearly listed with accompanying technical data. The preface reads as follows:

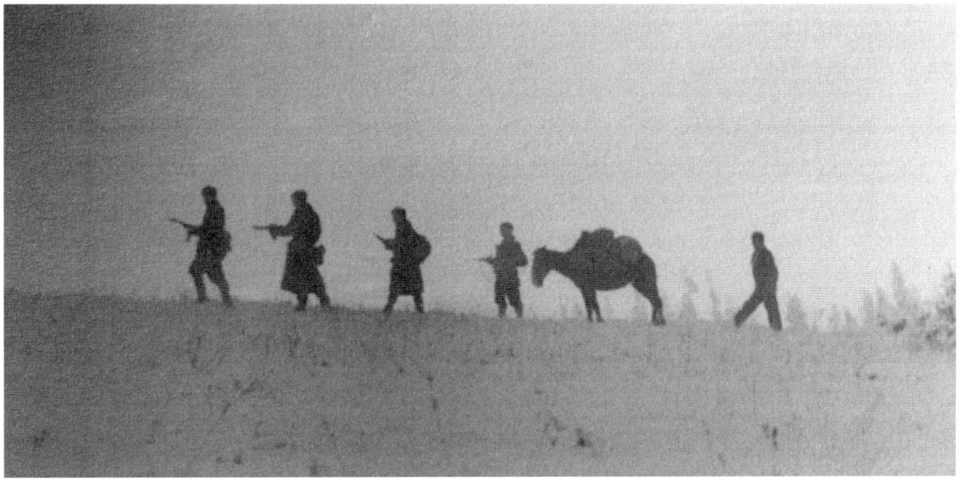

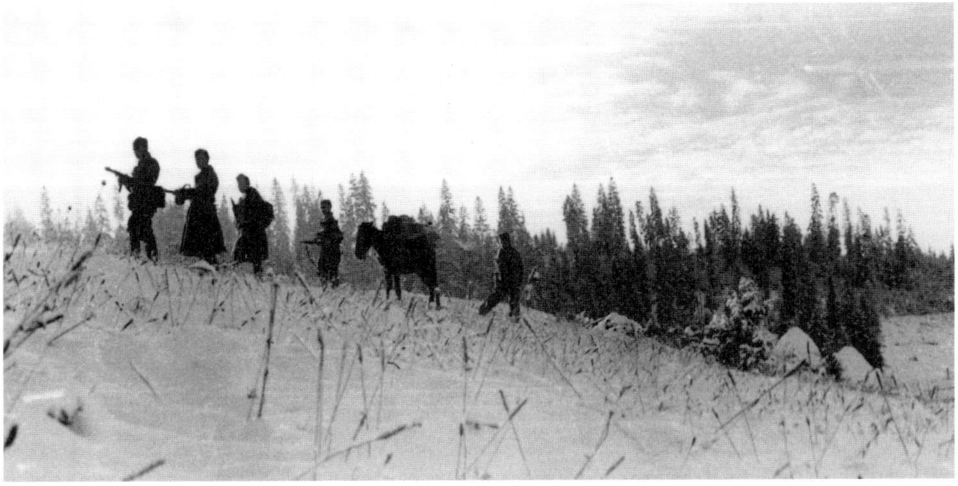

Unidentified scenes shot by photographer Drago Mažar. Archives of the Republic of Srpska, accession no. unknown.

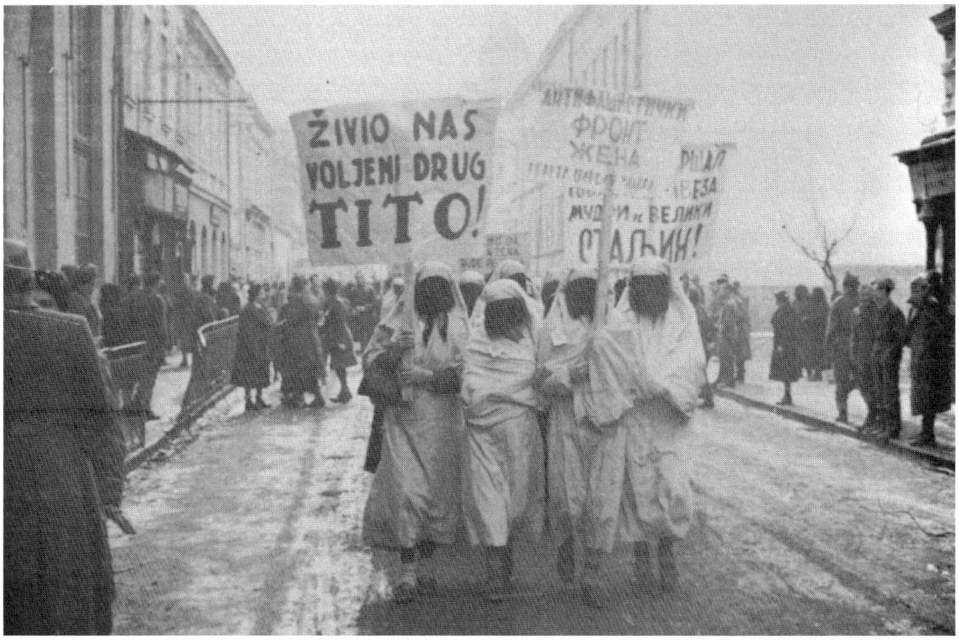

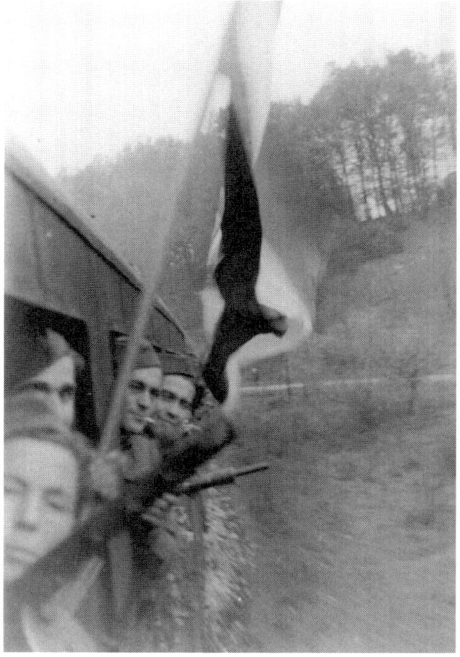

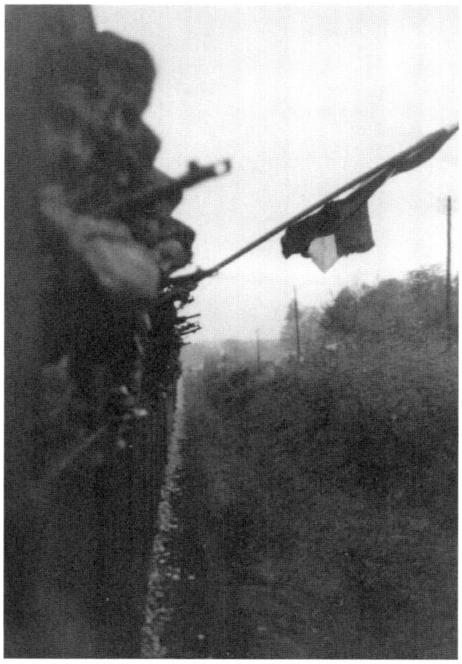

Unidentified scenes shot by photographer Drago Mažar.
Archives of the Republic of Srpska.

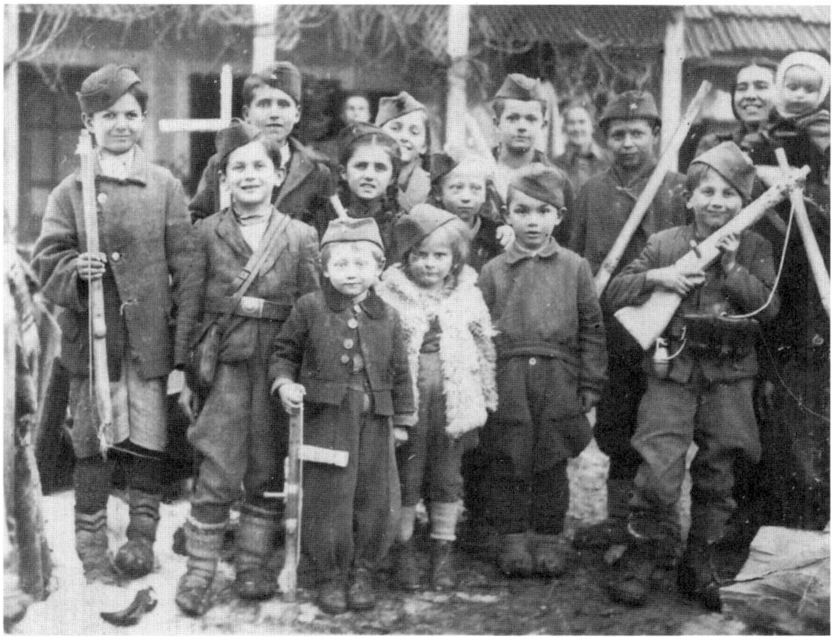

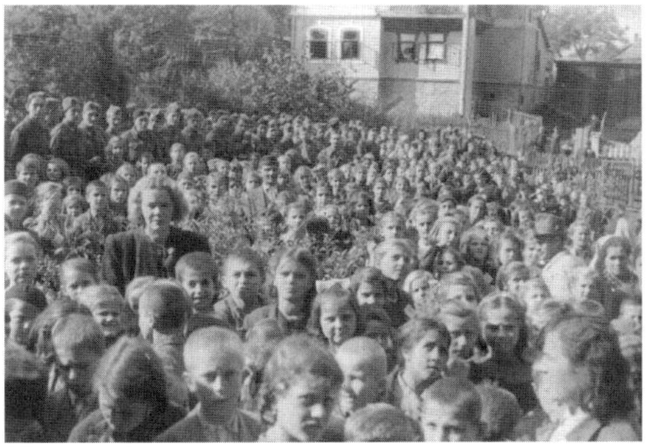

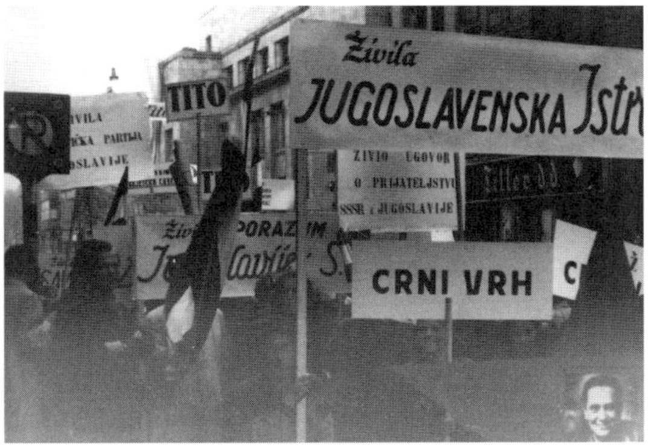

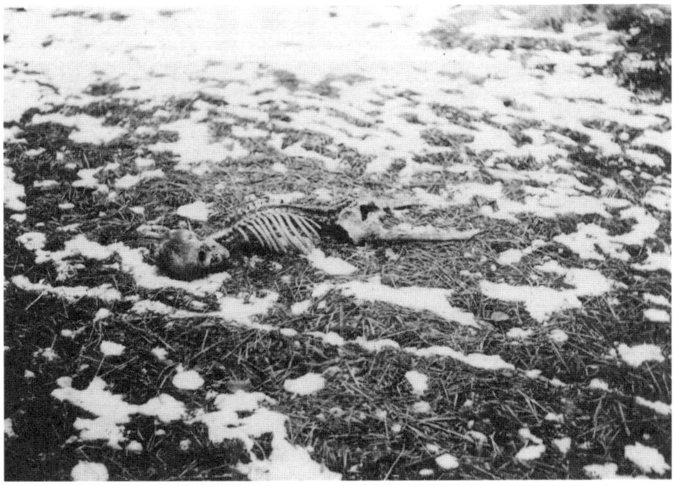

Unidentified scenes shot by photographer Drago Mažar.
Archives of the Republic of Srpska.

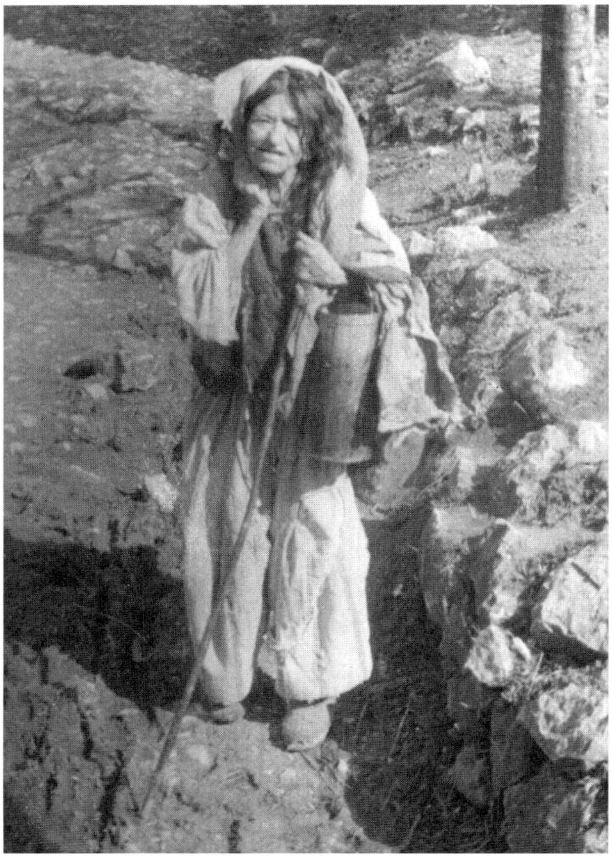

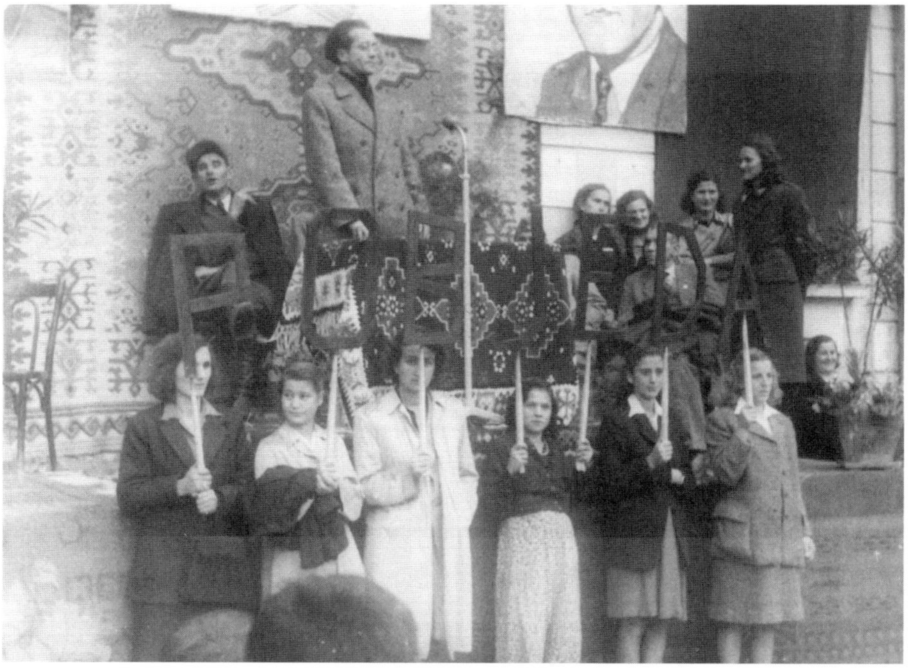

Unidentified scenes shot by photographer Drago Mažar.
Archives of the Republic of Srpska.

Photography doesn't record words, but it does convey the force of situations. These pictures are an important and inspirational confession of a 'photographer'. They are proof of our revolutionary principles and means, relations and opportunities. Yet, together in that powerful witnessing there is also poetry, sometimes with the hardly perceptible tone of an accident only just survived, and more often with the united enthusiasm of an equivalent hope.[79]

The main themes in his photography are freedom and emancipation. Mažar was a socially engaged photographer who captured horrifying scenes of suffering at Kozara in 1942 and the consequences of Operation Western Bosnia. In this operation, German and Ustashe forces, with the support of some Chetnik units, murdered 24,480 civilians, with as many as 8,893 being children under fourteen. According to data supplied by the Ministry of Health Associations and the Red Cross, a further 7,469 children were abducted from 138 villages in the Kozara area.[80]

Throughout the entire war, Savo Orović[81] photographed events in the Partisan movement by following units in Montenegro, Bosnia and Herzegovina, Dalmatia, Sandžak, Lika and Kordun. Vladimir Dedijer wrote in the preface to Orović's book *Photographs from the National Liberation War* (published in English in 1951):

In the first few months of the uprising, Partisan photography units were disorganised; there were just a few amateur photographers working with the scarce resources available. Unfortunately, many of these photographs were destroyed in offensives. How many fighters, how many amateur photographers were lost on the battlefields along with their cameras and films? How many precious pictures were destroyed due to the lack of necessary conditions for developing films?[82]

Skrigin also photographed Josip Broz Tito in Mlinište in September of 1942, while Orović was working on a portrait shoot of the commander. Later, they photographed many famous figures too, such as Koča Popović, Ivan Milutinović, Sava Kovačević, Milovan Đilas, Fjodor Mahin, as well as cultural workers such as Ivan Goran Kovačić, pictured in Livno, where he allegedly just finished writing the poem 'Jama'. As a professional officer, Orović took photographs with military precision. His framing was always extremely precise and his photo enlarging technique meticulous, although his camerawork is somewhat unadventurous in style. One of his most important photographs, depicting Tito injured with a hand on his bandage, and Dr Ivan Ribar, was taken on 9 June 1943 during the battle at Sutjeska, which the poet Kovačić did not survive.

79 Drago Mažar, *Partizanski album* (with preface by Jovo Popović), Belgrade 1981, unpaginated (4 July).

80 Dragoje Lukić, 'Zločini okupatora i njegovih saradnika nad decom kozarskog područja 1941–1945. godine', in: *Kozara u Narodnooslobodilačkoj borbi i socijalističkoj revoluciji: radovi za naučnog skupa održanog na Kozari (Mrakovica) 27. i 28. oktobra 1977. godine*, Zdravko Antonić and Joco Marjanović (eds.), Prijedor 1980, p. 283.

81 Savo Orović was a Montenegrin freedom fighter and officer in the army of the Kingdom of Montenegro, a Great War veteran, and later colonel in the Kingdom of Yugoslavia. At the outbreak of the Second World War, he established contact with Partisan units, but in 1942 after the Partisans' defeat in Montenegro, he retreated to Bosnia and Herzegovina. In May 1943 he was awarded the rank of lieutenant general.

82 Savo Orović, *Fotografije iz Narodnooslobodilačkog rata 1941–1945*, Belgrade 1951, p. 6.

Orović wrote a letter in December 1943 to Supreme Command, in which he spoke of the scarcity of photographic equipment. Attached to the letter were all photographs taken from December 1941 up to that point,[83] only 124 in total:[84]

Here you are, I am sending you the requested photographs of Partisan campaigns, of Partisan life itself, because the campaigns are mostly carried out at night, and so the most beautiful and pivotal moments of combat cannot be photographed. I am sending almost everything I have photographed and preserved, irrespective of its importance, but neglecting to send one part [that has remained] with the photographer in Bihać and Livno.[85]

His testimony speaks of strict Partisan rules that banned photographing Partisan hospitals,[86] with further restrictions on the photographing of Allied units, especially on Vis.[87] In contrast to Orović, the photographer Pavle Bojčević shot a series of photographs from a notably high angle. These shots taken by Bojčević are some of the most powerful photo-

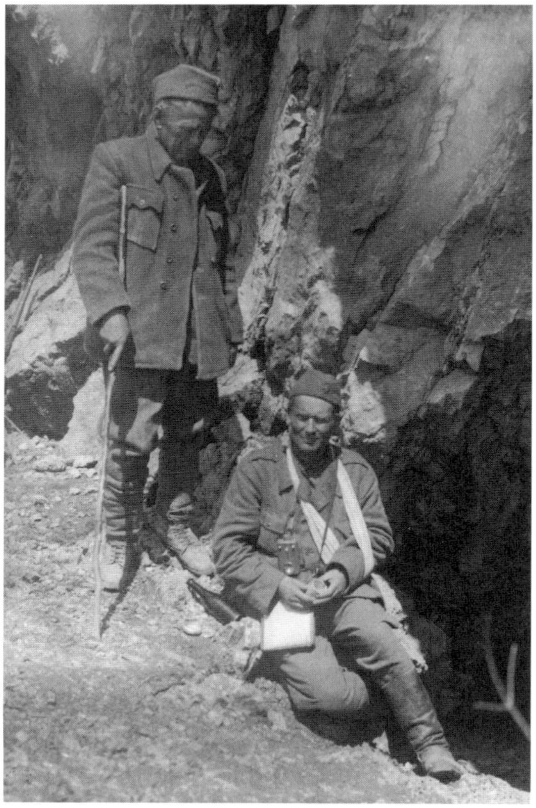

Josip Broz Tito injured at the Milinklada post at Sutjeska, with Dr Ivan Ribar. Photo: Savo Orović. Museum of Yugoslavia.

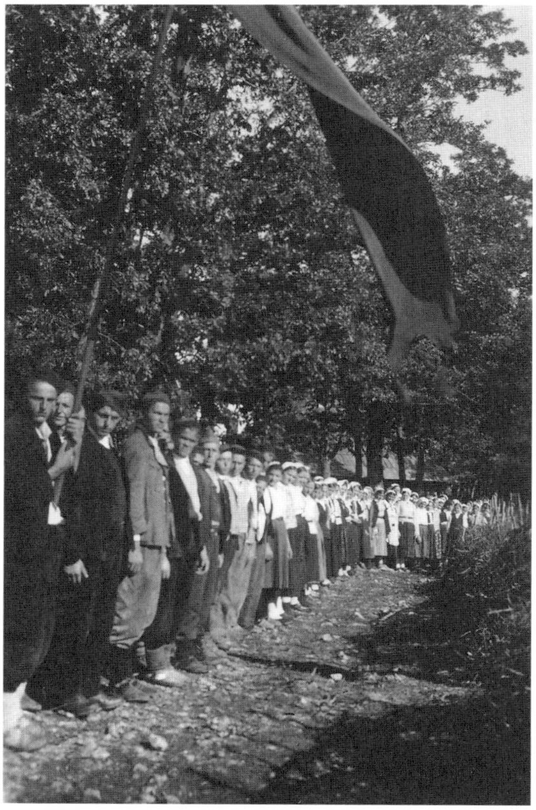

Youth troops at a meeting in Suvaja at Bosanski Petrovac on 25 October 1942 during elections for the District People's Committee. Photo: Savo Orović. Provided with the kind permission of Marko Strpić.

83 Ibid., p. 114.
84 Savo Orović, *Ratni dnevnik 1941–1945*, Belgrade 1972, p. 448.
85 Ibid., p. 448.
86 Ibid., p. 332.
87 Ibid., p. 584.

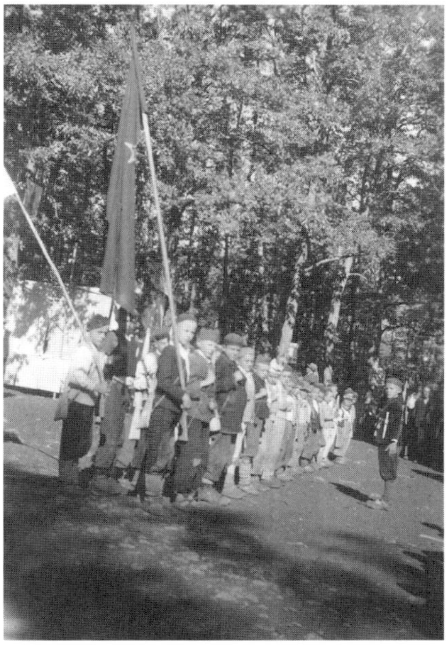

Youth troops at a meeting in Suvaja at Bosanski Petrovac on 25 October 1942 during elections for the District People's Committee. Photo: Savo Orović. Provided with the kind permission of Marko Strpić.

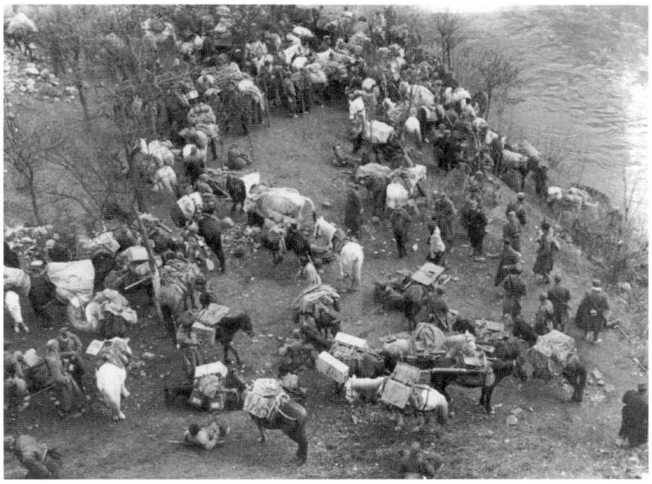

The Battle of Neretva, April 1943. Photo: Pavle Bojčević. Museum of Yugoslavia, MRNJ III – 4557.

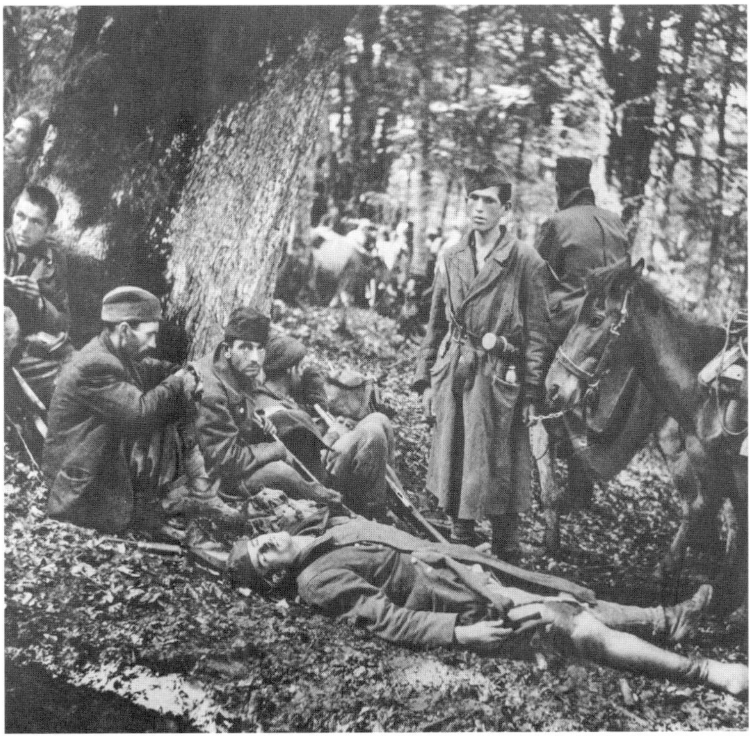

Milinklada at Sutjeska, 9 June 1943. Photo: Žorž Skrigin. Reproduced from the book Rat i pozornica (War and Stage), Belgrade Tourist Press, 1968.

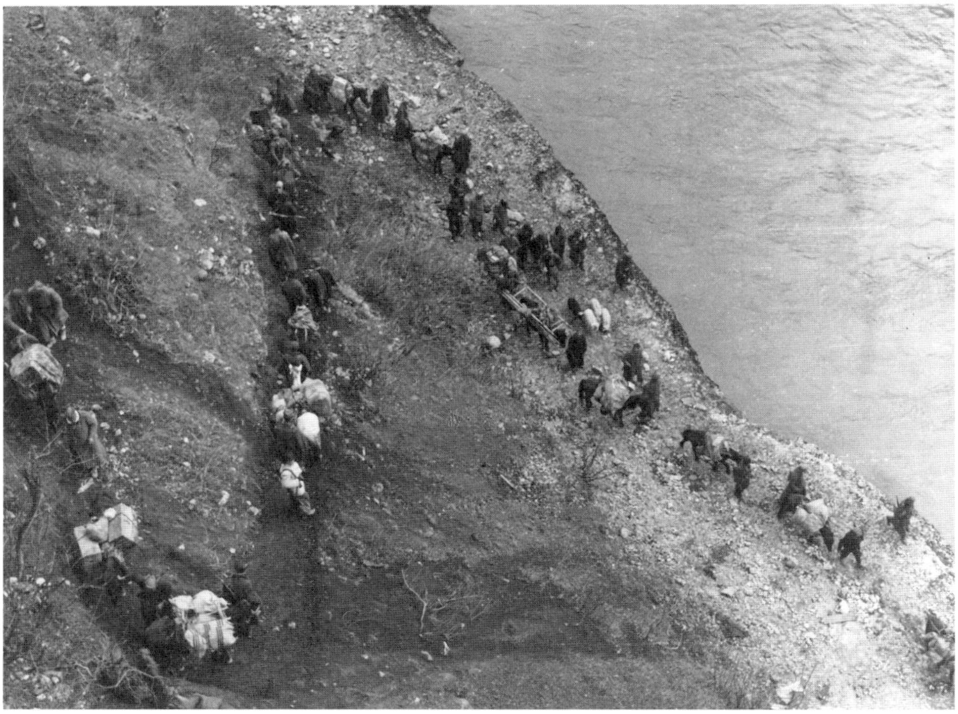

The Fourth Enemy Offensive, April 1943. Photo: Pavle Bojčević. Museum of Yugoslavia, MRNJ III – 4557

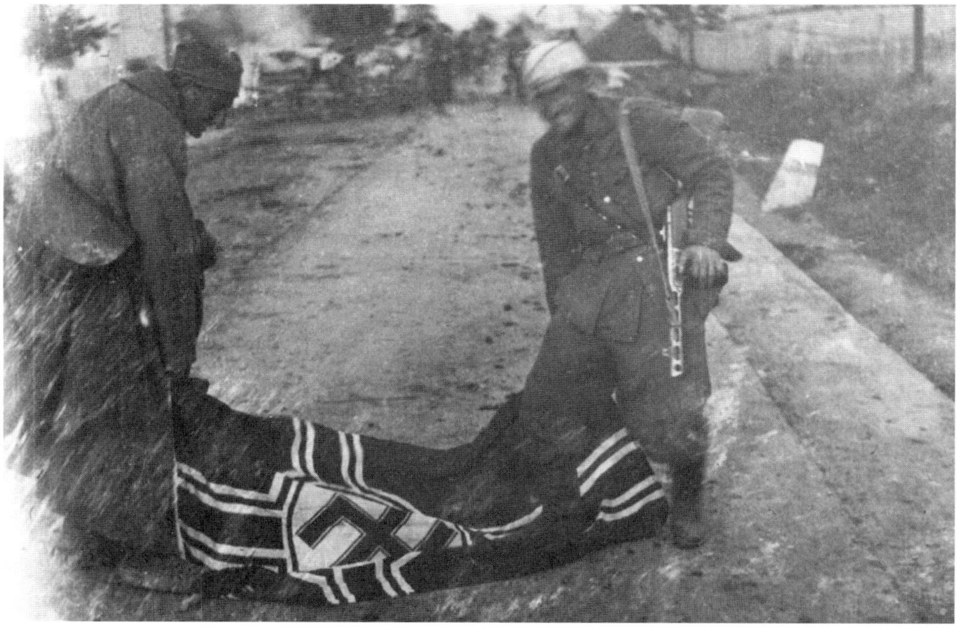

The Corps of the People's Defence of Yugoslavia in Macedonia, 1945. Photographer unknown. Military Museum Belgrade, 13290.

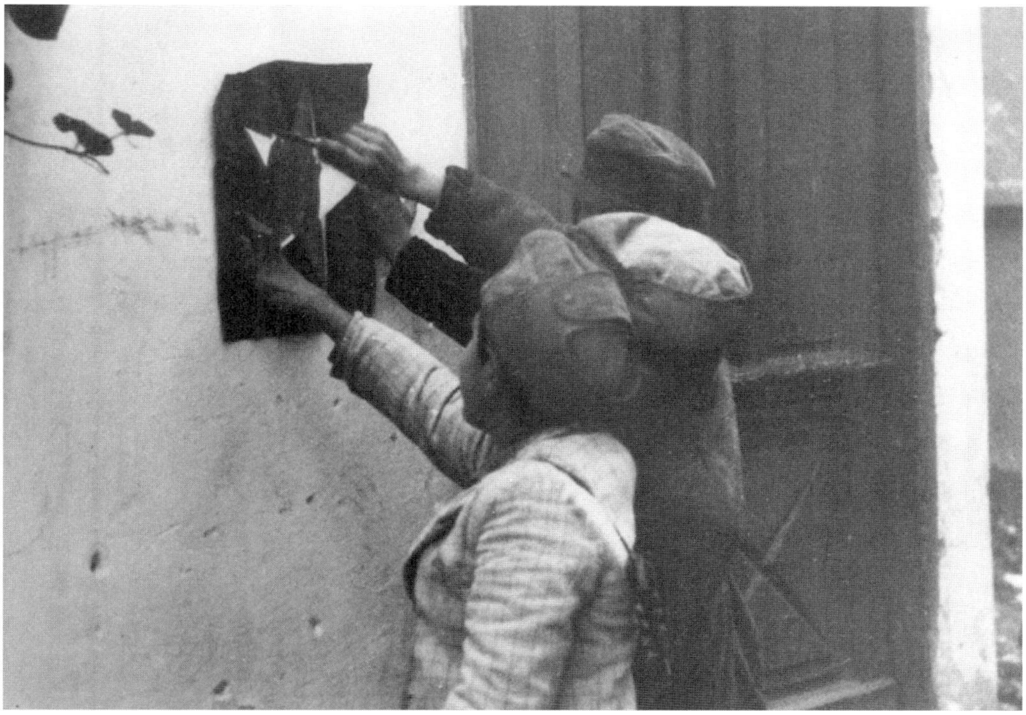

Pioneers paint five-pointed stars on the walls of houses, Skoplje 1945. Photographer unknown.
Military Museum Belgrade, 13288.

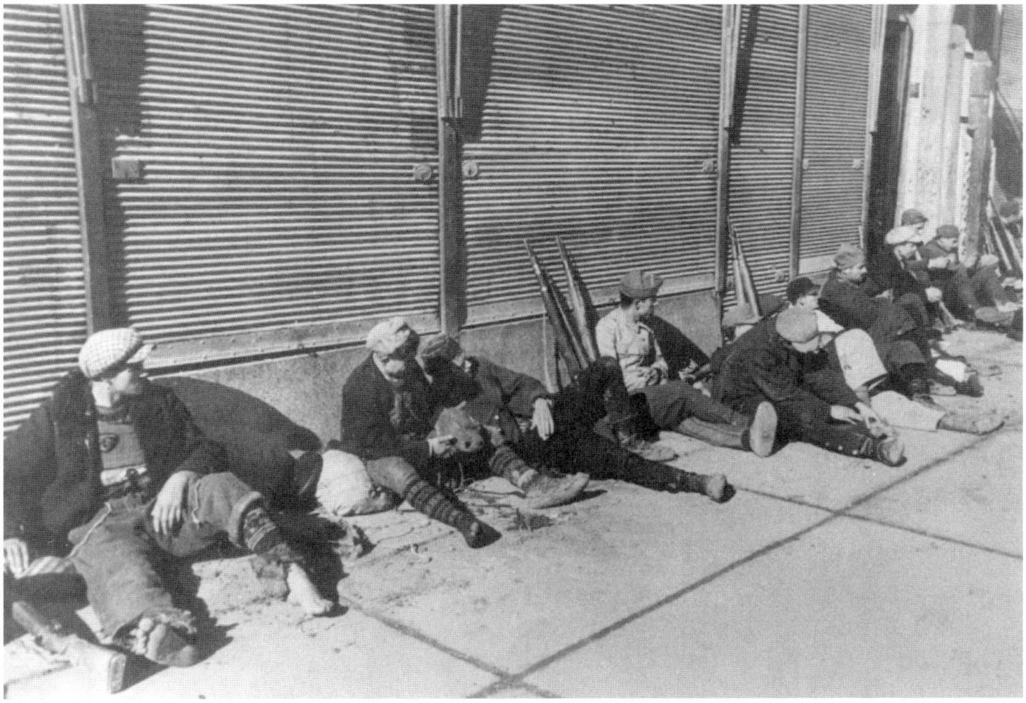

Off-duty soldiers from Macedonian units, November 1944. Skoplje. Photographer unknown.
Military Museum Belgrade, 413050.

graphs of Partisan columns and troop movements. The angle of his shots achieved a monumentality that resulted in filmic scenes that almost appear directed.

In Macedonia, the situation in publishing and cultural production was exceptionally bad. This was ascribed to the division of the state into a Bulgarian and Albanian component, and to the pro-Bulgarian leadership of the regional Communist Party of Yugoslavia, which was late in instigating an armed uprising. Although the Partisan movement itself became a mass movement in 1942, the Central Committee in Macedonia sent Svetozar Vukmanović-Tempo to organise and strengthen the actions of the Communist Party of Yugoslavia. Yet, in his report to the Central Committee of the Communist Party of Yugoslavia two years later, dated 22 April 1944, he mentions that in Macedonia there were only four newspapers to speak of, with only a handful of journalists and one opera singer from Sofia worth mentioning, but no photographers.[88] The same information is repeated in all subsequent reports sent during wartime.

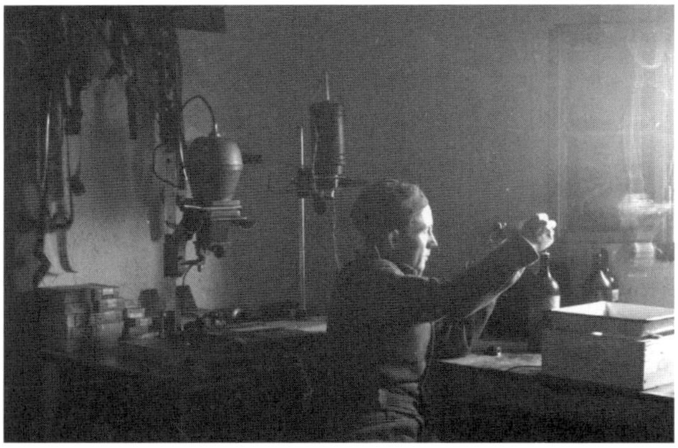

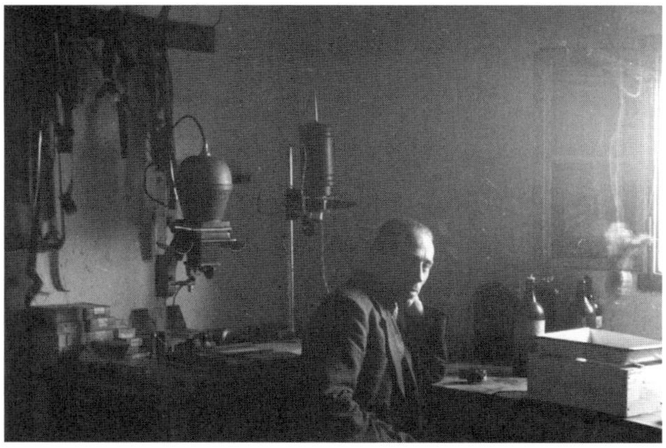

Franjo Veselko, head of the Slovenian war photography unit, at work in the film lab, 23 October 1944. Photo: Maksimilijan Zupančič. National Museum of Contemporary History of Slovenia, TN389/38

88 *Zbornik dokumenata/podataka o narodno-oslobodilačkom ratu jugoslovenskih naroda*, vol. II/12, Belgrade 1971.

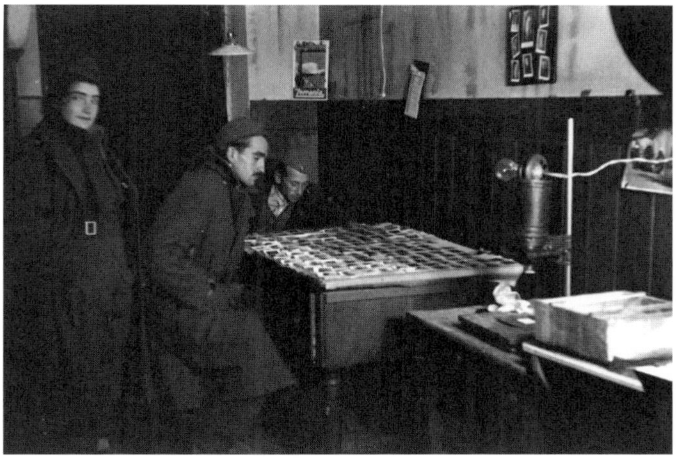

Photography unit of the Slovene People's Liberation Committee of Črnomelj. Photo: Alfred Kos. National Museum of Contemporary History of Slovenia, TN529/4.

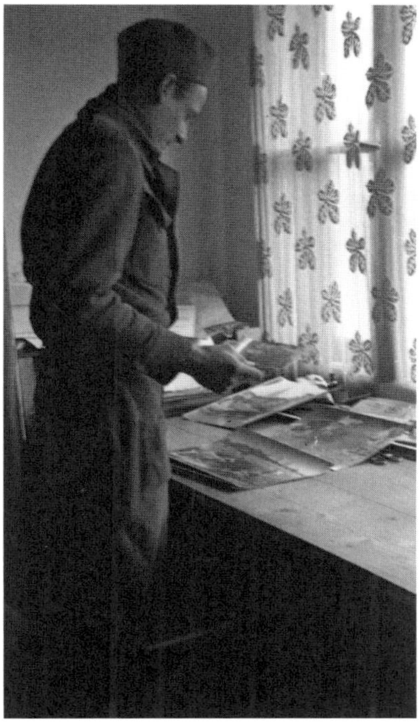

Work in the film lab, Črnomelj.
Photo: Alfred Kos. National Museum of Contemporary History of Slovenia, TN529/22.

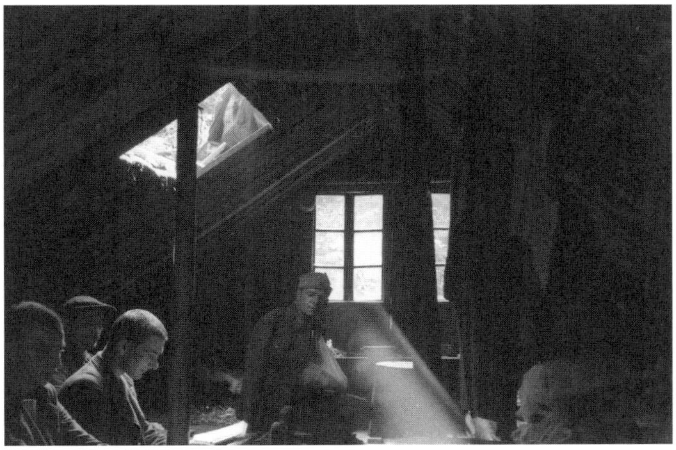

Partisan hospital Zgornji Hrastnik, spring 1944. Photo: Dr Janez Milčinski. National Museum of Contemporary History of Slovenia, 1227/15.

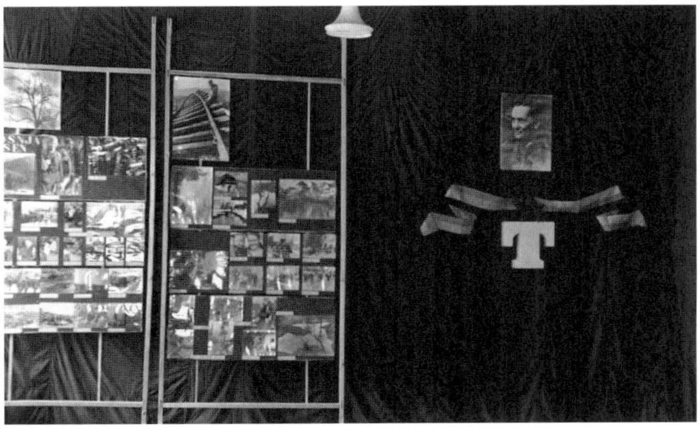

Photography exhibition in Črnomelj, 25–31 December 1944.
Photo: Jože Bitenc. National Museum of Contemporary History of Slovenia, TN526/1.

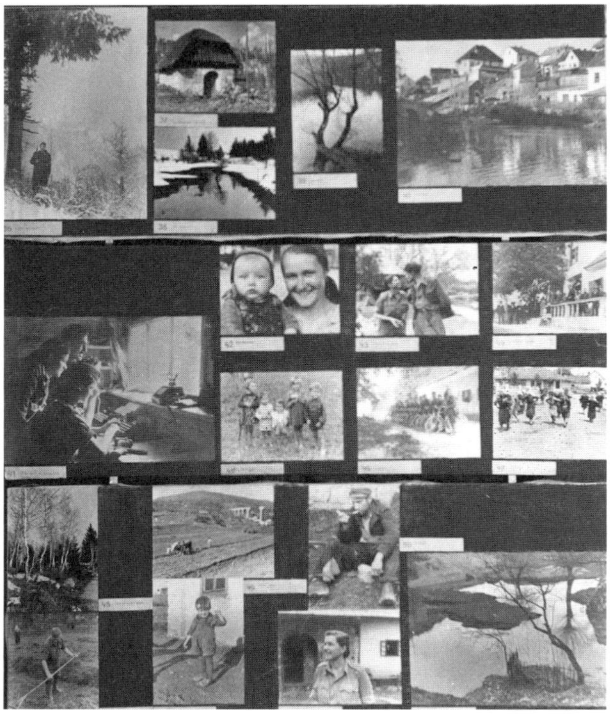

Photography exhibition in Črnomelj, 25–31 December 1944. Photo: Jože Bitenc. National Museum of Contemporary History of Slovenia, TN526/4.

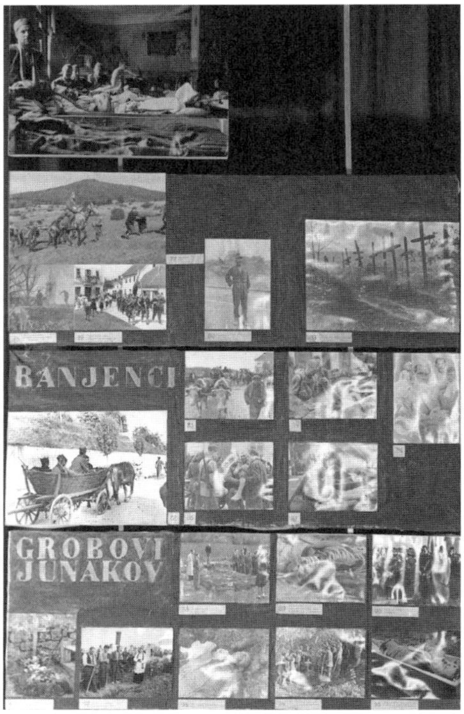

Photography exhibition in Črnomelj, 25–31 December 1944. Photo: Jože Bitenc. National Museum of Contemporary History of *Slovenia, TN526/2.*

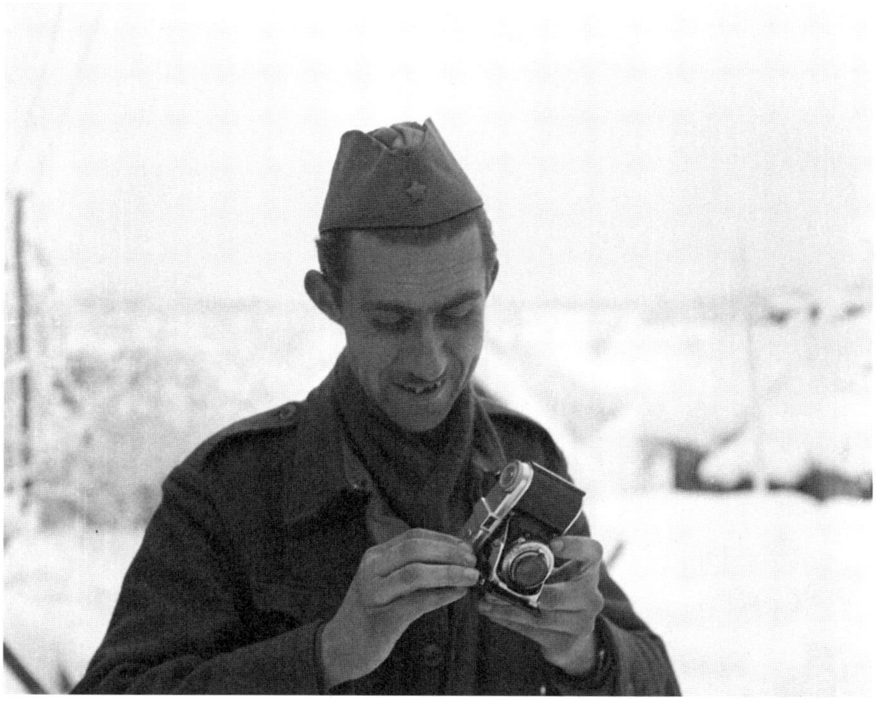

Comrade Stane Viršek at work with a new camera, during a breakthrough of enemy lines by the propaganda department of the People's Liberation Army and the Partisan Detachments of Slovenia, Črnomelj, 28 February 1945. Photographer unknown. National Museum of Contemporary History of Slovenia, TN1628/4.

After Italy's surrender on 8 September 1943 and the Fifth Enemy Offensive, the Partisans collaborated more closely with the Allies, especially the British. After several years of hesitation, Churchill's government finally recognised the reality on the ground. They recognised the Partisan movement as the only relevant Allied and anti-fascist movement on Yugoslav territory, actively fighting against German and quisling units. The now-open military alliance also resulted in fresh supplies of photographic equipment. The most notable uptick in photographic activities to ensue as a consequence was in Slovenia. This is substantiated by Tomaž Kladnik and Katarina Jurjavčić in their book *Vojne fotografije 1941–1945* with the following data:[89] In the winter of 1943 and in 1944, the events in Dolenjska were documented by Edi Šelhaus, Mirko Trobec, Miloš Brelih, Vinko Bavec and Gojko Pipenbacher, while events in Gorenjska were documented by Marjan Masterl, in Štajerska by Ivan Lipar-Iztok, in Primorska by Stane Lepardič-Žan and Miroslav Lilik, who were embedded with the Ninth Corps Čoro Škodlar. The Fourteenth Division's campaign, meanwhile, was recorded by Jože Petek. In that period, Alfred Kos, Stane Viršek and Frane Cerar worked as members of the photography unit of the Slovene People's Liberation Committee. The academic painter Božidar Jakac also took photos while in the Partisans, and the history teacher Franjo Veselko photographed the Cankar Brigade.[90]

The Slovenian Partisans boasted one of the best-organised photography units within the Partisan movement. After 1943 the number of photographers grew significantly, compared with the other Yugoslav republics, and exhibition activities intensified. In Cerkno on 23 February 1945, an important photography exhibition went on show marking the twenty-seventh anniversary of the Red Army's founding, organised by the propaganda department of the Ninth Corps.[91] Of the works made by Slovenian photographers, that of Jože Petek especially stands out. His observational approach, bravery, and uncompromising documentarism stands in the same league as the works of the eminent war photographer Robert Capa. The interesting works of Dr Janez Milčinski are also worthy of mention, as they present a kind of anthropological analysis of life in Partisan hospitals.

On 5 June 1944, the propaganda department of the General Staff of the People's Liberation Army and the Partisan Detachments of Slovenia showed an exhibition of 118 photographs that opened in Lakner's Salon in Črnomelj, before travelling to Metlika (9 June) and Semič (13 June) – all locations in south-east Slovenia.[92] The exhibition was split into four thematic blocks: the war crimes of the occupiers, the life and struggle of the Partisan army, caring for the injured and cultural performances. The exhibition attracted around 2,000 people at each venue.[93] The exhibit finally went on view in Dvor, with around 400 visitors (half of them soldiers). Visitors criticised the lack of photos depicting direct combat, and

89 Jurjavčič Dežman, Katarina Jurjavčič and Tomaž Kladnik, *Vojne fotografije, 1941–1945: Partizanske enote: iz fotografske zbirke Muzeja novejše Zgodovine Slovenije*, Ljubljana 2010.

90 Ibid., p. 22.

91 Mirko Ljubič-Bogo, 'Oris dejavnosti in služb', in: *Artilerija 9. Korpusa*, Boris Borivoj Lah (ed.), Ljubljana 1985, p. 260.

92 *Zbornik dokumenata i podataka o narodno-oslobodilačkom ratu jugoslovenskih naroda*, vol. IX/ 6: Partijsko-politička dokumenta 1943. Godine, Belgrade 1967.

93 Ibid.

the lack of a more detailed portrayal of Partisan life.[94] The Jesenje-Bohinj Detachment in Slovenia, acquired an envious photographic stock, even during wartime, thanks to the efforts of Slavko Smolej, who photographed the final push to victory in Koruška.[95]

The all-encompassing quality of Partisan cultural production and its broad, egalitarian quality led to art becoming open to all – to both the educated and the workers, peasants and artists alike. People who had never written poems became poets, while people who had never told stories became writers. Many photographers evolved into professionals in the wartime period, and many unknown amateurs took their first photographs. As with poets, writers, artists, dancers, sketch artists, musicians, sculptors and painters, photographers too depicted and commented on the world. Their photographs were made not merely to document events or to propagate a 'false' photographic truth. Rather, they were a means of producing their own artistic and political vision of the revolutionary struggle, a struggle that was intended to lead to a lasting peace. In this chapter, we have especially demonstrated that on the ground, under impossible conditions, the Partisans engaged in a lively photographic campaign of picture making, training, dissemination, archiving and exhibiting. The activities were specific to their time and place, determined principally by their role in the nurturing of revolutionary consciousness, yet also by the technical conditions in which Partisan photography evolved.

94 Ibid.

95 Mile Pavlin, *Jeseniško-bohinjski odred*, Ljubljana 1970, p. 317.

5. Photography and Propaganda

Today, the word 'propaganda' has negative connotations, often linked with manipulation and misuse of information. However, in the first few decades of the 20th century, it was understood as a structured process that used information to promote goals and drum up support. In this sense, it dealt with the control and transmission of information to an interested audience via the media.[1] The media in question is often, but not always, the mass media, as shaped by various political, cultural and profit-related interests.[2]

Indeed, photography is basically information. As the French cultural critic Roland Barthes might have put it – photojournalism is a message defined by its information source, transmitter, channel, receiver and destination.[3] From this perspective, the information source would be the members of a newspaper or magazine editorial board, the transmission channel would be the medium itself, and the receiver the audience.[4] If we apply such a system to Partisan photography, we could say that the information source is the photographer, war photography unit or cultural unit, the editorial board of a certain newspaper, the printing house or the photography and propaganda department. The transmission channels are Partisan newspapers. In these newspapers it was supremely difficult to publish high-quality photographic reproductions. Consequently, it was more common to see news boards containing clippings (photography alongside headlines and subheadings) or the developed prints of the photographs themselves.[5] And while other contemporary authors such as Allan Sekula have claimed that photography cannot be observed alone outside the context in which it is distributed, here the entire context underpinning the function of Partisan photography and its messages must be laid bare. This is because we are not speaking here of newspaper editorial offices with a staff of photographers and editors at work in comfortable conditions. Instead, we are dealing with printing presses found mainly in hideouts in forests or in liberated towns and villages. Not infrequently, the photographers were also acting alone.

1 Aristotle Kallis, *Nazi Propaganda and the Second World War*, New York 2005, p. 1.

2 Sebastiaan Faber, *Memory Battles of The Spanish Civil War*, Nashville, p. 30.

3 Roland Barthes, 'The Photographic Message', in: *A Barthes Reader*, Susan Sontag (ed.), New York, p. 124.

4 Ibid.

5 The poor distribution channels for photography become manifest after a meeting of Allied Command for the Middle East on Yugoslav soil, as shown in a letter, dated 19 June 1943, sent by Slovene Partisan Edvard Kardelj to Boris Kidrič and Franc Leskošek, informing them that they need to make political use of their photographs and get them printed in the newspaper *Poročevalec*. Aware of the limitations of such publications, he advises them to take the images directly into the surrounding country and show them to the peasants in the villages. In: *Zbornik dokumenata i podataka o narodno-oslobodilačkom ratu jugoslovenskih naroda*, vol. II/7: Dokumenta vrhovnog štaba Narodnooslobodilačke vojske Jugoslavije 1942–1943, Belgrade 1959.

When speaking of the context and channels of distribution, one interesting example is a photograph for which Chetniks posed together with German and Ustashe officers in Sanski Most, in a park where twenty-seven people had been hanged only a year earlier.[6] Another interesting example is the photographs in which members of the Ustashe pose with Chetniks on 15 May 1942 in Banja Luka, a town in northern Bosnia. After the Partisans had got their hands on these photographs through their connections and supporters of the Partisan movement, they distributed them among the local population, which helped garner even greater support for the Partisan movement. Vilko Vinterhalter was charged with this task. He was head of agitprop for Bosanska Krajina, and later editor of *Oslobođenje*, a newspaper still in circulation today.[7] Afterwards, the Ustashe units encountered increasing resistance from the local population. Stjepan Kovačević, the intelligence officer for the Fourth Infantry Division of the Independent State of Croatia, wrote about this in a report in great detail, as did a Chetnik colonel named Rade Radić:[8] 'The people attack us, me especially, violently, because of the concluded treaties.'[9]

Agitation, intrinsic to guerrilla movements (including the Partisans), is based on the assumption that political ideas are disseminated in words, letters and by many other means, and that this dissemination garners critical support for direct actions, or helps achieve a given political goal. Propaganda was understood to be the *planned* dissemination of political principles and knowledge allowing people to understand those principles. Culture presupposed a corpus of 'all the material and spiritual achievements of a single people or humanity over a certain period.'[10] The 'Instructions for the Operations and Organisation of Agitprop in Primorje-Gorenje Division' stated that in all units – in each platoon, company, battalion, brigade and, ultimately, division: 'You should always bear in mind that our army is stronger the more the fighters know, that is, the more politically aware, better informed, culturally advanced they are, in contrast to the fascist army, which is stronger the less the soldiers in it know, that is, the less politically conscious and informed and the more culturally backward they are.'[11] From its inception, the Communist Party of Yugoslavia believed culture and education to be an important aspect in the revolutionary struggle unfolding alongside the anti-fascist struggle. This idea is illustrated by slogans such as: 'Education leads to freedom'; 'Weapons aren't just guns and cannons, planes and tanks, but knowledge too'; and 'A book helps us gain freedom, freedom will ensure we win the book' [i.e., create a society that values literacy and education].[12] These slogans affirm the emancipatory potential of a struggle in which knowledge and education are the prerequisites for human liberation.

6 Branko J. Bokan, *Srez Sanski Most u NOB 1941-1945. godine*. Sanski Most 1980, p. 445.

7 Stevo Samardžija, *Četrnaesta srednjebosanska NOU brigada*, Banja Luka 1983, p. 233.

8 Ibid., p. 233.

9 Arhiv VII, NDH (Independent State of Croatia), box 101, reg. no. 2/4-1; see also Stevo Samardžija, *Četrnaesta srednjebosanska NOU brigada*, Banja Luka 1983.

10 *Zbornik dokumenata i podataka o narodno-oslobodilačkom ratu jugoslovenskih naroda*, vol. IX/3: Partijsko-politička dokumenta 1943. godine, Belgrade 1967.

11 Ibid.

12 Quoted from: Branko Petranović, *Istorija Jugoslavije 1918-1988*, Belgrade 1988, p. 357.

The Consolidation of Agitation and Propaganda Work

Agitprop became an increasingly important channel of communication for political agitation, emancipation and the struggle to create a new world, because of the opportunities it created for the easy transmission of messages via photography. Yet one of this book's key theses is that Partisan photography never entirely had a singular and exclusively propaganda-related function. This is because the centralised operations of the propaganda and cultural departments were only consolidated in the final two years of the war, in step with the combat-related and political tasks the Partisans had before them. In 1943 the agitation and propaganda apparatus began to be organised more systematically. A Culture and Education Committee was established, split into four sectors: political agitation, printing, cultural work and educational work. The latter two sectors included literacy-promotion, education, lectures, an amateur theatre section, choirs, a library, archival work – and photography:

Each agitprop brigade, in line with the opportunities and resources available to them (photographers, cameras and materials) should have a photojournalist who films combat, parades, exercises, learning, relaxation, entertainment, the seizing of enemy goods, prisons, enemy losses, our victims and work from the level of the brigade headquarters to the individual fighters, etc. They should bear in mind that photographs are the most objective images and documents of our struggle and that they are of invaluable historical value. They are also brilliant propaganda material. Photographs from the front lines portraying the struggle itself are of particular importance. This work should be approached as a matter of urgency: if the brigades lack the materials, they should let the agitprop division know, and they should report the number of cameras the brigade has available to use. All such recorded material belongs to the division staff and will be handed over as undeveloped film. The film stock will then be developed, and copies will be guaranteed for the brigade archive, and individual photographs will be presented to deserving individuals.[13]

The above description clearly shows that an awareness of photography-as-proof already existed. The writer believed in the power and truthfulness of photography, and viewed it as a more powerful medium at that time than written words, especially in terms of its propaganda potential. Such agitprop departments started indexing visual material by theme, thus laying the groundwork for the emergence of photographic archives. As for the topics chosen, their approach is strikingly bottom-up and non-hierarchical, celebrating and documenting common activities rather than only recording major events and figures. Leisure is important, as is every soldier, irrespective of their position in the military hierarchy.

Most photography units were organised following the directive issued by Supreme Command on 13 December 1944 on the organisation of propaganda and cultural and educational work in the People's Liberation Army of Yugoslavia. The photography units had to work in unison with the propaganda department of the Supreme Command, as well as

13 *Zbornik dokumenata i podataka o narodno-oslobodilačkom ratu jugoslovenskih naroda*, vol. IX/3: Partijsko-politička dokumenta 1943. godine, Belgrade 1967.

with the general staff of the divisions and brigades. Propaganda activity underwent its biggest upswing at the end of 1944. It permeated the entire military structure from the smallest formations, battalions and companies to the Supreme Command itself. The latter was now reorganised, with several new departments: propaganda, cultural and educational

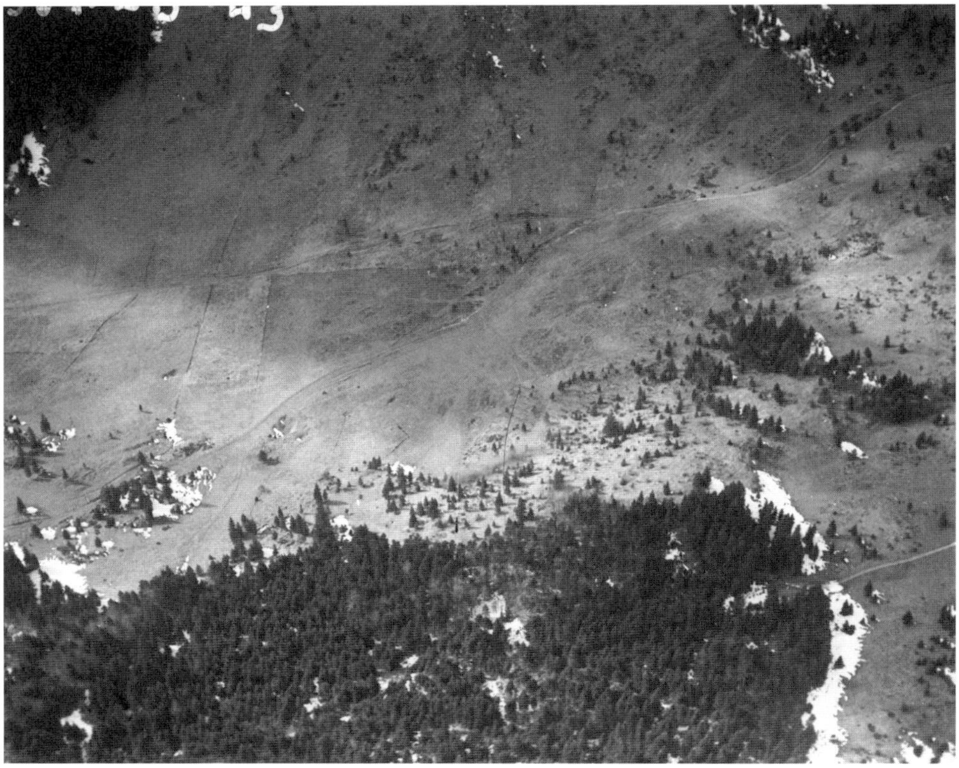

Uncaptioned. Most likely aerial reconnaissance from Allied plane, 1944–45. Photographer unknown. National Museum of Contemporary History (Slovenia), TN1119/8.

work, publishing, film, photography and historical and academic activities.[14] Criticism of this organisation structure was often directed at the 'one-size-fits-all approach to the various forms of work and the implementation of cultural and educational activities'.[15] At the same time, the cultural departments within the brigades were the torchbearers for agitation and propaganda work, cultural activities and educational activities. During these years, an aerial photography unit was set up, which proved of vital use to the land surveying section.[16] As Partisan aviation grew (the Partisans were the only resistance movement to form their own air force), so did the aerial photography unit, and its primary purpose was reconnaissance and intelligence. This was of crucial significance in preparing the final operations for the country's liberation. Aerial photos were enlarged and assembled into larger photomontages.

14 Ibid., p. 361.

15 Ibid., p. 362.

16 *Zbornik dokumenata i podataka o narodno-oslobodilačkom ratu jugoslovenskih naroda*, vol. V/26: Borbe u Hrvatskoj 1944. godine, Belgrade 1961.

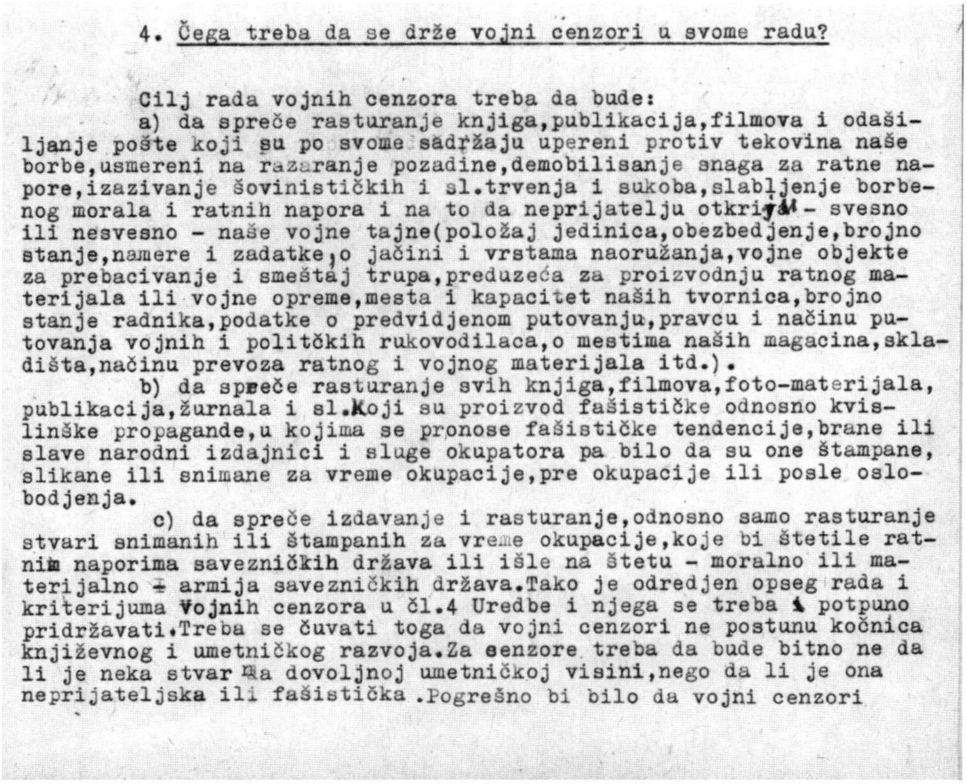

4. Čega treba da se drže vojni cenzori u svome radu?

Cilj rada vojnih cenzora treba da bude:

a) da spreče rasturanje knjiga,publikacija,filmova i odašiljanje pošte koji su po svome sadržaju upereni protiv tekovina naše borbe,usmereni na razaranje pozadine,demobilisanje snaga za ratne napore,izazivanje šovinističkih i sl.trvenja i sukoba,slabljenje borbenog morala i ratnih napora i na to da neprijatelju otkriju - svesno ili nesvesno - naše vojne tajne(položaj jedinica,obezbedjenje,brojno stanje,namere i zadatke,o jačini i vrstama naoružanja,vojne objekte za prebacivanje i smeštaj trupa,preduzeća za proizvodnju ratnog materijala ili vojne opreme,mesta i kapacitet naših tvornica,brojno stanje radnika,podatke o predvidjenom putovanju,pravcu i načinu putovanja vojnih i političkih rukovodilaca,o mestima naših magacina,skladišta,načinu prevoza ratnog i vojnog materijala itd.).

b) da spreče rasturanje svih knjiga,filmova,foto-materijala, publikacija,žurnala i sl.Koji su proizvod fašističke odnosno kvislinške propagande,u kojima se pronose fašističke tendencije,brane ili slave narodni izdajnici i sluge okupatora pa bilo da su one štampane, slikane ili snimane za vreme okupacije,pre okupacije ili posle oslobodjenja.

c) da spreče izdavanje i rasturanje,odnosno samo rasturanje stvari snimanih ili štampanih za vreme okupacije,koje bi štetile ratnim naporima savezničkih država ili išle na štetu - moralno ili materijalno - armija savezničkih država.Tako je odredjen opseg rada i kriterijuma vojnih cenzora u čl.4 Uredbe i njega se treba potpuno pridržavati.Treba se čuvati toga da vojni cenzori ne postunu kočnica književnog i umetničkog razvoja.Za cenzore treba da bude bitno ne da li je neka stvar na dovoljnoj umetničkoj visini,nego da li je ona neprijateljska ili fašistička .Pogrešno bi bilo da vojni cenzori

Letter headed 'What must military censors consider in their work?', People's Liberation Army of Yugoslavia, Military Archive Belgrade, K460C F2 20.

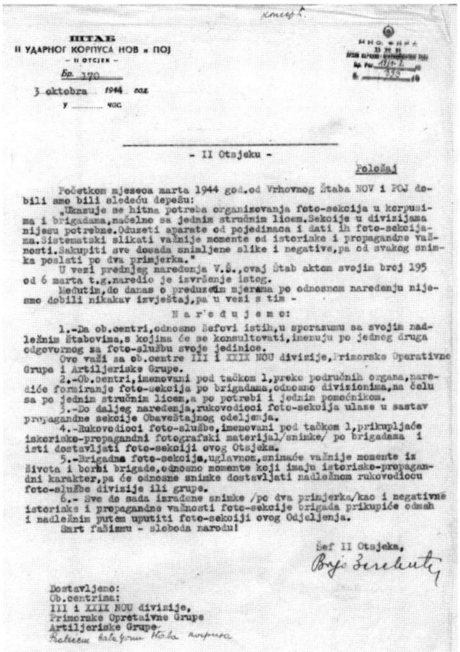

ШТАБ
II УДАРНОГ КОРПУСА НОВ и ПОЈ
- II ОТСЈЕК -
Бр. 170
3 oktobra 1944 год.
у ____ час.

- II Otsjeku -

Položaj

Početkom mjeseca marta 1944 god.od Vrhovnog Štaba NOV i POJ dobili smo bili sledeću depešu:

„Ukazuje se hitna potreba organizovanja foto-sekcija u korpusima i brigadama,načelno sa jednim stručnim licem.Sekcije u divizijama nijesu potrebne.Oduzeti aparate od pojedinaca i dati ih foto-sekcijama.Sistematski slikati važnije momente od istoriske i propagandne važnosti.Sakupiti sve dosada snimljene slike i negative,pa od svakog snimka poslati po dva primjerka."

U vezi prednjeg naređenja V.Š.,ovaj Štab aktom svojim broj 195 od 6 marta t.g.naredio je izvršenje istog.

Međutim,do danas o preduzetim mjerama po odnosnom naređenju nijesmo dobili nikakav izvještaj,pa u vezi s tim -

N a r e đ u j e m o:

1.-Da ob.centri,odnosno šefovi istih,u sporazumu sa svojim nadležnim štabovima,s kojima će se konsultovati,imenuju po jednog druga odgovornog za foto-službu svoje jedinice.

Ove važi za ob.centre III i XXIX NOU divizije,Primorske Operativne Grupe i Artiljeriske Grupe.

2.-Ob.centri,imenovani pod tačkom 1,preko područnih organa,narediće formiranje foto-sekcija po brigadama,odnosno divizionima,na čelu sa po jednim stručnim licem,a po potrebi i jednim pomoćnikom.

3.-Do daljeg naređenja,rukovodioci foto-sekcija ulaze u sastav propagandne sekcije Obaveštajnog odeljenja.

4.-Rukovodioci foto-službe,imenovani pod tačkom 1,prikupljaće istoriske-propagandni fotografski materijal/snimke/ po brigadama i isti dostavljati foto-sekciji ovog Otsjeka.

5.-Brigadna foto-sekcija,uglavnom,snimaće važnije momente iz života i borbi brigade,odnosno momente koji imaju istoriske-propagandni karakter,pa će odnosne snimke dostavljati nadležnom rukovodiocu foto-službe divizije ili grupe.

6.- Sve do sada izrađene snimke /po dva primjerka/kao i negativne istoriske i propagandne važnosti foto-sekcije brigada prikupiće odmah i nadležnim putem uputiti foto-sekciji ovog Odjeljenja.

Smrt fašizmu - sloboda narodu!

Šef II Otsjeka,

Dostavljeno:
Ob.centrima:
III i XXIX NOU divizije,
Primorske Opretaivne Grupe
Artiljeriske Grupe

Instructions issued by General Staff on setting up photography units in the corps and brigades, 3 October 1944, Military Archive Belgrade, NOVJ K393 F2 19.

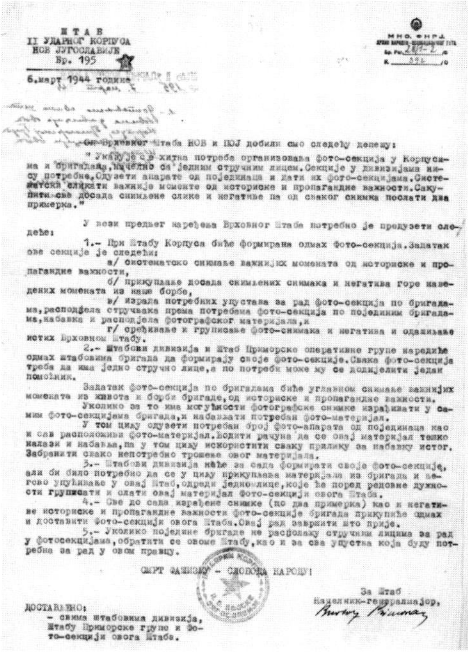

ШТАБ
II УДАРНОГ КОРПУСА
НОВ ЈУГОСЛАВИЈЕ
Бр. 195
6.март 1944 године

Од Врховног Штаба НОВ и ПОЈ добили смо следећу депешу:

" Указује се хитна потреба организовања фото-секција у Корпусима и бригадама,начелно са једним стручним лицем.Секције у дивизијама нису потребне.Одузети апарате од појединаца и дати их фото-секцијама.Систематски сликати важније моменте од историске и пропагандне важности.Сакупити све досада снимљене слике и негативе па од сваког снимка послати два примерка."

У вези предњег наређења Врховног Штаба потребно је предузети следеће:

1.- При Штабу Корпуса биће формирана одмах фото-секција.Задатак ове секције је следећи:

а/ систематско снимање важнијих момената од историске и пропагандне важности,

б/ прикупљање досада снимљених снимака и негатива горе наведених момената из наше борбе,

в/ израда потребних упустава за рад фото-секција по бригадама,расподјела стручњака према потребама фото-секција по појединим бригадама,набавка и расподјела фотографског материјала,и

г/ сређивање и груписање фото-снимака и негатива и одашиљање истих Врховном Штабу.

2.- Штабови дивизија и Штаб Приморске оперативне групе наредиће одмах штабовима бригада да формирају своје фото-секције.Свака фото-секција треба да има једно стручно лице,а по потреби може му се додијелити један помоћник.

Задатак фото-секција по бригадама биће углавном снимање важнијих момената из живота и борби бригаде,од историске и пропагандне важности.

Уколико за то има могућности фотографске снимке израђивати у самим фото-секцијама бригада,и набављати потребан фото-материјал.

У том циљу одузети потребан број фото-апарата од појединаца као и сав расположиви фото-материјал.Водити рачуна да се овај материјал тешко налази и набавља,па у том циљу искористити сваку прилику за набавку истог.

Забранити свако непотребно трошење овог материјала.

3.- Штабови дивизија неће за сада формирати своје фото-секције, али би било потребно да се у циљу прикупљања материјала из бригада и његово упућивање у овај Штаб,одреди једно лице,које ће поред редовне дужности груписати и слати овај материјал фото-секцији овога Штаба.

4.- Све до сада израђене снимке (по два примерка) као и негативе историске и пропагандне важности фото-секције бригада прикупиће одмах и доставити фото-секцији овога Штаба.Овај рад завршити што прије.

5.- Уколико поједине бригаде не располажу стручним лицима за рад у фотосекцијама,обратити се овоме Штабу,као и за сва упуства која буду потребна за рад у овом правцу.

СМРТ ФАШИЗМУ - СЛОБОДА НАРОДУ!

За Штаб
Начелник-генералмајор,

ДОСТАВЉЕНО:
- свима штабовима дивизија,
Штабу Приморске групе и фото-секцији овога Штаба.

Instructions issued by General Staff on setting up photography units in the corps and brigades, 6 March 1944, Military Archive Belgrade, NOVJ K392 F2 28.

The instructions for the correspondence service, written in March 1944, state that photographs are particularly important and that the correspondent's task is to gather all photography from the People's Liberation Movement, as well as photographs illustrating the consequences of enemy campaigns. Optimism was the order of the day, and the rules stated that Partisans should gather photographs in 'people's pockets, who will – for the needs of the movement – happily hand them over'.[17] The Supreme Command thus issued the order on 4 March 1944 to the General Staff of the NOV i POJ (People's Liberation Army and Partisan Detachments of Yugoslavia) stating that the brigades and the corps must each set up their own photography unit that would record significant events, and that they should do so urgently. As for any individuals in possession of a camera, they ordered that their cameras be requisitioned and handed to the photography units: 'Take photographs in a systematic manner of the more important moments of historical and propaganda-related importance and collect all the pictures shot so far, including negatives, sending two copies of each picture.'[18] The same order reached the remaining staffs over the following few days, and furthermore demanded of them to draft clear instructions and missions for each photography units' work.

The changes that gradually occurred in the propaganda and agitation apparatus led to the Communist Party of Yugoslavia deciding to establish a new propaganda service, with attempts made to centralise propaganda efforts in 1944:

The starting premise of the new organisation of the agitprop service of the Central Committee aimed at overcoming 'spontaneity and backwardness', at building an apparatus for propaganda and agitation, concentrating – directly or indirectly – the entire people's political, cultural, educational and intellectual life in the hands of Party institutions with the goal of generating mass Party membership and establishing the ideological basis of the new society.[19]

The final year of war and its end were a turning point for photography, which came under the complete control of the mass apparatus. After this point, we incrementally entered a period that the historian Branko Petranović has described as a period without 'critique, debate, plurality of viewpoints in the field of cultural creativity, except for the odd critically worded piece of a political nature issued from within the ranks of the "civic opposition"'.[20] This was the moment when Partisan photography fell into the hands of a centralised service. It would become an institution within the newly formed state that was attempting to establish sovereign control, including through the construction of dogmatic ideological positions across all of society. One of the reasons for such a turnaround is the fact that establishing a new state does not occur without resistance, or without problems, both in the country and abroad. After all, the Soviet Union presented a real threat of potential invasion.

17 *Zemaljsko antifašističko vijeće narodnog oslobođenja Hrvatske, zbornik dokumenata 1944 (od 10. svibnja do 31. prosinca)*, Institut za historiju radničkog pokreta Hrvatske, Zagreb 1975.

18 *Zbornik dokumenata/podataka o narodno-oslobodilačkom ratu jugoslovenskih naroda*, vol. II/12,Belgrade 1971.

19 Petranović 1988 (see note 12), p. 121.

20 Ibid., p. 24.

In 1945, the propaganda departments within the staffs of each brigade and division had their own section for political propaganda, a section for culture and education, a section for photography, as well as a press department. The propaganda department of each corps, meanwhile, had (like those of the brigades and divisions) a department for political propaganda and one for culture and education, but they also had their own sections for school learning, literacy courses and art, as well as departments for press reportage, film and photography. The Supreme Command of the NOV i POJ (from 1 March 1945 the General Staff of the Yugoslav Army) had a department for political propaganda and a department of culture and education. The latter had three sections: general education, literacy courses and artistic activities. There were also press departments, an institute for researching the People's Liberation War, a photography unit, and a department for foreign relations and personnel affairs.

Despite views commonly held today, military censorship was only introduced at the beginning of 1945 and was intended to control information-sharing *within* the army. According to the Supreme Command's documentation, the censors were established by the general staffs, and applied to the staffs of the corps and the corps' military fields and, when necessary, to the staffs of the brigades and detachments, too. The military censors fell under the command of the staffs, with a separate section tasked with censoring military postal correspondence. For the first time ever, there was an official list of forbidden books. Manuscripts and books arriving from abroad were tracked, and more detailed descriptions of their contents had to be given. There was a special list for movies. Besides their detailed description, reasons for their censorship had to be listed. Interestingly, no seized materials were allowed to be thrown away because of the scarcity of materials. Instead, they had to be preserved and, if necessary, later recycled. Censorship did not cover official letters, such as those of members of the Supreme Command, or letters by civilians to other civilians or soldiers. However, it did cover the journalists' reports, those of all correspondents and photographs sent to various official publications.

The aim of censorship was to prevent the distribution of enemy literature and quisling propaganda, the disclosure of military secrets and the distribution of material printed during the occupation that would in any way threaten the efforts of Allied units. The military censors were explicitly told not to stifle literary and artistic talent and that their task was not to assess the artistic merit of written or visual material, but instead to decide whether such works had an inimical or fascist intent.[21] In contrast to other military formations, both Allied and enemy, the censorship apparatus only came into being in the final year of war. As concerns photography, this is important because it was precisely the lack of coordinated supervision that contributed to the pluralism of ideas and approaches in style. Besides the difficult conditions of production, this pluralism was one of the most powerful defining features of Partisan photography. Broadly speaking, the democratic quality of the medium itself and of photographic production granted photographers a degree of autonomy from the authoritarian and bureaucratic practices that reigned

21 People's Liberation Army of Yugoslavia, Military Archive Belgrade, K24 F2 20.

elsewhere. Partisan photographers within the anti-fascist movement perhaps came closest to the ideal of a horizontal, 'bottom-up' anti-capitalist struggle in the sense that prevails today in various social movements the world over.

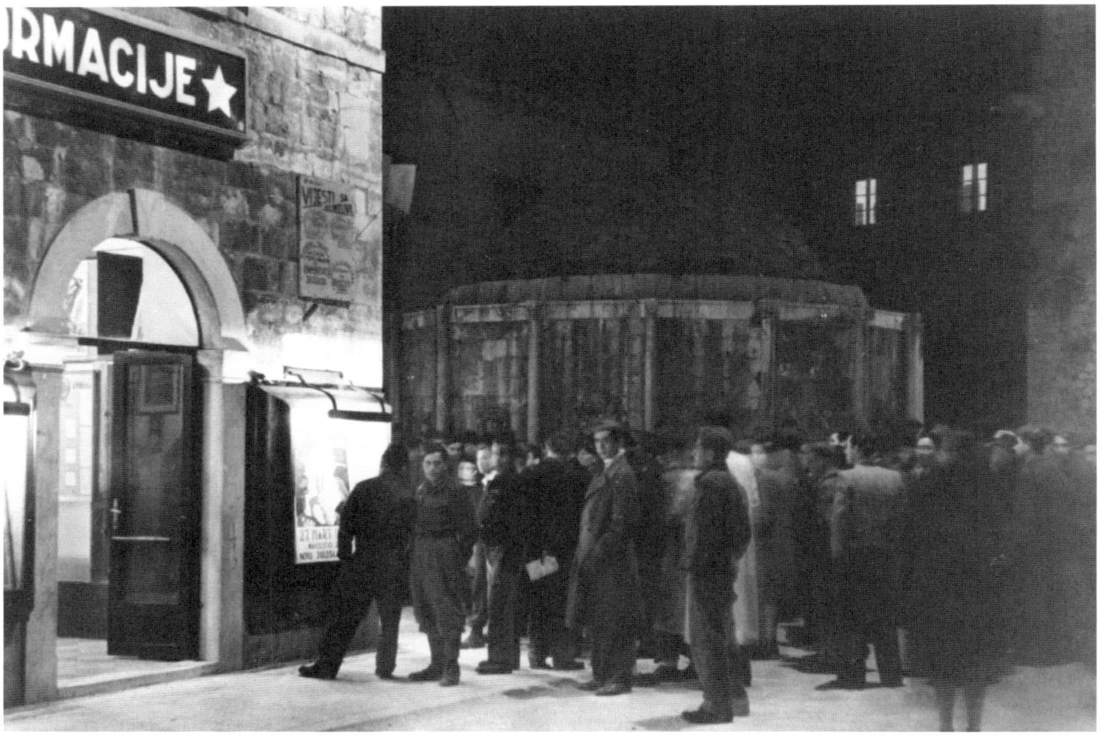

Waiting for radio news broadcast in front of the information office, Dubrovnik, 1945. Photo: Nikola Rupčić. Croatian History Museum, HPM/MRNH-F-8242.

Enemy Propaganda

Throughout the whole war, cultural and educational life on occupied territory was dedicated to fascist ideology and National Socialism, while the specific materials available were markedly anti-communist, antisemitic, and anti-Masonic. In the Independent State of Croatia they were also markedly anti-Serbian and anti-Yugoslav. German culture and Roman civilisation were glorified, and German, Italian, Bulgarian and Hungarian introduced as core languages.[22] Under the Italian occupation, an Institute of Fascist Culture was established in Split.

22 Petranović 1988 (see note 12), pp. 358–359.

In occupied Serbia, one of the biggest propaganda exhibitions negatively depicting the influence of Freemasons, communists and Jews was the *Anti-Masonic Exhibition*, organised by journalists with pro-fascist proclivities such as Milan Stojadinović (head of the propaganda department of the Government Presidency during occupation), and Đorđe Perić, head of state propaganda.[23] On posters and in the narratives of German – and especially quisling – propaganda in Yugoslavia, Partisans were depicted as arsonists and sexual perverts, prepared even to kill their own brothers.

In the Independent State of Croatia, photography fell under the responsibility of the State Reporting and Propaganda Office,[24] led from 1941 to 1943 by the writer and photographer Ivan Softa, with help from the head of the film department, Mladen Grčević.[25] The office's task was to gather all material for propaganda; by 1942 their picture library contained 3,000 photographs and negatives.[26] In autumn of 1943, a new propaganda structure was established under the Main Directorate for Propaganda. This included a department of printing and photography, in turn subdivided into a department of journalism, of photography and of film.[27] Propaganda photobooks were also published, such as *Lijepa naša domovino* (Our Beautiful Homeland). We can observe how propaganda functioned in the Independent State of Croatia by taking as an example the photographer Edmund Stoger, who was sent on assignment to Jasenovac concentration camp in early September 1942.[28]

Besides taking photographs during his eight-day-long stay in Jasenovac, Stoger filmed the propaganda film *Pozitivni rad u logoru Jasenovac* (Positive Work at the Jasenovac Concentration Camp), which was screened at the Zagrebački zbor, or ZZ, an autumn fair in Zagreb, that same year. Using the slogan 'Their earlier work was politics – our present-day politics is work', the fair even featured a replica of the barracks that simulated the conditions of life in the camp and its allegedly work-based and remedial character. The accompanying display showed artwork produced in incarceration, including drawings by the young Daniel Ozmo who was shot in September 1942, only a few days after his mother, brother and sister were also killed in Jasenovac.[29] Stoger shot propaganda stills in Jasenovac that did not show the camp's brutal conditions, or its primitive 'manufacturing', whereby it made use of the 'handicraft of the most developed form of cruelty'.[30]

The exhibition was shown in the original shed that had served as sleeping quarters for the camp prisoners. The shack was fenced off with wire on the outside, and a guard post was placed in each part in which the Ustashe kept guard. Indeed, the exhibition strived to give the most faithful picture, with everything organised just as it was in the concentration camp. At the entrance to

23 Milan Radanović, 'Antimasonska izložba', in: *Mesta stradanja i antifašističke borbe u Beogradu 1941–44. Priručnik za čitanje grada*, Milovan Pisarri and Rena Rädle (eds.), Belgrade 2016 (Rosa Luxemburg Stiftung Southeast Europe), p. 74.

24 Croatian: *Svjetlopisni ured Državnog izvještajnog i promičbenog ureda*.

25 Branka Hlevnjak and Rhea Ivanuš, *Hrvatska antiratna fotografija: Prvi svjetski, Drugi svjetski i Domovinski rat*, Zagreb 2008, p. 101.

26 Nataša Mataušić, *Koncentracioni logor Jasenovac*, Zagreb 2008, p. 46.

27 Alan Labus, 'Upravljanje medijima, cenzura, te položaj i uloga novinara u Nezavisnoj Državi Hrvatskoj', in: *Studia lexicographica, god. 3, no. 1–2(3–4)*, Damir Boris (ed.), Zagreb 2009, pp. 107–108.

28 Mataušić 2008 (see note 26), pp. 28–29.

29 Raphael Israeli, *The Death Camps of Croatia: Visions and Revisions, 1941–1945*, New Brunswick, New Jersey 2013, p. 166.

30 Mataušić 2008 (see note 26), pp. 171–172.

the shed where the exhibition was located, there was an Ustashe coat of arms, and beneath it the inscription: 'All for the leader [Ante Pavelić] – the Ustashe Defence.' [...] For years, Jews, Freemasons, and various other people like them have been a burden on the Croatian people. They have become absorbed into the lifeblood of the people, wishing to exploit the Croatian people as much as was humanly possible, to their own ends. This sea of people has placed a great strain on all our Croatian social strata, a sea it was impossible to defend oneself against, because those in power in Croatia at that time were themselves in their pockets, collaborating with them all the time, even when they were acting to the detriment of the Croatian people [...]. The exhibition *Godinu dana sabirnih logora Ustaške obrane* (One Year of the Concentration Camps of the Ustashe Defence) attracted the most attention among visitors to the ZZ. The wooden building in which the exhibition was located was constantly well attended and visitors looked around the various parts of the exhibition with particular interest. All necessary objects were purpose-built on site. One example is the bricks laid to make an oven for the camp to use, because they couldn't find the right kind of oven anywhere else.[31]

At the same time, the photographer Vice Lisičić was one of the few people granted permission to photograph the office of the Ustashe leader Ante Pavelić.[32] Speaking of taking Pavelić's portrait, Lisičić said:

Taking Pavelić's photo portrait was nothing but trouble, as in all photographs he came out just as he really was: gloomy and with that well-known gangster-like expression. Of course, his wife, Mara (dubbed 'the pharaoh's wife'), didn't like the photos so the shooting was repeated indefinitely on her explicit orders until the 'gracious Führer' got sick and tired of it all. Finally, she arrived at a solution about how best to make her husband look gentle in front of the photographers; she ordered that jokes be told to him while posing. I only ever noticed a natural smile on his face in other situations, when looking at his beloved son Velimir riding a horse or playing the violin.[33]

Ustashe propaganda spoke of the Partisans' moral degeneracy, with Jews leading the movement. One Ustashe ideologue, Julije Makanec, said that Partisan women had been stripped of their motherly function, claiming them to be former prostitutes, and 'unstable women who defied their female instincts and motherly role'.[34]

During the war, photographers in Zagreb continued their activities. In 1941, Fotoklub Zagreb put on the exhibition 'Our Beautiful Homeland' (accompanied by the eponymous publication mentioned above), with over 400 photographs on show. In occupied Slovenia, meanwhile, many Slovene Home Guard, Italian and German magazines were published. The first issue of the magazine *Slovensko domobranstvo* (Slovene Home Guard) serves as a striking example of photography seized from the Partisans and misappropriated. The issue includes an

31 *Hrvatski narod, Njihov prijašnji rad bila je politika – sadašnja naša politika jest rad, 9. IX. 1942*, no. 524; see also Nikica Mihaljević, 'Krvavi ustaški Disneyland: Srbi su lijeni, Židovi drski', in: *Express*, URL: (.express.hr/life/krvavi-ustaski-disneyland-srbi-su-lijeni- zidovi-drski-5978# (accessed 17 February 2017).

32 Hlevnjak/Ivanuš 2008 (see note 25), p. 105.

33 Aleksandar Vojinović, *Ante Pavelić*, Zagreb 1988, p. 16.

34 Rory Yeomans, *Visions of Annihilation: The Ustasha Regime and the Cultural Politics of Fascism, 1941–1945*, Pittsburgh 2013, pp. 315–316.

article, entitled 'The Communist Bourgeoisie and Their Proletariat', which attempts to discredit the poet Matej Bor by showing him in a bourgeois and faintly bohemian setting, holding a bottle of wine and surrounded by young women.

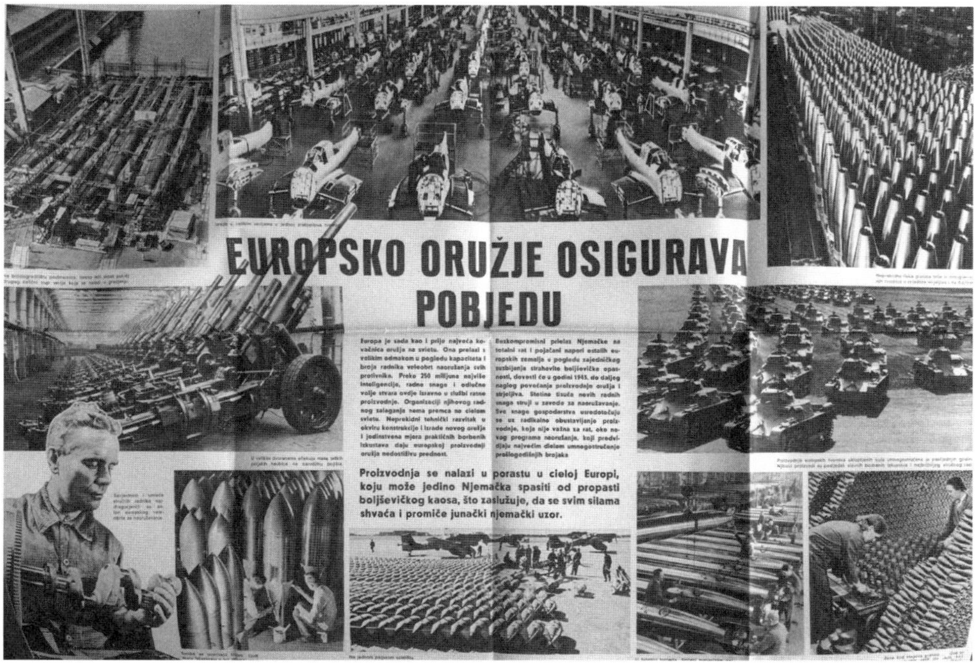

'European Weapons Secure Victory' poster. Archive of Bosnia and Herzegovina, FOND NDH.

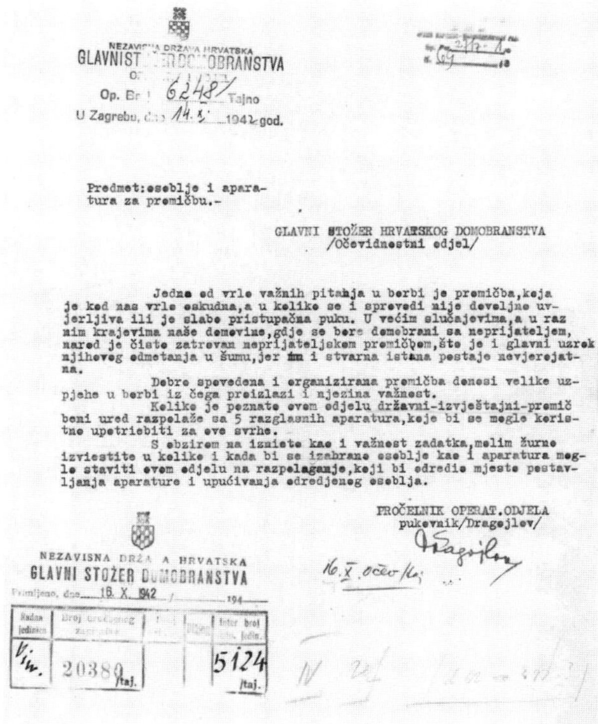

NEZAVISNA DRŽAVA HRVATSKA
GLAVNI STOŽER DOMOBRANSTVA
Op. Br. 6248/ Tajno
U Zagrebu, dne 14. X. 1942 god.

Predmet: osoblje i aparatura za promičbu.-

GLAVNI STOŽER HRVATSKOG DOMOBRANSTVA
/Očevidnostni odjel/

Jedno od vrlo važnih pitanja u borbi je promičba, koja je kod nas vrlo oskudna, a u koliko se i provodi nije dovoljno uvjerljiva ili je slabo pristupačna puku. U većim slučajevima, a u raznim krajevima naše domovine, gdje se bore domobrani sa neprijateljem, narod je čisto zatrovan neprijateljskom promičbom, što je i glavni uzrok njihovog odmetanja u šumu, jer im i stvarna istina postaje nevjerojatna.

Dobro provedena i organizirana promičba donosi velike uspjehe u borbi iz čega proizlazi i njezina važnost.

Koliko je poznato ovom odjelu državni-izvještajni-promičbeni ured raspolaže sa 5 razglasnih aparatura, koje bi se mogle korisno upotriebiti za ove svrhe.

S obzirom na izneseno kao i važnost zadatka, molim žurno izvjestiti u koliko i kada bi se izabrano osoblje kao i aparatura moglo staviti ovom odjelu na raspolaganje, koji bi odredio mjesto postavljanja aparature i upućivanja određenog osoblja.

PROČELNIK OPERAT. ODJELA
pukovnik /Dragojlov/

NEZAVISNA DRŽAVA HRVATSKA
GLAVNI STOŽER DOMOBRANSTVA
Primljeno, dne 16. X. 1942

Radna jedinica	Broj urudžbenog zapisnika			Inter. broj
V/iv.	20380/taj.			5124/taj.

Propaganda appeal issued by General Staff of the Independent State of Croatia. Military Archive Belgrade, NDH K69 F7 27.

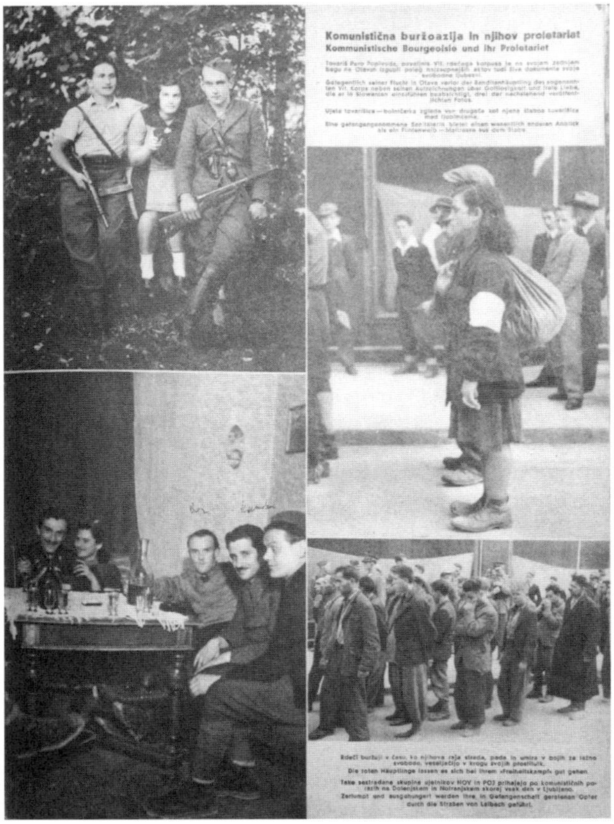

Komunistična buržoazija in njihov proletariat
Kommunistische Bourgeoisie und ihr Proletariat

Rdeči buržuji v času, ko njihova raja strada, pada in umira v bojih za lažno svobodo, veseljačijo v krogu svojih prostitutk.
Die roten Häuptlinge lassen es sich bei ihrem »Freiheitskampf« gut gehen.

Take sestradane skupine ujetnikov NOV in POJ prihajajo po komunističnih porazih na Dolenjskem in Notranjskem skorej vsak dan v Ljubljano.
Zerlumpt und ausgehungert werden ihre in Gefangenschaft geratenen Opfer durch die Straßen von Laibach geführt.

Slovene Home Guard, issue 1. Institute of Contemporary History (Ljubljana), accession no. unknown.

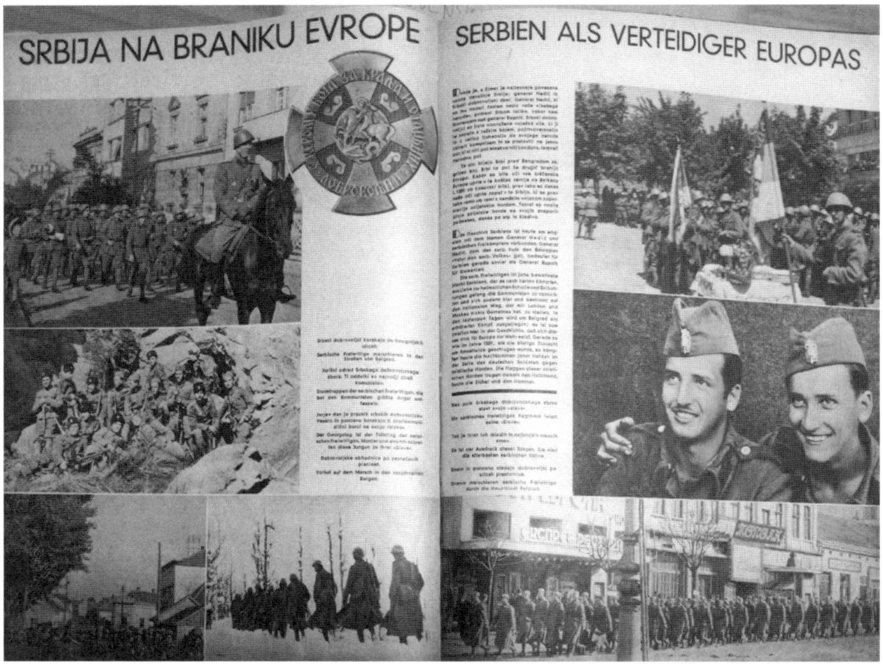

SRBIJA NA BRANIKU EVROPE

SERBIEN ALS VERTEIDIGER EUROPAS

Double-page spread, ‘Serbia as Defender of Europe’, from *Signal* magazine, published in Serbian and German. Date unknown.

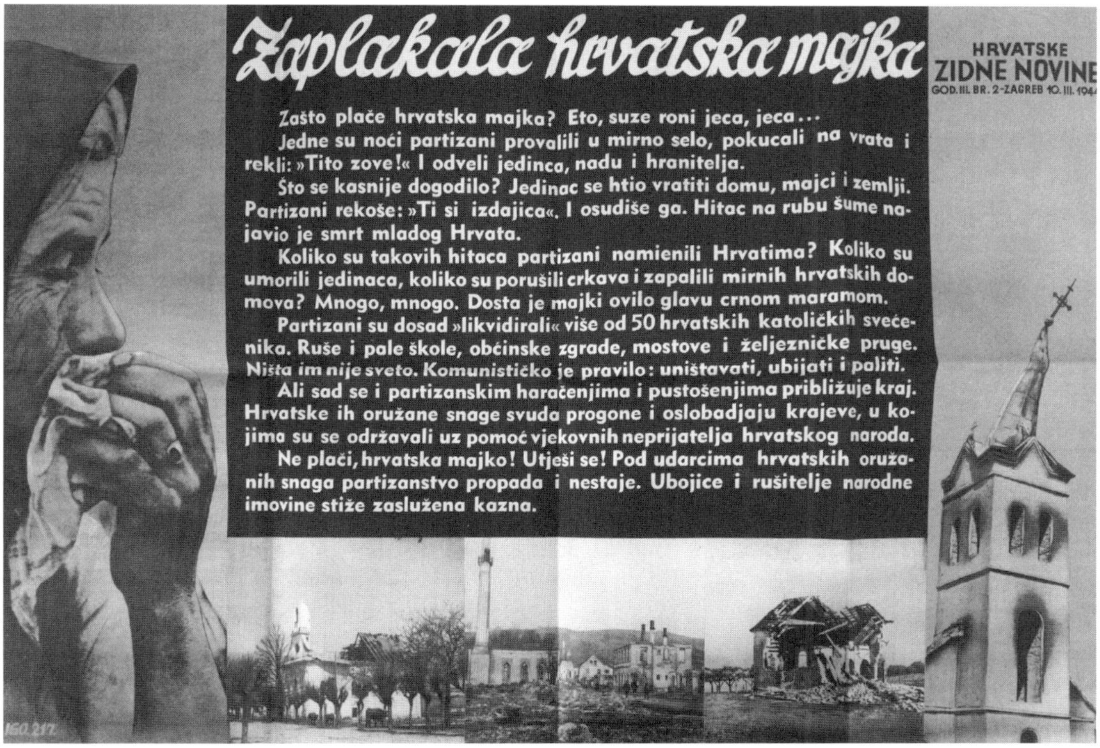

Poster with the heading 'Tears of a Croatian Mother'. Archive of Bosnia and Hercegovina, FOND NDH.

Founding the New Yugoslavia's Telegraph Agency

Telegrafska agencija nove Jugoslavije, or TANJUG for short, was founded on 5 November 1943. Its founding was an extremely important event for the Partisan movement, both for propaganda purposes and for the development of wartime photojournalism. It was founded during preparations for the Second Session of the AVNOJ in Jajce, Bosnia. At this session, the AVNOJ was recognised as a legislative body and the foundations were laid for the new Yugoslavia's federal form. The main advocate for establishing TANJUG was the painter Moša Pijade.[35]

Vili Šimunov-Barba took one of the first photographs of the TANJUG editorial team with his *Leica*. Besides him, several sources also mention Ernest Grgić, a photographer who worked as a radio-telegraphist. Grgić was one of the first to take photographs of TANJUG's audience – people listening to the radio as it broadcast news in English and Croato-Serbian. In September 1944 at the instigation of Moša Pijade, the agency succeeded in transmitting five photographic images by telegraph for the first time from the island of Vis. The wire-

35 For those interested in the founding staffers at TANJUG: Vladislav Ribnik was appointed director, Milan Gavrić and Mahmud Konjhodžić were correspondents, Veljko Dragićević, Jozo Butorac, Anđelko Gančević and Ante Runjić were radio-telegraphists, Aleksandar Tepavčević-Englez and Nikita Bakov were stenographers, Lepa Pijade, Olga Humo and Jara Ribnikar were translators, and Danilo Kabić and Vili Šimunov-Barba were photojournalists.

photo – a picture transmitted by electrical signals via telephone wires – marked a technological turning point for TANJUG, although in some respects it was playing catch-up, as other news agencies had already adopted wire photography in the 1930s. The Soviet newspaper *Komsomolskaya Pravda* published some of the TANJUG photographers' works, with the result that TANJUG images featured in a foreign news magazine for the first time.[36]

The radio station Slobodna Jugoslavija (Free Yugoslavia) started broadcasting on 2 November 1941, initially from the town of Ufa in the Ural mountains, and later from the Comintern building in Moscow. Its director, Veljko Vlahović,[37] stated that TANJUG's founding was of great importance for the development of photojournalism, too, and that the organisational prerequisites were finally in place for establishing a professional photojournalist service. Besides transmitting news by radiotelegraph, broadcasts by the AVNOJ's radio station were also planned. Also in the pipeline were photo-reportage assignments and war reporting, an exhibition, an illustrated weekly and a network of correspondents.[38] Within the agency, all manner of training courses were given, such as in handling portable radio equipment, encryption, handling cameras and developing negatives.[39]

TANJUG's task was to represent and promote the Yugoslav Partisan movement globally. This went hand in hand with the political struggle for the recognition of the People's Liberation Struggle – despite its communist and revolutionary character – as the only anti-fascist movement on the territory of Yugoslavia. Over time, the agency would evolve to become one of the most important and most professonal in this part of Europe. It collapsed during the 1990s when it fell under the control of the regime of Slobodan Milošević. In terminal decline ever since, it recently faced liquidation.

Trained professional photographers such as Stevan Benčić and Branko Savić joined TANJUG during the Second World War. Savić had trained in photography in Berlin and his father owned a photo shop in the centre of Belgrade.[40] His work includes some particularly interesting photojournalist shots taken during the liberation of Jasenovac which he wit nessed along with Peko Dapčević. These photographs were stored on several dozen TANJUG negatives dating from the period 1944 to 1947. The negatives and their contact prints were believed to be subsequently stored in the Office of Marshal Josip Broz Tito and were recently discovered by the curators of the Museum of Yugoslavia in Belgrade. The present publication features some of the undeveloped photographs that the curators found on the negatives, which are published here for the first time ever. Three photographers are mentioned by name: Branko Savić, Isak Koen and Pavle Obradović. Many years after the war, Savić described the conditions he found at the camp at Jasenovac on its liberation:

36 Veseljko Huljić, *Vis 1941–1945*, Split 1979, p. 268.

37 Valter Roberts, *Tito, Mihailović i saveznici 1941–1945*, Belgrade 2013, p. 82.

38 Veseljko Huljić and Milovan Dželebdžić, *Veze u Narodnooslobodilačkoj borbi 1943–1945*, vol. 2, Belgrade 1984, p. 145; Enver Ćemalović, *Mostarski bataljon*, Mostar 1986, p. 163.

39 Mihajlo Marić, 'Fragmenti iz okupiranog Beograda', in: *Veze u NOB-u 1941–1945. Ratna sećanja*, vol. 5, Esad Tihić and Momčilo Kalem (eds.), Belgrade 1981, p. 127.

40 Snežana Rovčanin, 'Kvadrati filma spojili i most', in: *Večernje Novosti*, URL: https://www.novosti.rs/vesti/naslovna/%20reportaze/aktuelno.293.html:197712-Kvadrati-filma-spojili-i-most (accessed 1 June 2021).

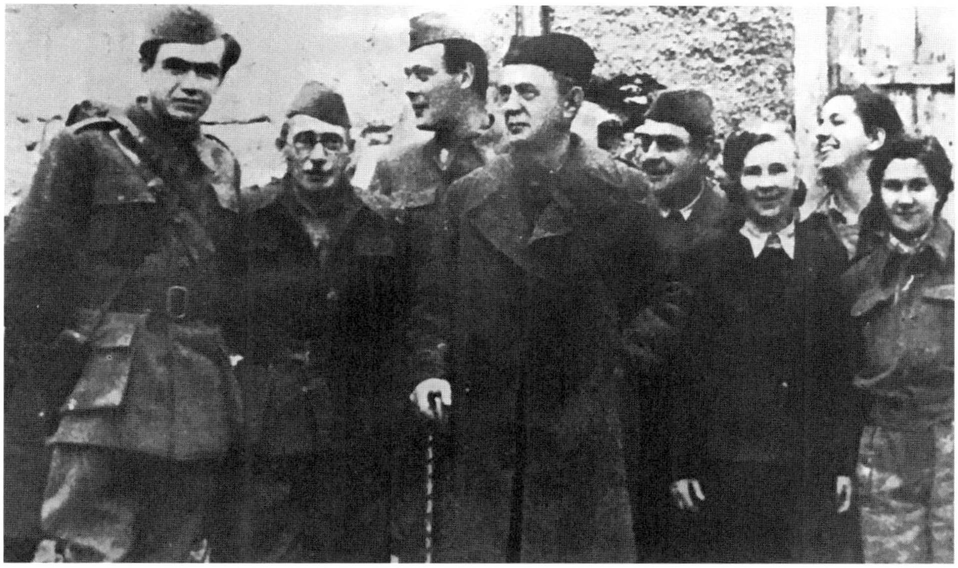

The founding TANJUG editorial staff in Jajce, with Ivo Lola Ribar (far left), Moša Pijade, Vladimir Velebit, Ivan Ribar, Vladislav Ribnikar, Lepa Pijade, Olga Humo and Jara Ribnikar (far right). Photographer nknown (Vili Šimunov-Barba?), from the book TANJUG 1943–1963, Belgrade 1963, p. 7.

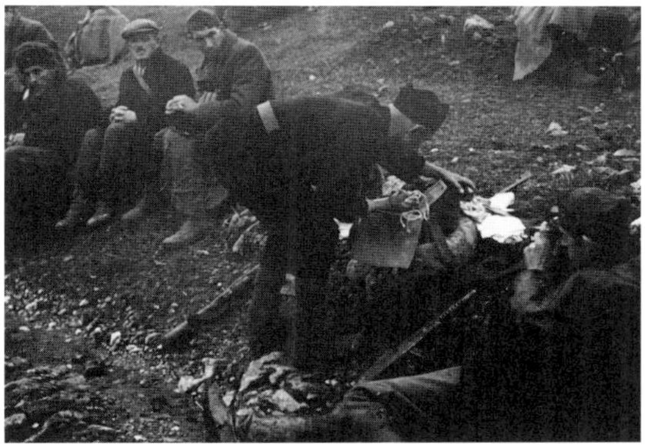

Delegates resting on the way to the Second Session of the AVNOJ, with Otmar Kreačić-Kultura (taking photo) and Dr Pavle Gregorić (centre), November 1943. Photographer unknown. Museum of Yugoslavia, III-225.

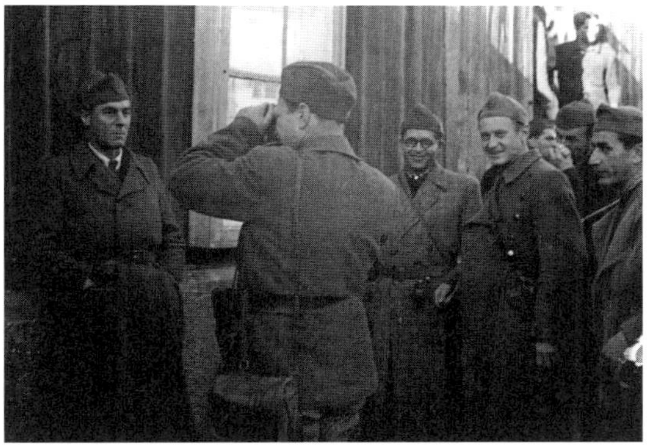

Photographer Vili Šimunov-Barba taking pictures of delegates at the Second Session of AVNOJ on the street in Jajce, November 1943. Photographer unknown. Museum of Yugoslavia, III-274.

Four of them were still alive. They were crawling along the wall of the brickyard when they heard shots approaching. They managed to save themselves. I took pictures for as long as I had enough film [...]. The waters of the river Sava retreated. There was a row of people chained up. All dead. Around fifteen to twenty of them in a line. Just when I thought everything was over, another massacre came to light. They had drowned them alive. When the water level dropped, you could see everything.[41]

41 Ibid.

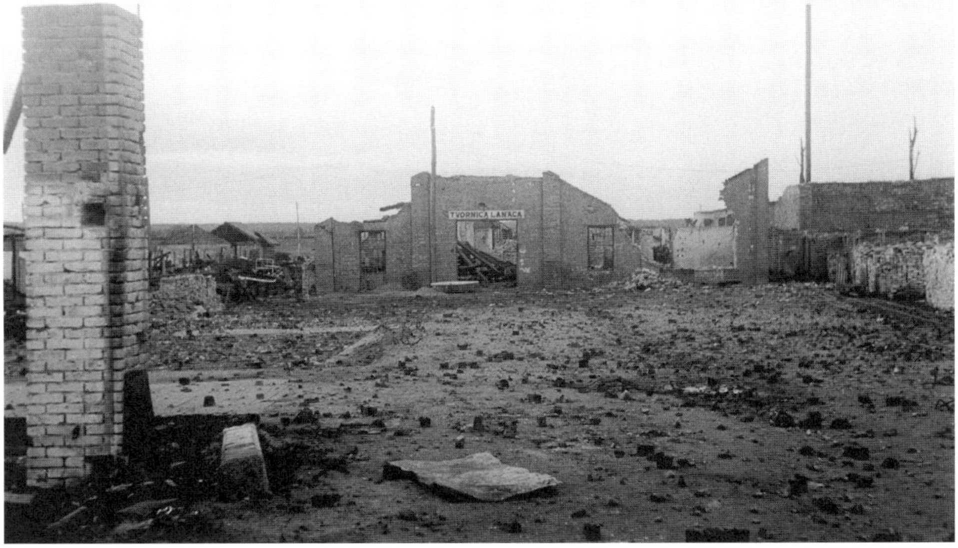

The Partisans entering Jasenovac concentration camp, deliberately destroyed by Ustashe in retreat, 5 May 1945. Photo: Branko Savić. Museum of Yugoslavia, VIS 286 04.

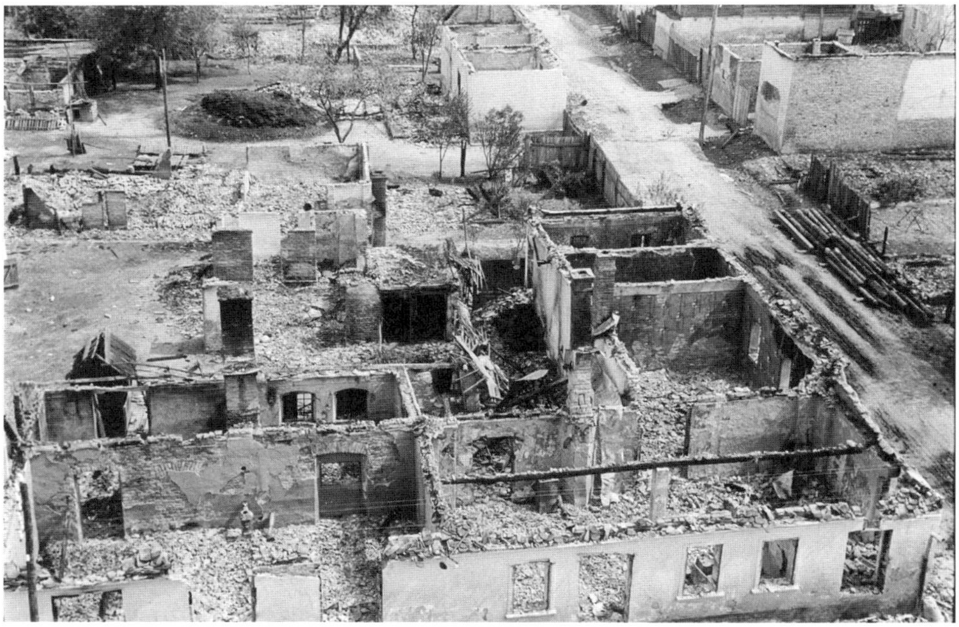

The ruins of the village of Jasenovac, as seen from the tower of the Catholic church, after the Ustashe had razed it to the ground in scorched-earth retreat. Photo: Branko Savić. Museum of Yugoslavia, VIS 286 14.

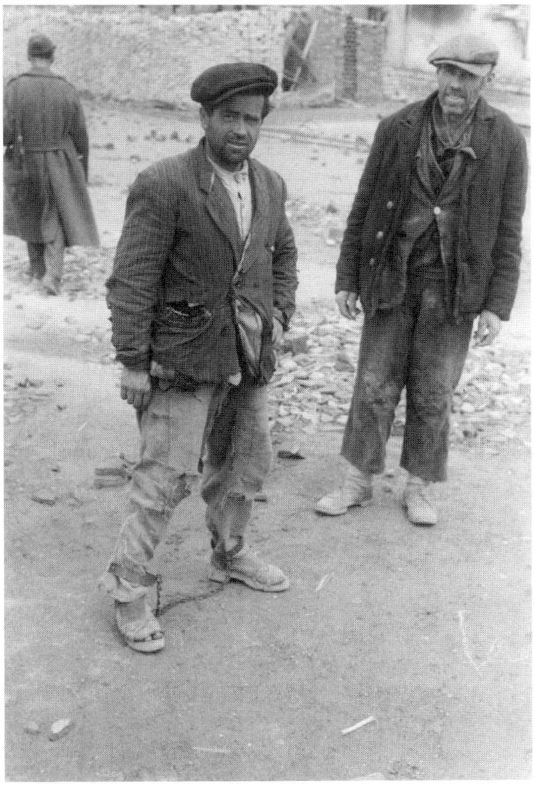

Former prisoners of Jasenovac concentration camp, image dates from same day as the previous two photographs. Museum of Yugoslavia, VIS 286 21.

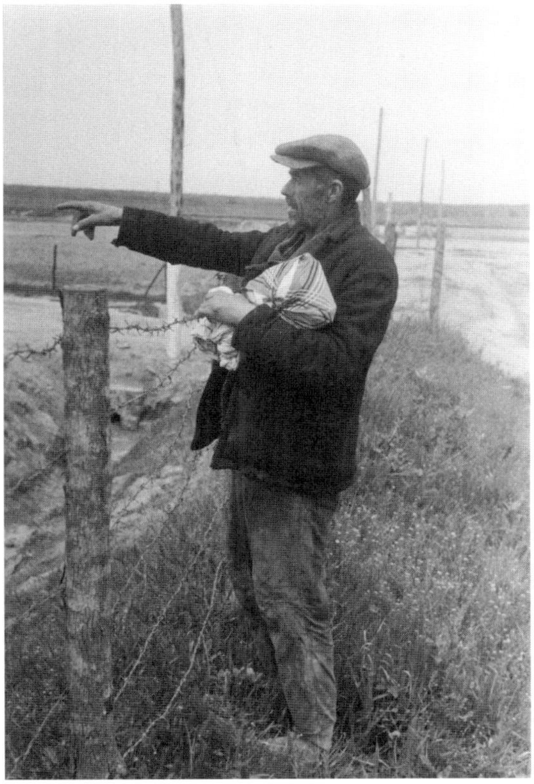

Eyewitness of the Jasenovac concentration camp, image dates from same day as previous photographs of Jasenovac. Museum of Yugoslavia, VIS 286 26.

At that same moment, Mato Tačković was also on the ground taking photographs of Jasenovac concentration camp.[42] He was a member of the photography unit of the Slavonia District People's Committee and entered Jasenovac with the Twenty-Eighth Slavonia Division, on 24 April 1945.

What happened to Savić's remaining negatives has not been clarified to this day, but it can be assumed that they were shot in the same period as the photographs depicted in this book. Partisan activities were strictly controlled at that time. Along with the district commissions for war crimes, corps commanders received orders to gather all data on the concentration camps and prisons in Jasenovac, Slavonski Brod, Savska Cesta, Đakovo, Slavonska Požega and Feričanci and to photograph them immediately after they had been liberated. All photos had to be delivered to the State Commission to Investigate Crimes Committed by the Occupiers and Their Collaborators.[43] These photos stand out in terms of their technical and photographic quality and are certainly comparable with the

42 Đorđe Mihovilović, *Jasenovac 1945–1947. Fotomonografija* Jasenovac 2016, p. 18.

43 *Zbornik dokumenata i podataka o narodnooslobodilačkom ratu jugoslovenskih naroda*, vol. V/34: Borbe u Hrvatskoj 1944. godine, Belgrade 1966.

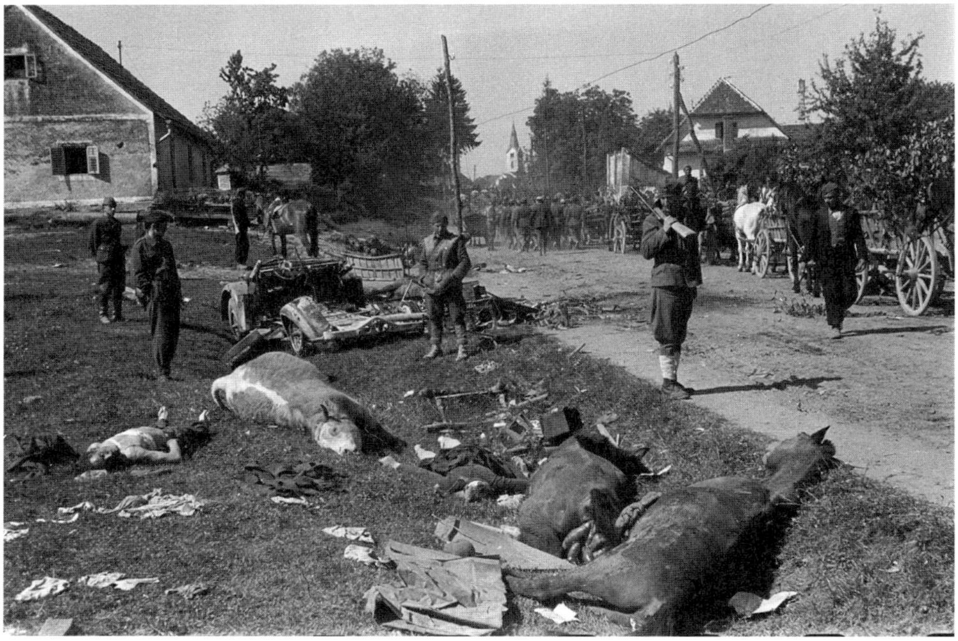

Yugoslav Army advancing on Zagreb, May 1945. Photographer unknown. Museum of Yugoslavia, VIS 287 0.

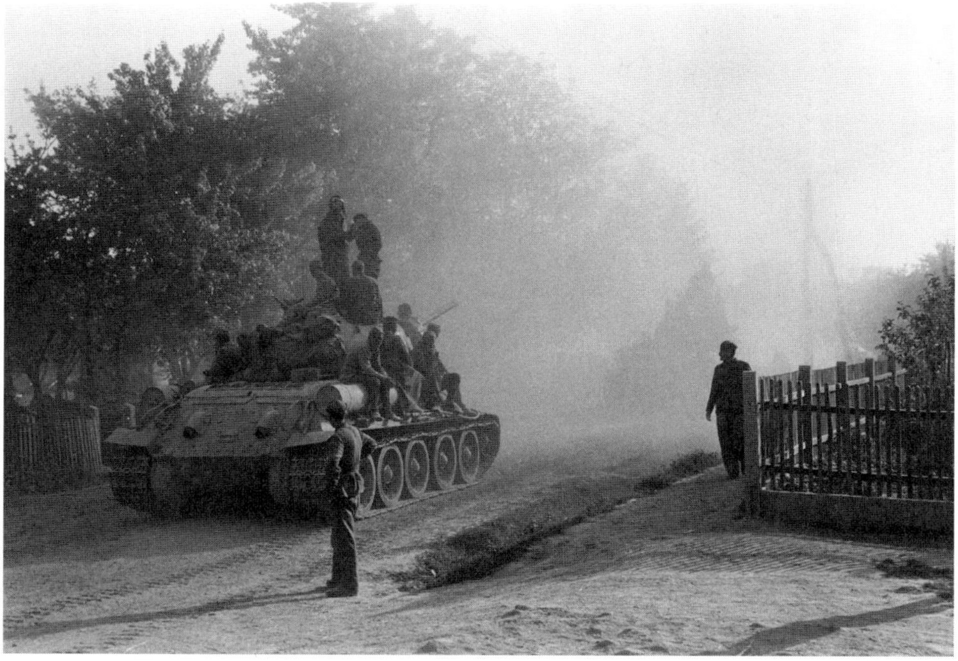

Yugoslav Army advancing on Zagreb, May 1945. Photographer unknown. Museum of Yugoslavia, VIS 288 19.

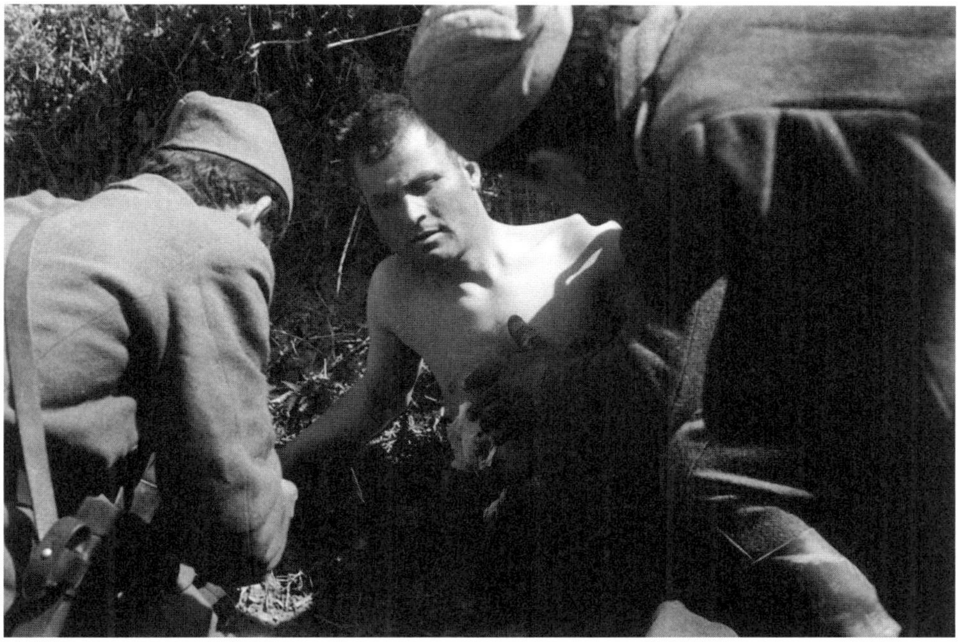

Wounded Partisan during push to take Zagreb, May 1945. Photographer unknown. Museum of Yugoslavia, VIS 289 0.

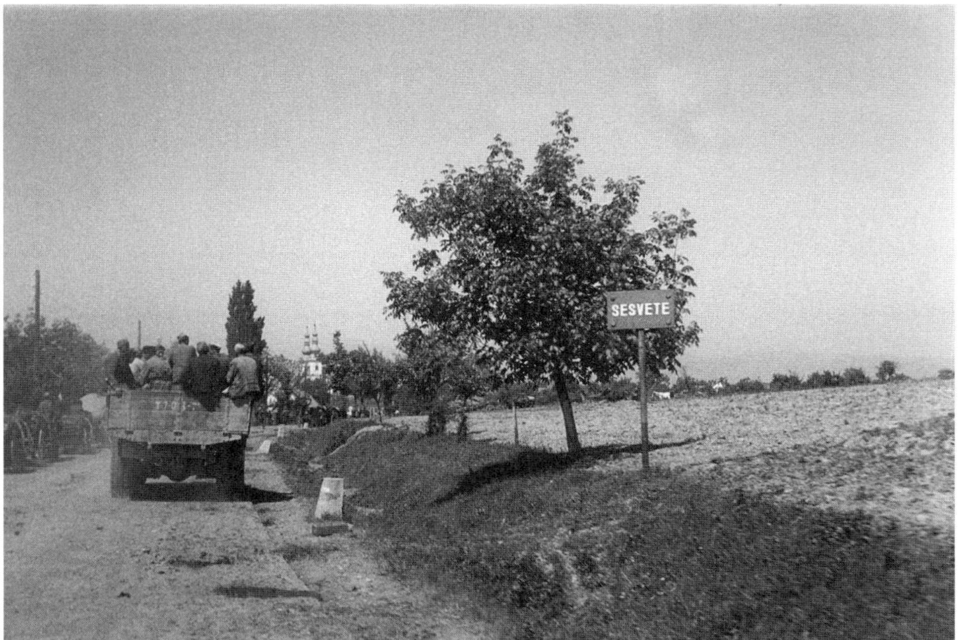

The Yugoslav Army advancing on Zagreb, May 1945. Photographer unknown. Museum of Yugoslavia, VIS 289 22.

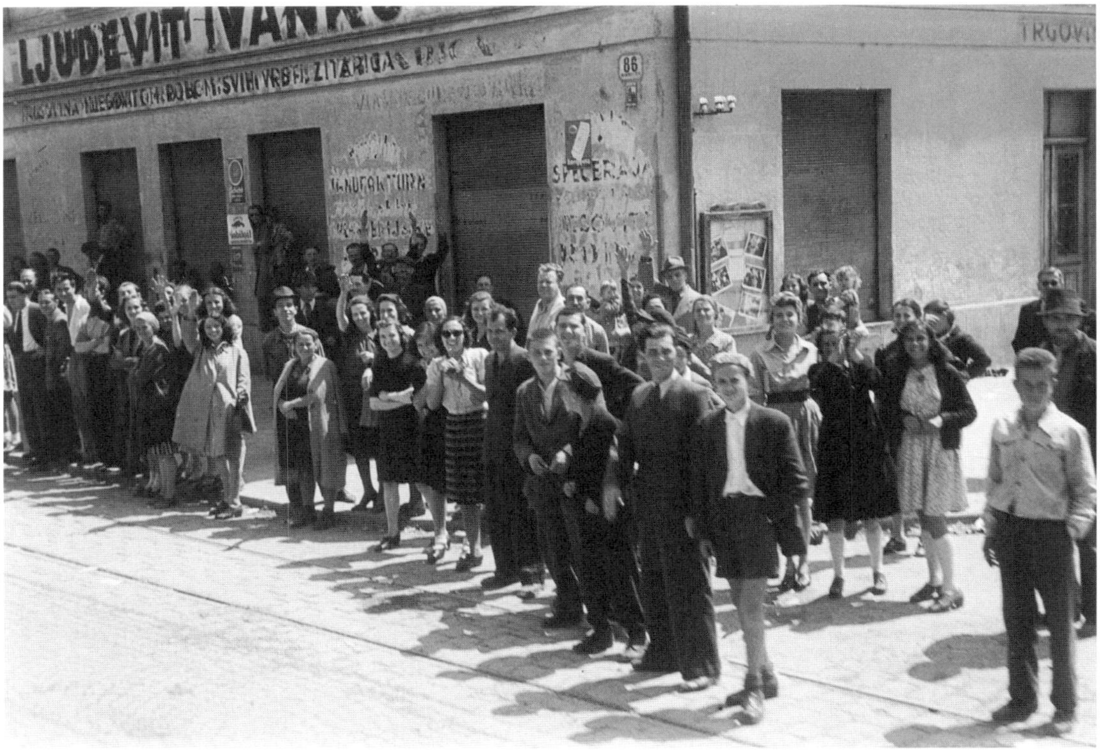

Civilians greeting the Yugoslav Army entering Zagreb, 8 May 1945. Photographer unknown.
Museum of Yugoslavia, VIS 290 12.

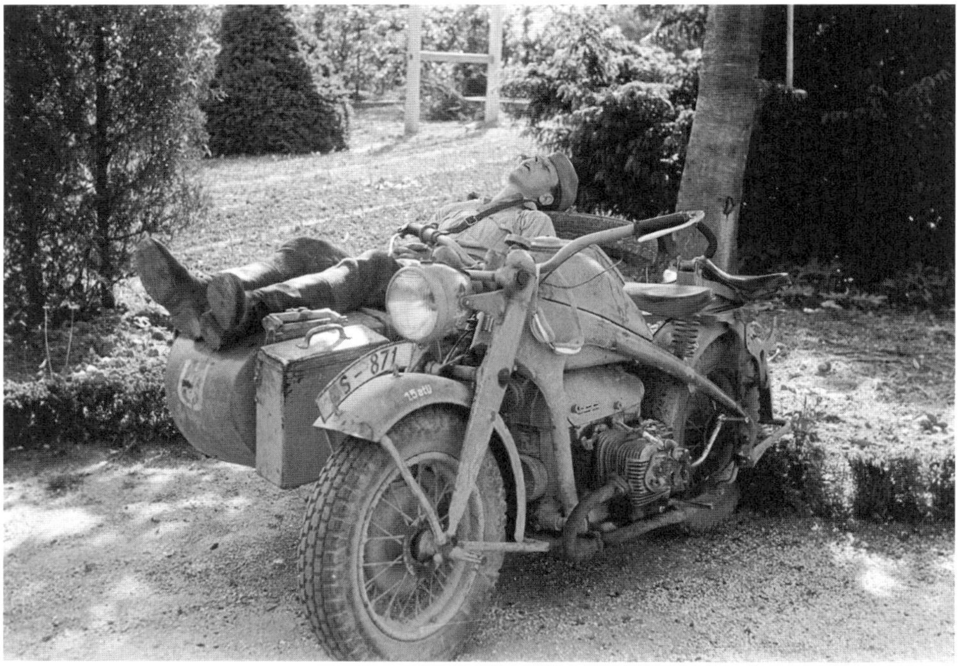

During push to take Zagreb, 8 May 1945. Photographer unknown.
Museum of Yugoslavia, VIS 291 23.

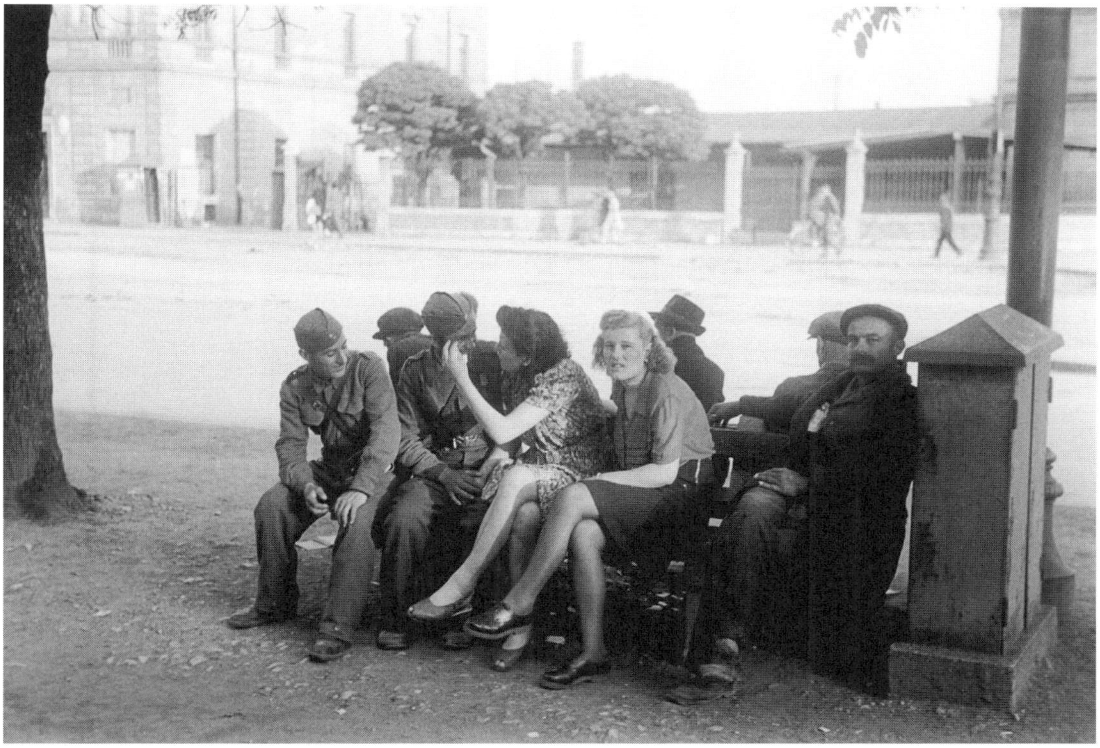

The Yugoslav Army entering Zagreb, 8 May 1945. Photographer unknown. Museum of Yugoslavia, VIS 291 35.

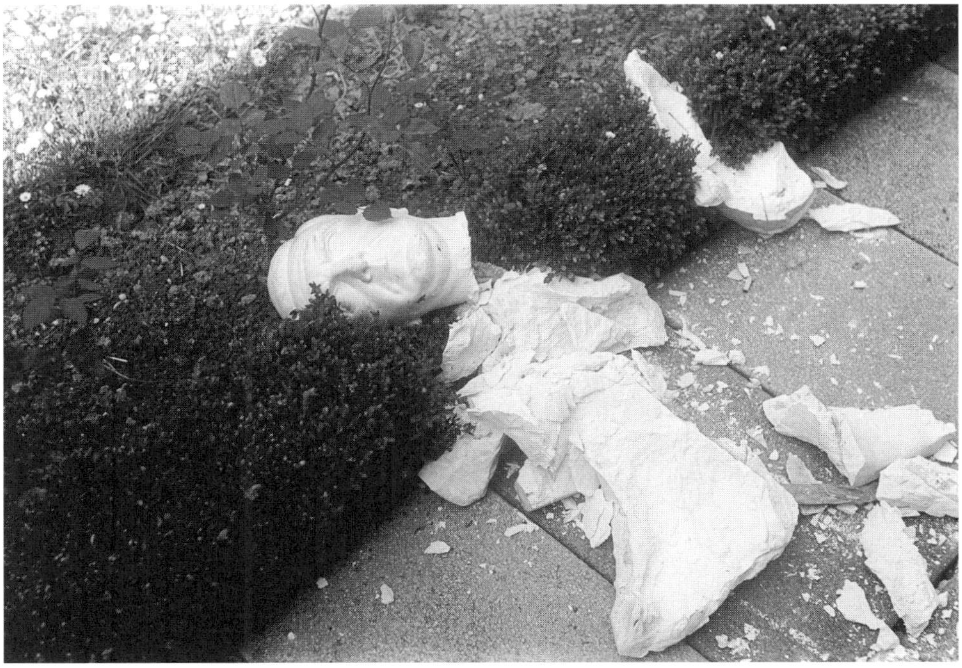

Toppled statue of Ante Pavelić in Zagreb, directly after the liberation, May 1945. Photographer unknown. Museum of Yugoslavia, VIS 293 35.

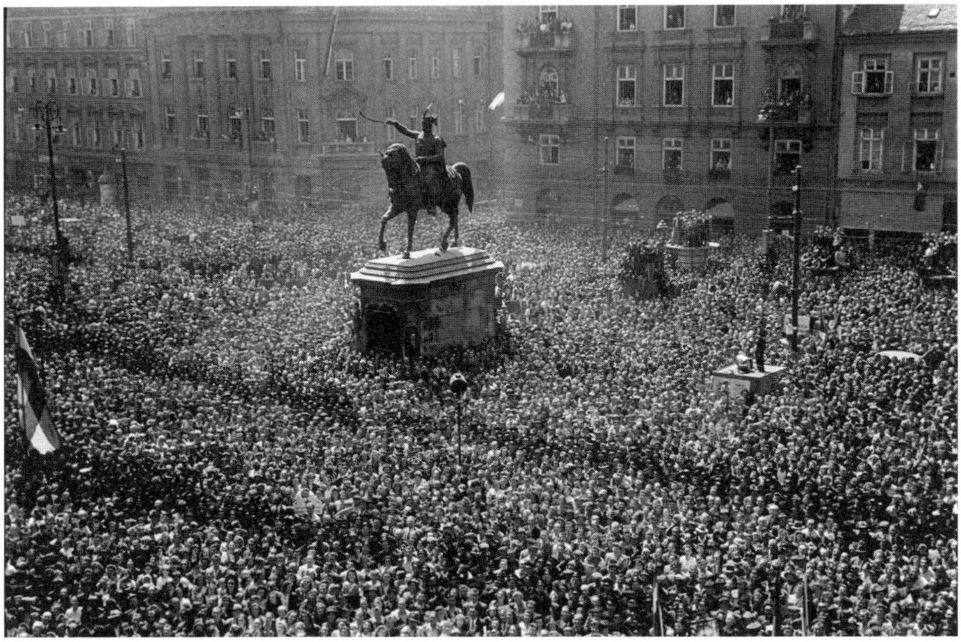

Crowds gather in Zagreb to mark the liberation of the country and the end of the war, 11 May 1945. Photographer unknown. Museum of Yugoslavia, VIS 292 13.

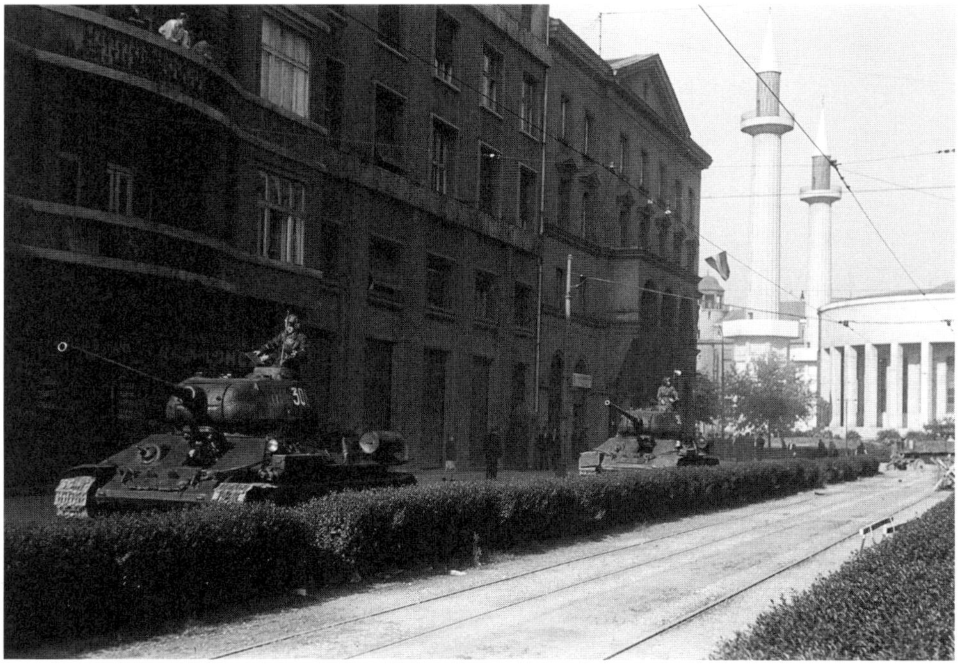

A military parade by the Yugoslav Army in liberated Zagreb, 13 May 1945. Photographer unknown. Museum of Yugoslavia, VIS 296 12.

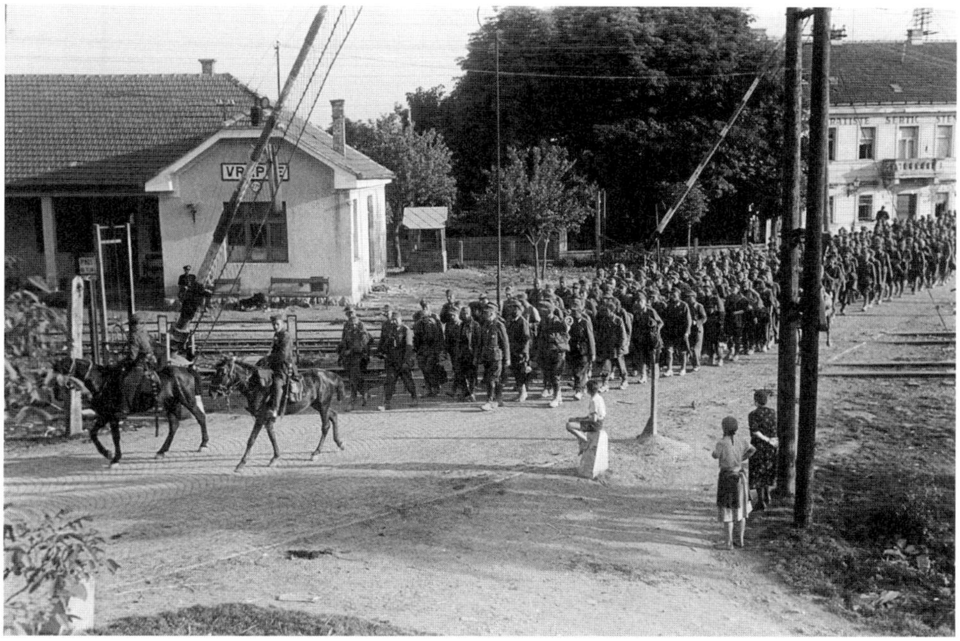

Defeated enemy soldiers captured in Zagreb, May 1945. Photographer unknown. Museum of Yugoslavia, VIS 294 24.

professionalism of Allied photographers' documentary work. The high photojournalistic quality is also visible in the photographs of the liberation of Zagreb, also published for the first time in this book.

On Propaganda's Impossibilities

Despite many orders and the establishing of a propaganda apparatus, photography remained beyond centralised control. Many photographers continued to develop their films privately, without supervision from propaganda departments. Even the officials in the propaganda departments themselves often left the decisions up to the photographers. Most reports acknowledge the success of photographic work, but poor technical production and material scarcity were also constantly mentioned as limiting factors, as was the lack of trained photographers. Guided by their own intuition and creative vision, photographers took pictures of subjects they considered important. But one consistent complaint from the propaganda departments was the persistent lack of combat photography, even in the final year of the war, as demonstrated in this report by the Ninth Corps:

We lack materials for negatives and positives, and we especially lack skilled photojournalists and photographic technicians. The number of combat photographs lags too far behind the number of everyday photographs. There are still too few daring photographs. The photography unit is thus overburdened with its current work and is not in a position to reproduce old shots in large numbers.[44]

The Ninth Corps received criticism that film stock was not getting to the units on time and that the film rolls that did arrive had sometimes been mistakenly used already. The instructions of the department of political education of the Twenty-Sixth Assault Division, dated 4 April 1945, and sent to the departments of political education of the brigades subordinate to it, came to the critical appraisal that precious film stock had been used up depicting unidentified columns, portraits or shots of leading military figures:

To this day, not a single brigade has sent a shot, article or biography of a prominent fighter or leader, fallen in battle, or even alive. [...] We need to stop thinking that the photographer is exclusively on hand for the brigades. This is not of significance for the brigade alone, but for our entire army! When the film stock has been developed, those pictures of value will be used for our

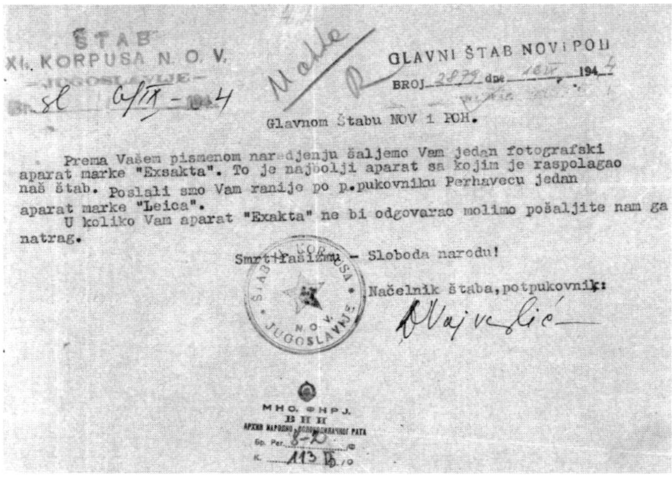
ŠTAB
XI. KORPUSA N. O. V.
JUGOSLAVIJE
Br. 81 6/IX-1944

GLAVNI ŠTAB NOV i POH
BROJ 2879 dne 1944

Glavnom Štabu NOV i POH.

Prema Vašem pismenom naredjenju šaljemo Vam jedan fotografski aparat marke "Exsakta". To je najbolji aparat sa kojim je raspolagao naš štab. Poslali smo Vam ranije po p.pukovniku Perhavecu jedan aparat marke "Leica".

U koliko Vam aparat "Exakta" ne bi odgovarao molimo pošaljite nam ga natrag.

Smrt fašizmu – Sloboda narodu!

Načelnik štaba, potpukovnik:

"In line with your written order, we have sent you one Exakta camera. It is the best camera that my headquarters has available. Earlier we sent a Leica camera to lieutenant colonel [illegible].
If the Exakta camera does not suit you, please return it. Death to Fascism, Freedom to the People."
Military Archive Belgrade, NOVJ K113B F2 8.

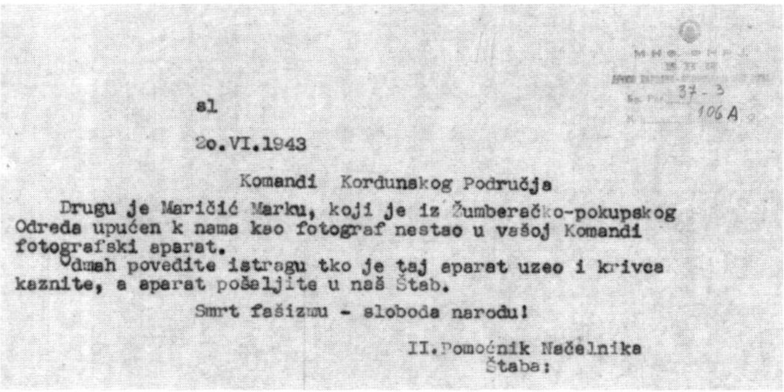
sl

2o.VI.1943

Komandi Kordunskog Područja

Drugu je Maričić Marku, koji je iz Žumberačko-pokupskog Odreda upućen k nama kao fotograf nestao u vašoj Komandi fotografski aparat.

Odmah povedite istragu tko je taj aparat uzeo i krivca kaznite, a aparat pošaljite u naš Štab.

Smrt fašizmu – sloboda narodu!

II. Pomoćnik Načelnika Štaba:

"To the Kordun region command, Comrade Maričić Marko from the Žumberak-Pokupsko division, directed to work with us as a photographer, lost his camera under your command.
Carry out an investigation immediately into who took the camera and punish the guilty party, and send the camera to our headquarters."
Military Archive Belgrade, NOVJ K113B F2 8.

44 *Zbornik dokumenata i podataka o narodno-oslobodilačkom ratu jugoslovenskih naroda*, vol. IX/3: Partijsko-politička dokumenta 1943. godine, Belgrade 1967.

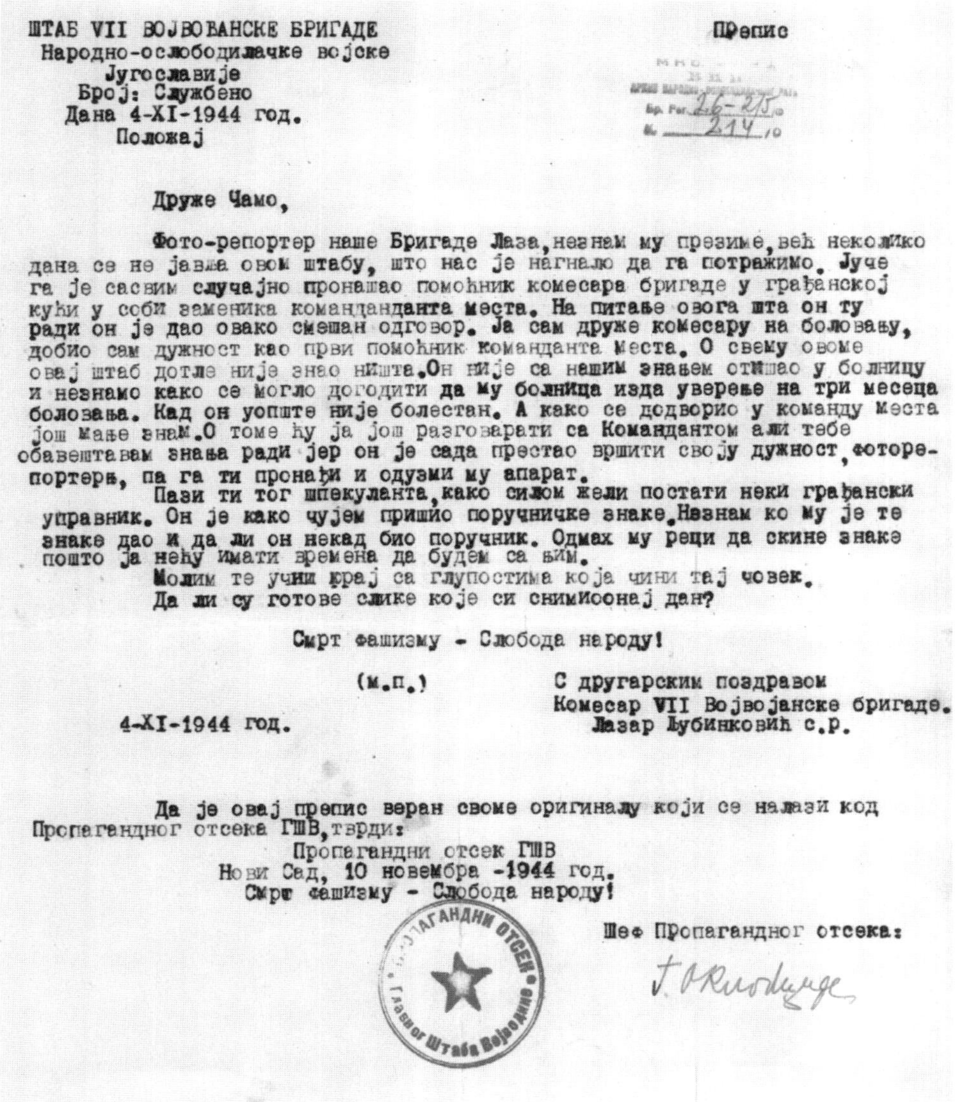

ШТАБ VII ВОЈВОВАНСКЕ БРИГАДЕ
Народно-ослободилачке војске
Југославије
Број: Службено
Дана 4-XI-1944 год.
Положај

Пpropis

Преpис

Друже Чамо,

Фото-репортер наше Бригаде Лаза, незнам му презиме, већ неколико дана се не јавља овом штабу, што нас је нагналю да га потражимо. Јуче га је сасвим случајно пронашао помоћник комесара бригаде у грађанској кући у соби заменика командандента места. На питање овога шта он ту ради он је дао овако смешан одговор. Ја сам друже комесару на боловању, добио сам дужност као први помоћник команданта места. О свему овоме овај штаб дотле није знао ништа. Он није са нашим знањем отишао у болницу и незнамо како се могло догодити да му болница изда уверење на три месеца боловања. Кад он уопште није болестан. А како се додворио у команду места још мање знам. О томе ћу ја још разговарати са Командантом али тебе обавештавам знања ради јер он је сада престао вршити своју дужност фоторепортера, па га ти пронађи и одузми му апарат.

Пази ти тог шпекуланта, како силом жели постати неки грађански управник. Он је како чујем пришио поручничке знаке. Незнам ко му је те знаке дао и да ли он некад био поручник. Одмах му реци да скине знаке пошто ја нећу имати времена да будем са њим.

Молим те учини крај са глупостима која чини тај човек.

Да ли су готове слике које си снимио онај дан?

Смрт фашизму - Слобода народу!

(м.п.)

С другарским поздравом
Комесар VII Војвојанске бригаде.
Лазар Љубинковић с.р.

4-XI-1944 год.

Да је овај препис веран своме оригиналу који се налази код Пропагандног отсека ГШВ, тврди:

Пропагандни отсек ГШВ
Нови Сад, 10 новембра -1944 год.
Смрт фашизму - Слобода народу!

Шеф Пропагандног отсека:

Message about a photographer with the Seventh Vojvodina Brigade reporting in sick, requesting to confiscate his camera. Military Archive Belgrade, NOVJ K214 F5 26.

central propaganda service: for the army, divisions and the brigades, so that the brigades can put on an exhibition tracing their history and so on. Shots of no great significance will be returned to you for archive purposes as originals with the negatives, while the more important shots will be returned in the 13 × 18 format. Pointless shooting that uses up material is forbidden in the brigades. You can only take pictures if you have an important propaganda goal, e.g., shots that interpret our struggle, important political and cultural moments, as well as upbeat encounters with the people being liberated etc.[45]

A report on the work of the photography and film section in the Fifth Serbian People's Liberation Assault Brigade relates the position of photographers in certain military units:

45 Ibid.

The section had three members, and in late February 1945, a further two photographers arrived. Due to a lack of expertise, a massive amount of photographic material was ruined at the hands of these photographers, and the head of the propaganda department reported the following: 'We can say that soon we will have more damaged than usable photographs. In most cases, the shots are blurred and show little artistry, i.e., were taken without any journalistic skill. Over this period, 154 different images were shot, of which 139 were a success, but not great, while 15 were a complete failure. Apart from that, much was left undeveloped on the films as it seemed that the photojournalists had not got to grips with the basic concepts of photography. In the brigade we do not have any better photojournalists and we must, of course, place stricter checks on their work and make do with them for the time being.'[46]

This particular brigade, the Fifth Serbian Assault Brigade, nevertheless managed to organise seven exhibitions that included, in total, eighteen photographs from combat positions, sixteen pictures of meetings of the engineer battalion, twenty-three photographs covering the celebrations of the Red Army's anniversary, and sixteen on brigade manoeuvres. As in the other brigades, photographs from the front lines and of direct combat were lacking. There were also rare cases in which certain photographers were punished for acts of cowardice and even treason before the enemy. Yet most often the problem lay in neglect.[47] The war photography unit of the Twenty-First Serbian Assault Brigade also had issues with individual photographers' personal conduct:

They drew special attention to their cameras, often hanging around outside the headquarters and photographing officers. The brigade's political commissar, Mirko Jovanović, did not like their milling around the headquarters and really wanted to see them in the line of fire, photographing fighters waiting in position, charging and repelling attacks.[48]

Instead of issuing strict orders to them, the political commissar managed to convince and motivate them to travel to the front line, and within ten days they managed to organise an exhibition that turned out to be a great success:

The arrival of photojournalists on the front line of combat, in the trenches and dug-outs, aroused a lively interest and curiosity among the fighters and leaders. In some places the fighters scorned them and made jokes. The photojournalists did not have time to respond to those who scorned them and just continued photographing. As luck would have it, some photojournalists even found themselves in the midst of the first exchange of fire and had their baptism of fire and shot pictures of historical value.[49]

46 'Izveštaj Propagandnog odsjeka 5. brigade od 15. ožujka 1945. godine o radu kulturno- prosvjetne sekcije od 15. veljače do 15. ožujka 1945. godine', in: *Peta srpska NOU brigada*, Stanimir Jovanović and Dragoljub Mirčetić (eds.), Belgrade 1989, p. 289.

47 People's Liberation Army of Yugoslavia, Military Archive Belgrade, K60B F5 22.

48 Milorad Gončin, *U rovovima Srema*, Belgrade 1981, p. 210.

49 Ibid.

The correspondence that the Supreme Command's propaganda department sent to the staff of the Fifth Corps on 1 December 1944 discussed the extent to which material and technical conditions influenced the organising of propaganda activities. In it, they requested that all Leica cameras 'found on persons and in use for personal satisfaction' be surrendered to them.[50] From the same document we also learn that the photography unit of the Supreme Command did not have a single good-quality camera available to use. This is why the staffs of the corps spent so much time searching for photography equipment.[51]

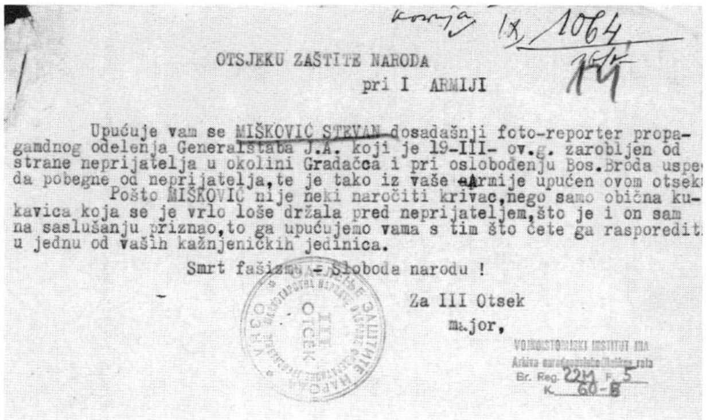

OTSJEKU ZAŠTITE NARODA
pri I ARMIJI

Upućuje vam se MIŠKOVIĆ STEVAN dosadašnji foto-reporter propagamdnog odelenja Generalštaba J.A. koji je 19-III- ov.g. zarobljen od strane neprijatelja u okolini Gradačca i pri oslobođenju Bos.Broda uspe da pobegne od neprijatelja,te je tako iz vaše armije upućen ovom otsek

Pošto MIŠKOVIĆ nije neki naročiti krivac,nego samo obična kukavica koja se je vrlo loše držala pred neprijateljem,što je i on sam na saslušanju priznao,to ga upućujemo vama s tim što ćete ga rasporedit u jednu od vaših kažnjeničkih jedinica.

Smrt fašizmu - Sloboda narodu !

Za III Otsek
major,

Report from General Staff of People's Liberation Army concerning the capture of a Partisan photographer by the enemy, his conduct while in custody and subsequent escape. Due to his 'cowardly manner' in enemy hands, the photographer is to be sent to a special department for punishment.
Military Archive Belgrade, K60B F5 22.

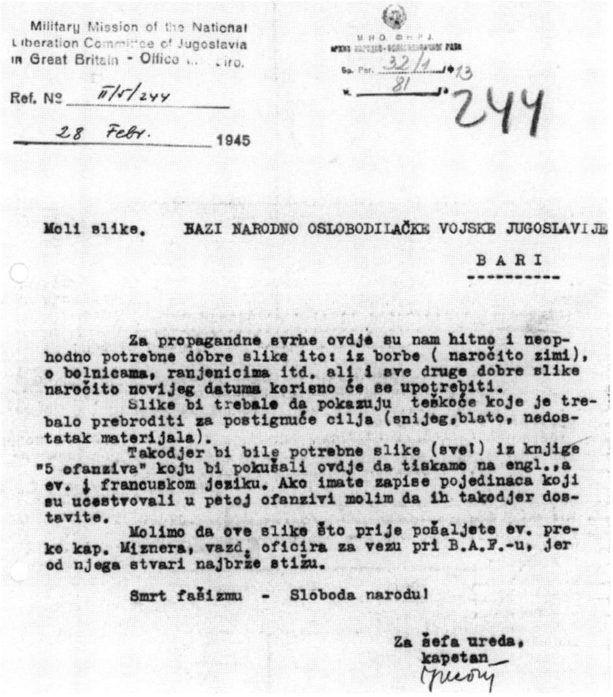

Military Mission of the National Liberation Committee of Jugoslavia in Great Britain - Office ... iro.

Ref. No II/5/244

28 Febr. 1945

Moli slike. BAZI NARODNO OSLOBODILAČKE VOJSKE JUGOSLAVIJE

BARI

Za propagandne svrhe ovdje su nam hitno i neophodno potrebne dobre slike ito: iz borbe (naročito zimi), o bolnicama, ranjenicima itd. ali i sve druge dobre slike naročito novijeg datuma korisno će se upotrebiti.

Slike bi trebale da pokazuju teškoće koje je trebalo prebroditi za postignuće cilja (snijeg,blato, nedostatak materijala).

Takodjer bi bile potrebne slike (sve!) iz knjige "5 ofanziva" koju bi pokušali ovdje da tiskamo na engl.,a ev. i francuskom jeziku. Ako imate zapise pojedinaca koji su ucestvovali u petoj ofanzivi molim da ih takodjer dostavite.

Molimo da ove slike što prije pošaljete ev. preko kap. Miznera, vazd. oficira za vezu pri B.A.F.-u, jer od njega stvari najbrže stižu.

Smrt fašizmu - Sloboda narodu!

Za šefa ureda,
kapetan

Request from Allied base in Bari asking the People's Liberation Army to supply pictures for propaganda purposes, especially of hurdles (shortages, snow, mud) that have been overcome in the push for victory, as well as images from a book on the Fifth Offensive that can be reproduced in a foreign-language edition for English- and French-speaking readers. Military Archive Belgrade, K113B F2 8.

50 People's Liberation Army of Yugoslavia, Military Archive Belgrade, K460C F29 8.

51 Ibid.

Interestingly, in early 1944, the propaganda section of the General Staff of Slovenia and the Slovene People's Liberation Committee separated their war photography unit from their civilian photography service. Photographers in uniform and in active military duty were generally tasked with documenting war operations. These photographers were constantly on the move and in direct combat with the enemy. Another subset of the unit was tasked with taking pictures of liberated territory. The most frequent subjects included the consequences of enemy devastation and the destruction of civilian and commercial facilities. According to the Rules on the Operation of Photography Units, they had to send

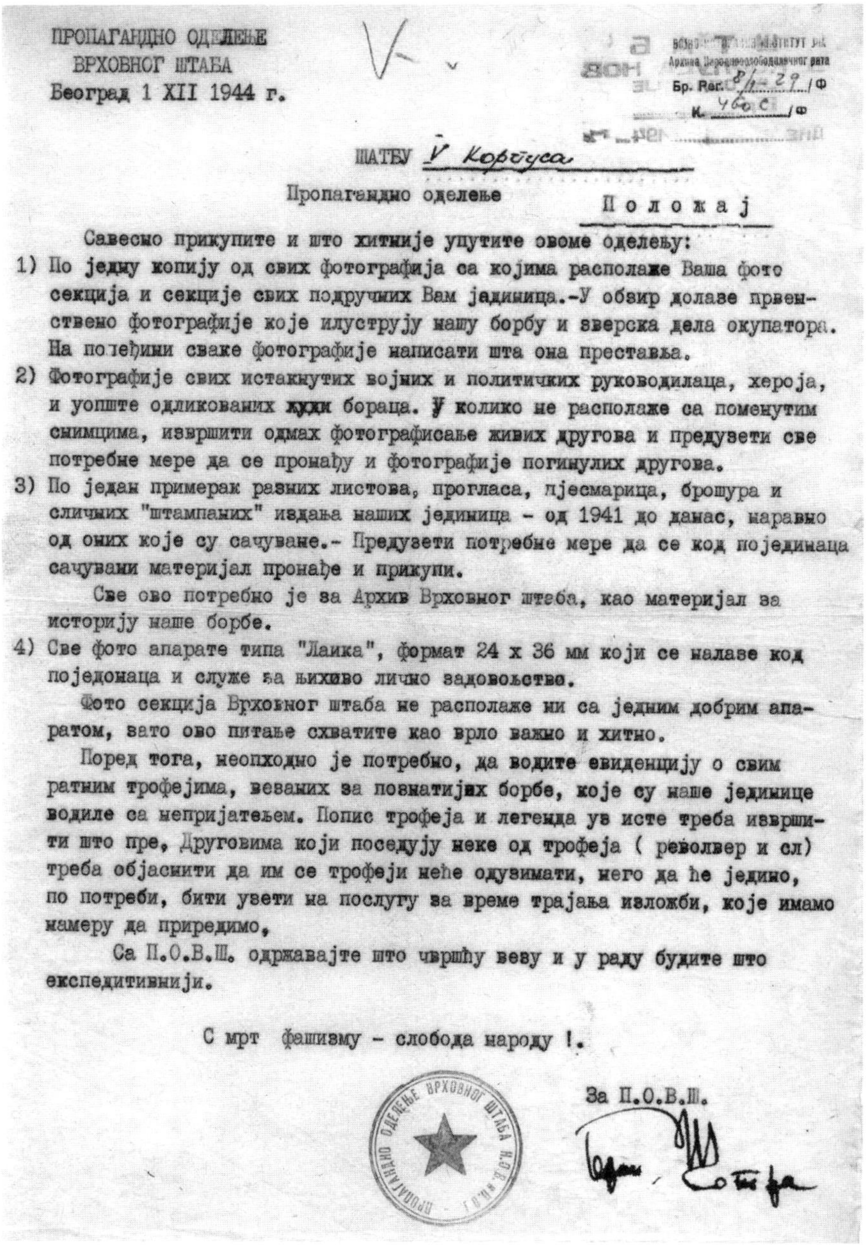
ПРОПАГАНДНО ОДЕЛЕЊЕ
ВРХОВНОГ ШТАБА
Београд 1 XII 1944 г.

Бр. Рег. 8/1-29 / Ф
К. 460 С / Ф

ШТАБУ V Корпуса

Пропагандно оделење

Положај

Савесно прикупите и што хитније упутите овоме оделењу:

1) По једну копију од свих фотографија са којима располаже Ваша фото секција и секције свих подручних Вам јединица.-У обзир долазе првенствено фотографије које илуструју нашу борбу и зверска дела окупатора. На полеђини сваке фотографије написати шта она преставља.
2) Фотографије свих истакнутих војних и политичких руководилаца, хероја, и уопште одликованих људи бораца. У колико не располаже са поменутим снимцима, извршити одмах фотографисање живих другова и предузети све потребне мере да се пронађу и фотографије погинулих другова.
3) По један примерак разних листова, прогласа, пјесмарица, брошура и сличних "штампаних" издања наших јединица - од 1941 до данас, наравно од оних које су сачуване.- Предузети потребне мере да се код појединаца сачувани материјал пронађе и прикупи.

Све ово потребно је за Архив Врховног штаба, као материјал за историју наше борбе.

4) Све фото апарате типа "Лаика", формат 24 x 36 мм који се налазе код појединаца и служе за њихиво лично задовољство.

Фото секција Врховног штаба не располаже ни са једним добрим апаратом, зато ово питање схватите као врло важно и хитно.

Поред тога, неопходно је потребно, да водите евиденцију о свим ратним трофејима, везаних за познатијих борбе, које су наше јединице водиле са непријатељем. Попис трофеја и легенда уз исте треба извршити што пре, Друговима који поседују неке од трофеја (револвер и сл) треба објаснити да им се трофеји неће одузимати, него да ће једино, по потреби, бити узети на послугу за време трајања изложби, које имамо намеру да приредимо,

Са П.О.В.Ш. одржавајте што чвршћу везу и у раду будите што експедитивнији.

С мрт фашизму - слобода народу !.

За П.О.В.Ш.

Letter from the Propaganda Department of the General Staff instructing recipient to send urgently needed photographic supplies and Leicas. Military Archive Belgrade, NOVJ K113B F2 8.

negatives directly to the General Staff so as to create a central photo archive.[52] According to various estimates, around 150 photographers were active in the Slovenian Partisan movement.

A report issued on 1 May 1945 by the propaganda department of the General Staff of the People's Liberation Army and the Partisan Detachment of Slovenia, addressed to the propaganda department of the Supreme Command, states that the units sent fifteen copies of the exhibition *Sahrana generallajtanta Franca Rožmana-Staneta* (The Burial of the General Lieutenant Franc Rožman-Stane) mounted on canvas with appropriate captions provided.[53] During this same period, an exhibition was held on successful sabotage actions, entitled *Rušimo komunikacije* (We Are Destroying Communications). Later, there was an exhibition on the Twenty-Fourth Italian Division named *Fontanot*, and another entitled *Pohod XIV. Divizije* (March of the XIV Division) that included photographs by Jože Petek. However, materials were lacking for the exhibition, especially photographic paper for blow-ups.[54] The crisis of scarcity continued and a report by the same propaganda department dated 1 February 1945 mentions the shortage of photography supplies. Nevertheless, the work of the Slovenian photography unit was particularly lively and in Črnomelj, a town in south-east Slovenia, from 14 January to 24 January that year, an exhibition of the Fourteenth Division went on view, while the General Staff of the People's Liberation Army and Partisan Detachment of Slovenia compiled a photo album with all the images gathered from the unit, which was later sent to Supreme Command.[55] The report from the following month states that the unit had survived the supply crisis and that a photography workshop had included 4,023 shots of various sizes that included scenes of combat, work and civilian life.[56] The Twenty-Sixth Assault Division held an exhibition in Tržič (in northern Slovenia), with captions translated into Italian and English. The exhibition was accompanied by a mobile library. Two-hundred photographs – in the formats of 16 × 24, 18 × 24, 26 × 38 and 13 × 18 cm – were pasted onto fifteen cardboard panels.

Trained amateur photographers participated in the work of Partisan photography units right to the end of the war, as evidenced in the report of the Operations Staff of Istria, dated 23 April 1944. As concerns opportunities in the field, the report says:

Cultural and educational work is not organised in a planned manner but is rather implemented ad-hoc. [...] We intend to establish a photography unit. We already have a workshop for producing, duplicating and developing photos. The squadrons have their own amateur photographers. We need one good photographer for our staff.[57]

52 Franc Fabec, 'Photography During the Slovene National Liberation Struggle', in: *Resistance, Suffering, Hope: The Slovene Partisan Movement 1941–1945*, Jože Pirjevec and Bože Repe, Ljubljana/Trieste 2008, pp. 97–99.
53 *Zbornik dokumenata*, vol. IX/3: Partijsko-politička dokumenta.
54 Ibid.
55 Ibid.
56 Ibid.
57 *Zbornik dokumenata i podataka o narodno-oslobodilačkom ratu jugoslovenskih naroda*, vol. V/26: Borbe u Hrvatskoj 1944. godine, Belgrade 1961.

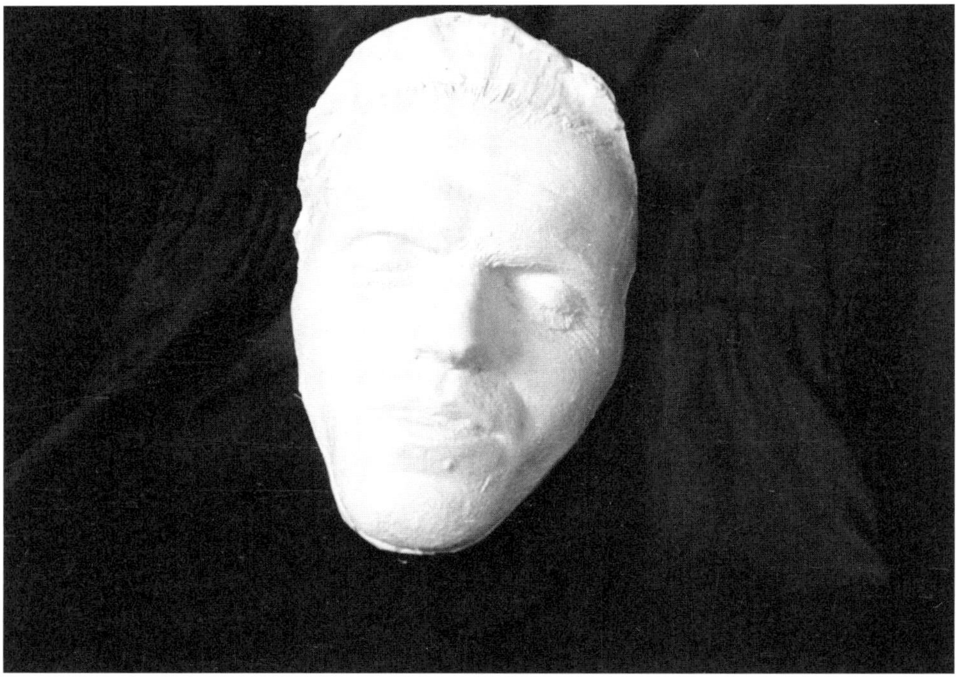

Franc Rozman's ('Commander Stane's') death mask, Črnomelj, 8 November 1944. Photo: Peter Jelič. National Museum of Contemporary History (Slovenia), TN440/16.

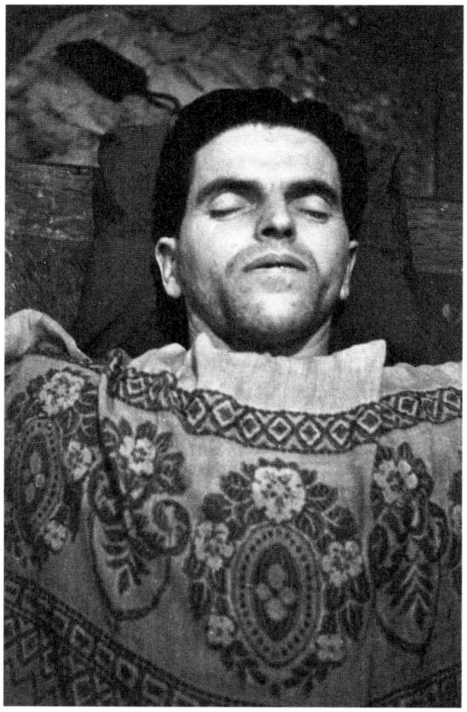

The late Franc Rozman ('Commander Stane') on a bier, Črnomelj, 8 November 1944. Photo: Peter Jelič. National Museum of Contemporary History (Slovenia), TN440/16.

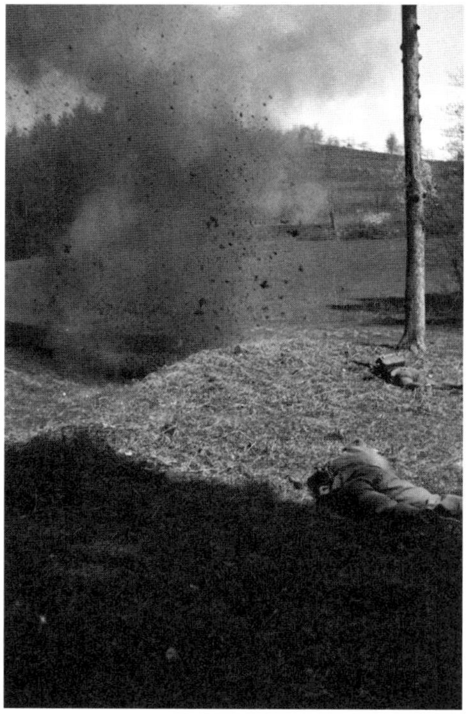

Grenade explosion, August 1943. Photographer unknown. National Museum of Contemporary History (Slovenia), TN27/40.

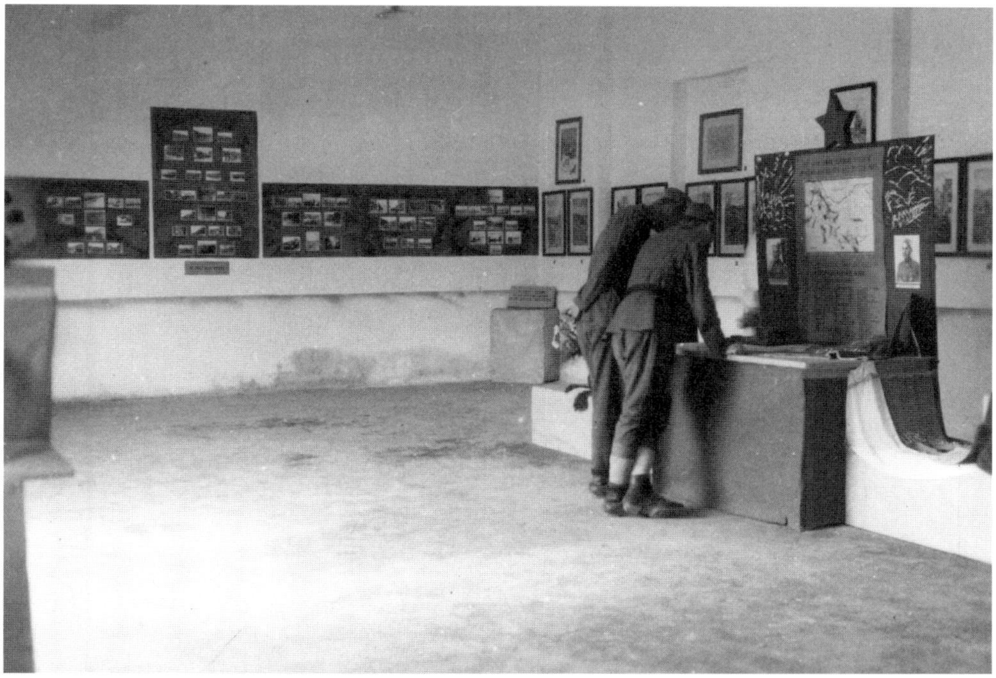

Exhibition in Samobor, 6 June 1945. Photo: Vlado Potočnjak. Croatian History Museum, HPM/MRNH-F-9155.

In recent years, other authors have covered the topic of Partisan art from 1941 to 1945. They have analysed the archives available today in detail and the many works by Partisan artists. Partisan art is difficult to categorise as cultural production in the present-day sense. However, we can classify it as a special form of political activity that generated a certain amount of autonomy despite the centralised nature of the People's Liberation Struggle.[58] Partisan photography's importance lies in this autonomy, because the political language and mechanisms used during the People's Liberation Struggle resulted in an emphasis on its activist potential, which is also important today.

All this means that Partisan photography cannot be labelled as purely propaganda photography. Nor can it be viewed only as a part of the propaganda apparatus. As we have seen so far, while the idea of a centralised system (within which each photography unit would operate) existed from the very beginning, the situation on the ground from 1941 to 1943 was quite different. In this period, Partisan photography existed primarily thanks to the bravery and enthusiasm of key individuals. In the final chapter of the war, 1944 and 1945, a whole series of regulations were passed that attempted to specify the role of photography units within the propaganda system. This came fully into force only after the end of the war in 1945 when many photographers stopped working or volunteering. Photographers' materials then fell under the control of a centralised archive. The entire

58 Gal Kirn, 'On the Specific (In)existence of the Partisan Film in Yugoslavia's People's Liberation Struggle', in: *Partisans in Yugoslavia: Literature, Film and Visual Culture*, Miranda Jakiša and Nikica Gilić (eds.), Bielefeld 2015, p. 207.

system's centralisation was strongly influenced by the new state's consolidation of the levers of power, along with the foreign office's security assessments warning of a potential Soviet occupation. Only after Cominform's resolution and the split with the USSR did Yugoslavia throw out 'dogmatic views in the field of education and culture taken on from the Soviet experience'.[59]

59 Petranović 1988 (see note 12), p. 319.

6. Partisan Photography's Revolutionary Perspective

The previous chapter explored how Partisan photography was defined by the 'impossible' conditions in which it emerged. But it was also defined by its production techniques. Partisan photographs were published using printing presses, as no machines for stacking, stencilling, hot-metal typesetting and rotation existed at that time and place. Instead, cyclostyles were mainly used for printing. A cyclostyle or *Gestetner* is a machine for duplicating text stencilled from typewriter copy. When roll paper was replaced by kraft paper (which, because the colour usually ran, was better suited for wrapping perishables rather than as printing paper), it became practically impossible to print papers more than two pages long. For this reason, many news-sheets were written by hand on regular paper and then duplicated. Yet even for this, ink and fountain pens were also in short supply. Typewriters were few and far between, as were *Gestetners*.[1] The Communist Party of Yugoslavia relied on their pre-war experience and on scarce technical provisions to work undercover.

Campaigns against the more powerful and better-equipped enemy were often carried out under the cover of night, which made it more difficult to document them photographically. A report from the staff of the Eighteenth Division described one such experience, namely a campaign to destroy the train tracks between the two Slovenian villages of Preserje and Goričica. An unnamed American photojournalist wanted to photograph the operation, but was unsuccessful:

> The American journalist counted the explosions with delight. He wasn't able to take photographs using magnesium flash powder, as this would have given away the position of the minelayer who was on the tracks, laying the mines. He would likely have given away his own position too, and would surely have become an easy target for enemy fire from automatic weapons and mortars. He was able to figure this out for himself and didn't even attempt to take photographs. Photographing the explosions was thus not possible for technical reasons.[2]

1 Fabijan Hrvačić, 'Listovi, brošure i leci – ubojito oružje protiv neprijatelja u Pokuplju i *Žumberku*', *in: Četvrta godina narodnooslobodilačkog rata na području Karlovca, Korduna, Like, Pokuplja i Žumberka*, Đuro Zatezalo (ed.), Karlovac 1981, p. 134.
2 *Zbornik dokumenata i podataka o narodnooslobodilačkom ratu jugoslovenskih naroda, vol. V/4: Borbe u Hrvatskoj 1944. godine, Belgrade 1961.*

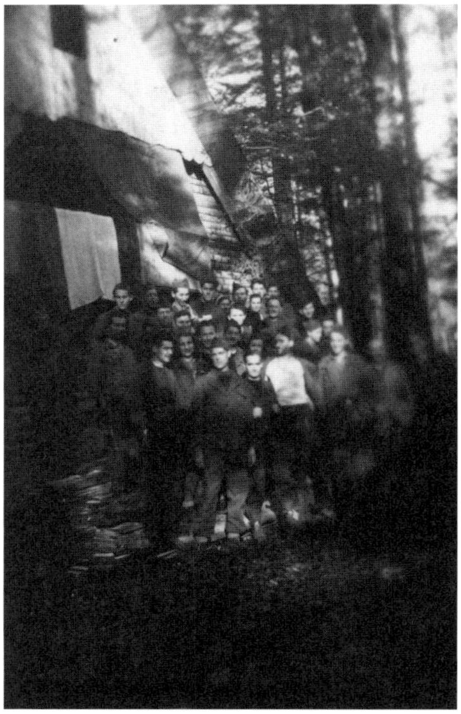

The Naprijed printing-press collective, Drežnica, 1944. Photo: Marija Kreačić. Croatian History Museum, HPM/MRNH-F-3517.

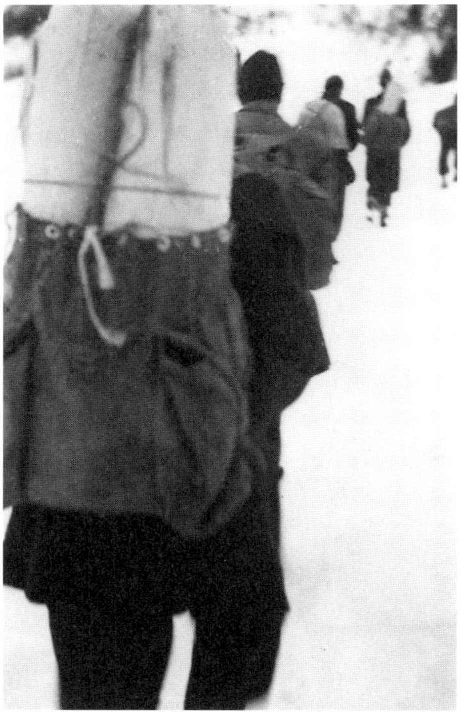

Walking in column. Photographer unknown. Croatian History Museum, HPM/MRNH-F-3569.

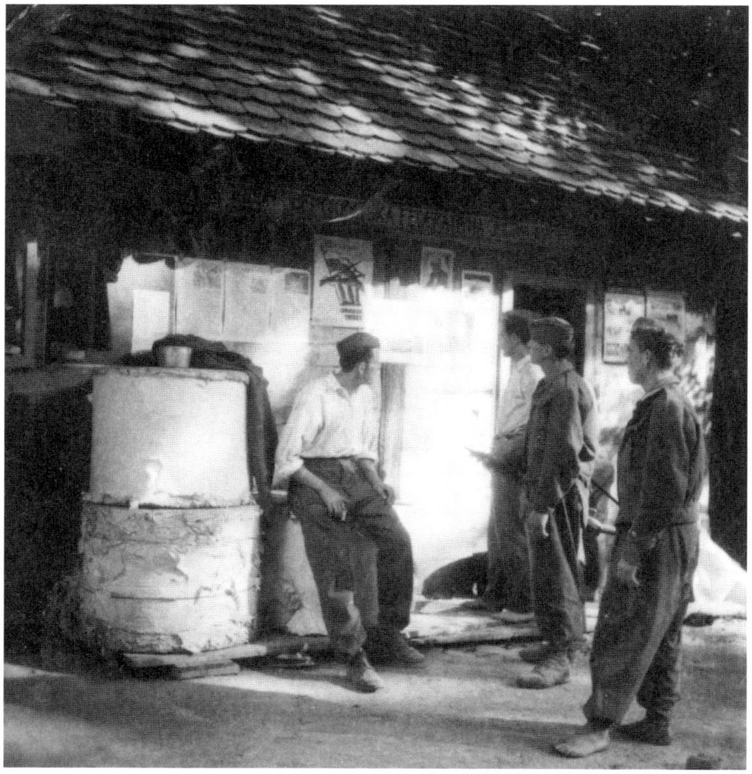

Bales of paper delivered after an ambush of a Ustashe train at Koprivnica, Kordun, 1944. Photographer unknown. Croatian History Museum, HPM/MRNH-F-4808.

At night, the films were developed and fixed, most often in pots for rationing food that had previously been well-scrubbed with sand. For developing photos, pots with a lid, developing spirals, measuring jugs, a thermometer, and film rolls were all in short supply. The fact that even high-ranking officers in the Partisan movement failed to notice this scarcity is a sign of how widespread the situation was. Supreme Commander Josip Broz Tito discussed it in a letter to Svetozar Vukmanović-Tempo, in which he asked him to deliver cigarettes and film:

If it's possible to get the film rolls I sent to Sarajevo developed, can you please send them, and if the images turn out more or less okay, duplicate as many as possible. Besides film for my camera, if there are any cigarettes in Sarajevo, especially 'Neretves', please don't forget us paupers.[3]

Shot film could only be developed on especially dark nights with no moonlight; they were dried with the help of ordinary sponges and checked by holding them up to the light of a fire.[4] Such conditions naturally shaped the photographs' final appearance. Indeed, they were its defining feature as Partisan photography's self-reliant, independent quality contrasted with the German and Ustashe's superior propaganda machinery and technical means of production. In the face of the difficult conditions, Partisan photography resulted in a whittling down of the production process. The Partisans were forced to devise new means of production and – most importantly – of distribution, which did not proceed from the top-down, but rather from the bottom-up. The weak control over propaganda made this possible, as did the decentralised nature of the propaganda system during the first few years of war. Portions of the population that had previously been excluded, both socially and politically, were further empowered by becoming literate and trained in using the technology. It is worth emphasising that the photojournalism that emerged after the First World War was based on a highly professionalised photojournalistic industry, which led to a separation of object and subject. In times of crisis, such as wartime, this rule was suspended by all sides, and 'objectivity' became unattainable. In contrast to war photographers embedded in the military units on all sides, the Partisan photographers often established their own rules, and the Partisan viewer looked towards the photographer as their surrogate: rejoicing in the victories and successes and grieving at Partisan losses.[5] Partisan photography was consumed differently to Axis photography, as the former was not intended for the civic classes of western European states. It could not be found alongside regular adverts for consumer products, which is why we can fairly make the claim that Partisan photography turned the struggle against poverty and misery into the object of consumption.[6]

3 *Zbornik dokumenata i podataka o narodno-oslobodilačkom ratu jugoslovenskih naroda*, vol. II/ 6: Dokumenta vrhovnog *štaba* Narodnooslobodilačke vojske Jugoslavije 1941–1942, Belgrade 1954.

4 *Žorž* Skrigin, *Rat i pozornica, Belgrade 1968, p. 23.*

5 Martha Rosler, *Decoys and Disruptions: Selected Writings, 1975–2001*, Cambridge, Massachusetts 2004, pp. 226–227.

6 Walter Benjamin, *Eseji*, Belgrade 1974, p. 107.

The lack of indexing or signed photographic images can also be viewed as a collective practice. For most photographers, a signature was not important, as the work was experienced collectively. Bearing this in mind, one photograph presently in the Croatian History Museum is particularly interesting. It was discovered on one of the negatives found on a Partisan casualty. The picture was shot while crossing a destroyed bridge on the river Neretva. Taken on the move and out of focus, its lack of style gives it potency. Its technical shortcomings speak of the photographer's class and economic background. Today, the 'lowly' aesthetics of smartphone photography tell a similar story, as described by Hito Steyerl when he writes that focus is the concern of class and privilege, and resolution is an unnecessary object of fetishisation.[7]

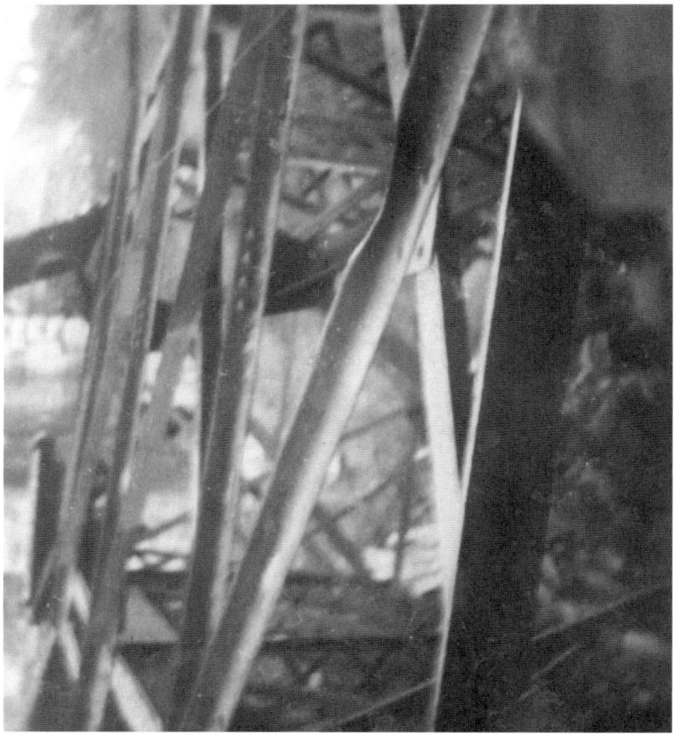

Crossing the river Neretva. Photographer unknown. Croatian History Museum, HPM-MRNH-F-830.

One of the few Partisan photographers still alive today, Franjo Cvrtila (95), now lives in Zagreb and once stated that he never received an order that made assumptions about choice of subject, except for an order forbidding the taking of pictures of Partisan casualties, as such images could be used for enemy propaganda purposes. He joined the Partisans in 1943 as a sixteen-year-old soldier in the Joža Vlahović Sixteenth Youth Brigade. After the war, he photographed the Third Congress of the Alliance of Anti-Fascist Youth of Yugoslavia.

7 Hito Steyerl, 'In Defense of the Poor Image', in: *e-flux Journal #10*, URL: https://www.e-flux.com/journal/10/61362/in-defense-of-the-poor-image (accessed 1 June 2021).

I belonged to the working class. I was a servant and life was hard. I was looked down on as a child. I was working as an apprentice in a construction-painter firm, when they started hanging people in Koprivnica. My sister was working for the International Red Aid at the time, and my two other brothers were in the Ustashe. I managed to escape to the Partisans with a mouth organ and a Kodak *Retina* camera in 1943. During the fighting in the Žumberak hills against the Ustashe units, a great number of us died and I lost all my photographs. Before engaging in combat, I gave them to a hospital nurse to take care of, and I instructed her to burn them if [the notorious Ustashe unit] the Black Legion showed up. I survived the battle, but she didn't and she burned all the photographs before she died. Photographing slain Partisans was forbidden.[8]

During the war, Žorž Skrigin encountered a similar situation when in enemy territory in Jadovnik, with fighters from the Seventh Corps and the British-Soviet military mission, which included Randolph Churchill and Stojan Pribićević. They issued the order that all personal documents and photographs had to be destroyed, due to the very real threat of being captured.

I was shocked. Should I destroy the negatives? I understood the order and it was logical that such documents mustn't fall into enemy hands. But how could I destroy what I had worked so hard to make and had kept for so long? Hadn't I managed to carry them over the river Bosna? Hadn't I been lucky enough to get them out of Drvar again? And how was I supposed to destroy them now? No way! I wasn't going to do that! I decided to wait until the last moment. In my mind I had already made a plan: I would destroy the negatives like this, by blowing them to pieces with my *Schmeisser.*[9]

Besides the fact that photographic material could be easily destroyed in combat, damp presented an additional set of problems as the wet and decomposing negatives could often not be dried out quickly enough and so were sometimes irreparably lost. When crossing a river, while the fighters carried their clothes in bundles over their heads to keep them dry, photographers were often forced to wade through the water fully clothed, all the while preserving their camera equipment, negatives and photographs by holding them above their heads.[10] Photographic supplies would be placed in secret locations or buried in the woods, a practice mentioned in the Report on the Fifth Operative Zone to the General Staff of the Croatian Detachment of the People's Liberation Movement, dated 29 May 1942.[11] When film was sent off for development, it was advised to always write on the envelopes: 'Photographic film, do not open in sunlight!' Films and photographs sent via the Partisan postal service, which operated throughout the war via a network of undercover agents, secret channels and couriers who relayed (on foot) bundles of photographs, letters, newspapers, packages and even dental supplies.[12] It was crucial that the negatives not fall into enemy hands, as this would have put the families of Partisans in occupied territory in mortal danger.

8 The conversation with Franjo Cvrtila took place on 13 December 2017 in Zagreb.

9 Skrigin 1968 (see note 4), p. 257.

10 Ibid., p. 213.

11 *Zbornik dokumenata i podataka o narodno-oslobodilačkom ratu jugoslovenskih naroda*, vol. V/4. Borbe u Hrvatskoj 1942. godine, Belgrade 1954.

12 Mahmud Konjhodžić, 'Različite veze', in: *Veze u NOB: Ratna sećanja 1941–1945, vol. 4, Esad Tihić and Momčilo Kalem (eds.), Belgrade 1981, p. 44.*

Many negatives were destroyed in enemy bombardments and attacks, as was the case with the German bombardment of the hospital in the Croatian town of Korenica, when as many as 1,500 negatives were destroyed, as described by Franjo Mosinger in his photo diary. The most important collection of Partisan photographs was destroyed when Ivo Lola Ribar died on 27 November 1943 in Glamočko polje. The loss occurred as a result of a German air raid. The entire photo archive went up in smoke after a Partisan plane caught fire and crashed to the ground. Vili Šimunov-Barba, Ernest Grgić and by some accounts Žorž Skrigin had been working on it for months. They had planned to use the photographs as magazine illustrations and to assemble an exhibition representing the Partisan movement to the Allies, due to go on show first in Cairo, then London. Around 300 painstakingly selected photographs were lost in the flames in that single incident.[13] One day later, the Partisan leader Moša Pijade charged Skrigin with developing his photographs once again. He then took them to Vladimir Velebit and Miloje Milojević in Cairo. During that period, some of his photographs were published in *The New York Times* and the British newspaper *News Chronicle*.[14]
Educational programmes for teaching propagandists and novice photographers intensified during 1944. Perhaps one of the best examples was *Fotografski priručnik*, a handbook written by the Slovenian Partisan lieutenant Milan Štok. He was the leader of the photography unit in the propaganda department of the Seventh Corps. The introduction to the handbook, printed using a cyclostyle, states that the guide is intended for photojournalists in the People's Liberation Army tasked with photographing important and interesting events. Film processing, meanwhile, was left to the photography unit of the General Staff. Štok's handbook is a valuable document. On its first page, it clarifies why education and a familiarity with photographic techniques are important:

> Certainly, the greatest success cannot be attained exclusively by mastering technique, but those who do not master it will never be successful. This handbook covers the materials that photojournalists (many of whom are still unskilled photographers) urgently need in order to meet the needs of contemporary photography [...]. Consequently, this booklet's goal is to get every photojournalist intimately familiar with their camera. They must also know how to use it at night, must know the basic principles and procedures for lighting, depth of field, know about film stock and its characteristics, and, more generally, know what makes an image. The war photography service plays an important role in our army. It was entrusted with capturing pictures of all our fighting, from the smallest missions upwards, all our problems and suffering, and also the joy that shines in our ranks, especially now, as we approach the final victory.[15]

Thanks to this handbook, we learn that the most frequently used film formats among Partisan photographers were 24 × 36 mm, and 4 × 4, 6 × 6, 6 × 3 and 9 × 12 cm. The cameras most often used were manufactured by Leica, Contax and Kodak, along with two medium-format cameras, the *Rolleiflex* and *Rolleicord*. In the Partisan units (at least in the Slovenian units) you could find cameras using 6 × 9 cm film and the American rangefinder camera *Kodak 35*, which the US Army perfected in 1938 for its own use. The *Kodak 35* was advertised as 'your

13 Skrigin 1968 (see note 4), p. 216.
14 Ibid.
15 Milan *Štok, Fotografski priručnik*, Propagandni odsjek Sedmog korpusa 1944, pp. 3–5.

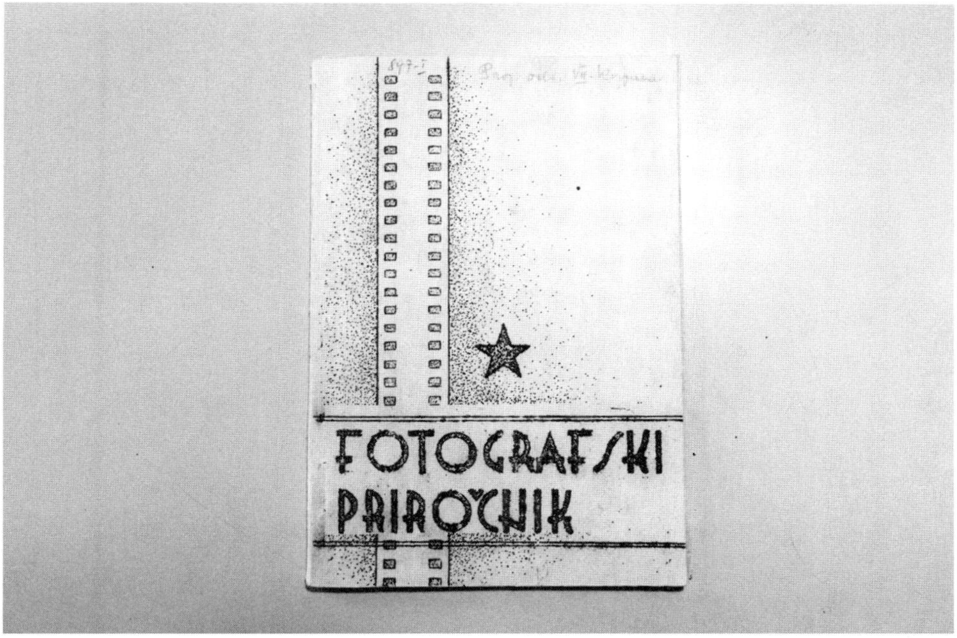

Cover of Milan Štok's Fotografski priručnik, the Partisan photography handbook, 1944. Photo: Davor Konjikušić.

civilian miniature' and was a favourite among hobby photographers. During the war Kodak even released an edition in olive-grey to match army uniform. Because of its technical properties and compact design, the camera was a great choice for military units that were constantly on the move.[16] In his handbook, Štok emphasised how cameras using 35 mm film had a great advantage, as such cameras could take as many as thirty-six frames while boasting a greater depth of field compared with cameras in the 6 × 9 cm format, thus making them especially suited to photographing military action and campaigns.[17]

The handbook pays special attention to technical training. For instance, the author understands one particular problem to be that the subject in Partisan photography is often too far away, the composition messy, with resulting images that are 'all over the place'.

The handbook suggests that every photograph should be composed systematically, made up of a central area, a surrounding area and a background. The author states that small-format cameras are worth considering for pictures with foregrounded action and close surroundings.[18]

In winter, show small buildings amid large snowdrifts. Each picture with snow has to have an especially clear foreground – traces of skis or feet, ski poles pricked into the snow, a snowy fir tree or fence etc. [...] The sun must never shine directly on the lens. Tip: Take a picture by shading the lens with your hand, with a piece of paper or by standing in a shaded spot.[19]

16 *Life Magazine*, 8 May 1944, p. 59.
17 *Štok* 1944 (see note 15), p. 7.
18 Ibid., p. 40.
19 Ibid., p. 39.

Štok's text has a textbook character. Written with precision, it is easy to follow and makes basic technical knowledge available to all interested, for instance on depth of field, measuring light, exposure and the more complex physical properties of the lens. Despite being written more than seventy years ago, this handbook is still relevant for analogue photography today. Štok obviously possessed a great deal of background knowledge from the field of physics, and his explanation of the function of the shutter, the aperture, and how the photographic images themselves are made would not disappoint even today:

When light falls on the film layer, it penetrates the tape. The silver-bromide layer is exposed to the light that strikes it. From outside, on the film layer of the tape, nothing changes: the picture is still invisible, hidden (latent). Only with the help of various developers does the picture become visible: that which is naturally white is black on the negative, and vice versa. The negative is

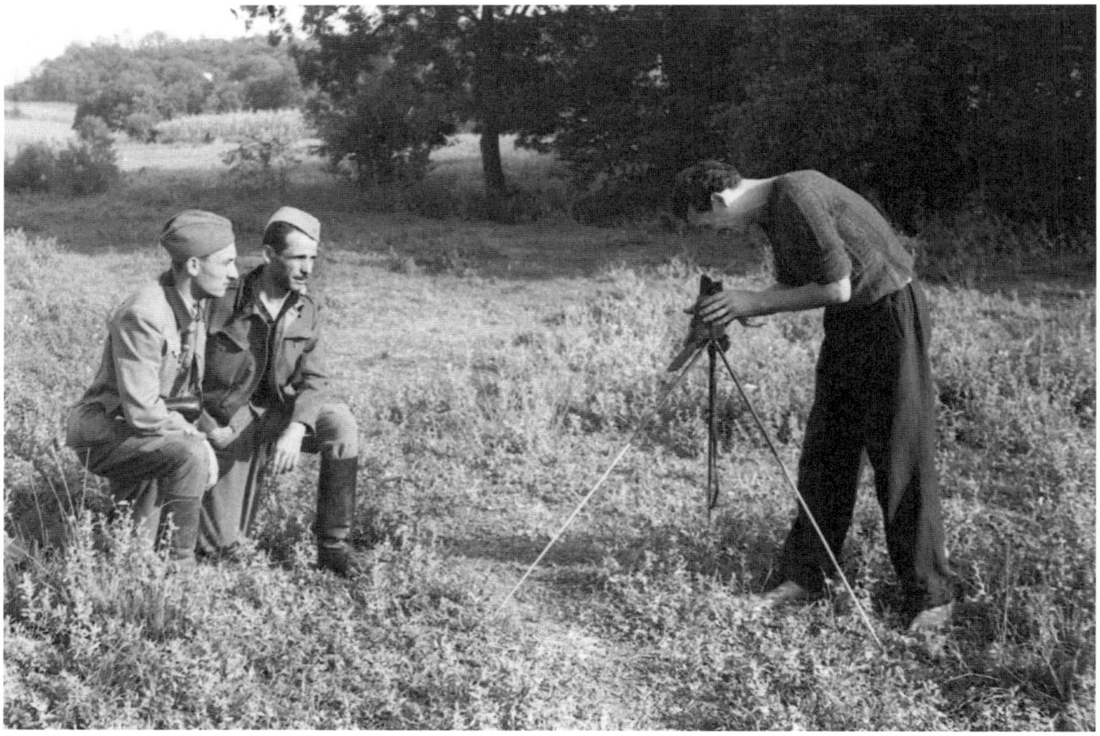

An ethnic Slovenian photographer from Slavonski Brod at work after joining the Partisans with his wife and working in the propaganda department of the District People's Committee for Slavonski Brod, Breznica, 1944. Photo: Pero Dragila. Croatian History Museum, HPM-100522/36.

transferred onto light-sensitive photographic paper, which transforms the image into a positive. Light sets off the chemical process in the silver-bromide layer of the tape, and this process is only made manifest by developing the image using chemicals. The developer can distinguish bromide from the lightened silver-bromide parts. The bromide is transferred to the developer, while the original silver-bromide changes into the metal silver. These innumerable particles of silver-bromide are what make the image. The non-exposed silver-bromide particles remain untouched by the developer. The metal silver particles are 'grains', and the picture is made up of these grains.[20]

The handbook also reveals that panchromatic emulsion was used more frequently than orthochromatic emulsion, and it was of exceptional importance in photographing the Partisans. Panchromatic films were sensitive to more colours, or more wavelengths of light, and provided a greater range of grey tones compared with orthochromatic films. The latter were exceptionally difficult to isolate, so that the red five-pointed star would only be visible against a green background. Štok devotes special attention to how you can obtain fine-grained images when developing a film and explains the optimal chemical proportions for different films and developers.

The most important part of this handbook, and one of the most important artefacts linked to Partisan photography, concerns choice of photographic subject. Despite Štok's suggestions on how the Partisan movement ought to be depicted, he expects every photographer to take the initiative in choosing the subjects they capture on film – in other words, he expects them to be auteur photographers. He recommends photographing combat, brigade parades, meetings and consultations, as well as depicting military conveys, weaponry and

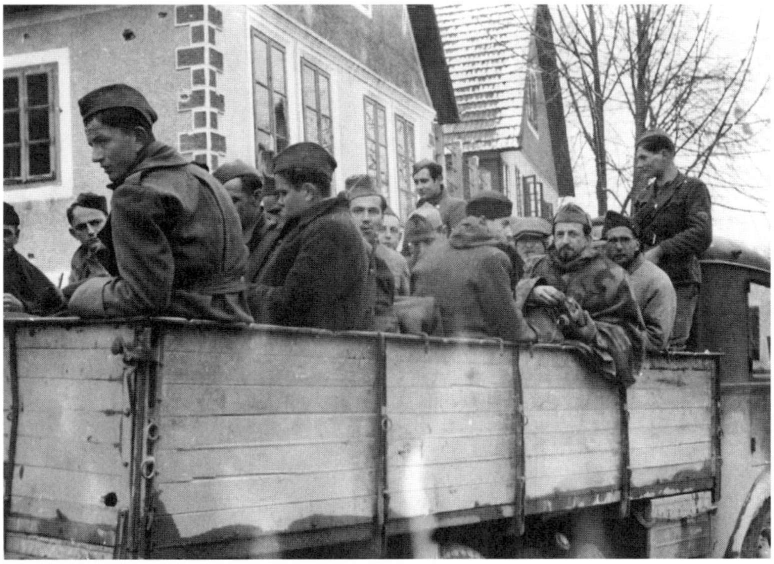

Delegates of the Second Session of the AVNOJ in transit between meetings (with Slovene artist Božidar Jakac, third from right, facing camera), Jajce, 29–30 November 1943. Photographer unknown. Museum of Yugoslavia, III-180.

20 Ibid., pp. 37–38.

radiotelegraph activities. Štok foregrounds photography's propaganda function, but on the next page discusses artistic expression. The photography handbook even ends with a story about Leonardo da Vinci, with the author emphasising the need to photograph snapshots of Partisan life, moments of calm with a semblance of normality.

During 1944, as the Allies' aid mission to the Partisans started to arrive, so too did larger amounts of photographic supplies. This galvanised photographic activities further. The value of goods delivered up to 15 April 1945 from the USA, Great Britain and Canada was in excess of 10.25 million US dollars. The largest portion of goods consisted of food, engine oil, gasoline, petroleum, ambulances, construction materials for building bridges, railway equipment, clothes and – of course – photographic materials.[21] Packages arrived from Gorica, Trieste, Milan, Bari and Rome. Precision-engineering workshops started to operate more intensively. They were now better placed to repair all manner of precision instruments, including cameras.[22] It is therefore unsurprising that the emergence of this photography handbook coincided with greater Allied help, and also with the Partisan movement becoming the only anti-fascist resistance movement to be recognised by the Western Allies. Despite better supplies, chiefly linked with Allied political recognition of the Partisan movement, sporadic shortages of photography supplies continued.[23] Even the well-known Slovenian painter and photographer, Božidar Jakac, then in the Fifteenth Brigade, ran out of film when photographing the Second Assembly of Activists of the Liberation Front on 4 and 6 September 1944 in Črnomelj, which 600 delegates attended.[24]

Besides the technical conditions in which Partisan photography emerged and the points discussed above, as with the rest of the movement, Partisan photographers faced the real threat of loss of life. Numerous photographers died, and we will never find out anything about many of them. Many died taking photographs on the front line. While photographing the enemy retreat at Lovas, for instance, the photographer Dragić Radivojević from the Fourth Serbian Assault Brigade was killed, as was Ljubo Anđelić, earlier in the year, on 10 June, while attempting to record the German airstrikes near Ljubin Grob at Tjentište. Most of his photographs were destroyed, too. But sometimes life was a fate worse than death, in periods of starvation and illness, as the following description clearly attests:

First the horses started to drop, because there was almost no food for them. After the horses, the Italians began to drop – the prisoners – and then our fighters. I watched the horses die, and only a few minutes later they disappeared into the prisoners' bags. Our soldiers followed suit. It would have been unthinkable to see our men eat fallen livestock, yet on this march we witnessed precisely that. Everything we experienced, all the deaths and the utter desperation, had a devastating effect on the more dispirited. It wasn't unheard of that, in desperation, a person would resort to taking their own life. I looked at how in the columns that moved from Krstača towards

21 Branko Petranović, *Istorija Jugoslavije 1918–1988*, Belgrade 1988, pp. 355–356.

22 Vida Tom-Lasič, 'Slovenačke partizanske radio-stanice', in: *Veze u NOB: Ratna sećanja 1941–1945*, vol. 4, Esad Tihić and Momčilo Kalem (eds.), Belgrade 1981, p. 425.

23 People's Liberation Army of Yugoslavia, Military Archive Belgrade, K24 F2 20.

24 Mile Pavlin, *Petnajsta brigade, Ljubljana 1969, p. 277.*

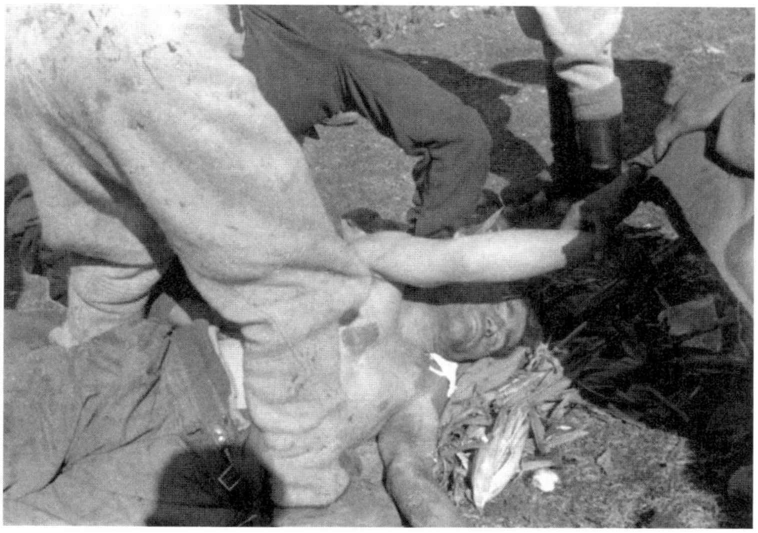

Wounded soldier in First Dalmatian Brigade shortly before dying from injuries, Konjic, Idbar valley, Bosnia and Herzegovina, 1943. Photo: Mladen Iveković. Croatian History Museum, HPM/MRNH-A-6337/66.

the valley of Idbar, one fighter (I don't know his name) strapped an Italian bomb to his chest and detonated it; in the valley I came across a man who killed his own female comrade and then himself. Between Lake Boračko and Konjice, after one very violent clash, I came across my injured fighter (still bearing the wounds he had suffered in Banija), Uroš Dmitrović, who was lying languidly, groggy and sure that he would go no further. I forced him to come to his senses and keep moving, but he made it clear to me that for him the journey was over and that he couldn't go any further.[25]

One other problem existed within the troops themselves, between soldiers and photographers. Tensions sometimes rose unnecessarily, often also producing tragicomic situations, such as those in the Mostar Battalion:

Salko Zebić picked up a camera for the first time in his life and managed to open it. As he didn't know how to close it again, mockery of our 'photojournalist' ensued, who subsequently hurled the camera into a stream.[26]

During combat in the Rama valley in Bosnia and Herzegovina, just before the battle of Prozor, the Mostar Battalion lost Luka Knežić, a photographer from Mostar and a pre-war communist. He had sent three rolls of film to Enver Ćemalović before catching typhoid fever. Yet when the commander was searching for papers, he came across the rolls and unspooled them: 'All three rolls were irrevocably lost, I am certain that they were the most precious photographic documents of our battalion. When I saw what had happened, we argued and almost fought. In his typhoid agony, Luka took his own life.'[27]

25 Obrad Egić, 'Treći bataljon Pete dalmatinske brigada', in: *Neretva, zbornik radova*, vol. 3, Svetislav Savković (ed.), Belgrade 1965, p. 451.

26 Enver *Ćemalović, Mostarski bataljon*, Mostar 1986, p. 163.

27 Ibid., p. 175.

Partisan photography emerged under such difficult conditions as these, and was the product of the technical parameters that defined it. We can say that throughout the entire war, Partisan photography – particularly in the first three years – was itself engaged in a struggle for survival. Over time, however, Partisan photographers learnt to adapt to the dangers of disappearance and destruction. As with Partisan art, photography 'breached its own impossibility', as Miklavž Komelj has demonstrated with respect to Partisan poetry.[28] Sharing the fate of the Partisan movement and the art within it, Partisan photography had one more tragic destiny: it found itself caught between genres as documentary material, art or propaganda. However, the most important task of Partisan photography was to successfully represent the anti-fascist and revolutionary struggle, including its vision and humanity, all the while using equipment with significant technical limitations. In this struggle, faced with the impossible, Partisan photographers – in contrast to Allied and Entente photographers – managed to liberate their own political potential in Walter Benjamin's sense of the phrase. They strengthened their alliances and struggles, and they attacked the enemy. Partisan photography, with all its technical failings as part of a guerrilla movement fighting an asymmetrical war, became a practice of revolutionary viewing.

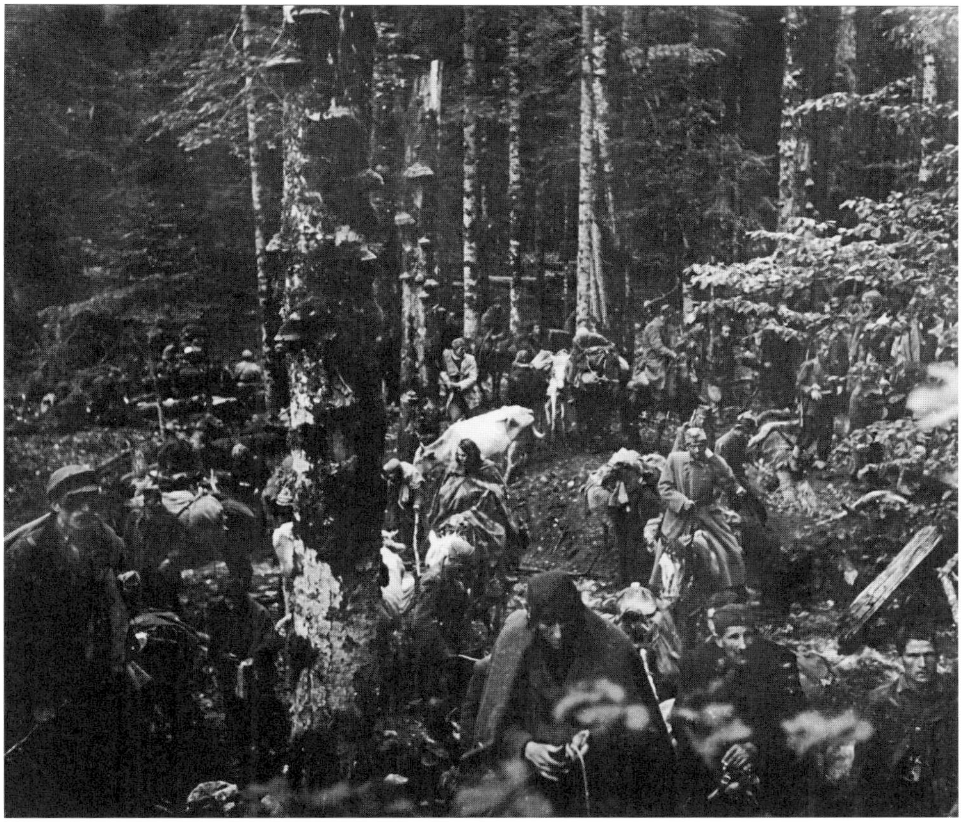

Casualties from the Second Division taking a short rest on Mount Balinovac, Battle of Sutjeska, 1943.
Photo: Žorž Skrigin. Museum of Yugoslavia, III-3429.

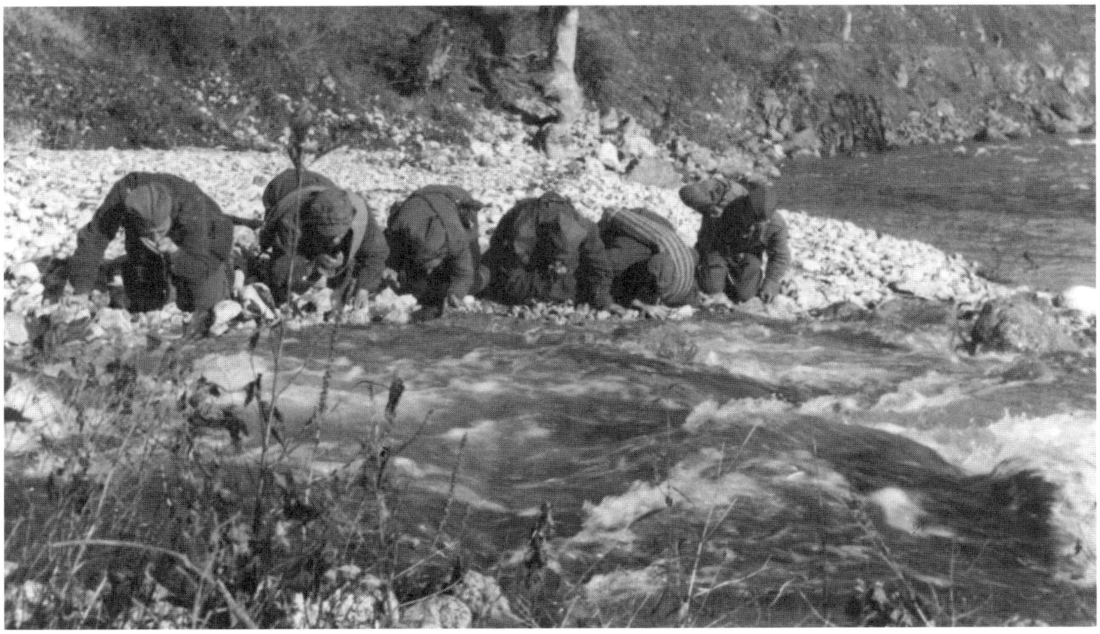

Quenching thirst at a clear stream, Croatia, 1944. Photographer unknown. Croatian History Museum, HPM/MRNH-F-1056.

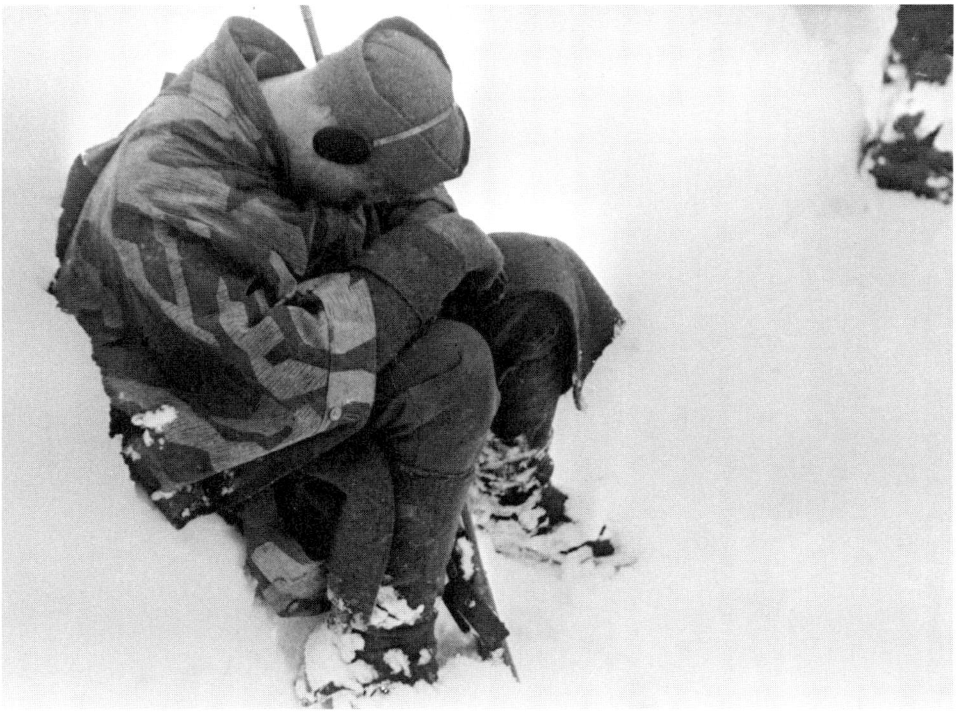

Soldier fights the cold during march of the Fourteenth Division of the People's Liberation Movement in Croatia. Photo: Jože Petek. National Museum of Contemporary History of Slovenia, PL1476.

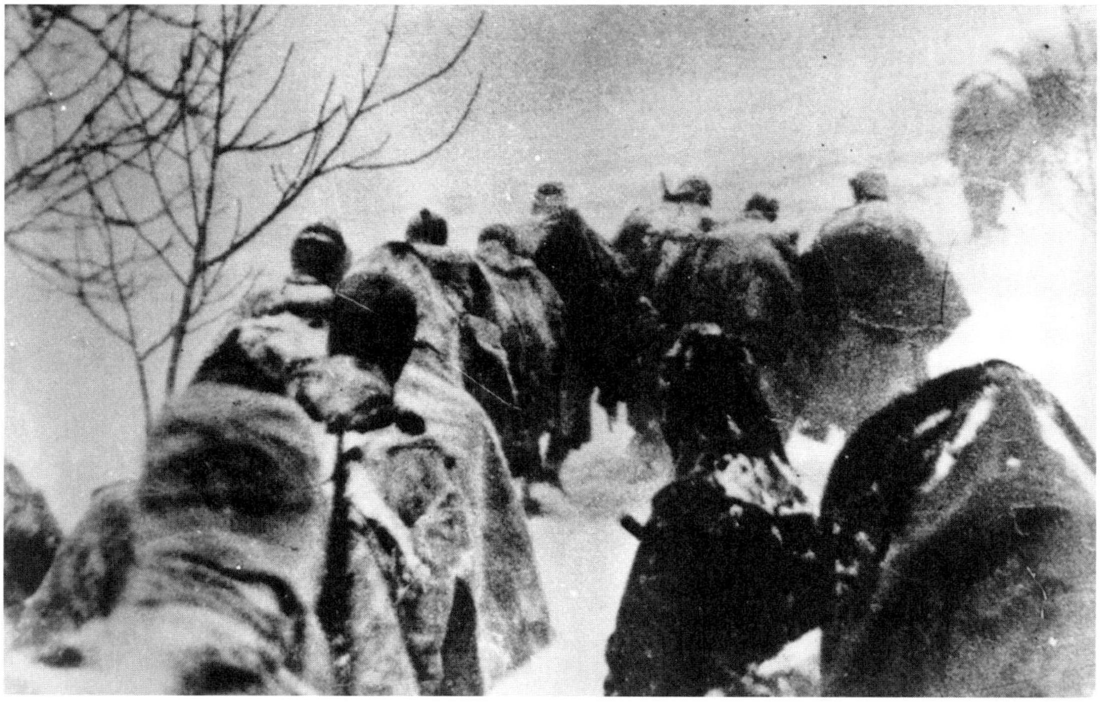

Transporting the injured, 1944. Photo: Jože Petek. Museum of Recent History, Celje, FZ2/801. XIV.

7. Iconic Photographs

An iconic picture is an image recognised and understood by many people in different cultures and times. To a greater or lesser extent, such a picture has transcended its initial purpose and parameters, especially in relation to its 'production, function, context and meaning'[1] A great example of an iconic photograph is that of Ernesto 'Che' Guevara, shot by the Cuban photographer Alberto Korda. This photograph has found its way into popular culture, art and the mass media. Its global dissemination only occurred after Che Guevara's murder, during the student demonstrations of 1968, first in May at the Sorbonne in Paris, then in October in Mexico City[2] and in the Yugoslav student movement. The Italian publisher Giangiacomo Feltrinelli was the person responsible for this image's wide distribution. In 1967 he travelled to Cuba, where Korda gave him two copies of the famous revolutionary's portrait.[3] Korda had no qualms with his close-up of Guevara's face being used in various political struggles, as long as it would not be used for commercial purposes, which unfortunately did become the norm over time. This photograph is perhaps the clearest example of how a photograph can be semiotically transformed into a universally recognisable symbol, that is, into an icon.[4]

As concerns the Partisan movement, surely one of the most instantly recognisable iconic photographs was one taken by the Yugoslav Partisan photographer Žorž Skrigin in late 1943.[5] His photograph *Majka Knežopoljka* was named after Skender Kulenović's poem 'Stojanka majka Knežopoljka' (Stojanka, Mother from Knežopolje). He took the photograph when civilians were fleeing from Kozara. The photograph displays Milica Tepić, wife of the fallen People's Hero Branko Tepić, with her son Branko and daughter Dragica. The Croatian art historian and curator, Želimir Koščević, justifiably compared this very photo with the famous picture *Migrant Mother* that the US photographer Dorothea Lange shot in 1936 during the Great Depression.[6] Koščević believed that Skrigin's photograph had not been taken with propaganda purposes in mind, and he knew it was free from the kind of censorship that

1 Martin Kemp, *Christ to Coke: How Image Becomes Icon*, New York 2012, p. 3.

2 Antigoni Memou, *Photography and Social Movements: From the Globalisation of the Movement (1968) to the Movement against Globalisation (2001)*, Manchester 2013, p. 74.

3 Phyllis Passariello, 'Desperately Seeking Something: Che Guevara as Secular Saint', in: *The Making of Saints Contesting Sacred Ground*, James Hopgood (ed.), Tuscaloosa 2005, p. 84.

4 Ibid., p. 89.

5 Several different publications and recorded oral accounts state that the photograph was likely shot in January 1944.

6 Želimir Koščević, *U fokusu: ogledi o hrvatskoj fotografiji*, Zagreb 2006, p. 74.

prevailed in the magazines of Allied countries or Nazi Germany.[7] However, it is important to emphasise that while these two photographs are comparable in terms of content and iconography, in no sense is the position of these two photographers comparable. In contrast to Skrigin, Lange was commissioned by the state, in this case the Farm Security Administration, to shoot photographs for propaganda purposes during the Great Depression.

Together with the other photographers commissioned by the state programme (Walker Evans and Russell Lee among them), her job was to take photographs of the deprived social classes to garner public support for large federal subsidies. In contrast to Lange, Skrigin was not engaged by the state to shoot these photographs. Instead, serendipity gave rise to these shots, which were unplanned, as the force of the scene unfolded before him. Skrigin's negatives, and indeed all the photographs in this series, can now be found in the Museum of Yugoslavia, Belgrade. Researching them allows the viewer to gain a more detailed analy-

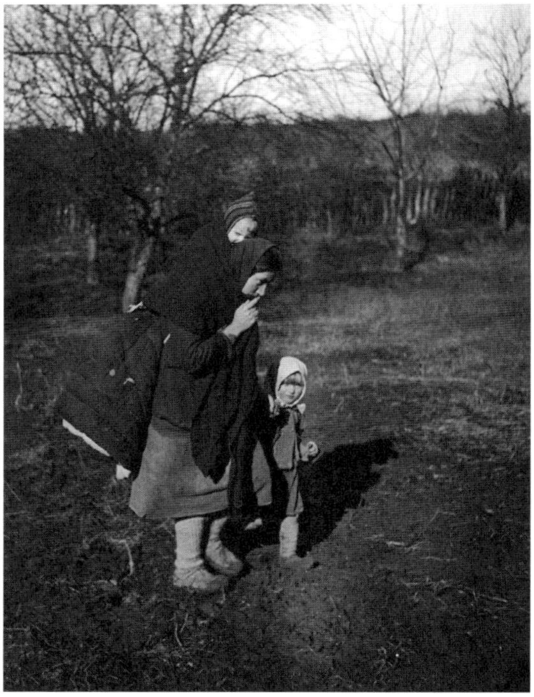

The 'Mother from Knežopolje' (Milica Tepić and her children), fleeing the village of Knežopolje after it was razed to the ground by members of the Russian Liberation Army, fighting on the Axis side, during the Sixth Enemy Offensive, January 1944. Photo: Žorž Skrigin. Museum of Yugoslavia, III-802.

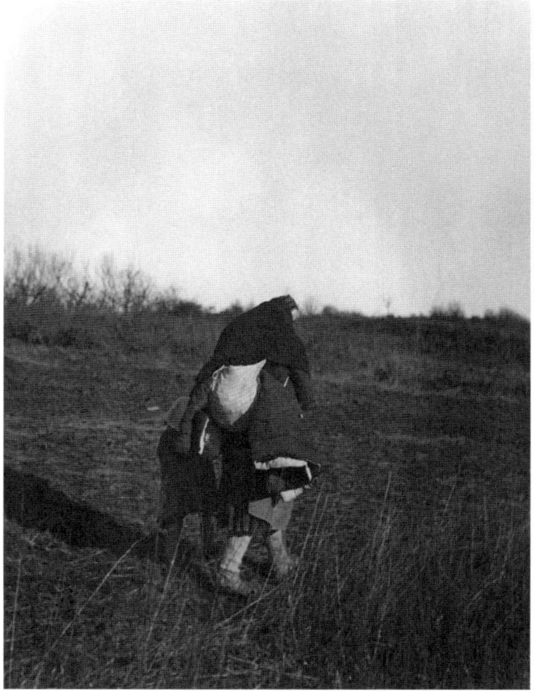

The 'Mother from Knežopolje' (Milica Tepić and her children), fleeing the village of Knežopolje. Photo: Žorž Skrigin. Museum of Yugoslavia, III-803.

7 Ibid., p. 78.

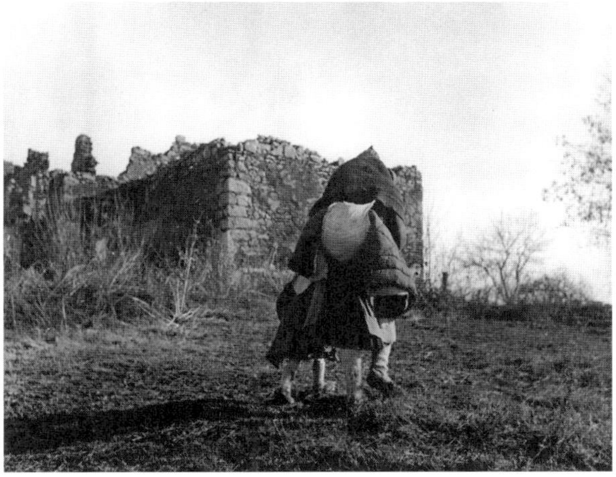

The 'Mother from Knežopolje' (Milica Tepić and her children), fleeing the village of Knežopolje. Photo: Žorž Skrigin. Museum of Yugoslavia, III-806.

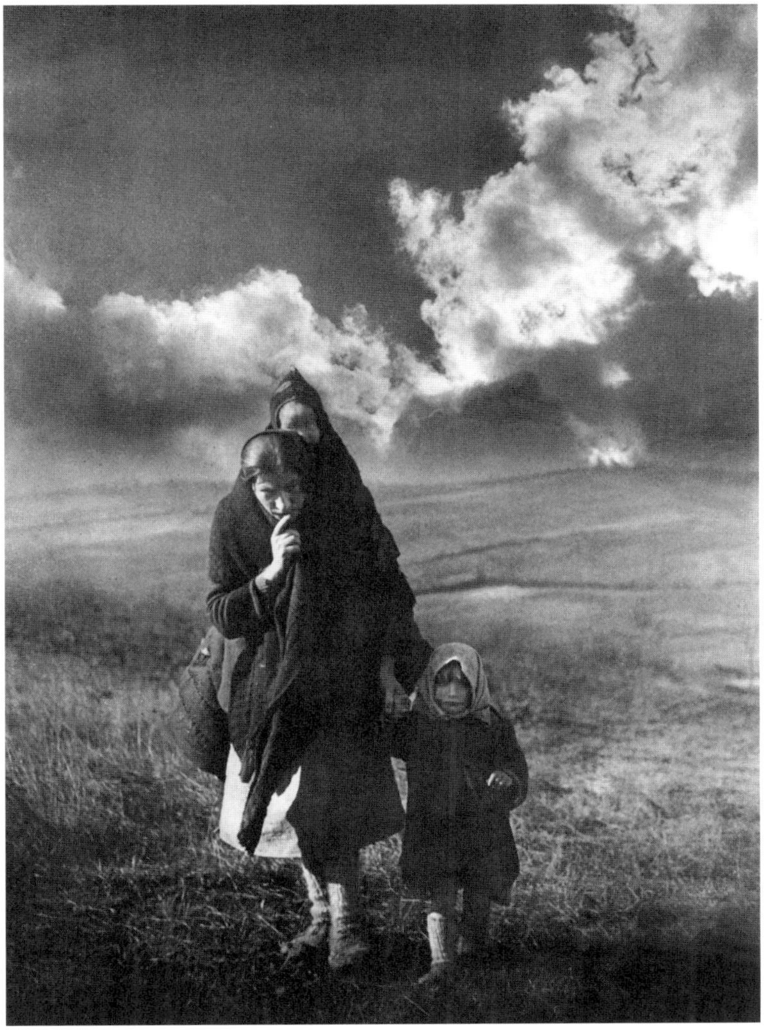

The 'Mother from Knežopolje' (Milica Tepić and her children), fleeing the village of Knežopolje after it was razed to the ground by members of the Russian Liberation Army, fighting on the Axis side, during the Sixth Enemy Offensive, January 1944. Photo: Žorž Skrigin. Museum of Yugoslavia, III-807.

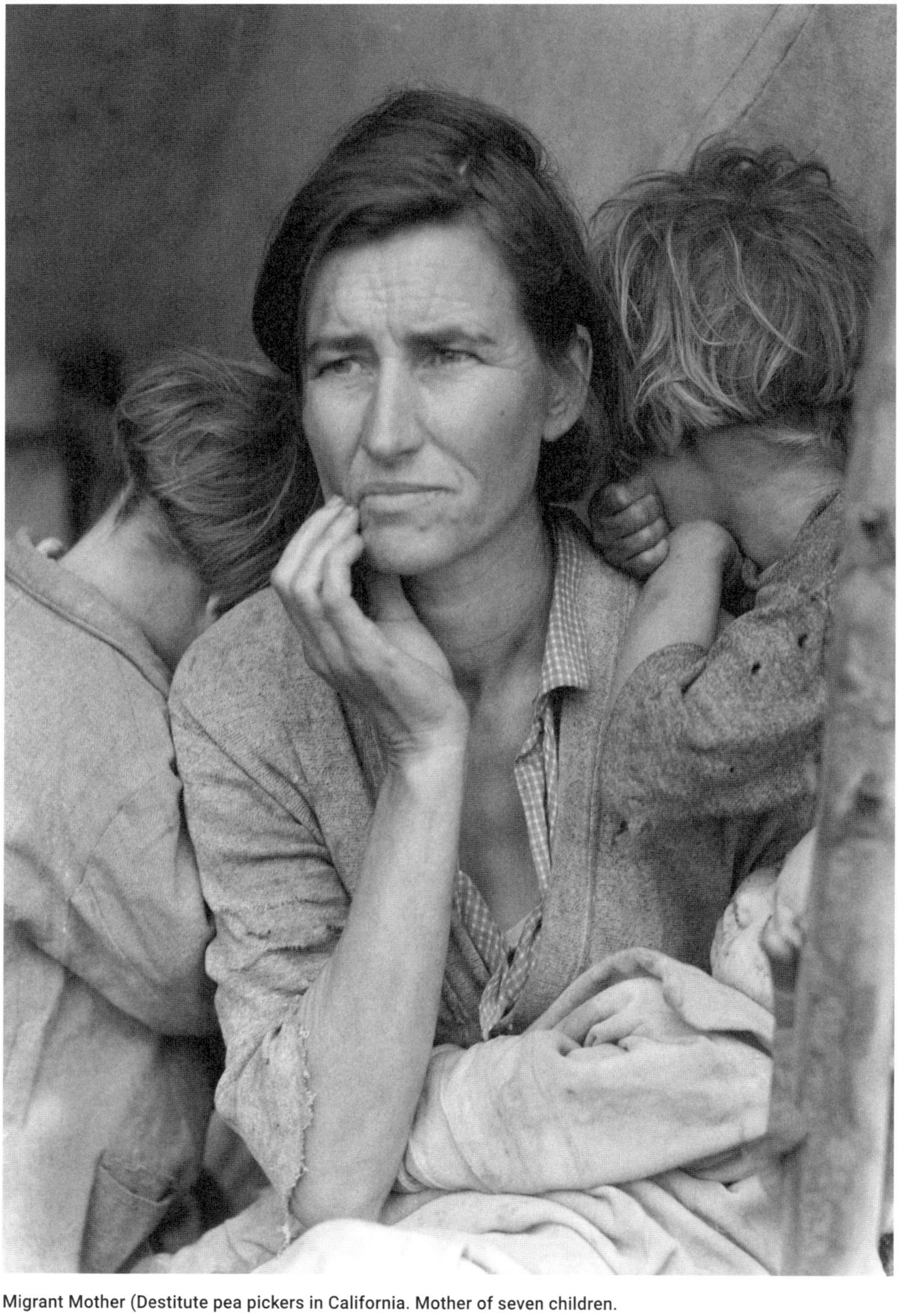

Migrant Mother (Destitute pea pickers in California. Mother of seven children. Age thirty-two. Nipomo, California), February/March 1936. Photo: Dorothea Lange. Library of Congress Prints and Photographs Division, fsa 8b29516.

sis of the photographer's approach and working methods. While lacking film and materials, the photographer decided to take numerous pictures while still seeking the right angle. After several unsuccessful attempts, he took some frontal shots of the mother, thus isolating her amid a never-ending expanse of wasteland and dereliction. In the style of a documentary filmmaker, he did not influence or direct his subject, but pursued it while searching for a decisive moment, believing that in this way he would be able to take a photograph with the greatest significatory and emotive charge.

I dismounted the pony, which was only irritating me now, and I let him free. I ran around 20 metres in front of her and lay in the grass, waiting for her to pass. Deep in thought, she approached, still holding her hand to her face. And finally, the expression I wanted to capture, it was before me. A step or two more and I pressed click.[8]

Behind the young mother and widow, the warm sun was peeping through dark clouds. Skrigin later brightened these clouds in his film lab to heighten the contrast and dramatic quality of the action. Working in conditions a world away from those of the Allied and German photographers, he created an image that would gain further iconic value over time, largely because it successfully combined elements recognisable in the history of art. Skrigin knew these elements well and successfully applied them here thanks to his rich pre-war photography experience. This is a photograph that undoubtedly managed to communicate a message outside the Yugoslav context too. It is a good example of how a photograph can disseminate certain messages – in this case, of civilian casualties and the horrors of war – but also the heroic efforts as represented in the archetypical figure of the mother.

In the photograph, as in the poem, her role as an epic heroine comes to the fore. This is a common stylistic feature in the epic (folk) poetry of the region. An excellent example of this is the poem 'Smrt majke Jugovića' (Death of Mother Jugović). Its title and central figure is a mother who loses her husband and seven sons in the 1389 Battle of Kosovo, a battle of great importance for Serbian national myth-making, linked to ideas of victimhood and a 'noble defeat'. As Jelena Batinić claims, it is this model of the traditional heroine which is praised in the most famous poem about the Partisan struggle, 'Stojanka, Mother from Knežopolje'.[9] Skrigin translated this literary trope into a photograph, something the title also hints at. Elevating an isolated figure to the level of archetype was not merely the reserve of Partisan photographers alone. Indeed, the photographer John Phillips shot a practically identical image in El Shatt. His photograph was superior in a technical sense, but the content was the same.

8 Žorž Skrigin, *Rat i pozornica*, Belgrade 1968, p. 244.
9 Jelena Batinić, *Women and Yugoslav Partisans*, Stanford 2015, p. 51.

Skrigin shot a second iconic photograph, in the same period, at the same location, on the fringes of Knežopolje in December 1943. The photograph was of Milja Marin (neé Toroman), who had been taken to the concentration camp in Sisak as a fifteen-year-old girl during the 1942 Enemy Offensive. From there she was sent to Nuremberg instead of Jasenovac, and worked for a German woman named Margit in her home. Wanting to return as quickly as possible to Yugoslavia, her new hosts decided to help her, and they procured the necessary permits for her to depart for Slovenia. She joined the Partisans in Cerovljani, Bosnia and Herzegovina, after which she reached the Eleventh Krajina Brigade, in which she worked as a hospital nurse. In contrast with the photograph *Majka Knežpoljka*, this time Skrigin carefully directed his subject.

Skrigin needed to find a beautiful and charming young woman for this shot. Of all the hospital nurses, he chose Milja, whom he carefully prepared for the photograph: a cap was

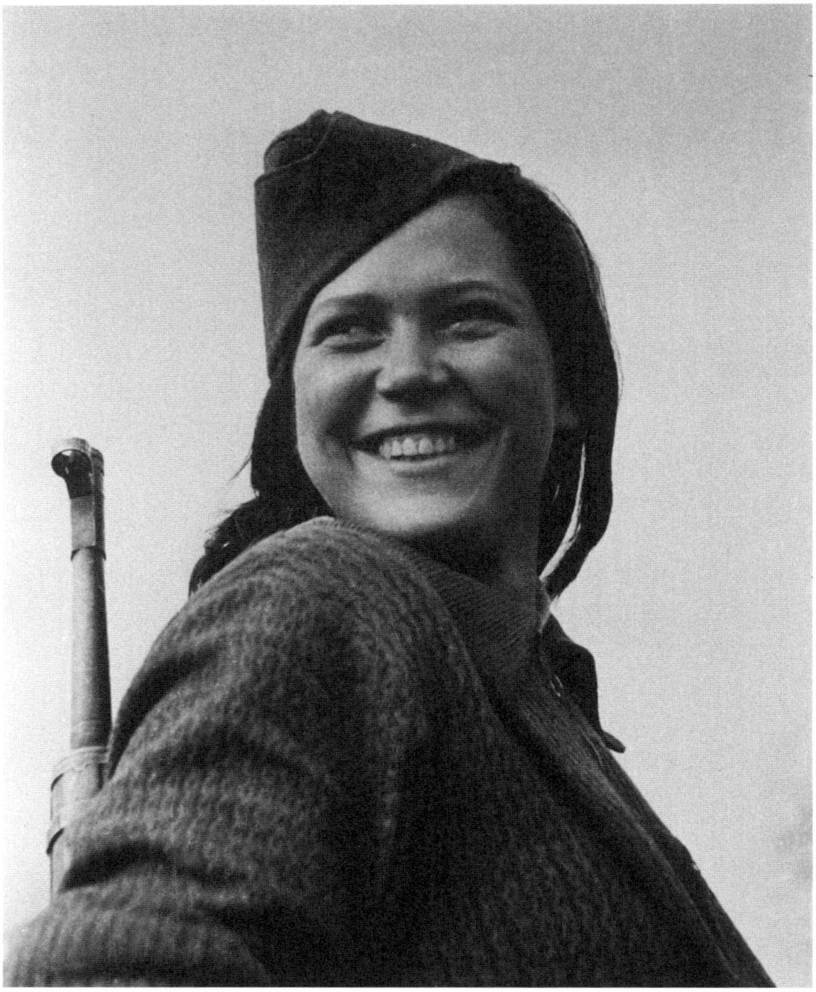

Milja Toroman from Kozara, hospital nurse in the Eleventh Krajina Brigade of the People's Liberation Army of Yugoslavia, winter 1943/44. Photo: Žorž Skrigin. Museum of Yugoslavia, VIS 554 25.

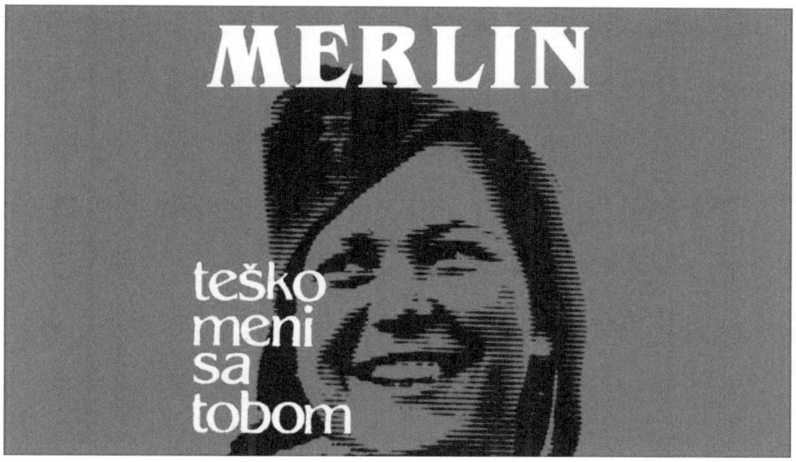

Album cover of Teško meni sa tobom, a još teže bez tebe by singer-songwriter Dino Merlin, design by Design Trio, released on the Diskoton label, 1986.

placed on her head and the barrel of the rifle between her shoulders.[10] Her hair was clean and neatly brushed. When shooting this photograph, Skrigin had enough time to direct the scene and make decisions regarding how best to express and convey the required message. He chose a slight low-angle shot to isolate the subject against the background and make the young woman appear more imposing and taller than she was. Her youth, her wide smile and her femininity dominate the composition, in stark contrast to overtly masculine depictions of male combatants. The rifle on her back only emphasises the special quality of the Partisan movement that many women had joined, the movement's importance in the struggle for equality and its uniqueness in relation to other military formations. In many ways, Skrigin's photograph strongly resembles that of seventeen-year-old Marina Ginestà, and we can only speculate as to whether the Serbian photographer was familiar with what has become one of the most iconic photographs of the Spanish Civil War, taken by the Spanish photographer Juan Guzmán. In Guzmán's shot, Marina Ginestà also poses with her rifle protruding from between her shoulders.

Unlike his earlier photograph of the mother from Knežopolje, this image had an afterlife in post-war pop culture. In 1948, postcards were printed with the young Partisan woman's face, along with the words 'Seja s Kozare' (sister from Kozara). The photograph also appeared in school textbooks and featured on the album sleeve of *Teško meni sa tobom, a još teže bez tebe*, an album by the Bosnian pop musician Dino Merlin.

From a present-day perspective, the photograph of Milja Toroman is strikingly reminiscent of images of Kurdish women favoured by Western media. The same idea lies behind the photographs showing women who have joined an armed struggle and stand shoul-

10 Unknown author, 'Fotografija partizanke Milje Marin: Simbol svega pozitivnog', in *Buka*, 9 May 2014, URL: http://www.6yka.com/novost/55806/fotografija-partizanke-milje-marin-simbol-svega-pozitivnog (accessed 1 June 2021).

der-to-shoulder with men. There is emancipatory potential in such images as they offer a change from the traditional paradigm. These kinds of women become relevant subjects, attempting to forge their own destiny.[11] One such contemporary photograph was taken by the Egyptian photographer Asmaa Waguih. Many of her photographs have found their way into the Western media. Her image made the Kurdish struggle more visible, and the Kurdish question too. Nevertheless, as far as the social position of these women is concerned, most of the articles framing the image in Western publications were simplified, colonially tinged, misogynous and patronising. Indeed, they neglected to discuss the full complexity of questions surrounding women's emancipation and gender rights in a deeply patriarchal society.[12] In the Turkish and Iranian media, these women's credibility was often called into question through tales of their seductive quality and sexually promiscuous behaviour,[13] in a fashion similar to how the enemy printing presses – be they German, Ustashe, Slovene Home Guard or Chetnik – discredited Partisan women. It should also be mentioned that despite the many women who joined the Partisan movement, only a few were photographers, and women photographers were not tasked with taking photographs on the front line, with the result that there are few images of female Partisan soldiers captured through the lens of a female photographer.

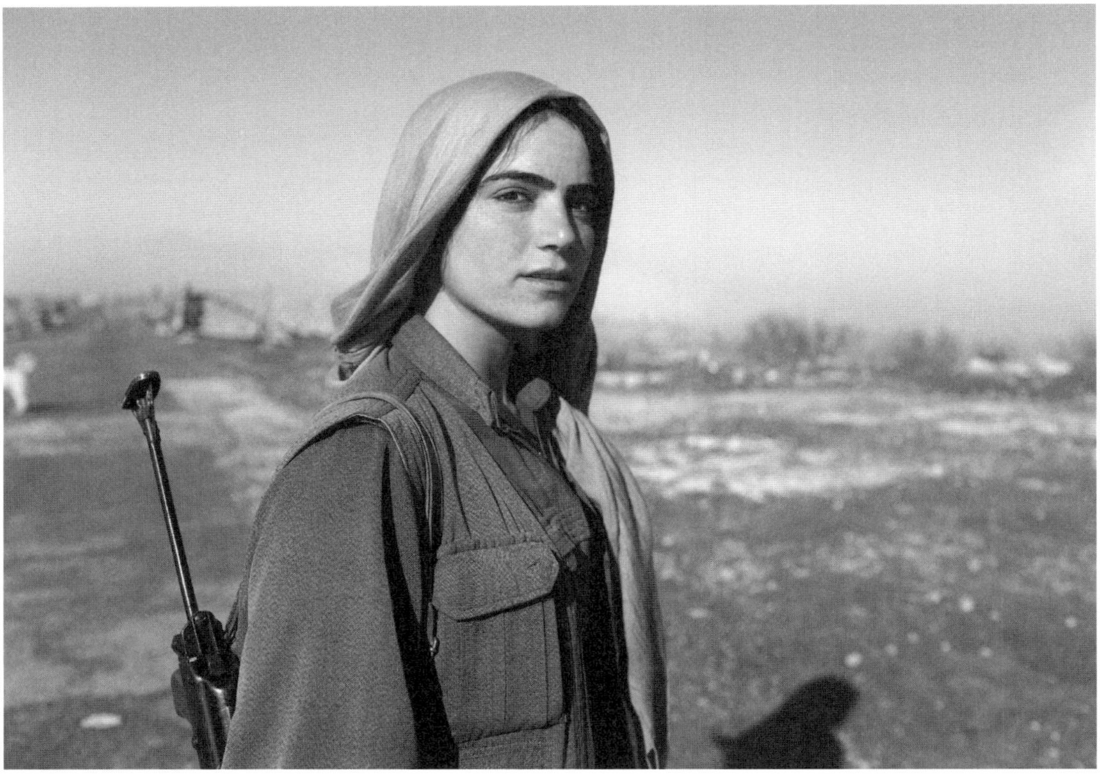

Soldier in the Kurdistan Workers' Party (PKK) at security post, Sinjar (Iraq), March 2015. Photo: Asmaa Waguih. We thank Reuters for kind permission to reproduce this photograph.

11 This question goes beyond the research topic covered here, but it leaves open the possibility of a more thorough future analysis that relates to the construction of social identities and questions of representation.
12 Dilar Dirik, 'The Representation of Kurdish Women Fighters in the Media', in: *Kurdish Question*, URL: http://kurdishquestion.com/oldarticle.php?aid=the-representation-of-kurdish- women-fighters-in-the-media (accessed 4 November 2017).
13 Ibid.

One Partisan photograph that has transcended regional borders is that of Stjepan Filipović, known in Serbia as Stevan Kolubarac. He was born in Opuzen, a small town near Dubrovnik, Croatia. He came to Serbia with his family as a young man. An active pre-war trade unionist, he joined the Partisans at the beginning of the uprising, first as deputy commander of the Kolubara Company, and, after that, as a political commissar for the Mačva Detachment. After his capture, the Chetniks handed him over to the German forces who decided, as a warning to others, to hang him publicly in the centre of Valjevo on 22 May 1942. The photograph showing him beneath the gallows, with a rope around his neck and arms raised, was taken just moments before his life was taken from him. Brought before around 3,000 people in the town's central square, instead of humiliation he showed defiance, and addressed the people gathered around him, saying: 'Don't just look on; fight this scum! Grab your rusty rifles. If you just look on, this scum will kill us one by one.'[14]

To silence him and prevent his speech from getting any longer, the German officer gave the signal to execute Filipović fifteen minutes earlier than planned. That same afternoon, a photograph of his execution appeared in the window display of a photography shop named Kosara in Valjevo. The picture showing this twenty-six-year-old man defiantly holding his clenched fists high in the air became a symbol of resistance, defiance and bravery. Instead of his death intimidating and inhibiting people, his raised arms motivated many of the citizens gathered there to resist the occupiers. The story of his defiant act began to spread among the people.

The photograph of Stjepan Filipović with outstretched arms on the gallows was published publicly for the first time on the front page of the daily newspaper *Politika* on 4 November 1944. It then became an iconic photograph of the resistance. After the Second World War, the exact burial location of the executed proletarian was never found, and this photograph's negative was not preserved. Only a few positive copies were found, kept safe by the citizens of Valjevo. Notably, one copy was even found in the archives of the Serbian Gestapo in Belgrade. Indeed, Milan Nedić's government handed Filipović over to the Gestapo, and Filipović was kept prisoner for a time in the Gestapo headquarters in Belgrade.[15] It was only long after the war, as late as 1983, that the backstory to the image emerged.[16]

The most likely version of the story is that Stjepan Filipović's execution was captured by Slobodanka Vasić, then a young seventeen-year-old girl and trainee in the above-mentioned Kosara photo studio. Immediately after the execution, that same afternoon, she made

14 Nebojša Radišić and Milana Pejić, 'Herojska Lekcija Koju Ne Smemo Da Zaboravimo Hrvat koji je želeo da umre sa Srbima', in: *Blic*, 22 May 2017, URL: https://www.blic.rs/vesti/drustvo/herojska-lekcija-koju-ne-smemo-da-zaboravimo-hrvat-koji-je-zeleo-da-umre-sa-srbima/7enh5k3 (accessed 1 June 2021).

15 Milan Radanović, 'Stjepan Filipović: heroj radničke i antifašističke borbe: 70 godina od smrti', in: *Poseta Starom sajmištu*, 21 May 2012, URL: http://www.starosajmiste.info/blog/stjepan-filipovic-heroj-radnicke-i-antifasisticke-borbe-70-godina-od-smrti/ (accessed 1 June 2021).

16 A comprehensive study of the life of Stjepan Filipović and this historical photograph has been published in Radivoje Davidović and Mirjana Belić-Koročkin-Davidović's book, *Stevan Filipović, istina o istorijskoj fotografiji*, published by Belgrade-based publisher Čigoja in 2012.

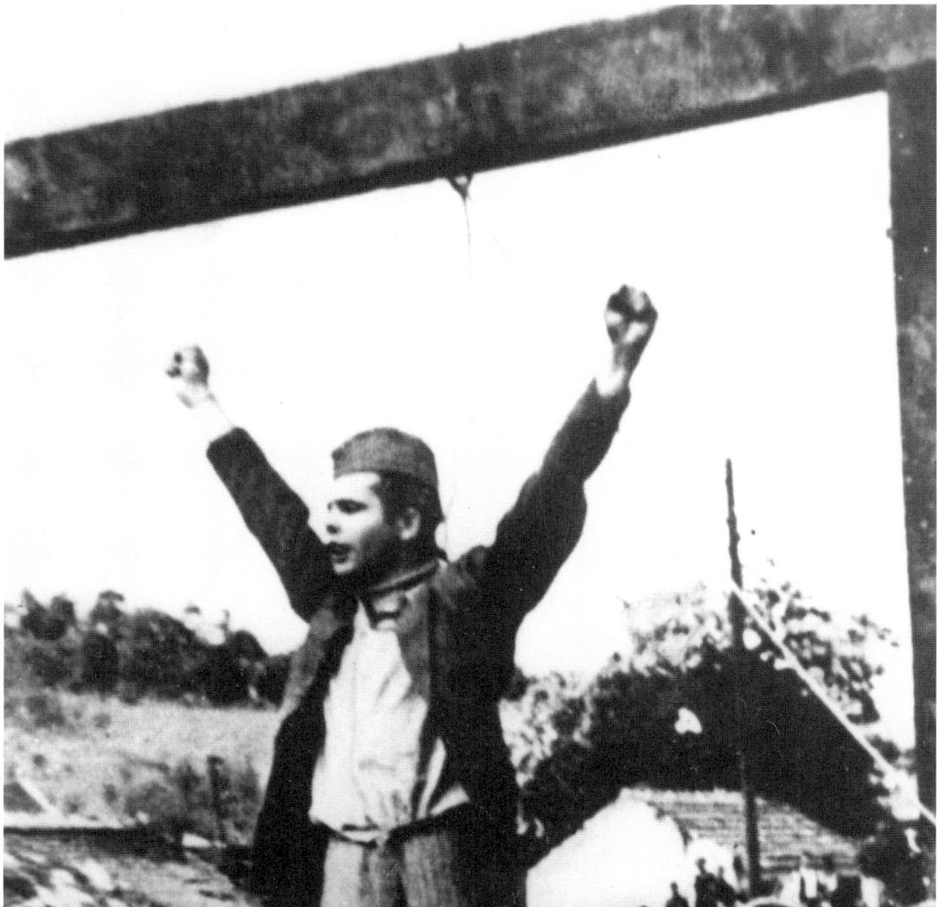

Stjepan Filipović, posthumously declared a People's Hero, immediately before his hanging, 22 May 1942. Photo: Slobodanka Vasić. Museum of Yugoslavia, accession no. unknown.

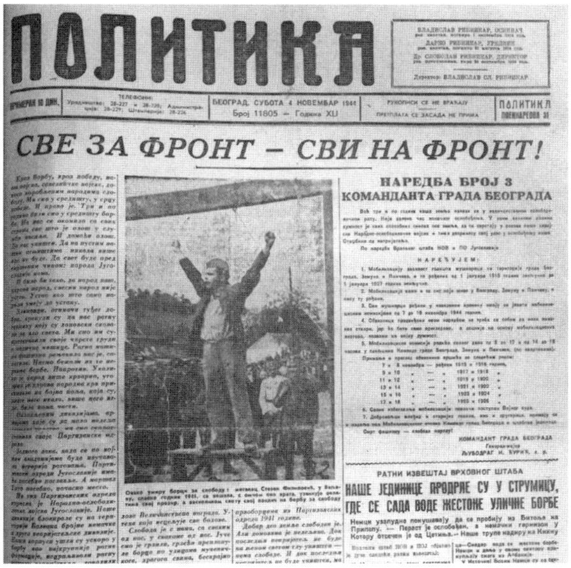

ПОЛИТИКА

БЕОГРАД, СУБОТА 4 НОВЕМБАР 1944
Број 11805 — Година XLI

СВЕ ЗА ФРОНТ – СВИ НА ФРОНТ!

НАРЕДБА БРОЈ 3
КОМАНДАНТА ГРАДА БЕОГРАДА

КОМАНДАНТ ГРАДА БЕОГРАДА

РАТНИ ИЗВЕШТАЈ ВРХОВНОГ ШТАБА

НАШЕ ЈЕДИНИЦЕ ПРОДРЛЕ СУ У СТРУМИЦУ, ГДЕ СЕ САДА ВОДЕ ЖЕСТОКЕ УЛИЧНЕ БОРБЕ

Немци узалудно покушавају да се пробију из Битоља на Прилепу. — Перast је ослобођен, а немачки гарнизон у Котору отсечен је од Цетиња.— Наше трупе надиру ка Никшићу

Front page of the daily newspaper Politika, 4 November 1944, Ljubljiana, Institute of Contemporary History.

copies of the photograph and displayed them for sale in the shop window until the German occupiers caught wind of it and put a stop to the display.[17] Many years later, Vasić explained to journalists how her celebrated photograph came about:

Steva [Stjepan] was carried off with his hands tied. He stepped out with his head proudly raised. Accompanied by a guard, they took him to the market where a crowd had already gathered. I was clicking my camera the whole time. When they raised him onto the footstool, I got close to him at a distance of four or five metres and took around ten shots. I didn't notice anyone else with a camera, not even among the Germans. After he had been executed, I quickly ran to the shop, developed the film, and made photographs of the event. We set out the pictures on a drawing board in the window display. People soon started gathering around the window. Many came inside and bought pictures. As the shop was positioned opposite the German Military Command, the Germans noticed that something was up. After some time, Germans entered the shop with the military police and carried out a search, seizing all pictures, including the film.[18]

In a second version of the story, the photograph was taken by Bata Antić, the son, then fourteen years old, of the shop's owner, Milka Antić.[19] After the war, this photograph was often published in the media, featured in school textbooks, and was blown-up to life-size proportions and even exhibited in the United Nations Building in New York.[20] Its iconic power, as

17 Jovana Gligorijević, 'Što čekate? Što trpite?', in: *Vreme*, 8 November 2012, URL: http://www.vreme.com/cms/view.php?id=1081728 (accessed 1 June 2021).

18 Radivoje Davidović, 'S "lajkom" na zadatak', in: *Front*, 1983, quoted from: *Yugopapir*, URL: http://www.yugopapir.com/2016/01/slobodanka-vasic-autor-istorijske.html (accessed 1 June 2021).

19 Ibid.

20 Stanislav Soldo, 'Ovo je Stjepan Filipović, hrvatski heroj kojemu se u UN-u klanjaju, ali u rodnom Opuzenu ga ne žele: Svjetski državnici ga veličaju, a ovdje za njega nema mjesta. I spomenik su mu minirali!', in: *Slobodna Dalmacija*, 2017, URL: https://www.slobodnadalmacija.hr/dalmacija/dubrovnik/clanak/id/487162/ovo-je-stjepan- filipovic-hrvatski-heroj-kojemu-se-u-un-u-klanjaju-ali-u-rodnom-opuzenu-ga-ne-zele-vjetski-drzavnici-ga-velicaju-a-ovdje-za-njega-nema-mjesta-i-spomenik-su-mu-minirali (accessed 22 May 2017).

with the other photographs mentioned here, perhaps lies in the fact that this photograph is easy to read in societies the world over: with the noose already around one's neck, one would expect the accused to pray for their life rather than spurn death. This fundamental element of rebellion is immediately relatable and can be read by almost everyone.

Montenegro provided the backdrop for a similar photograph of defiance and resistance, in which the People's Hero Čedomir Ljubo Čupić is seen giving a faint smile just before his execution. He was the commissar of the Đuro Đaković Company in Nikšić, and was executed by Chetniks on 9 May 1942, two weeks before Filipović. This picture, too, is significant as, although it depicts a young man immediately prior to execution, there is little sense that this will be the last image taken of the man alive. Although his hands are clearly shackled and his situation is evidently no laughing matter, we gradually realise that his smile is a form of resistance – to the photographer and the executioners. It is as if he were saying: 'You can't hurt me; I am untouchable.'

In the early 1990s, a monument to Stjepan Filipović in Opuzen was demolished by explosives, while the statue in Valjevo by the sculptor Vojin Bakić continues to stand, albeit in a state of disrepair. The photographs presented here have more than a common documentary value because they point to something that goes beyond ordinary photographic representation. Within them, they carry – as the scholars Robert Hariman and John Louis Lucaites have clearly noticed – an aura of history, humanity and self-determination. They represent 'sacred pictures for a secular society',[21] as does the picture of Che Guevara from the beginning of this chapter.

21 Robert Hariman and John Louis Lucaites, *No Caption Needed: Iconic Photographs, Public Culture, and Liberal Democracy*, Chicago 2007, p. 2.

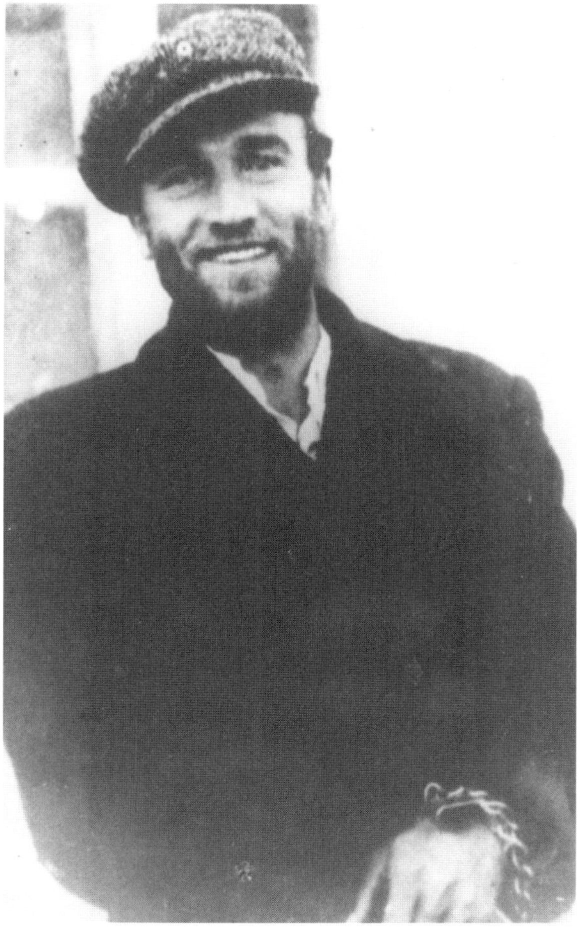

Čedomir 'Ljubo' Čupić, law student and member of the Communist Party of Yugoslavia who joined the People's Liberation Struggle in 1941, shortly before execution by Chetnik forces, Nikšić, May 1942. Photographer unknown. Museum of Yugoslavia, 12426.

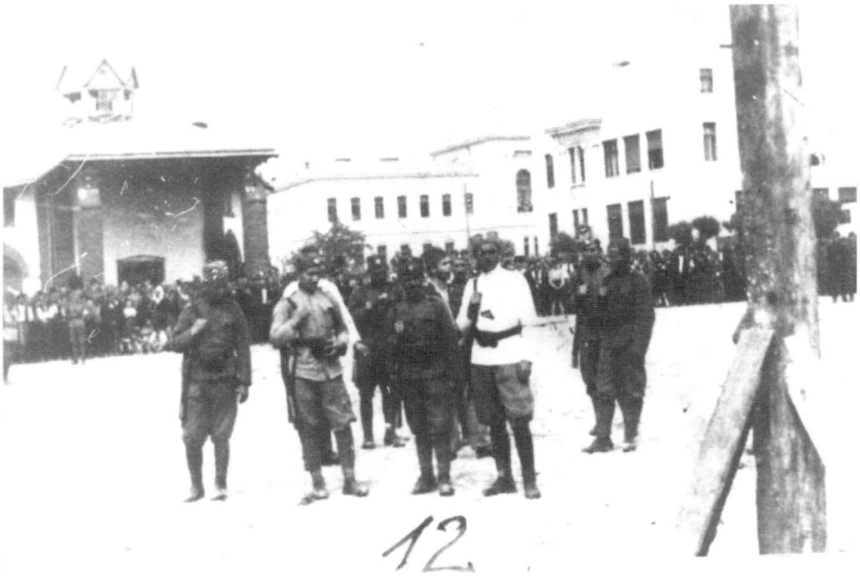

Stjepan Filipović, People's Hero, just before his hanging, Valjevo, 22 May 1942. Museum of Yugoslavia, A-948/22.

8. Intelligence Uses of Photography and Trophy Photos of Atrocities

In October 1942, the Supreme Command issued instructions on the importance and possible use of seized enemy documents. All written official orders, letters, propaganda material, brochures, newspapers, books and especially photographs (be they of individuals, groups or buildings) fell into this category.[1] In the early days of intelligence gathering, the first data arrived in reports from members of the resistance movement who were active in urban locations, as well as from supporters of the Partisan movement, while informants in the units gathered information by analysing the objects and photographs delivered to them.[2]

For certain groups under the German and Ustashe occupation, owning a camera was strictly forbidden. And for those strands of population targeted by the race laws, being caught with a camera could have fatal consequences. From the moment of the quisling Independent State of Croatia's inception, cameras were confiscated from the homes of Jews and Serbs, as were radio receivers and binoculars.[3] In the ancient city of Zadar on the Adriatic coast, even typewriters were seized from the homes of certain individuals,[4] while in other parts of the Independent State of Croatia, all Jews were ordered to surrender their bicycles and cars to the authorities.[5] The trade in photographic chemicals was overseen by the military authorities. They demanded that every seller maintain a record of their customers. The Belgrade photographer Branko Savić recalls this period:

I travelled three times to Ustashe-occupied Zagreb to acquire photo supplies during the period of the Independent State of Croatia, when there weren't any materials available in Belgrade. Sometimes [I travelled] with fake papers, sometimes without them. The police always inspected the 'wrong' suitcase: the one with personal effects inside, rather than the smuggled supplies. On one occasion after the police check I returned to a friend in the waiting room. She said: 'Branko, you're as pale as a ghost.'[6]

1 *Zbornik dokumenata i podataka o narodno-oslobodilačkom ratu jugoslovenskih naroda*, vol. II/6: Dokumenta vrhovnog štaba Narodnooslobodilačke vojske Jugoslavije 1942, Belgrade 1957.

2 *Zbornik dokumenata i podataka o narodno-oslobodilačkom ratu jugoslovenskih naroda*, vol. II/10: Dokumenta vrhovnog štaba Narodnooslobodilačke vojske Jugoslavije 1943, Belgrade 1962.

3 Dušan Lukač, *Ustanak u Bosanskoj krajini*, Belgrade 1967, pp. 56–57.

4 *Zbornik dokumenata i podataka o narodno-oslobodilačkom ratu jugoslovenskih naroda*, vol. IX/ 3: Partijsko-politička dokumenta 1943. godine, Belgrade 1967.

5 Stjepan Iveković (ed.), *Građa za povijest narodnooslobodilačke borbe u sjeverozapadnoj Hrvatskoj 1941–1945*, vol. 1, Zagreb 1981.

6 Snežana Rovčanin, 'Kvadrati filma spojili i most', in: *Večernje Novosti*, 7 May 2007, URL: https://www.novosti.rs/vesti/naslovna/reportaze/aktuelno.293.html:197712-Kvadrati-filma-spojili-i-most (accessed 1 June 2021).

Acting in strict secrecy was perhaps most difficult for those photographers in the resistance movement operating in fascist-occupied territory. Their main task was to falsify identification cards,[7] needed for people to move beyond the city and enter liberated territory. If they were found out, it was imperative that not a single photograph fall into enemy hands. The undercover agents were strictly forbidden from having any photographs of other members of the Partisan movement on them, as we learn from a letter dated 24 June 1942, written by Koloman Barany, a member of the Varaždin District Committee of the Communist Party of Croatia. The letter demonstrates that members were acutely aware that, in the wrong hands, such photographs threatened blowing the cover of the Partisan's underground network.[8] In Zagreb, the plan for getting people out of occupied territory and into the Partisan units was drawn up by the respective local committee of the Communist Party and was implemented through the activities of five District Committees, with the railway representing a 'district' of its own. Among these committees, a special group was responsible for transferring people and delivering various materials to the liberated territory. In the first year of the war alone, around 25,000 residents of Zagreb left to join Partisan units, using fake identification cards that had been forged by hand.[9]

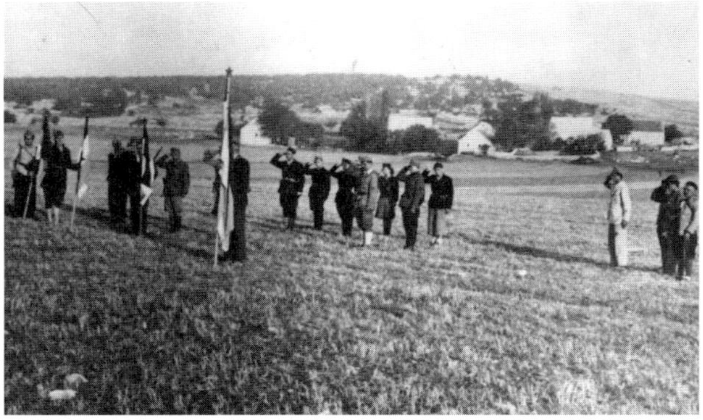

Photograph showing Partisans handing over the flag of the First Dalmatian Brigade, Livanjsko polje, Bosnia and Herzegovina. Photographer unknown. Military Archive Belgrade, K82 F3 16.

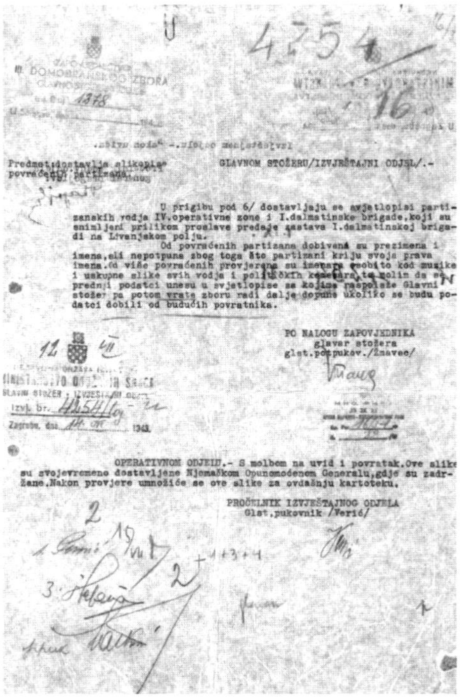

III. DOMOBRANSKOG ZBORA

Broj 1378

Predmet: dostavlja slikopise povraćenih partizana.

GLAVNOM STOŽERU/IZVJEŠTAJNI ODJEL/.-

U prigibu pod 6/ dostavljaju se svjetlopisi partizanskih vodja IV. operativne zone i I. dalmatinske brigade, koji su snimljeni prilikom proslave predaje zastave I. dalmatinskoj brigadi na Livanjskom polju.

Od povraćenih partizana dobivena su prezimena i imena, ali nepotpuna zbog toga što partizani kriju svoja prava imena. Od više povraćenih provjerena su imena osobito kod muzike i uskupne slike svih vodja i političkih komesara, te molim da se prednji podatci unesu u svjetlopise sa kojima raspolaže Glavni stožer pa potom vrate zboru radi dalje dopune ukoliko se budu podatci dobili od budućih povratnika.

PO NALOGU ZAPOVJEDNIKA
glavar stožera
glst. potpukov./Žnavec/

GLAVNI STOŽER - IZVJEŠTAJNI ODJEL
Izvj. br. 4454/
Zagreb, dne 14. VII 1943.

OPERATIVNOM ODJELU.- S molbom na uvid i povratak. Ove slike su svojevremeno dostavljene Njemačkom Opunomoćenom Generalu, gdje su zadržane. Nakon provjere umnožiće se ove slike za ovdašnju kartoteku.

PROČELNIK IZVJEŠTAJNOG ODJELA
Glst. pukovnik /Verić/

Correspondence accompanying the seized Partisan photograph below, identifying Partisans shown therein. Military Archive Belgrade, K82 F3 16.

7 Norbert Veber, 'Delatnost u okupiranom Zagrebu', in: *Veze u NOB: Ratna sećanja 1941–1945*, vol. 4., Esad Tihić and Momčilo Kalem (eds.), Belgrade 1981, p. 54.

8 Iveković 1981 (see note 5), vol. 2.

9 Mato Putrić, 'Kako se odlazilo u partizane', in: *Večernji list*, 26/27 April 1975.

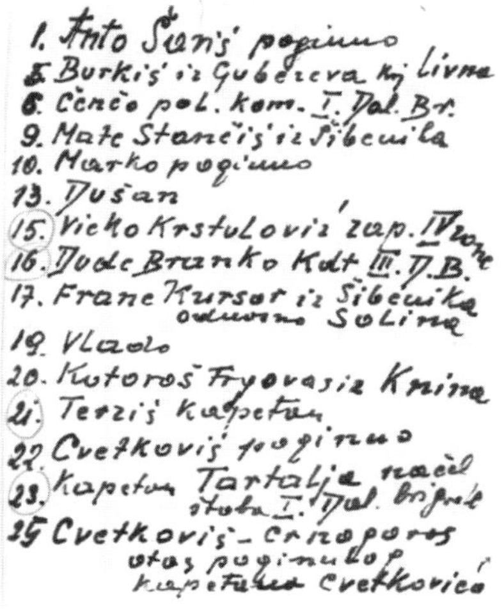
1. Anto Šanić poginuo
5. Burkić iz Gubereva kod Livna
6. Čenčo pol. kom. I. Dal. Br.
9. Mate Stančić iz Šibenika
10. Marko poginuo
13. Dušan
15. Vicko Krstulović zap. IV zone
16. Dude Branko Kdt. III. D.B.
17. Frane Kursar iz Šibenika odveden Solina
19. Vlado
20. Kotoroš Frgovasić Knina
21. Terzić kapetan
22. Cvetković poginuo
23. Kapetan Tartalja načel. štaba I. Dal. brigade
25 Cvetković – Crnogorac otac poginulog kapetana Cvetkovića

List of members of the Partisan movement identified using seized Partisan photographs taken during a flag-handover ceremony of the First Dalmatian Brigade. Military Archive Belgrade, K82 F3 16.

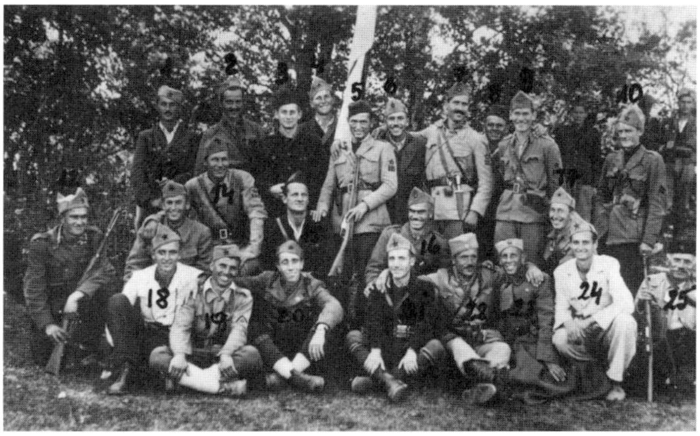

Seized Partisan photograph used to visually identify Partisans. Military Archive Belgrade, K82 F3 16.

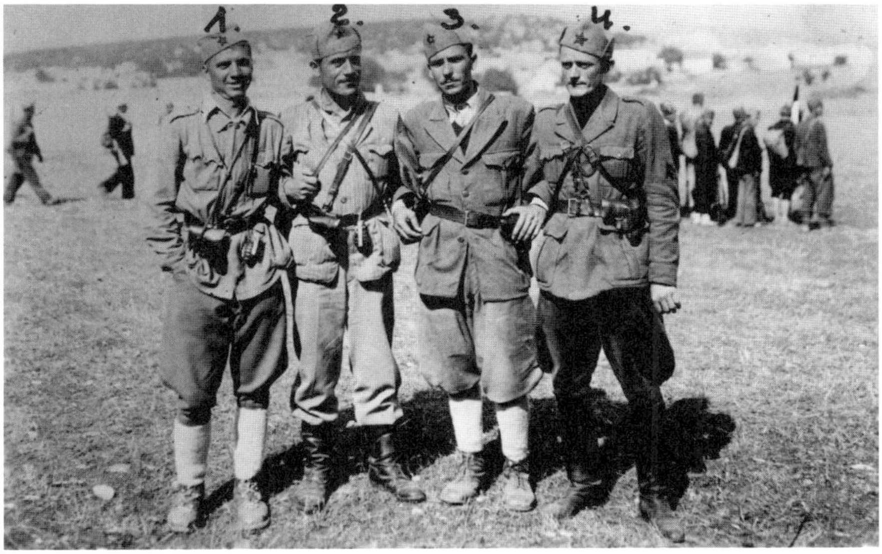

Seized Partisan photograph used to visually identify Partisans. Military Archive Belgrade, K82 F3 16.

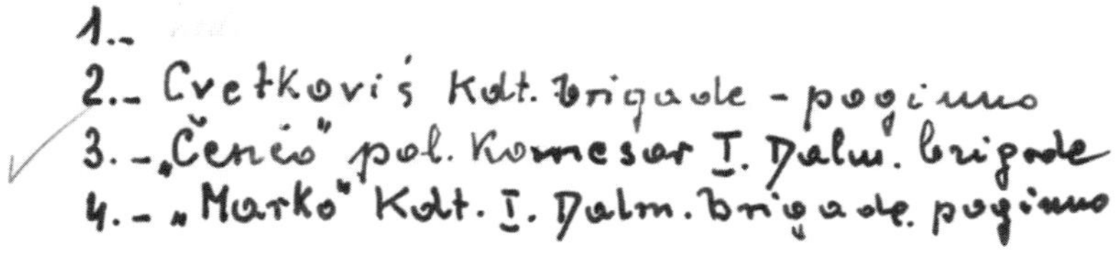
1.–
2.– Cvetković Kdt. brigade – poginuo
3.– „Čenčo" pol. komesar I. Dalm. brigade
4.– „Marko" Kdt. I. Dalm. brigade. poginuo

List of members of the Partisan movement identified using seized Partisan photographs taken during a flag handover-ceremony of the First Dalmatian Brigade. Military Archive Belgrade, K82 F3 16.

In Zagreb, the first wartime apparatus for producing forged identification documents was located in Dragutin Susović's flat at the address Derenčinova no. 21d. Assisting Susović was a person named Maks Durjava, and it was he who acquired the necessary photographic materials.[10] Local committee meetings were often held in the flat of photographer Srećko Delhuni, at the address Ilica St. no. 124.[11] As photographic equipment was all but impossible to acquire unnoticed, the Partisans used existing legitimate channels as a cover instead, through sympathisers employed at photographic supply stores, such as Foto Corsa and the Agfa representative on Ilica St.[12] When it was no longer possible to get hold of blank identification papers, special substances were used to erase the ink on existing papers, allowing new names to be written in their place.[13] After producing the photographic prints, all negatives were destroyed. It was the responsibility of undercover agents living in Zagreb to take stealth photographs of notable members of the Ustashe and have the photographs smuggled out to liberated territory. Over time this became a regular practice in other Croatian towns and cities too. It was one way of making an archive to help identify potential double-agents and Ustashe collaborators who had infiltrated the ranks of the Partisans.

Enemy intelligence activities were well-organised and rigorous. On 22 February 1942 in Zagreb, the chiefs of the German military intelligence service, the Abwehr, compiled an ' Album of [Communist] Party and Partisan Leaders',[14] while the police produced enlarged

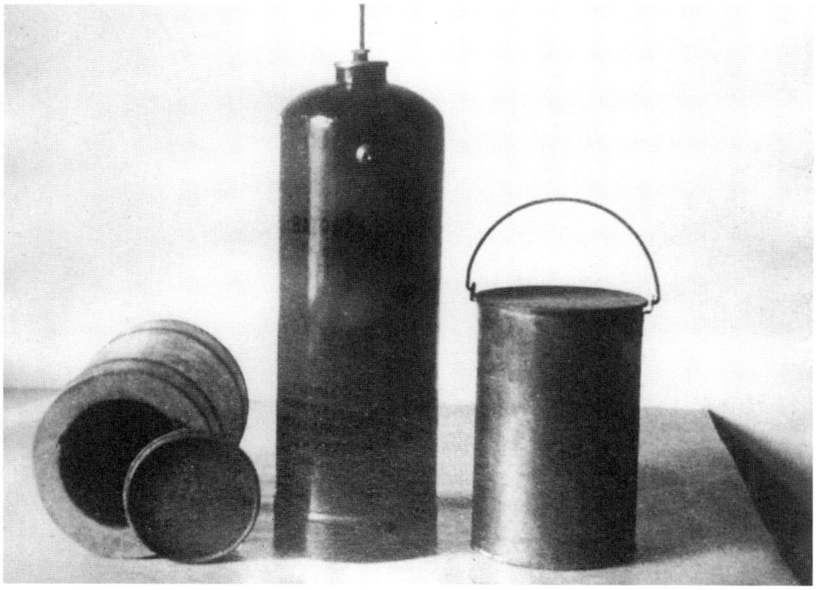

Objects with a false bottom to conceal illegal materials during the occupation, Slovenia. Photographer unknown. Objects now held at National Museum of Contemporary History of Slovenia, Ljubljana, 10902.

10 Stipe Ugarković, 'Partijska tehnika u okupiranom Zagrebu', in: *Ustanak naroda Jugoslavije 1941*, Belgrade 1964, p. 86.
11 Perica Dozet, 'Moj dolazak u Zagreb', in: *Zbornik sjećanja Zagreb 1941–1945*, vol. 4, Josip Malić (ed.), Zagreb 1984, p. 20.
12 Dragutin Susović, 'U partijskoj tehnici', in: idem, vol. 3, p. 223.
13 Mila Čobanski, Zvonimir Golubović and Živan Kumanov, *Novi Sad u ratu i revoluciji 1941–1945*, Novi Sad 1976, p. 419.
14 Nemačka obaveštajna služba (Abwehr, German military secret service), IX.

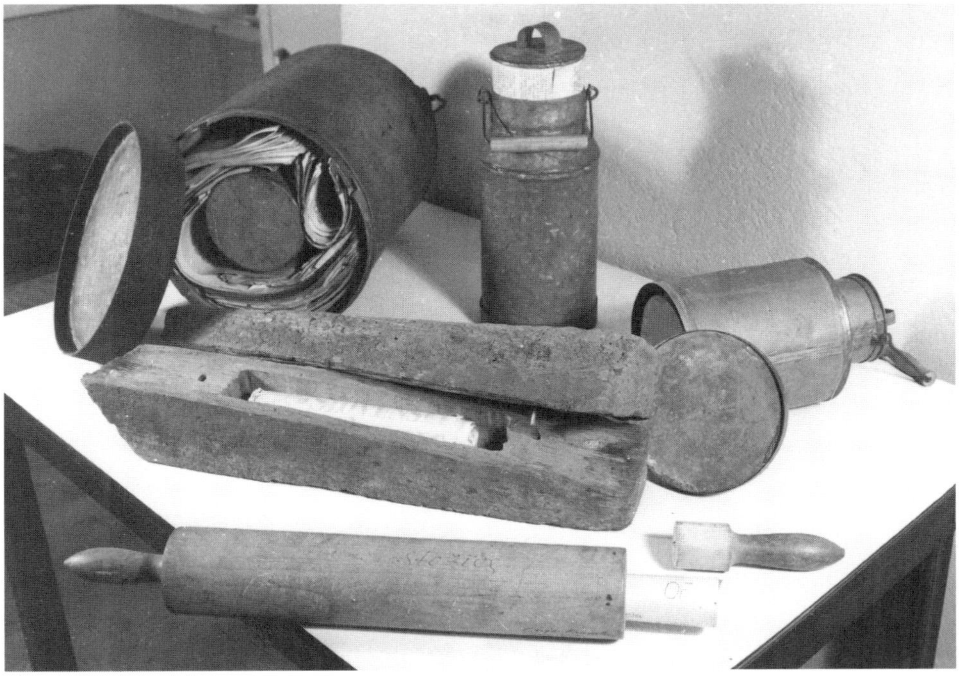

Objects for hiding and passing on secret messages and literature, Slovenia. Photographer unknown. Objects now held at National Museum of Contemporary History of Slovenia, Ljubljana, 10903.

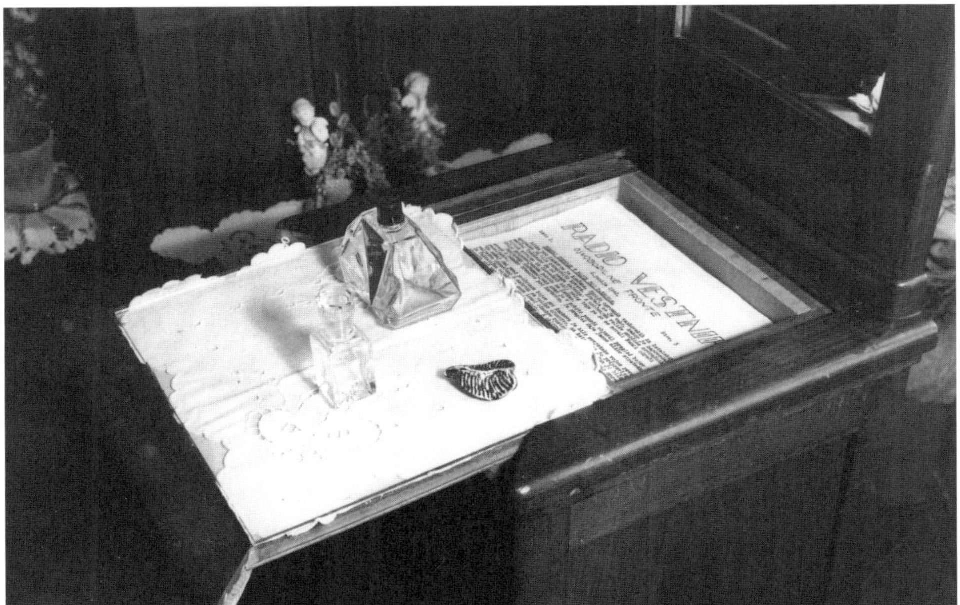

Objects for hiding and passing on secret messages and literature, Slovenia. Photographer unknown. Objects now held at National Museum of Contemporary History of Slovenia, Ljubljana, 10904.

photos of suspected members of the anti-fascist resistance movement. The photographs and accompanying information gathered on potential resistance suspects were distributed by a network of plain-clothes agents, who had the right to shoot any suspect without warning.[15]

One example of the use of photography in undercover resistance work and counter-espionage is known to us in Rijeka. The photographer Karlo Lau Ritz, resident of Sušak in Rijeka worked for the Gestapo. He was originally from Bela Crkva in Vojvodina (a town in present-day Serbia) and was the owner of the photography shop Foto Desa, which had forged links with the German intelligence service even before the Second World War. He justified his frequent journeys to the German Reich as vocational training during which he attended photography courses. During the war he broadened his intelligence activities by assisting in the arrest of resistance members and even interrogating them in custody.[16] Meanwhile, the resistance movement in Rijeka had an agent named Miculinić working undercover in the police records department. On Mondays and Fridays he would smuggle confidential police records on agents and collaborators out of the office. The photographer Simo Milković would then secretly photograph these papers in a barber shop owned by a certain Živko Jović. He would then develop the prints and send them to the village of Kostrena, where a Partisan courier would pick them up and bring them over the border to liberated territory.[17]

Intelligence and propaganda material also travelled in the other direction – from the liberated territory to the occupied towns and cities. Photographs portraying Partisan successes and war victories were distributed in occupied territory and had an especially disturbing effect on the enemy. The photographs usually chosen were those deemed most impactful[18] or useful in attracting new recruits or winning over sympathisers.[19]

During the occupation of Zagreb, organisations linked to the League of Communist Youth of Yugoslavia were active in high schools. This organisation included around forty female members and around a hundred female sympathisers. So as not to arouse suspicion, the female members of the League held meetings on Sundays after mass. As part of their regular activities, they organised days out, reading groups and communal trips to the cinema and to academic lectures at the Public Open University (POUZ), an adult-learning centre. After these meetings they also held private debating sessions to discuss what they had heard in the lectures. Notably, in contrast to the other organisations in the League, the girls in this local chapter also formed their own amateur photography group.[20] Zorka Fak, a pupil at the First Girls' Grammar School, was responsible for distributing photographs of Ustashe crimes.

15 Lepa Perović, 'Ilegalni partijski rad u Zagrebu', in: Malić 1984 (see note 11), vol. 4, p. 11.

16 Radule Butorović, *Sušak i Rijeka u NOB*, Rijeka 1975, p. 341.

17 Ibid., p. 429.

18 *Zbornik dokumenata i podataka o narodno-oslobodilačkom ratu jugoslovenskih naroda*, vol. V/4: Borbe u Hrvatskoj 1942. godine, Belgrade 1954.

19 *Zbornik dokumenata i podataka o narodno-oslobodilačkom ratu jugoslovenskih naroda*, vol. V/30: Borbe u Hrvatskoj 1941–1942. godine, Belgrade 1963.

20 'Djevojke iz treće ženske', in: *Revolucionarni omladinski pokret u Zagrebu 1941–1945*, vol. 2, Esad Tihić (ed.), Zagreb 1984, p. 150.

It's difficult to say today how images of the brutal torture of communists, Jews and Serbs in the Ustashe concentration camps got to Zagreb in late 1941. They were horrific testimony to the crimes of the occupiers and their local lackeys [the Croatian Ustashe]. The photographs had to be duplicated and distributed across the city. Comrade Zorka Fak (from the First Girls' Grammar School) turned up at school one day with several such photographs and her fellow pupils set about the task of duplicating them. They turned the pantry in the flat of one pupil living at Deželićeva no. 60 into a small film lab. A few days later, two female members of the League of Communist Youth distributed small packages containing several hundred photographs via their 'connections'.[21]

At that time, the resistance movement also had a stronghold in Dalmatia. Many photographers there were involved in the movement, such as the Split photographer Marcel Njegovan, from Plinarska St. no. 14. On 18 June 1942 the Italian authorities arrested him for smearing black paint over newly erected street signs in Italian.[22] Information on the first campaigns against the Italian occupiers was published on a fairly regular basis by the fascist paper *Il popolo di Spalato*. In contrast to the German-occupied zone, the Italian military administration chose to distribute photographs of public executions, not realising that such images often only served to antagonise and foment resistance among the local population. Such photographs, taken by or for the occupiers themselves, proved to be excellent source material for Partisan propaganda. Vicko Krstulović obtained several collections of such enemy photographs, and in Donji Lapac, where the editorial offices of the newspaper

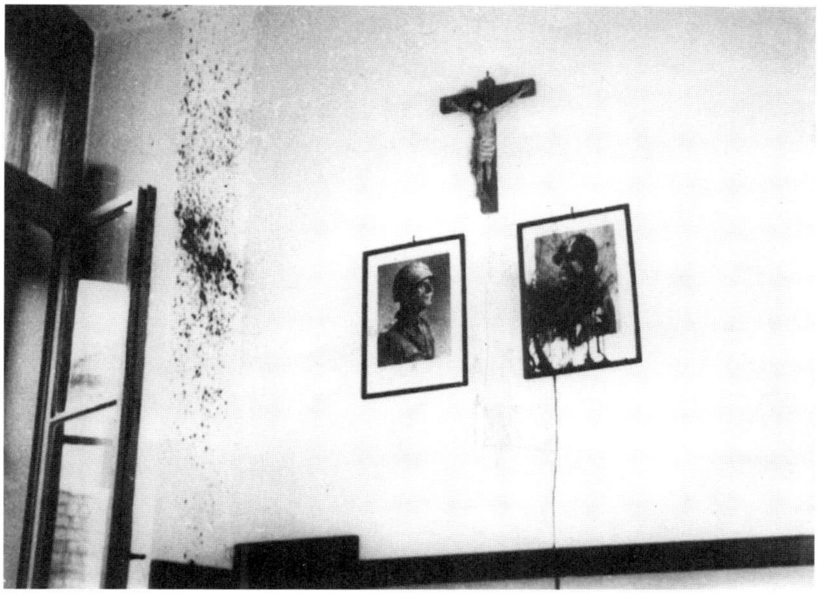

Defaced portrait of 'Il Duce', Benito Mussolini, Split, October 1941. Photographer unknown. Croatian History Museum, HPM/MRNH-R-5740.

21 Sofija-Maša Pavičić and Zorka Fak-Horvatić, 'Borbena Prva ženska gimnazija', in: ibid., p. 147.
22 Arhiv VII K 533, reg. no. 38/8-1.

Vjesnik were situated at the time, he handed over incriminating photographs to Otmar Kreačić-Kultura and Vjera Jurić. These photographs, dated 26 August 1941, documented the execution of members of the Split Detachment.[23]

In Sarajevo, members of the League of Communist Youth of Yugoslavia had been targeting photography exhibitions even before the war. One of the better-known attacks occurred in spring of 1938 when a group of young men led by Vasa Miskina decided to sabotage a photography exhibit organised by the People's Radical Party of Serbia (NRS). The Radical Party's president was Milan Stojadinović, then-ruling prime minister of the Kingdom of Yugoslavia. He enjoyed strong support from Nazi Germany. The members of the League descended on the exhibition and managed to take off with most of the photographs on display, which they then publicly ripped up on the street in front of Sarajevo city hall.[24]

Sarajevo was occupied by the Ustashe at the beginning of the war. On 23 June 1941, the head of the Ustashe headquarters, Ivan Zovko, issued orders to strip Jews and Serbs of their cameras and radios, remove Serbian Cyrillic from signs, and to install Ustashe representatives in Jewish and Serbian-owned businesses. Jewish and Serbian citizens also had their cars, typewriters, bicycles and other valuables taken off them.[25] Yet at this same moment, Partisan photographs and slogans began to appear in the city, distributed under the cover of night, put up mainly by young men who were members of the League. They included Stevo Nevjestić – a photographer employed in local policing – and Ivica Lisac, who was responsible for the illegal duplication of photographs:[26]

Suddenly, as typically happens in such situations, the League of Communist Youth of Yugoslavia meetings were held, group schedules made, material was distributed and the secretaries were responsible for ensuring their members actively participated in the night-time campaigns, quickly, in synchrony and without losses. The next day, Sarajevo residents found photographs in their letterboxes, on their stairwells, beneath windows, in courtyards, in conspicuous places, thoroughfares and in factories.[27]

Gathering intelligence data in Sarajevo was the important job of the Home Guard captain Muhamed Šefkić, and the lieutenant colonel Šefket Hasandedić, who surreptitiously photographed military plans and sketches, before sending them via a go-between to the headquarters of the Tenth Division, delivering exceptionally important intelligence information.[28] Šefkić and Hasandedić were also responsible for supplying Partisan units with photographic equipment and cameras, and for making fake identification cards. All the material was secretly stored, right under the enemy's nose, in the warehouse of a photo studio

23 Vicko Krstulović, *Memoari jugoslavenskog revolucionara I*, Sarajevo 2012, p. 287.

24 Josif Radić, 'Borba omladine željezničke zanatske škole', in: *Sarajevo u revoluciji. U borbi do punog oslobođenja (novembar 1943–april 1945)*, Nisim Albahari et al. (eds.), Sarajevo 1981, p. 366.

25 Arhiv VII, NDH (Independent State of Croatia) Special Collection, box 171, reg. no. 2/18-1.

26 Mario Mikulić, 'Plakati i Titove slike širom okupiranog Sarajeva', in: Albahari et al. 1981 (see note 24), p. 232.

27 Ibid., p. 233.

28 Milan Đokić, 'O radu posebnog centra V korpusa NOVJ za informacije iz Sarajeva', in: ibid., p. 366.

called Foto Karahasanović, located opposite the Sarajevo Gestapo's headquarters in Hotel Gaza. Besides these two men, a studio named Foto Enis was also used to forge identification papers. In Sarajevo, the first Partisan police photo archive was established in spring 1945. It was the only one of its kind and included 4,000 records with data on suspects of war crimes.[29]

As far as important pre-war photographers are concerned, the Croatian photographer Milan Pavić deserves a special mention. He was a pre-war correspondent for the biggest Yugoslav daily, *Politika*. At the start of the war, Pavić lived and worked in the Croatian town of Daruvar. Active in the Partisan movement, he was responsible for smuggling people over the border into liberated territory and for making fake ID. However, his group's activities were very quickly uncovered by the Ustashe. After his arrest and a prison sentence, Pavić was released. He soon began working for the Ustashe Photography Service of the Independent State of Croatia in Zagreb as an infiltrator. Risking his own life, he continued to work undercover for the anti-fascist movement throughout the war, primarily on intelligence jobs. He also managed to provide the movement with photography equipment, chiefly photochemicals and paper, and later medicines, too.[30] Midway through 1944 he started working as a Zagreb correspondent for the Partisan press. He secretly gathered information from the very highest levels of the Ustashe administration, at first once a week, then twice, then even three times a week, recording the material in secret code. He wrote his reports in his flat at Buconjićeva St. no. 6/1, as if reporting from liberated territory and not the heart of occupied Zagreb. The reports were then surreptitiously handed over to his go-between, an engineer named Machaček who lived at Istarska St. no. 17. He, in turn, handed them over to a radio-telegraphist named Ljerka Dulčić who lived in another neighbourhood of Zagreb.[31] In April 1945, Pavić worked with Machaček and Bishop Gabrijel Bukatko in secretly photographing the Jasenovac concentration camp for Allied reconnaissance, giving the Allies knowledge of the camp's precise location and thus preventing Allied bombs from falling on camp prisoners. Pavić was responsible for the transcript of the Ustashe memorandum of surrender sent by Ustashe leader Ante Pavelić to the Western Allies seeking protection.[32]

There was one point at which Pavić should have left Zagreb and joined the ZAVNOH along with a larger group of anti-fascists, but the Ustashe authorities uncovered his plan and stopped him from leaving Zagreb for liberated territory. Pavić remained in Zagreb and at the start of 1945, the Ustashe authorities gave him the task of following and filming the journey of the Ustashe Guard to the Jasenovac concentration camp, while the Partisans simultaneously tasked him with secretly taking pictures of the camp.[33]

29 Zvonko Grbac, 'O vojnoobavještajnom radu za NOP u neprijateljskim vojnim i drugim institucijama', in: ibid., p. 619.

30 Milan Pavić, 'Kamera je zabilježila posljednje događaje u Zagrebu', in: Malić 1984 (see note 11), p. 394.

31 Ibid., p. 395.

32 Ibid., pp. 395–396.

33 Ibid., p. 394.

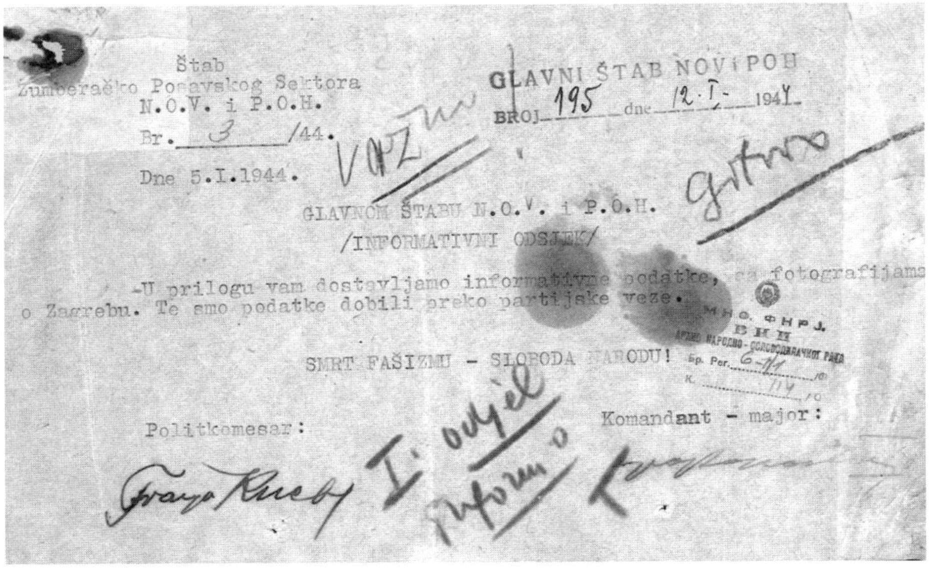

Štab
Žumberačko Posavskog Sektora
N.O.V. i P.O.H.
Br. 3 /44.
Dne 5.I.1944.

GLAVNI ŠTAB NOV i POH
BROJ 195 dne 12.I. 1944

GLAVNOM ŠTABU N.O.V. i P.O.H.
/INFORMATIVNI ODSJEK/

-U prilogu vam dostavljamo informativne podatke, sa fotografijama o Zagrebu. Te smo podatke dobili preko partijske veze.

SMRT FAŠIZMU - SLOBODA NARODU!

Politkomesar: Komandant - major:

Intelligence data with photographs of Zagreb. Military Archive Belgrade, K114 F1 6.

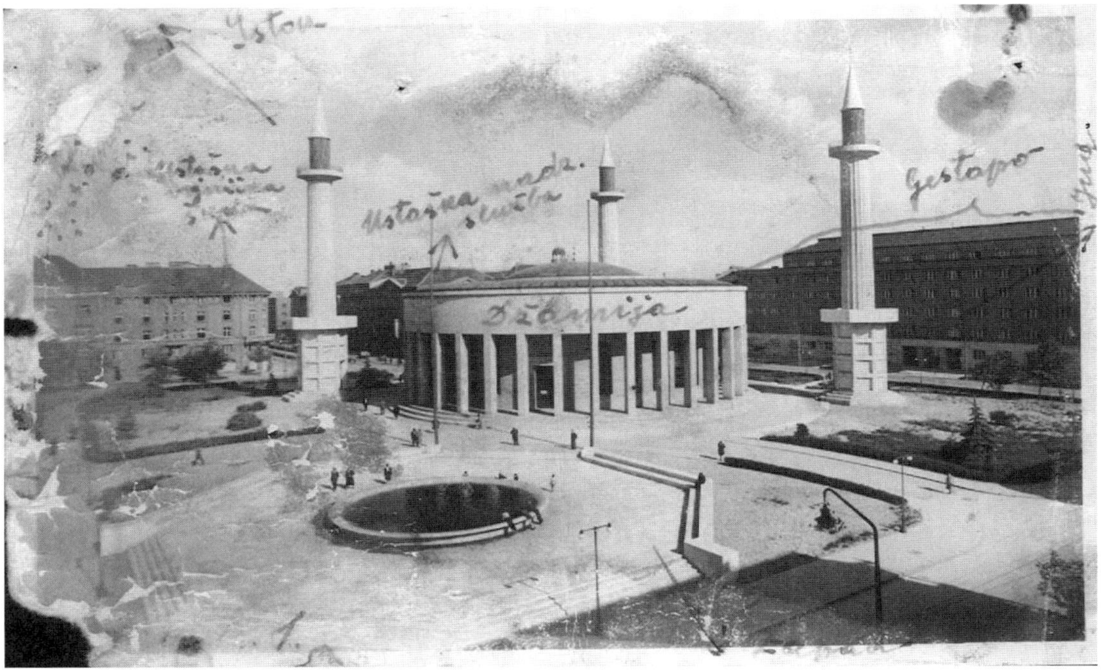

Intelligence data with photographs of Zagreb. Military Archive Belgrade, K114 F1 6.

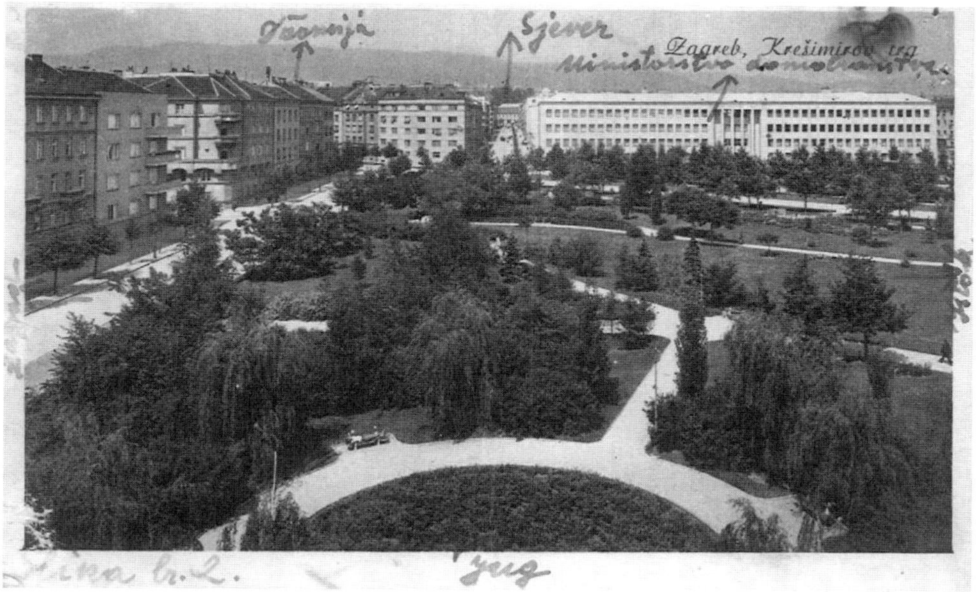

Intelligence data with photographs of Zagreb. Military Archive Belgrade, K114 F1 6.

Commandant Luburić banned us from filming, but he said that if we saw something positive that could be used for propaganda, then we should ask him or his deputy, Colonel Džala, about each shot, and if we didn't ask, then he'd have us locked up in the concentration camp for the rest of our lives. From the control tower at the entrance to the camp (height 18 m), with Džala's permission I took three panoramic shots (negatives 6 x 6 cm) of the entire camp. That day, the local prefect Servaci Maks Luburić was awarding medals marking the fourth anniversary of the Ustashe Inspectorate, which he gave to his next-in-command and fellow henchmen, the colonels Pavlović, Džala and others. I used this opportunity to take a portrait photograph of Luburić (whose picture had not appeared in the press up to that point), and each of his abettors in the slaughter, one by one. Upon returning to Zagreb, I printed the photographs in 13 x 18 cm format, together with photos of the entire concentration camp (a montage of three shots). I handed everything over to my case officer (Duško Doder), and he smuggled them to the liberated territory. All shots (negatives) were put in the propaganda photo archive, and the shots of the concentration camp from the tower were put in the top-secret archive.[34]

34 Ibid., p. 395.

As with Branko Savić's camerawork, Pavić's photographs of Jasenovac appear not to have survived. The part of the Ustashe photo archive that Pavić managed to preserve ended up at the Photo-Documentation Agency (Agencija za fotodokumentaciju), but it would seem these particular photographs of his were lost. Near the end of the war, Pavić was tasked with setting up a Partisan photography unit in Zagreb capable of producing photographs for press and propaganda purposes:

Eight days before the liberation [of Zagreb] I received an order from a high-ranking agent to establish undercover contact with the photographer Tošo Dabac who had a studio and film lab at Ilica St. no. 71/1. I was supposed to ask him whether he would be willing to make his lab available for propaganda purposes after the liberation, in the event of the propaganda building being blown up, which was a distinct possibility then. I approached Dabac, as a fellow photographer and an acquaintance, on what is now the Square of Brotherhood and Unity [since renamed Cvjetni Trg] and set out the demands of the People's Liberation Movement. He looked at me first in disbelief and amazement, and then agreed without reservation to put his lab at our service.[35]

Throughout the war it was strictly forbidden for anyone to take photographs of concentration camps, both from inside and outside without a permit; the offence was punishable by death.[36] Despite this, certain individuals deliberately risked their lives by breaking this law, as was the case with the railway engineer Mato Đukić, who took pictures of the Jasenovac concentration camp from a distance. Meanwhile, 'insider' photographs are known to have existed: Several camp prisoners stated on record that Dominik 'Hinko' Piccili – the Ustashe lieutenant colonel and infamous commander of the section Ciglana III (Brickyard III) who had a primitive crematorium built to incinerate prisoners, some while still alive[37] – used to walk around the camp with his *Leica* taking pictures of prisoners.[38] In Belgrade, the deputy director of the Banjica concentration camp, Peter Kriger, renowned for his especially inhuman and cruel behaviour, was known to ride around the camp on a bicycle, similarly photographing camp prisoners whenever anything seemed suspicious to him.[39]

The members of the underground resistance movement often themselves did not even know who other members were. In 1943 Pavić could not have assumed that Tošo Dabac (the photographer mentioned earlier with a film lab at Ilica St. no. 71/1) was increasingly distancing himself from propaganda jobs he had done for the Ustashe regime and had in fact switched sides, delivering photography equipment and material to the Partisans. Dabac donated his *Contax II* camera, photometer and photographic supplies worth 20,000 kunas at that time – which landed him in prison in September 1944.[40] In the last month of war, on 5 April 1945, Partisan agents in Zagreb managed to secretly photograph and smuggle out to Tito's Ministry of People's Defence (as it was already known by then) the

35 Ibid., p. 396.

36 Nataša Mataušić, *Koncentracioni logor Jasenovac*, Zagreb 2008, p. 30.

37 Unknown author, 'Dominik Hinko Piccili (Pićili) ustaški pukovnik', in: *Jasenovac Memorial Site*, URL: http://www.jusp-jasenovac.hr/Default.aspx?sid=6248 (accessed 1 June 2021).

38 Mataušić 2008 (see note 36), pp. 28–29.

39 Sima Begović, *Logor Banjica 1941–1944*, vol. 2, Belgrade 1989, p. 102.

40 Iva Prosoli, *Monografska obrada umjetničkog opusa Toše Dabca*, doctoral thesis, Filozofski fakultet Sveučilišta u Zagrebu, Zagreb 2018, pp. 137–138.

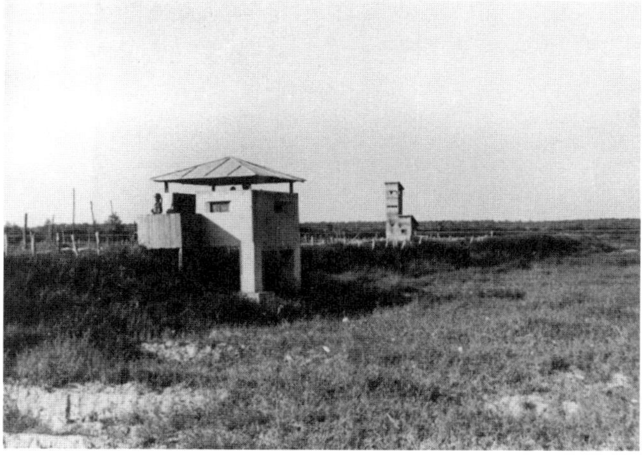

The Jasenovac concentration camp tower, equipped with floodlights and machine guns. Photographer unknown. History Museum of Bosnia and Herzegovina, FNOB 2029.

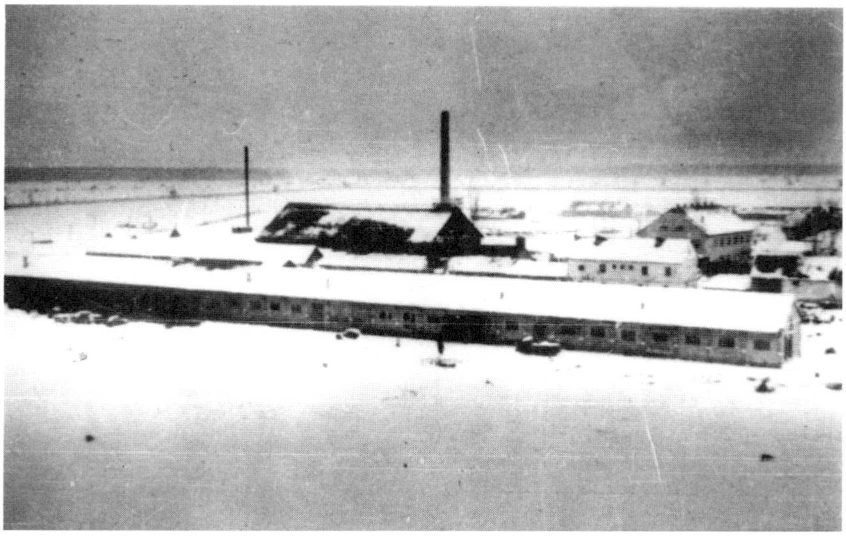

Jasenovac concentration camp in winter. Photographer unknown. Yad Vashem, 42913.

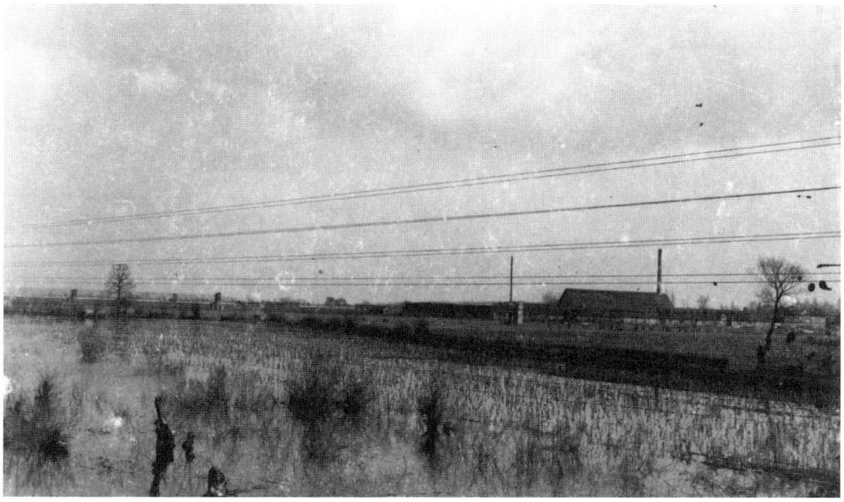

Jasenovac. Photograph taken by railway engineer Mato Đukić, 1942.
Jasenovac Memorial Site, accession no. unknown.

Ustashe plans for mounting a last defence of the city.[41] Pavić's photographs of the liberation of Zagreb include some of the most important photographs recording the liberation on 8 May 1945 and the period immediately before it. According to eye-witness accounts, during those eight days, Chetniks, broken German formations, civilians, Home Guard and Ustashe passed through Zagreb day and night, while the citizens were gripped by an indescribable fear. Some photographs of Zagreb's liberation were also shot by the underground agent Stjepan Puba Cerjan, who narrowly avoided arrest when trying to say goodbye to his parents just before leaving to join the Partisans.[42] Besides Cerjan, the only other person to attain a permit to take pictures of the Partisan units entering Zagreb was Tošo Dabac, who notably approached the task with a critical eye and sense of detachment.

In the Slovenian capital of Ljubljana, the Anti-Imperialist Front was founded in late April 1941 and soon changed its name to the Liberation Front of the Slovenian People. The first Liberation Front campaigns were recorded by the photographers Miran Pavlin, Dr Jakob Prešern,[43] Viktor Kramar and Jože Stajer, and their film rolls were sent to Partisan units on liberated territory. Similar networks involving photographers were set up in other Slovenian cities.[44] The Liberation Front operated illegally, organising the printing of propaganda pamphlets, and their photographers also carried out the technical work required to make passport photographs for fake identification. One especially interesting detail about the campaign in Slovenia is that many photography studios took the brave decision to secretly make copies of photographic material that the Italian and German occupying authorities brought to them. Such 'intelligence gathering' began very early on, in 1941. Following an order by the poet Karel Destovnik-Kajuh, Stane Viršek organised a group of fifteen people to carry out this work.[45] Edi Šelhaus in Škofja Loka documented occupier war crimes in the same way,[46] and in Celje, Josip Pelikan, working as an official photographer for the Germans, managed to keep photographs of the execution of civilians incarcerated in Stari Pisker. The question of who shot these photographs has never been entirely clarified, but Pelikan was the person responsible for the photo archive that documented the terrible conditions that prevailed during the German occupation of Celje, and his archive has been preserved to this day.

The Stari Pisker prison wing is presently part of Celje Prison, and its courtyard has been turned into a memorial space open to the public. During the war, around 10,000 people are estimated to have passed through this prison, and executions were carried out on at least six occasions in its courtyard. The greatest known atrocity occurred on 22 July 1942, when units from the German SS decided to murder all prisoners in detention at that moment in

41 *Zbornik dokumenata i podataka o narodno-oslobodilačkom ratu jugoslovenskih naroda*, vol. II/15, Belgrade 1982.

42 Stjepan Cerjan, 'Ustaj, evo ustaša!', in: Tihić 1984 (see note 20), p. 95.

43 Franc Fabec, 'Photography during the Slovene National Liberation Struggle', in: *Resistance, Suffering, Hope: The Slovene Partisan Movement 1941–1945*, Jože Pirjevec and Bože Repe, Ljubljana/Trieste 2008, p. 95.

44 For a detailed list of names, see the book by Franc Fabec and Dejan Vončina, *Slovenska odporniška fotografija 1941–1945*, Ljubljana 2005.

45 Ibid., p. 23.

46 Fabec 2008 (see note 43), p. 95.

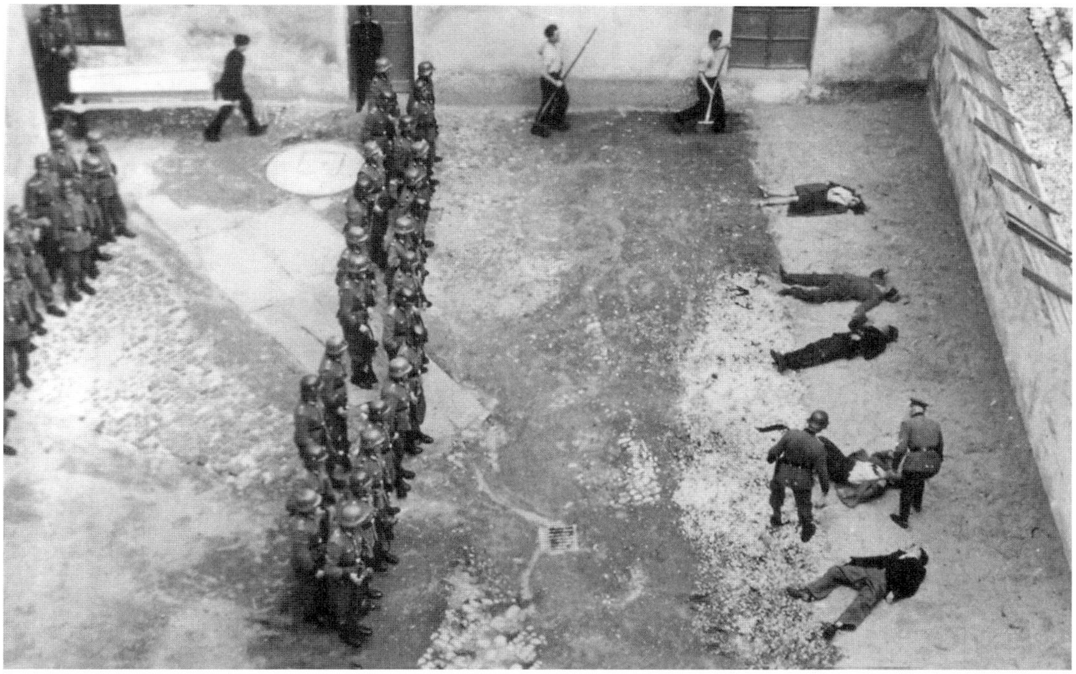

After an execution by firing squad at Celje, 22 July 1942. Photographer unknown. Museum of Recent History, Celje, VF 96.

an act of retaliation. To this day, the Museum of Recent History, Celje has preserved their farewell letters, which are distressing testimonies of Nazi brutality.

In 1942, Pelikan also took photographs of the so-called 'shaming' of the Partisans. These practices included displaying the dead bodies of killed Partisans, while their captured comrades were forced to stand above them, wearing humiliating placards as civilians and German soldiers walked by to observe the spectacle. One of the photographs shows Tončka Čeč (a Partisan with the codename Roza), a pre-war communist and member of the Liberation Front who died in Auschwitz on 3 November 1943 as a result of a typhus infection. One photograph depicting her is particularly haunting:

Dead bodies are strewn across the pavement, while civilians and German soldiers pass them by. Only the gentlemen in suits are relaxed. They are chatting. Their bodies show no sign of tension. Pelikan is neat, focused and pays attention to the composition. He chooses a wide shot that captures the dead, the living and those being tortured. He includes everything in the frame. He can jump over the rope and enter the protected area. He moves the lens to the right and on the right-hand side he foregrounds a woman whose face is difficult to distinguish. Her head is gently raised and turned to her left. And she stands proud. You feel her strength, despite the fact she is captured and her hands are tied.[47]

47 Davor Konjikušić, 'Nacistički zločini celjski', in: *Novosti*, issue 746, 7 April 2014, URL: http://arhiva.portalnovosti.com/2014/04/nacisticki-zlocini-celjski (accessed 2 June 2021).

In Serbia, meanwhile, the illegal printing press of the Central Committee of the Communist Party of Yugoslavia operated throughout the entire war, publishing the *Glas Jedinstvenog narodno-oslobodilačkog fronta Srbije* (Voice of the United People's Liberation Front of Serbia).

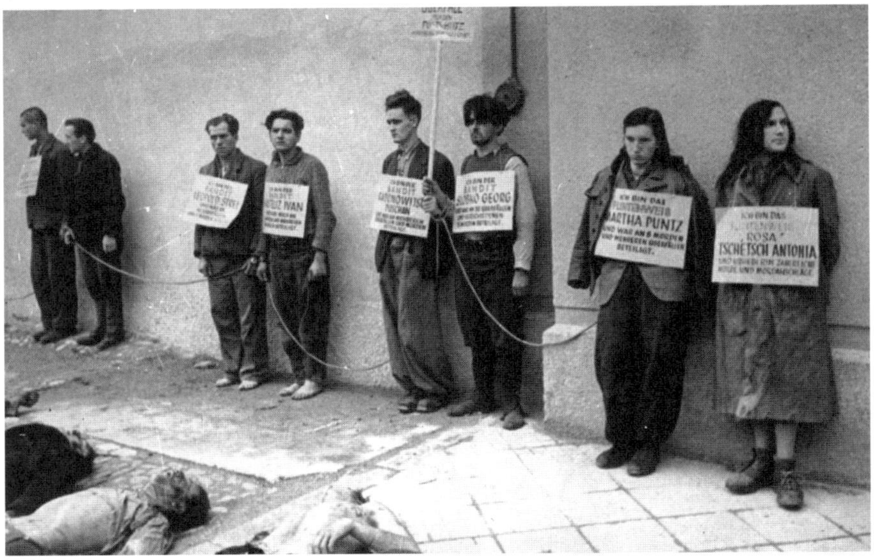

Tončka Čeč (right), Celje, 1942. Photographer unknown. Museum of Recent History, Celje.

Many members and supporters of the anti-fascist movement collaborated on the paper – writers, artists and journalists. Despite many arrests, the underground printing press was active from the beginning of the war up until 28 July 1944, when members of the special police, the Gestapo and the quisling gendarmerie raided its secret location, then at a house at Daničareva no. 24. The typesetters Slobodan Jović and Branko Đonović first set about destroying secret documents, before putting up armed resistance. Finding themselves trapped, the two friends turned their guns on themselves, each firing a lethal shot at the other after a count of three, so as to evade police capture. The married couple Ratka and Milutin Blagojević also died in the raid.[48]

* * *

German units in occupied Yugoslavia carried out mass executions that were documented by the German propaganda unit *Propaganda-Abteilung Südost* which was active in the Yugoslav region from October 1941 onwards. Stationed in Belgrade, the unit's task was to produce propaganda material intended for the local population.[49] In the German troops, there was a clear hierarchy of photographic production from the very beginning: from acquiring photographic material, taking photographs, developing film and making positives, to the distribu-

48 Milan Radanović, 'Ilegalna štamparija Pokrajinskog komiteta KPJ za Srbiju Daničareva 24', in: *Mesta stradanja i antifašističke borbe u Beogradu 1941–1944. Priručnik za čitanje grada.* Milovan Pisarri and Rena Rädle (eds.), Belgrade 2016 (Rosa Luxemburg Stiftung Southeast Europe), pp. 109–111.

49 Daniel Uziel, *The Propaganda Warriors: The Wehrmacht and the Consolidation of the German Home Front*, Bern 2008, p. 287.

tion of photographs. An order by the counter-intelligence department of the Oberkommando der Wehrmacht (OKW), dated 28 November 1941, labelled 'confidential', states that it is explicitly forbidden to photograph the faces of those sentenced to death by firing squad:

1. Taking photographs of shootings after sentencing by military court is forbidden in general. If, in certain exceptional cases, it is necessary to make photographic images for purely military goals, approval can only be granted by an officer of a rank no lower than division commander. Used film that has not been developed should be submitted to superiors as 'Confidential OKW/W. Pr [Wehrmachtpropaganda]', with the concurrent request that certain images be produced.
2. In striving to carry out this order, military organs ordered to carry out executions of death by firing squad are required to take all necessary precautionary measures to ensure that there are no viewers. Any images and negatives already in existence from previous executions should be removed from circulation, and if possible, be submitted to the Oberkommando des Heeres.

Contrary to this order, pictures of war crimes were often to be found on German soldiers – trophy photographs that they collected as proof of the struggle against the 'bandits' – their name for the Partisan units, as they refused to recognise them as a legitimate military organisation. Making photo albums, of themselves but also of their victims, was an especially popular pastime among German soldiers. Such albums depicted deportations, executions, public hangings and the debasement of the occupied peoples, along with routine acts of violence.[50] One such example is a postcard showing three hanged civilians with the caption 'Trees in Blossom, Serbia 1941'.[51] While writing to their families in Germany, some German soldiers even sent trophy photographs of war crimes, even though this directly violated paragraph 25 of the German Military Code, which penalised such behaviour as failing to respect military secrets, and paragraphs 90d and 90e of the Penal Code relating to acts of treason.[52]

The National Museum of Contemporary History of Slovenia in Ljubljana is home to the photo albums of several SS officers. These are painstakingly made scrapbooks of brutality that include composite photographs of crimes against Partisan soldiers, arranged in a linear montage. Such photographs sometimes became special trophies, as was the case with pictures of the German SS battalion in the Slovenian village of Masor, when two civilians and three Partisans from the Vojko Brigade were killed. This was also the case with photographs dated 20 March 1945 and taken in the village of Sedej next to a settlement called Idrijske Krnice.

In Croatia, data on trophy photographs can be found in the report of the Staff of the Third Operative Zone to the General Staff of the People's Liberation Army and the Partisan Detachment of Croatia. The report, dated 23 May 1943, covers the work of the intelligence

50 Sandra Vitaljić, *Rat slikama. Suvremena ratna fotografija*, Zagreb/Mostar 2013, p. 93.
51 *Trials of War Criminals Before the Nuremberg Military Tribunals Under Council Law*, no. 10, vol. XI, United States Government Printing Office Washington 1950, p. 1147.
52 Valter Manošek, *Holokaust u Srbiji. Vojna okupaciona politika i uništavanje Jevreja 1941–1942*, Belgrade 2007, p. 90.

service. It states that in an attack on Slavonski zdrug at Voćin, the captured officers had photographs of war crimes on their person.[53] Similar photographs were found on German officers, especially at Kozara.[54]

Civilians were hanged, often as an act of retribution, all over Yugoslavia. Yet one of the most brutal atrocities committed were the mass killings in the city cemetery in Pančevo on 22 April 1941, photographed by Gerhard Gronefeld in a company of the Wehrmachtpropaganda service. Gottfried Kessel, a second member in this company, recorded the hangings and murders on camera using colour film. Years later, Gronefeld said that these photographs had haunted him for the rest of his life.[55] The victims were degraded even in death, their bodies put on show to German soldiers and crowds of civilians. Hats were placed on their heads as a macabre insinuation that only dead and hanged like this were they afforded the status of proper gentlemen, being peasants otherwise. This is reminiscent of the communists whose bodies were put on public display, degraded and photographed after the collapse of Paris Commune. It also calls to mind the Slovenian communists who were

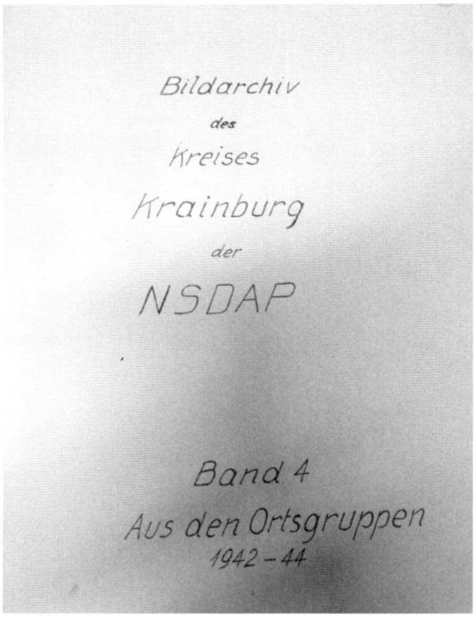

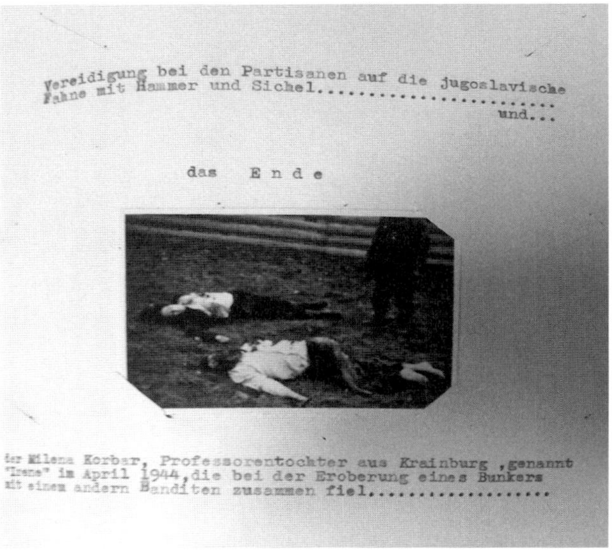

Photo album: 'Picture Archive of the District of Krainburg [Kranj] of the National Socialist German Workers' Party. Volume 4. From the local groups'. National Museum of Contemporary History of Slovenia.

53 *Građa za historiju NOP u Slavoniji, knjiga*, vol. 5 (1.4.–31.5.1943.), Slavonski Brod 1966.

54 Ljubomir Borojević, Dušan Samardžija and Rade Bašić, *Peta kozaračka brigada*, Belgrade 1973, p. 215.

55 Associated Press, 'Eyes of Victims in '41 Massacre Haunt German', in: *Deseret News*, 7 March 1997, URL: https://www.deseretnews.com/article/547366/eyes-of-victims-in-41-massacre-haunt-german.html (accessed 2 June 2021).

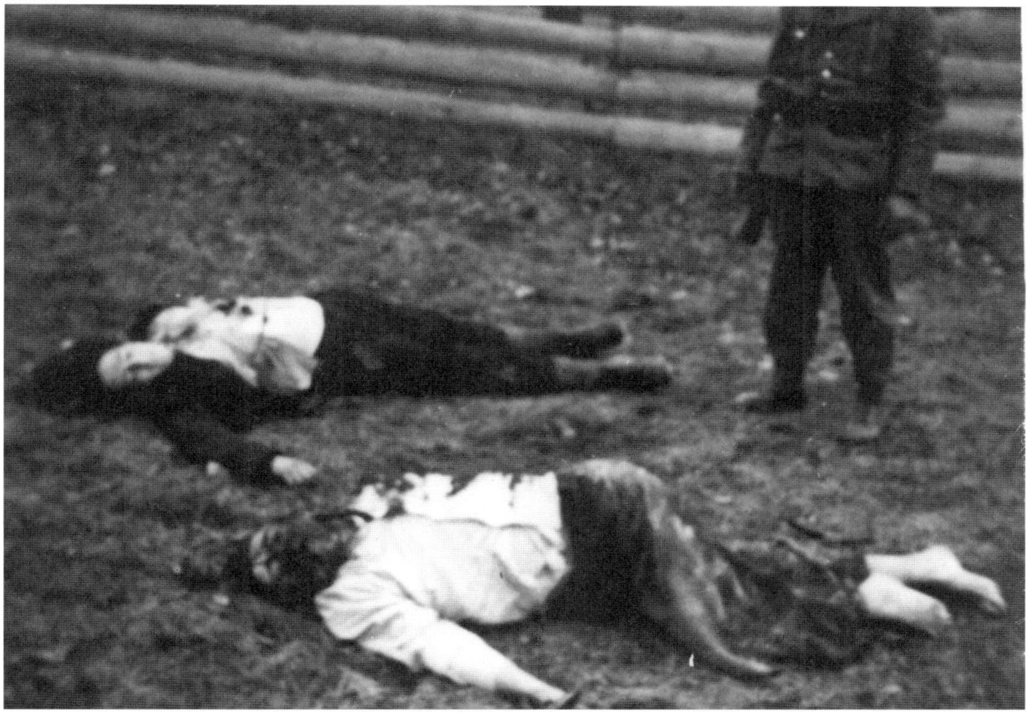

Image from the Nazi album 'Bildarchiv des Kreisses Krainburg', vol. 4. National Museum of Contemporary History of Slovenia.

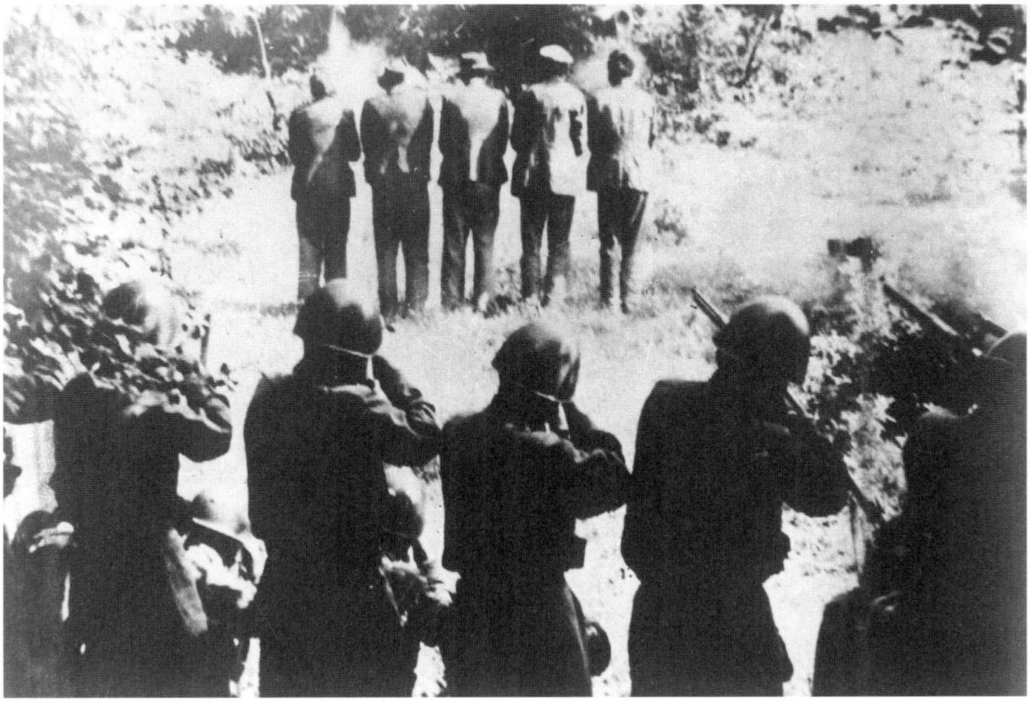

Execution of prisoners Franc Žnidaršič (left), Janez Krajc, France Škerbec, Feliks Žnidaršič, Edvard Škerbec (right). Križna Gora, Loška valley, 31 June 1942. Photographer unknown. National Museum of Contemporary History of Slovenia, 1818.

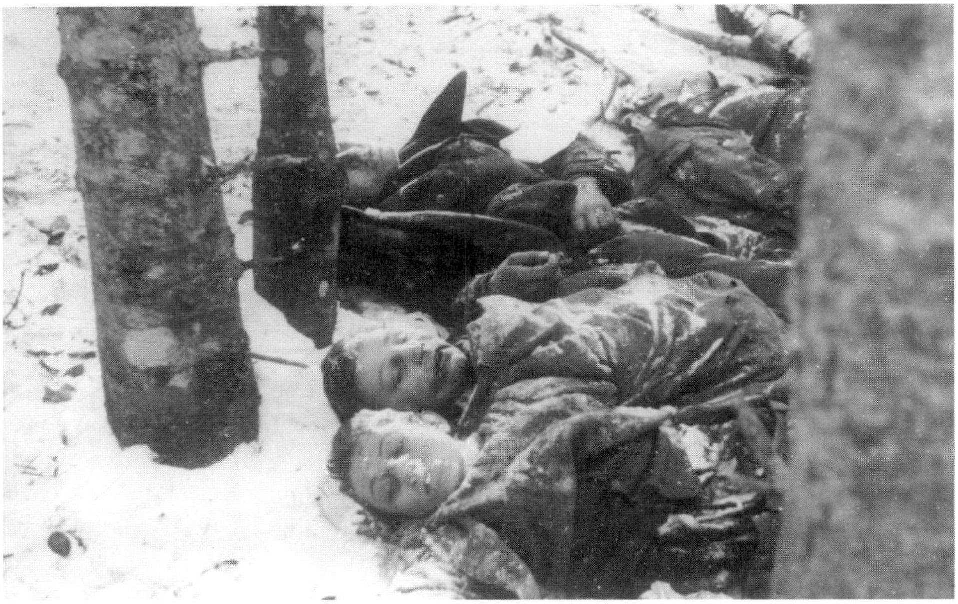

Killed Partisans from the Pohorski Battalion, including child soldiers Vanček Šarh (first from front, age 12) and Pepček Šarh (age 14), sons of the Partisan soldier Alfonz Šarh, who was also killed. Photographer unknown. National Museum of Contemporary History of Slovenia, 4973/9.

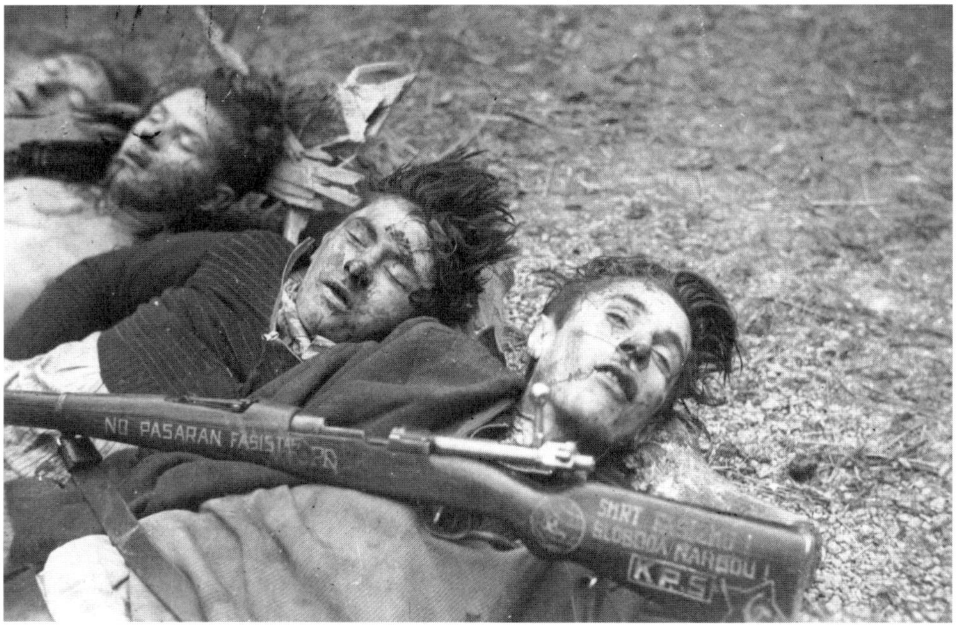

Four fighters from the Brezice Company: Ivan Milavec (left), Marjan Cerjak, Draško Hlebec and Milan Kovačič (right foreground), Podsreda, Slovenia, 28 November 1941. Photographer unknown. National Museum of Contemporary History of Slovenia, pl8864a.

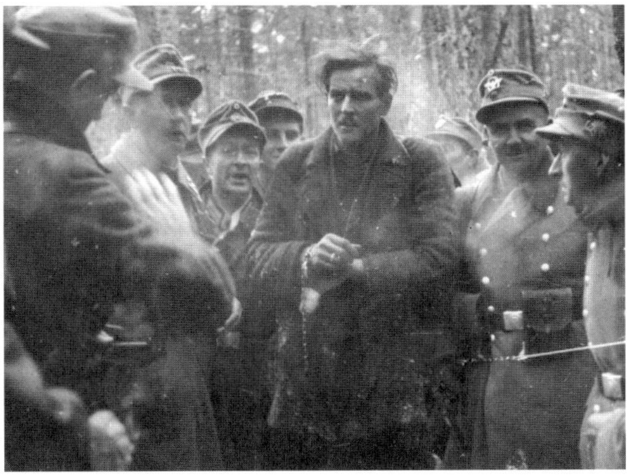

Franc Kunaver, captured fighter from the Pohorski Battalion, with German police, Pohorje, 8 January 1943. Photo: Ordelt Delti. National Museum of Contemporary History of Slovenia, Di1085/1.

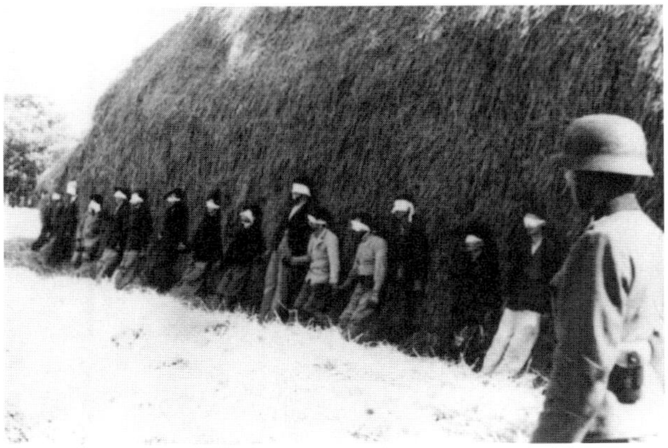

Death by firing squad of 17 communists in Smederevska Palanka, Serbia, 20 July 1941. Photographer unknown. Military Museum Belgrade, 1069.

publicly humiliated in front of their comrades' bodies that were strewn around them. Public hangings and executions were methods used to inculcate terror among the population. Retribution killings and exterminations were especially prevalent in South-East Europe, where large swathes of the population fell victim to the race laws. Images of these executions became proof of military orders acted out,[56] and served to coerce the population further. Throughout history, public hangings have been intended mainly for underprivileged social

The horrific photograph of the hanging of the seventeen-year-old girl Lepa Radić came to be perhaps the most well-known image of suffering, a symbol of the atrocities committed on Yugoslav soil. As a member of the Second Krajina Detachment, Radić, a young hospital nurse, was responsible for evacuating injured soldiers and the civilian population during the Fourth Enemy Offensive in 1943. In the evening of 8 February 1943, her camp was discovered by units of the notorious Seventh SS Volunteer Mountain Division 'Prinz Eugen'. After having shot her final round of ammunition, Lepa was overpowered by being struck in the head with a gunstock and led away to Bosanska Krupa, where, after three days' impri-

56 Sanja Horvatinčić, 'Ballade of the Hanged: The Representation of Second World War Atrocities in Yugoslav Memorial Sculpture', in: *Art and Its Responses to Changes in Society*, Ines Unetič et al., Cambridge 2016, pp. 188–189.

sonment, she was publicly hanged from a false acacia tree not far from the railway station. The art historian Dragoje Lukić, known for researching the deaths of children and civilians from nearby Bosanska Krajina, published an article in *Ilustrovana Politika* in 1968 on Lepa Radić. The article revealed that the negatives of the photographs of her execution were found on a German soldier who fell on Ilica St. during the liberation of Zagreb. For years, the identity of the girl in the photograph remained unknown and was revealed entirely by chance by a visitor to what was then called the Museum of the Revolution in Mostar.[58] Thanks to the discovery of these trophy photographs found on the fallen German soldier, we now have further visual evidence of the brutality of the public hanging of this young member of the League of Communist Youth. The expression on her face is defiant, without a trace of fear. But rather than having a galvanising effect, as is the case with the image of Stjepan Filipović on the gallows, these photographs – showing a girl surrounded by a group of men who would, moments later, eagerly remove her shoes and jacket as 'war spoils' –

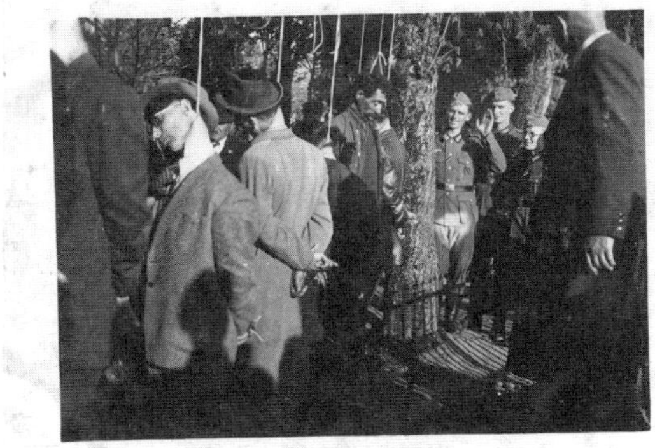

The hanging of civilians, Pančevo, 22 June 1941. Photograph found on a dead German soldier. Photographer unknown. Yad Vashem, 8053985.

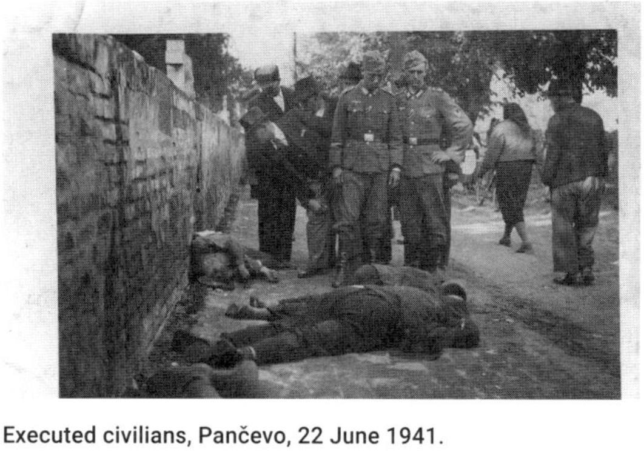

Executed civilians, Pančevo, 22 June 1941. Photograph found on a dead German soldier. Photographer unknown. Yad Vashem, 8053996.

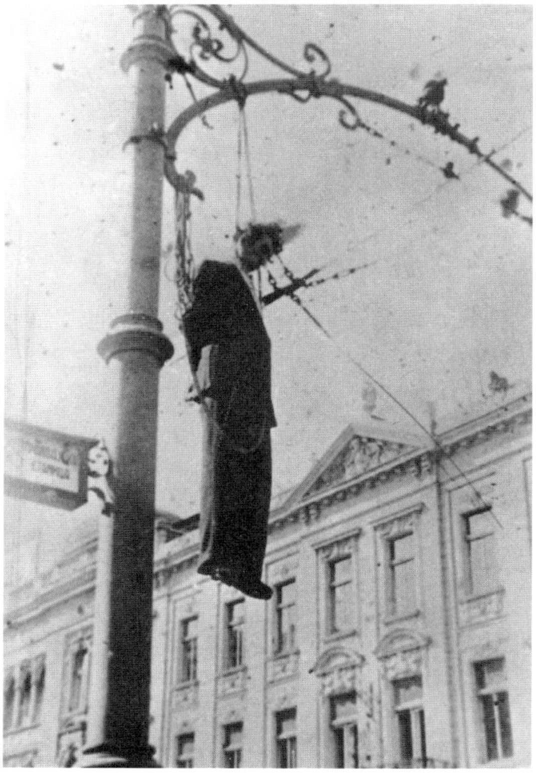

Jovan Janković, a tailor from Belgrade, hanged by the German occupiers on Terazije, a central square in Belgrade, 17 August 1941. Photographer unknown. Military Museum Belgrade, 1022.

57 Ibid., p. 190.

58 Dragoje Lukić, 'Lepa Radić 1943. nije imala ni 18 godina: Kako su otkriveni potresni snimci vešanja mlade partizanke', in: *Ilustrovana Politika*, 1968, quoted from: *Yugopapir*, URL: http://www.yugopapir.com/2017/10/lepa-radic-43-nije-imala-ni-18-godina.html (accessed 2 June 2021).

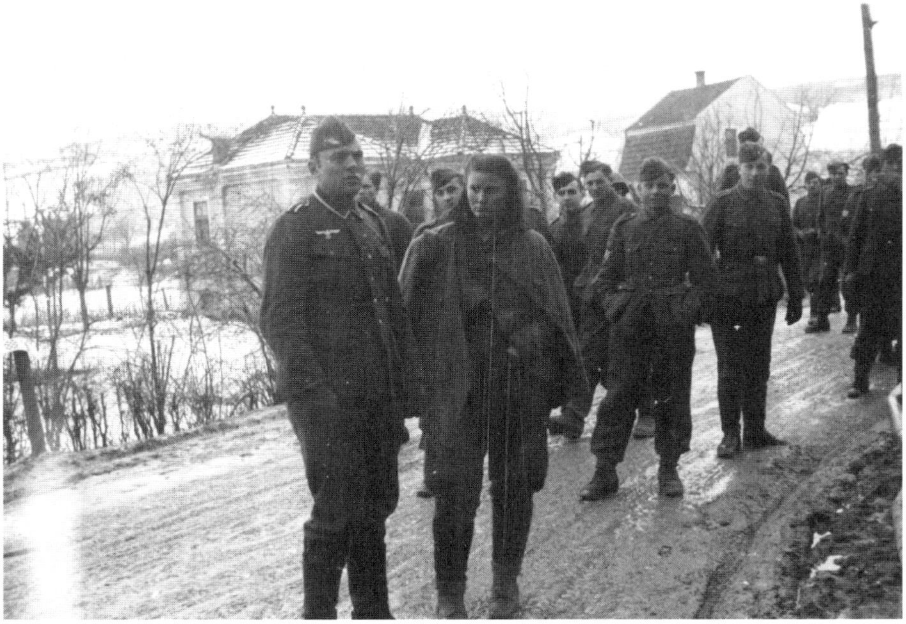

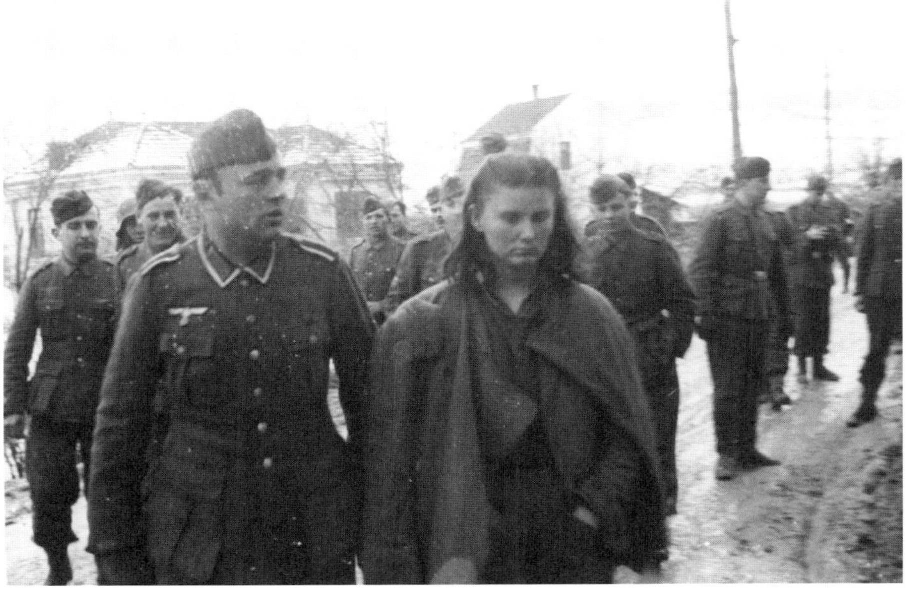

Lepa Radić, later declared a People's Hero, immediately before her hanging, at age 17, in Bosanska Krupa, 8 February 1943. Photographer unknown. Photograph donated by Dragoje Lukić.

leave the viewer with an overriding sense of helplessness and convey the 'banality of evil'. Although the Axis powers primarily used photography to terrify and coerce the civilian population under occupation, once they fell into Partisan hands, these same photographs had the exact opposite effect. Photographic evidence of atrocities underscored a heroic narrative of human sacrifice so that 'despite high risks and the threat of violence, they served as a sign of the groundswell of resistance among the people and their determined resolution to join and support a resistance movement led by the Communist Party of

Yugoslavia, which laid the foundations for the future political and social order after the war'.[59] Instead of being intimidating, photographs of war crimes only hardened the resolve of soldiers and fighters to take an even stronger stand against the enemy. It is therefore unsurprising that by 20 October 1942, the head of the temporary administrative section of the Supreme Command, Moša Pijade, had already asked that Partisans gather all proof of enemy war crimes. He stressed that such photographs could even be acquired from within occupied Zagreb.[60] Some of the first examples of photographs taken by the occupying forces but published by Partisans appeared in the paper *Borba*, issue 15, 29 November 1944, under the heading 'We avenge the blood and suffering of our brothers from the Slovenian Littoral'.[61]

It is important to mention here, once again, that Partisan photography emerged within the Partisan movement, whose right to exist was denied by the German occupiers and quisling authorities.[62] The only route out of this situation was armed resistance to preserve and maintain the civilizational and emancipatory achievements of modern humankind.[63] The Partisans did not revere and fetishise death in their photographs, a key point of difference

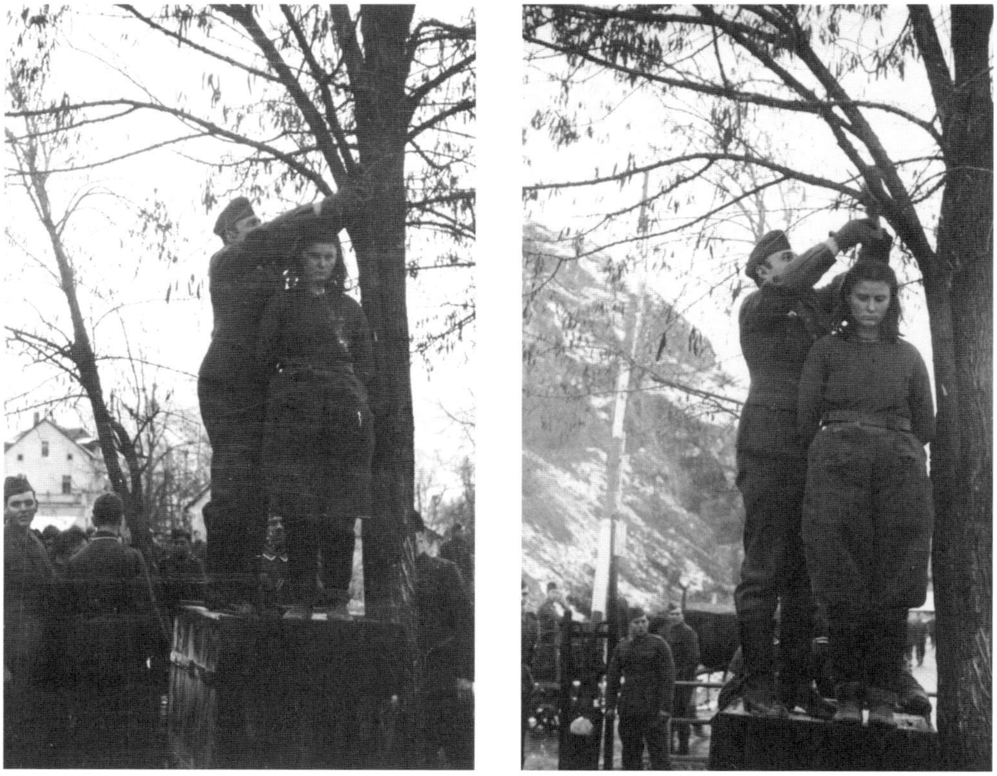

Lepa Radić, later declared a People's Hero, immediately before her hanging, at age 17, in Bosanska Krupa, 8 February 1943. Photographer unknown. Photograph donated by Dragoje Lukić.

59 Horvatinčić, p. 191.

60 *Zbornik dokumenata i podataka o narodno-oslobodilačkom ratu jugoslovenskih naroda*, vol. II/6: Dokumenta vrhovnog štaba Narodnooslobodilačke vojske Jugoslavije 1942, Belgrade 1957.

61 Sandra Vitaljić, *Rat slikama. Suvremena ratna fotografija*, Zagreb/Mostar 2013, p. 92.

62 Krunoslav Stojaković, 'Revolucionarno nasilje u narodnooslobodilačkom ratu', in: Milan Radanović, *Kazna i zločin: Snage kolaboracije u Srbiji*, Belgrade 2014 (Rosa Luxemburg Stiftung Southeast Europe), p. 21.

63 Ibid., p. 24.

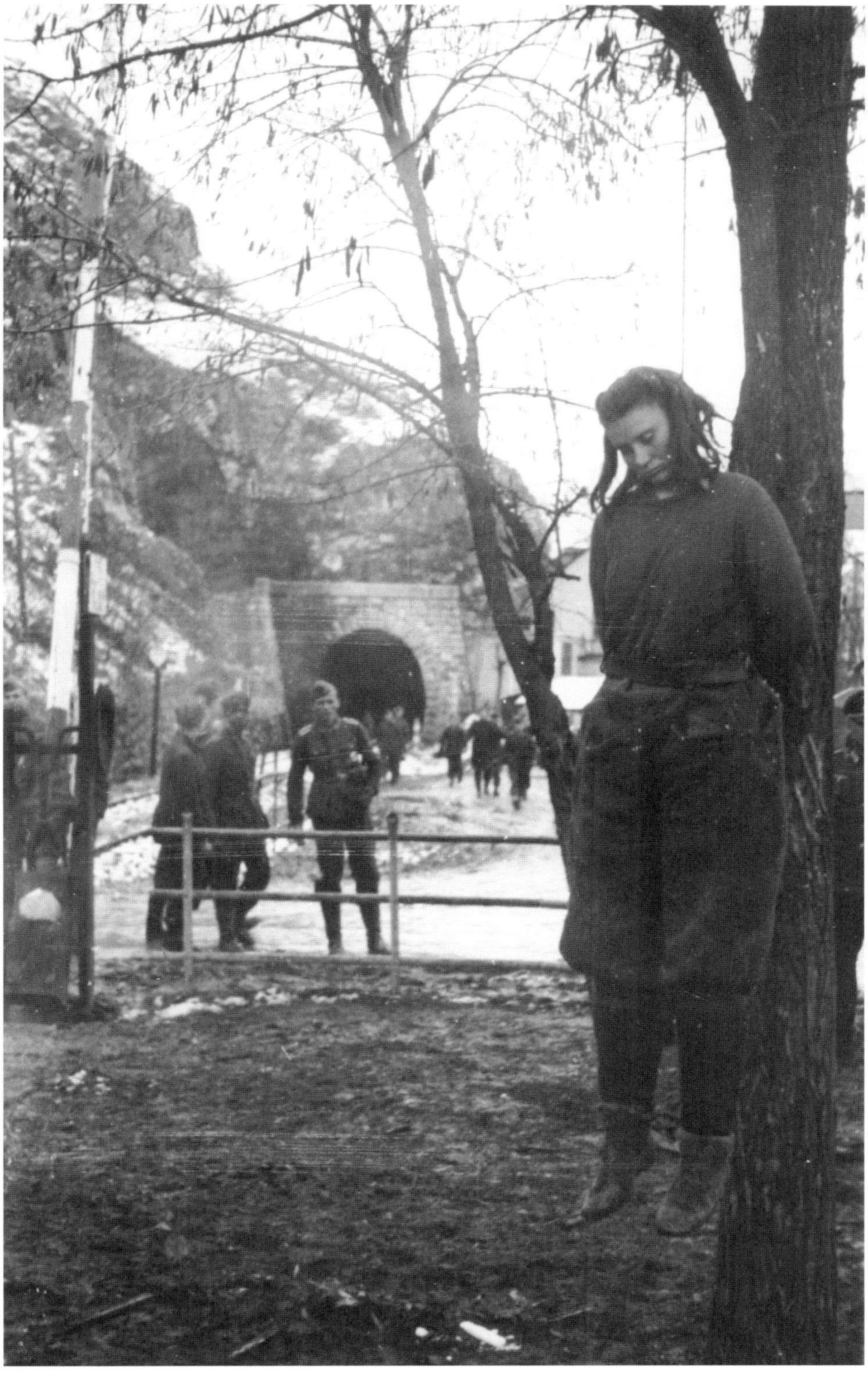

Lepa Radić was executed at age 17, in Bosanska Krupa, 8 February 1943. Photographer unknown.
Photographs donated by Dragoje Lukić.

with Nazi and fascist ideology and culture. The Nazi reverence of death is evidenced in their use of such imagery as skulls (for example the skull-and-crossbones insignia of the SS), bones, knives, etcetera, and also through various occult rituals that gained traction in certain Nazi circles. Ultimately, Hitler, whose favourite opera coincidentally was Wagner's *Götterdämmerung*, saw death as valiant and a higher form. With a death cult prevailing in Nazi Germany, not just in political discourse but also in art, it was therefore entirely logical that the Germans used photographs of their own dead for propaganda purposes. The Partisans, by contrast, did not photograph their dead, as for them death in and of itself was not a symbol of pride, but rather defeat, and this was an important difference in their everyday practice.

Photographs of Partisan executions of captured enemy soldiers were forbidden in a series of orders from 1941 onwards. One of the rare examples of such photographs was shot by Croatian photographer Hugo Fischer Ribarić during the struggle for the liberation of Rijeka. It was shot above Vežica, not far from the astronomy centre there today. As an established photographer, he certainly knew that he was breaking all the war regulations, but irrespective of this, he decided to photograph the execution of German soldiers and publish the photographs. He most likely did so to express his objections against his superiors' decision to execute prisoners of war.

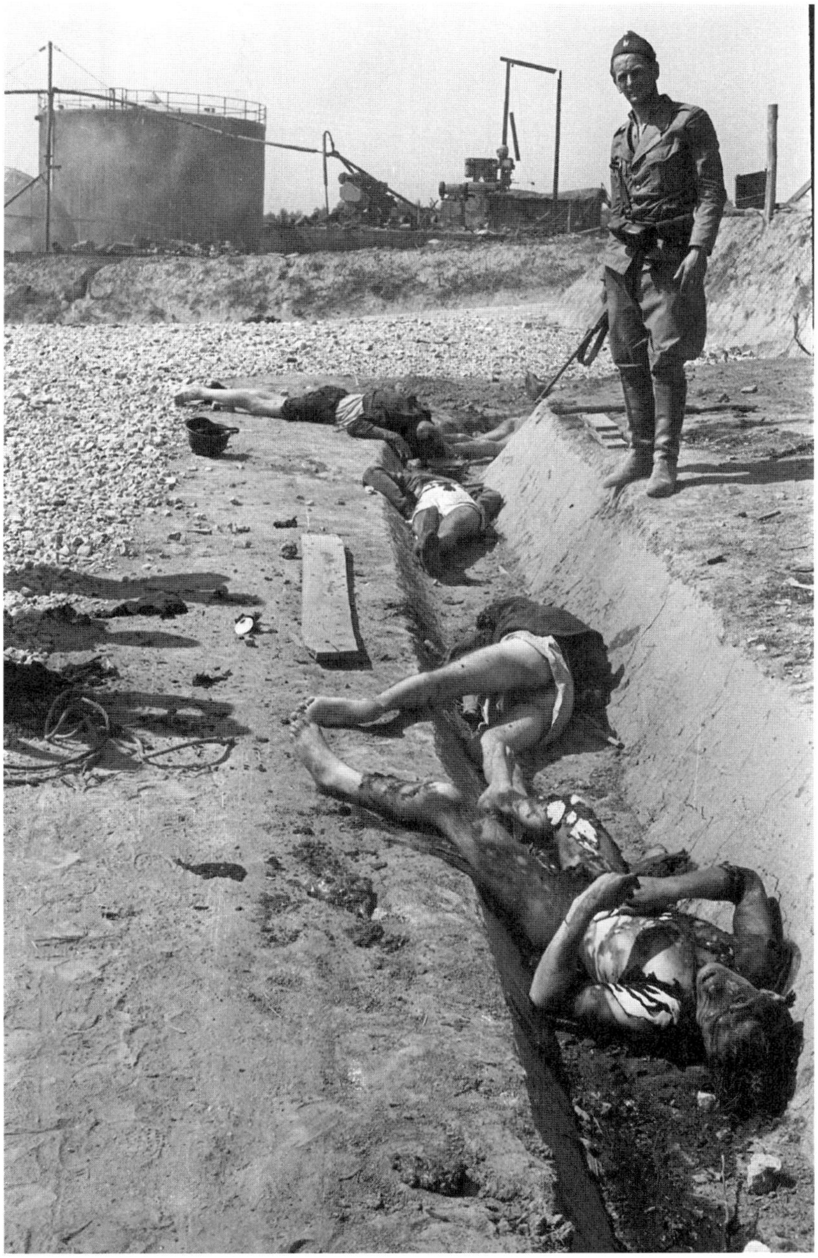

A Ustashe soldier stands above his victims after the Partisan ambush on Gojlo, 6 September 1942. Photo: Dragutin Rajterić (Croatian Film Service). Croatian History Museum, HPM-MRNH-N-6751.

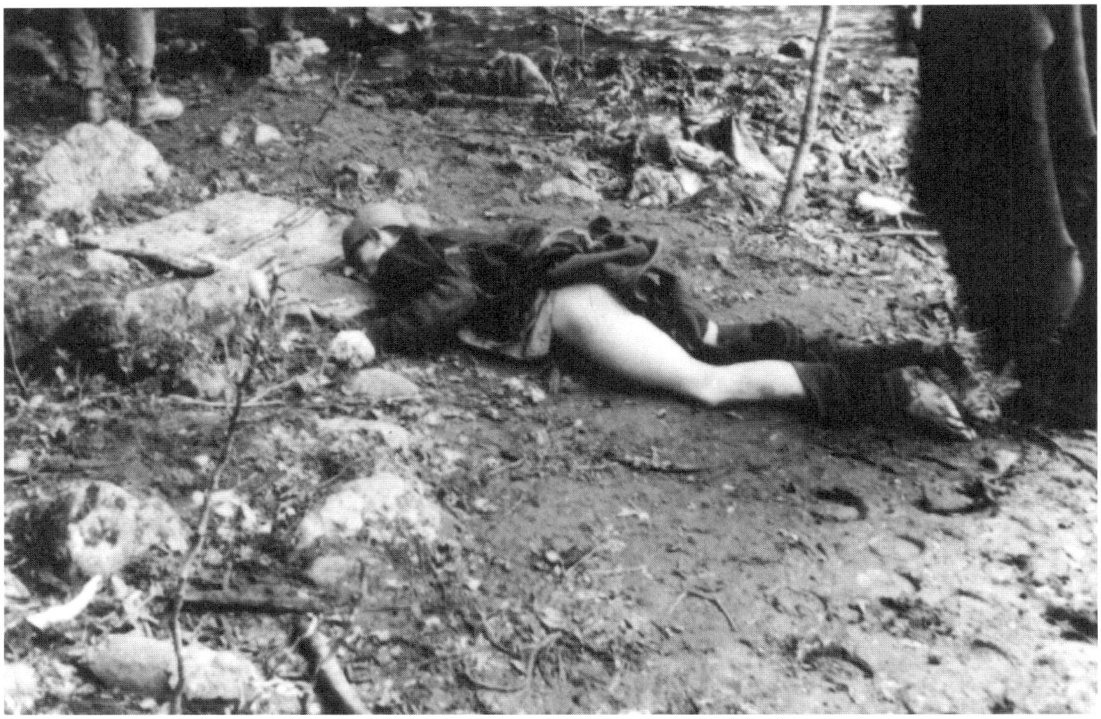

Unknown victim, Bosnia and Herzegovina, 1943. Photo: Mladen Iveković. Croatian History Museum, HPM-MRNH-A-6337 165.

9. Photo Archive: The Themes and Subject Matter of Partisan Photography

As photographs are taken and begin to pile up, an archive quickly emerges. This chapter therefore presents – as a kind of photo album or record book – the fragments of the photo archive that emerged while investigating the historical material. During this research, the subject matter covered in the various photographs hinted strongly at several themes that I have grouped into the twenty-one units presented here. These units offer a critical overview of how the members of the Partisan movement saw themselves as well as their ideology, convictions, beliefs and values. The French philosopher Louis Althusser quite rightly believes that one of the communication channels for an ideology (or an idea, myth or concept) is through photographs. Such representation is largely unconscious, and we do not think about it in great detail; ideology features as society's representation of itself to itself. If we interpret the photographic medium semiotically, then we can say that photography, as with language itself, lies at the epicentre of ideological tensions. Croatia and the post-Yugoslav region more widely have again reached a point in time when political tensions could boil over. We find ourselves in a moment when attempts are being made to change the meaning of a signifier – in this case the Partisans. The motives behind such attempts are predominantly revisionist – they aim to alter representations of the past. Photographs are exceptionally important in such a struggle over meanings, as they construct the world of which we speak.

Moving on from the examples that this book has provided so far, we will begin this chapter with several sections from the magazine *Liberation*. This magazine was established by pro-Yugoslav emigrants in the USA during the Second World War. Their editor was Louis Adamic, an American writer with Slovenian roots who, in 1942, became actively involved in the propaganda war that was raging in the American press. This war entailed a desperate struggle for representation between those who supported the exiled Yugoslav government – in other words, the Chetniks – and those who supported the Partisans and the anti-fascist struggle.[1]

1 Walter R. Roberts, *Tito, Mihailović and the Allies, 1941–1945*, New Brunswick 1973, p. 75.

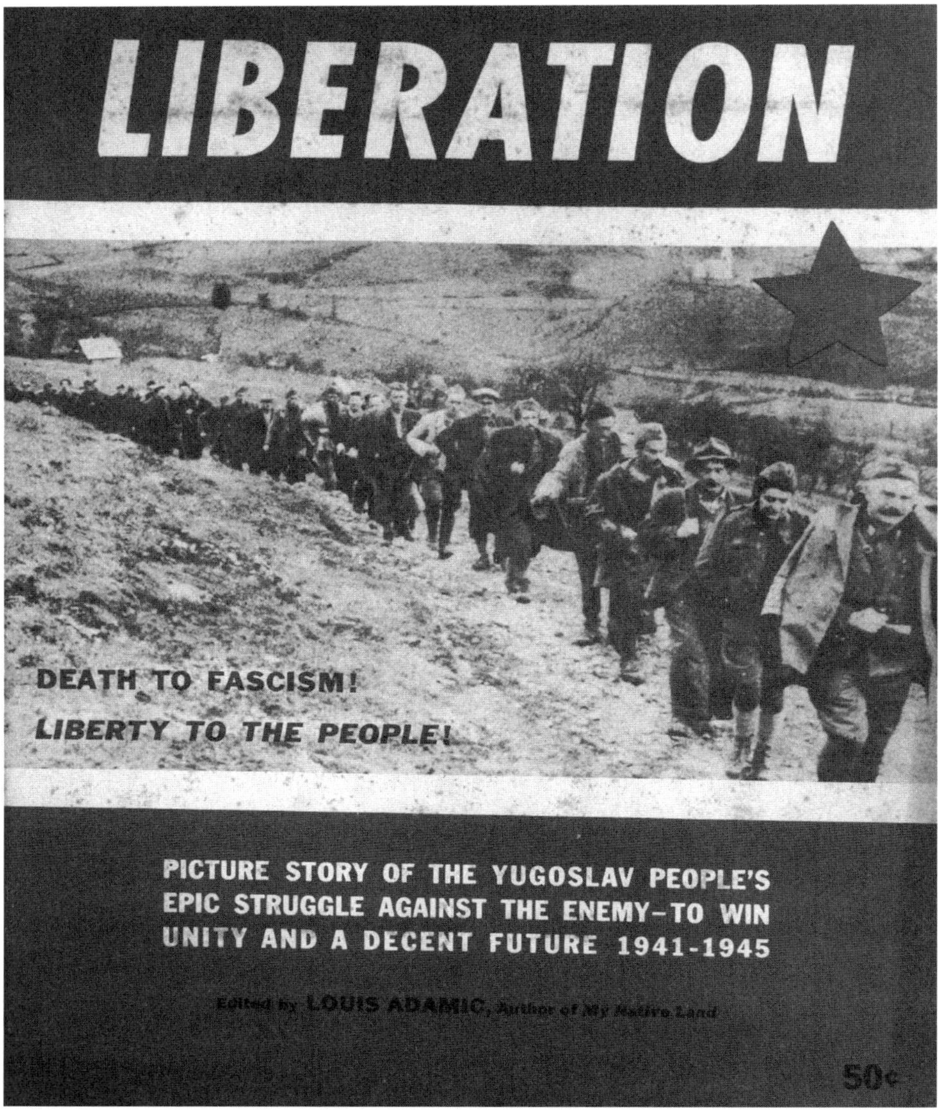

Cover of the magazine *Liberation*, undated. Institute of Contemporary History, Ljubljana.

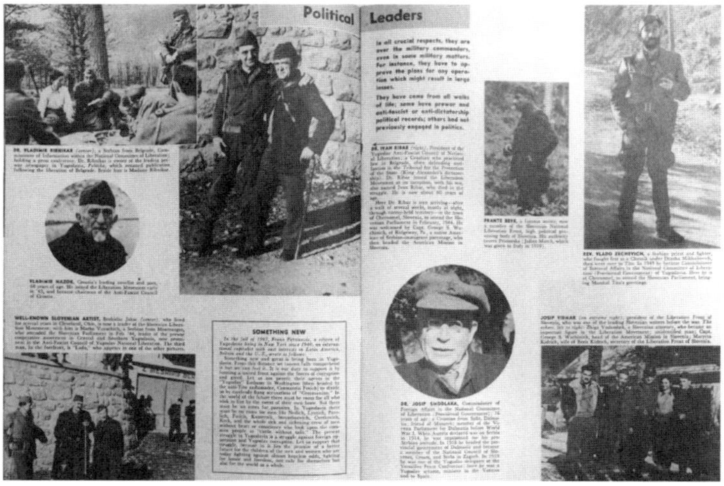

Double-page spread from Liberation, undated. Institute of Contemporary History, Ljubljana.

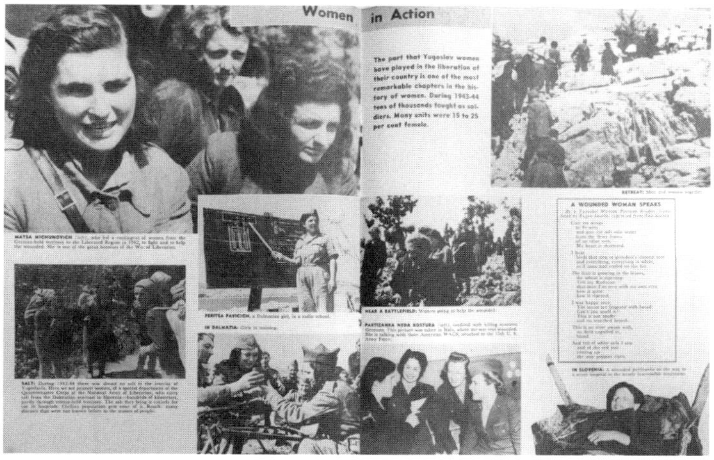

Women in Action

The part that Yugoslav women have played in the liberation of their country is one of the most remarkable chapters in the history of women. During 1943-44 tens of thousands fought as soldiers. Many units were 15 to 25 per cent female.

Inside spread from Liberation. Institute of Contemporary History, Ljubljana.

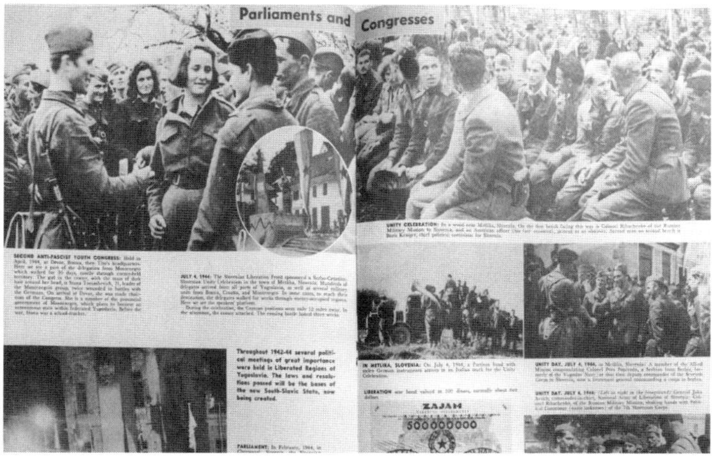

Parliaments and Congresses

Throughout 1942-44 several political meetings of great importance were held in Liberated Regions of Yugoslavia. The laws and resolutions passed will be the bases of the new South-Slavic State, now being created.

Inside spread from Liberation. Institute of Contemporary History, Ljubljana.

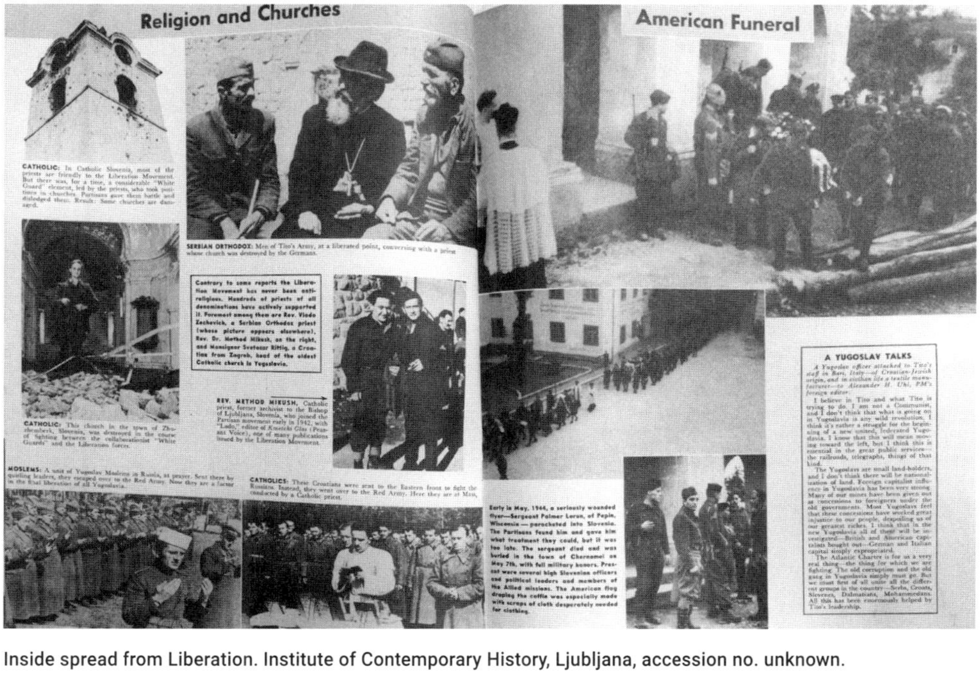

Religion and Churches

Contrary to some reports the Liberation Movement has never been anti-religious. Hundreds of priests of all denominations have actively supported it. Foremost among them are Rev. Vlado Zechevich, a Serbian Orthodox priest (whose picture appears elsewhere), Rev. Dr. Method Mikush, on the right, and Monsignor Svetozar Rittig, a Croatian from Zagreb, head of the oldest Catholic church in Yugoslavia.

REV. METHOD MIKUSH, Catholic priest, former archivist to the Bishop of Ljubljana, Slovenia, who joined the Partisan movement early in 1942, with "Lado," editor of *Kmetski Glas* (Peasant Voice), one of many publications issued by the Liberation Movement.

SERBIAN ORTHODOX: Men of Tito's Army, at a liberated point, conversing with a priest whose church was destroyed by the Germans.

American Funeral

Early in May, 1944, a seriously wounded flyer—Sergeant Palmer Loren, of Pepin, Wisconsin—parachuted into Slovenia. The Partisans found him and gave him what treatment they could, but it was too late. The sergeant died and was buried in the town of Chernomel on May 7th, with full military honors. Present were several high Slovenian officers and political leaders and members of the Allied missions. The American flag draping the coffin was especially made with scraps of cloth desperately needed for clothing.

A YUGOSLAV TALKS

Inside spread from Liberation. Institute of Contemporary History, Ljubljana, accession no. unknown.

Photographs of Partisan Life

At the beginning of the essay 'The Mass Ornament', the German cultural critic Siegfried Kracauer claimed that an epochs' position in the historical process can best be identified, not by that epoch's own judgements of itself, but by its 'surface-level expressions' which: 'provide unmediated access to the fundamental substance of the state of things. Conversely, knowledge of this state of things depends on the interpretation of these surface-level expressions. The fundamental substance of an epoch and its unheeded impulses illuminate each other reciprocally.'[1] We also find an abundance of these expressions on the photographic surfaces of images of Partisan life and leisure, materials that have so far been of little interest to historians and other researchers. These surfaces reflect a different reality than those preserved in the photographs of Nazi, Ustashe and Chetnik soldiers, whose bodies and outer appearance, especially in the case of the German SS and Wehrmacht, were strongly imprinted by ideology, as evidenced, for example, in the Hugo Boss design of their uniforms, their stylised gestures and their poses. In the case of the Germans, their ideology is also apparent in the political rituals and festivities in which their collective body was formed. As mentioned much earlier in chapter 2, the work of August Sander was notably one of the first picture publications to be censored in Nazi Germany. August Sander had opposed the Nazified collective body and permitted individuality, had torn to shreds the physiognomy-related myth about the superiority of the Aryan 'race', the so-called *Übermensch*. There was no place in Nazism for a typology of German society of the kind that Sander had spent years recording.

Partisan photography, on the other hand, established an often-unexpected contrast with the war environment in which it emerged. Indeed, in tone, it also offered a surprising contrast to the very real threat of elimination of the entire Partisan movement. Some of these photographs hint at a normality not present in wartime, as if such photographs wanted to deny the horrors of war and the history of the atrocities committed. Looking at the 'surface-level expressions' in photographs of Partisan life, we often see relaxed and smiling faces, scenes of happiness at the sight of the first snowfall or the chance to go bathing outdoors. The figures' bodies are relaxed and, despite the military uniforms, often individuated.

1 Siegfried Kracauer, *The Mass Ornament, Weimar Essays*, Cambridge, Massachusetts 1995, p. 75.

Photographs of Partisan life are also valuable because they offer us direct insights into how people lived in the temporary communities founded on liberated territory, the habits, the atmosphere, the relationship between the military and civilians, the first coordinated work actions, religious freedom and conscientious objection. If one delves beneath the surface of the photographs by analysing them more attentively, for instance by enlarging them, a great deal more can be revealed. One can uncover what Partisan food looked like, or try and decode the expressions on the screwed-up faces of children and the mien of people to whom fate had dealt a heavy blow.

In a sense, the photographs presented here can also be considered as an expanded family album. The familial angle certainly explains many of the recurring themes: marriages, childbirth, important events, anniversaries, funerals. Photographs also became cinematic sequences, templates for scriptwriters of documentary or experimental film. And the creator of the Partisan photography handbook, Milan Štok (see chapter 6), did indeed emphasise that Partisan photographers should record scenes from life, such as breakfast, exercise, sport, music and dance, sports matches, workshops, even soap factories. He even believed that photographers should especially record the ordinary side of life of Partisan officers, as there were not enough decent photographs of them. This all speaks to the thesis that the choice of Partisan themes and motifs was truly democratic. The photographs often exude the humour of the people behind the lens, too, or offer a direct commentary on their situation.

Certain photographs stand out for their visual appeal and thematic scope. Examples include pictures of people sleeping, people with animals, snowball fights, bathing – all activities that tease out moments of special happiness and joy.

This evening's experience was like a dream. The Fourth Battalion went to the baths at Toplice. I was in a lazy mood but not lazy enough not to join them. The journey took us through green fields and grass, now growing beautifully. Because of the difficult situation and the lack of cattle and workforce, the fields had barely been ploughed. [...] We arrived in Toplice where we found many comrades from our brigade. There were so many bathers, all happily surrendered to the pleasure of bathing. One of the comrades who had been there for longer led me to a special room with a bath. When I opened the door, I almost gasped. The whole room was shimmering from the white marble. I let out a laugh like a child, thinking that rich people had bathed here before, while today the poor Partisans were visiting. What a miracle![2]

Žorž Skrigin also wrote in his diary of a bathing experience:

We wanted to bathe here, as we hadn't even washed our legs for over a month. We chose a small spot where we could bathe in the nude. Our spirits were buoyed up even higher by the beautiful sunny day. We took our clothes off, splashing around in the shallow water. I thought the sheer pleasure of being in the water would never stop. But the next moment, over the hill a fighter plane suddenly appeared. We hadn't heard the sound of its engine at all. It immediately spotted us and like a sparrowhawk it dashed towards us, its machine gun blazing. We didn't even have time

2 Archives of the Republic of Slovenia, Ljubljana, AS 1887, Zbirka NOB tiska–brošure, 1062–1065.

to pick up our uniforms, and – as naked as the day we were born – made a run for the trees. The woodland there was sparse, which made us a fine target. To protect ourselves from our attacker, each one of us hid behind the thickest tree trunk we could find. And as the plane circled us, shooting, we went in circles around our tree, hugging it closely, as if by command. The pilot seemed to think it was funny that he had caught us all naked, and so he continued with his entertainment. And our 'tragedy' took on a new dimension, when we heard a guffaw from the woods – from a woman no less! Several of our female comrades, being more cautious, had managed to scramble to shelter and had been observing us the whole time! I don't know how much longer we would have kept going in circles around the tree trunks, like on some merry-go-round, had the pilot at some point not used up all his ammunition. He extended his arm outside the cockpit, making a Hitler salute. And having greeted us like this, he then made one more circle and departed.[3]

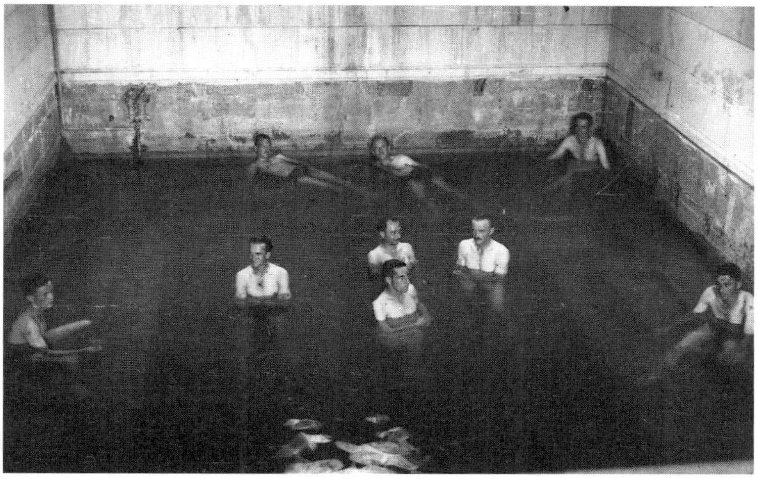

A group of severely injured fighters from a unit in the Ninth Notranjska Corps, Slovenia, September 1944. Photographer unknown. National Museum of Contemporary History of Slovenia, TN319/8.

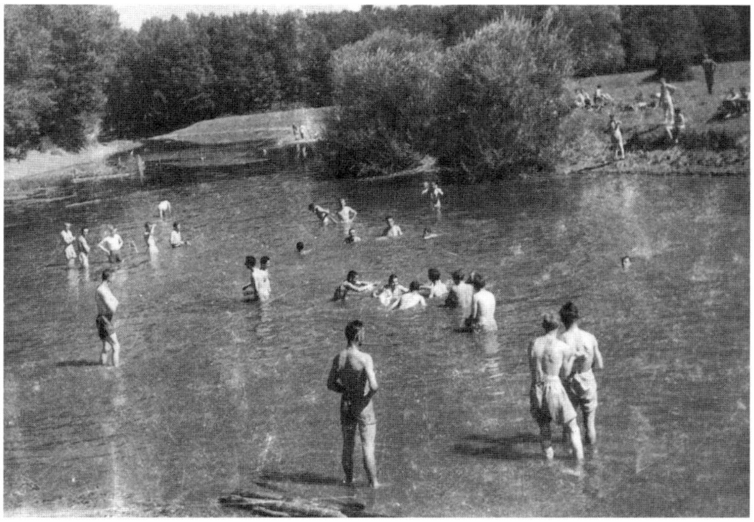

Bathing scene. Photographer unknown. Zagreb City Museum.

3 Žorž Skrigin, *Rat i pozornica*, Belgrade 1968, p. 207..

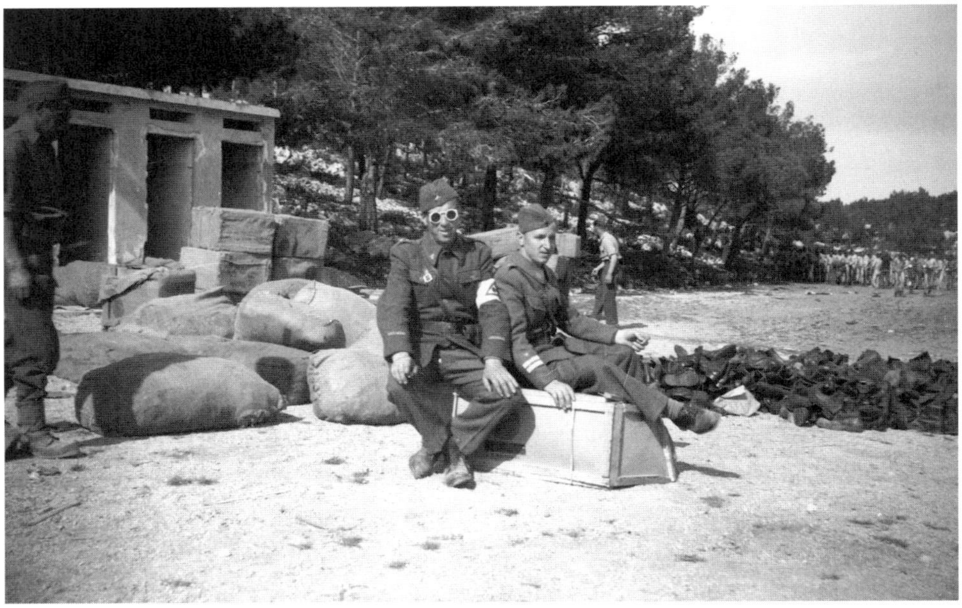

Fighters from a Macedonian brigade bathing before combat continues, Biograd na Moru, Croatia, April 1945. Photo: Peter Jelič. National Museum of Contemporary History of Slovenia, TN710/1.

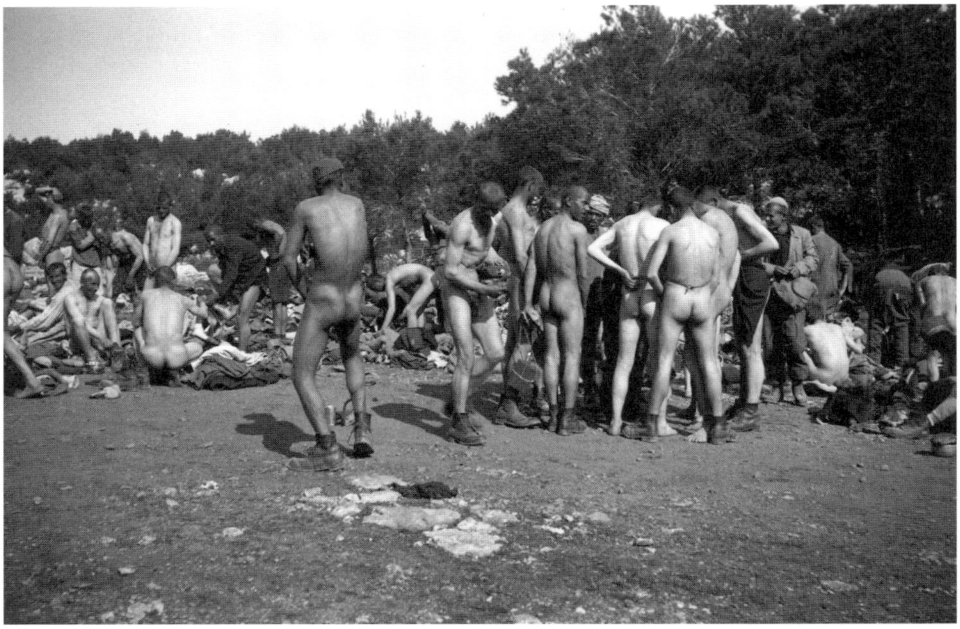

Fighters from a Macedonian brigade in Zadar, Croatia 1945. Photographer unknown. National Museum of Contemporary History of Slovenia, TN618/2.

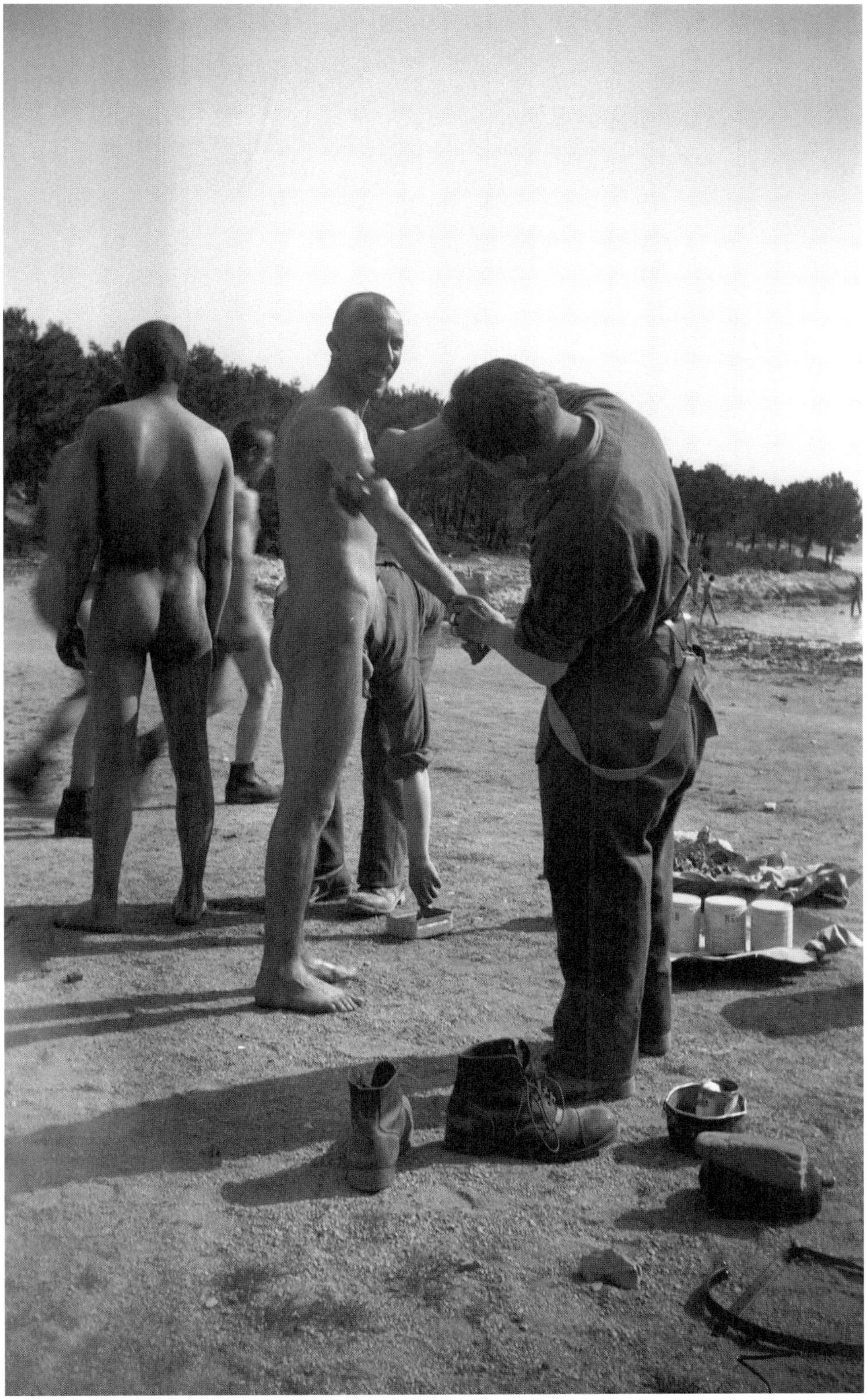

Fighters from a Macedonian brigade bathing before fighting resumes, Biograd na Moru, April 1945.
Photo: Peter Jelič. National Museum of Contemporary History of Slovenia, TN710/2.

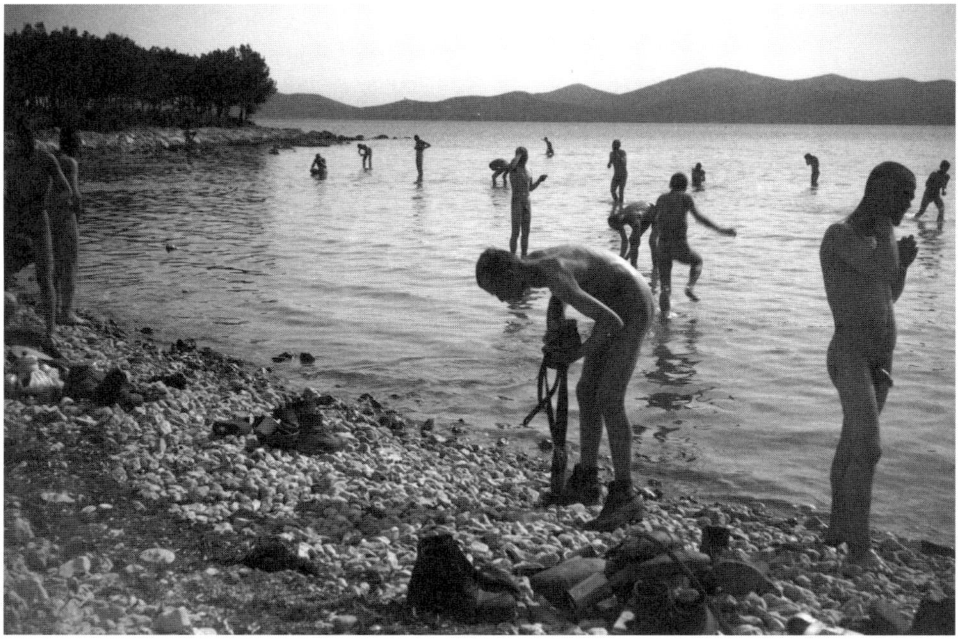

Fighters from a Macedonian brigade bathing before fighting resumes, Biograd na Moru, April 1945.
Photo: Peter Jelič. National Museum of Contemporary History of Slovenia, TN710/5.

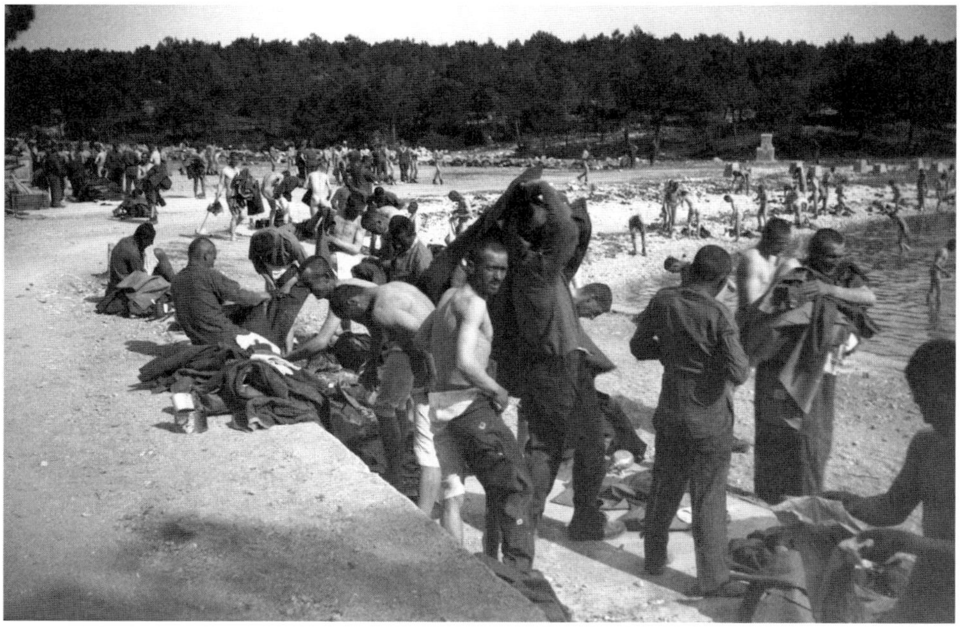

Fighters from a Macedonian brigade bathing before fighting resumes, Biograd na Moru, April 1945.
Photo: Peter Jelič. National Museum of Contemporary History of Slovenia, TN710/6.

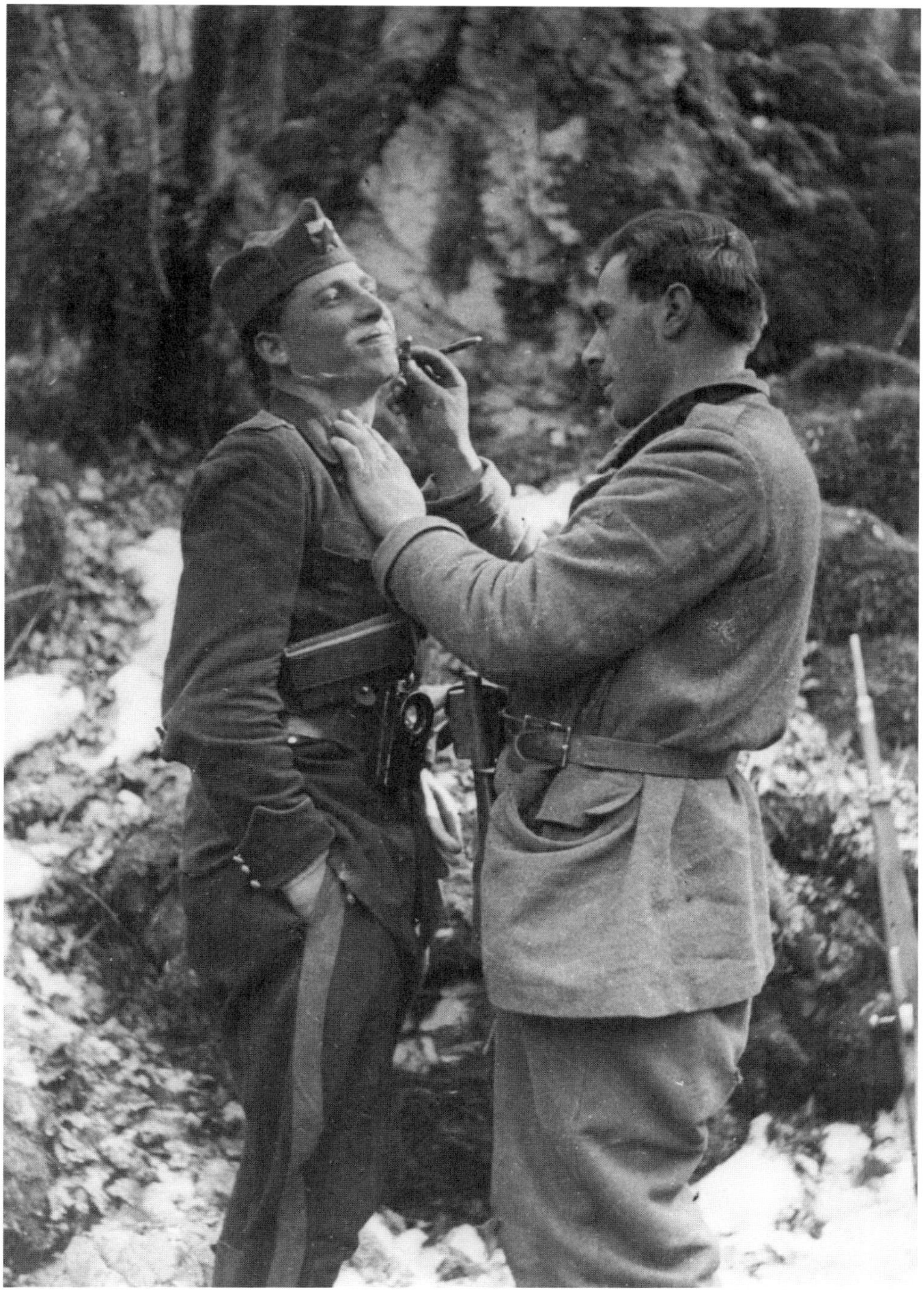

Inside the camp of the First Company of the First Battalion of the North Littoral Detachment at Dabar (Šentviška plateau, Slovenia), 3 April 1945. Photographer unknown. National Museum of Contemporary History of Slovenia, 5410/b.

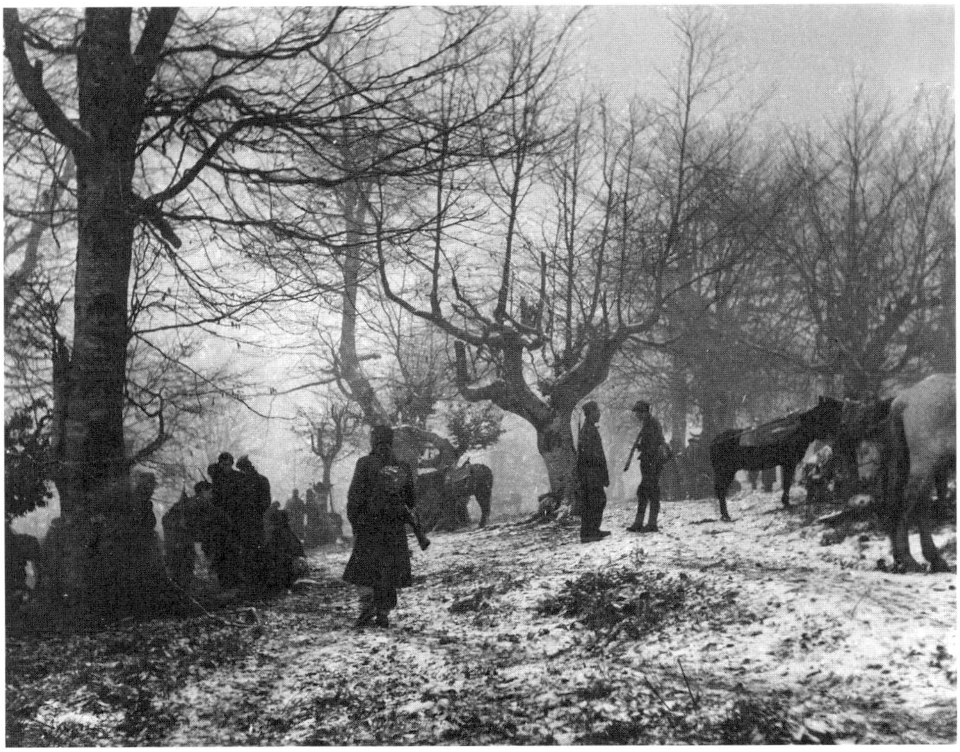

Frontier soldiers taking a short break, Kozara, Maslin Bajir peak, Bosnia and Herzegovina, Sixth Enemy Offensive, late 1943. Photographer unknown. Museum of Yugoslavia, III-1273.

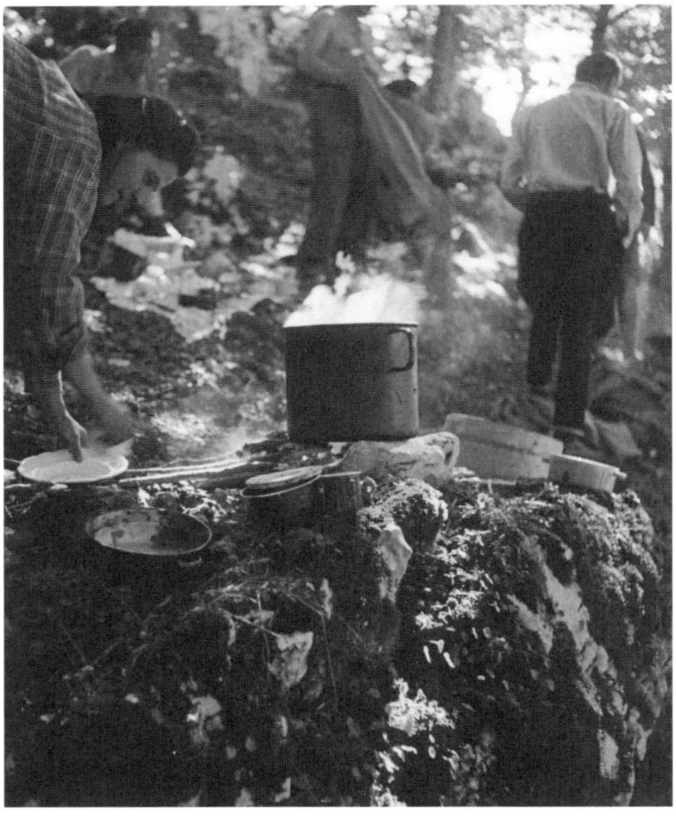

Preparing lunch for fighters in the People's Liberation War in Herzegovina, May 1943. Photographer unknown. Museum of Yugoslavia, III-3469.

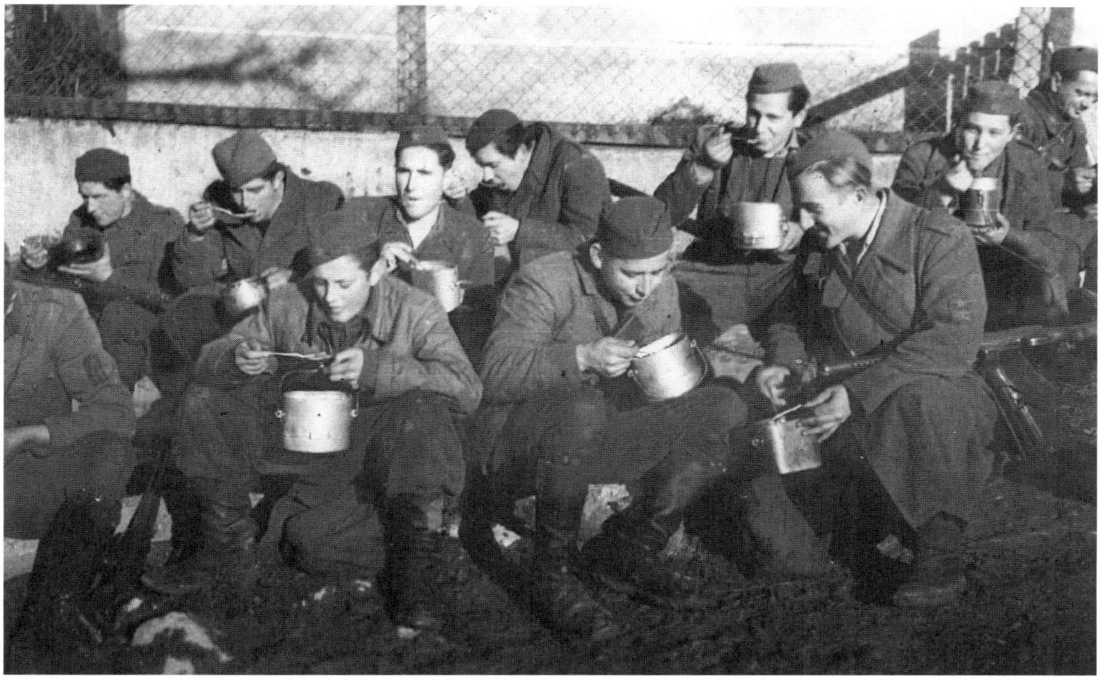

Members of Tomšič Brigade enjoying their rations in the settlement of Hinjah, Slovenia, 19 December 1943.
Photo: Miloš Brelih. National Museum of Contemporary History of Slovenia, TN53/40a.

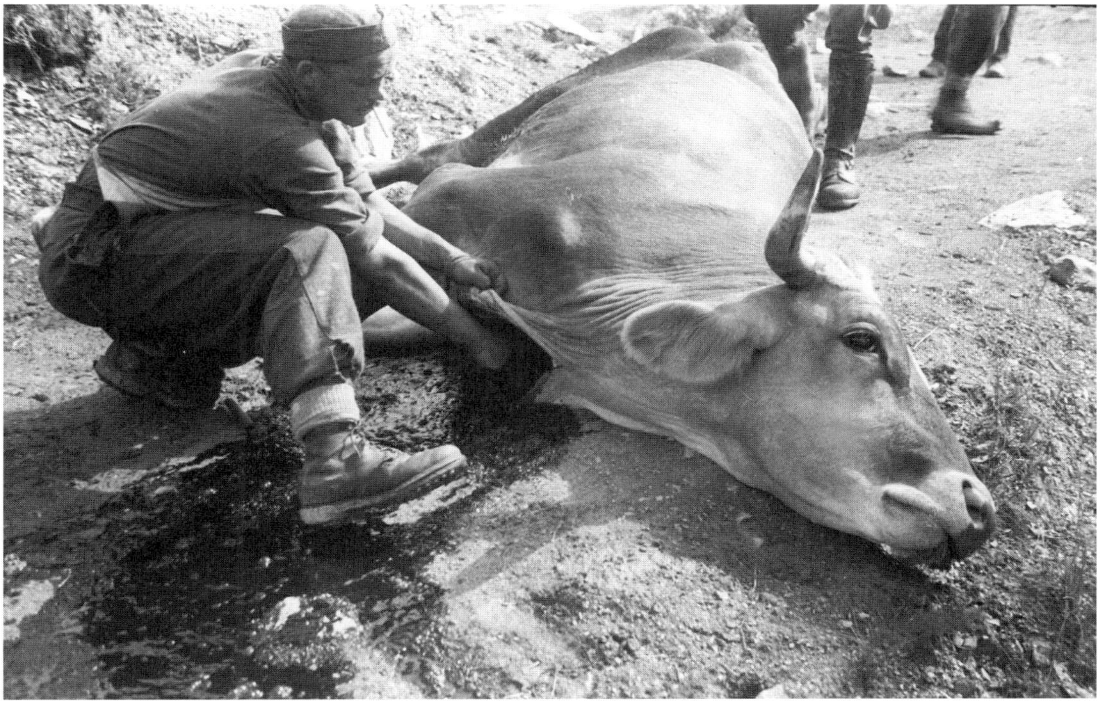

A butcher slaughtering a bull, Lokve, Slovenia, July 1944. Photo: Čoro Škodlar.
National Museum of Contemporary History of Slovenia, TN218/7.

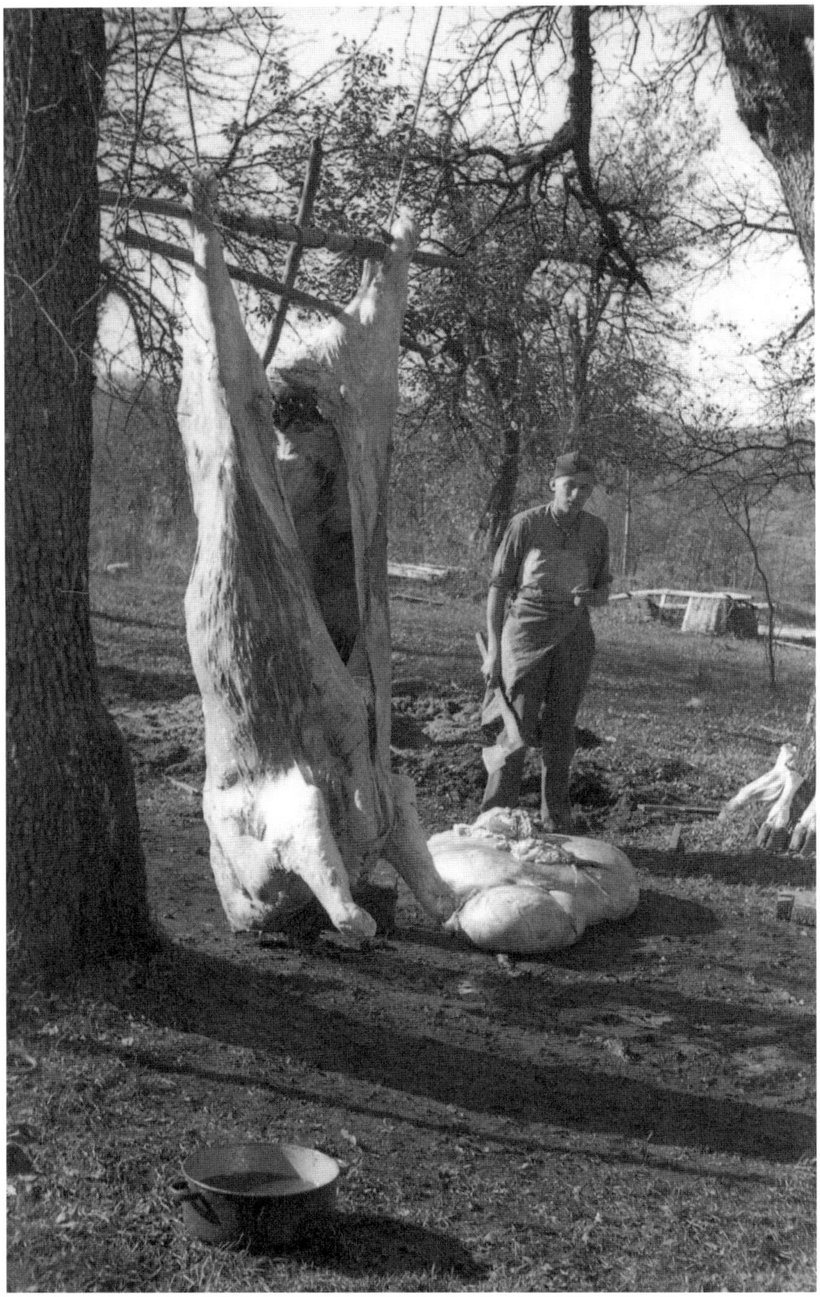

Hanging freshly slaughtered cattle in Komarna Vas, Slovenia, winter 1943–44.
Photo: Dr Janez Milčinski. National Museum of Contemporary History of Slovenia, 1227/5.

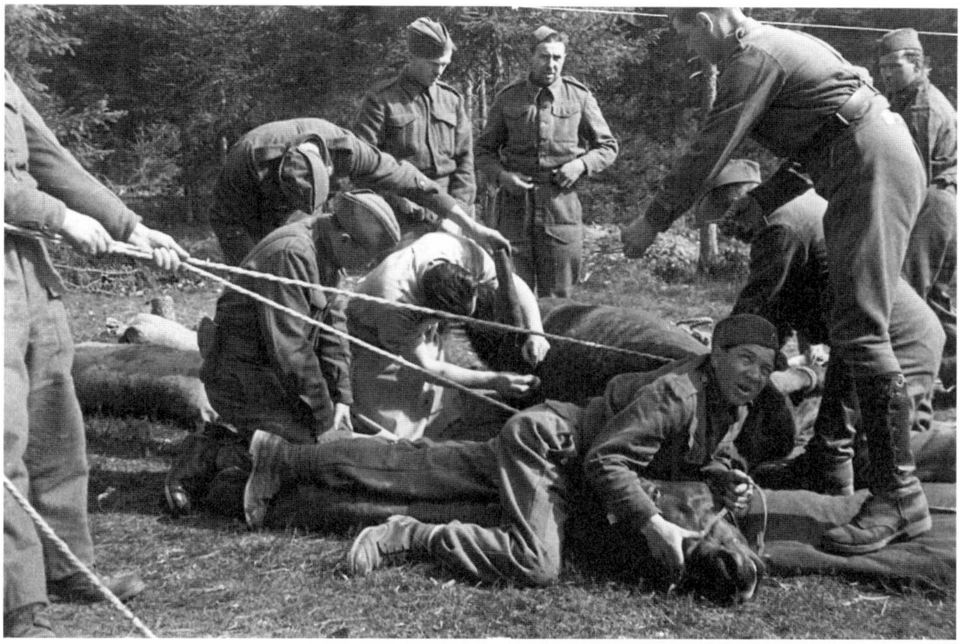

Operation on a horse, Kanižarica, Slovenia, April 1944. Photo: Franjo Veselko.
National Museum of Contemporary History of Slovenia, TN792/12.

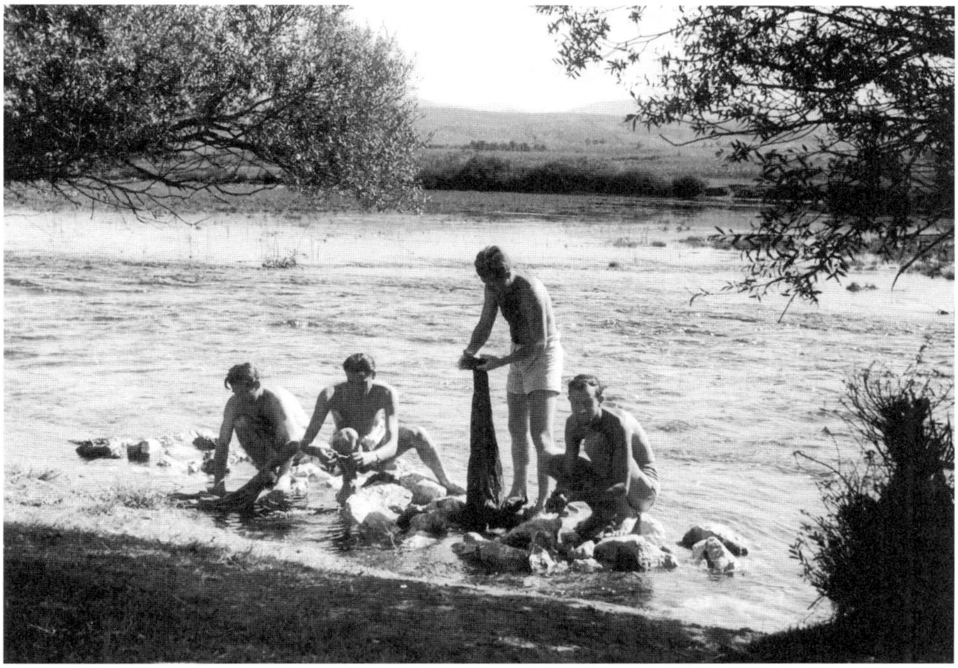

Pilots from the First Air Base of the NOV i POJ, washing clothes, Sanski Most, Bosnia and Herzegovina 1944.
Photographer unknown. Museum of Yugoslavia, III-3292.

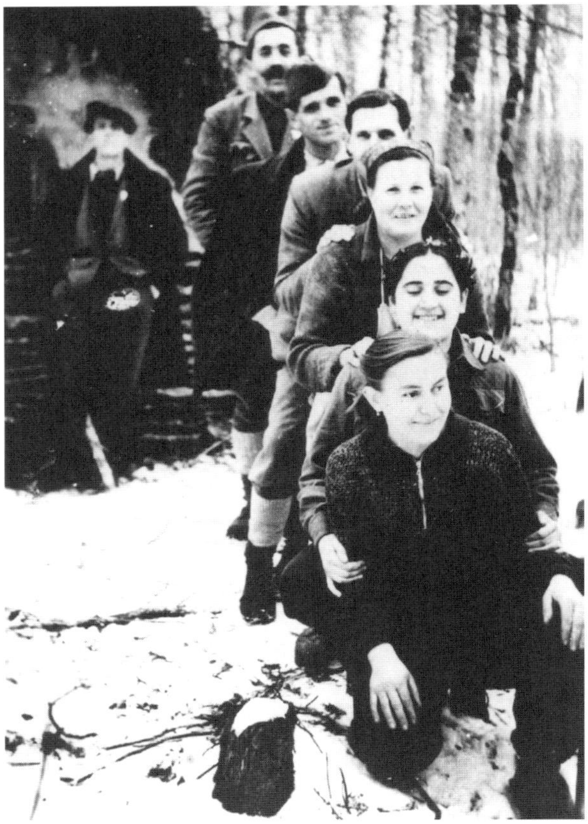

Members of the Tenth Zagreb Corps, February 1945. Photographer unknown. Zagreb City Museum.

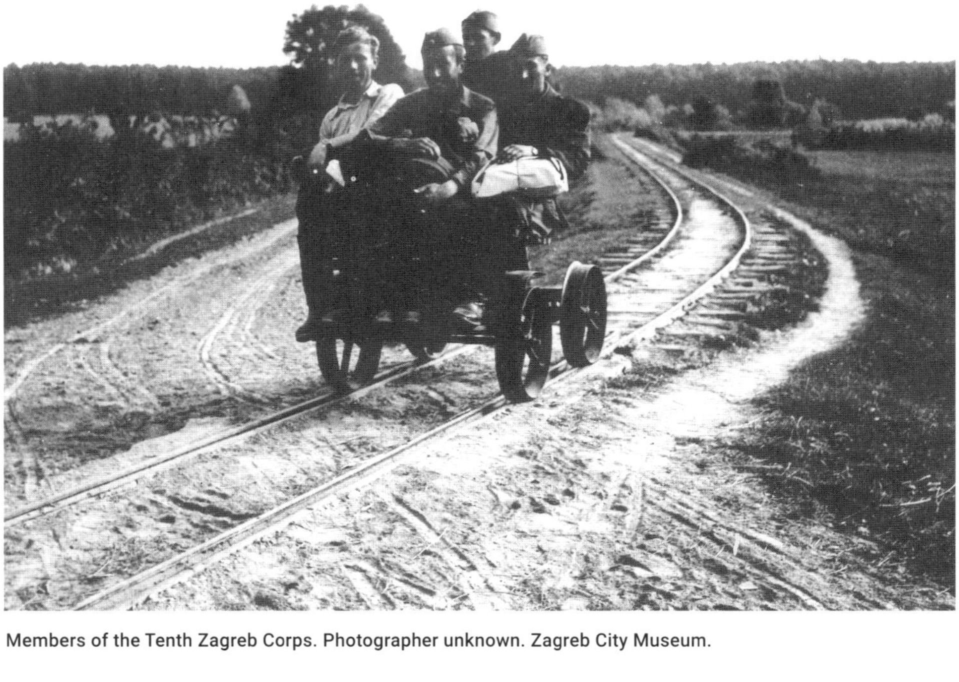

Members of the Tenth Zagreb Corps. Photographer unknown. Zagreb City Museum.

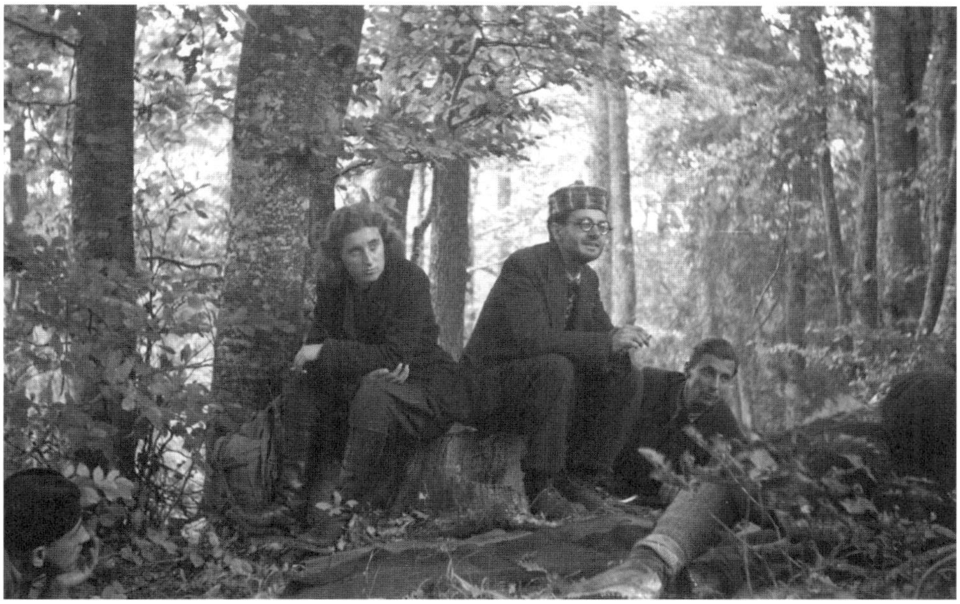

Members of Cankar Brigade, Dr Zwitter and wife Janja (centre), October 1943.
Photo: Franjo Veselko. National Museum of Contemporary History of Slovenia, TN45/11.

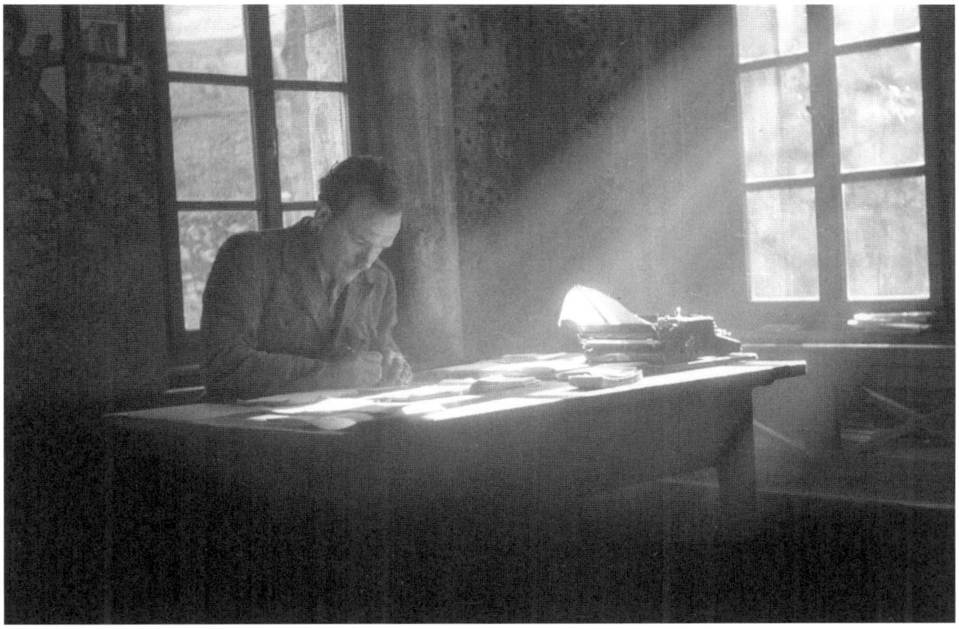

Unknown senior officer in Cankar Brigade, Dolž, February 1944. Photo: Franjo Veselko.
National Museum of Contemporary History of Slovenia, TN48/27.

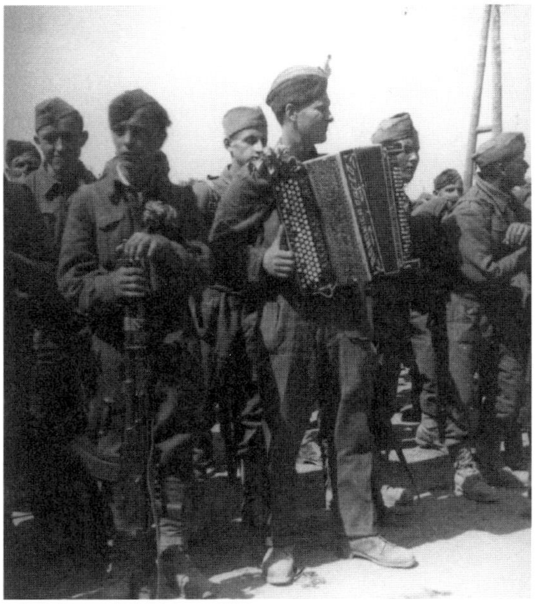

Fighters in the Fifth Overseas Brigade in Črnomelj, Slovenia, 1945. Photographer unknown. Museum of Recent History, Celje, FZ2B.

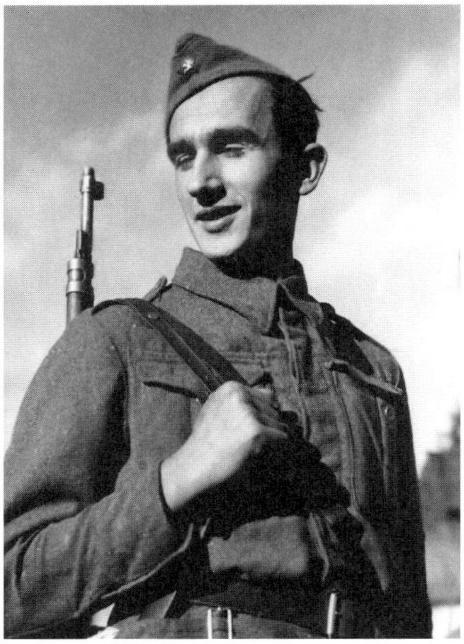

Gvozden Đukanić, fighter in the Supreme Command support company. Photographer unknown. Museum of Yugoslavia, III-433.

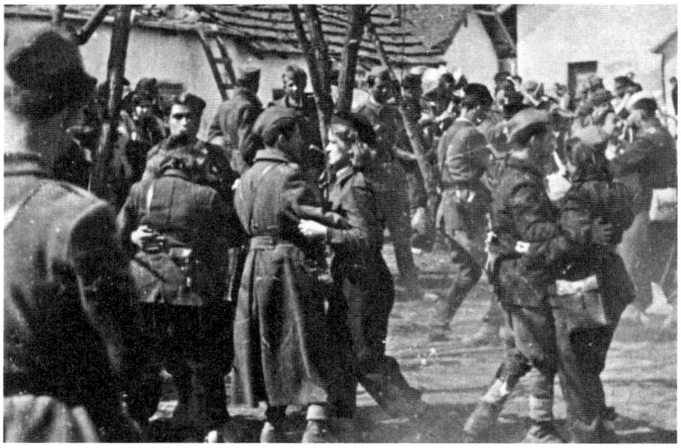

First Krajina Brigade enjoying a respite just before the battle to take Bijeljina, Šabac, Serbia, 1945. Photographer unknown. History Museum of Bosnia and Herzegovina, FNOB 17419.

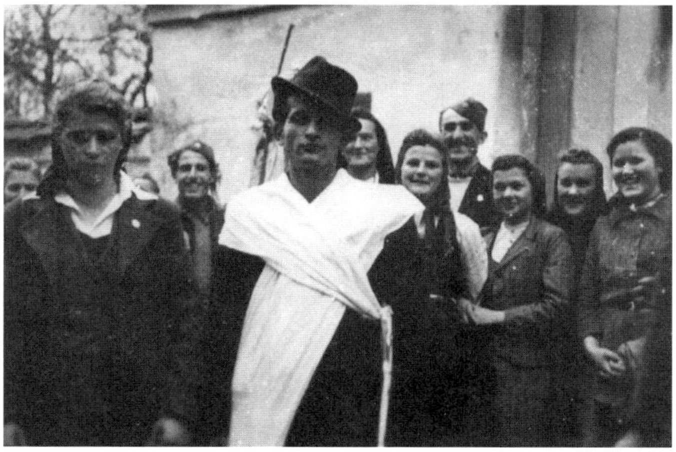

Partisan wedding in the village of Krasnić near Glina, Croatia. Photographer unknown. Croatian History Museum, HPM-MRNH-R-366.

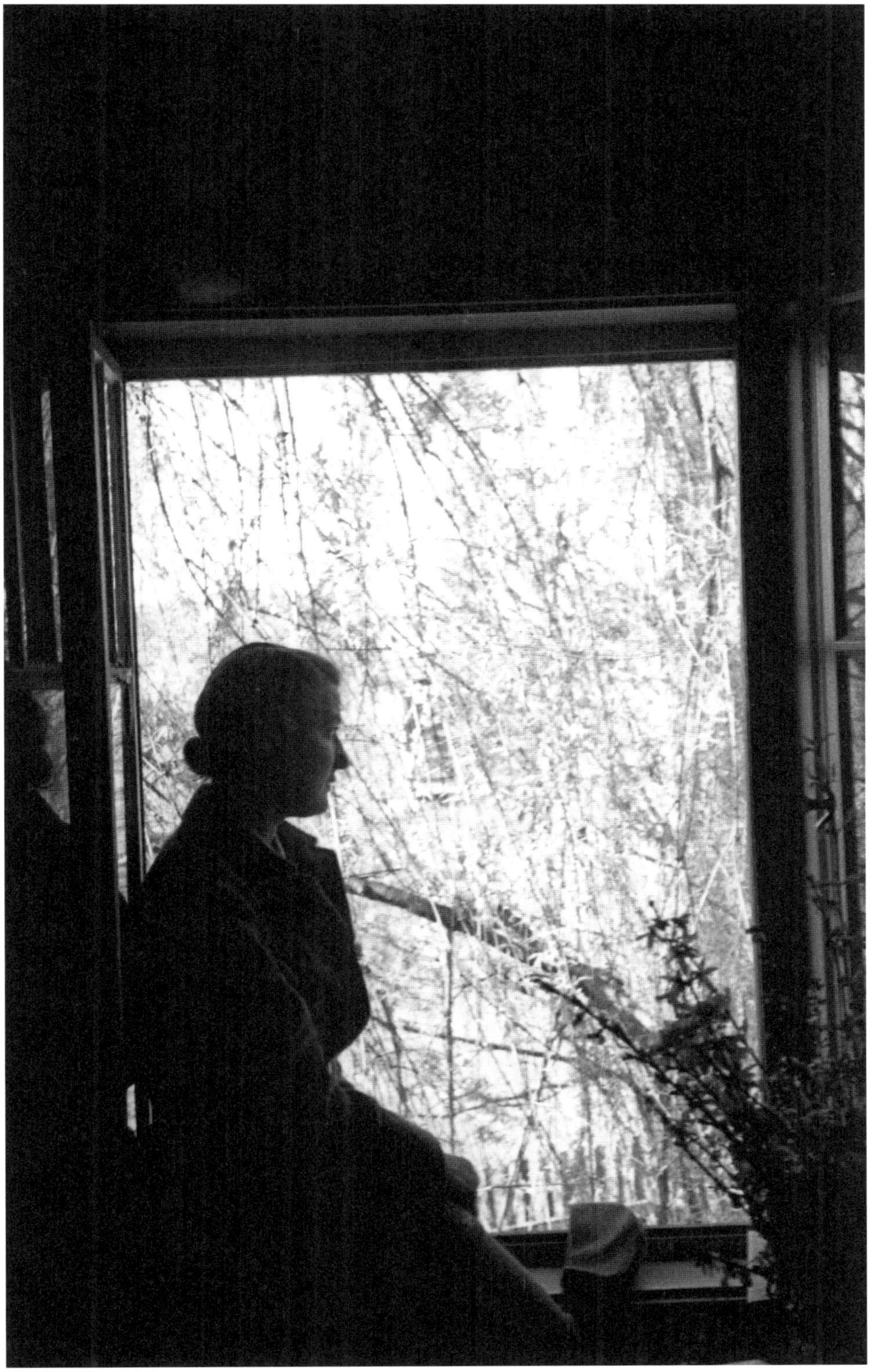

Vera Hreščak on her wedding day, Vojna vas, Slovenia, 3 April 1945. Photo: Stane Lenardič.
National Museum of Contemporary History of Slovenia, TN728/8.a.

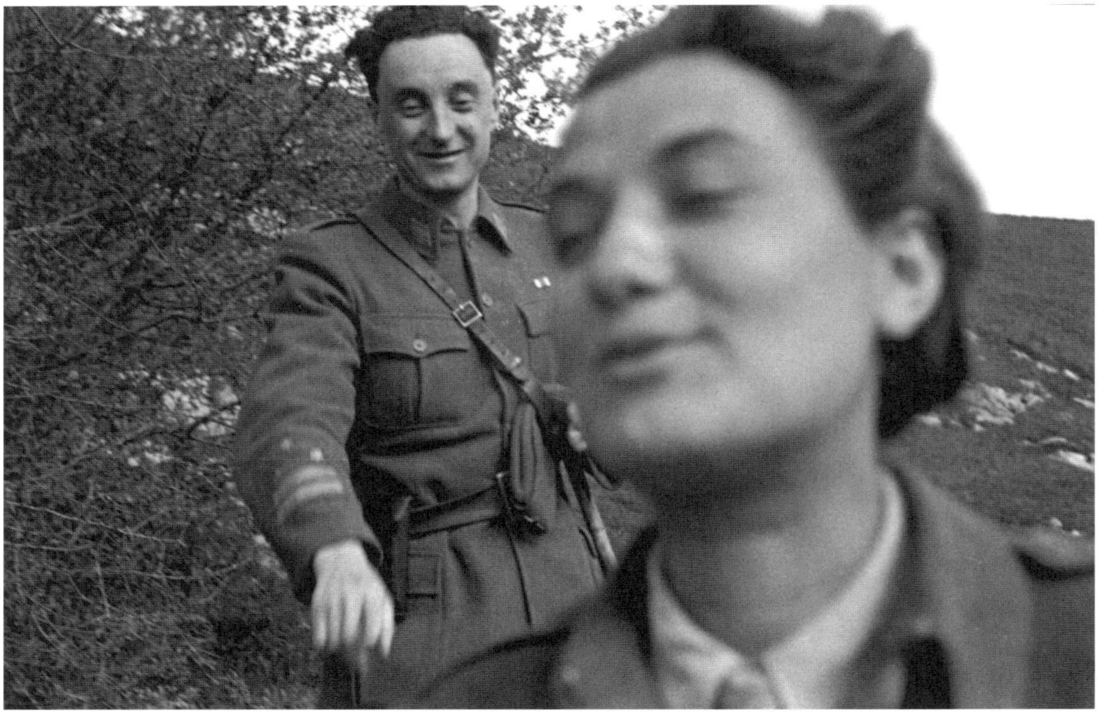

Vera Hreščak and Aleša Beblerja on their wedding day, Vojna vas, Slovenia, 3 April 1945. Photo: Stane Lenardič.
National Museum of Contemporary History of Slovenia, TN728/28.

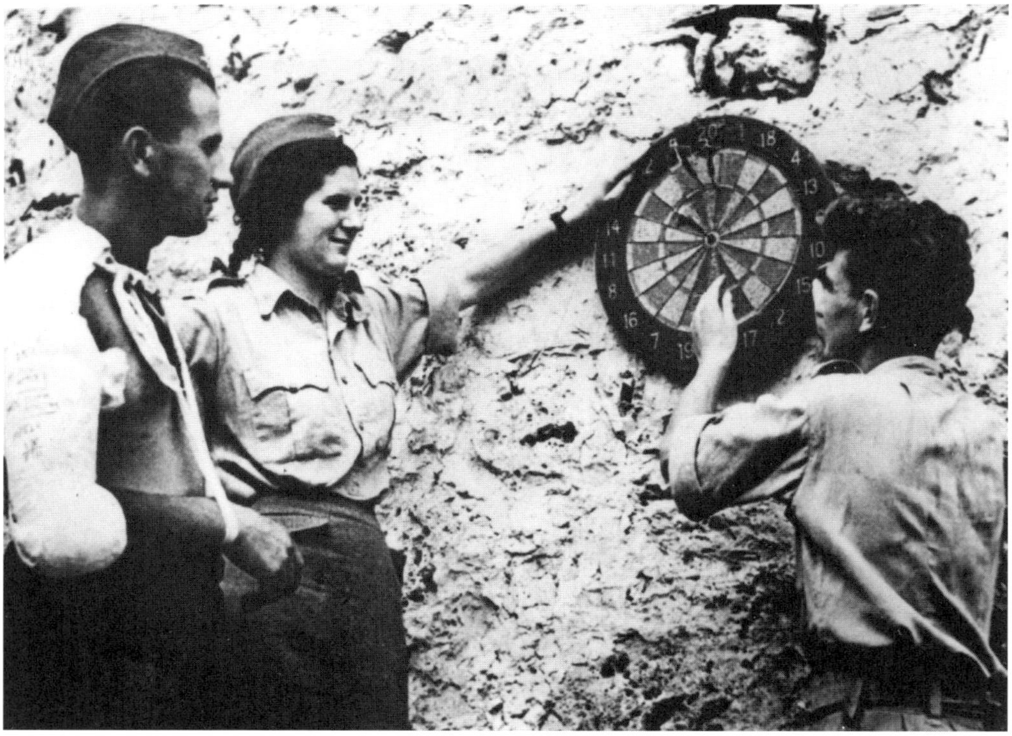

Two nurses relaxing with a patient, playing darts, 1944. Photographer unknown.
History Museum of Bosnia and Herzegovina, FNOB 1349.

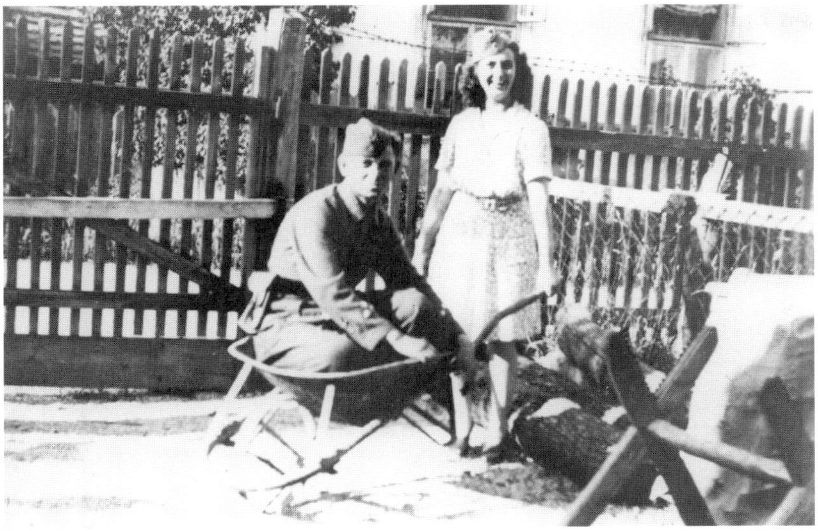

'Leading the charge on Zagreb' – light-hearted caption to a scene showing a Third Company sergeant and unknown woman, 1945. Photographer unknown. Zagreb City Museum, TN45/11.

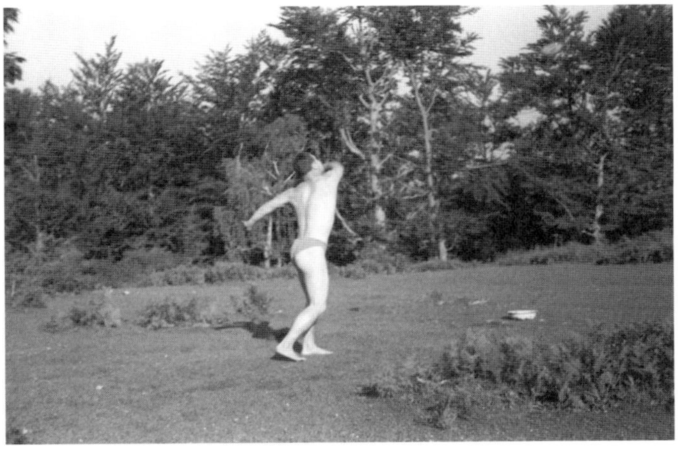

Leader of physical training in the Thirteenth Primorje-Gorenje Division, a trained athlete named Šoić, 1944. Photographer unknown. Croatian History Museum, HPM-MRNH-A-2603-f14 030.

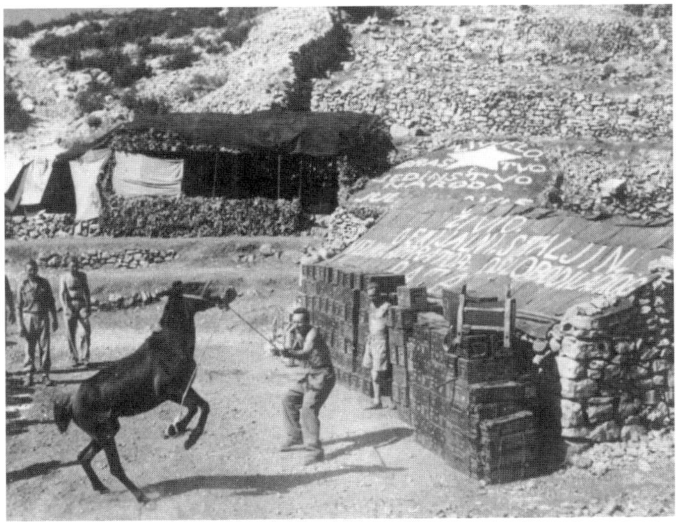

Breaking in a horse in a Partisan unit, Vis, 1944. Photographer unknown. Source unknown.

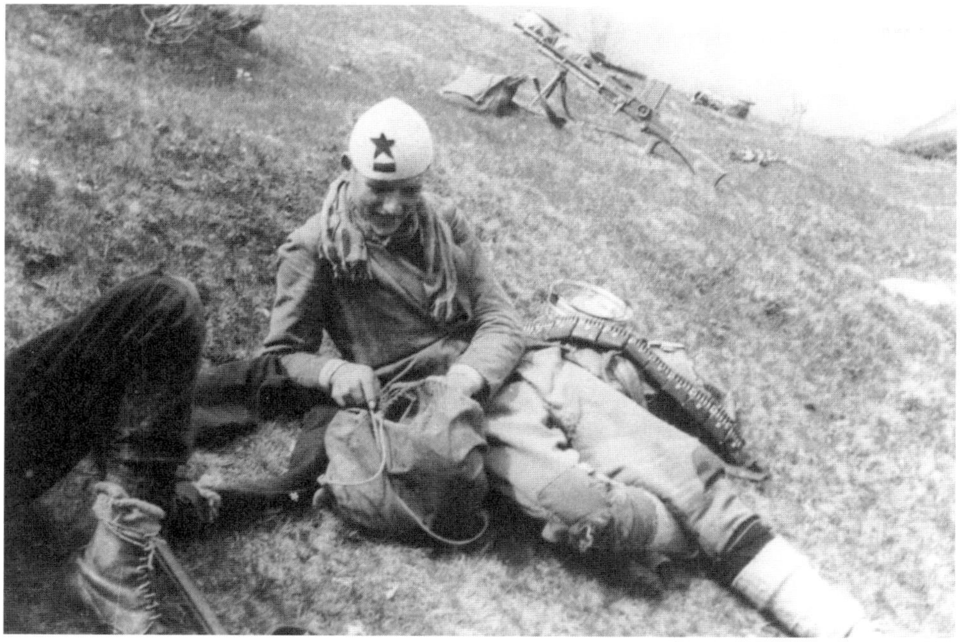

Fighters from the Šara Mountain Partisan Detachment, Mount Šara, 1943. Photographer unknown.
Military Museum Belgrade, 1295.

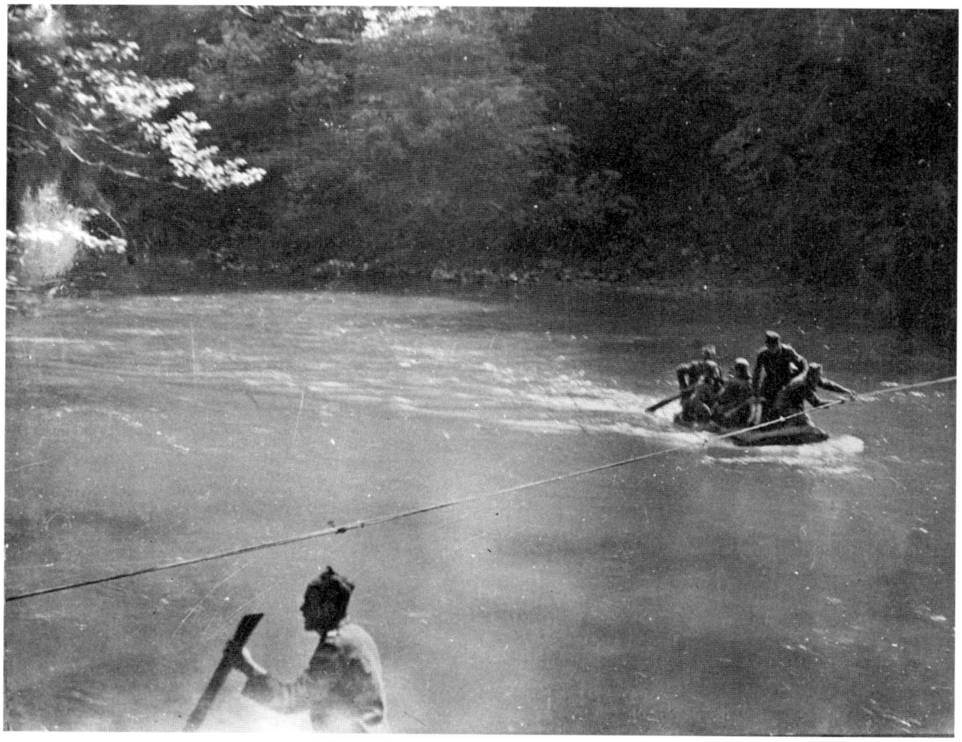

The Second Proletarian Division crossing the river Piva, 1943. Photographer unknown.
History Museum of Bosnia and Herzegovina, FNOB 17737.

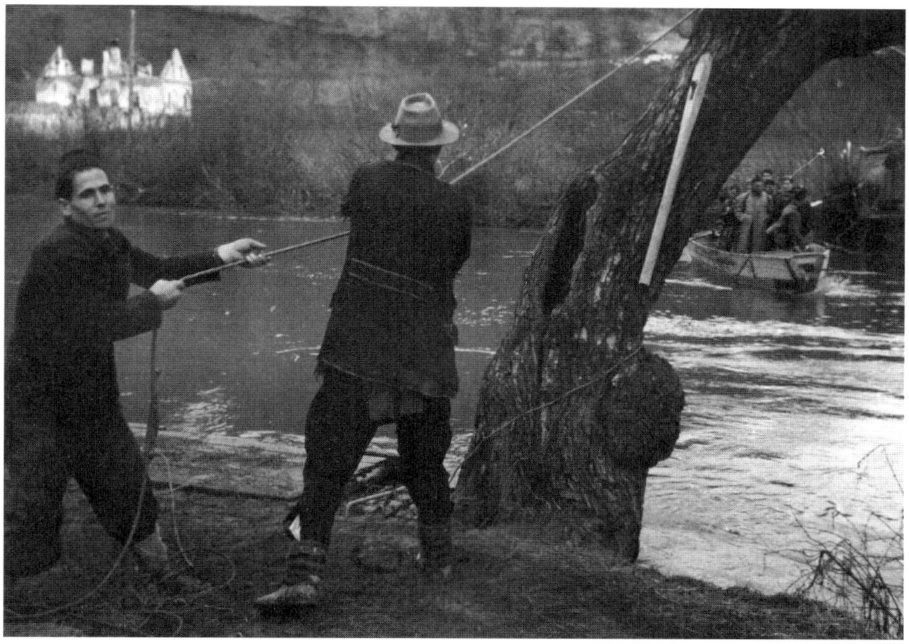

Delegates returning from the Second Session of the AVNOJ, crossing the river Sanica at Ključ, Bosnia and Herzegovina. Photographer unknown. Museum of Yugoslavia, accession no. unknown.

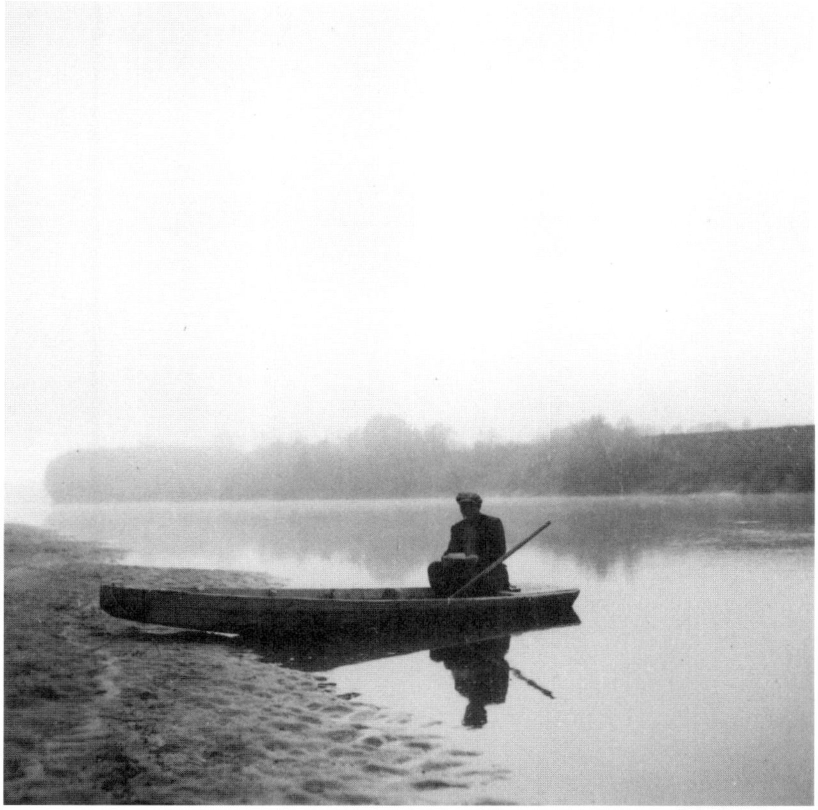

The boatman Đuro Jambrek after transporting Partisans over the Kupa, Croatia. Photo: Emil Vičić. Croatian History Museum, HPM/MRNH-F-4069.

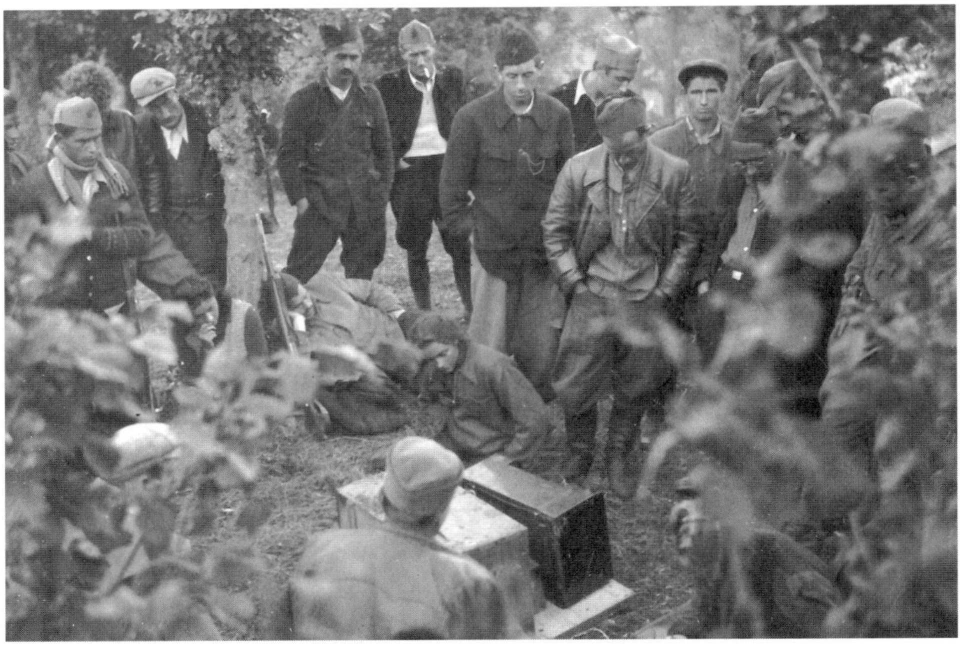

Fighters from the Fourth Montenegrin Brigade listening to a news broadcast during the Battle of Sutjeska, 1943. Photographer unknown. Military Museum Belgrade, 4394.

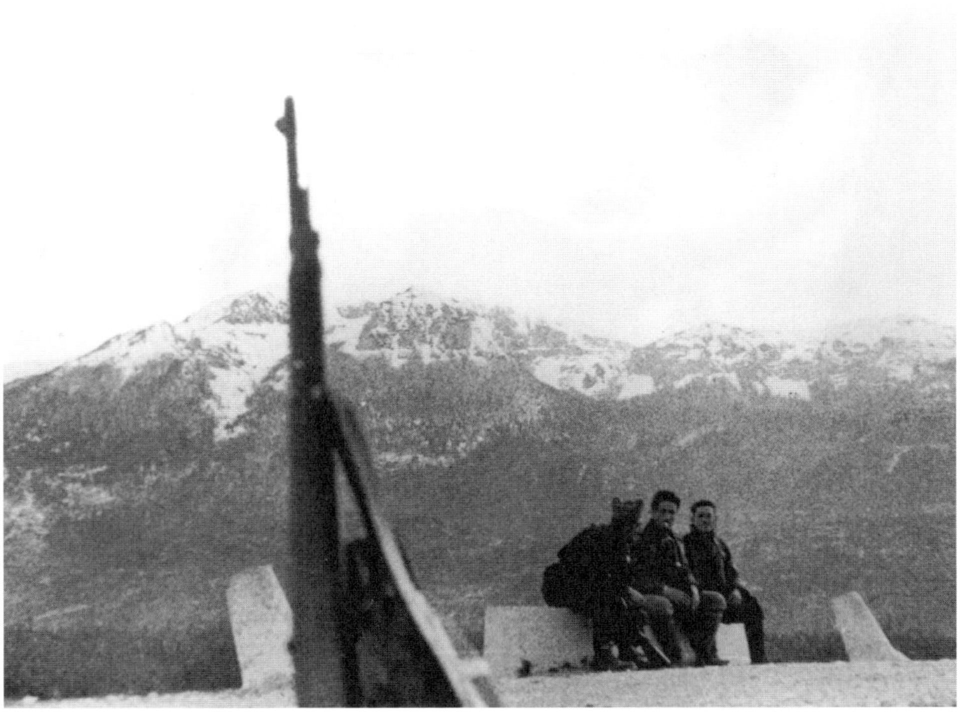

The first couriers operating between the Dalmatian and Krajina Detachments, taking a break in Livanjsko polje with Mount Troglav in background, Bosnia and Herzegovina, May 1942. Photographer unknown. Published in Crveno Zvezda (Red Star), 7 June 1956, History Museum of Bosnia and Herzegovina, FNOB 10843.

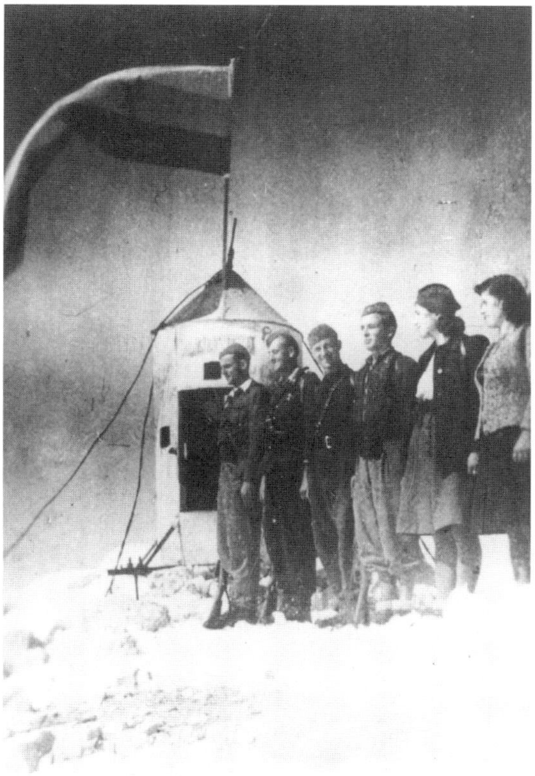

The third temporary route up Mount Triglav, Slovenia, October 1944. Photo: Bogo Tavčar. National Museum of Contemporary History of Slovenia, 2214/1.

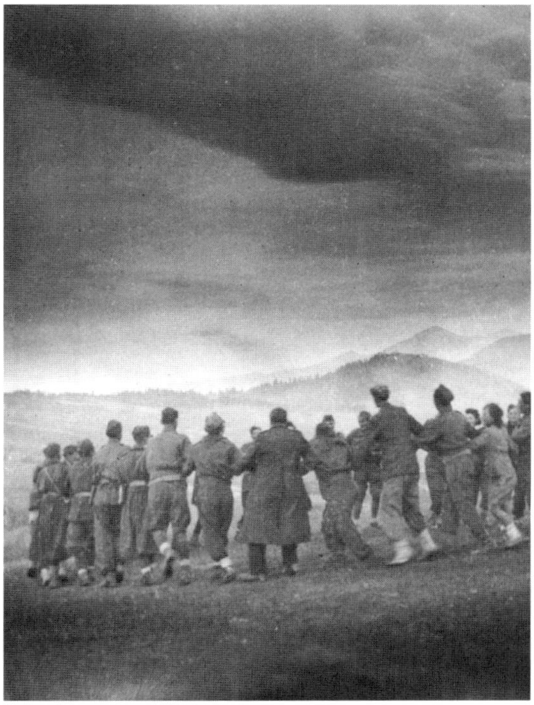

Folk dancing in uniform. Photographer unknown. History Museum of Bosnia and Herzegovina, FNOB 207.

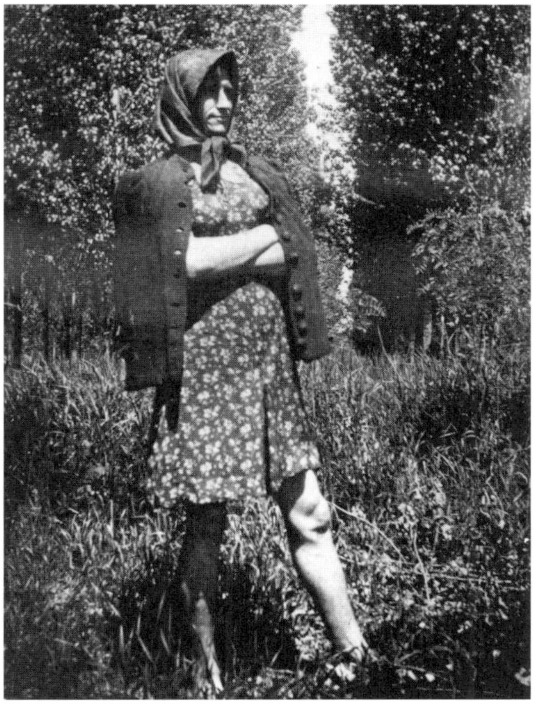

Underground agent Lazar Tešić disguised as a woman, Tuzla. Photographer unknown. History Museum of Bosnia and Herzegovina, FNOB 14741.

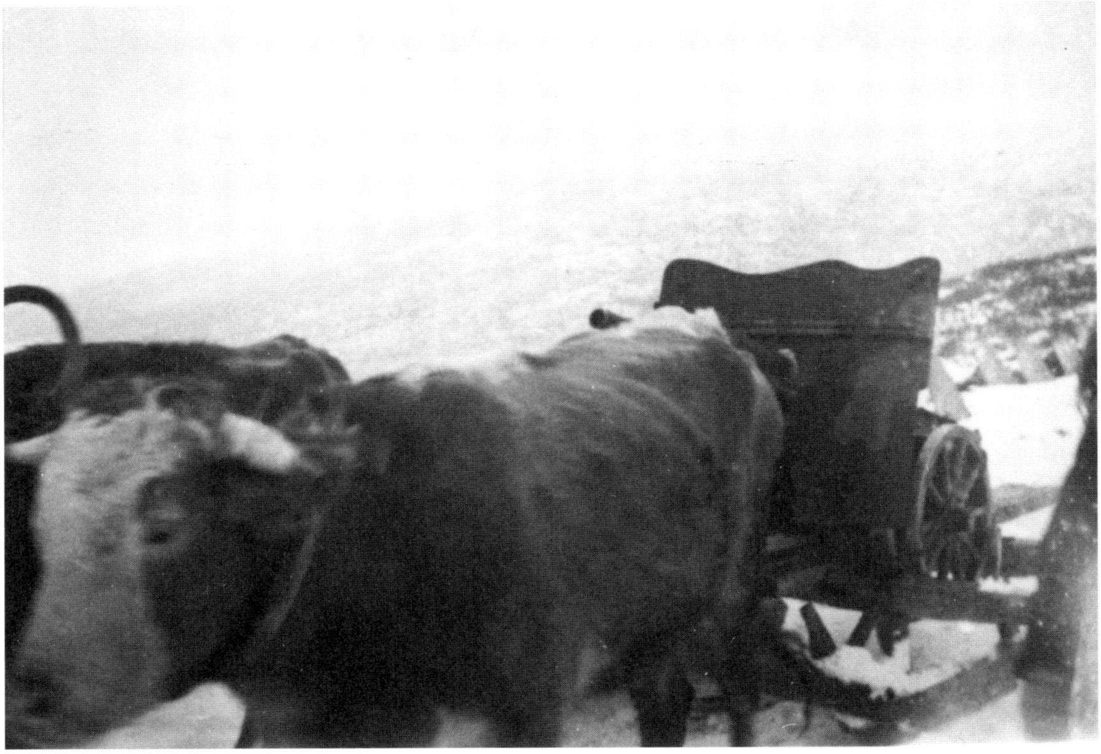

Oxen pulling the first flak artillery sent by Supreme Command to Podgora to defend the Adriatic coast, Korićani, between Glamoč and Livno, 17 January 1943. Photographer unknown. History Museum of Bosnia and Herzegovina, FNOB 14533.

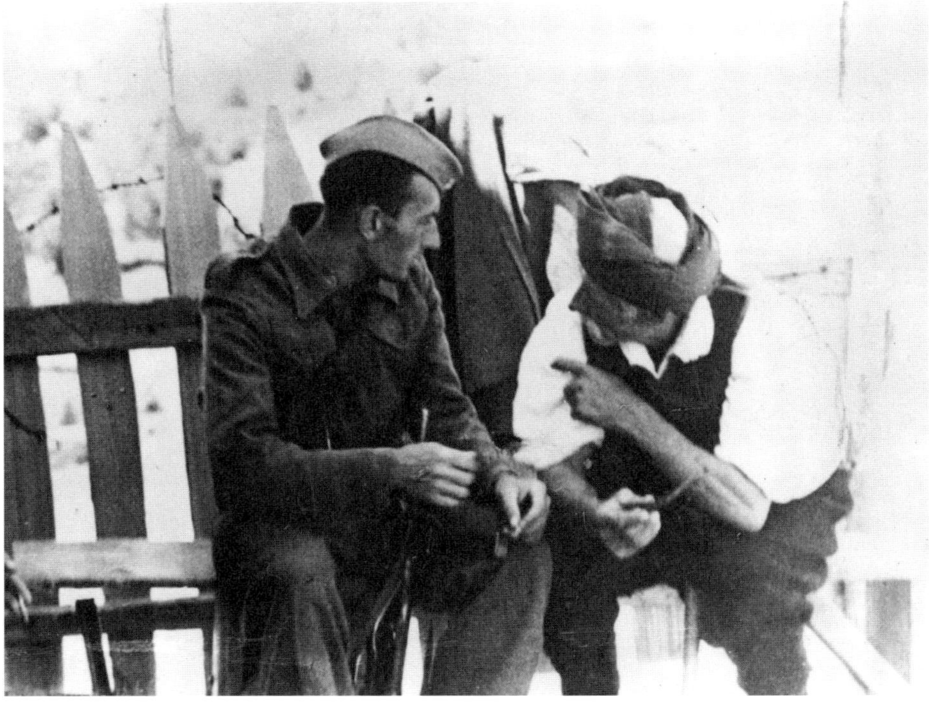

A meeting between father and son, outside Tuzla, 1943. Photographer unknown. History Museum of Bosnia and Herzegovina, FNOB 16418.

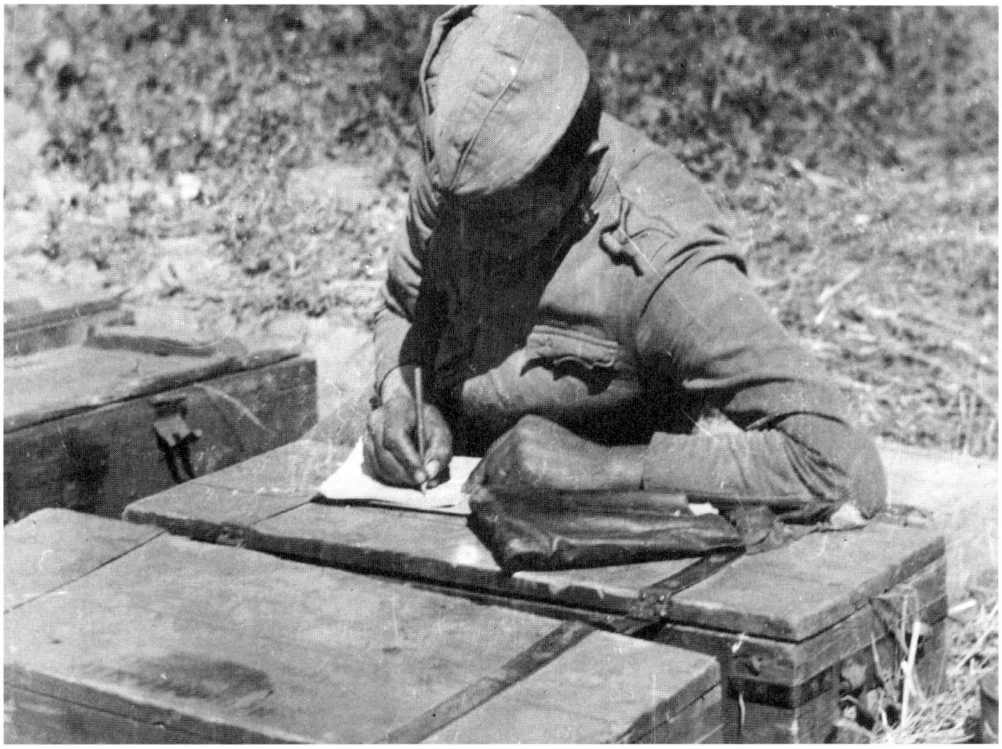

Fighter from the First Krajina Brigade writing a letter to family on a break, Srijemski (Syrmian) Front, an Axis line of defence, final weeks of war, 1945. Photographer unknown. History Museum of Bosnia and Herzegovina, FNOB 18856.

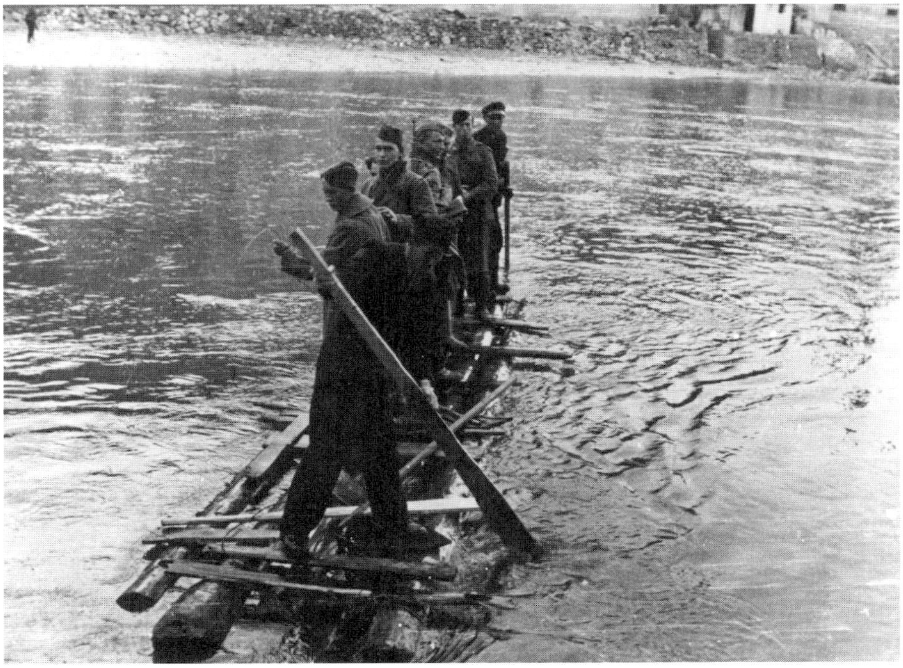

Members of Second Herzegovina Brigade crossing to left bank of the river Neretva on a makeshift raft, Konjic, Bosnia and Herzegovina, 18 February 1945. Photographer unknown. History Museum of Bosnia and Herzegovina, FNOB 16695.

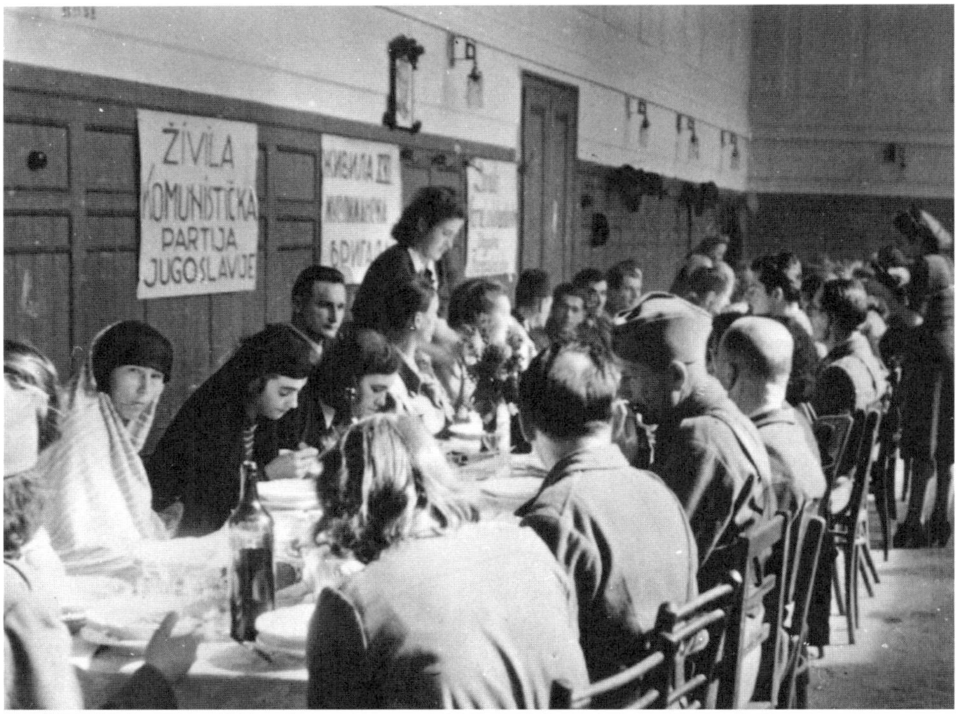

Celebrations marking anniversary of the founding of the Sixteenth Muslim Brigade, 21 September 1944. Photographer unknown. History Museum of Bosnia and Herzegovina, FNOB 17201.

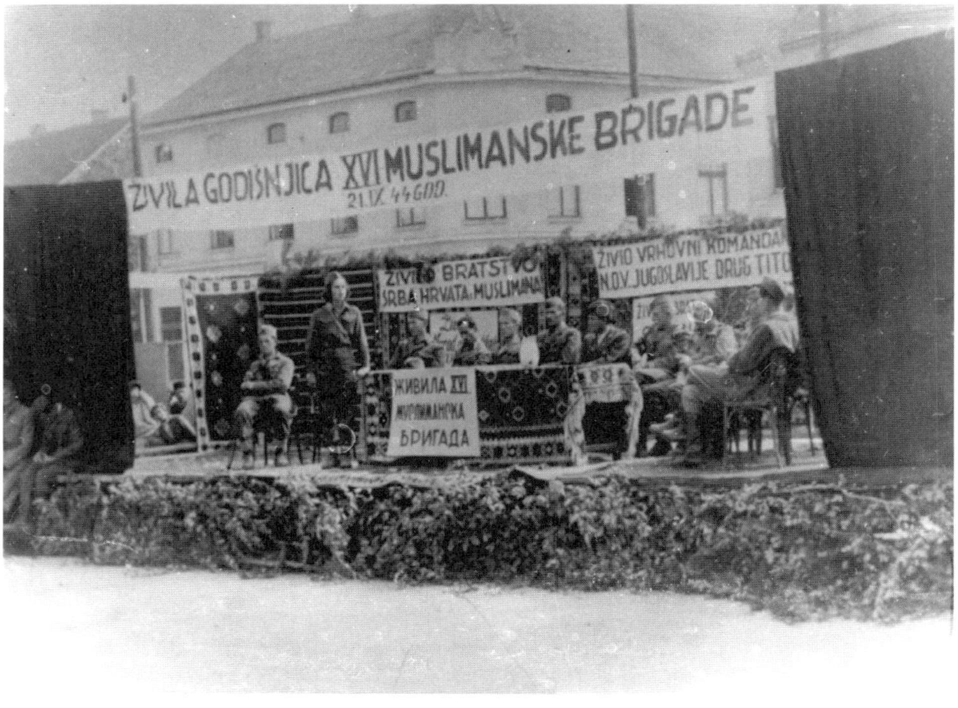

Celebrations marking anniversary of the founding of the Sixteenth Muslim Brigade, 21 September 1944. Photographer unknown. History Museum of Bosnia and Herzegovina, FNOB 17202.

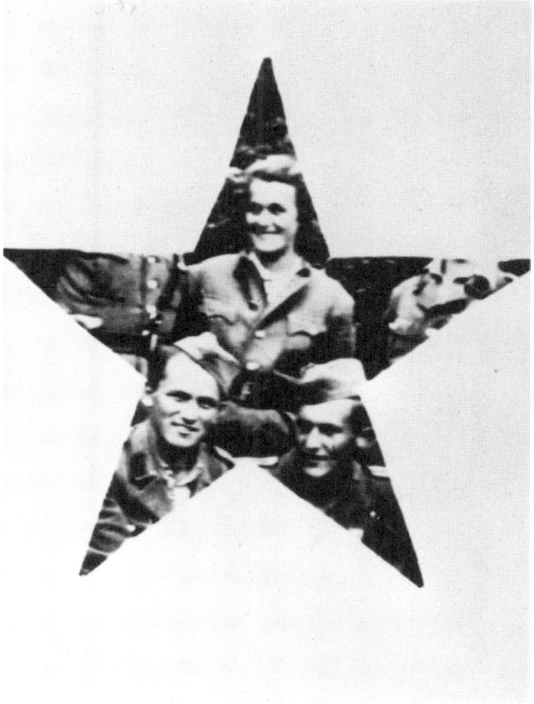

Fighters from the Twelfth Krajina Brigade. Photographer unknown. History Museum of Bosnia and Herzegovina, FNOB 18689.

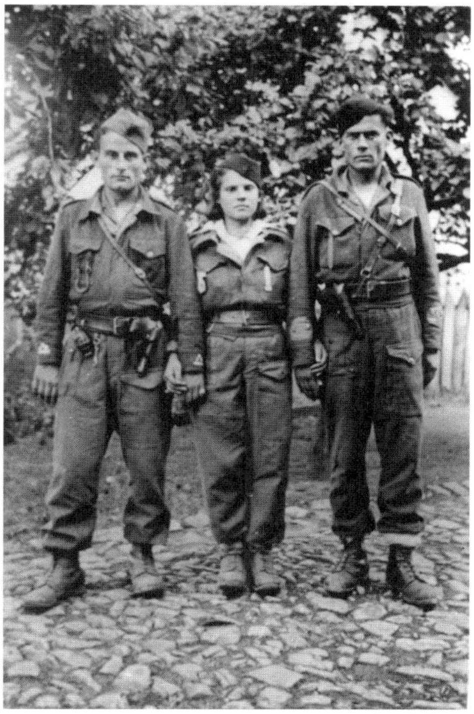

Nikola Kalanj, nurse Fatima Hanzić and battalion commander Nikola Lučić from the Third Krajina Brigade of the Third Battalion. All three lost their lives just weeks before the end of the war, in March 1945, in Dragaljevac Donji near Bijeljina, Bosnia and Herzegovina. Photographer unknown. History Museum of Bosnia and Herzegovina, FNOB 18080.

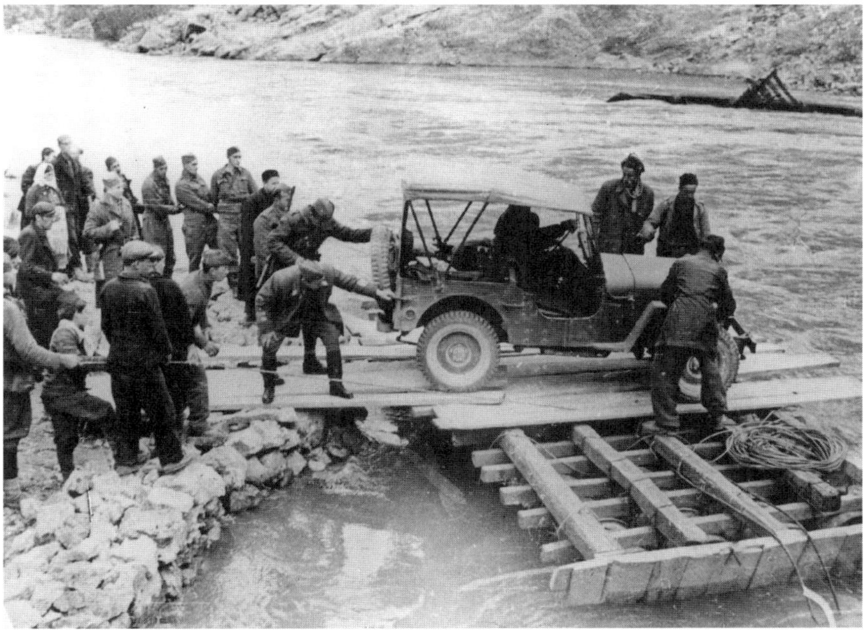

Moving a jeep across the river Neretva on a newly built raft. Photographer unknown. History Museum of Bosnia and Herzegovina, FNOB 18198.

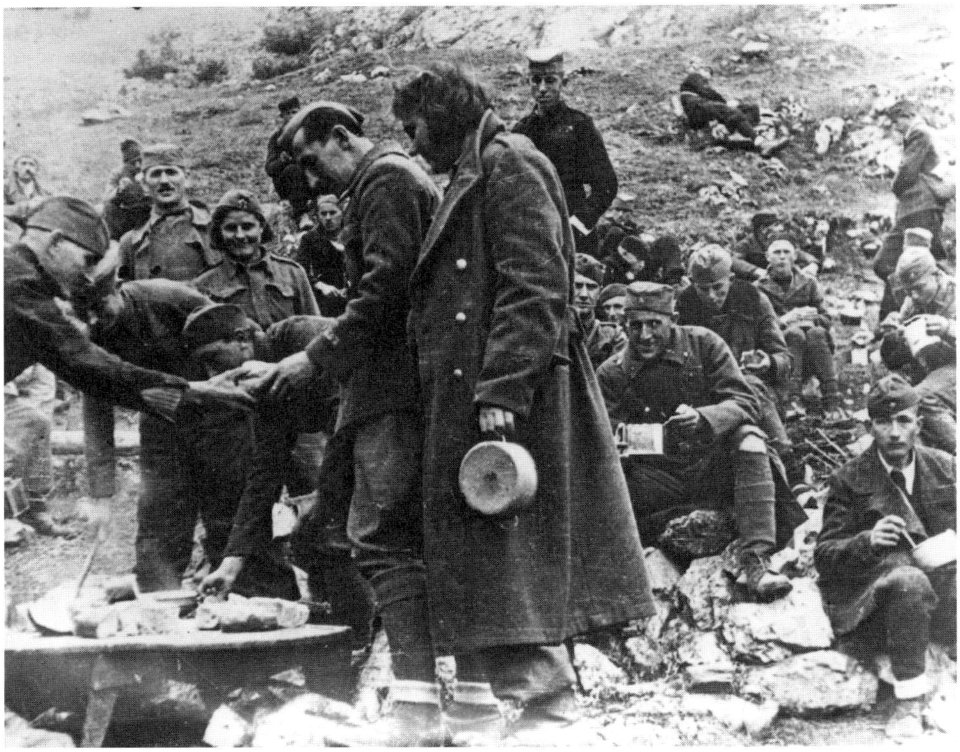

Lunch being dished out on the red rock slopes of Trnovo, near to firing positions during the liberation of Sarajevo, late March 1945. Photographer unknown. History Museum of Bosnia and Herzegovina, FNOB 18748.

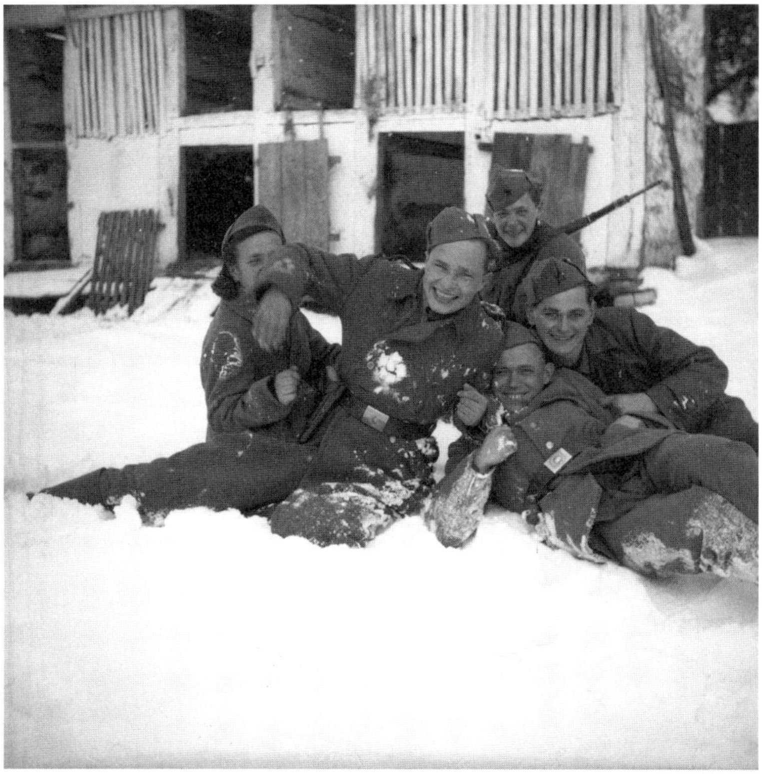

Unknown Partisans in the snow. Photo: Photography unit of the District People's Liberation Committee for Slavonia. Croatian History Museum, HPM-MRNH-A-2203 1695.

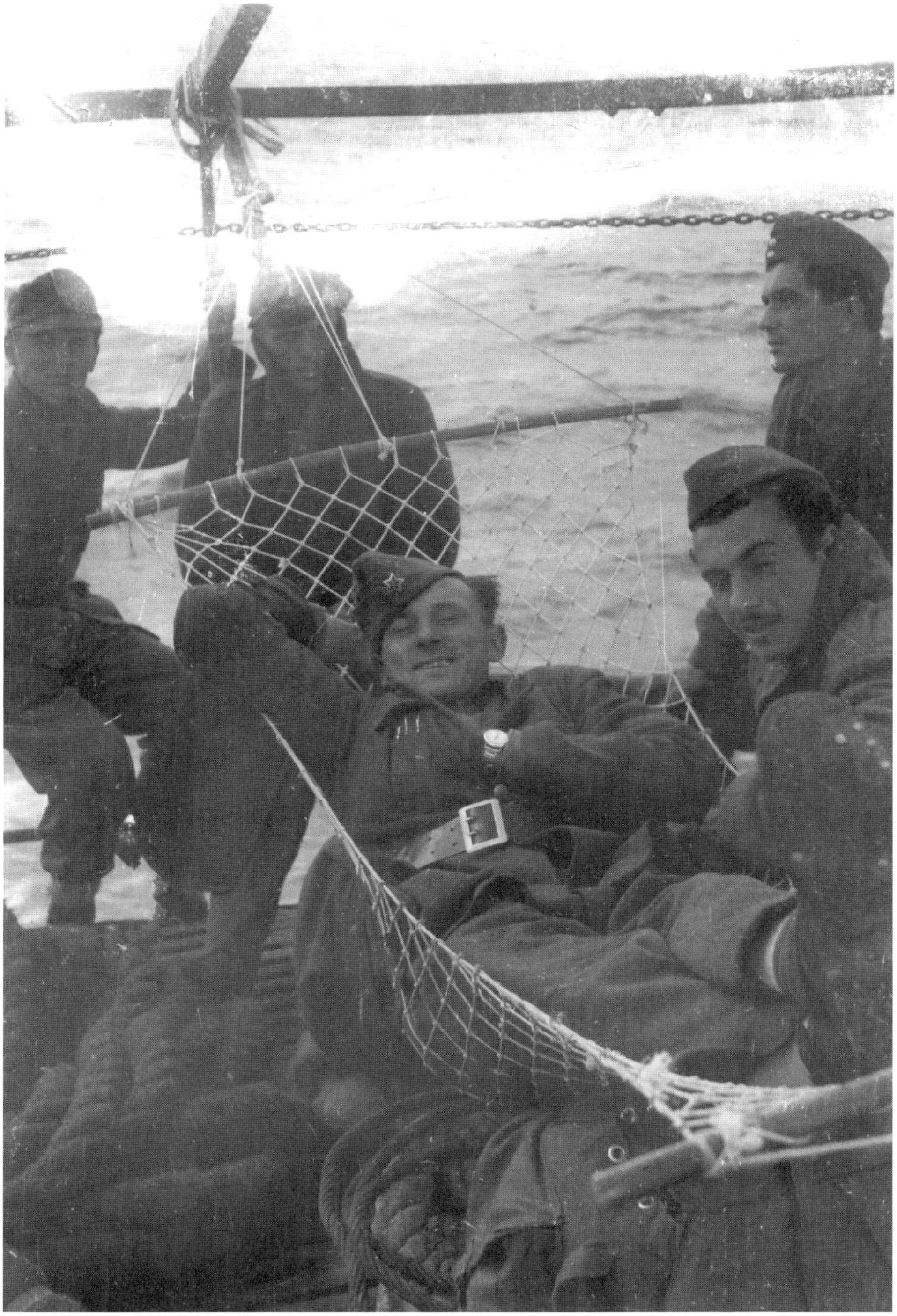

Pilots from the People's Liberation Army on a boat off Korčula, Croatia, 1944.
Photographer unknown.

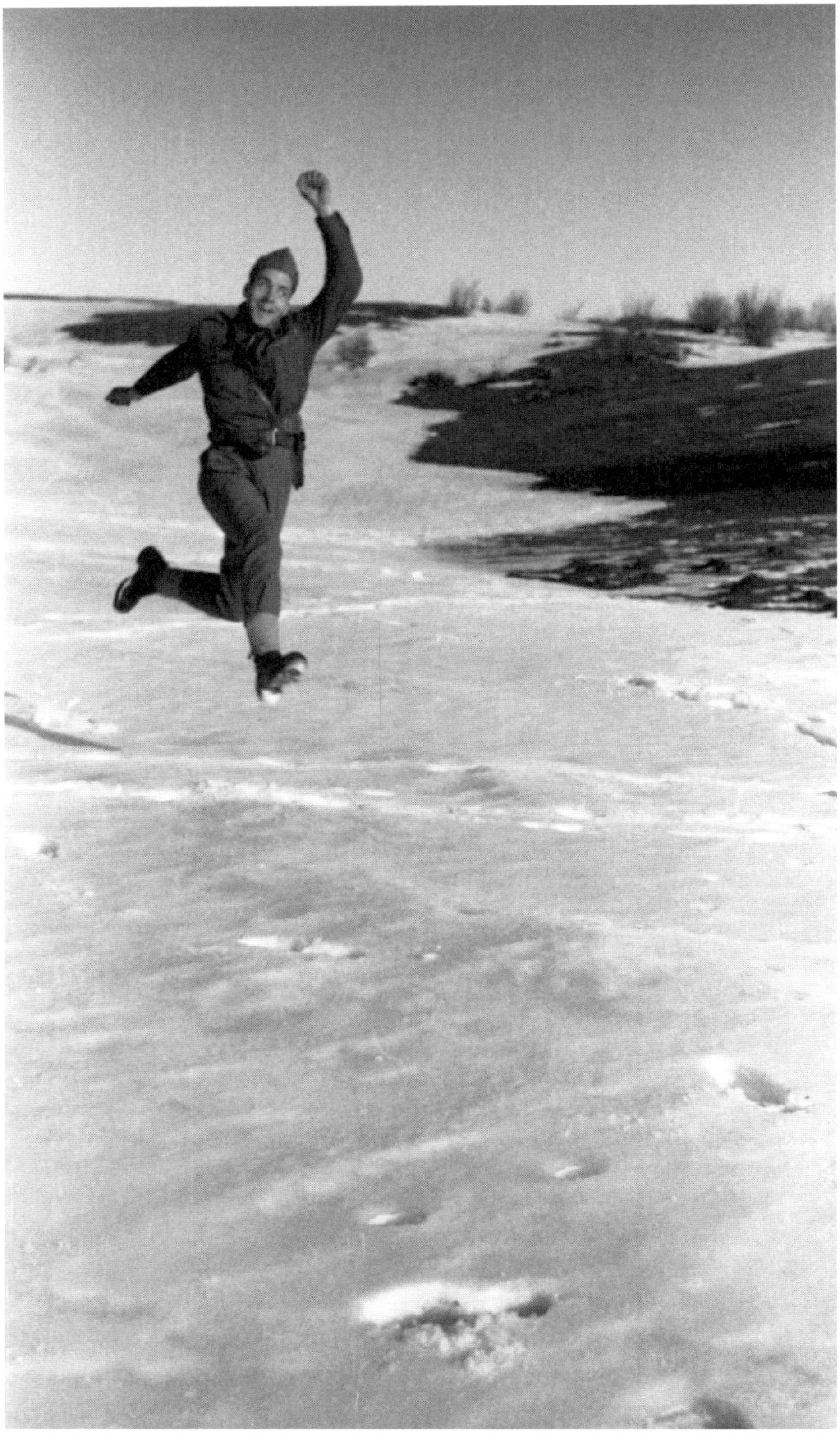

Unknown radio-telegraphist for Croatian Command, Lika, winter 1943. Photographer unknown.
Croatian History Museum, HPM-MRNH-A-2603-f123 23A.

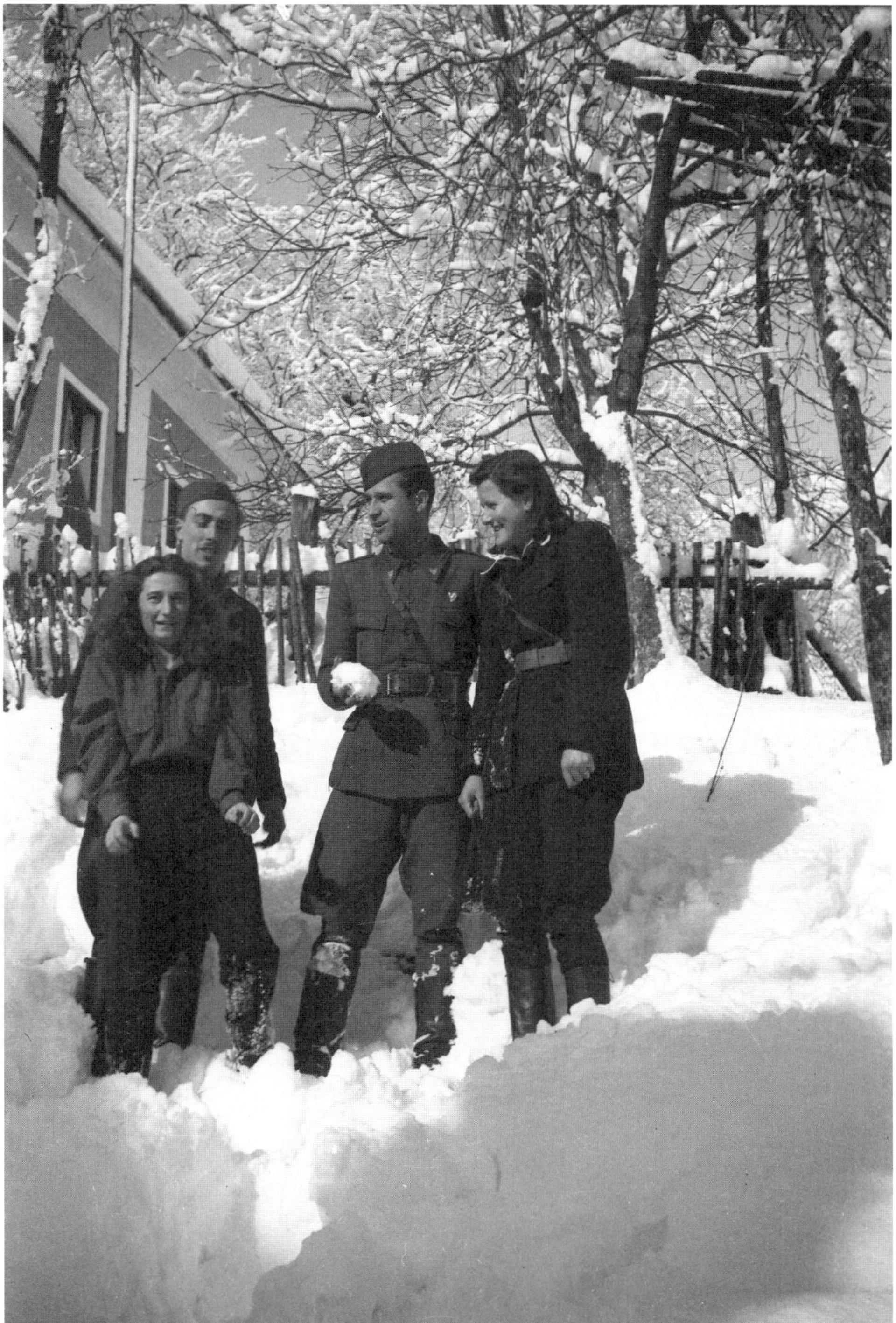

Iva Valenti, operations administrator of the Ninth Corps; Stanko Gorjanc, leader of the geodetic section; lieutenant Mitar Raičević alongside unknown female operations administrator of the Ninth Corps who later left to work as a primary-school teacher, all standing in front of the house that served as Ninth Corps HQ, Poljane, Slovenia, 21 January 1945. Photo: Aleksander Jesenovec. National Museum of Contemporary History of Slovenia, SJ2/6.

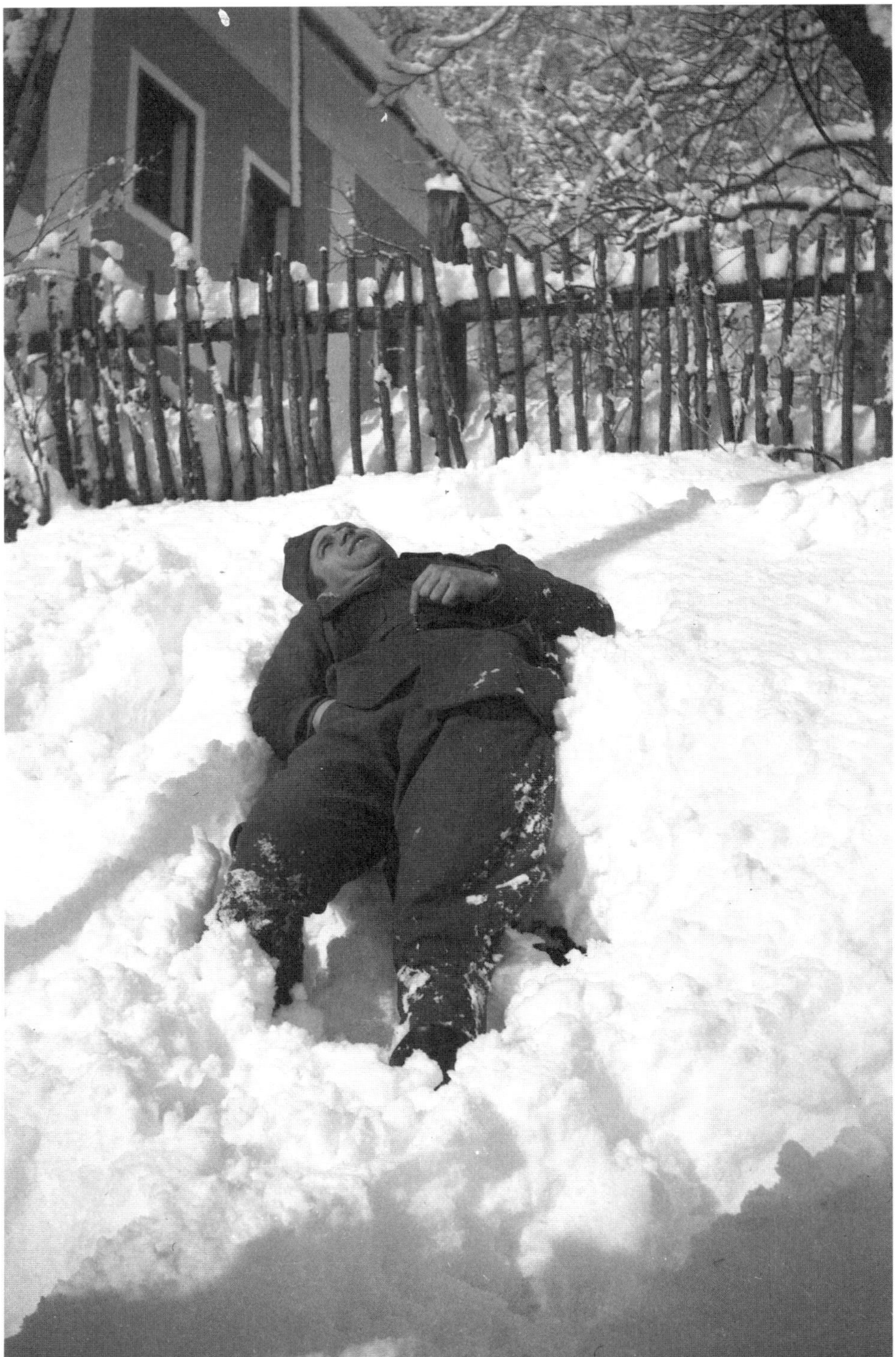

Lieutenant Mitar Raičević posing in the snow with Ninth Corps HQ in the background, Poljane outside Cerkno, Slovenia, 21 January 1945. Photo: Aleksander Jesenovec. National Museum of Contemporary History of Slovenia, SJ2/5.

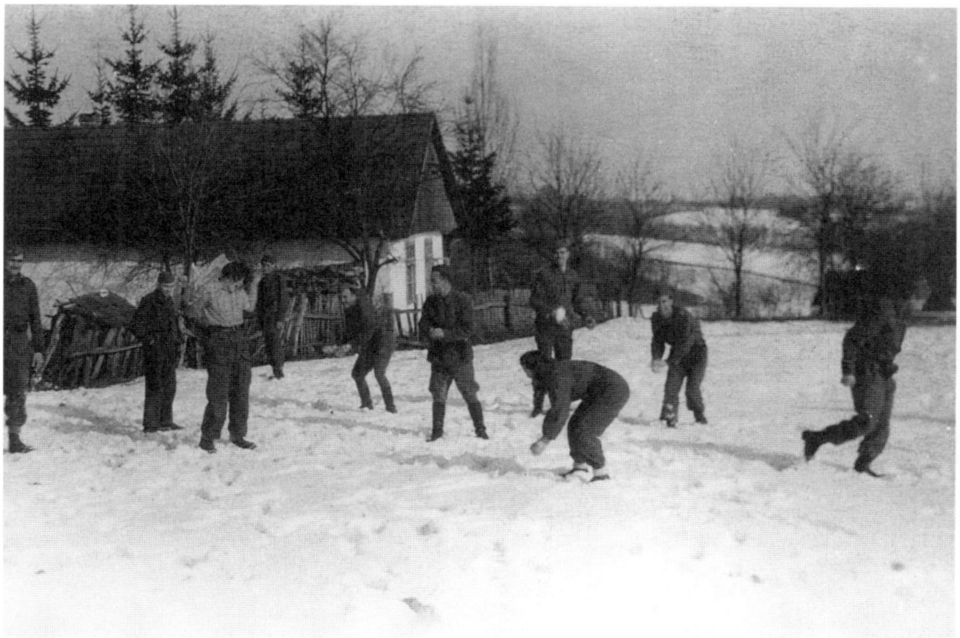

Surgical team of the Thirty-Third Division, Tenth Zagreb Corps, Bilogora, Croatia, late 1944. Photographer unknown. Donated to Zagreb City Museum by Ibrahim Balta and Zvonko Šubat, September 1980.

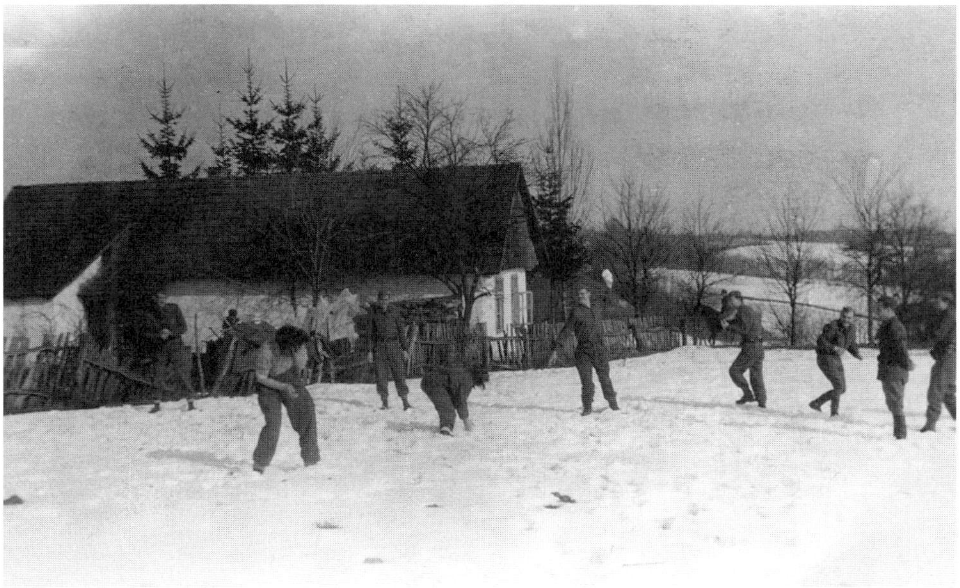

Snowball fight by surgical team of the Thirty-Third Division, Tenth Zagreb Corps, Bilogora, Croatia, late 1944. Photographer unknown. Zagreb City Museum.

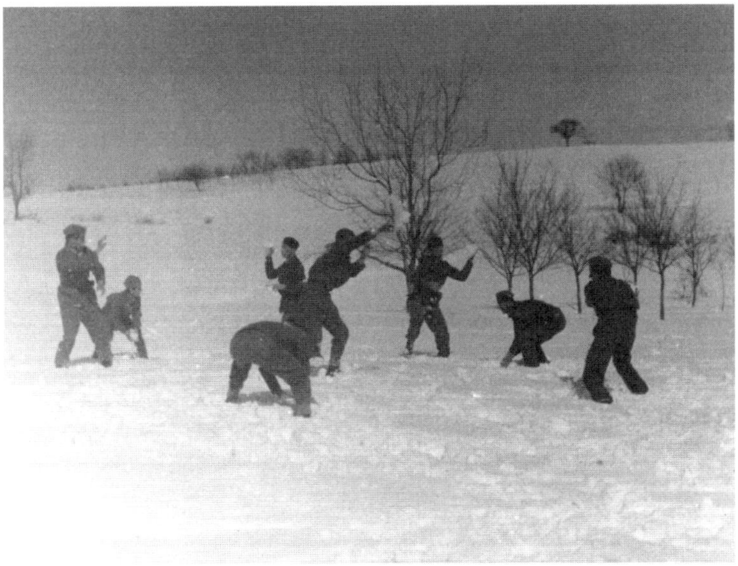

Undated winter scene.
Photo: Drago Mažar. Archives
of the Republic of Srpska, Banja Luka.

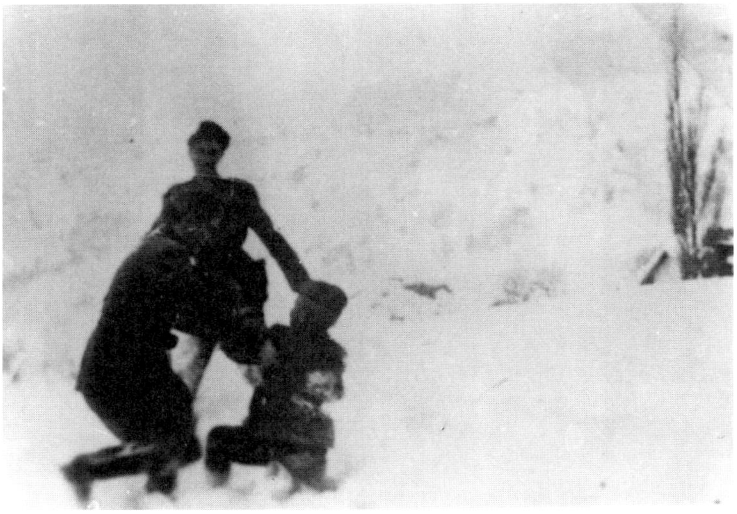

Soldiers from Eleventh Krajina
Brigade, Gučja Gora, Travnik, Bosnia
and Herzegovina, winter 1944–45.
Photographer unknown. History
Museum of Bosnia and Herzegovina,
FNOB 17306.

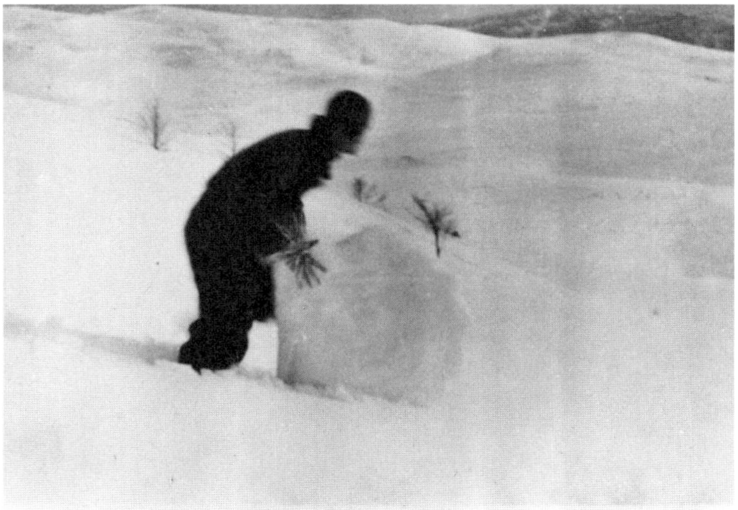

Comrade Čedomir Perić making a
giant snowman during a break in the
fighting, Dinara mountains, 10 March
1942. Photographer unknown. History
Museum of Bosnia and Herzegovina,
FNOB 17674.

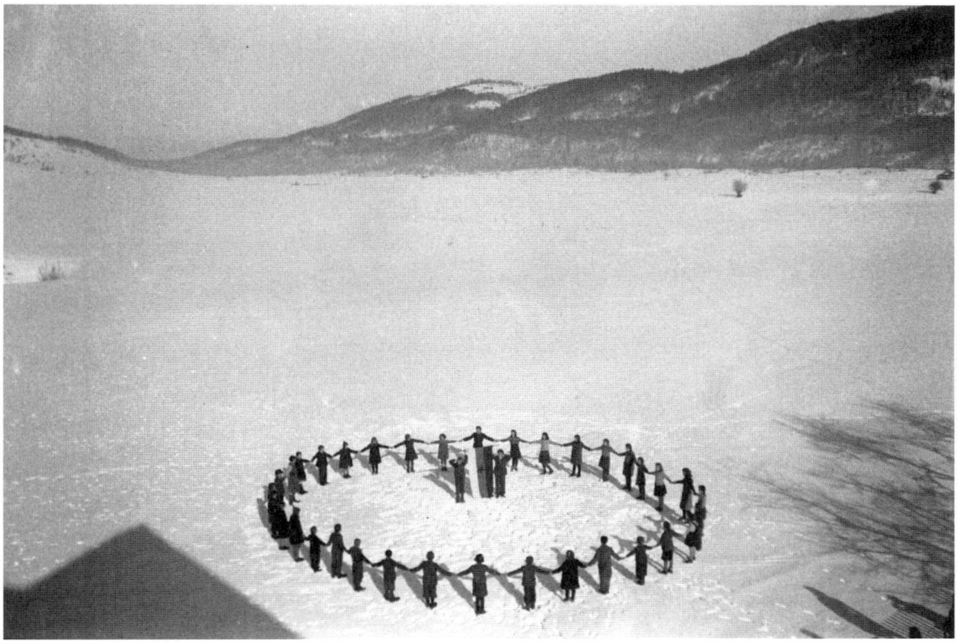

School pupils from Babno Polje performing the 'Titovo kolo', a dance in honour of Tito, 1945. Photo: Edi Šelhaus. National Museum of Contemporary History of Slovenia, TN957/6.

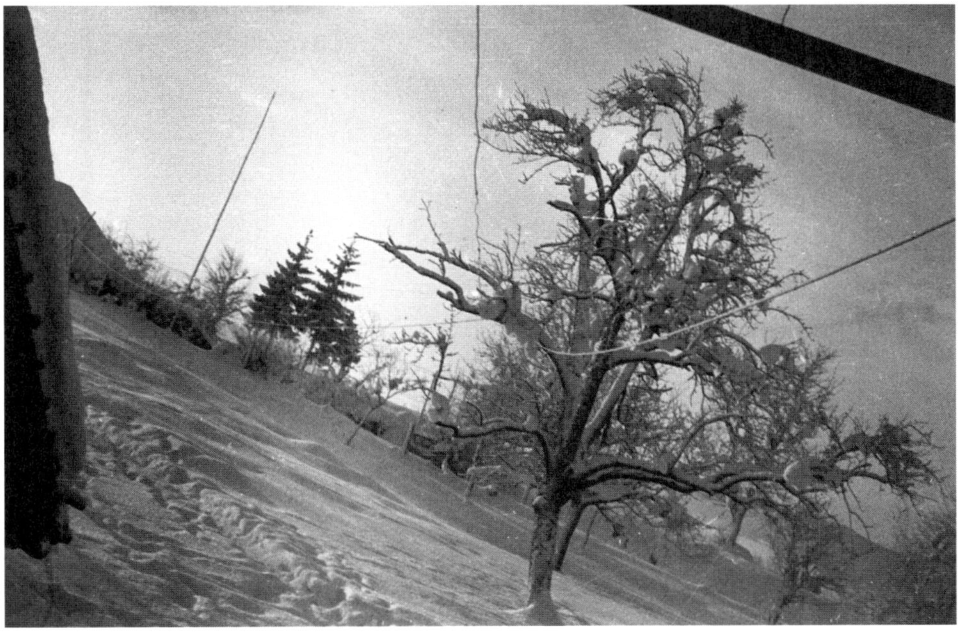

Winter scene on the outskirts of Otovec, Bela Krajina, Slovenia, January 1945. Photo: Klis. National Museum of Contemporary History of Slovenia, TN912/18.

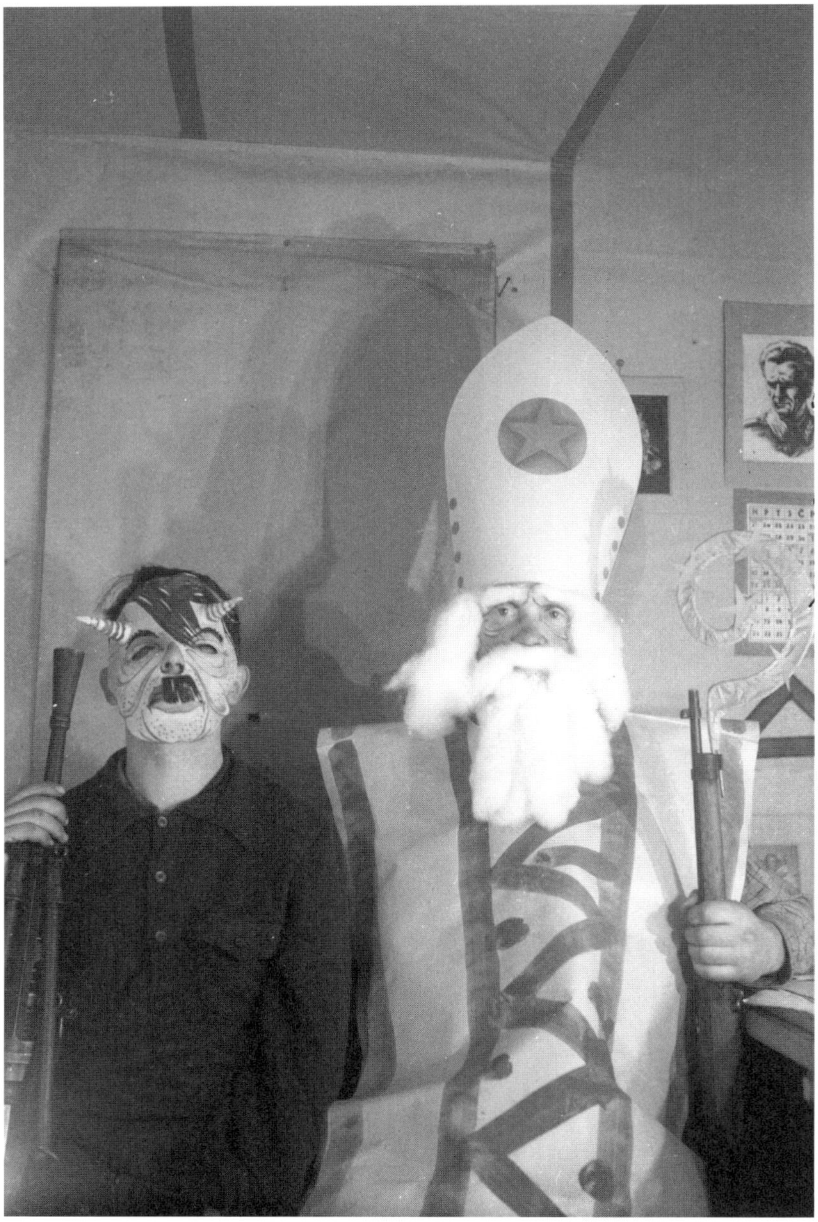

Unknown Partisan soldiers dressed up for satirical performance.
Photographer unknown. National Museum of Contemporary History of Slovenia, TN1205/4.

Partisans at Rest

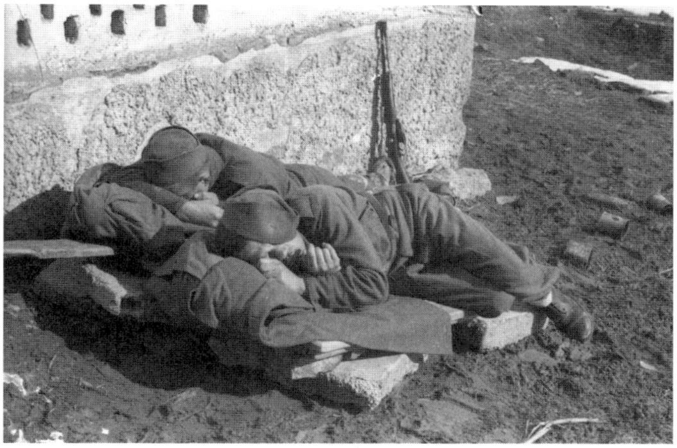

During evacuation of Bela Krajina to the Zadar peninsula, 25 February 1945. Photo: Dr Janez Milčinski. National Museum of Contemporary History of Slovenia, 1236/20.

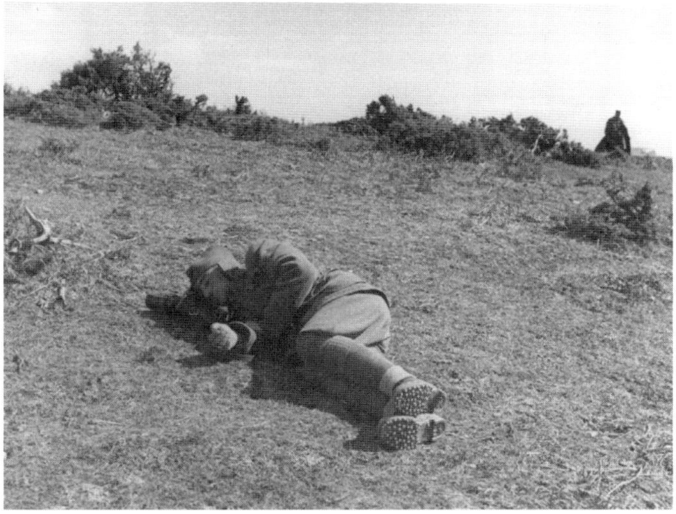

Uncaptioned. Photo: Drago Mažar. Archives of the Republic of Srpska, Banja Luka, no accession no.

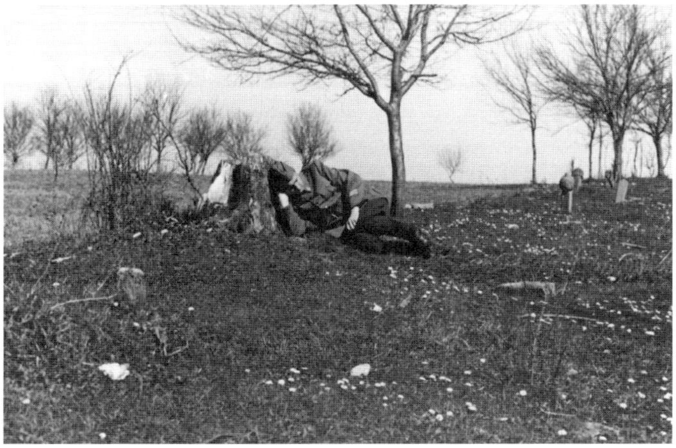

Uncaptioned. Photo: Drago Mažar. Archives of the Republic of Srpska, Banja Luka, no accession no.

Colour Photographs and News Boards

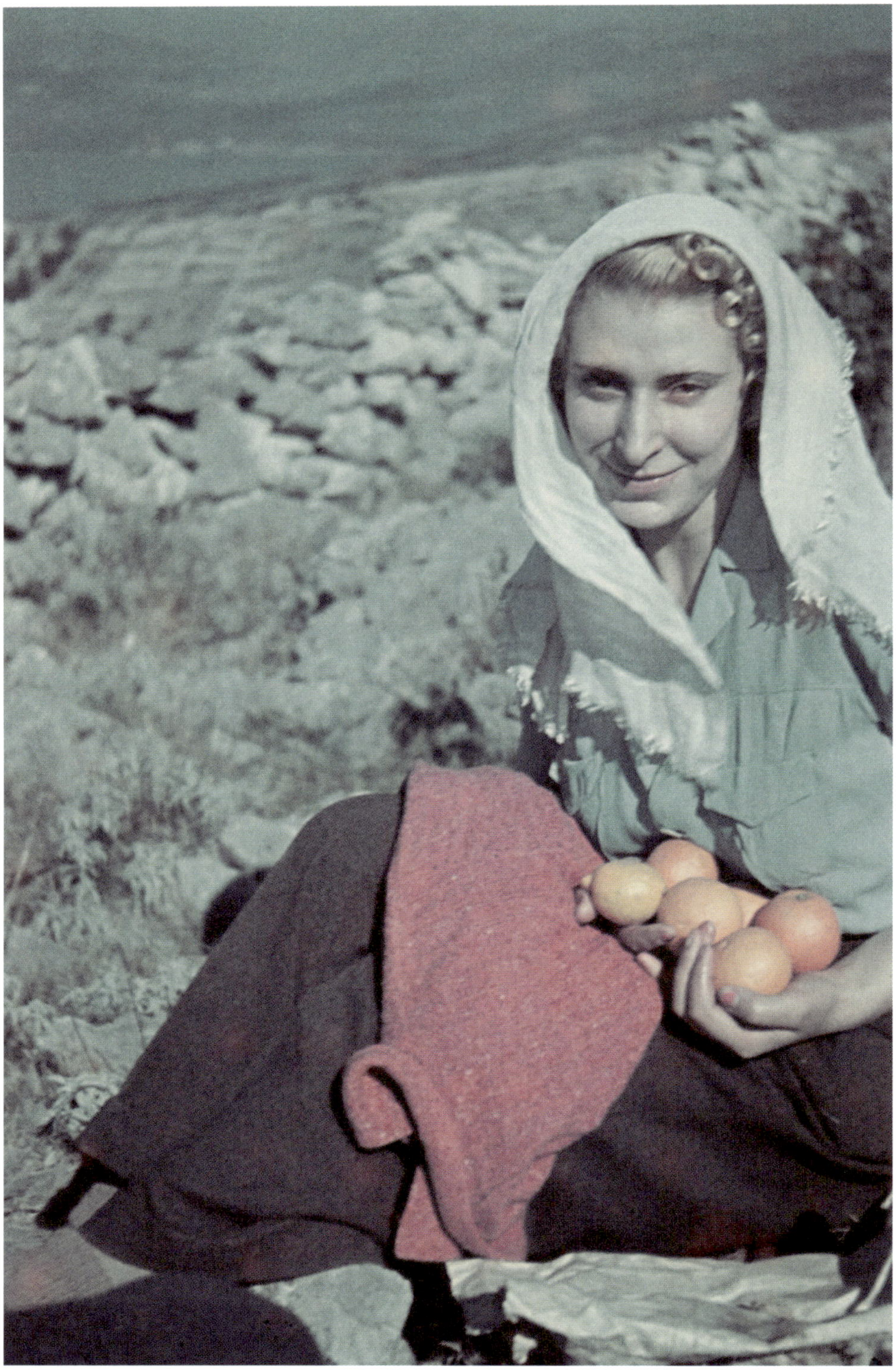

A woman holding oranges, Čiovo, 1942. Photo: Živko Gattin. Photograph reproduced with the kind permission of Ingrid Gattin Pogutz.

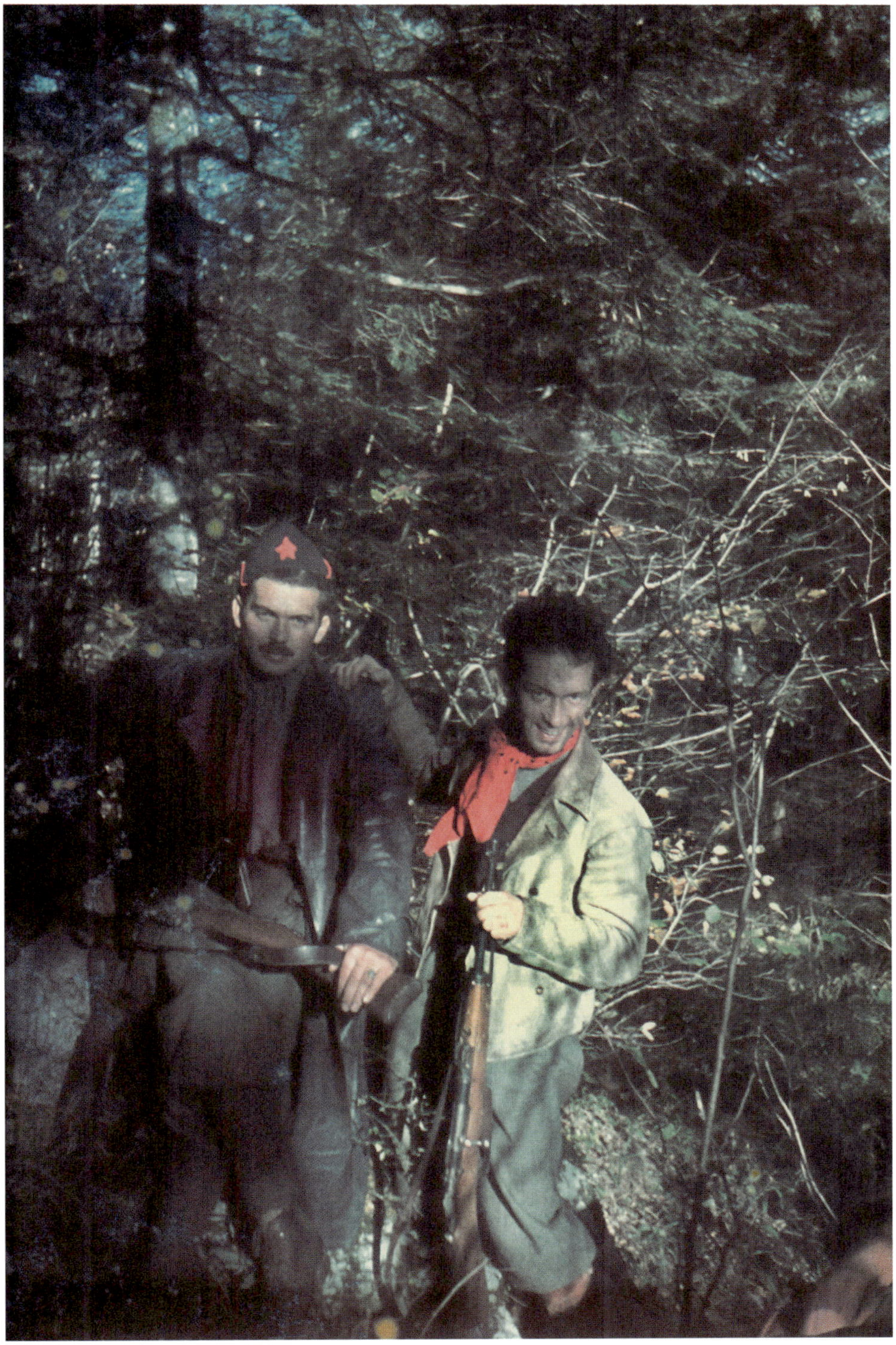

Yugoslav painter Čoro Škodlar (right) with unknown Partisan soldier, summer 1944. Photographer unknown. National Museum of Contemporary History of Slovenia, DP72DP64.

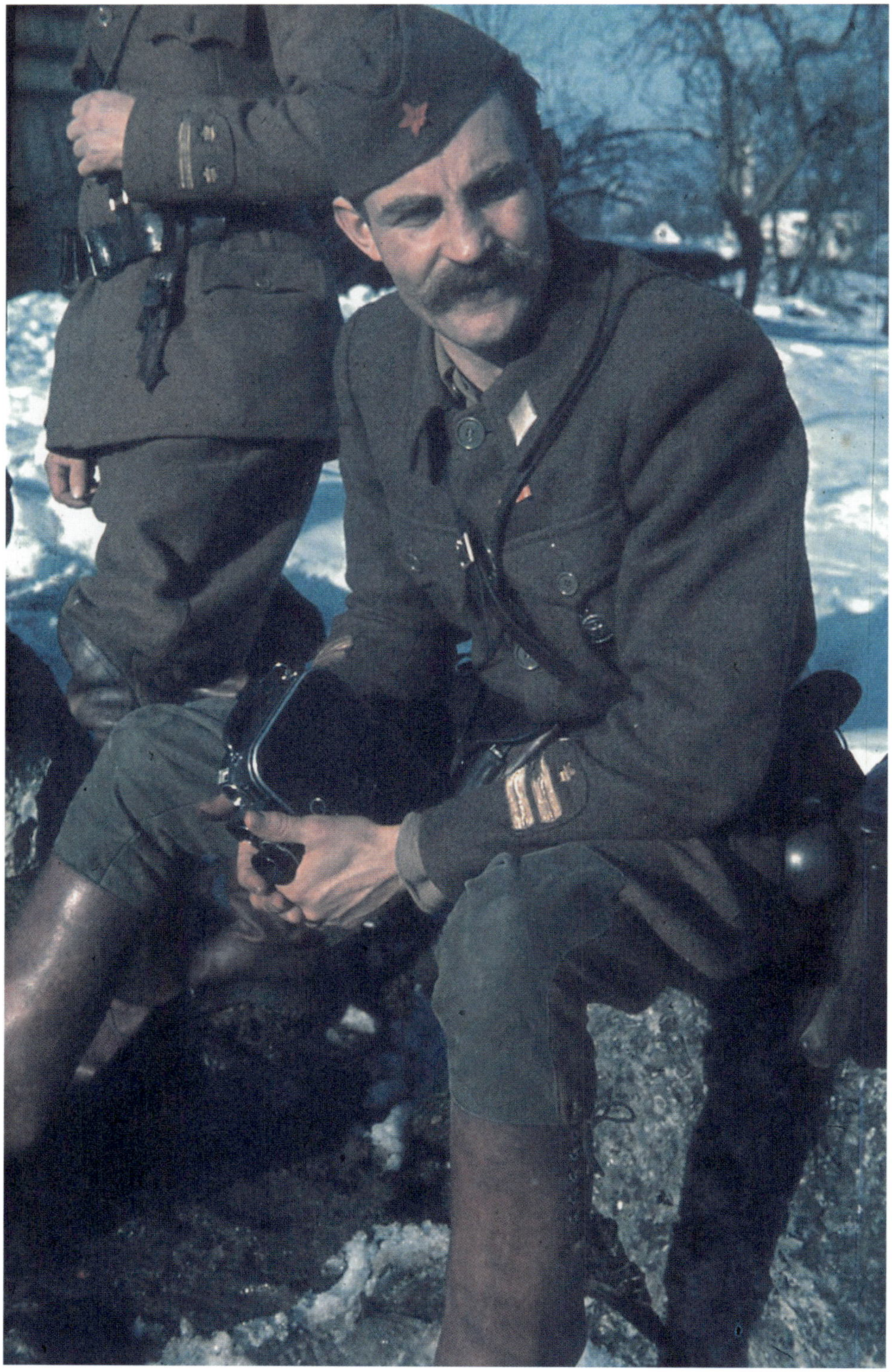

A Partisan commander with a 16 mm movie camera, winter 1944–45.
Photographer unknown. National Museum of Contemporary History of Slovenia, DP3.

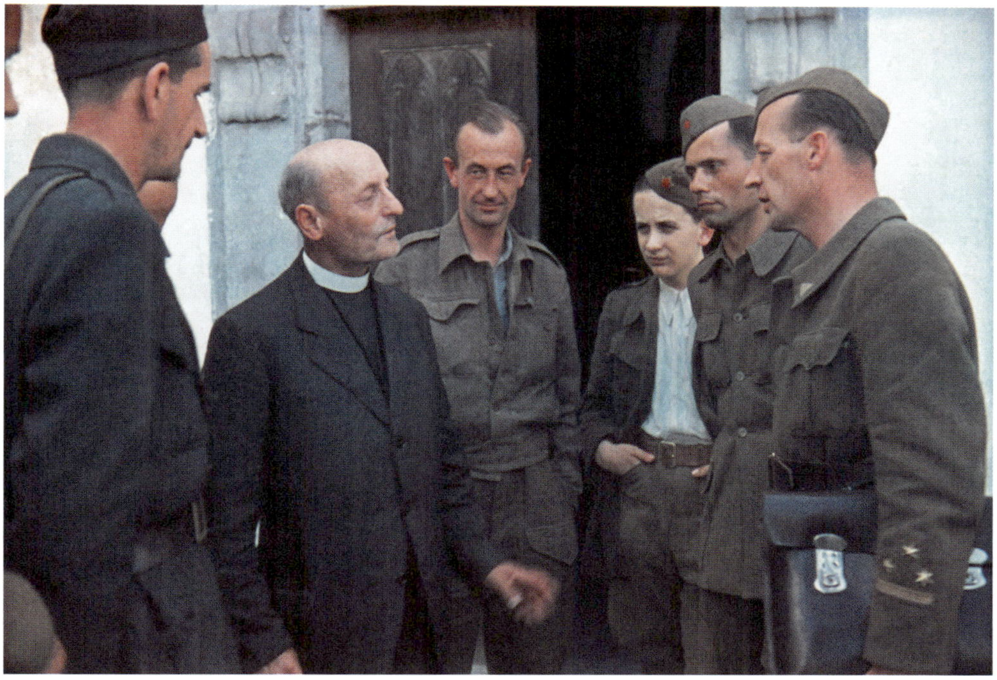

The priest Ksaver Meško with Ciril Kosmač (centre), an unknown female Partisan, Miško Kranjec and Mile Klopčič (right), Stična Monastery, Slovenia, summer 1944. Photographer unknown. National Museum of Contemporary History of Slovenia, DP72.

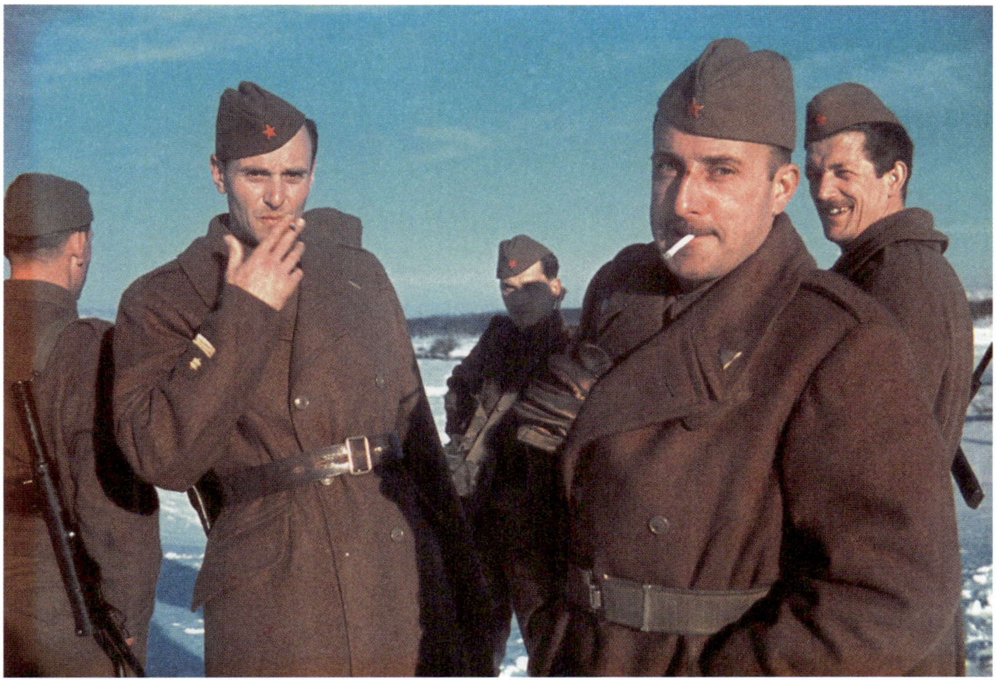

Partisans in winter 1944–45. Photographer unknown. National Museum of Contemporary History of Slovenia, DP72.

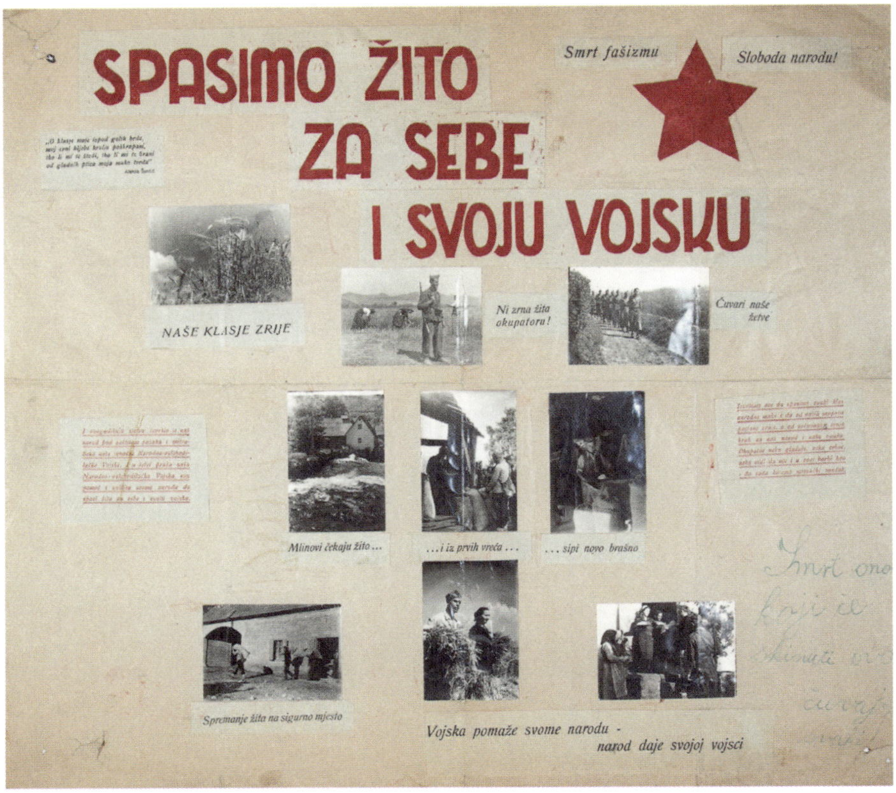

News board display with the heading 'Save the Grain for Us and Our Army'. Photo: Photography service of the People's Committee of Dalmatia. Croatian History Museum, HPM/MRNH-F-11963.

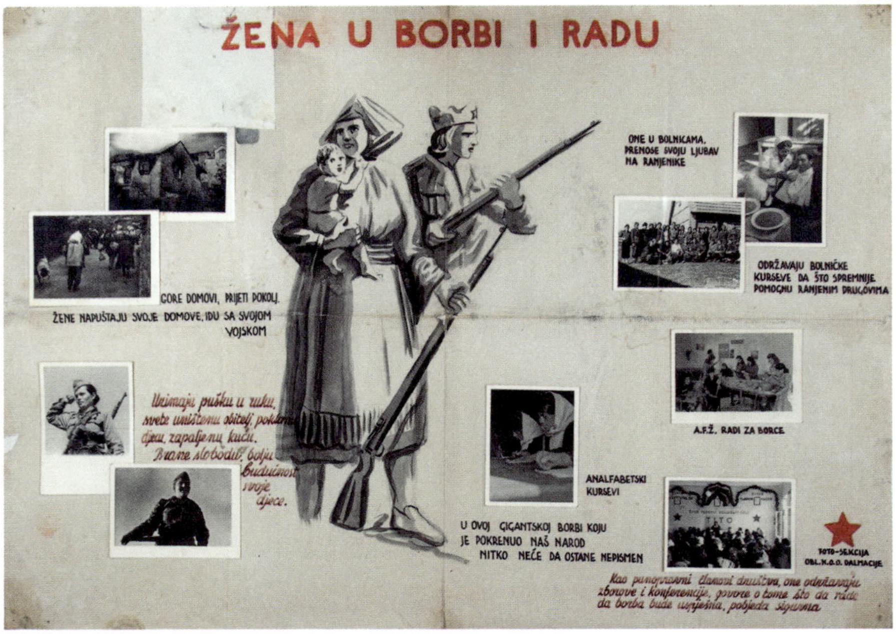

News board display with the heading 'Women in Combat and at Work'. Photo: Photography service of the People's Committee of Dalmatia. Croatian History Museum, HPM/MRNH-F-11963.

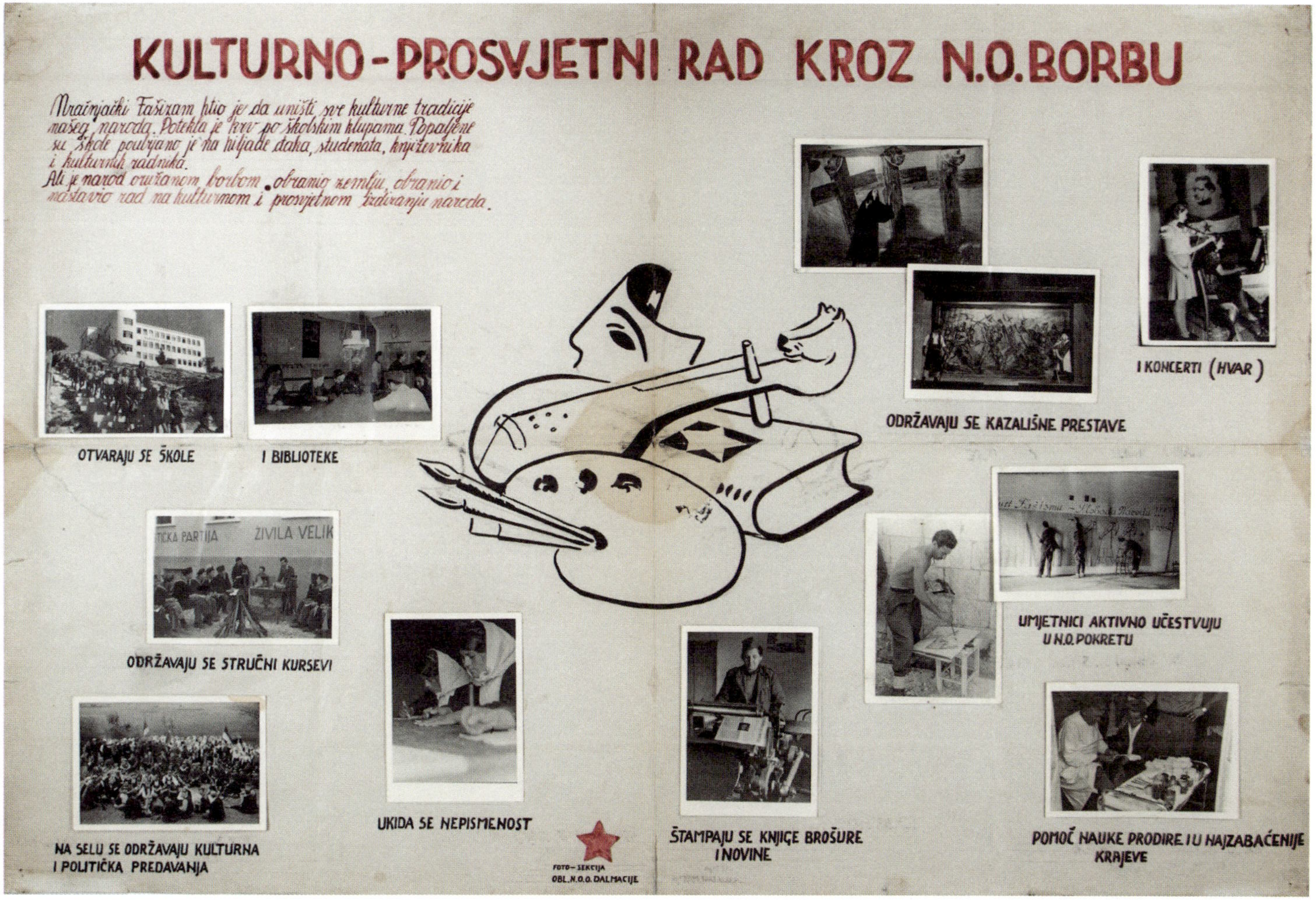

'Cultural education through the People's Liberation Struggle'. Photo: Photography service of the People's Committee of Dalmatia. Croatian History Museum, HPM/MRNH-F-11962.

Beneath the Cross

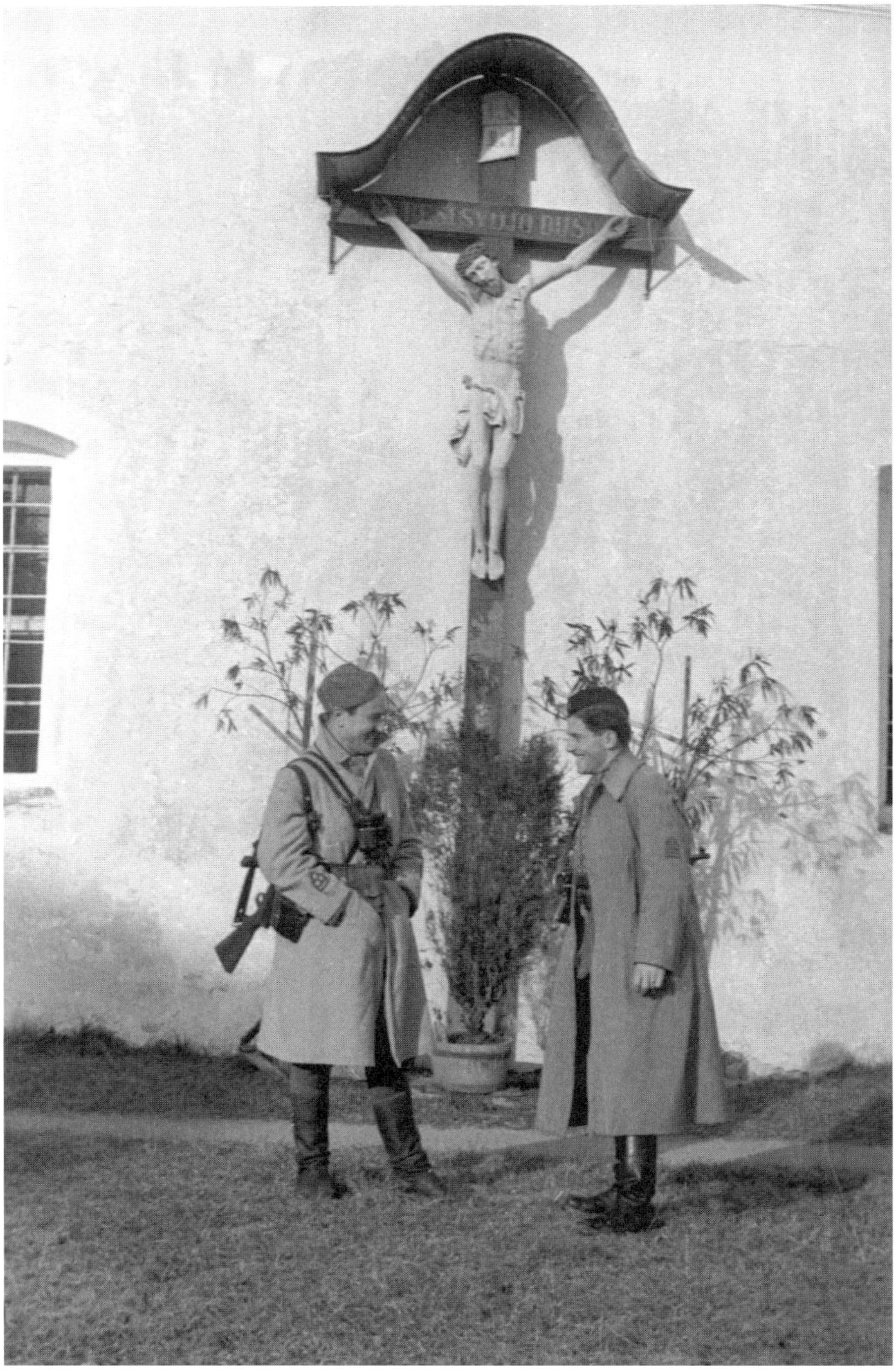

Partisans meeting beneath the cross, Notranjska, Slovenia, 1944. Photo: Vinko Bavec.
National Museum of Contemporary History of Slovenia, TN126/21.

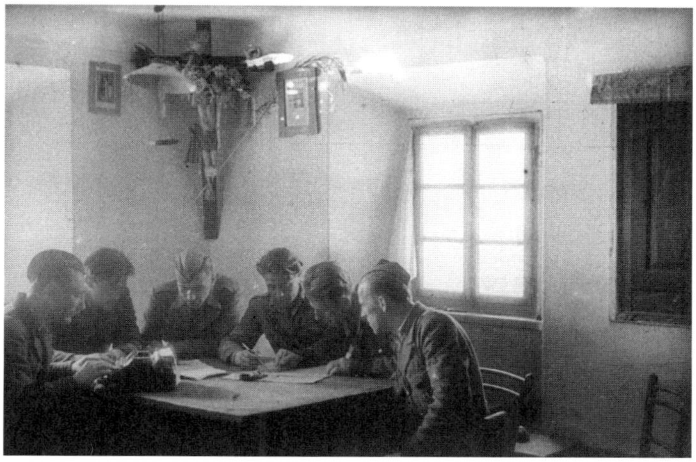

Meeting of the staff of the Twelfth Brigade (Stojan Petrovič, Stane Sever, Ivan Groznik, Bogomil Gaberc, Niko Šilih and Tomaž Slapar), Trebnje, Slovenia, 1944. Photo: Maksimilijan Zupančič. National Museum of Contemporary History of Slovenia, TN 106/21.

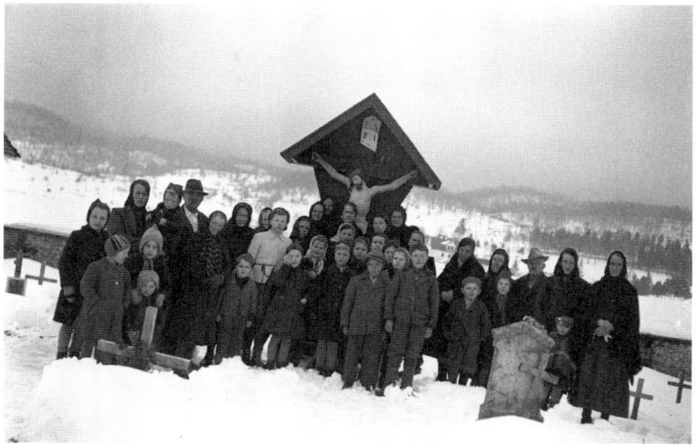

In Babno polje, 1944. Photo: Edi Šelhaus. National Museum of Contemporary History of Slovenia, TN941/4.

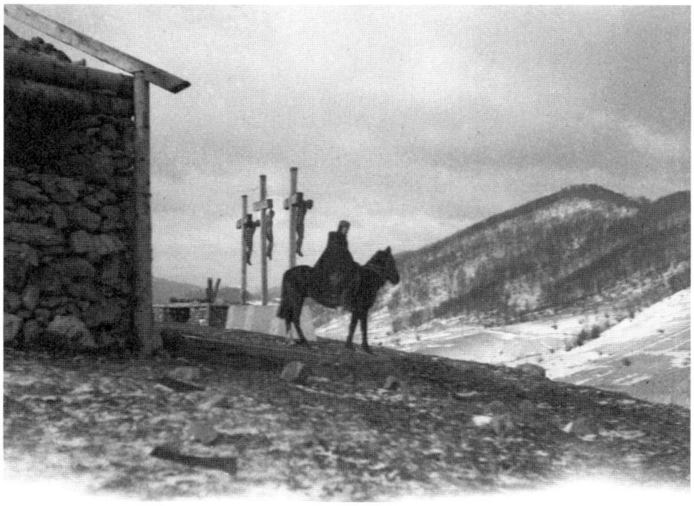

Member of the Partisan cavalry at an Italian fortress at Kalvarija, winter 1944–45. Photo: Edi Šelhaus. National Museum of Contemporary History of Slovenia, TN1659/6.

People and Animals

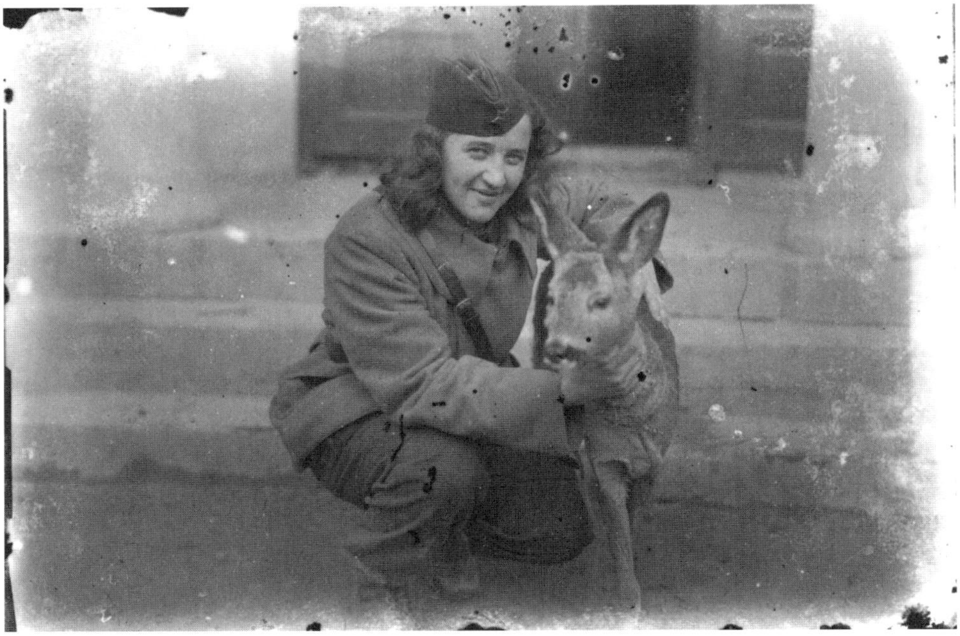

Partisan from the Posavina Partisan Detachment with deer. Photo: Stjepan Šubek. Croatian History Museum, HPM-MRNH-F-10814.

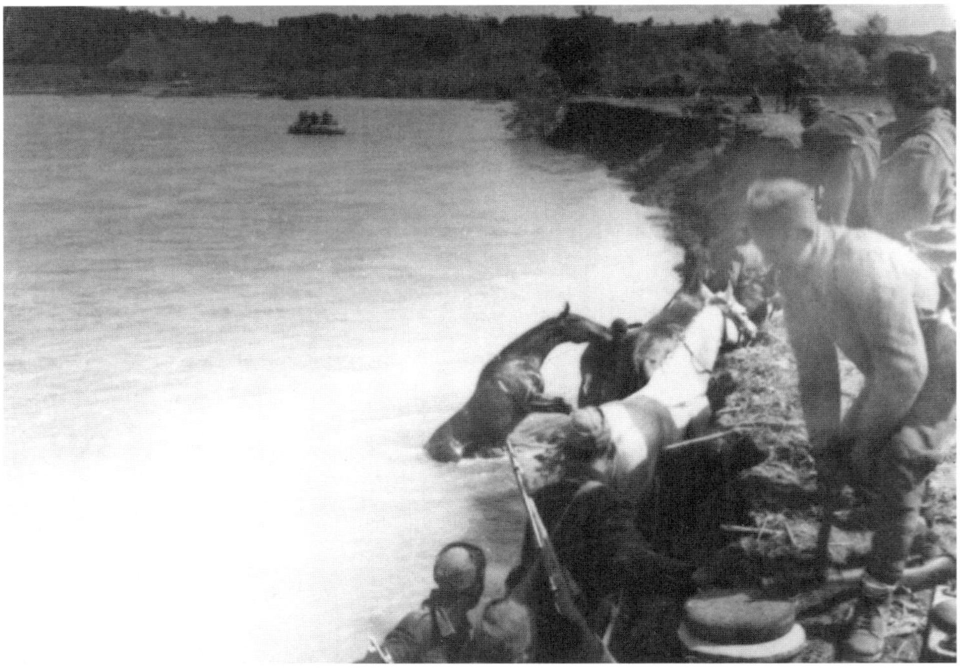

A unit from the Twenty-Eighth Division crossing the river Vrbas outside village of Kukulje, Bosnia and Herzegovina, 23 April 1945. Photographer unknown. Military Museum Belgrade, 6764.

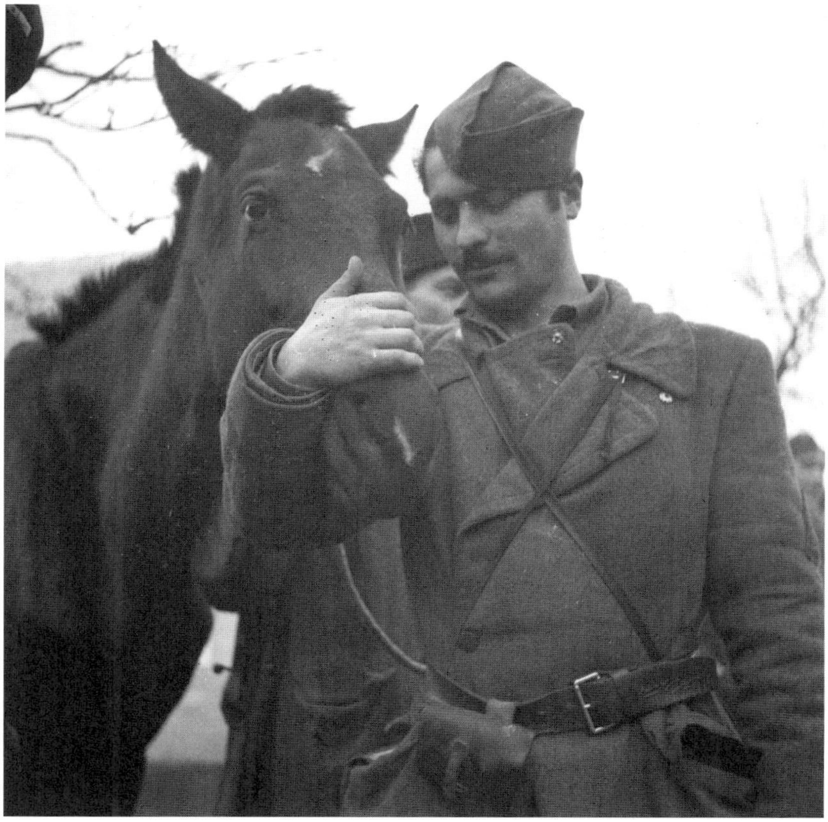

Uncaptioned. Photo: Mirko Trobec. National Museum of Contemporary History of Slovenia, T/34.

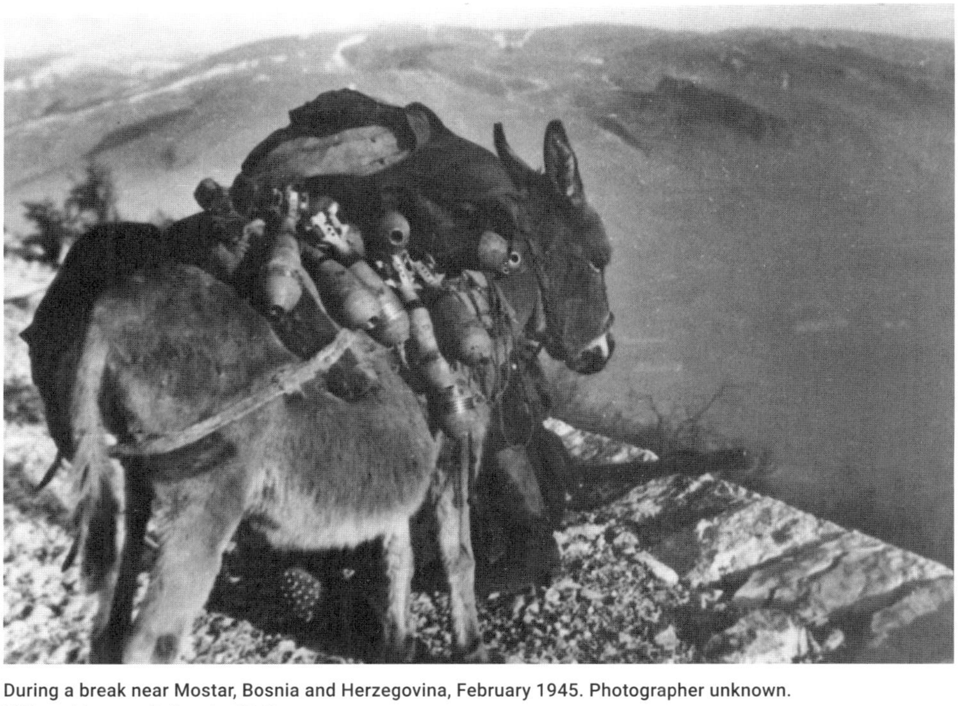

During a break near Mostar, Bosnia and Herzegovina, February 1945. Photographer unknown.
Military Museum Belgrade, 6218.

Children

At the outbreak of the Second World War, the League of Communist Youth of Yugoslavia had around 35,000 members; during the war that number rose to 70,000. As members of the League and the United Alliance of Anti-Fascist Youth of Yugoslavia, *pioniri* (pioneers) were involved in the war effort and often completed supplementary tasks or worked as couriers. Many were also active as bombers, saboteurs and front-line soldiers. In east Bosnia, in the Birač region, young fighters even formed the first Pioneer Division.

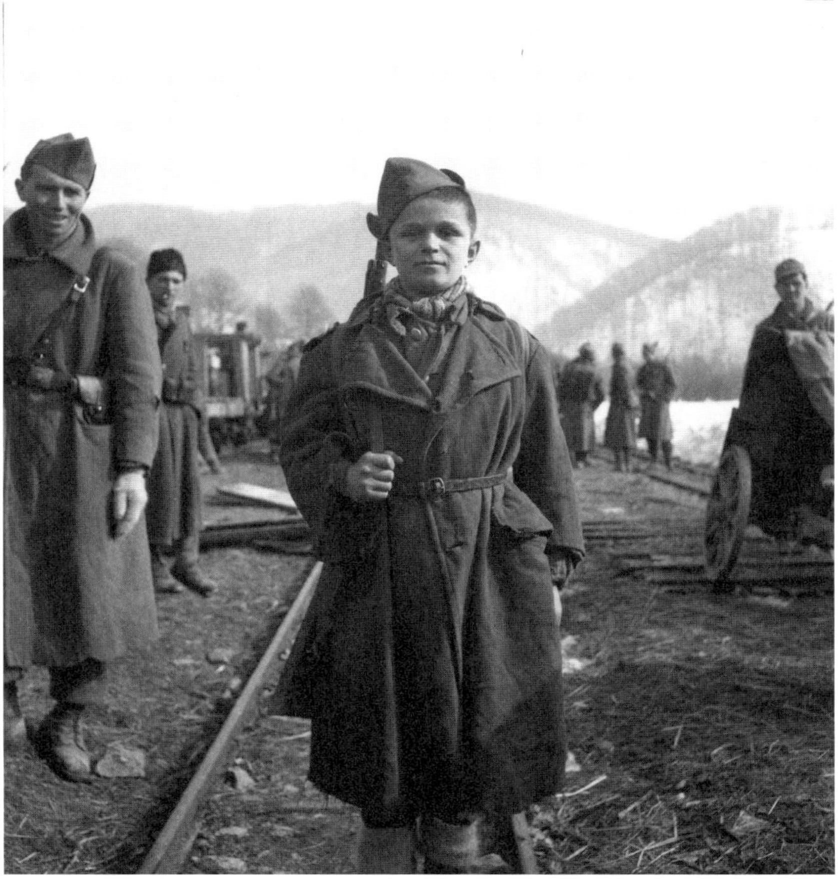

Milan Ostojić from Lađevac near Okučani (Croatia), member of the Joža Vlahović Youth Brigade, January 1944, a year before he was killed in battle in 1945. Photographer unknown. Croatian History Museum, HPM-MRNH-A-2201 556.

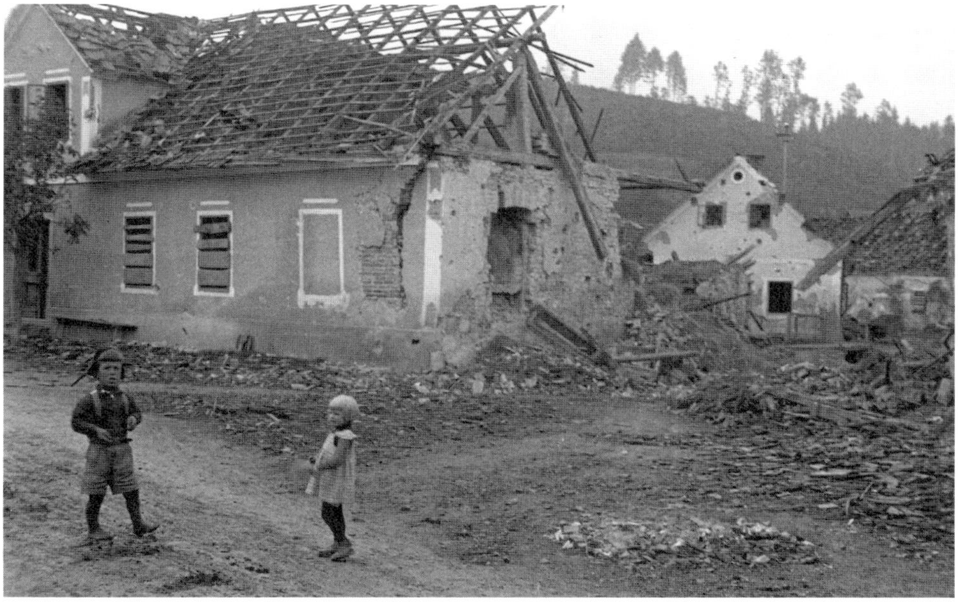

Village children in front of devastated house belonging to the Škod family after the attack on Mokronog, Slovenia, September 1943. Photo: Maksimilijan Zupančič. National Museum of Contemporary History of Slovenia, TN36/16.

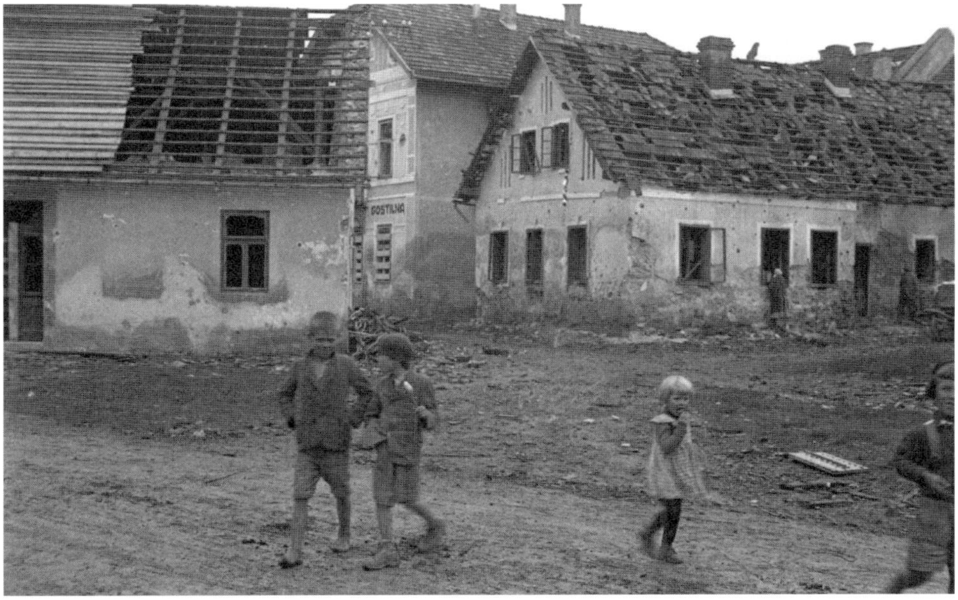

Village children after attack on Mokronog, with the Škod family home in background, September 1943. Photo: Maksimilijan Zupančič. National Museum of Contemporary History of Slovenia, TN36/17.

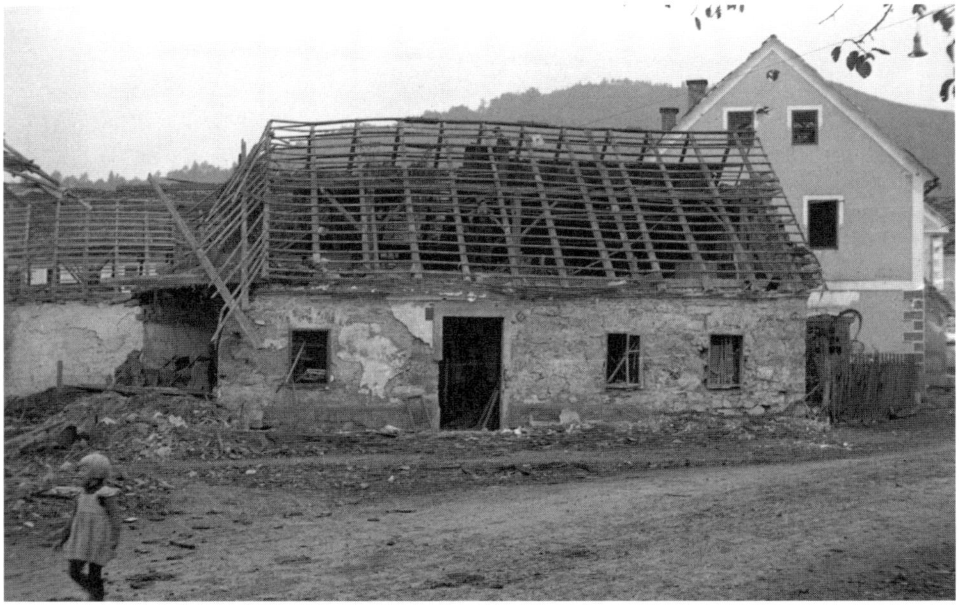

Documenting the devastation to the Škod family home, Mokronog, Slovenia, September 1943.
Photo: Maksimilijan Zupančič. National Museum of Contemporary History of Slovenia, TN36/20.

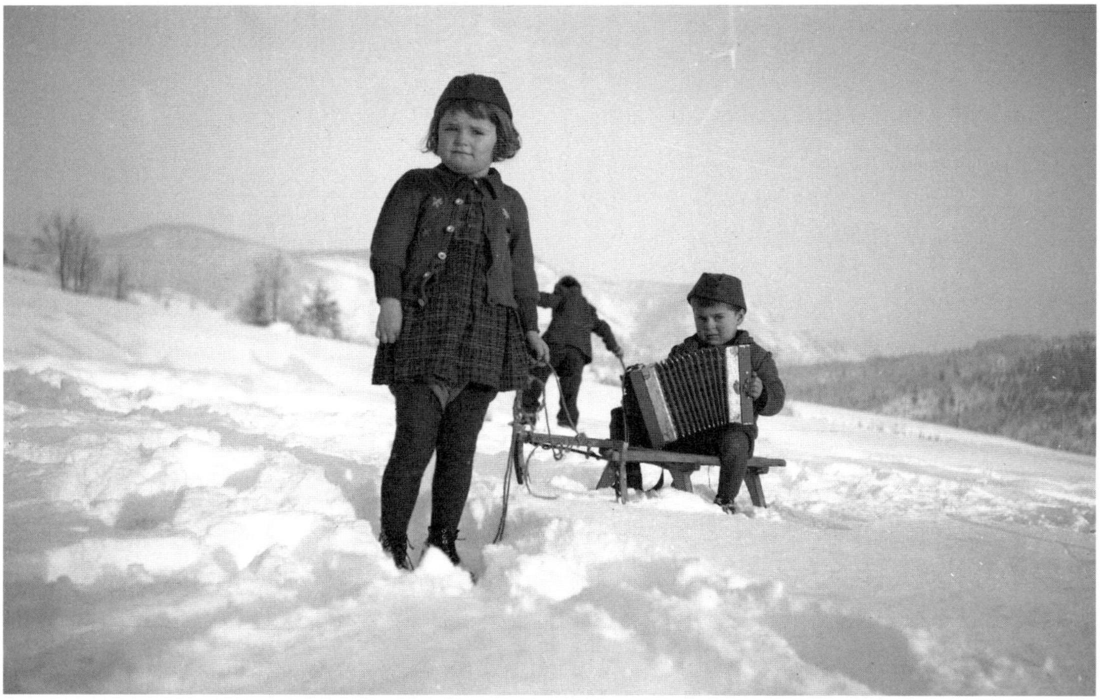

Two of the youngest Pioneers from the village of Potok, Kočevje, Slovenia.
Photo: Edi Šelhaus. National Museum of Contemporary History of Slovenia, TN577/5.

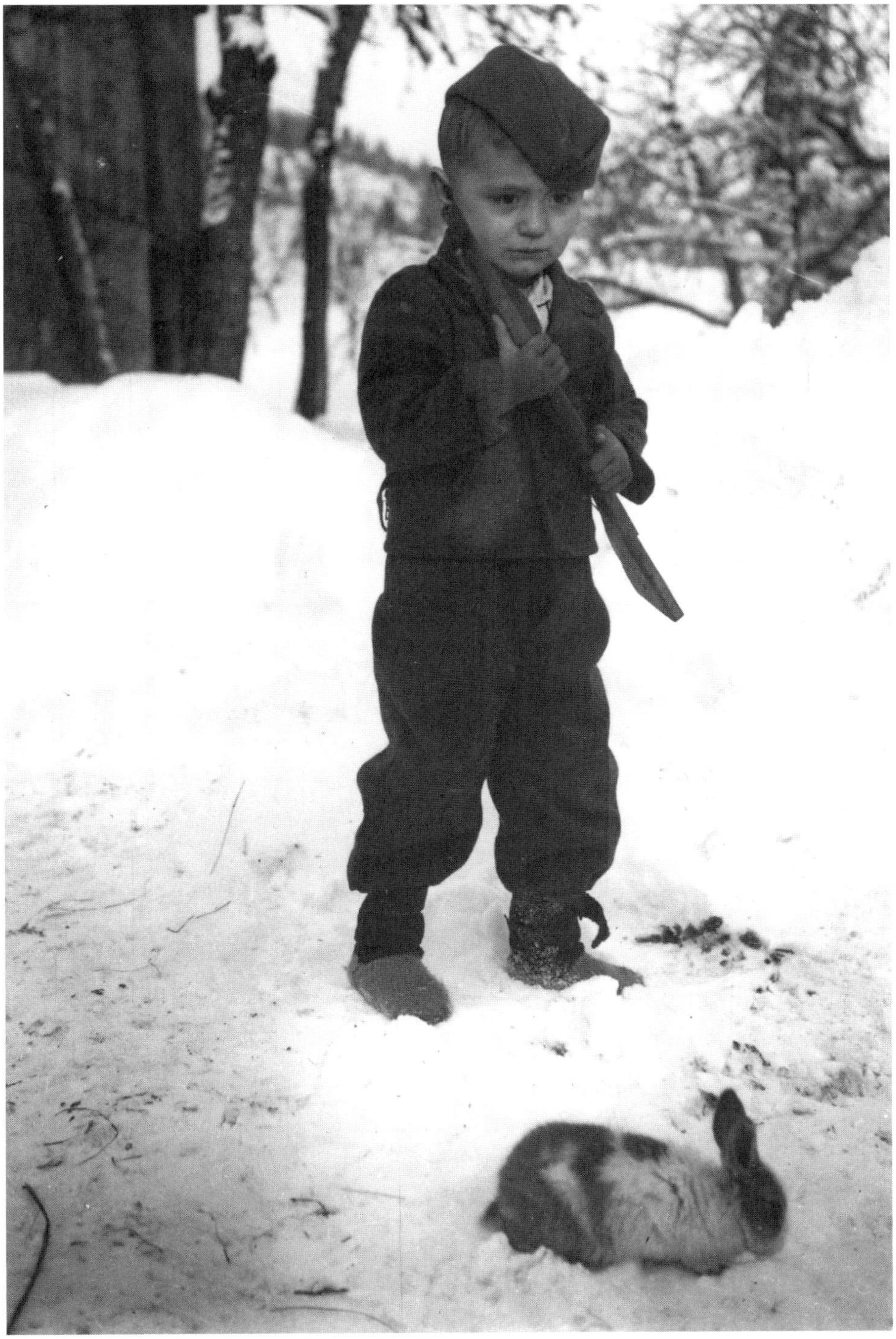

Pioneer from Kočevje with a rabbit. Photographer unknown.
Private collection.

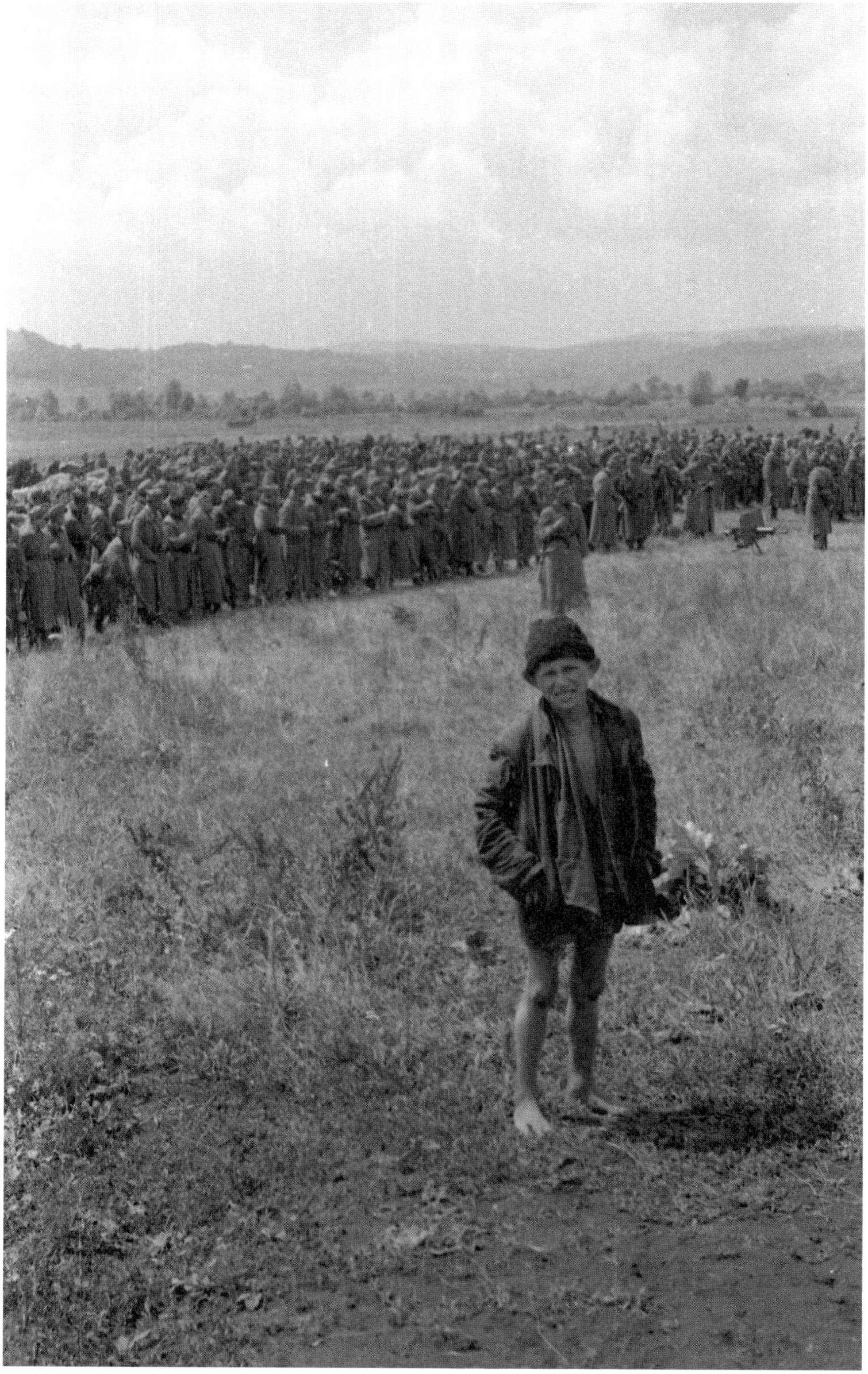

Celebrations marking the second anniversary of the founding of the Twelfth Slavonian Brigade, Levanjska Varoš, near Osijek, Croatia, October 1944. Photographer unknown. Croatian History Museum, HPM-100525 027.

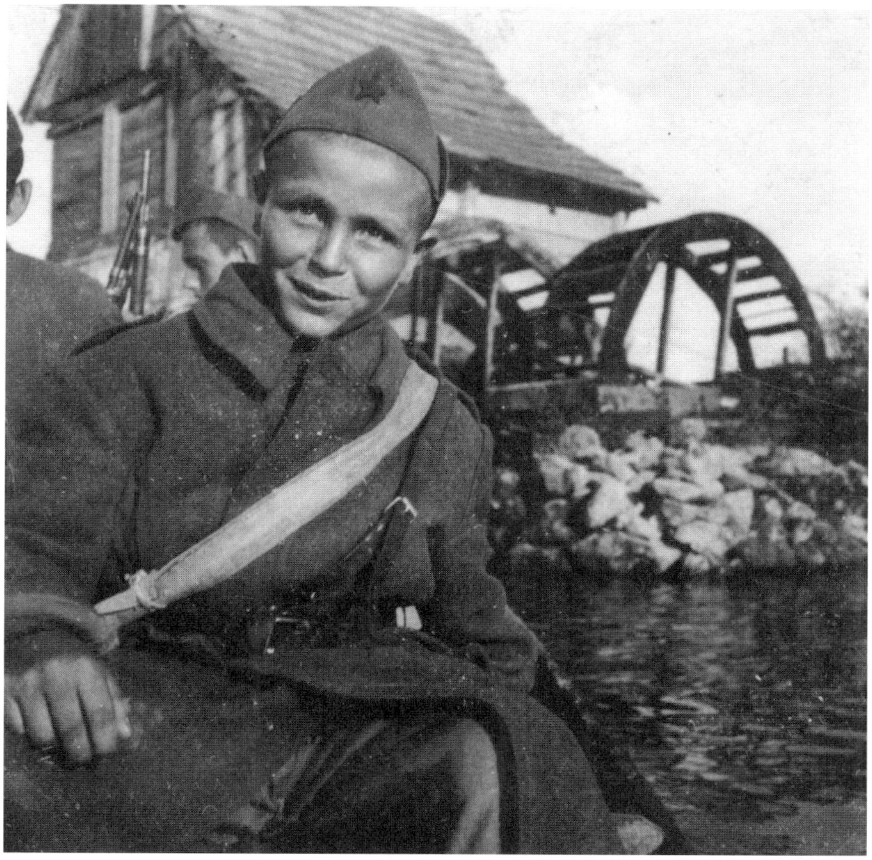

Miloš Brkić, the youngest fighter in a company of the Seventh Kordun Division before the attack on Duga Resa, approx. 65 kilometres from Zagreb, June 1944. Photo: Mahmud Konjhodžić. Croatian History Museum, HPM-MRNH-F-4723.

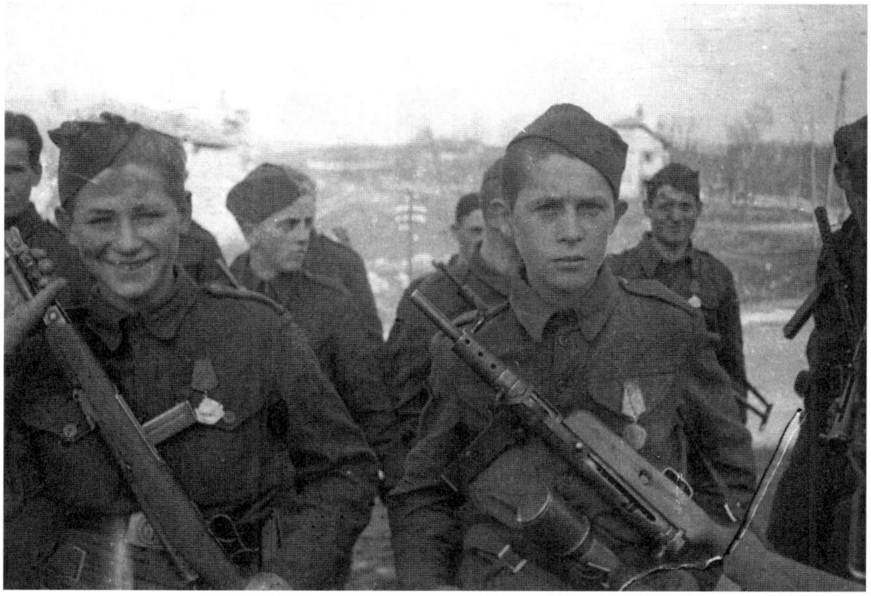

Members of First Proletarian Corps marching to Šid, a town in Vojvodina, Serbia, near the Croatian border, on the Srijemski (Syrmian) Front, an Axis line of defence, December 1944. Photo: Pavle Bojčević. Museum of Yugoslavia, accession no. unknown.

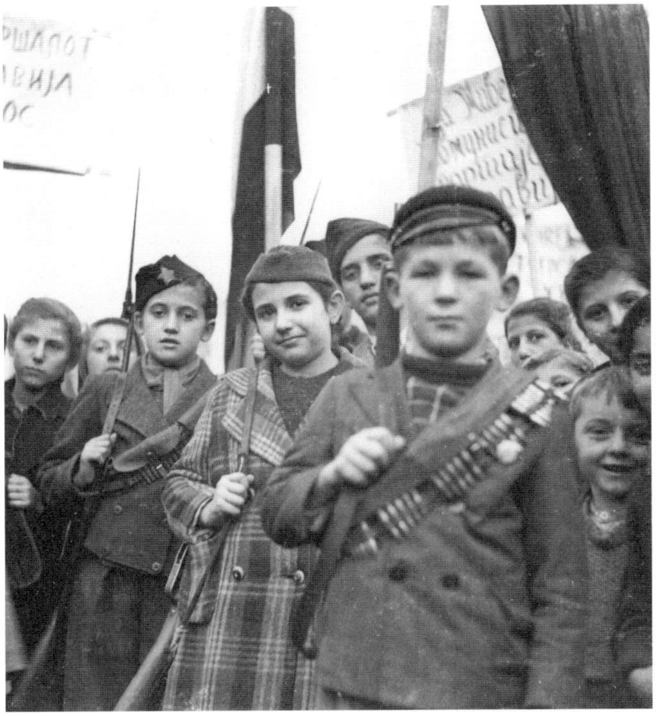

A youth meeting in Skopje, Macedonia, 1944.
Photographer unknown. Museum of Yugoslavia.

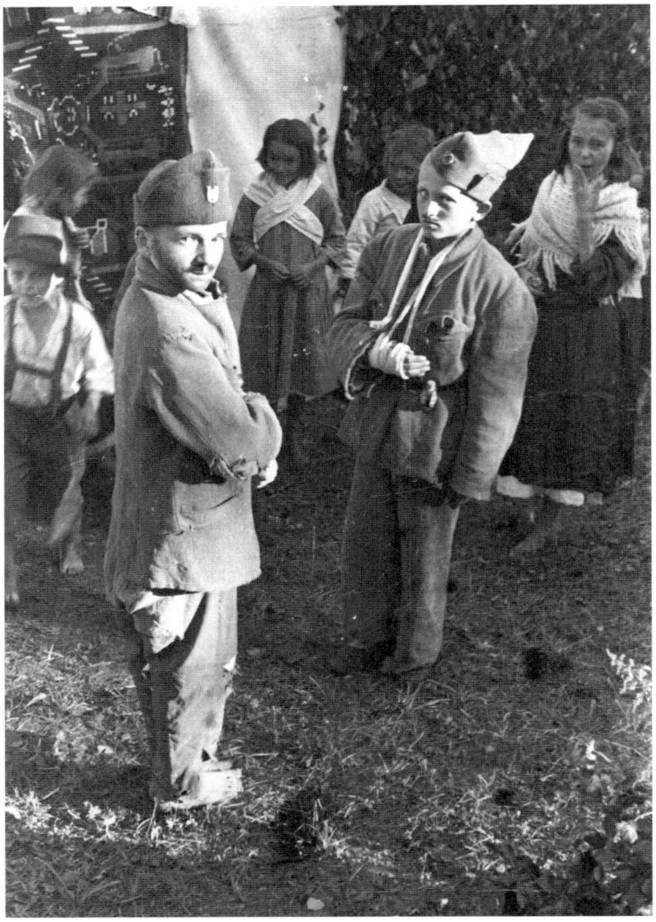

A children's theatre group, Psunj, 1944.
Photo: Pero Dragila. Croatian History Museum, HPM-100544–003.

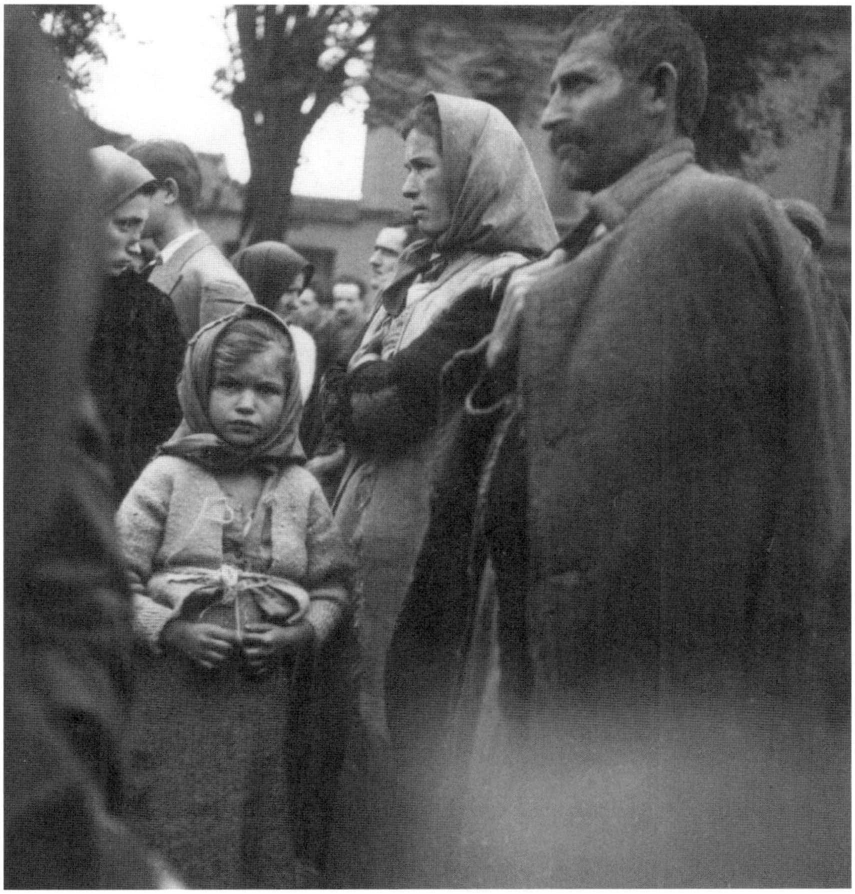

At flag-presentation ceremony of the newly founded Obilić choir society, held in tribute to the victims of fascist terror on the ruins of a church in Glina (site of a Ustashe massacre of Serbs in August 1941), Glina, Croatia, October 1944. Photo: Mahmud Konjhodžić. Croatian History Museum, HPM-MRNH-F-4777.

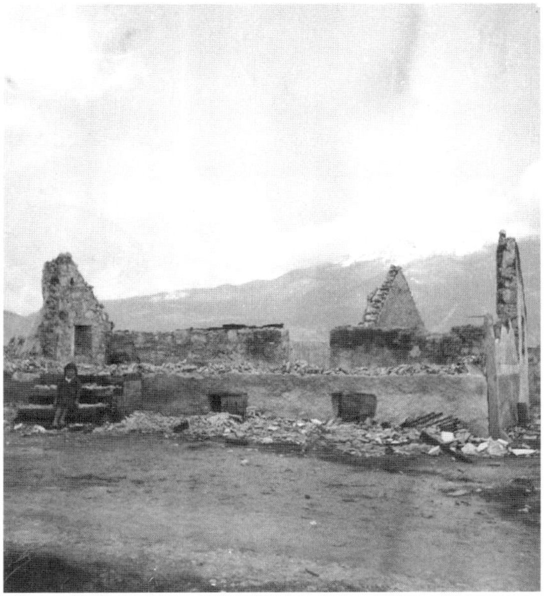

A child on the doorstep of its former home, Kamenica, Bosnia and Herzegovina. Photo: Žorž Skrigin. Museum of Yugoslavia, accession no. unknown.

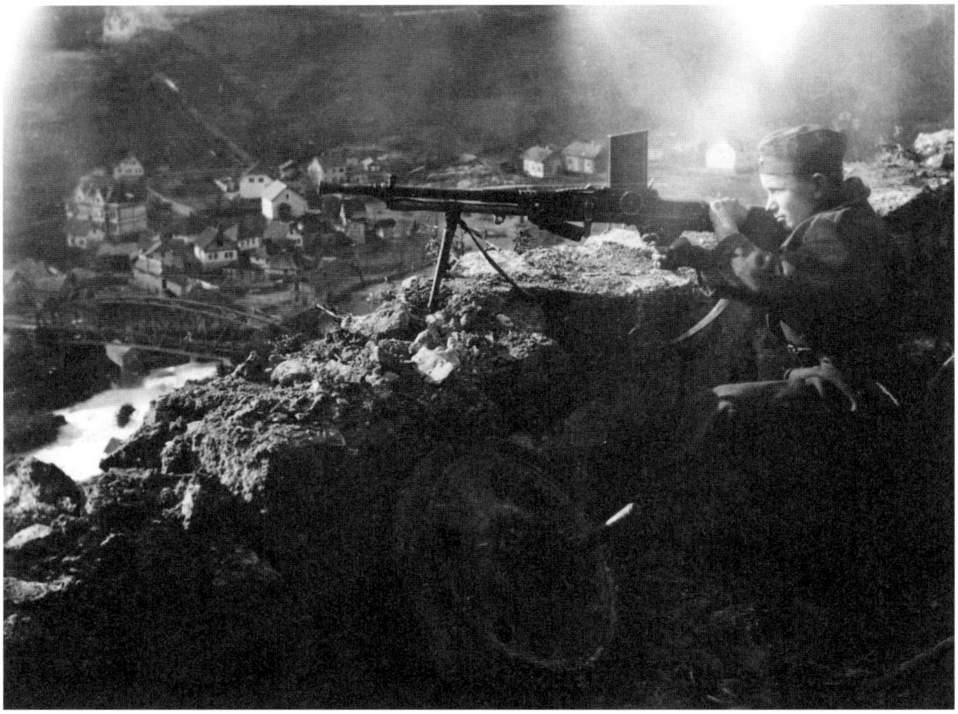

Artillery gunner in a tower in Jajce, Bosnia and Herzegovina, during Second Session of the AVNOJ, July 1943. Photographer unknown. Museum of Yugoslavia, III-204.

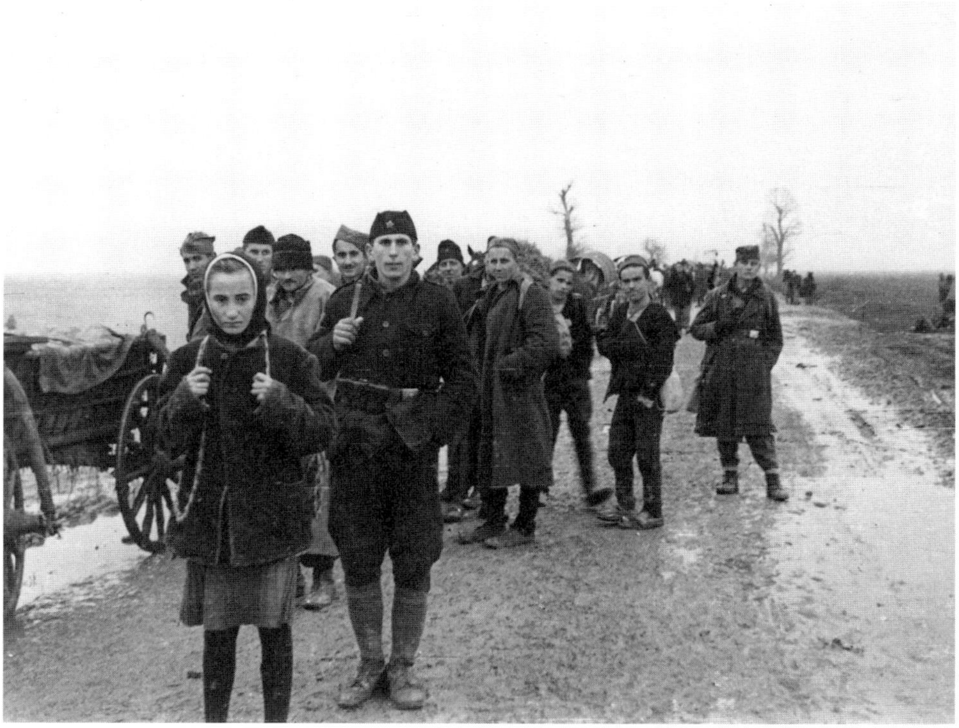

First Proletarian Corps on the march to Šid, on the Srijemski (Syrmian) Front, an Axis line of defence, December 1944. Photo: Pavle Bojčević. Museum of Yugoslavia.

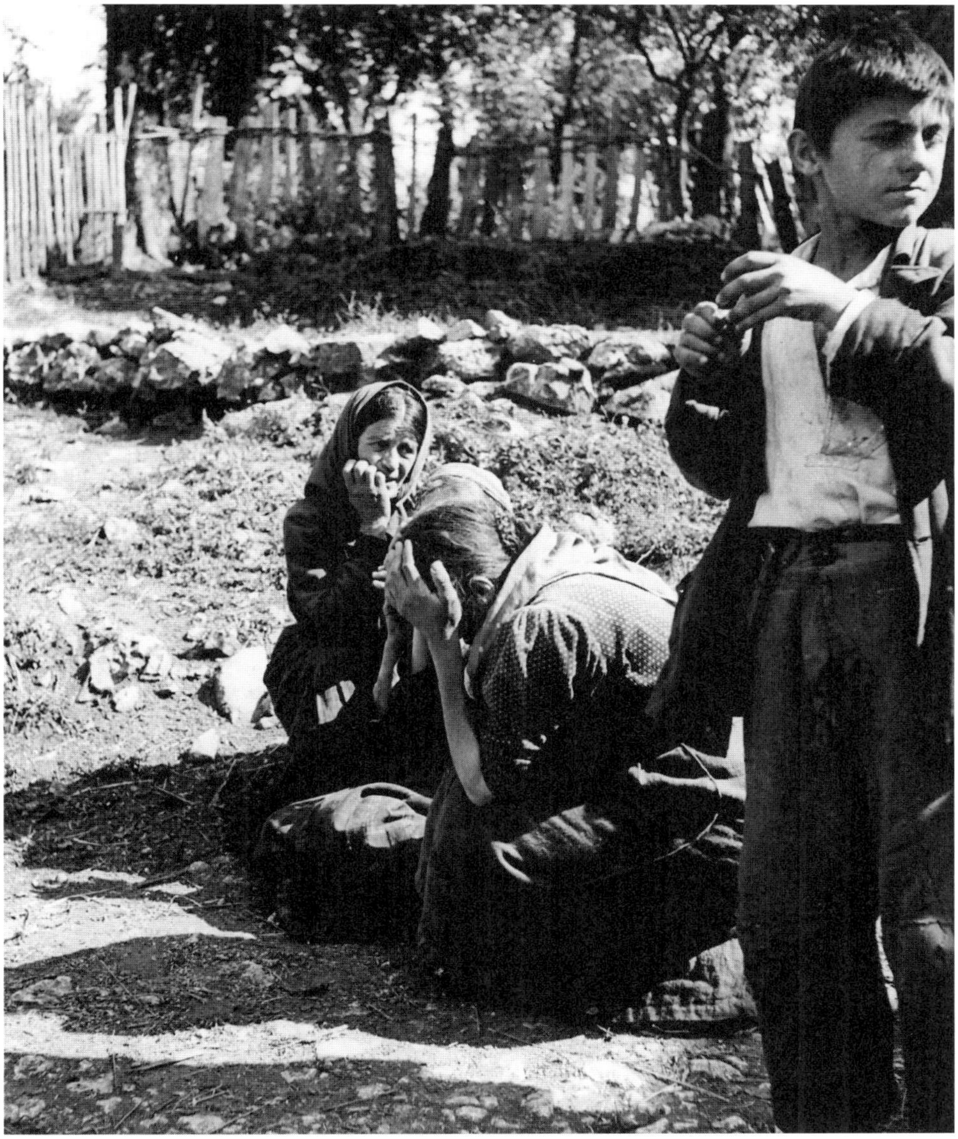

A family left homeless after the bombardment of Drežnica, July 1942.
Photographer unknown. Museum of Yugoslavia, III-3705.

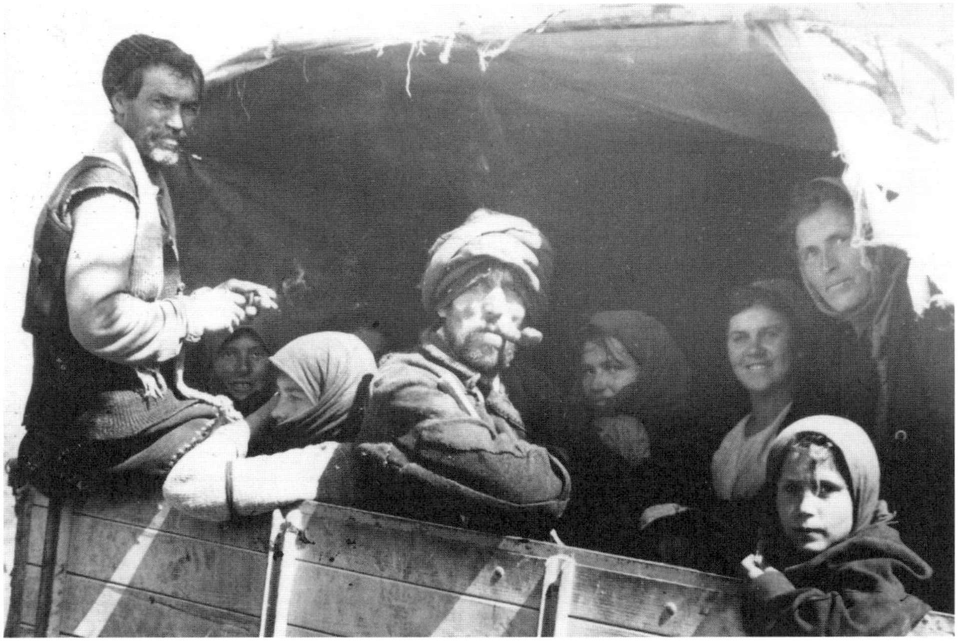

Uncaptioned. Photo: Drago Mažar. Archives of the Republic of Srpska, Banja Luka.

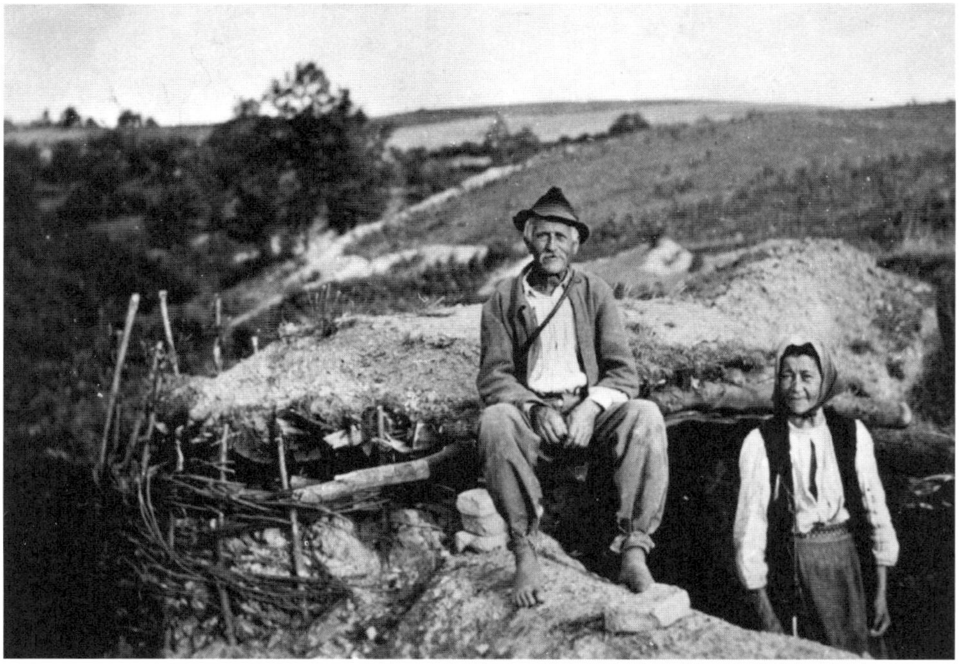

Displaced people from Podgrmeč, north-west Bosnia and Herzegovina, April 1945. Photographer unknown. History Museum of Bosnia and Herzegovina, FNOB 16223.

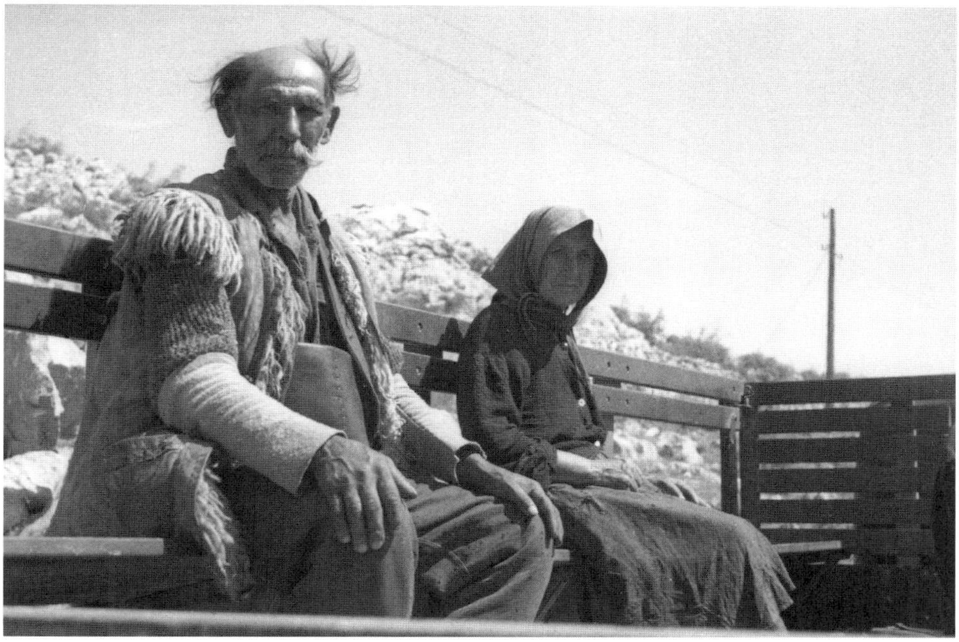

On the Adriatic coast road, May 1945. Photo: Dr Janez Milčinski. National Museum of Contemporary History of Slovenia, 1239/5.

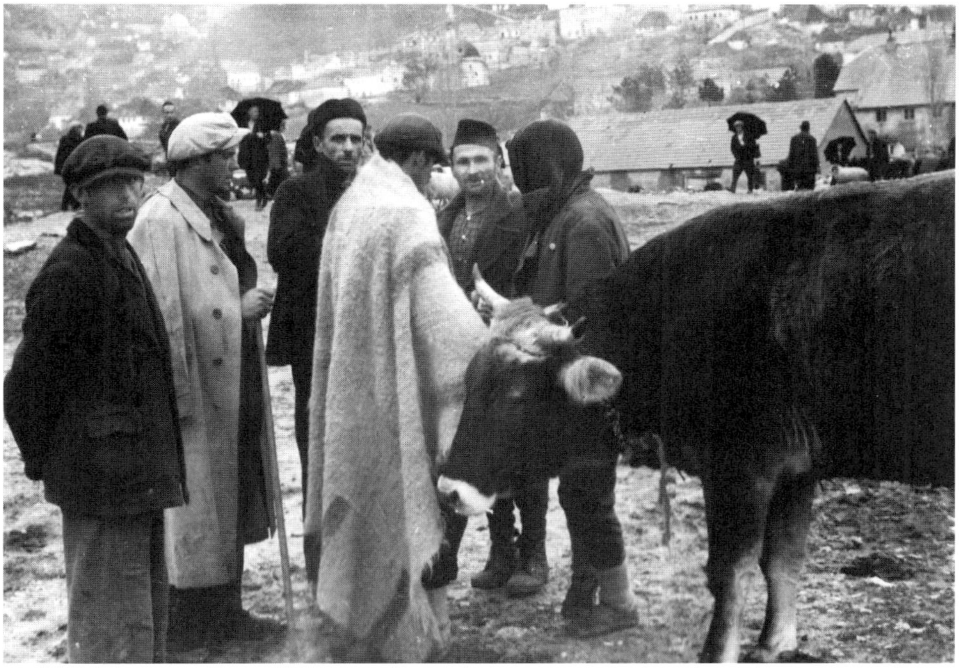

Market scene, Livno, Bosnia and Herzegovina, 1943. Photographer unknown. Museum of Yugoslavia, III-1812.

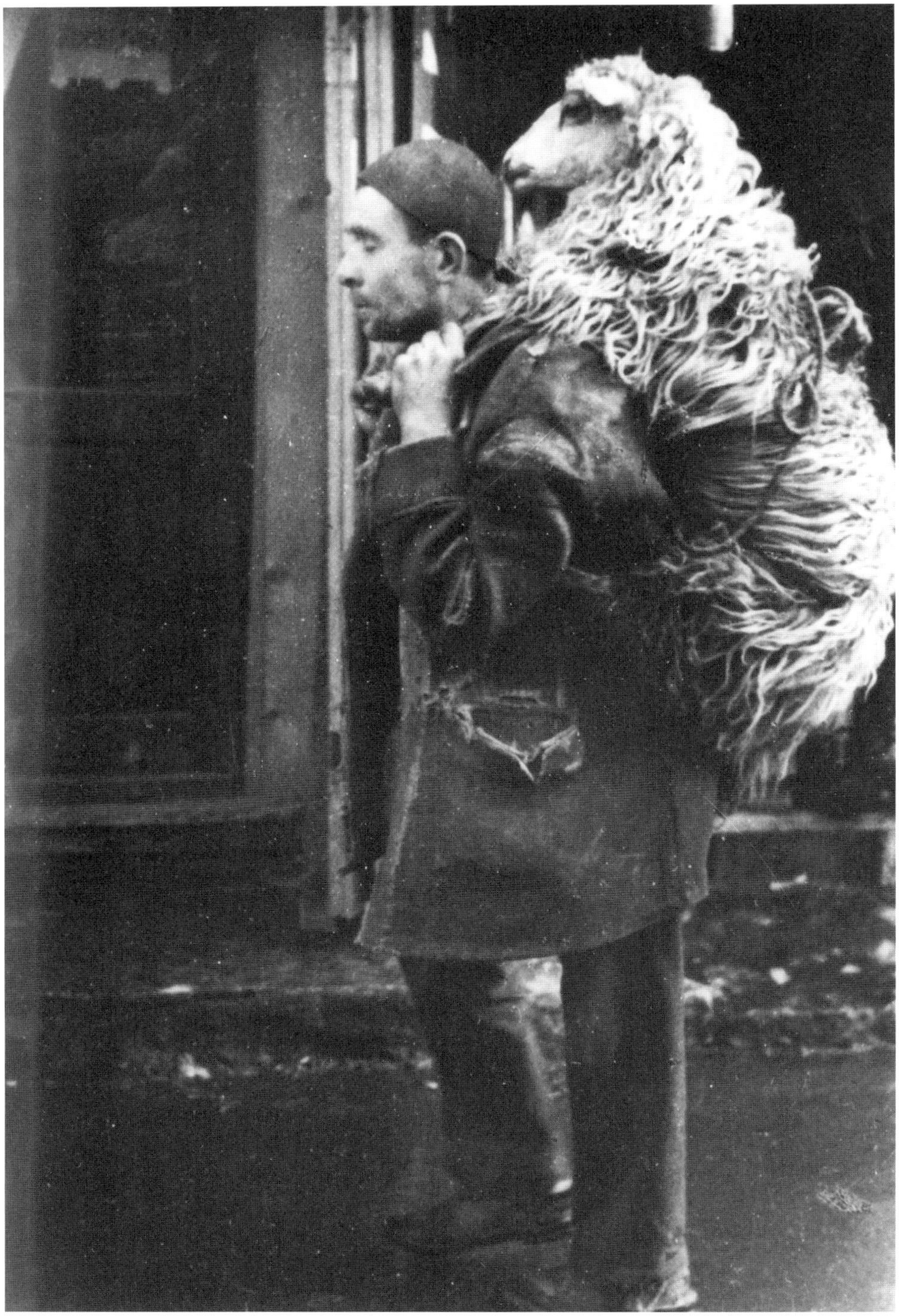

Displaced man from east Bosnia carrying one of his possessions. Photographer unknown.
History Museum of Bosnia and Herzegovina, FNOB 1994.

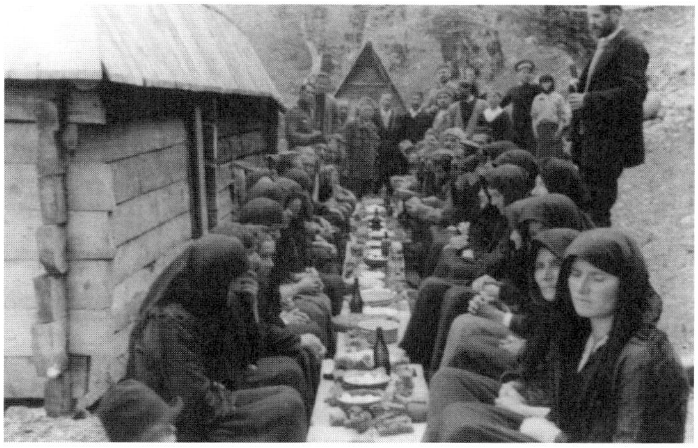

Wake with Dr Ivan Ribar and Dr Simo Milošević standing at far end of table, Zaglavak, Sandžak, Serbia, 16 May 1943. Photo: Dr Mladen Iveković. Croatian History Museum, HPM-MRNH-A-6337 149.

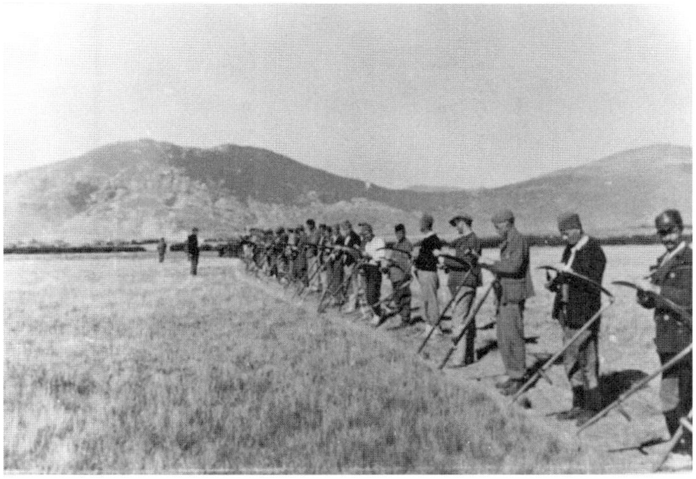

Staff battalion of the Thirty-Ninth Division helping locals make hay in Kupreško polje, Bosnia and Herzegovina, April 1944. Photographer unknown. History Museum of Bosnia and Herzegovina, FNOB 17704.

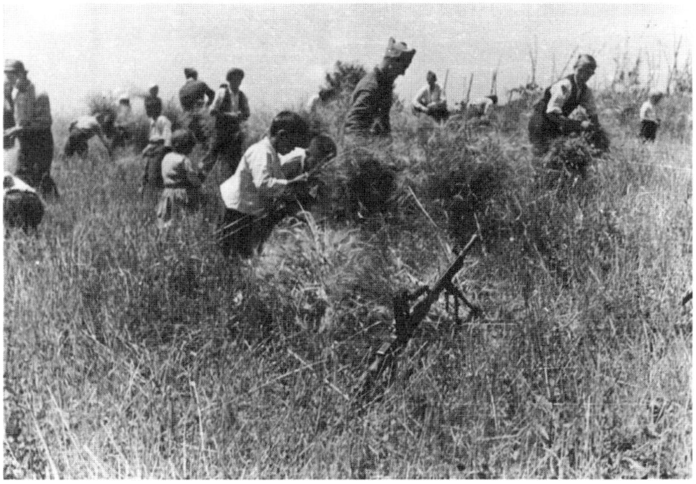

Tenth Zagreb Corps helping with the harvest, summer 1944. Photographer unknown. Zagreb City Museum, accession no. unknown.

Liberated Territory

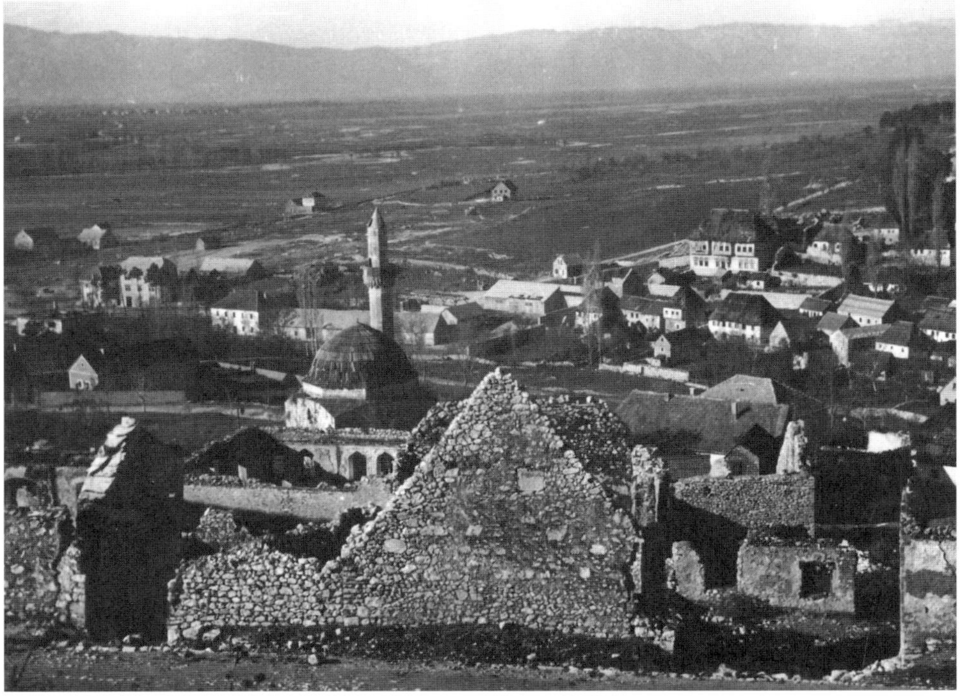

Panoramic shot of Livno, Bosnia and Herzegovina, 1943. Photographer unknown.
Central Committee of League of Communists of Yugoslavia Collection (CK SKJ), accession no. unknown.

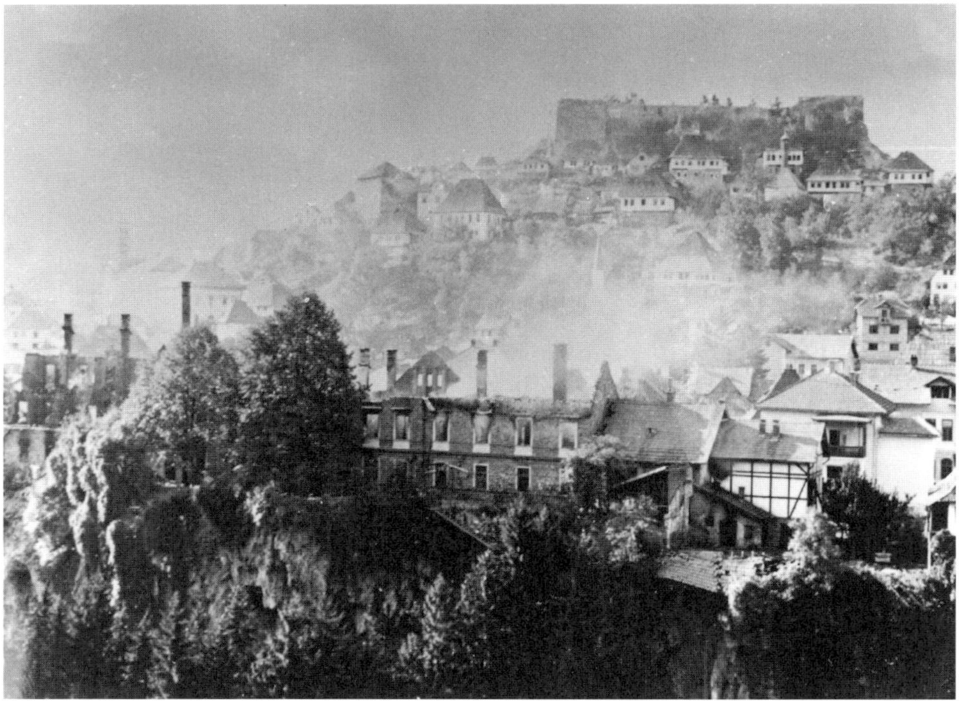

Bosnian town of Jajce during the Second Session of the AVNOJ. Photographer unknown.
History Museum of Bosnia and Herzegovina, FNOB 17882.

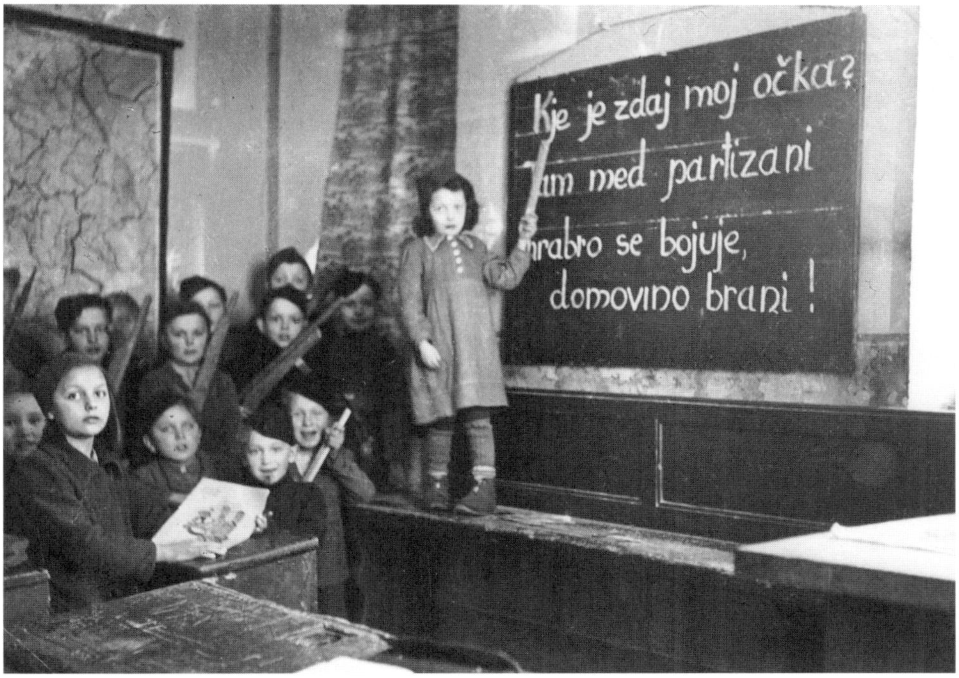

Children in school, Podprel, Kočevje, Slovenia, 1944. Photographer unknown.
National Museum of Contemporary History of Slovenia, accession no. unknown.

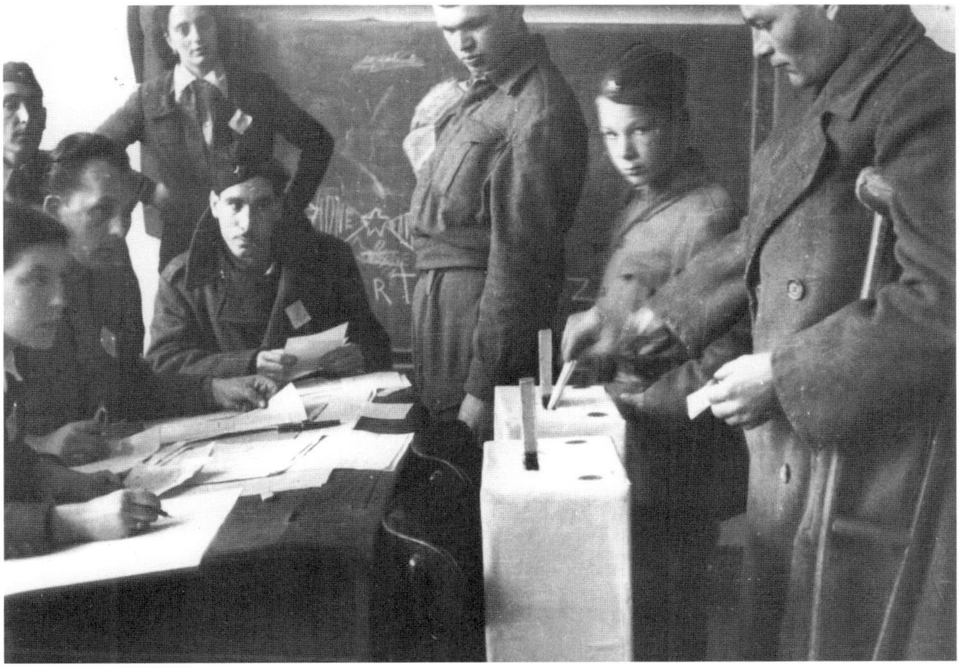

Elections for the people's liberation committees in Split, Croatia, March 1945.
Photographer unknown. Croatian History Museum, 4963.

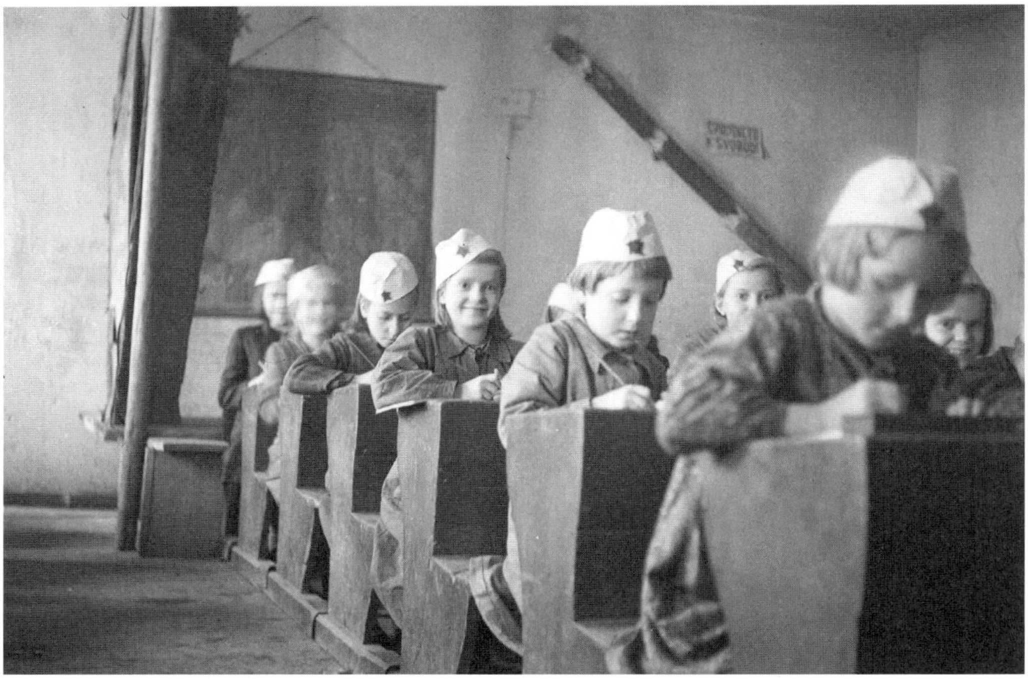

School lesson in Osilnica, Slovenia, 23 March 1945. Photo: Edi Šalhaus.
National Museum of Contemporary History of Slovenia, TN829/5.

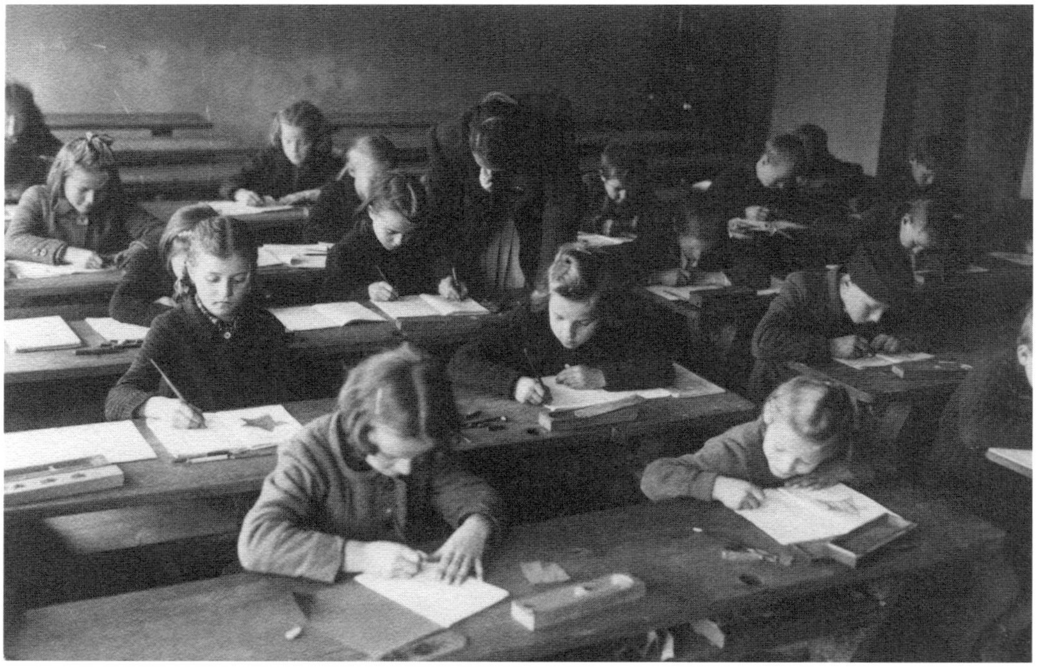

A Partisan school in Ljubno, Savinja valley, north Slovenia, autumn 1944. Photographer unknown.
Museum of Recent History, Celje FZ2 1612.

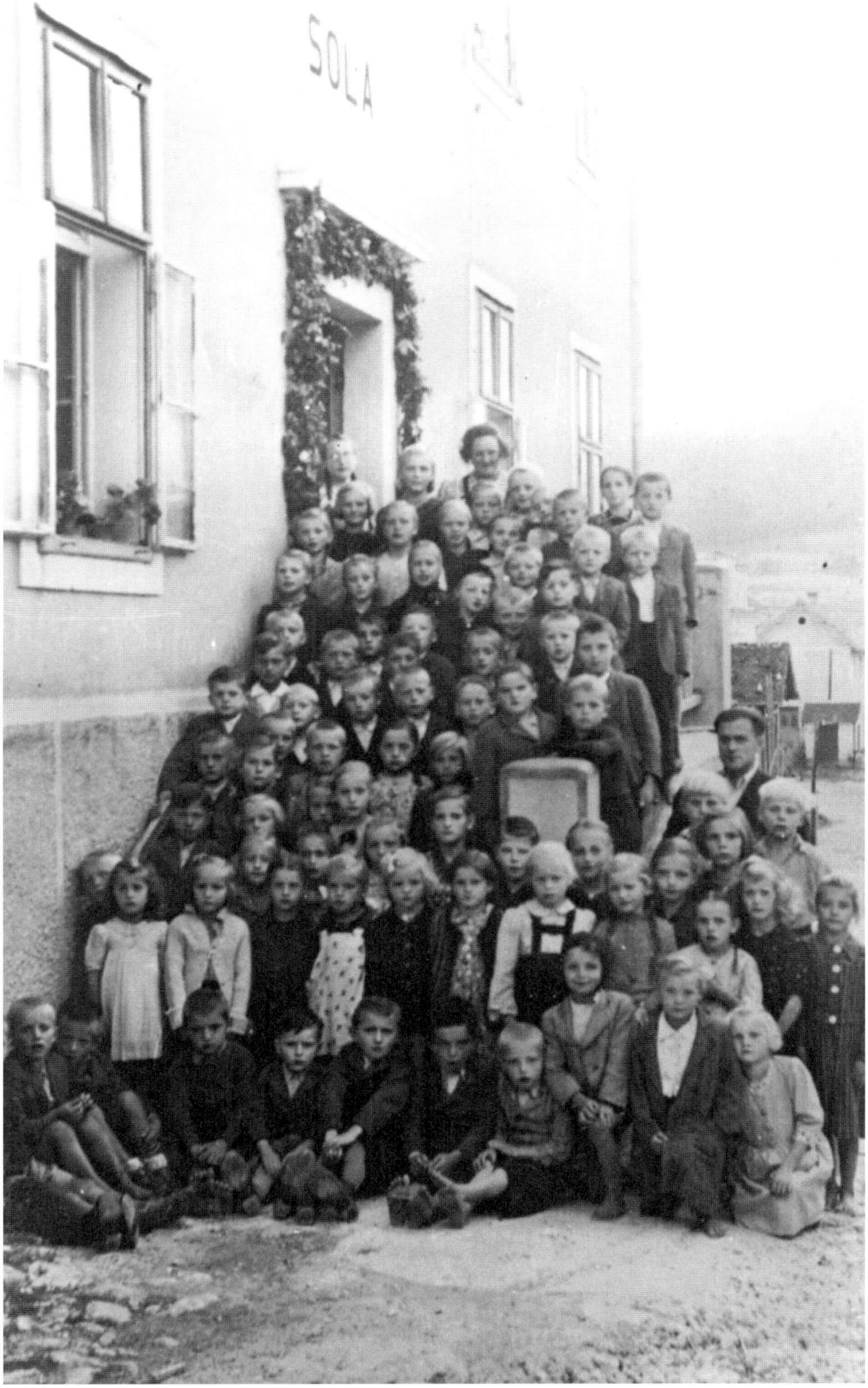

A Partisan school, Kozjansko, Slovenia, 1944. Photographer unknown.
Museum of Recent History, Celje, FZ2 A.

Rallies

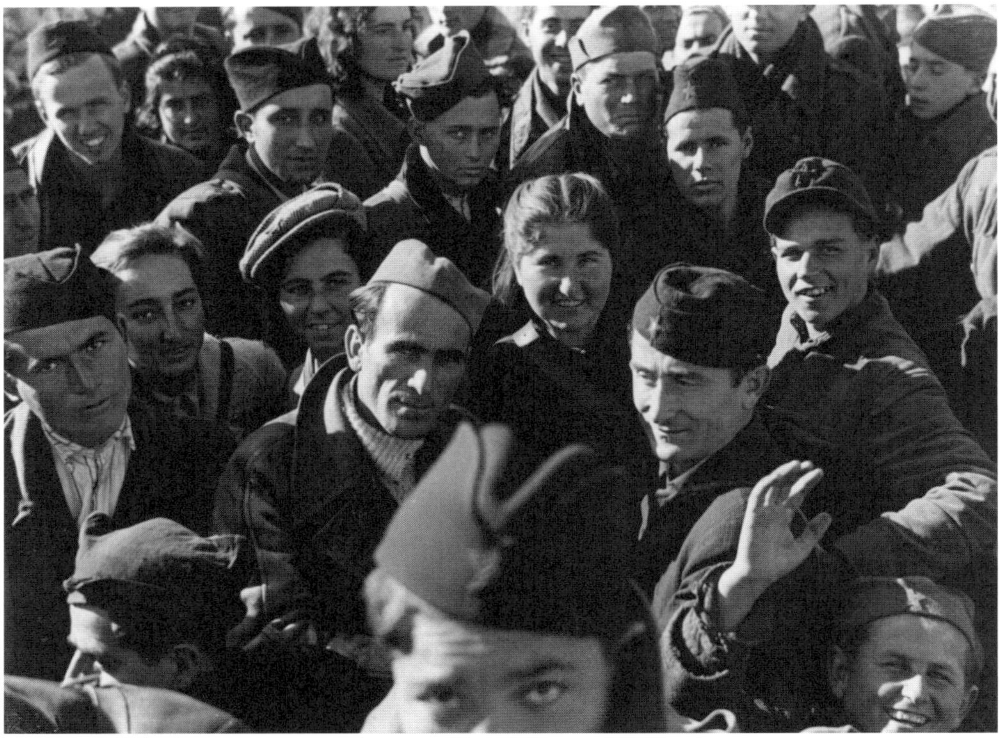

Youth delegation from the Second Proletarian Division on the way from Livno to Glamoč to attend the First Congress of the USAOJ, 22 December 1942; among them: Stana Tomašević, Jurica Ribar, Dragica Đurašević, Grozdana-Zina Belić Penezić, Zaga Stojilović, Boško Buha and Pavle Bojčević. Photographer unknown. Museum of Yugoslavia, III-11983.

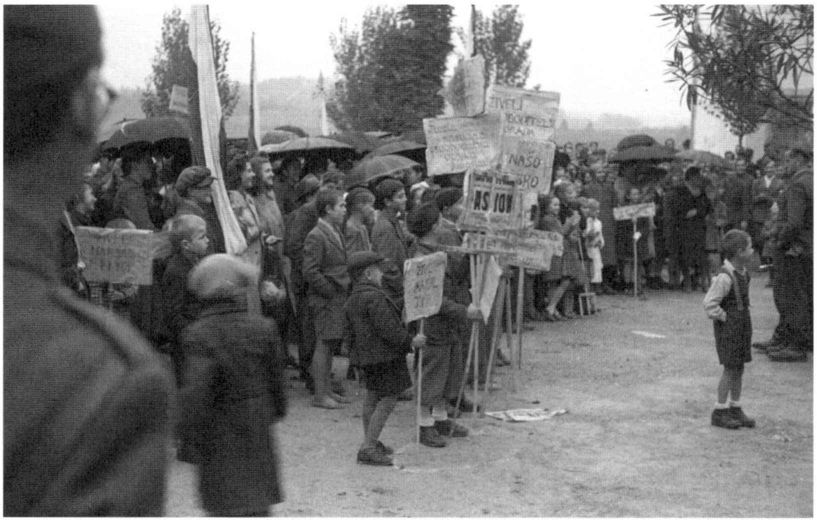

Youth delegation, carrying placards, arriving at meeting grounds, Črnomelj, Slovenia, 22 October 1944. Photo: Franjo Veselko. National Museum of Contemporary History of Slovenia, TN376/901.

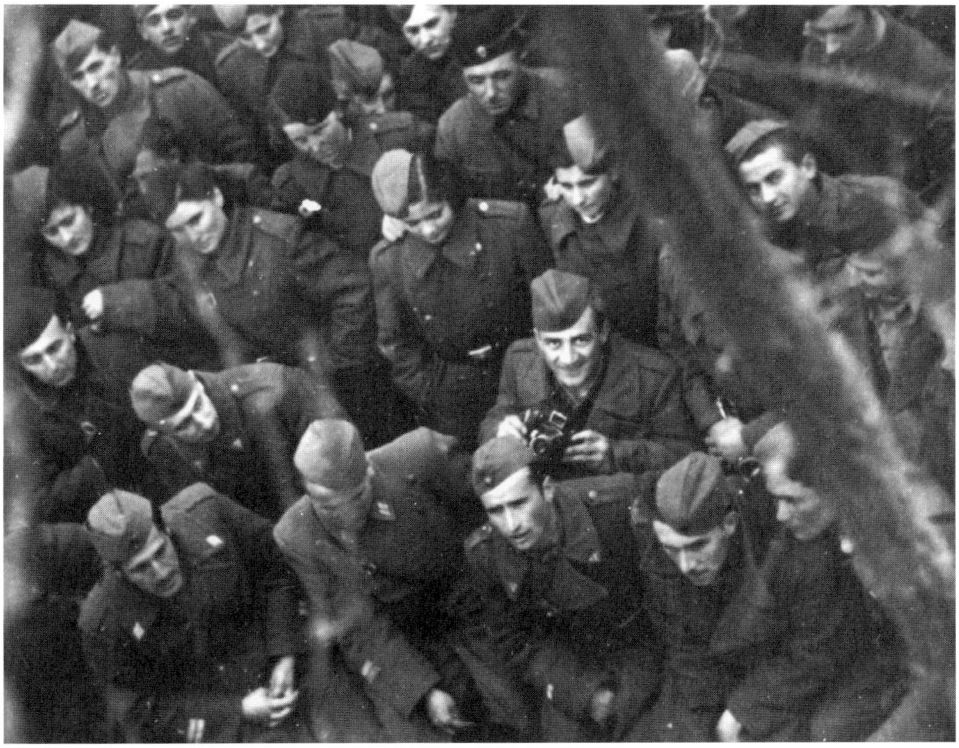

An event held by the First Krajina Brigade on the Srijemski (Syrmian) Front, autumn 1944. Photographer unknown. History Museum of Bosnia and Herzegovina, FNOB 18826.

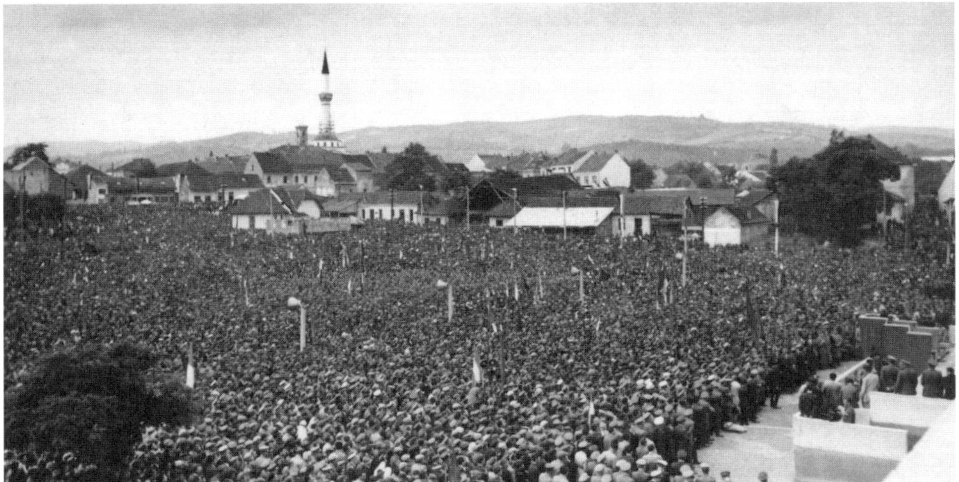

Rally in Banja Luka. Photo: Drago Mažar. Archives of the Republic of Srpska, Banja Luka.

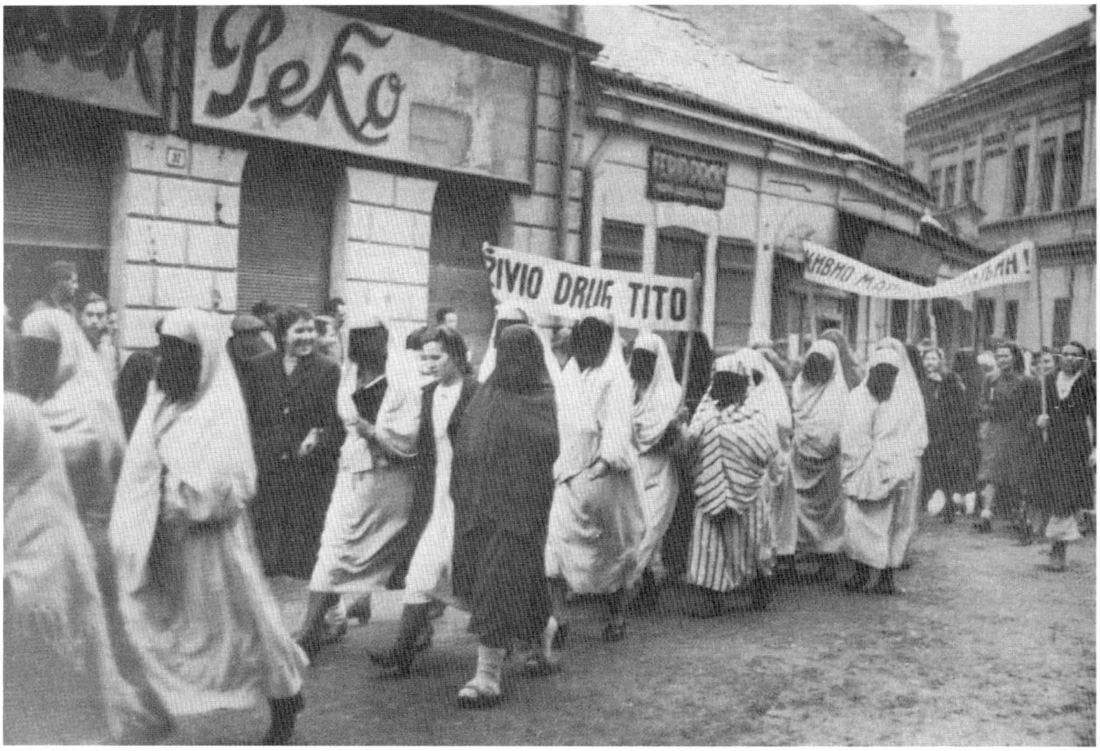

An anti-fascist meeting of women in Tuzla, eastern Bosnia and Herzegovina.
Photo: Drago Mažar. Archives of the Republic of Srpska, Banja Luka.

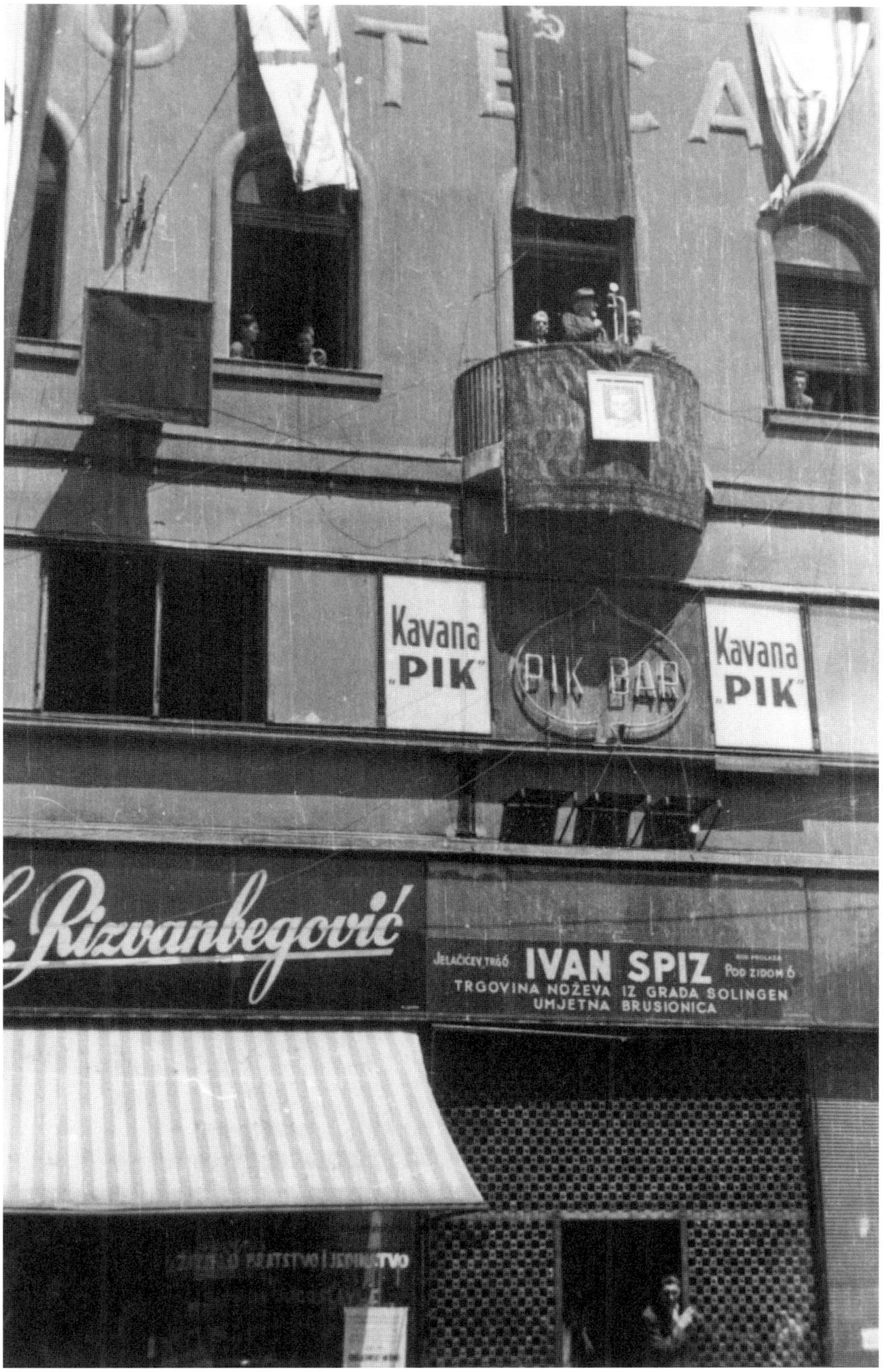

Vladimir Nazor addresses the masses from a balcony featuring a portrait of Josip Broz Tito, on what is nowadays called Ban Jelačić Square in the Croatian capital, Zagreb, 16 May 1945. Photo: Milan Blašković. Croatian History Museum, HPM-MRNH-F-2407.

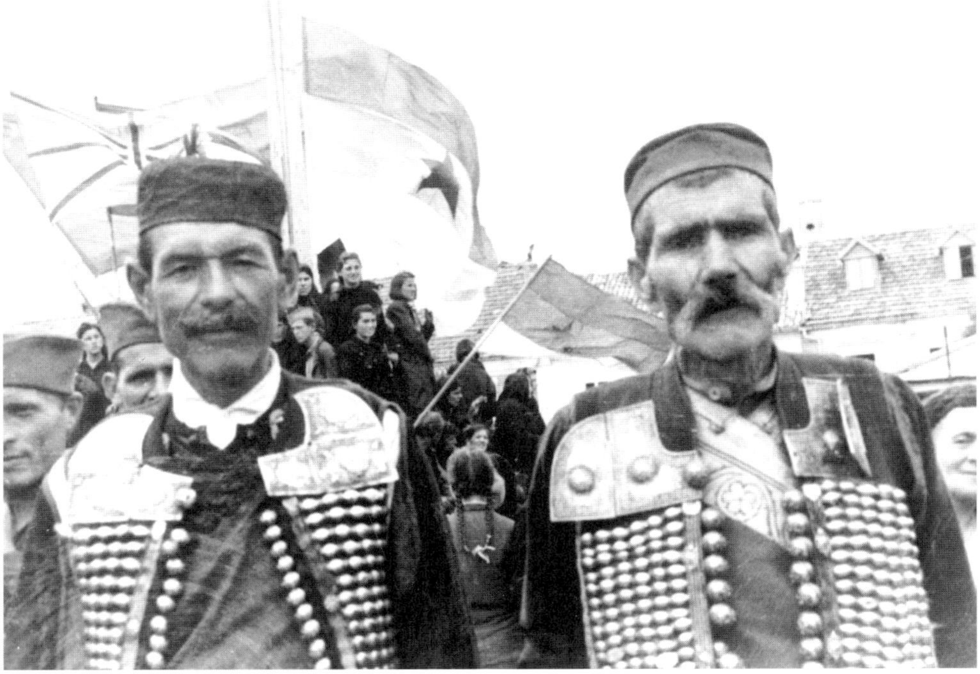

Old veterans celebrating the October Revolution in Nikšić, Montenegro, 1944.
Photographer unknown. Military Museum Belgrade, 12683.

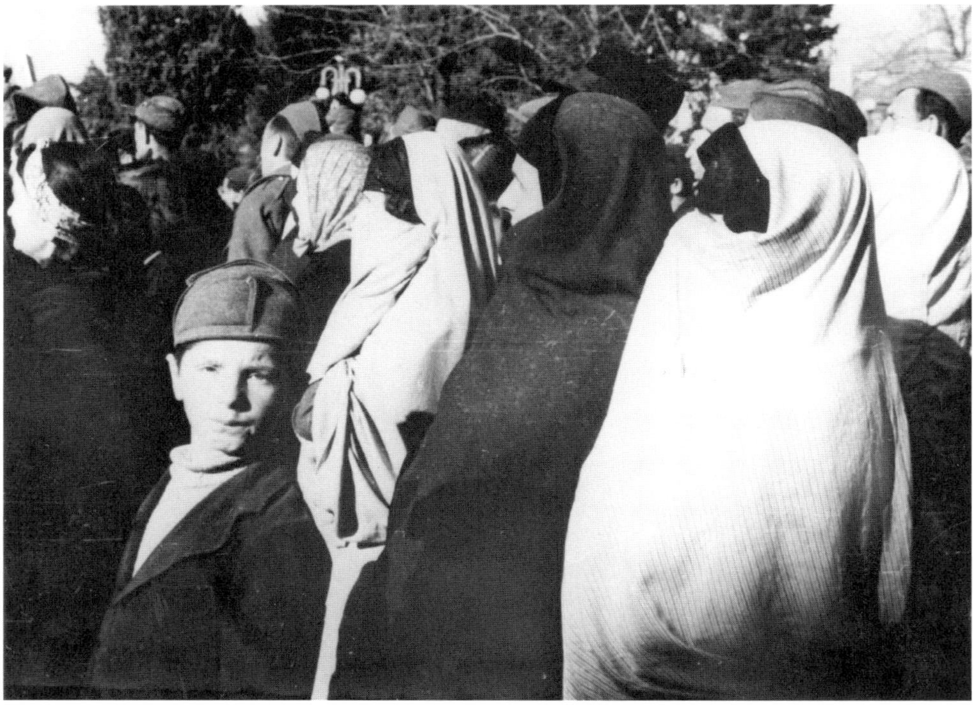

Picture from a meeting in liberated Mostar, Bosnia and Herzegovina, 16 November 1945.
Photographer unknown. History Museum of Bosnia and Herzegovina, FNOB 11209.

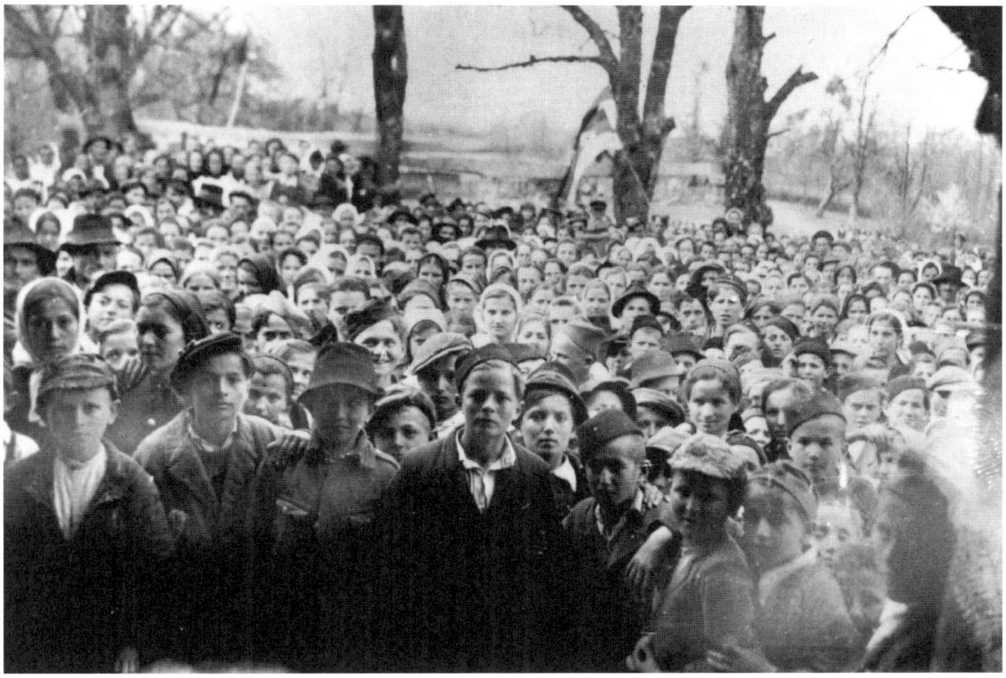

A rally in Brekinja, Kozarska Dubic, Bosnia and Herzegovina. Photographer unknown.
History Museum of Bosnia and Herzegovina, FNOB 2982.

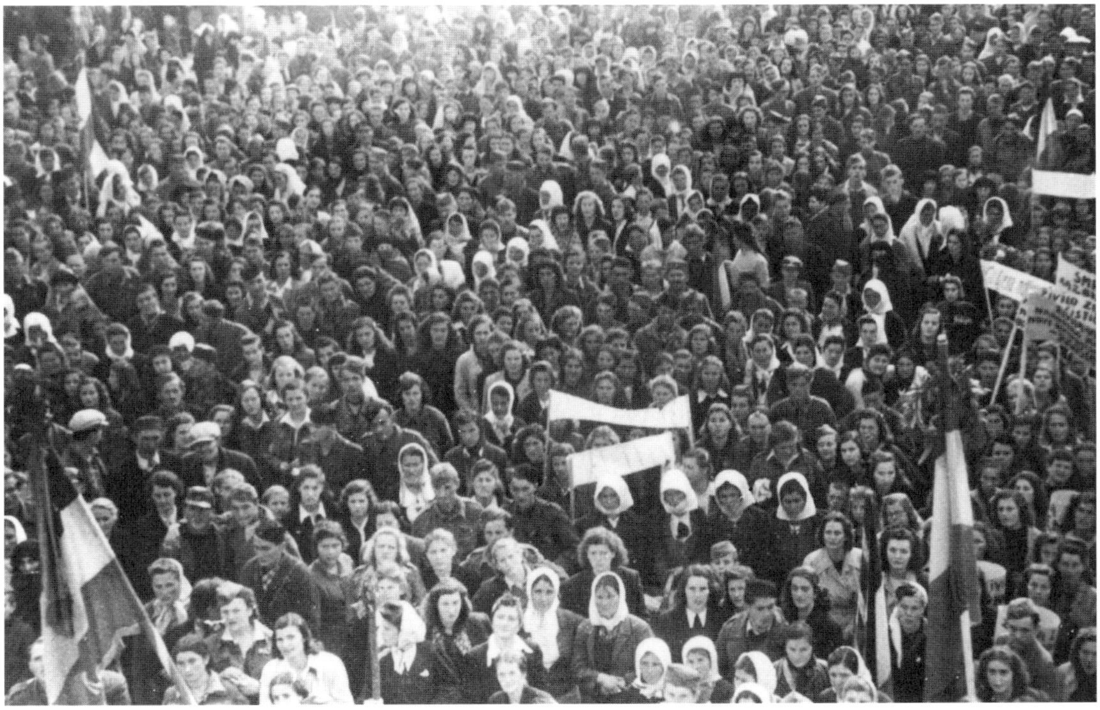

A meeting in Trebinje, Bosnia and Herzegovina, opposing the return of King Peter II to Yugoslavia, 1944.
Photographer unknown. History Museum of Bosnia and Herzegovina, FNOB 19351.

Graffiti

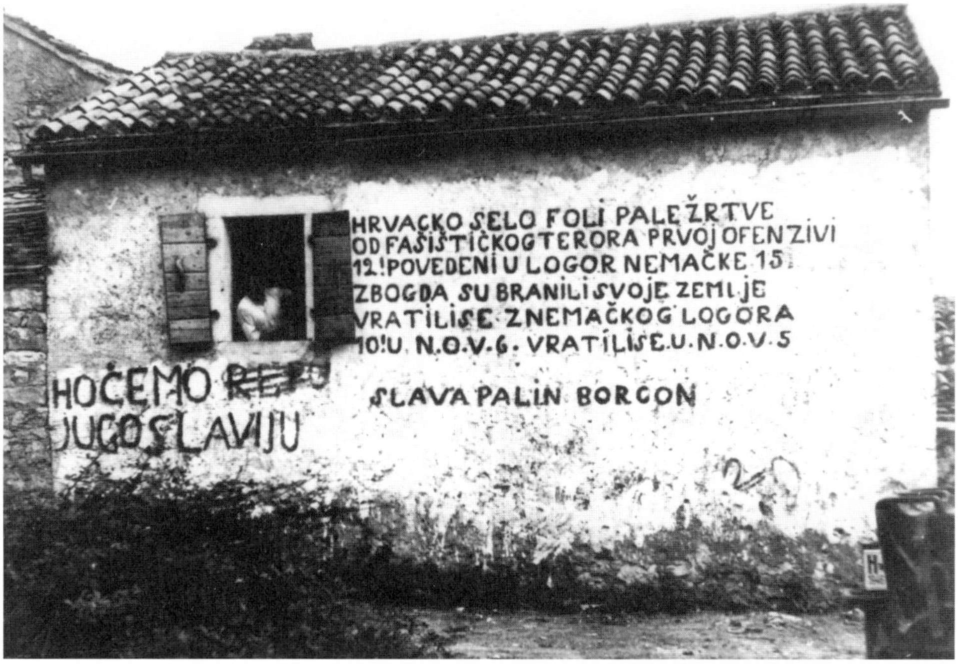

Slogans on house in an Istrian village: besides 'We want Yugoslavia' (left), the text on the right describes the deportation of Croatian villagers by Italian fascists to a German camp. Photographer and date unknown.

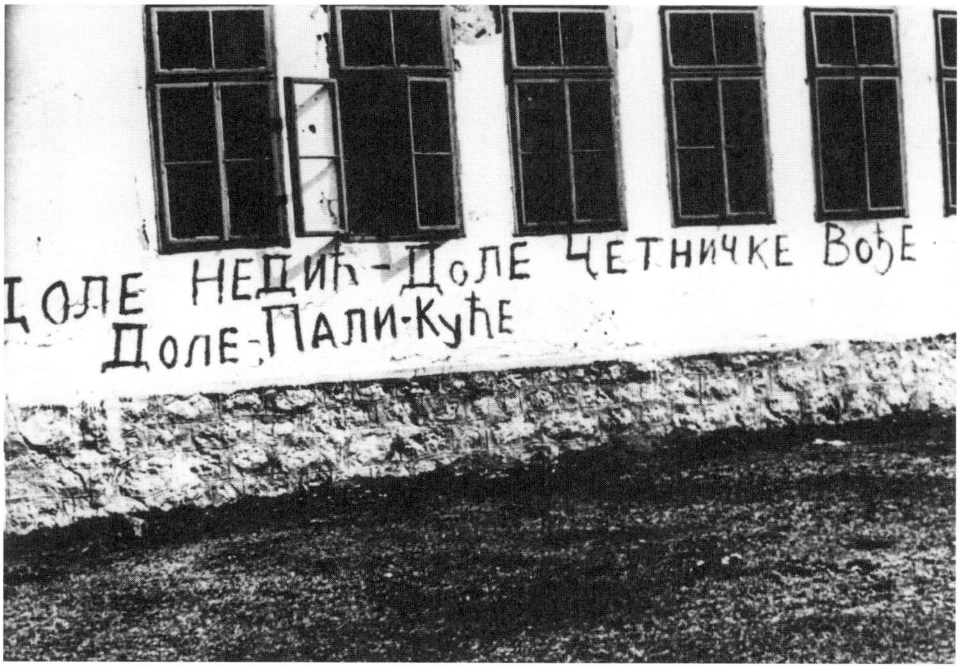

Slogans on a building on the way from Sarajevo to Zvornik: 'Down with Nedić. Down with the arsonists. Burn down houses'. Bosnia and Herzegovina. Photographer unknown. History Museum of Bosnia and Herzegovina, FNOB 38.

Religious Freedom

Historical photographs revealing insights into religious freedom and the right to practice one's religion within the Partisan movement seem especially important in the present moment. These photographs show that many priests were involved in the People's Liberation War. Priests who joined or supported the Partisan movement are visible in the photographs, where they are seen observing religious festivals, holding mass, assisting soldiers, teaching, blessing Partisan flags, putting up religious symbols, and getting involved in other faith-related activities. Many Partisans were given a religious burial, as demonstrated by the example of a funeral of twenty-seven Partisan casualties killed by the Ustashe between 12 and 13 September 1943 while being treated in hospital in Otočac. Their funeral service was held by the priest Grga Starčević.

When it had become clear that war was on the horizon, Josip Broz Tito published an article in *Proleter*, the newspaper of the central committee of the Communist Party of Yugoslavia. The article was titled 'Communists and Catholics'. In it, drawing on Comintern's decision to establish a joint anti-fascist front, Tito stated:

> Without losing sight of what separates us, we must look and search for what brings us closer to them [Catholics]. And what brings us closer, above all else, is our common struggle for our daily bread. The common struggle for peace and freedom, against war and fascism. The common struggle for equality and freedom of the Croatian and Slovenian people. The common struggle against the 6 January fascist cliques [the 6 January Dictatorship] who have exiled and imprisoned not only communists but also Catholic leaders and organisations. The common struggle for the life of a dignified person. Faced with the dangers of the hellish forces of war and fascism, we hold out our hands to jointly defend the peace and wellbeing of all humanity.[1]

The key document on arrangements for religious services in Partisan units was an order from the Supreme Command given on 23 June 1942 to the headquarters of the Proletarian brigades. It dealt with arrangements for religious officials responsible for keeping records of fallen comrades, the promotion of the People's Liberation War and holding religious rituals if the people so demanded.

1 Josip Broz Tito, 'Komunisti i katolici', in: Proleter, 1936.

One of the most prominent figures in the Partisan movement was the Serbian Orthodox priest Vlada Zečević, who joined the Partisans after the Chetniks started collaborating with German forces. The largest concentration of Orthodox priests who assisted the Partisans was in Montenegro.[2] In Croatia, the Catholic priest Svetozar Rittig had an especially prominent role. He was the pre-war parish priest at St Mark's (Crkva sv. Marka) in Zagreb and had been embroiled in a long-running conflict with Ustashe leader Ante Pavelić since 1929. After the founding of the Independent State of Croatia, Rittig left for Novi Vinodolski, then for the island of Krk, where he requested that the bishop of Krk seek out two young priests with whom he could perform religious services on liberated territory. The bishop rejected his request, but Rittig left to join the Partisans anyway. In all, 147 Catholic priests joined Partisan ranks.

As concerns religious freedom, the situation in Macedonia is particularly interesting, as the republic administration installed an officer for religion in Macedonia. The liberated territory hosted the Council of Orthodox Priests in July 1943 and such events as a religious celebration of Saint Sava. The council demanded autocephaly (religious independence) from the Serbian Orthodox Church.

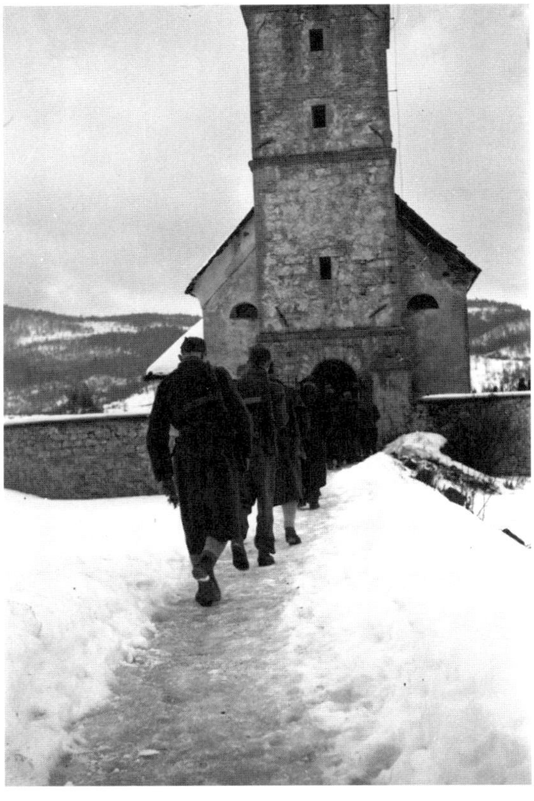

Partisans leaving for church in Babno Polje, Slovenia. 1945. Photo: Edi Šelhaus. National Museum of Contemporary History of Slovenia, TN964/1.

2 Jozo Tomasevich, *Rat i revolucija u Jugoslaviji 1941. – 1945. Okupacija i kolaboracija*, Zagreb 2010, p. 581.

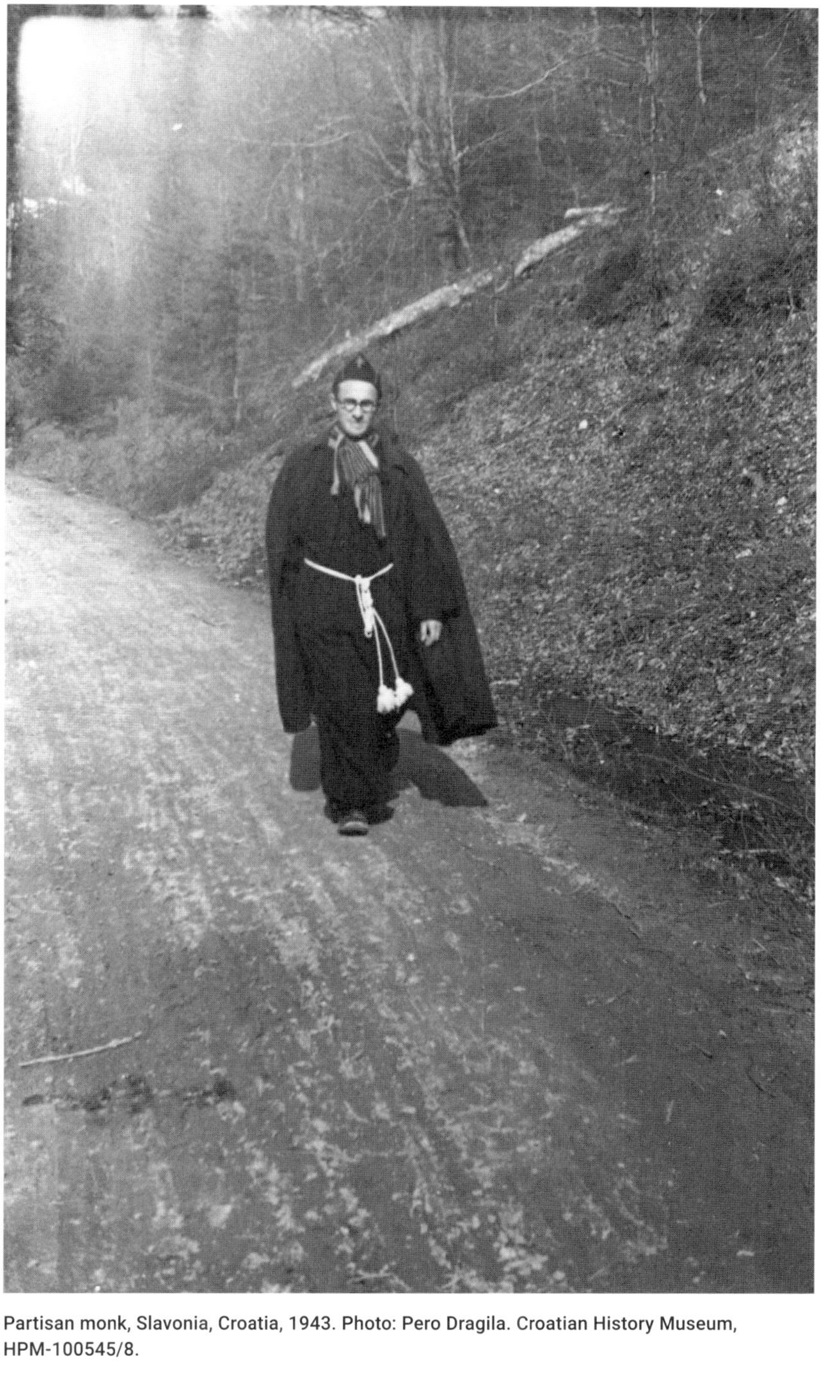

Partisan monk, Slavonia, Croatia, 1943. Photo: Pero Dragila. Croatian History Museum, HPM-100545/8.

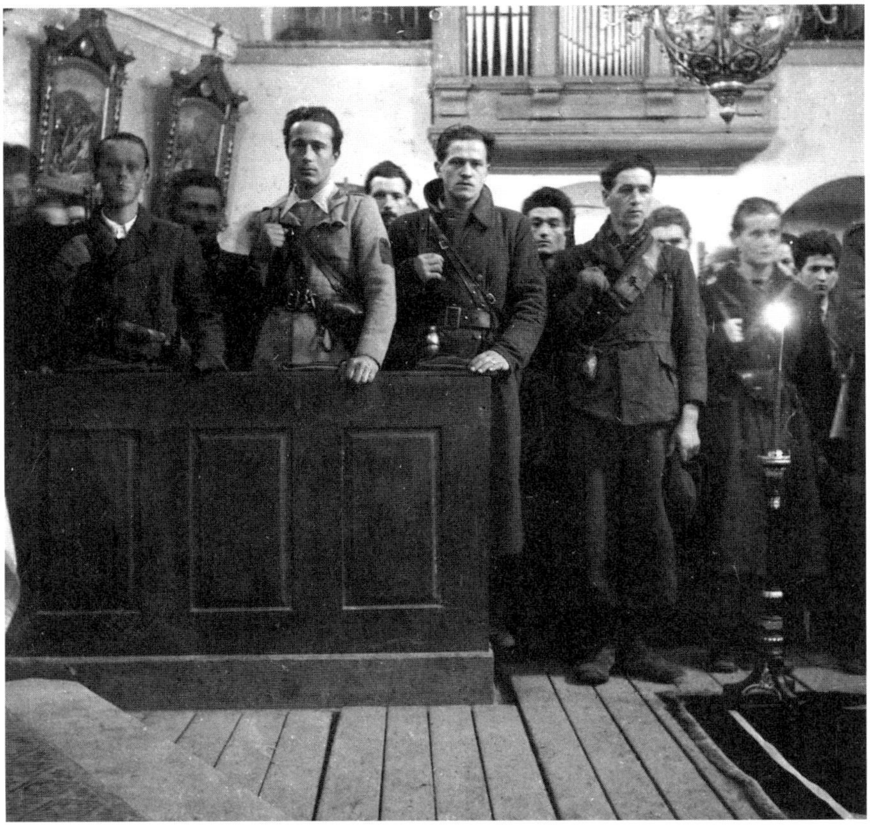

During service (with colonel Ivan Gošnjak second from right). Photo: Mirko Trobec. National Museum of Contemporary History of Slovenia, T/31.

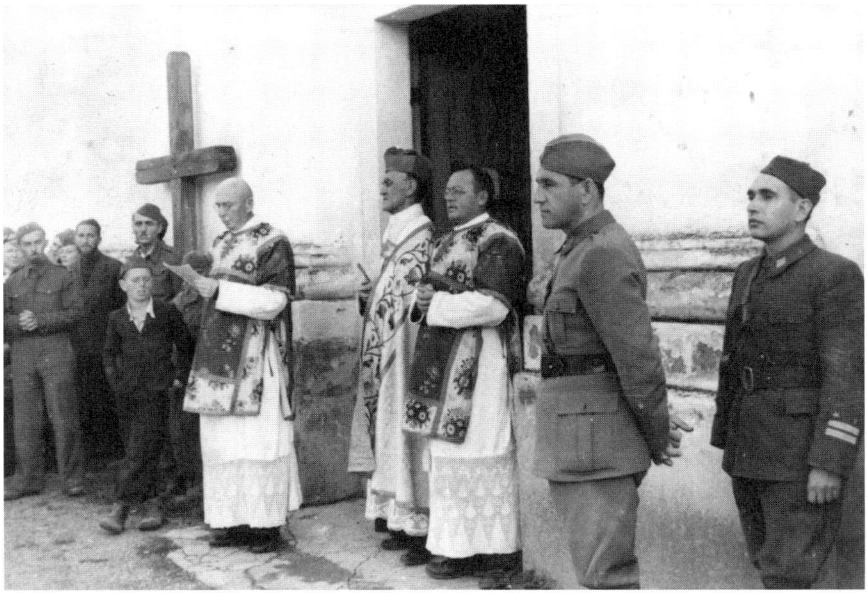

Monsignor Svetozar Rittig holding mass to celebrate the liberation of Belgrade, Topusko, Croatia, October 1944. Photo: Photography Service of the ZAVNOH, Croatian History Museum, HPM-MRNH-A-2602 f8 21a s.

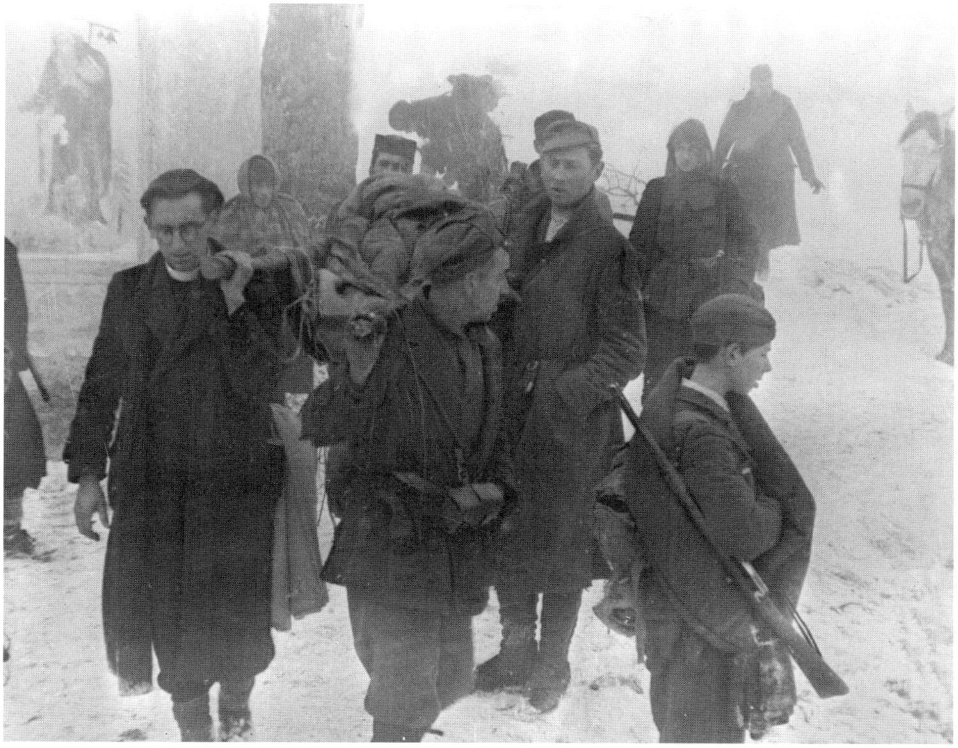

Carrying the injured of the Fourteenth Division, with the division's religious officer, Jože Lampret, shouldering the stretcher. Photo: Jože Petek. National Museum of Contemporary History of Slovenia, 1734.

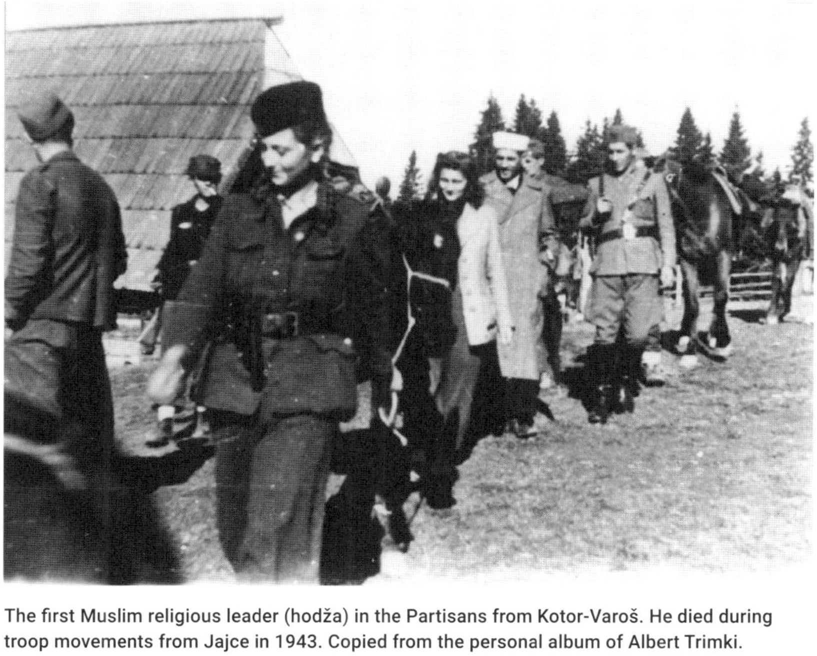

The first Muslim religious leader (hodža) in the Partisans from Kotor-Varoš. He died during troop movements from Jajce in 1943. Copied from the personal album of Albert Trimki. History Museum of Bosnia and Herzegovina, FNOB 19545.

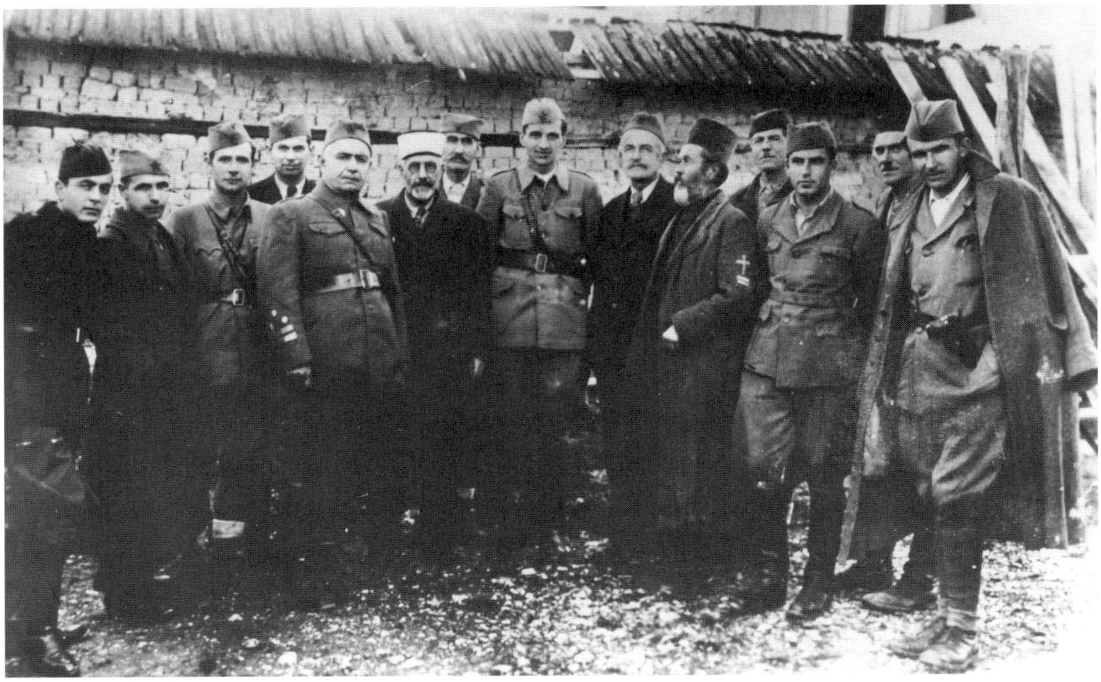

The staff of the People's Liberation Movement of Sandžak and executive committee of the Anti-Fascist Council for the People's Liberation of Sandžak, including Priest Jevstatije Karamatijević from Nova Varoš and the Dervish mufti Šećerkadić from Pljevlja, Pljevlja, Montenegro, November 1943. Photographer unknown. The original photograph was in the collection of the former Institute of the Worker's Movement of Serbia.

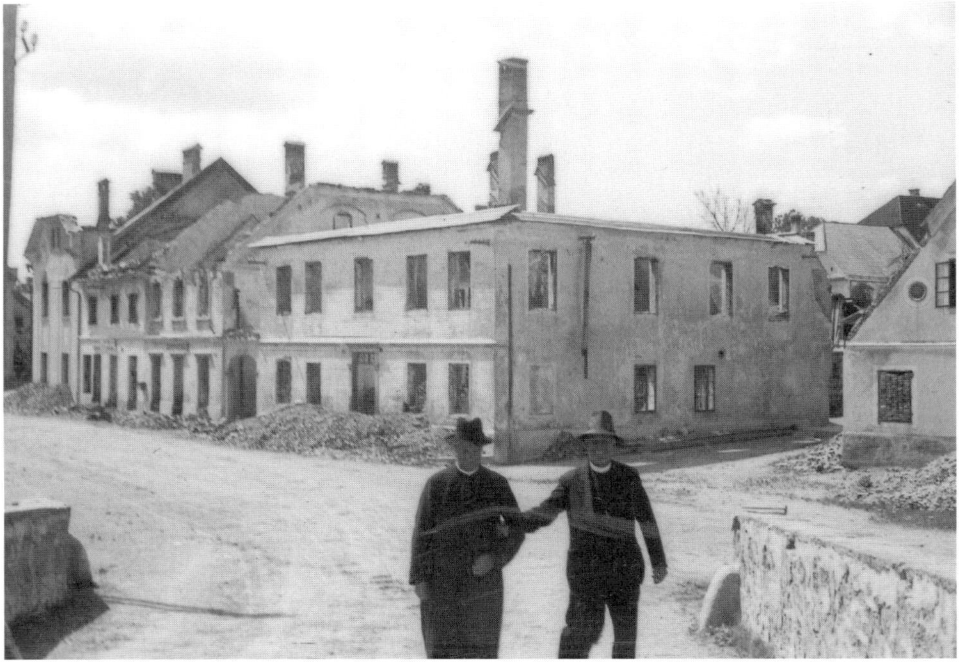

The ruins of the Žumer Hotel in Cerknica, Slovenia, 1944. Photo: Vinko Bavec. National Museum of Contemporary History of Slovenia, TN173/15.

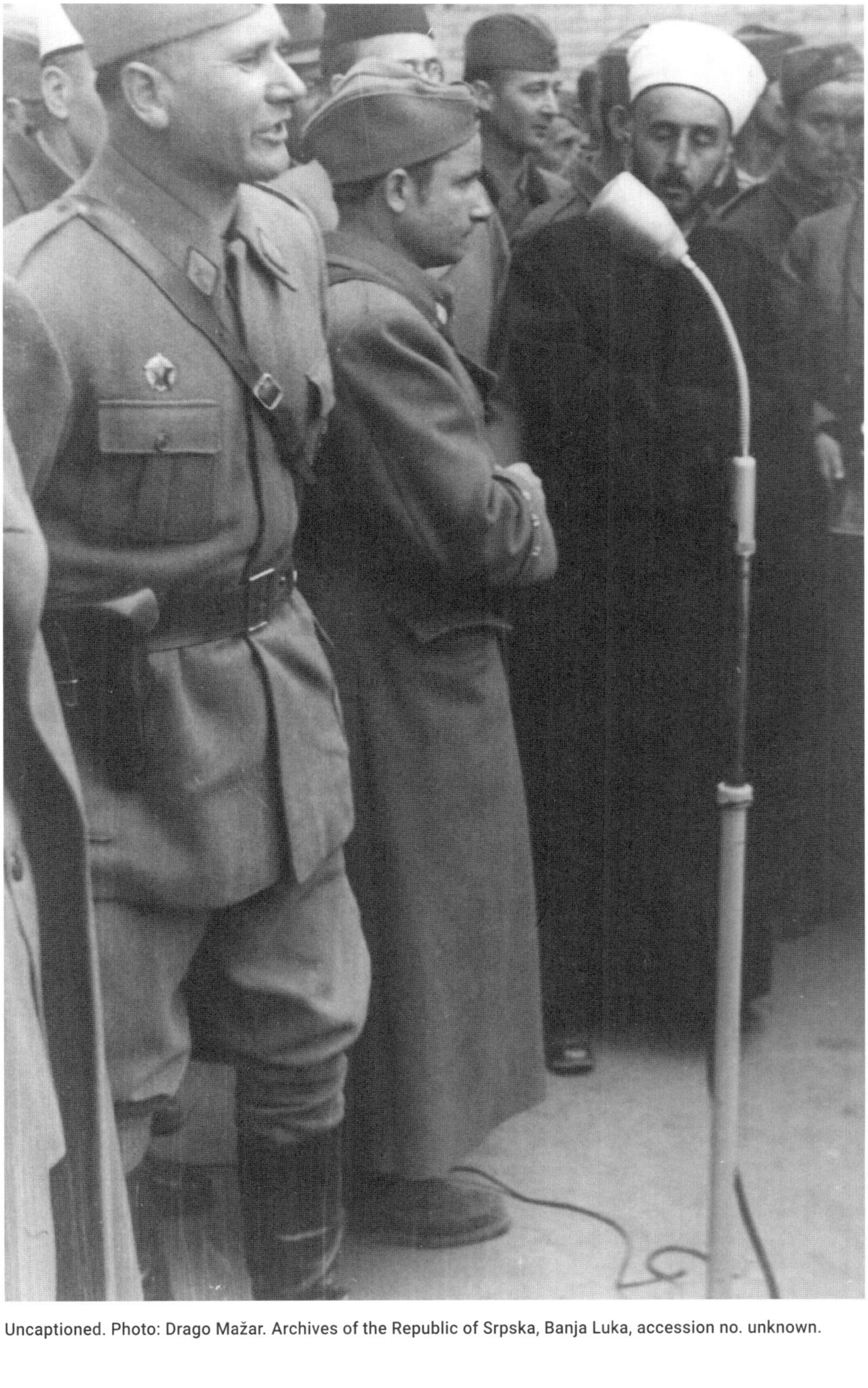

Uncaptioned. Photo: Drago Mažar. Archives of the Republic of Srpska, Banja Luka, accession no. unknown.

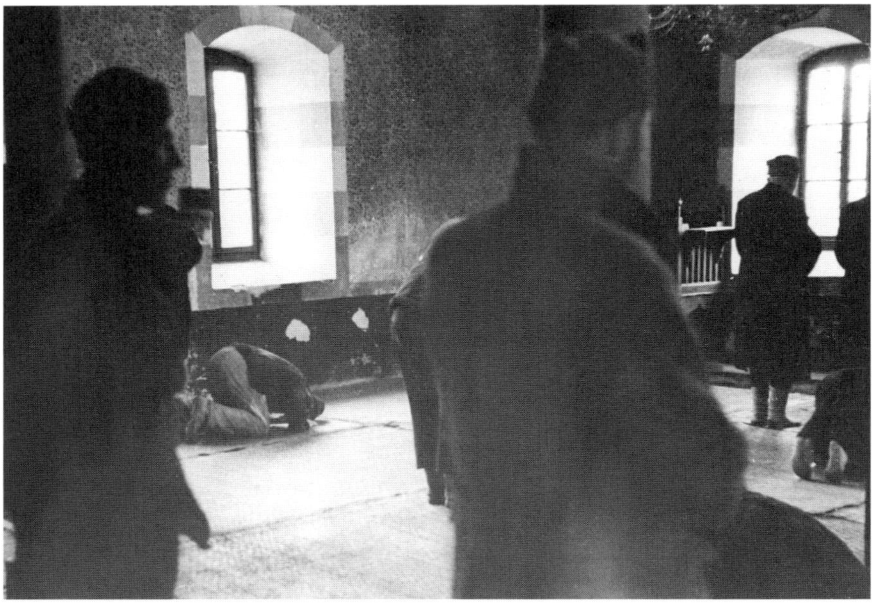

Prayer in a mosque. Mrkonjić-Grad, Bosnia and Herzegovina, 1943. Museum of Yugoslavia, III-1780.

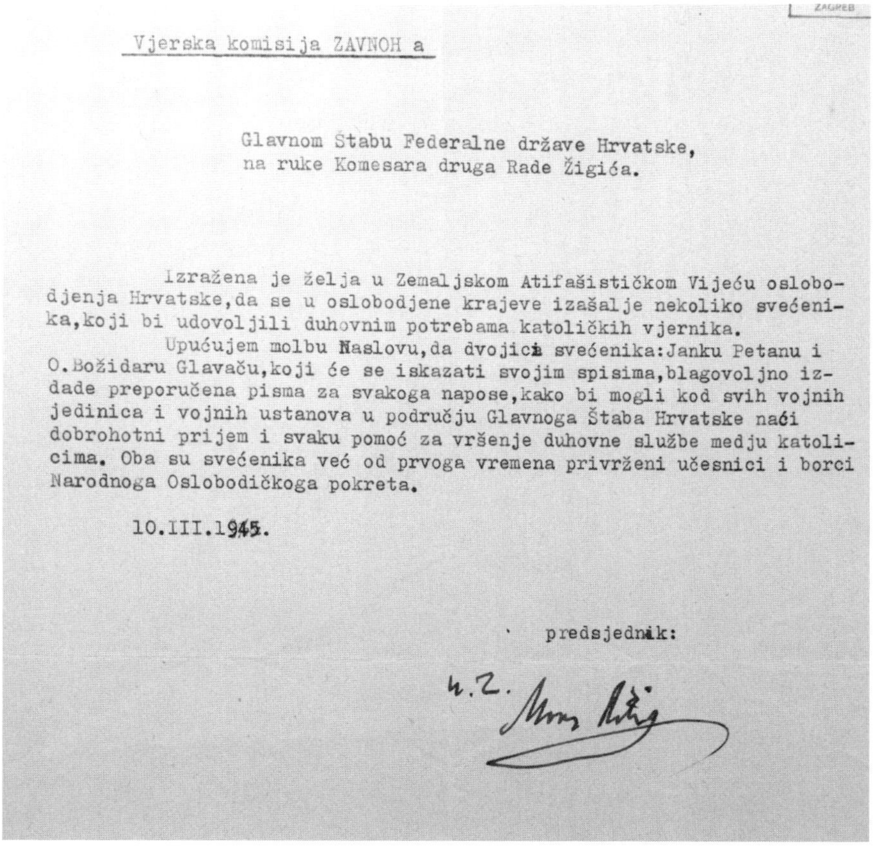

Vjerska komisija ZAVNOH a

Glavnom Štabu Federalne države Hrvatske,
na ruke Komesara druga Rade Žigića.

Izražena je želja u Zemaljskom Atifašističkom Vijeću oslobodjenja Hrvatske,da se u oslobodjene krajeve izašalje nekoliko svećenika,koji bi udovoljili duhovnim potrebama katoličkih vjernika.

Upućujem molbu Naslovu,da dvojici svećenika:Janku Petanu i O.Božidaru Glavaču,koji će se iskazati svojim spisima,blagovoljno izdade preporučena pisma za svakoga napose,kako bi mogli kod svih vojnih jedinica i vojnih ustanova u području Glavnoga Štaba Hrvatske naći dobrohotni prijem i svaku pomoć za vršenje duhovne službe medju katolicima. Oba su svećenika već od prvoga vremena privrženi učesnici i borci Narodnoga Oslobodičkoga pokreta.

10.III.1945.

predsjednik:

Request by the Faith Commission of the ZAVNOH to the General Staff of the (liberated) Federal Republic of Croatia to send clergymen to the predominantly Catholic territory, 10 March 1945. Zagreb, Croatian State Archives, ZAVNOH archive.

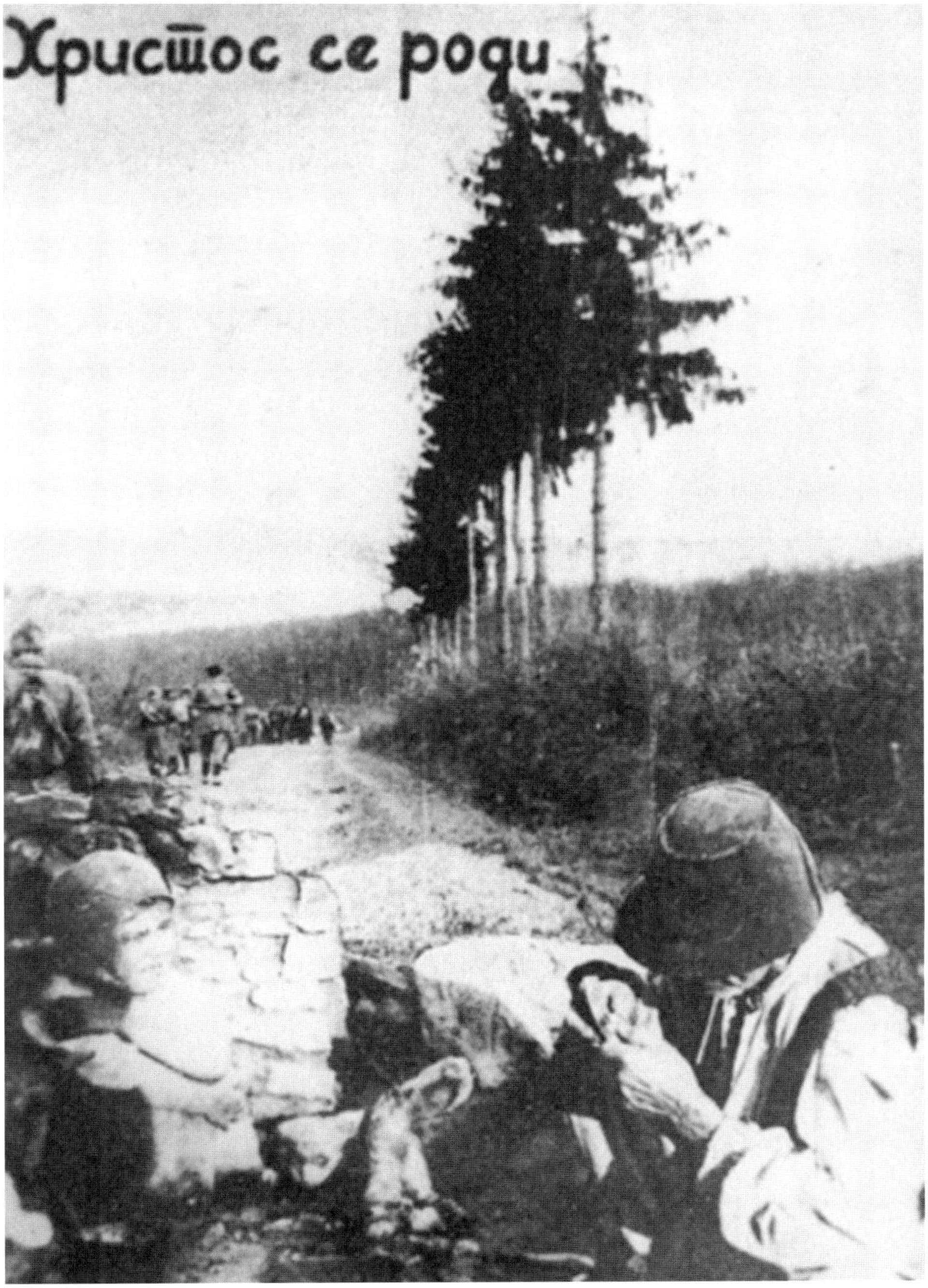

A photomontage celebrating Orthodox Christmas made by the photography unit of the Slavonian People's Liberation Committee. Private collection.

Partisan Funerals

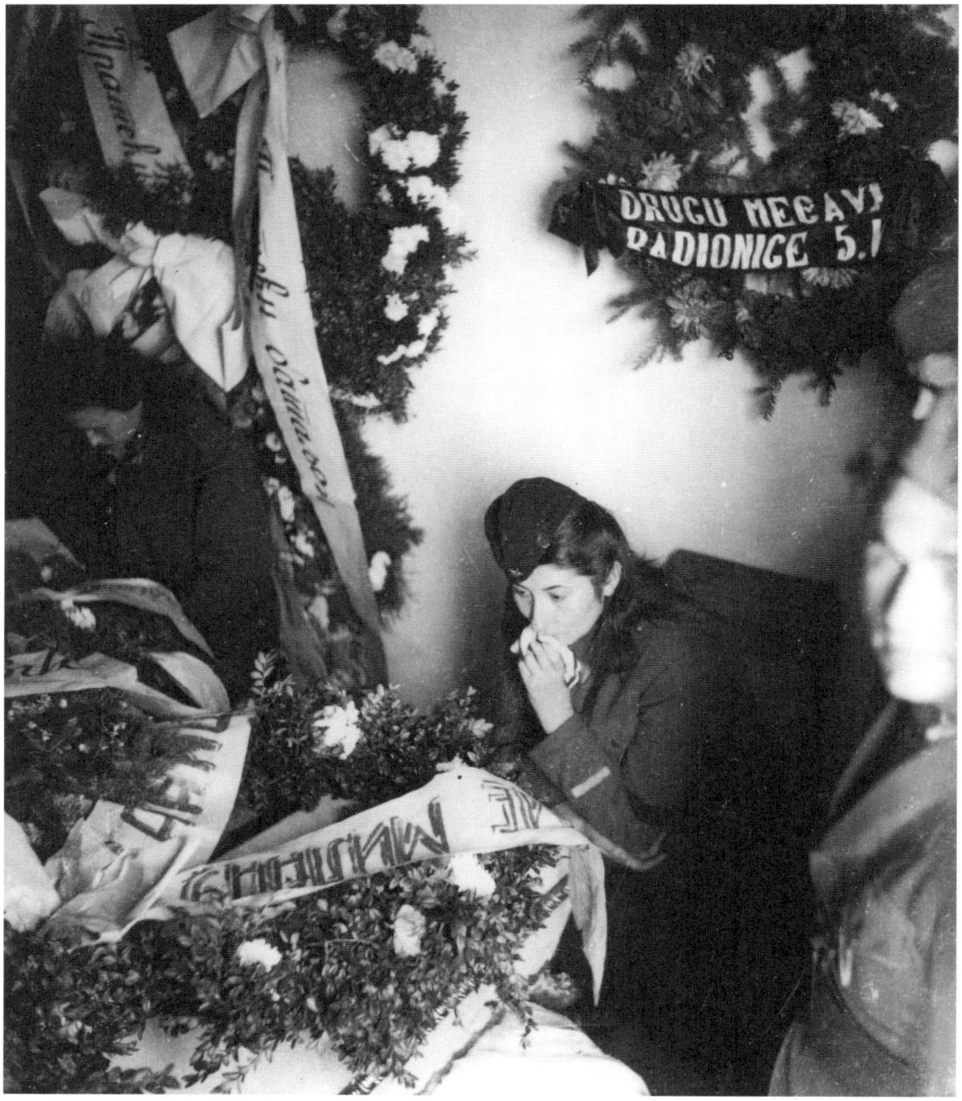

Funeral of the People's Hero Petra Mećave, Travnik, Bosnia and Herzegovina, October 1944.
Photographer unknown. History Museum of Bosnia and Herzegovina, FNOB 4920.

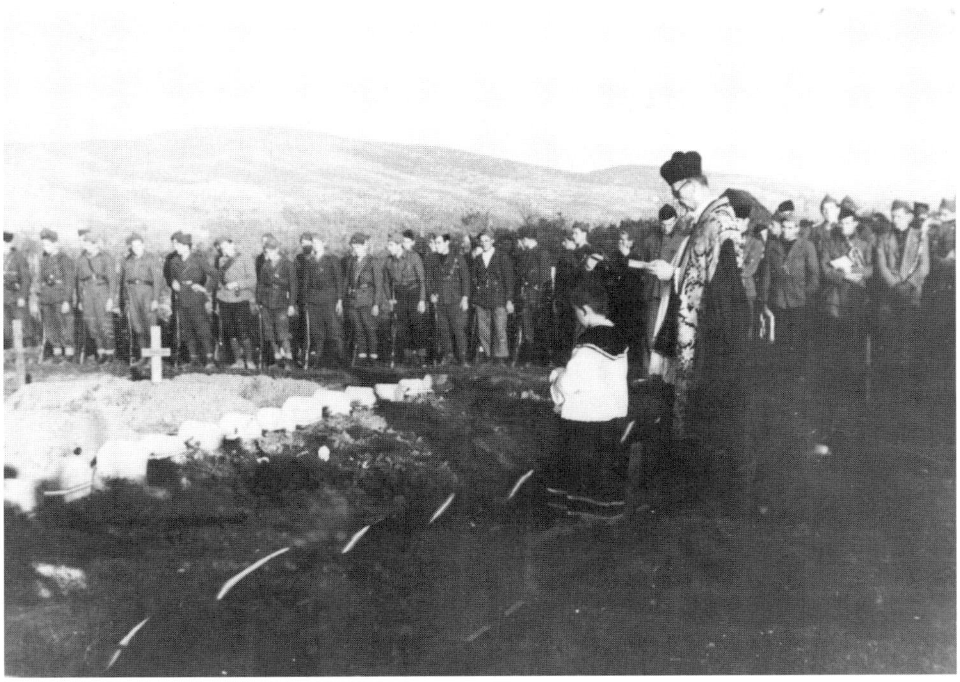

Burying the Partisans killed by the Ustashe while being treated in the Otočac hospital, Croatia, September 1943. Photographer unknown. Croatian History Museum, HPM-MRNH-A-2601 f22 12 s.

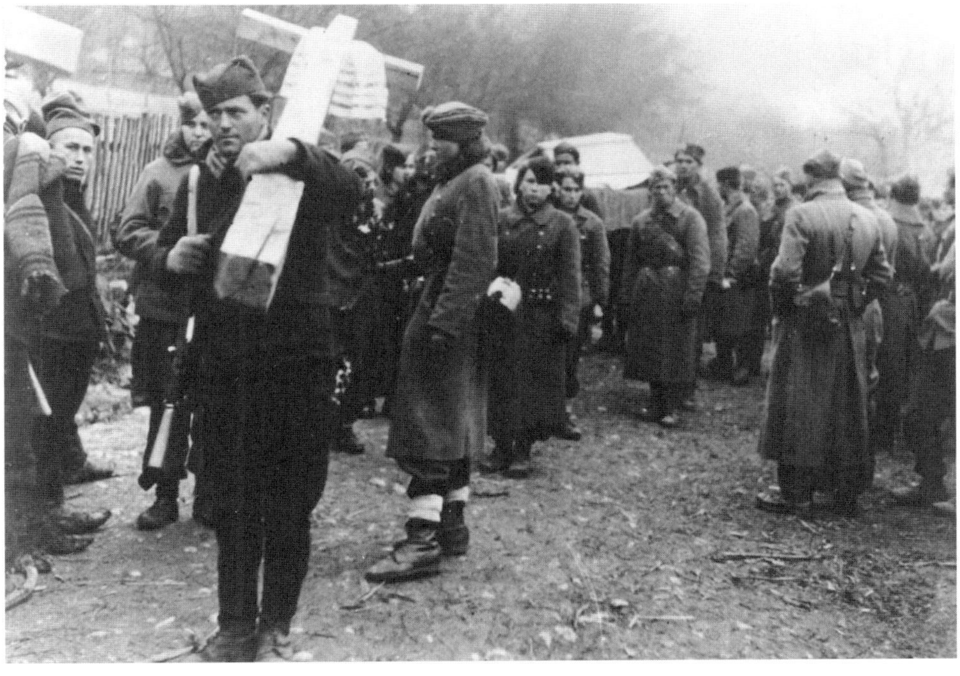

Funeral of Branko Kuprešanin, commissar of the Twenty-First Assault Brigade, Twenty-Eighth Assault Division, Pilice, Bosnia and Herzegovina, January 1945. Photographer unknown. Military Museum Belgrade, 6770.

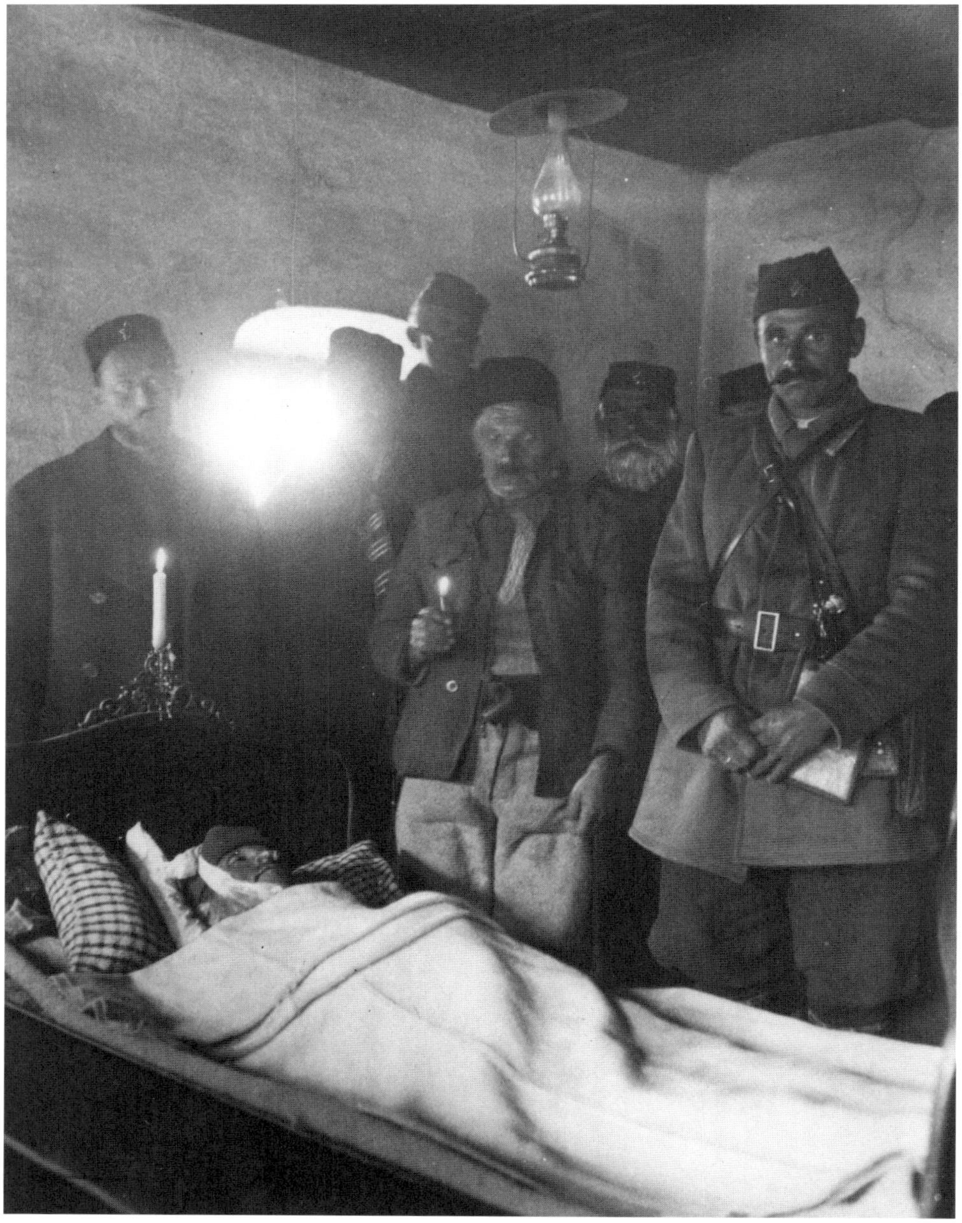

Body of Pero Ćetković, commander of the Fourth Division, killed during the Fourth Offensive, with Ćetković's father holding a candle (centre), People's Hero Sava Kovačević beside him (right) and People's Hero Đoko Pavićević between the two in the background, outskirts of Nevesinje, Bosnia and Herzegovina. Photo: Žorž Skrigin. History Museum of Bosnia and Herzegovina, FNOB 214.

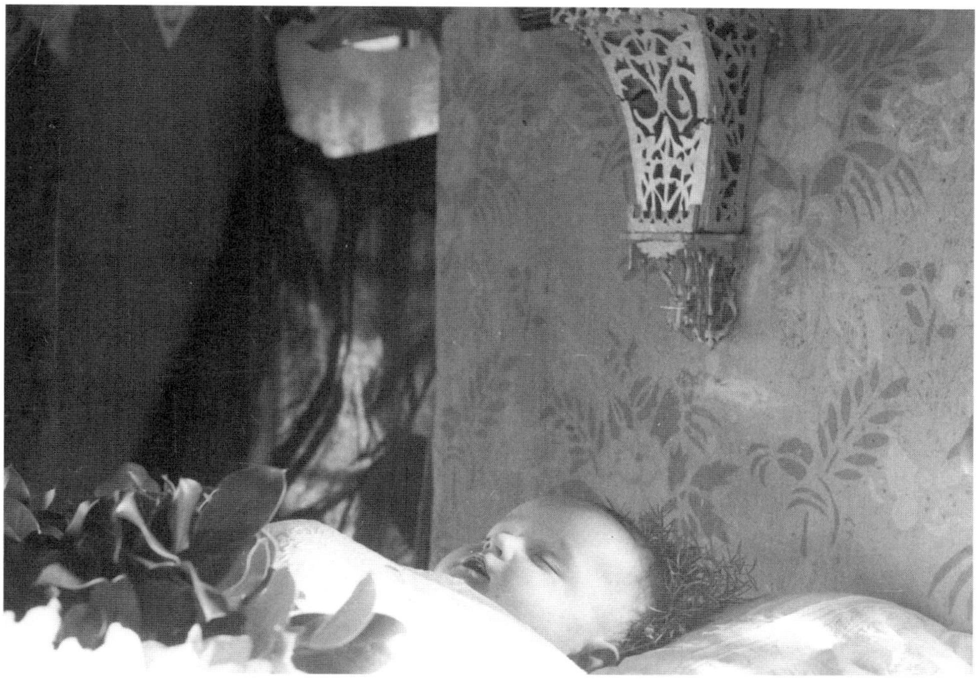

Child on a bier. Photo: Dr Janez Milčinski. National Museum of Contemporary History of Slovenia, 1226/29.

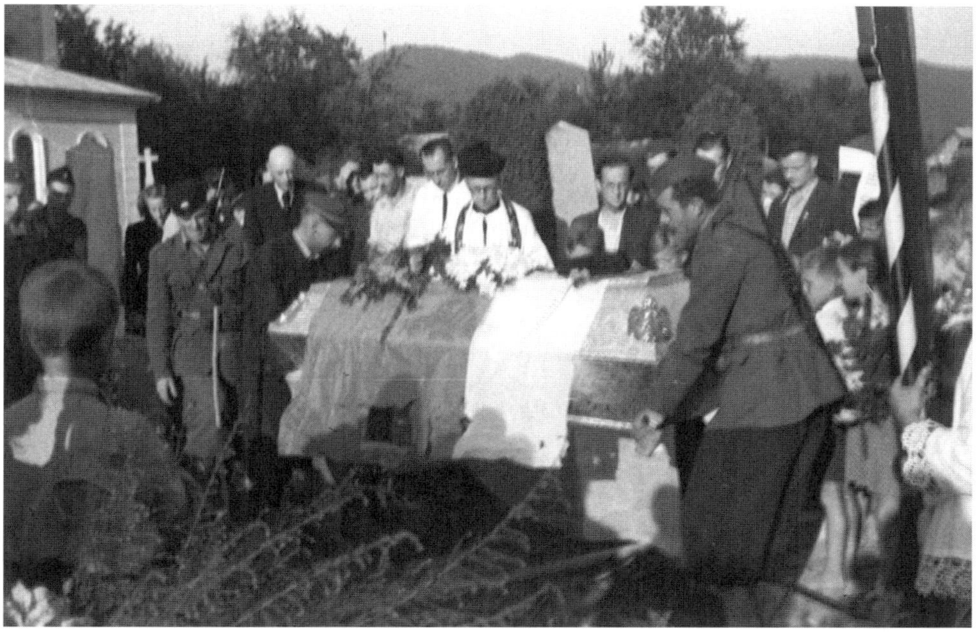

Funeral of a fallen Partisan priest from the village of Gorenja near Ribnica, September 1943. Photo: Vinko Bavec. National Museum of Contemporary History of Slovenia, TN39/19.

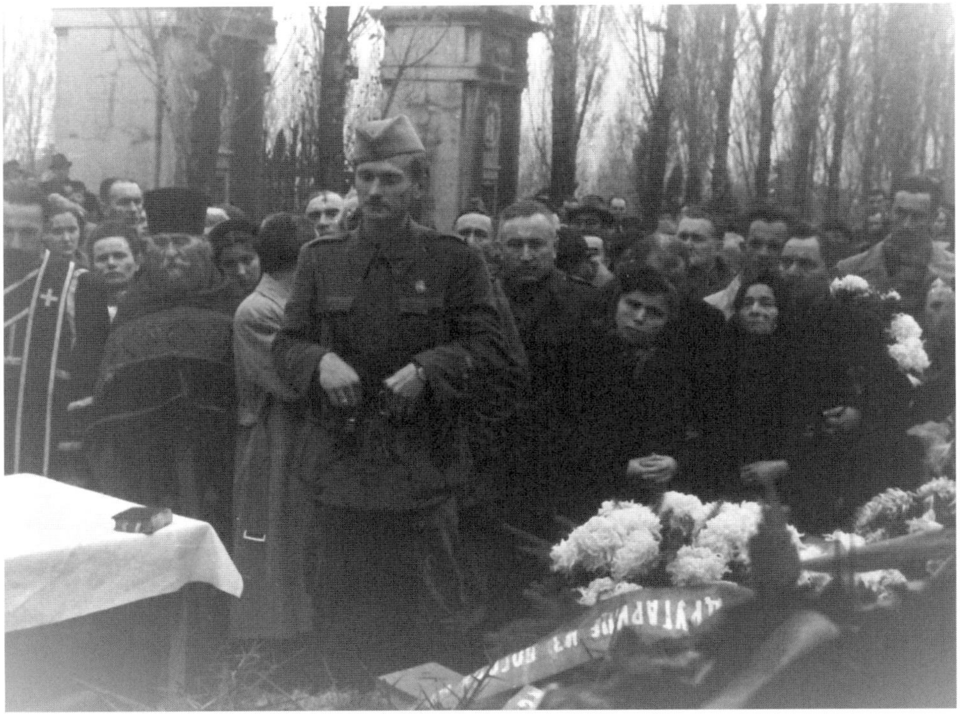

Funeral for victims of Banjica concentration camp at the New Cemetery, Belgrade, November 1944.
Military Museum Belgrade, 18431.

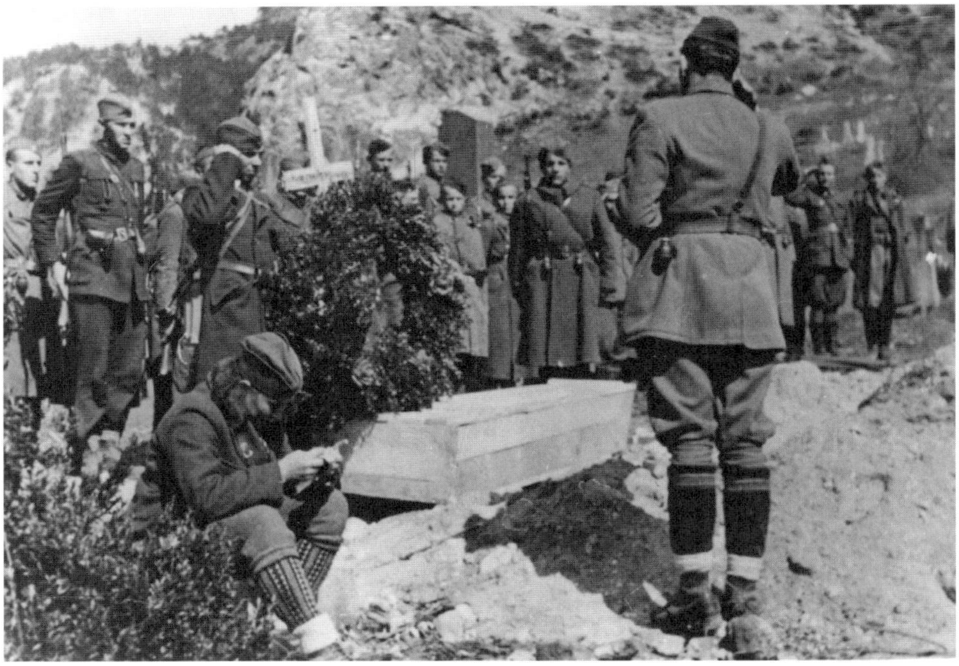

Funeral of Rajko Milošević, commissar of the Third Battalion of the Twelfth Herzegovinian Brigade.
Photographer unknown. History Museum of Bosnia and Herzegovina, FNOB 16367.

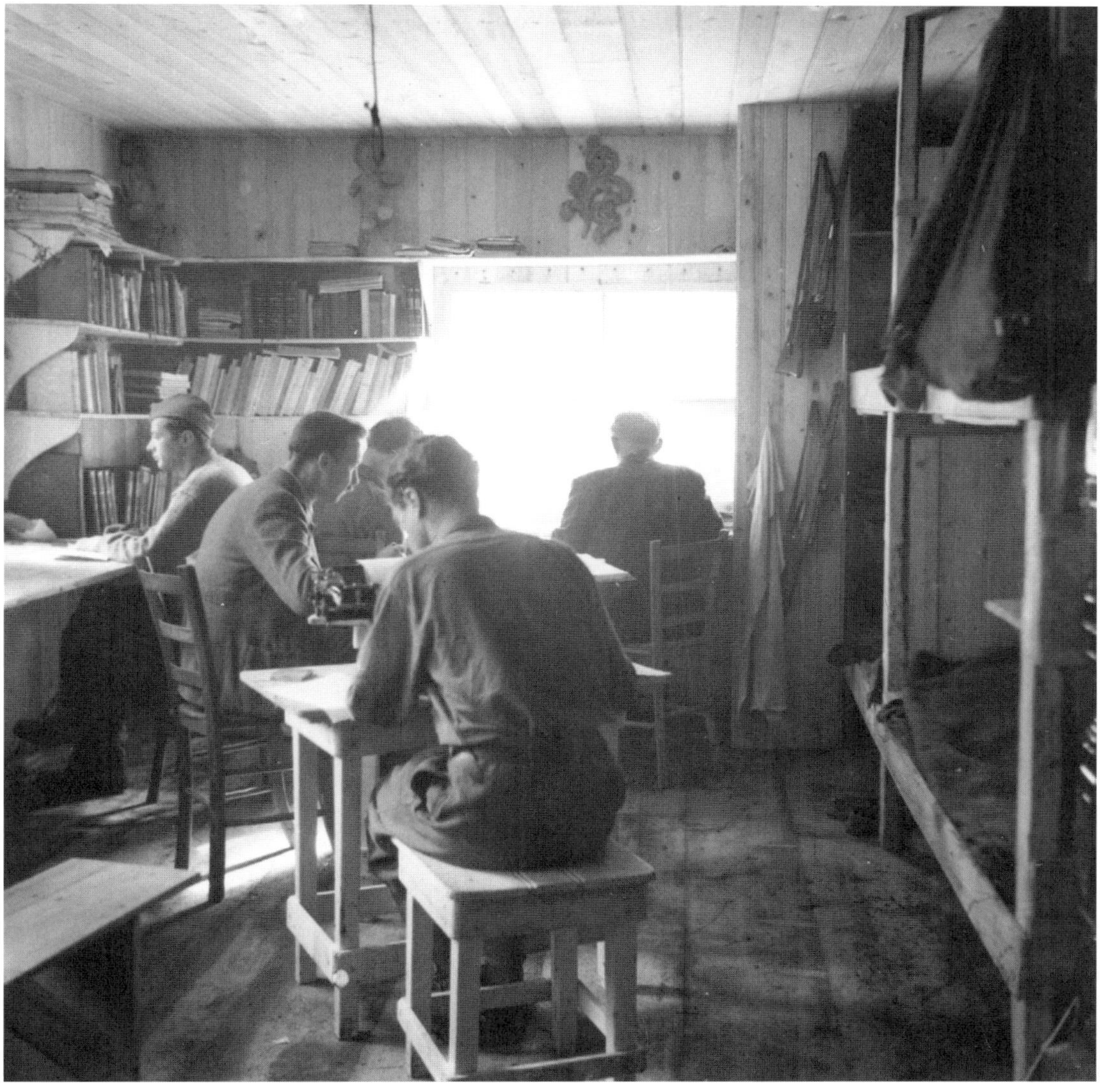

Members of the Academic Institute at work in Kočevski Rog, Slovenia, 1944. Photographer unknown.
National Museum of Contemporary History of Slovenia, TN364/5.

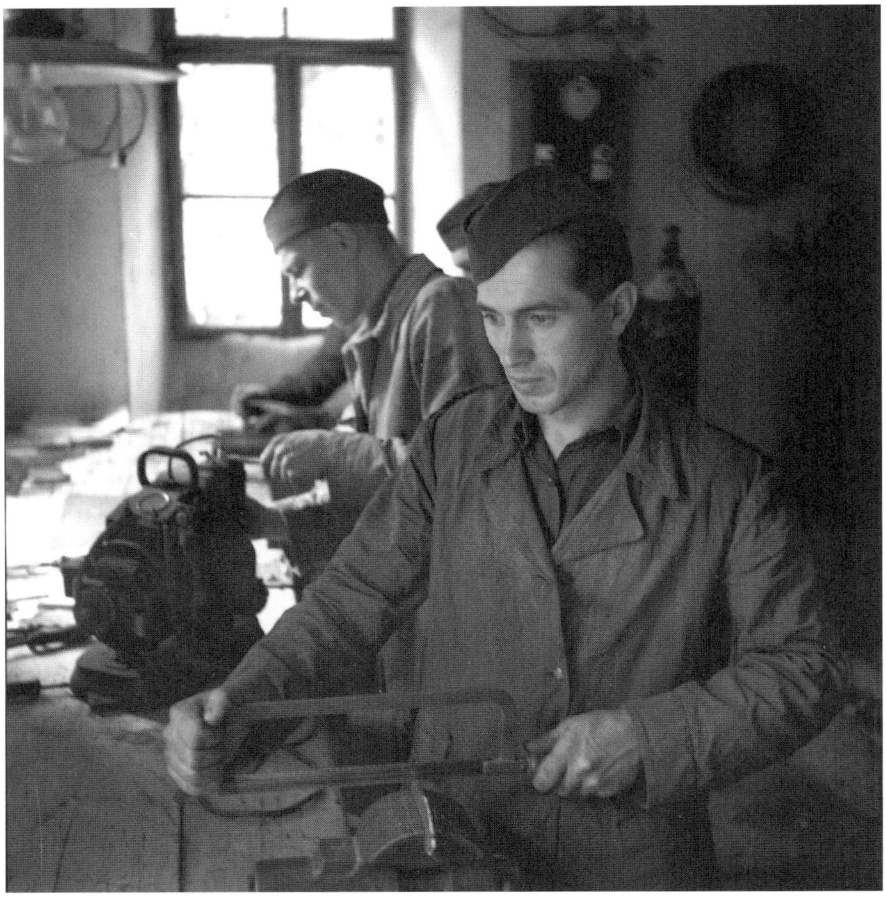

One of many mechanical workshops for repairing bicycles, motors and even cars (in this case an electronics workshop) at the headquarters of the People's Liberation Army and Partisan Detachments of Slovenia, Stare Žage, 1944. Photo: Stane Viršek. National Museum of Contemporary History of Slovenia, TN117/2.

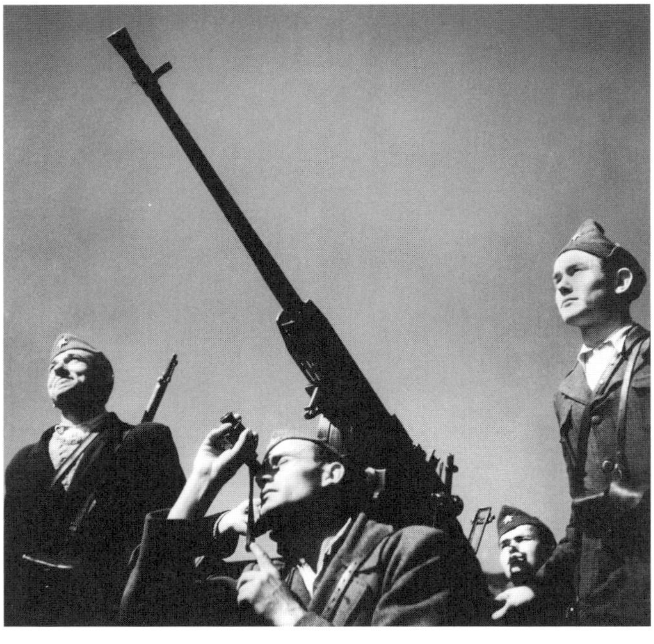

Manoeuvres at the officers' school (with Ivan Gošnjak), Lapac, Croatia, 1942. Photographer unknown. Museum of Yugoslavia, III-5541.

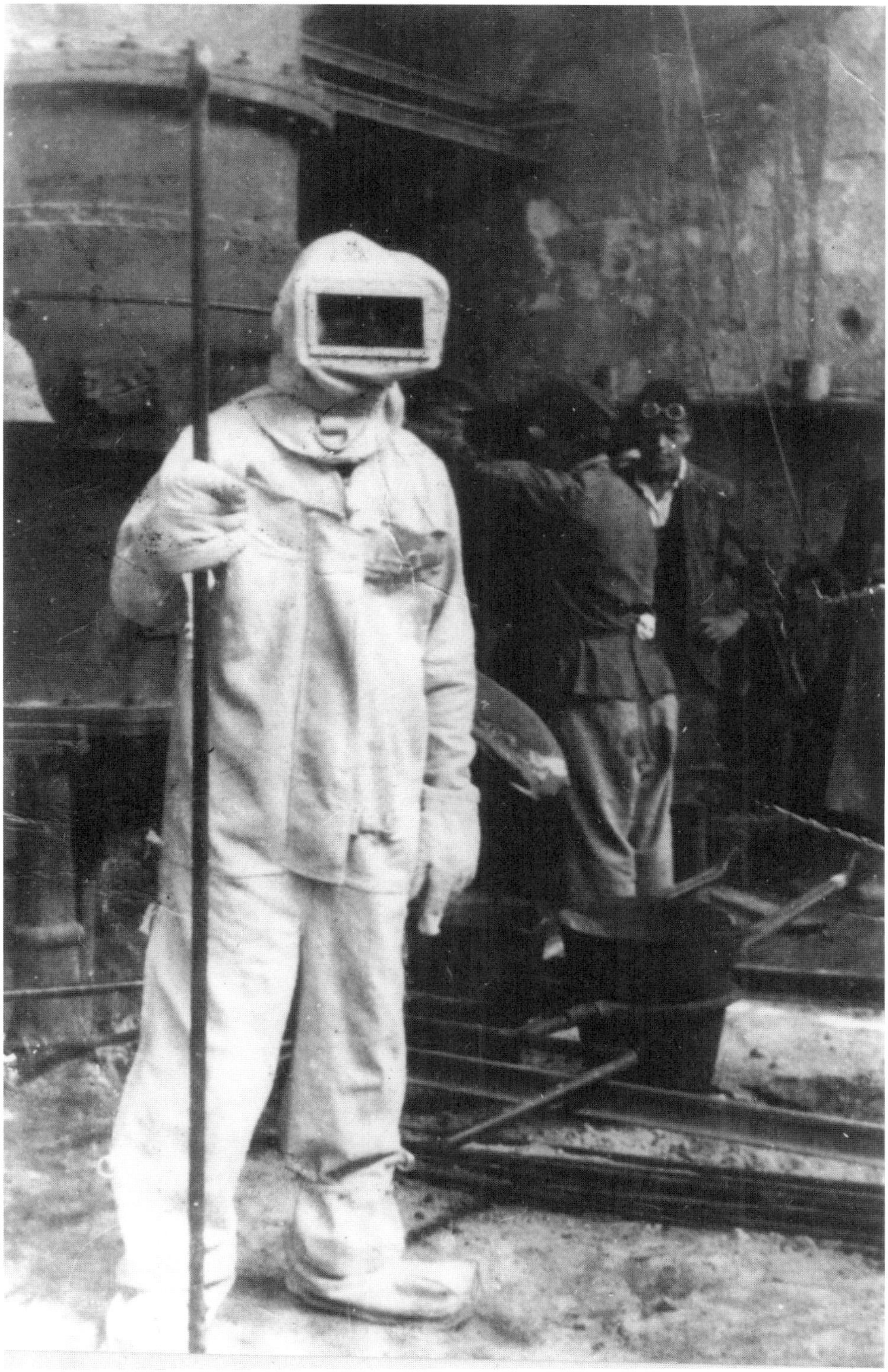

Scene from a Partisan incendiary workshop for manufacturing and repairing munitions, Drvar, Bosnia and Herzegovina, 1941. Photographer unknown. History Museum of Bosnia and Herzegovina, FNOB 2681.

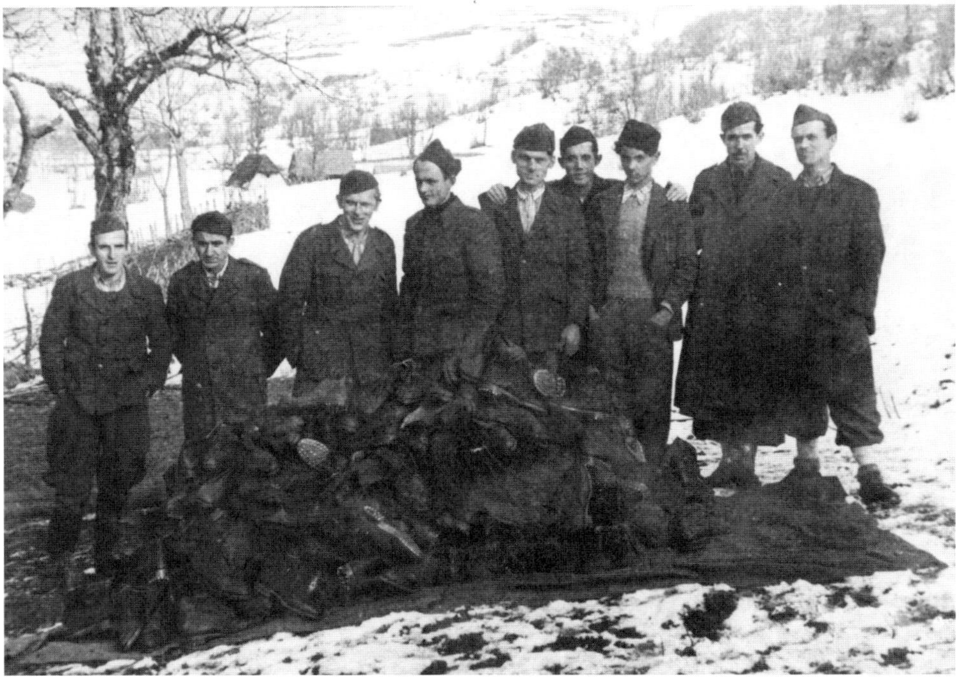

Fighters and workers from the Third Central Cobblers' Workshop at Croatian HQ, Turjanski, Vrhovine in Lika, Croatia, February/March 1944. Photographer unknown. Croatian History Museum, HPM-MRNH-A-2601 f82 25 s.

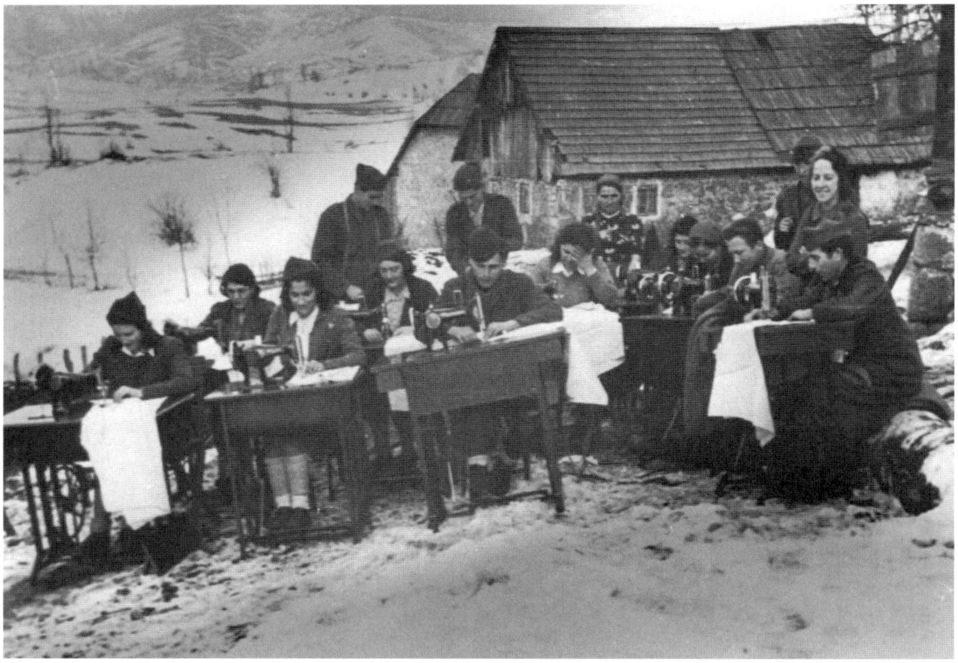

Women from the Croatian region of Lika on sewing machines as part of a coordinated work action, winter 1944–45. Photographer unknown. Croatian History Museum, accession no. unknown.

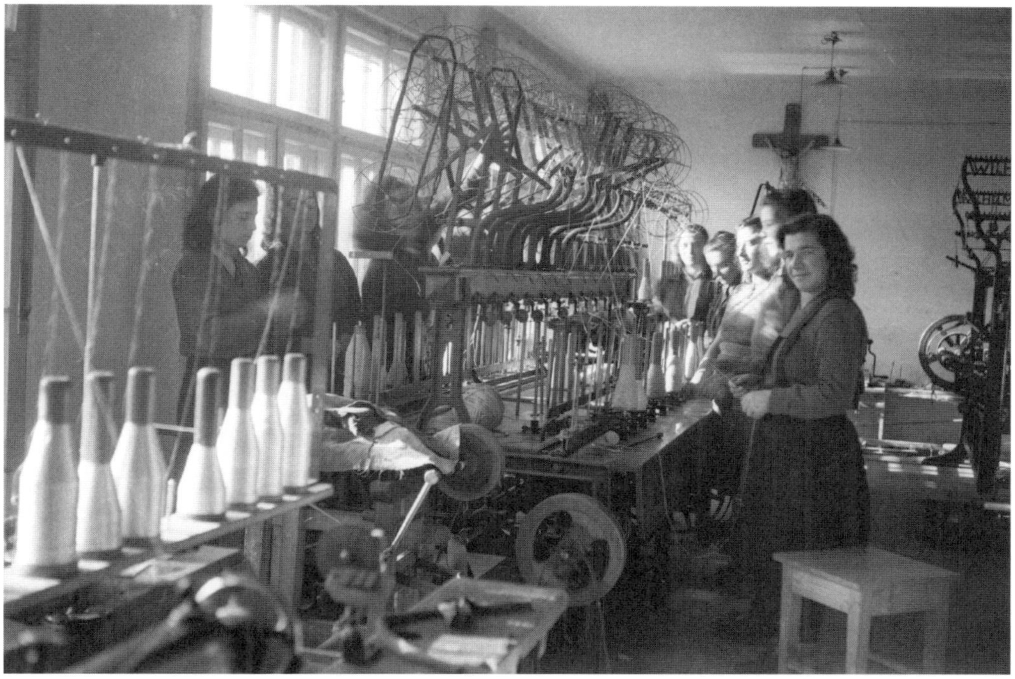

A Partisan sewing room in Črnomelj, Slovenia, October 1944. Photo: Edi Šelhaus. National Museum of Contemporary History of Slovenia, TN387/2.

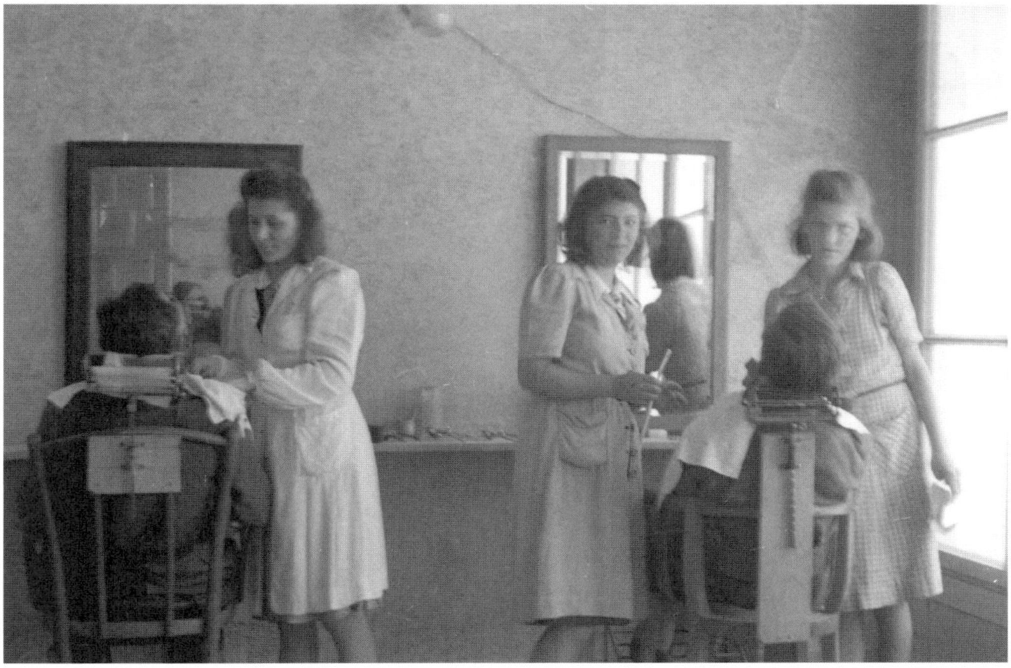

Partisans in a barber's shop in Črnomelj, Slovenia, 1944. Photo: Maksimilijan Zupančič. National Museum of Contemporary History of Slovenia, TN389/32.

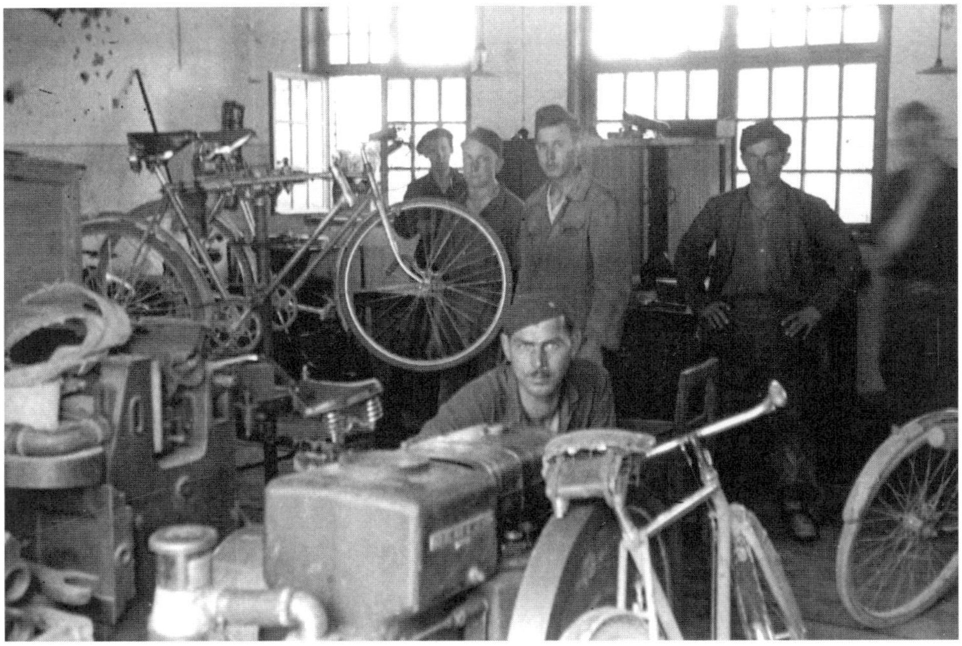

Župančič's mechanical workshop, August 1944. Photo: Alfred Kos. National Museum of Contemporary History of Slovenia, TN213/14.

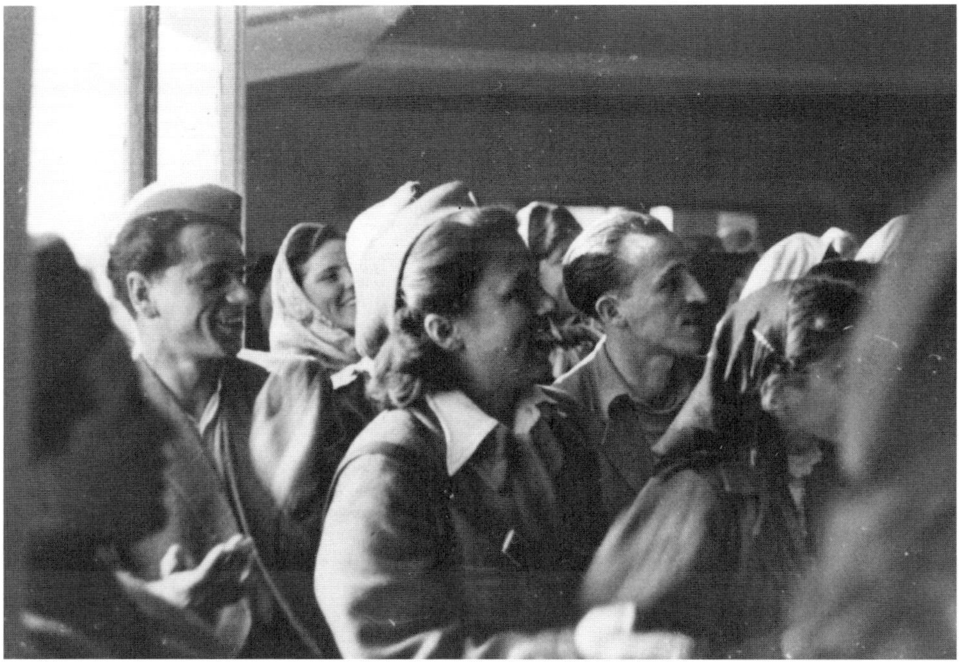

Partisan training. Photo: Drago Mažar. Archives of the Republic of Srpska, Banja Luka.

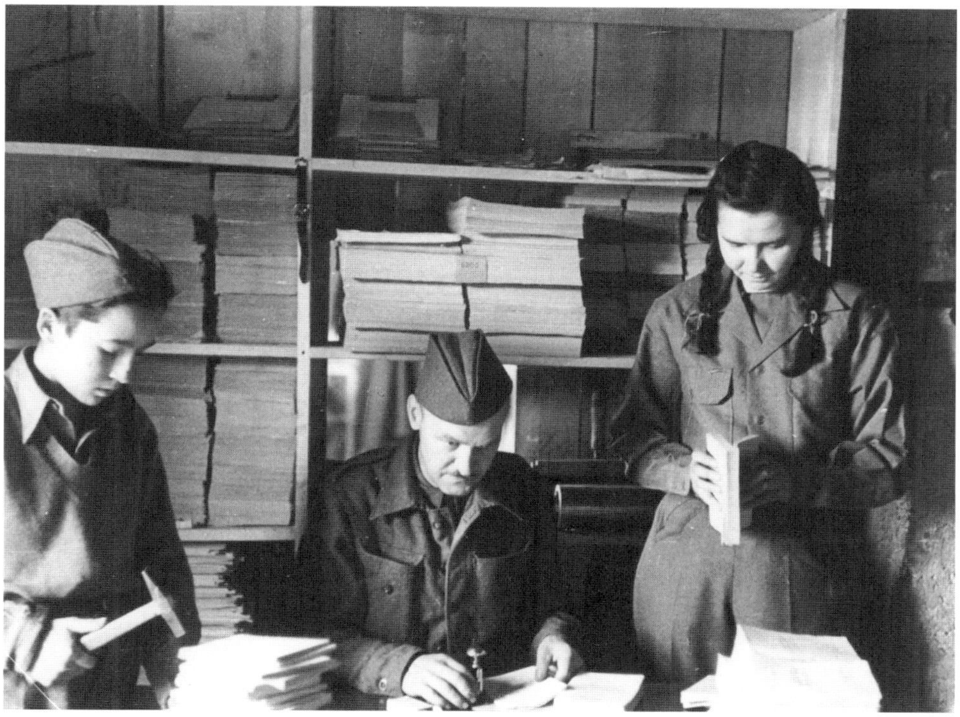

Partisan printing office, bindery, Slovenian HQ, 1945. Photographer unknown.
National Museum of Contemporary History of Slovenia.

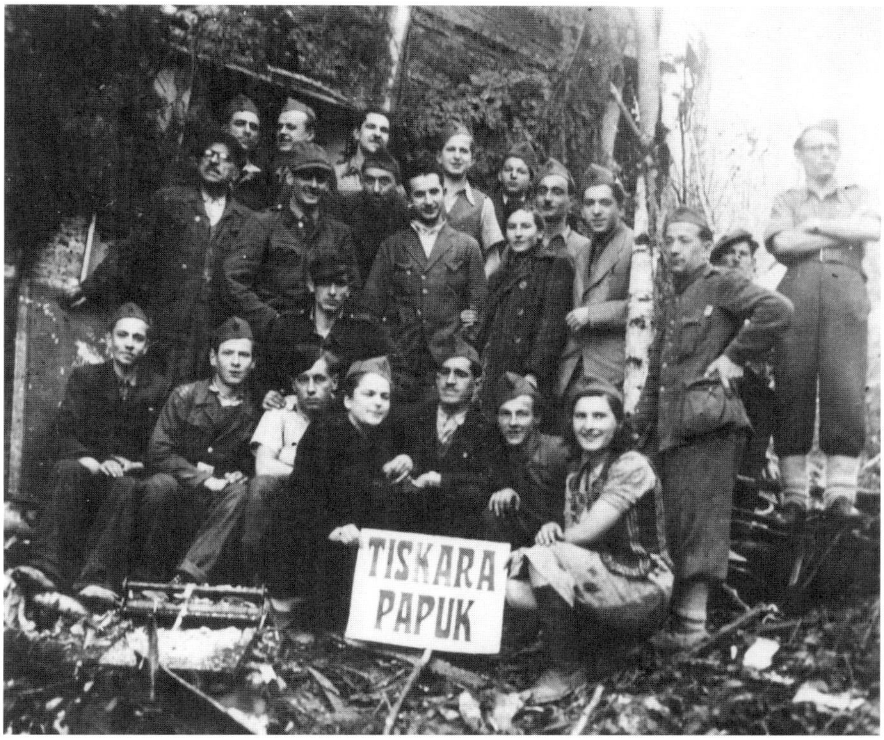

First proof on a large printing machine at the printing press on Mount Papuk, Croatia. Photographer unknown.

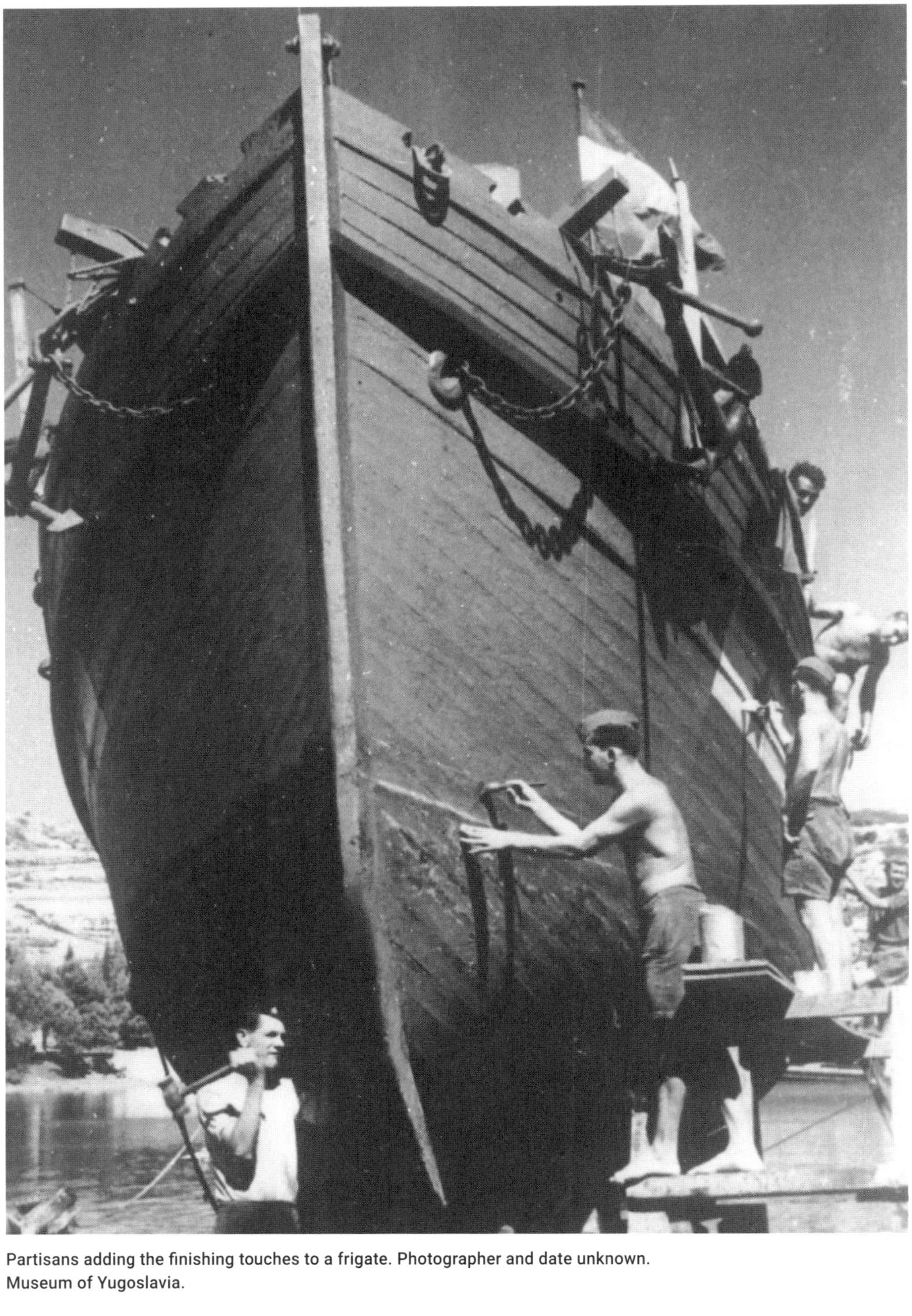
Partisans adding the finishing touches to a frigate. Photographer and date unknown.
Museum of Yugoslavia.

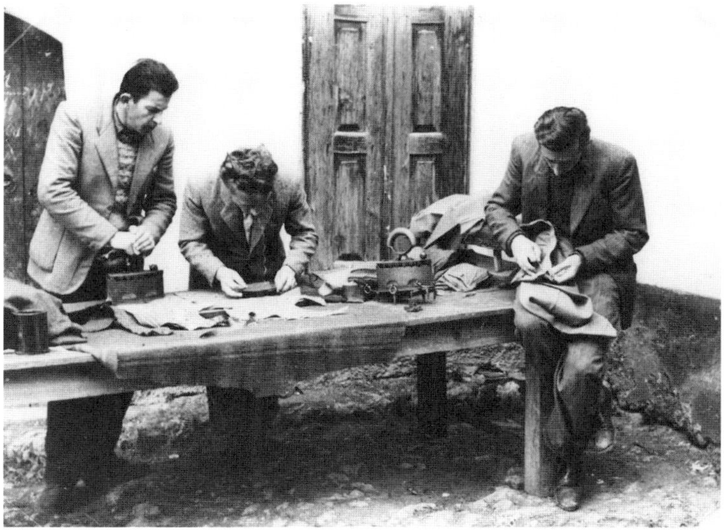

A sewing workshop in Pljevlja, Montenegro.
Photographer unknown.

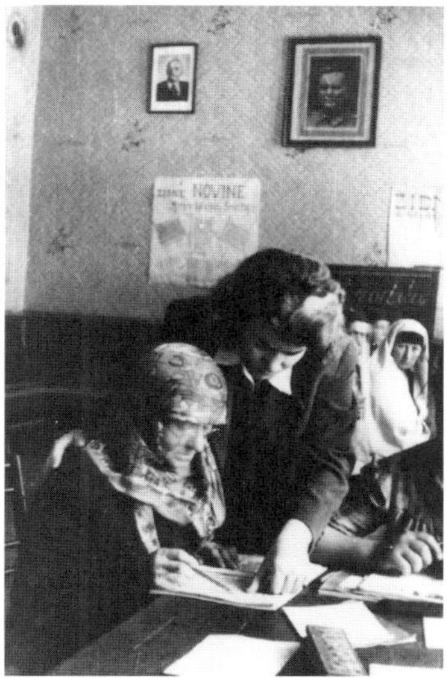

Literacy course in the district of Radion Zahum, Mostar, Bosnia and Herzegovina.
Photographer unknown.

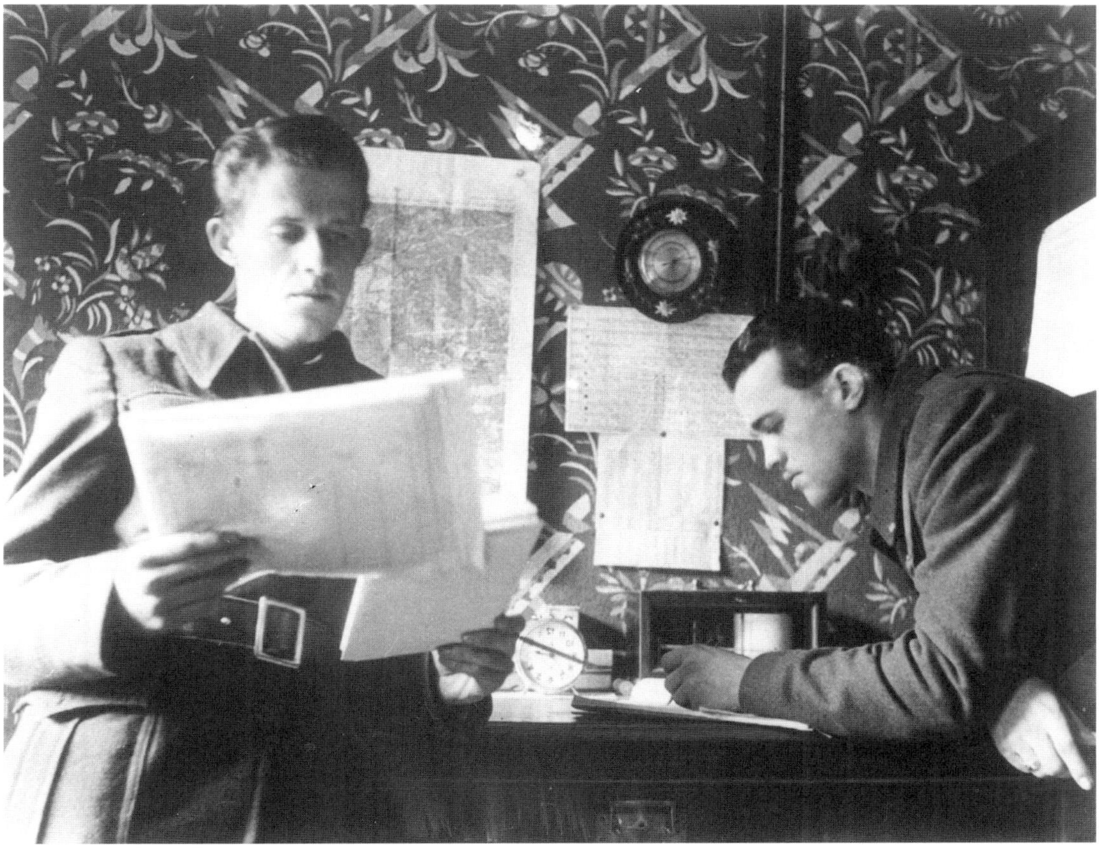

Dare Dodič and Mirko Župančič at the Ninth Corps radio-telegraphy and weather station, Cerkno, Slovenia, March/April 1944. Photographer unknown. National Museum of Contemporary History of Slovenia, TN1066/11.

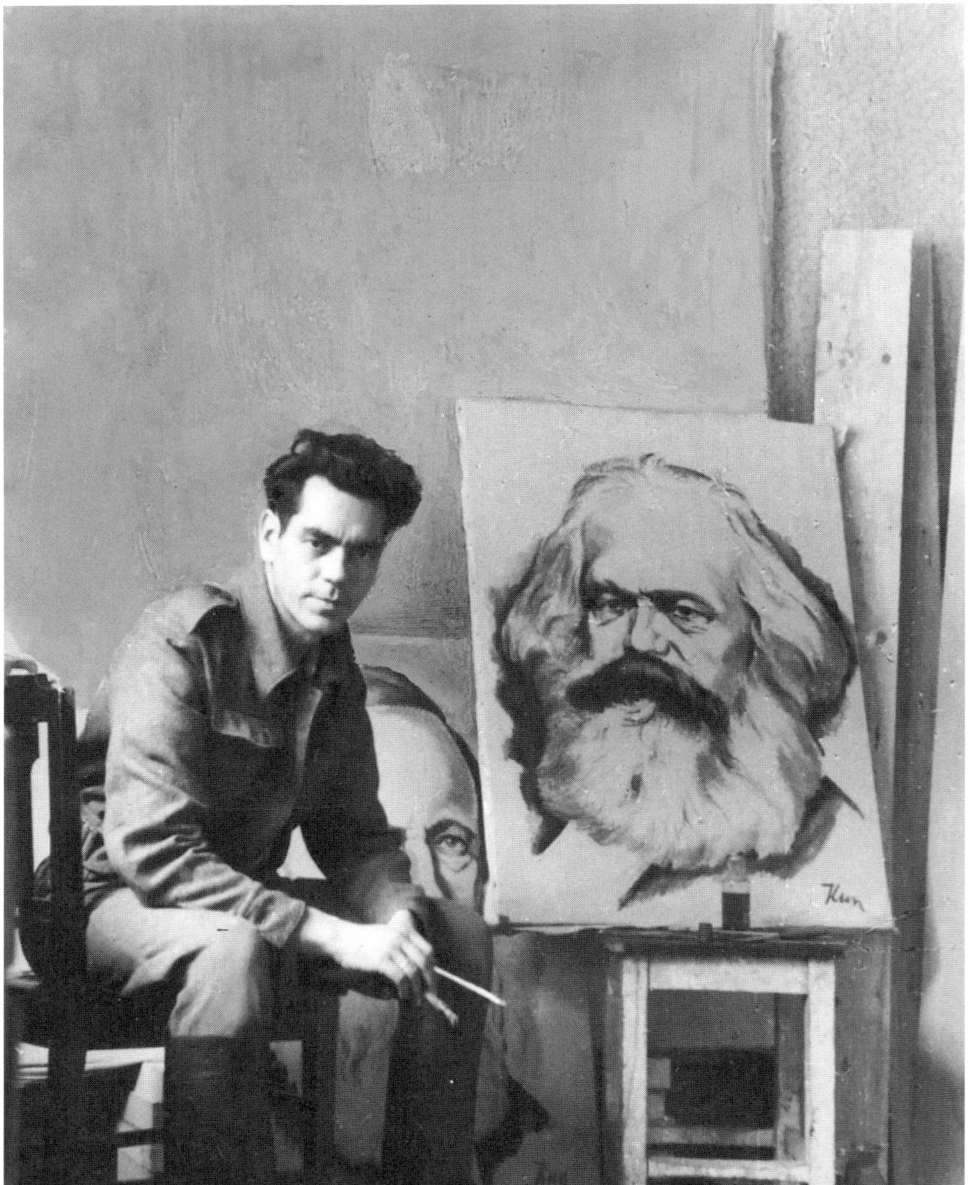

Painter Đorđe Andrejević-Kun in his studio in a factory building, September 1943. Photographer unknown.
Central Committee of League of Communists of Yugoslavia Collection (CK SKJ), accession no. unknown.

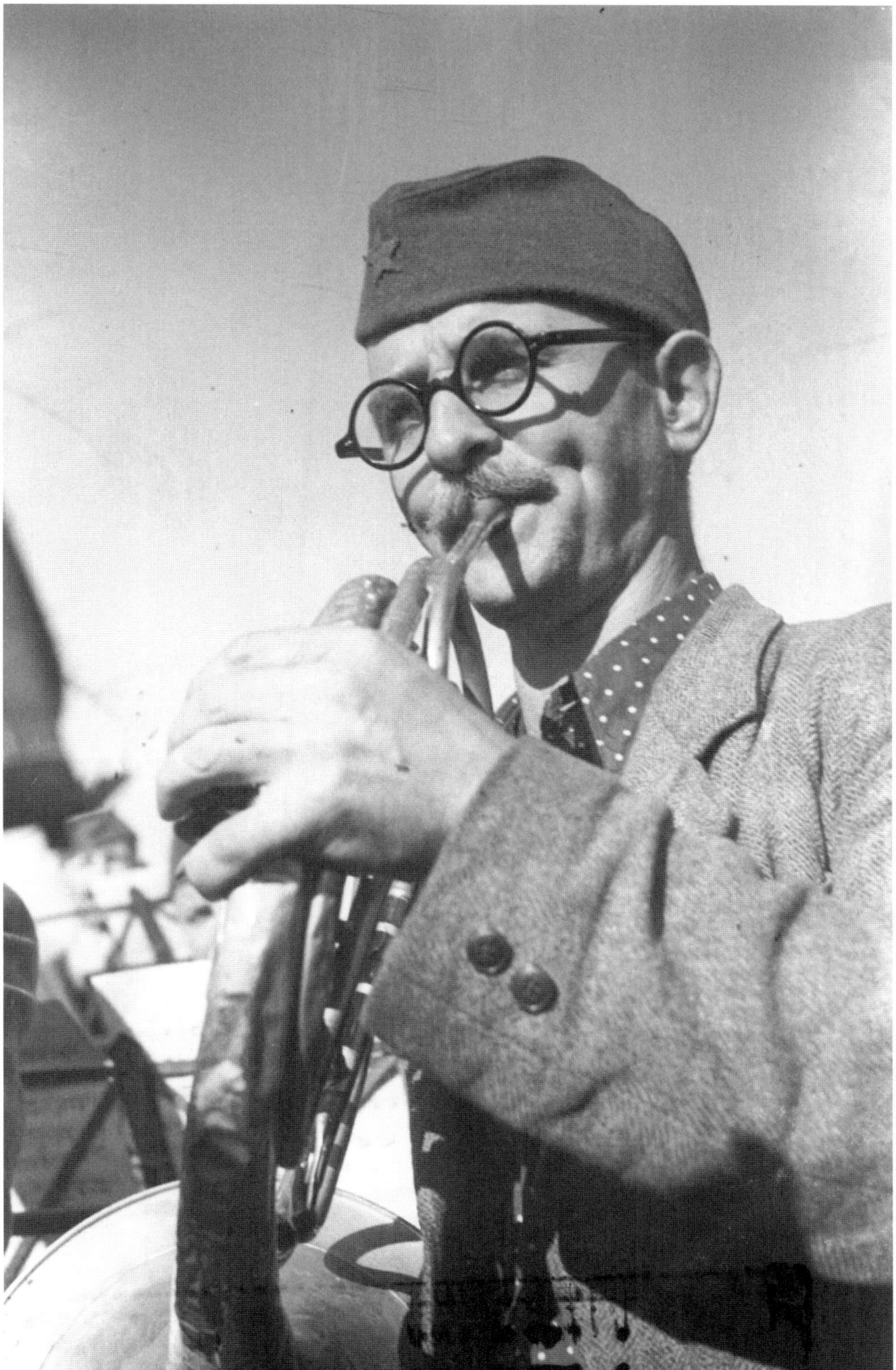

Horn-playing, Srednja Vas, Slovenia, 1944. Photo: Franc Cerar.
National Museum of Contemporary History of Slovenia, TN321/39.

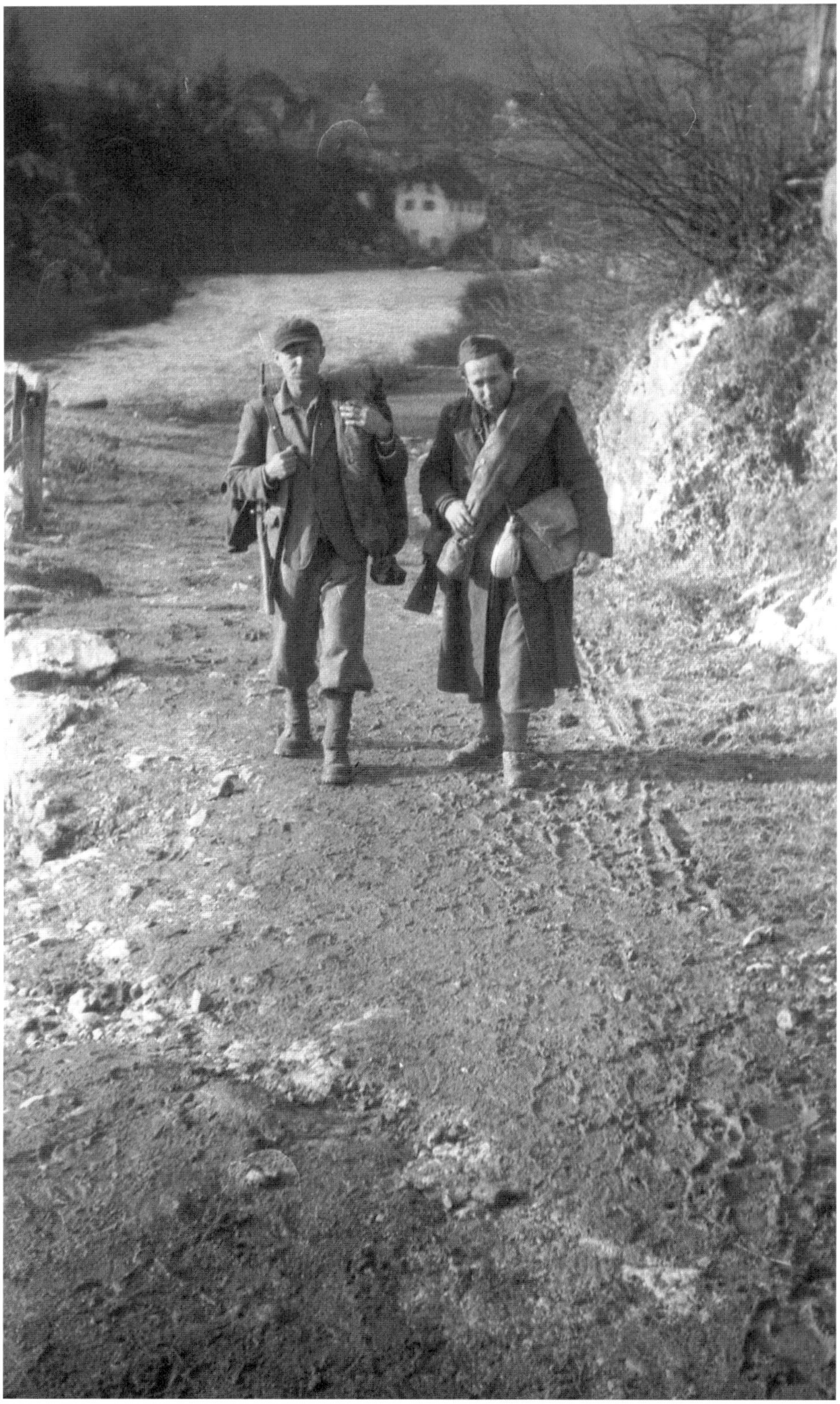

Prof. Franček Veselko and Ivan Kronovšek of the cultural group and economic department of Cankar Brigade, after the German Offensive, Zagradec, November 1943. Photo: Franjo Veselko. National Museum of Contemporary History of Slovenia, TN56/21.

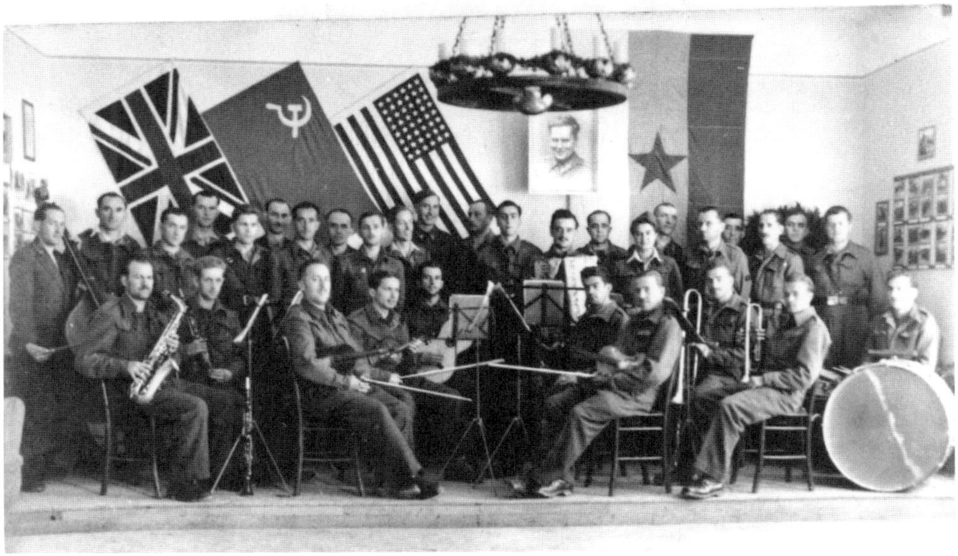

Performance in Ljubno, Savinja valley, Slovenia. Photographer unknown.
Museum of Recent History, Celje FZ25539.

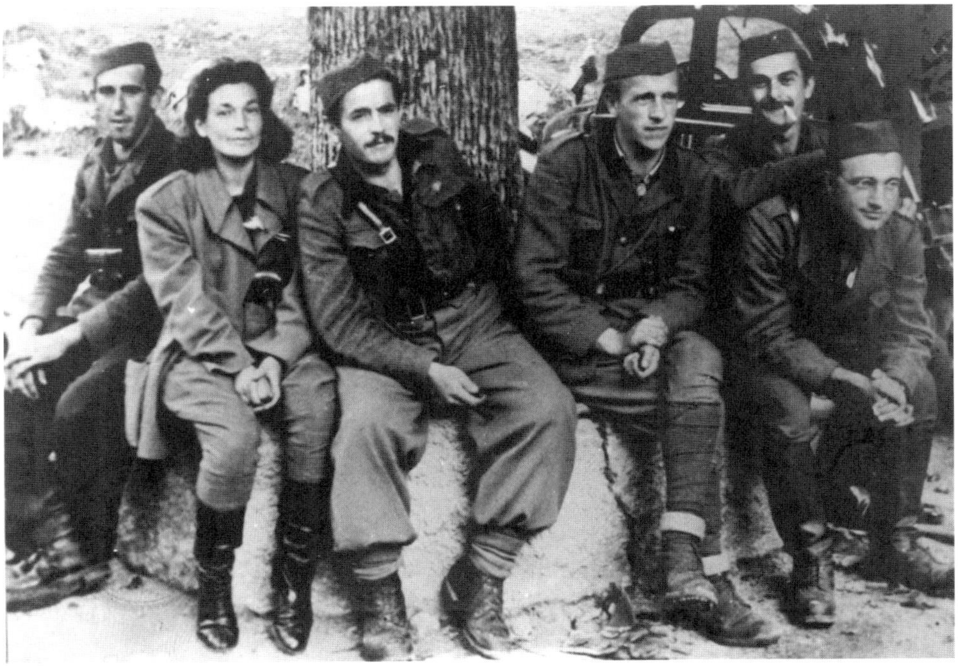

The Fourteenth Division's cultural group. Photographer unknown.
Museum of Recent History, Celje FZ2836.

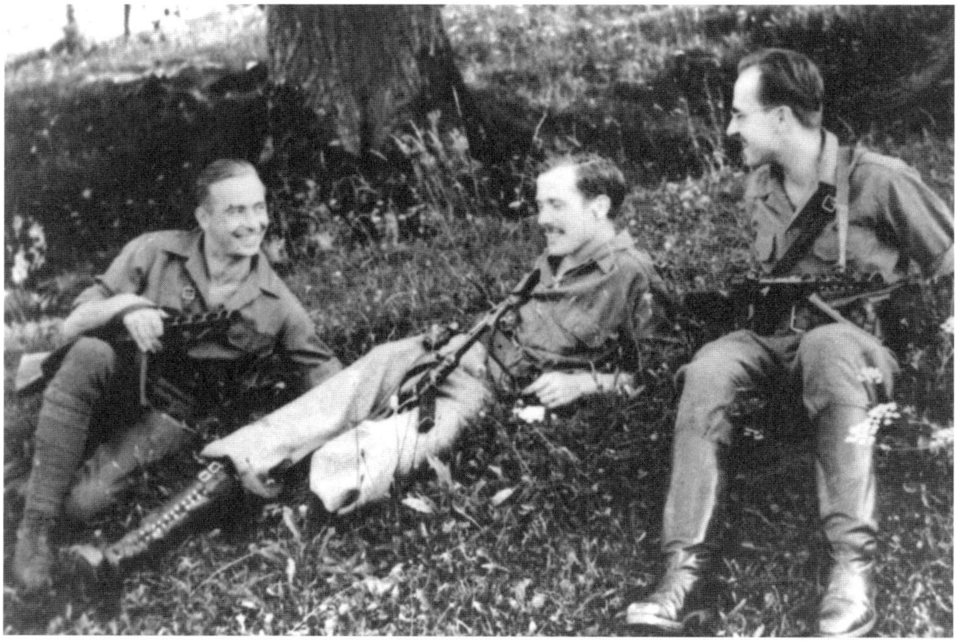

Ivo Lipa Iztok (left) from the agitprop group of the Fourteenth Operative Zone, Milan Venišik and Jože Petek (right), photographer for the Fourteenth Division. Photographer unknown. Museum of Recent History, Celje FZ2876.

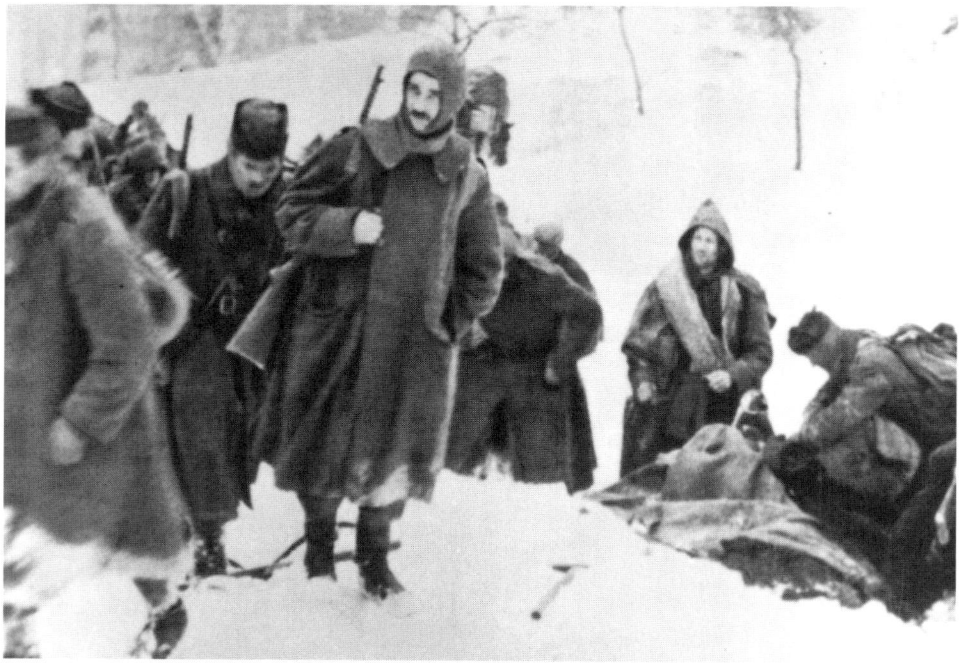

One of the last photographs of Karel Destovnik-Kajuh, Paški Kozjak, Slovenia, 16 February 1944. Photo: Jože Petek. Museum of Recent History, Celje FZ2910.

Political Leaders

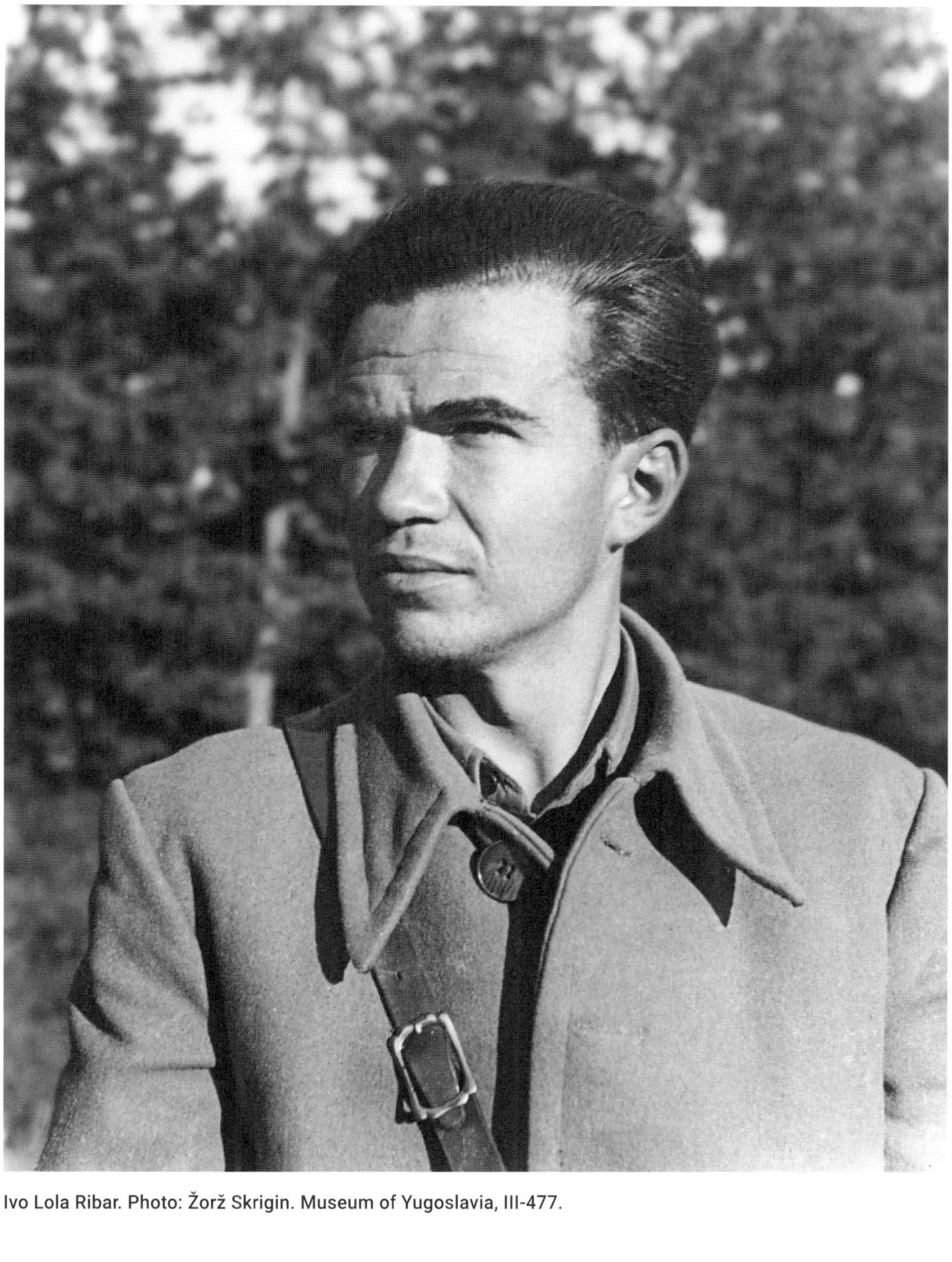

Ivo Lola Ribar. Photo: Žorž Skrigin. Museum of Yugoslavia, III-477.

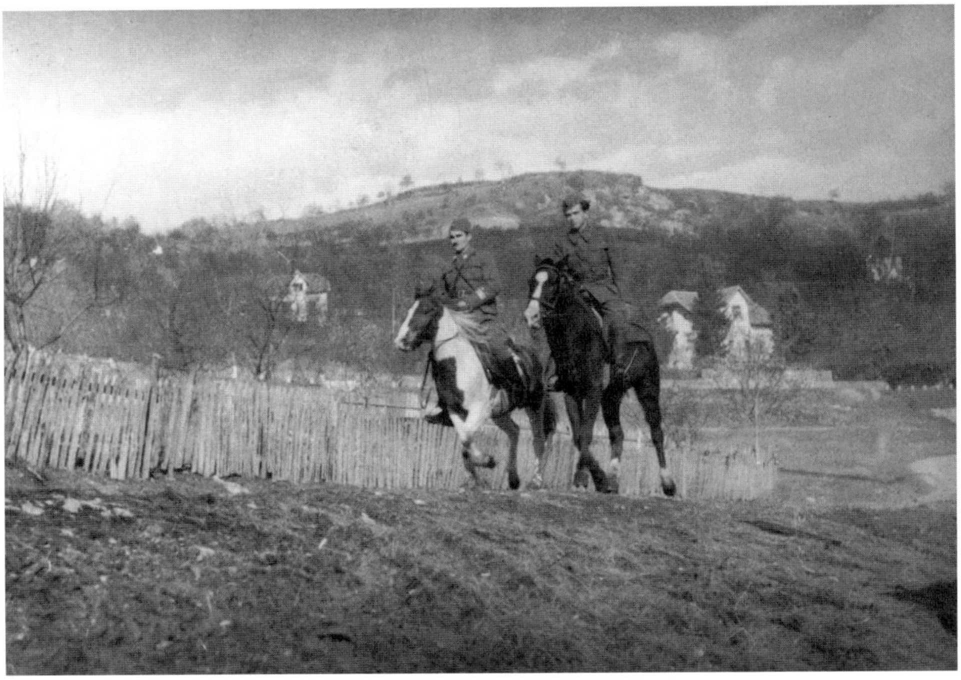

Ivo Lola Ribar and Miloje Milojević of the military mission of the Supreme Command of the NOV and POJ, during a meeting of Allied Command for the Middle East, before flying to Cairo and Ribar's death at Glamočko polje, 27 November 1943. Photographer unknown. Croatian History Museum, HPM-MRNH-F-1073.

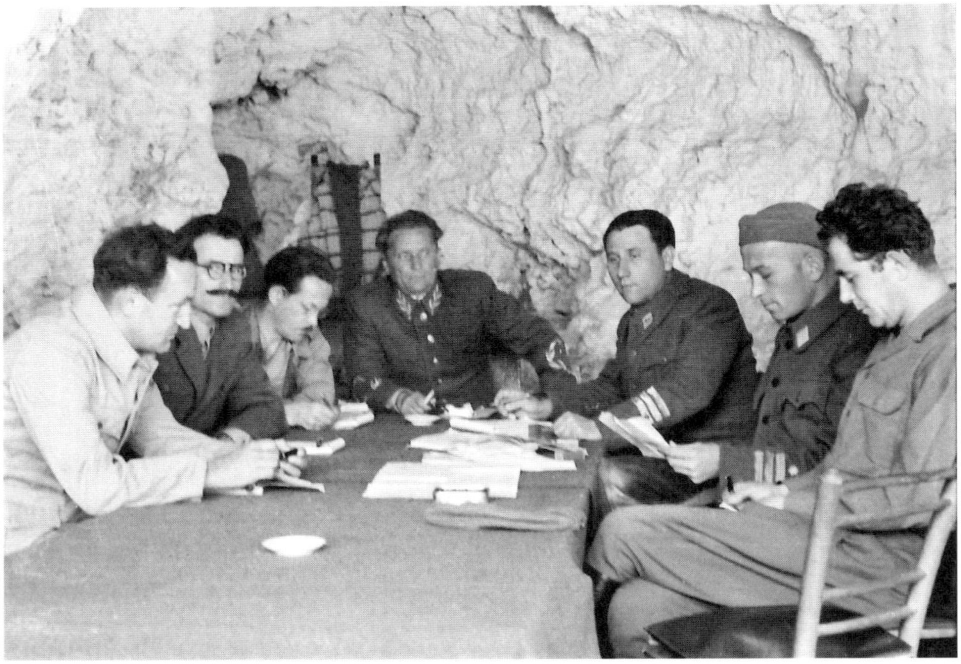

Vladimir Bakarić (left), Ivan Milutinović, Edvard Kardelj, Josip Broz Tito (head of table), Aleksandar Ranković, Pavle Gregorić, Milovan Đilas, Vis, Croatia 1944. Photographer unknown. Military Museum Belgrade, 18679.

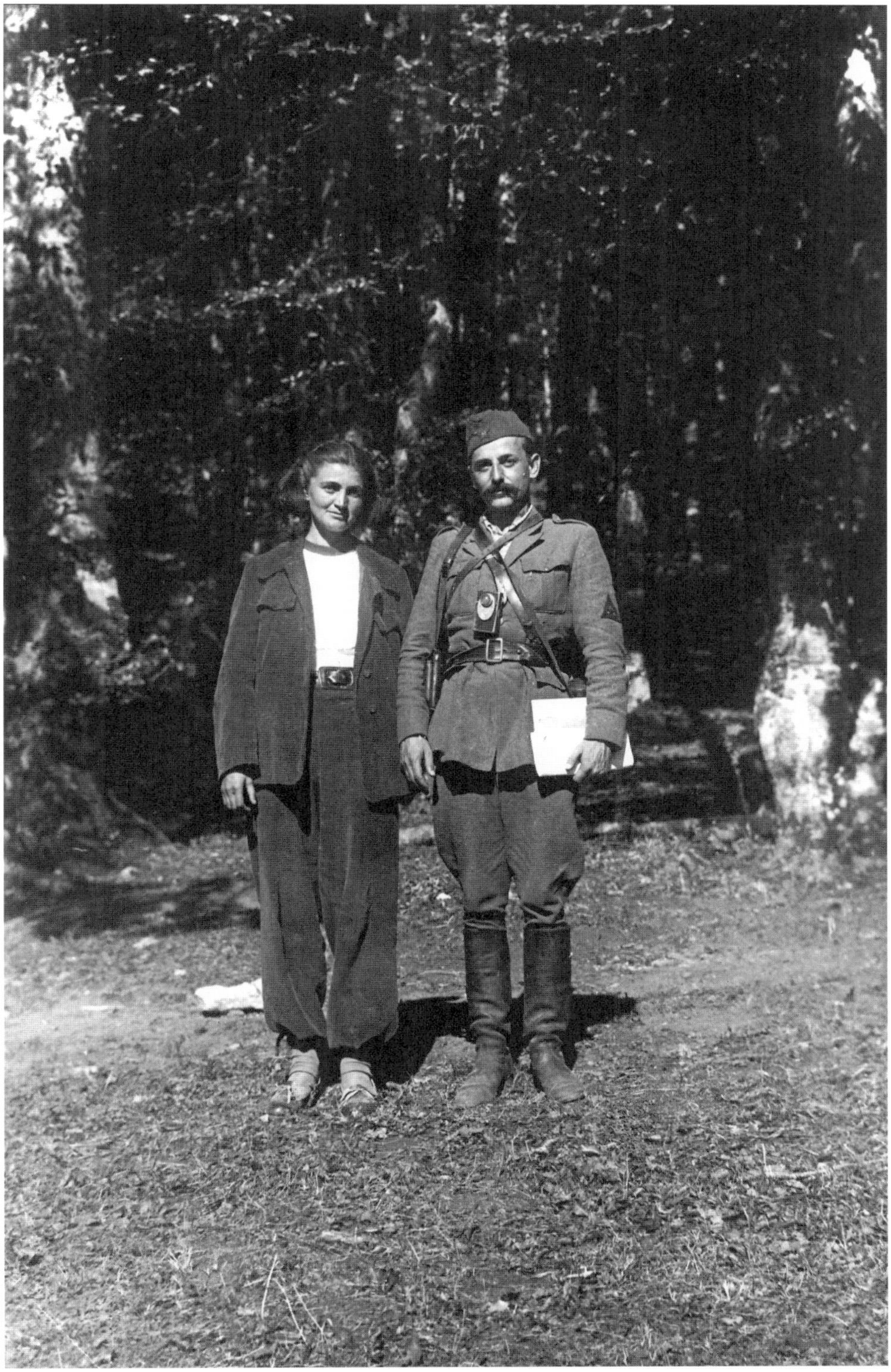

Koča Popović on arrival at Supreme Command for a consultation, beside him comrade Beba, Oštrelj, Bosanska krajina, Bosnia and Herzegovina, September 1942. Photo: Savo Orović. Museum of Yugoslavia, III-8852.

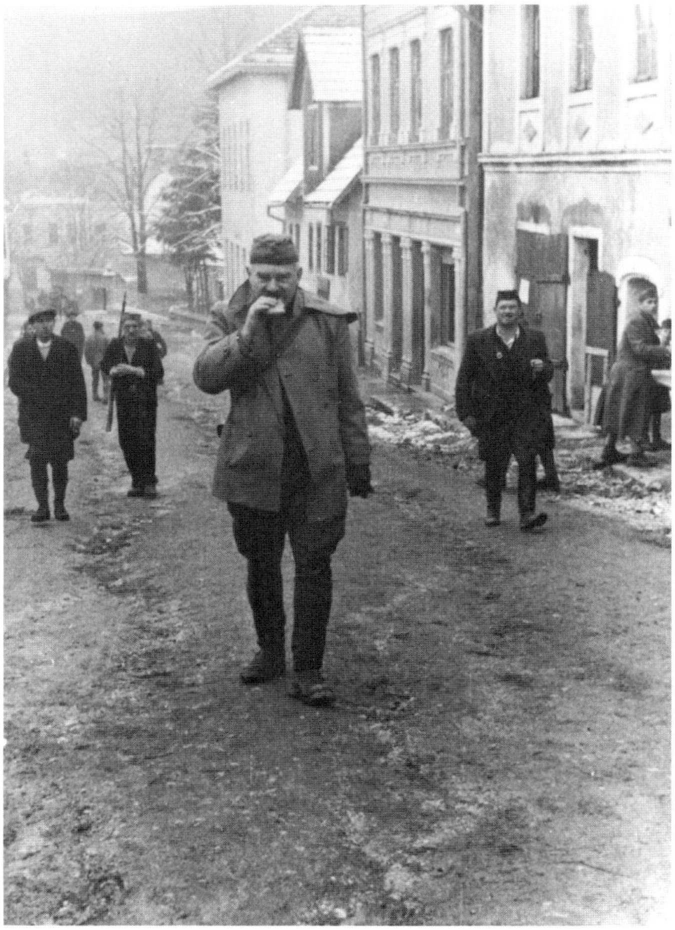

Colonel Jakov Avšič, an AVNOJ councillor from Slovenia, Jajce, Bosnia and Herzegovina. Photographer unknown. History Museum of Bosnia and Herzegovina, FNOB 721.

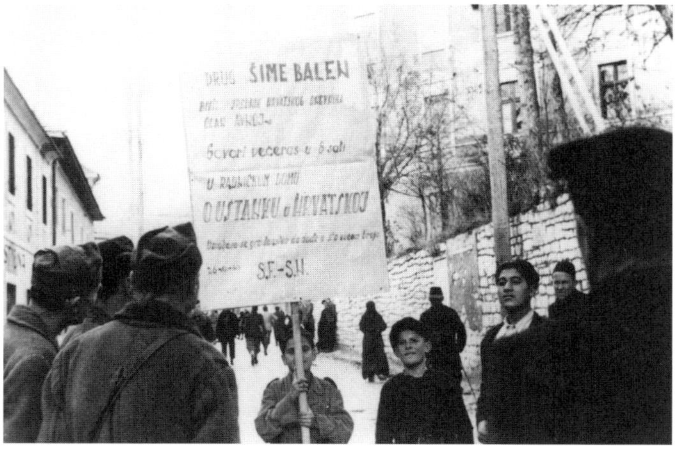

A rally in Livno, Bosnia and Herzegovina, at the Second Session of the AVNOJ, 26 November 1943. Photographer unknown. History Museum of Bosnia and Herzegovina, FNOB 726.

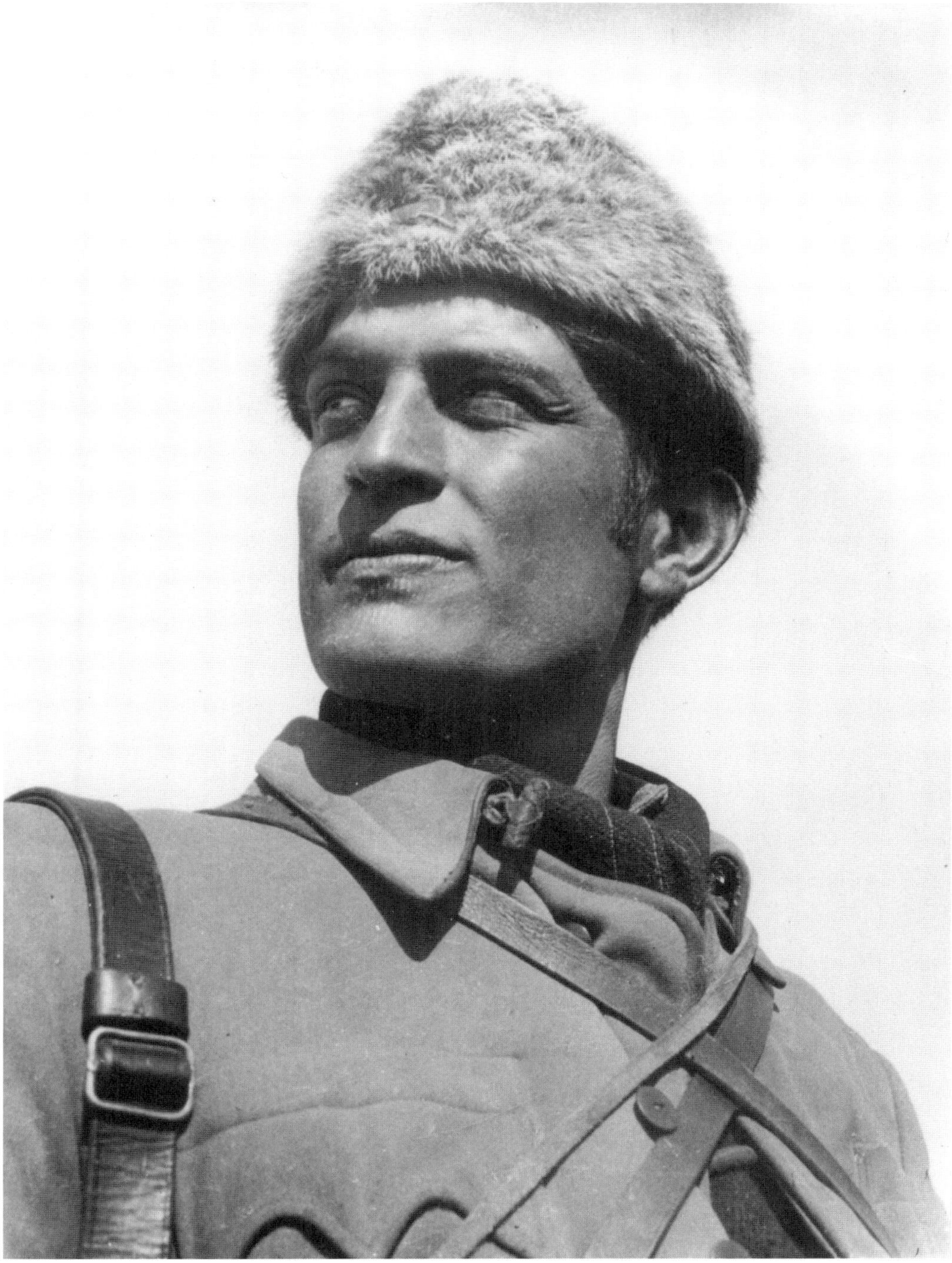

Dragiša Ivanović, political commissar of the Fifth Montenegrin Brigade during the Battle of Neretva (Operation Weiss II), Nevesinje, Bosnia and Herzegovina. Photo: Žorž Skrigin. History Museum of Bosnia and Herzegovina, FNOB 6476.

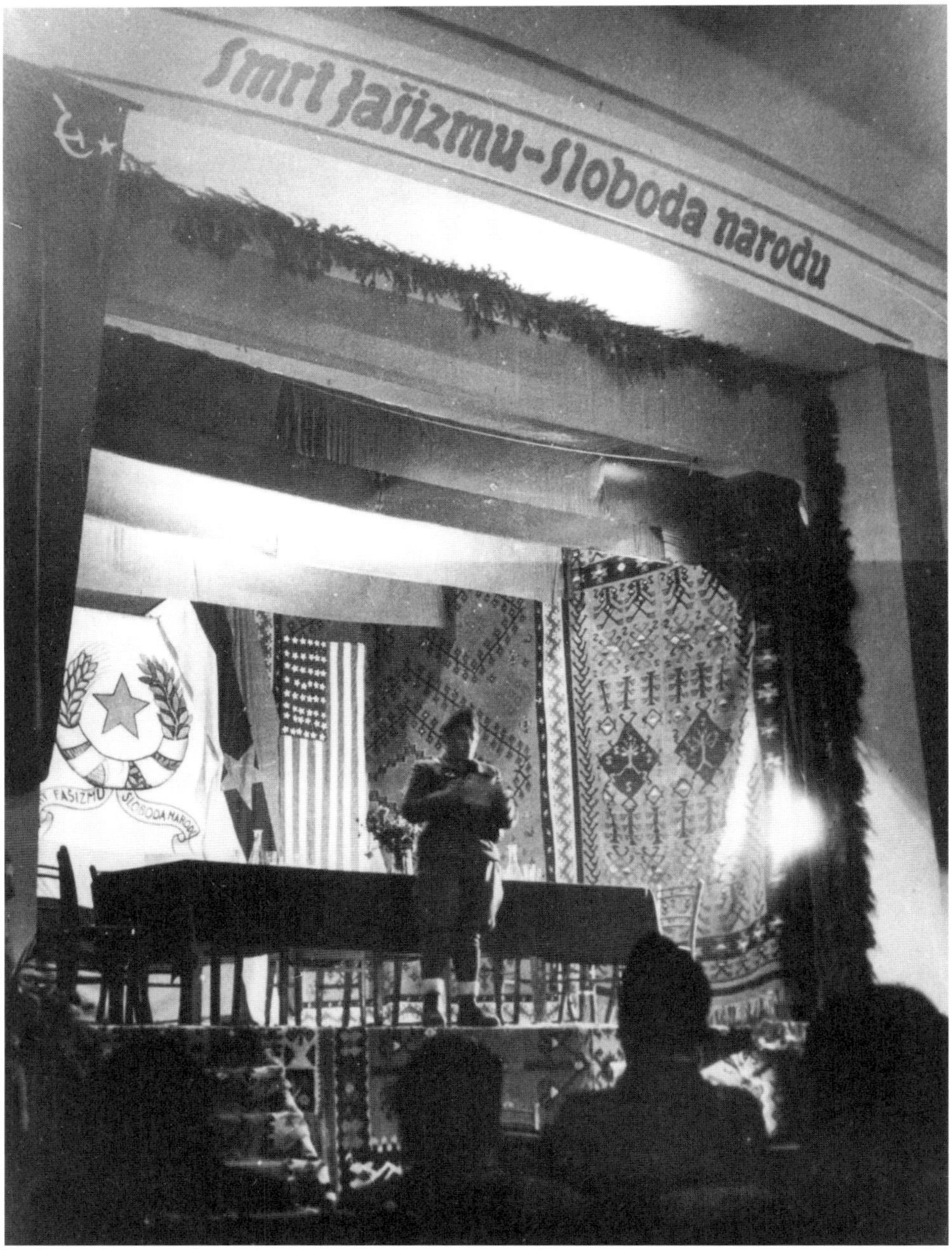

First Session of the AVNOJ, 26–27 November 1942. Photo: Žorž Skrigin. History Museum of Bosnia and Herzegovina, FNOB 6490.

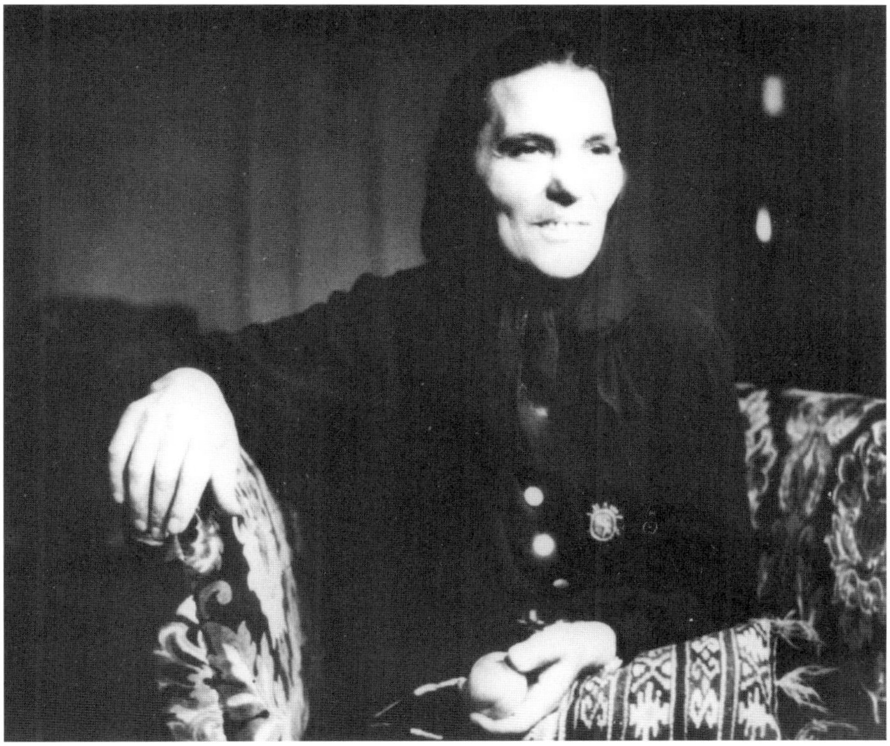

Kata Pejnović, president of the Anti-Fascist Women's Front of Croatia, 1945. Photographer unknown. History Museum of Bosnia and Herzegovina, FNOB 10701.

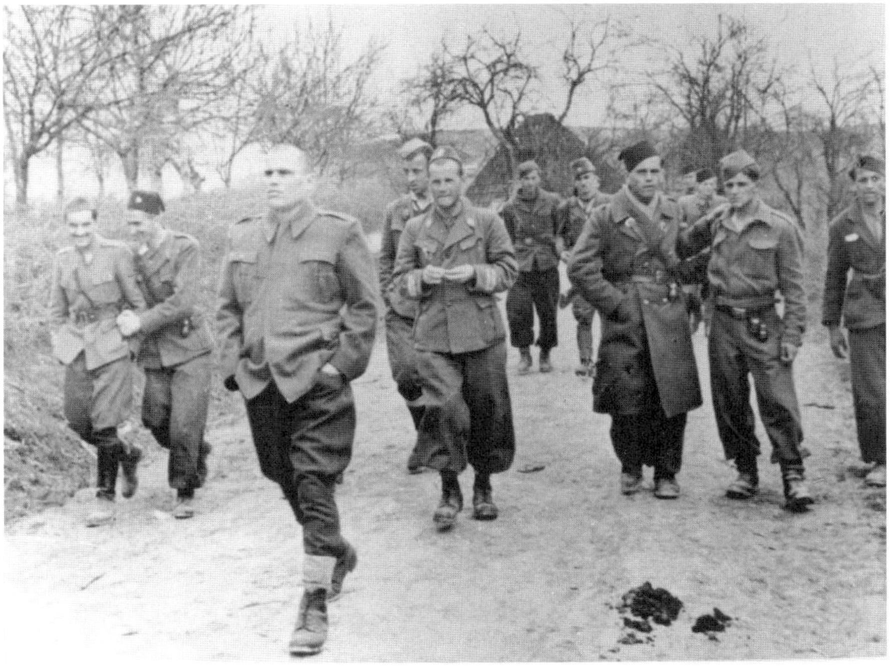

Officers and staff members of the Una Operative Group, with Husko Miljković (with shaved head and no badges) right after joining the People's Liberation Movement, spring 1944. Photographer unknown. History Museum of Bosnia and Herzegovina, FNOB 16176.

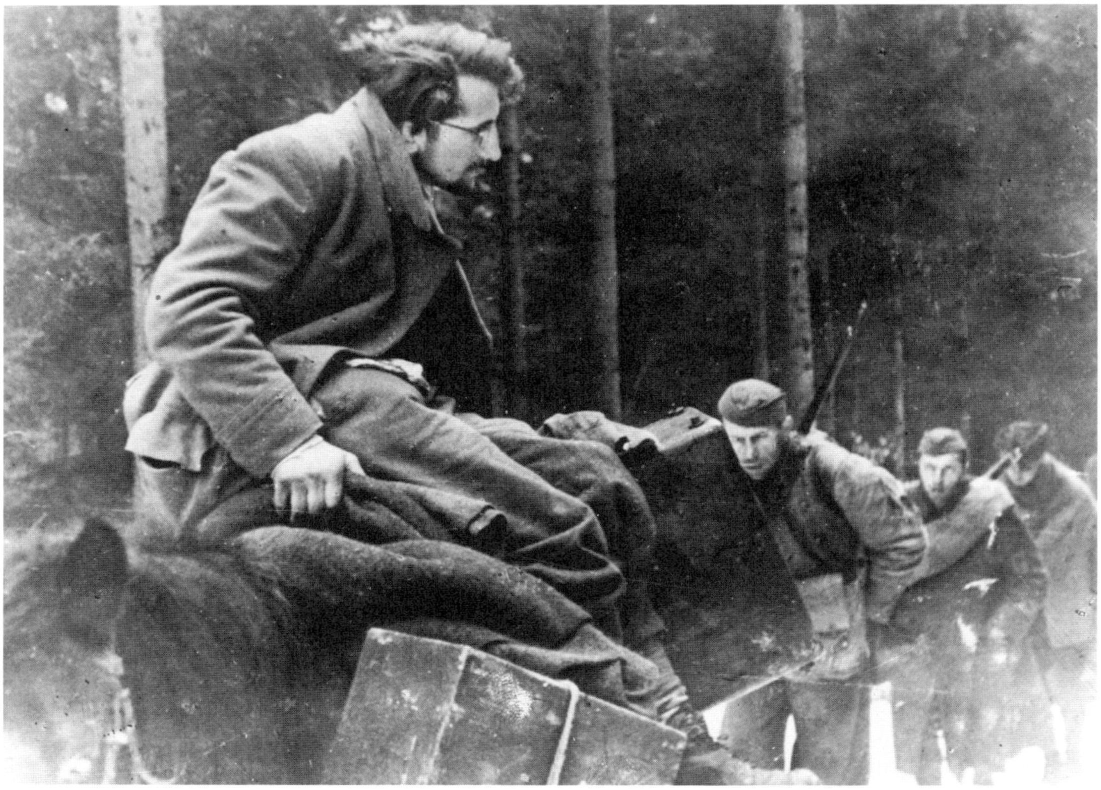

Injured political commissar of Bračič Brigade, Franc Šlajph, being carried after Partisans penetrated German positions on the road from Šoštanj to Črna, 22 February 1944 (shortly before his capture and killing). Photo: Jože Petek. National Museum of Contemporary History of Slovenia, pl7898a.

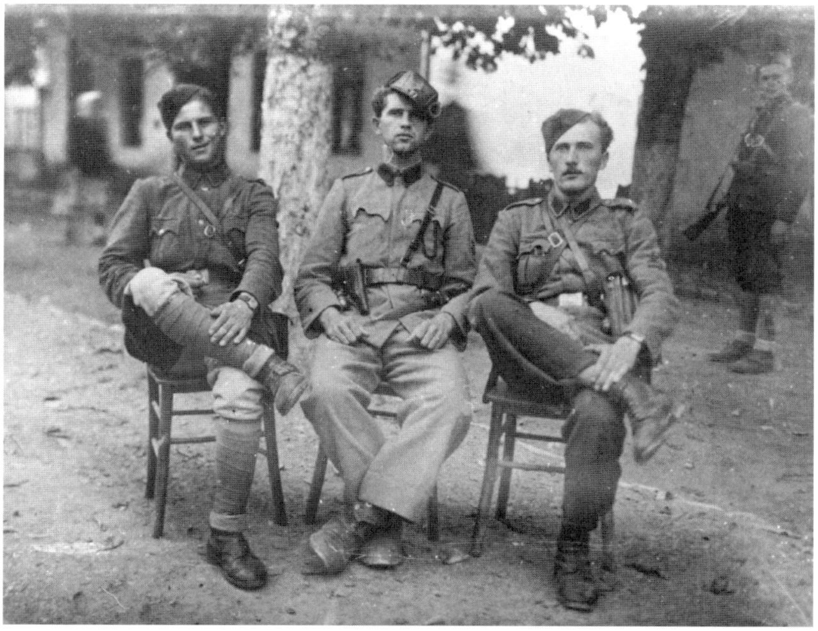

Dragan Milašin (left), battalion commander of the Fourteenth Central Bosnian Brigade, Brane Babić and a fighter named Milan, Central Bosnia, 1944. Photographer unknown. History Museum of Bosnia and Herzegovina, FNOB 16969.

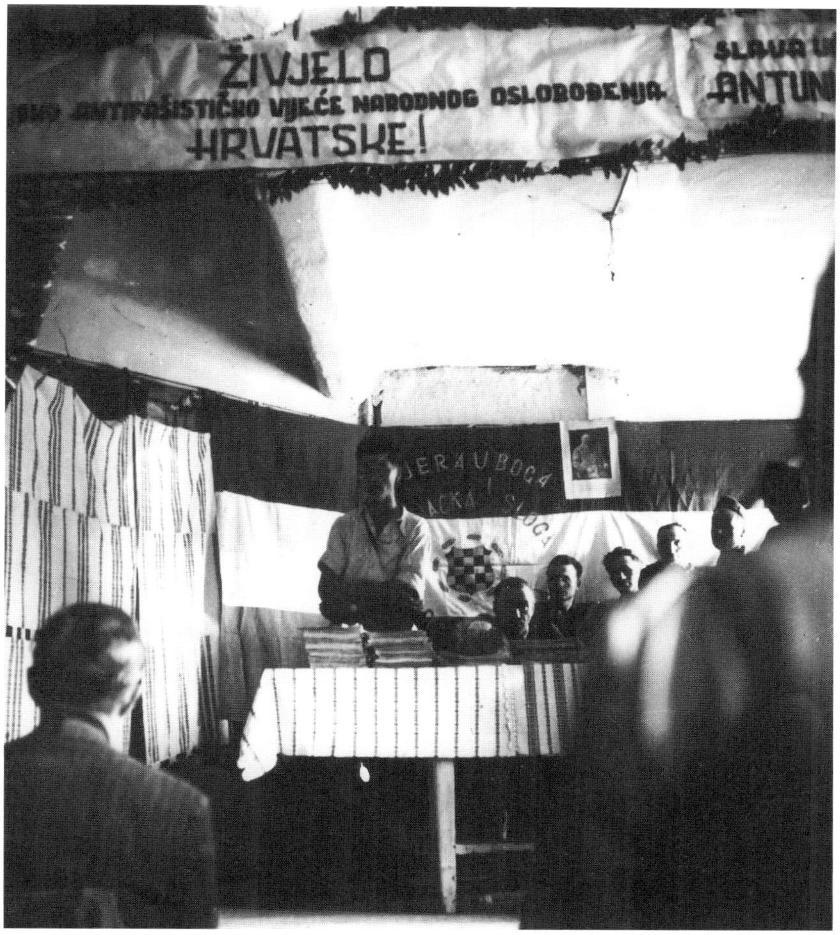

Conference with representatives of the Croatian Peasant Party, Voćin, 1943. Photographer unknown.

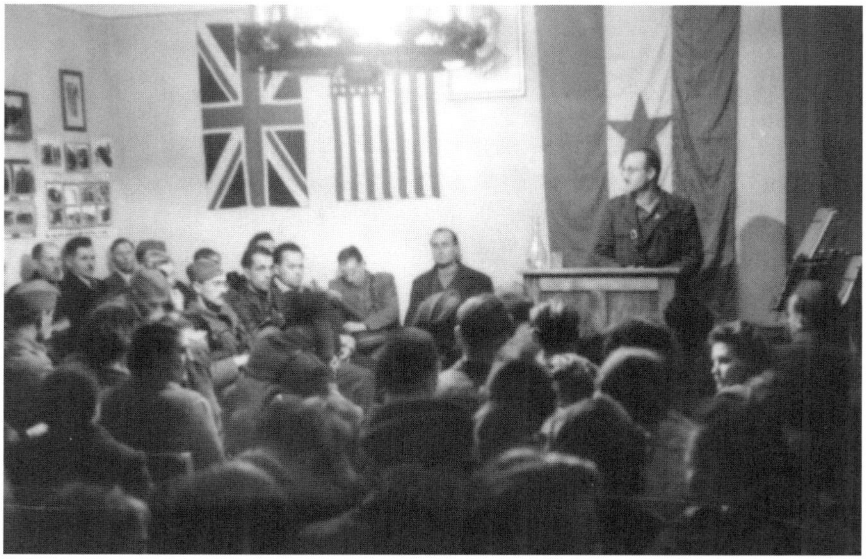

Assembly of propaganda writers for the People's Liberation Army and the Partisan Liberation Front of Štajerska (Slovene Styria), with Dušan Bole speaking, Gornji Grad, Savinja valley, Slovenia. Photographer unknown. Museum of Recent History, Celje FZ2 1587.

Representing Josip Broz Tito

Representations of the Partisan Supreme Commander Josip Broz Tito changed significantly over the course of the Second World War. When the war started, many Partisans didn't actually know what Tito looked like (the same was not true of enemy informants, however). This was because of his years-long position in the clandestine political underground, where he had been hiding under a pseudonym, as an engineer named 'Slavko Babić'. The first photograph of Tito in the Partisans dates from 1942 in Foča. There was much speculation over who the person hiding behind the byname 'Tito' really was. One of the strangest explanations suggested that the name was an acronym for 'Third International Terrorist Organisation'.

His photograph was published for the first time in the paper *Borba* on 6 December 1942, while in the Allied media it was published in *The New York Times* on 5 December 1943. Žorž Skrigin was among the first to photograph Josip Broz Tito on 14 September 1942 in Mlinište, as was Savo Orović. Certain historians (such as Nikolina Kurtović) have since asserted that Partisan photography was not suitable for publication in the Western media as its look and feel was 'not contemporary' and of too low quality for the commercial newsstands. According to Nikolina Kurtović and her recent research, the editors of *Life* magazine claimed that Partisan photography looked strange and was unsuitable for its readership, while Skrigin's 'Pictorialism was outdated, and Orović's amateur approach did not display enough personal style and formal polish'.[1] Kurtović has also stated that the Partisans inherited the tradition of the Uskoks and Hajduks (irregular soldiers in the borderlands between the Austro-Hungarian and Ottoman Empires, variously perceived as bandits or guerrilla fighters) even though, in fact, this was a key theme in the Chetnik[8] and Ustashe movements – and least of all in the Partisans.

These kinds of interpretations of Partisan photography ought to be read bearing in mind the conditions of production in which Partisan photography was made. Importantly, Skrigin enjoyed notable international success before the war. He won many prizes, including the prize for the photograph *Proljeće* (Spring) at the Golden Gate International Exposition in San Francisco in 1939. As with most other photographers, Skrigin also found his own style during the war and distanced himself from earlier Pictorialist themes. In

1 Nikolina Kurtović, *Communist Stardom in the Cold War: Josip Broz Tito in Western and Yugoslav Photography, 1943–1980*, doctoral thesis, University of Toronto 2010, pp. 66–67.

contrast to many Western photographers, his approach to the medium was guided by artistic intuition and knowledge of photography gained *before* the war. As a member of the Zagreb School of Photography, he was certainly influenced by Pictorialism, but undoubtedly also by the New Objectivity of the Weimar years.

As concerns the relationship between Western photojournalism and Partisan photography, it is interesting to compare Skrigin's photograph *Majka Knežopoljka* (see chapter 7) with a photograph, also of a woman with children, taken by the Reuters photographer John Phillips. Both photographers approached their topic in the same way. The only difference was that Phillips's photograph is superior in a technical sense because of the better production conditions in which he was able to work. In the Allied media, the Partisan movement was perceived through a colonial prism, and the Partisans were often referred to as disorganised guerrilla groups, which was far from the truth.

Before Tito's photographs were published, rumours circulated of an 'invisible' supreme commander. Such accounts assumed an almost mythic dimension, and enemy propaganda called into question his very existence. Ustashe propaganda claimed that the Partisan movement was splintered and on the verge of collapse, while the German newspaper *Signal* in fact printed the first photographs of the supreme commander. The Communist Party, forced to operate in secrecy for years even before the war, decided to published Tito's photographs for three reasons: To confirm his existence and refute tales of a purely fictitious person, to prevent the further creation of unfounded myths about the Supreme Command and to attempt to raise morale among the fighters. Further down the line, these photographs opened the path to the creation of a personality cult. Decades later, the Zapatistas in Mexico constructed the personality of Subcomandante Marcos because they required a media spectacle, but they did so without revealing his identity. 'Zapatistas covered their faces with balaclavas and bandannas from the earliest days of the uprising; they became anonymous, supressing any outer sign of leadership', wishing, in this way to create the impression of a collective, rather than emphasising a charismatic leader.[2]

Skrigin photographed Tito for the second time in 1943 during the Second Session of the Anti-Fascist Council for the People's Liberation of Yugoslavia (AVNOJ). He described the encounter in his personal records in detail:

> It was cloudy and a fine rain was falling, and so I explained to Old Man Janko [Moša Pijade] that I couldn't guarantee the photograph would come out well. 'There you go again! Ever the artist! You'll just have to photograph him today, not when the sun's out!' There was no point arguing with the Old Man any further. [...] The weather and lighting didn't suit the portrait because the gloomy clouds and rain covered the sky. I started taking pictures anyway, trying my utmost to make use of certain techniques to overcome the poor lighting.[3]

2 Antigoni Memou, *Photography and Social Movements*, Manchester 2013, p. 35.

3 Žorž Skrigin, *Rat i pozornica*, Belgrade 1968, p. 218.

On this occasion, Skrigin photographed Tito from a low angle to give the impression of a resolute leader on the day when Tito was declared marshal. Through this approach, Skrigin wanted to hint at his size and at his vision (by having him look into the distance), and strong lighting was used to emphasise the sharp lines of his face, thus highlighting his determinism.

In terms of representation, Tito's transformation into a state leader is most visible in the photographs taken on the island of Vis, dated 12 July 1944, shot by John Philips who had travelled there together with Stojan Pribićević at Vladimir Dedijer's invitation. The idea was to take photographs that would slip through the Allied news blackout that had prevailed up to that point.[4] In Phillips's photographs, Tito is staged as a powerful and masculine supreme commander as would be played by a Hollywood star: intelligent, glamorous, with a refined and decisive character. Some photographs were taken while he was playing chess, alluding to his strategic skills. Indeed, he is staged as an American pop celebrity of the time. The Vis photographs show him posing with his dog, a German shepherd called Tiger. This followed a trend among many leaders of that time – Roosevelt posed with his Scottish terrier, and Churchill with his poodle.

When in front of the camera, Tito was very much aware of his personal appearance, of the meanings attached to representation and the unseen audience he was really addressing. He looks completely different in each of these photographs, compared with the Tito photographed in Foča in 1942. He told Phillips at the time: 'You can photograph me the whole day, but please don't ask me to pose for you. It will have an unnatural effect.'[5] Phillips kicked off his report with this tagline, albeit in a slightly altered version, published months later in *Life*.[6] In his first meeting with Winston Churchill, Tito notably did not wear the insignia of marshal. He rectified this at their second meeting, when he received a present from the British prime minister, a hand-signed photograph of Churchill, a sign that Tito and the Partisans had finally been recognised as allies.[7]

As we have already shown, throughout the war, the Partisan movement were not only engaged in an armed struggle, but also in the battleground of representation, at home but also abroad. For example, in mid-1942 in the USA, photographs of Dragoljub Draža Mihailović started being displayed in certain public spaces alongside portraits of President Franklin Roosevelt.[8] Tito was valued as a leader and politician who behaved self-confidently in front of the camera, while Walter Bernstein claimed that Tito performed as a good actor would.[9] After four years of having ignored the Partisan movement, the American press gradually elevated Tito in their pages to an icon of the anti-fascist struggle in Yugoslavia. Phillips continued to photograph and work in Yugoslavia even after the end of the war.

4 John Phillips (Dzon Filips), *Jugoslovenska priča*, *Jugoslovenska revija*, Belgrade 1983, p. 31.

5 Ibid., p. 34.

6 John Phillips, 'Marshal Tito', in: *Life*, 16, no. 17, 1944, pp. 35–38.

7 Fitzroy Maclean, *The Life and Times of Josip Broz-Tito*, New York 1957, p. 211.

8 Branko Petranović, *Istorija Jugoslavije 1918-1988.: treća knjiga Socijalistička Jugoslavija 1945–1988.*, Belgrade 1988, p. 186..

9 Walter Bernstein, 'Interview with Tito of Yugoslavia', in: *Yank, The Army Weekly*, pp. 8–9.

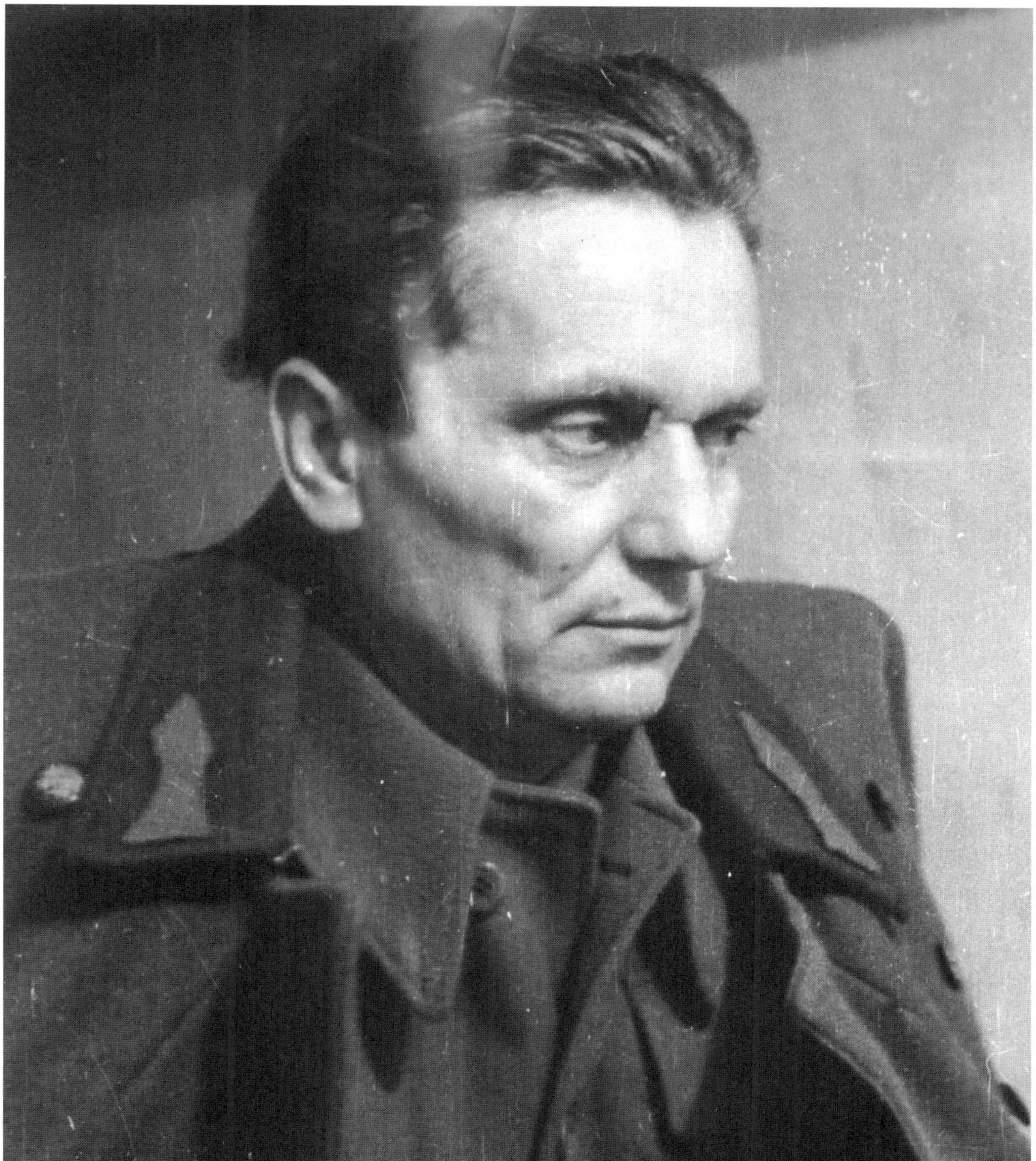

Josip Broz Tito zur Zeit der Zweiten Sitzung des Antifaschistischen Rats der Volksbefreiung Jugoslawiens am 29. und 30. November 1943 in Jajce. Foto: Žorž Skrigin. znaci.net.

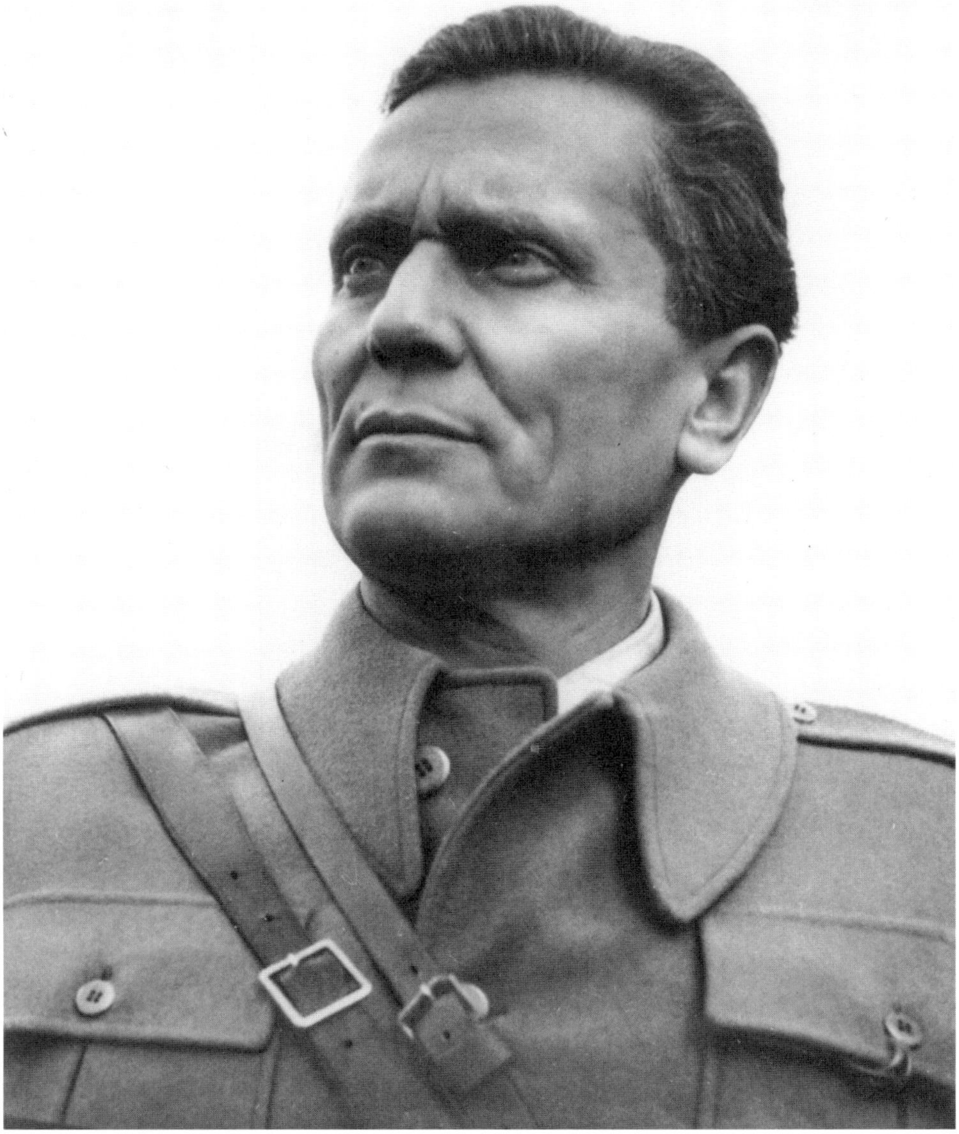

Portrait study of Josip Broz Tito during the Second Session of the AVNOJ in Jajce on 29–30 November 1943. Photo: Hugo Fischer Ribarić.

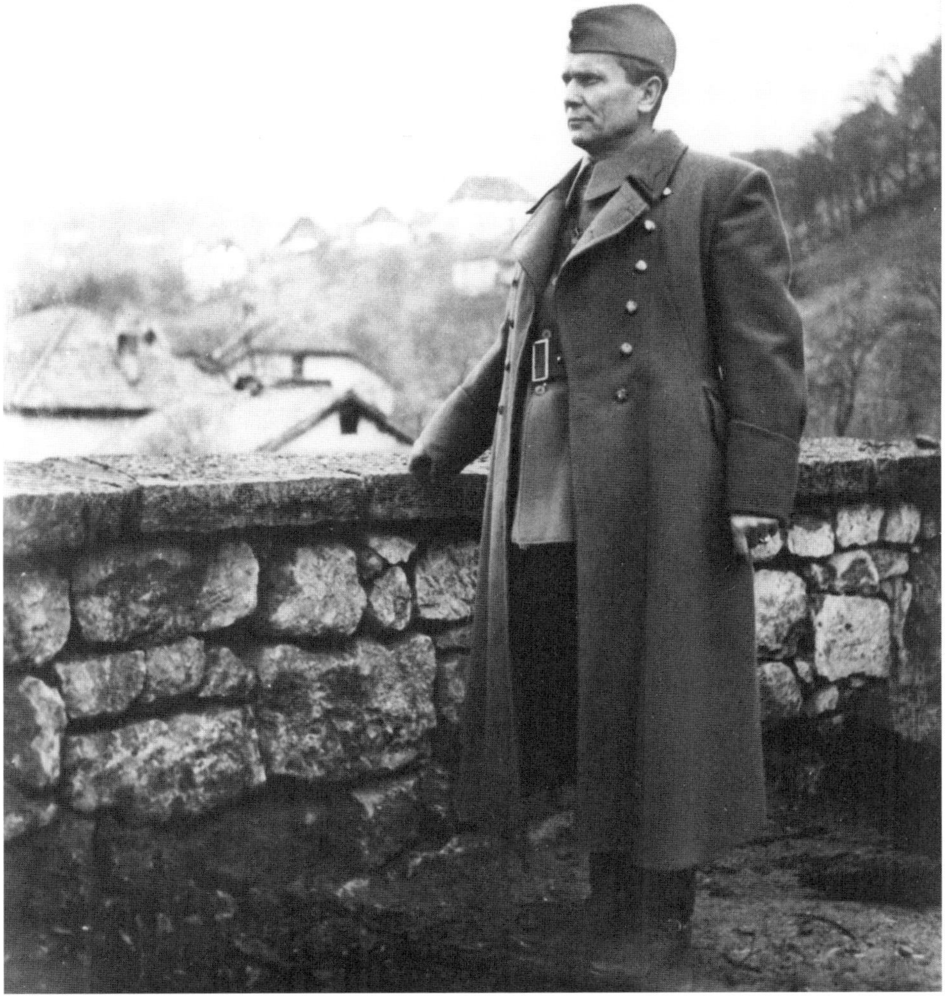

Josip Broz Tito on the day when he was named Marshal of Yugoslavia in Jajce on 29 November 1943. Photo: Žorž Skrigin. History Museum of Bosnia and Herzegovina, FNOB 2954.

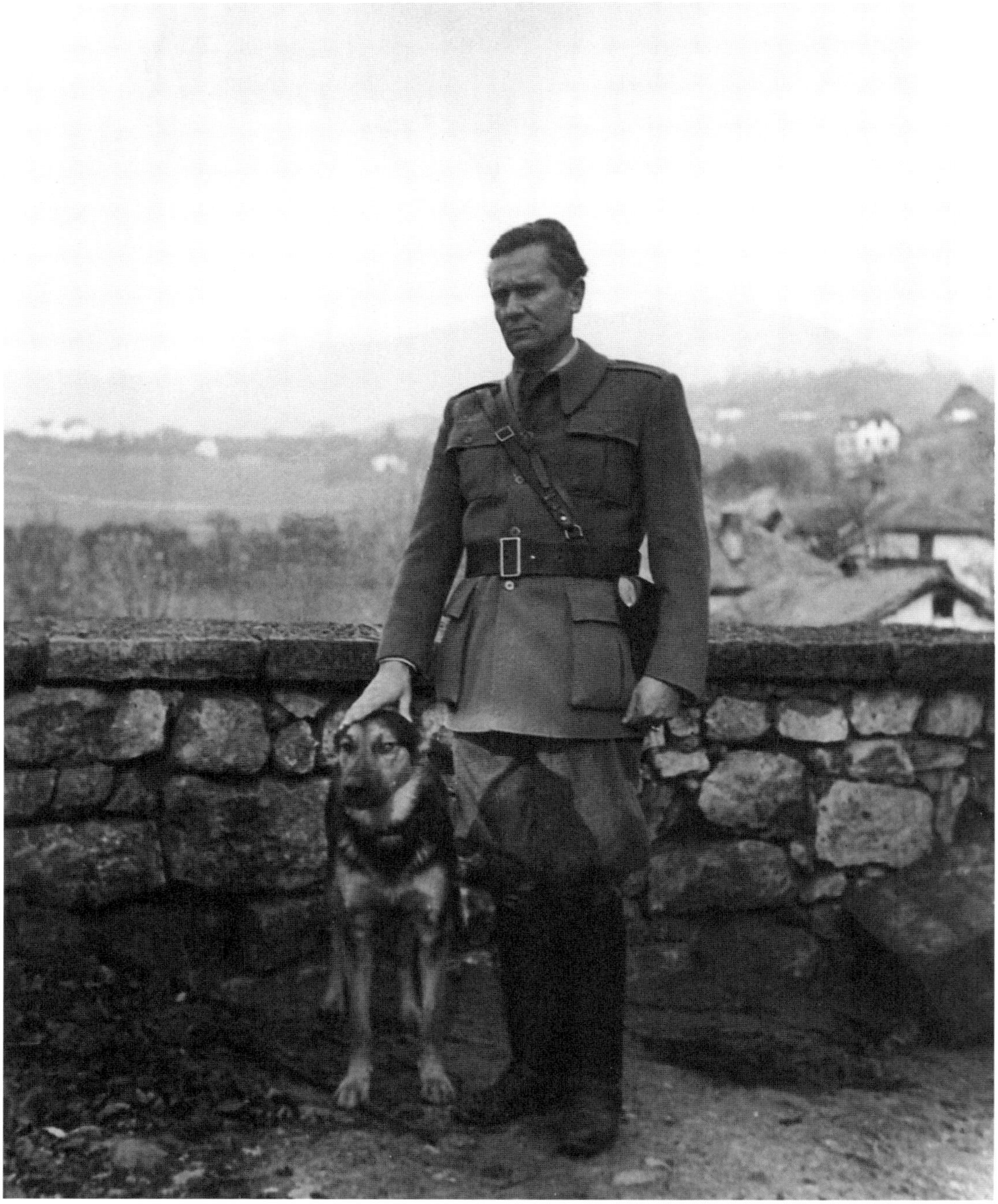

Josip Broz Tito and his dog, Jajce, 29 November 1943. Photo: Žorž Skrigin.
Museum of Yugoslavia, III-444.

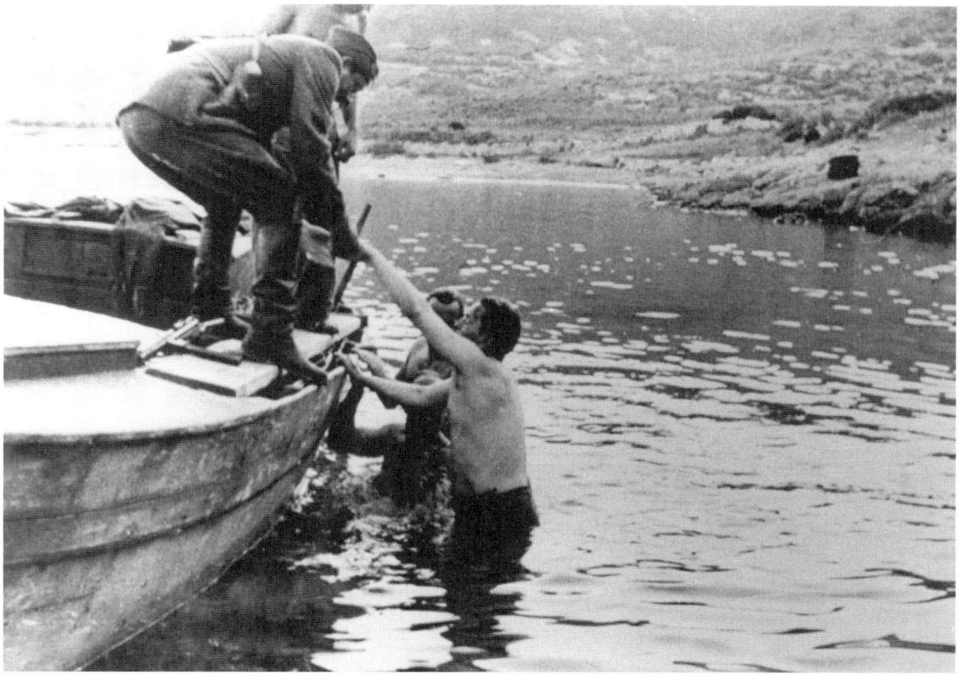

Josip Broz Tito on the Croatian island of Vis, July 1944. Photographer unknown.
Croatian History Museum, album III/2 serija 126 (16).

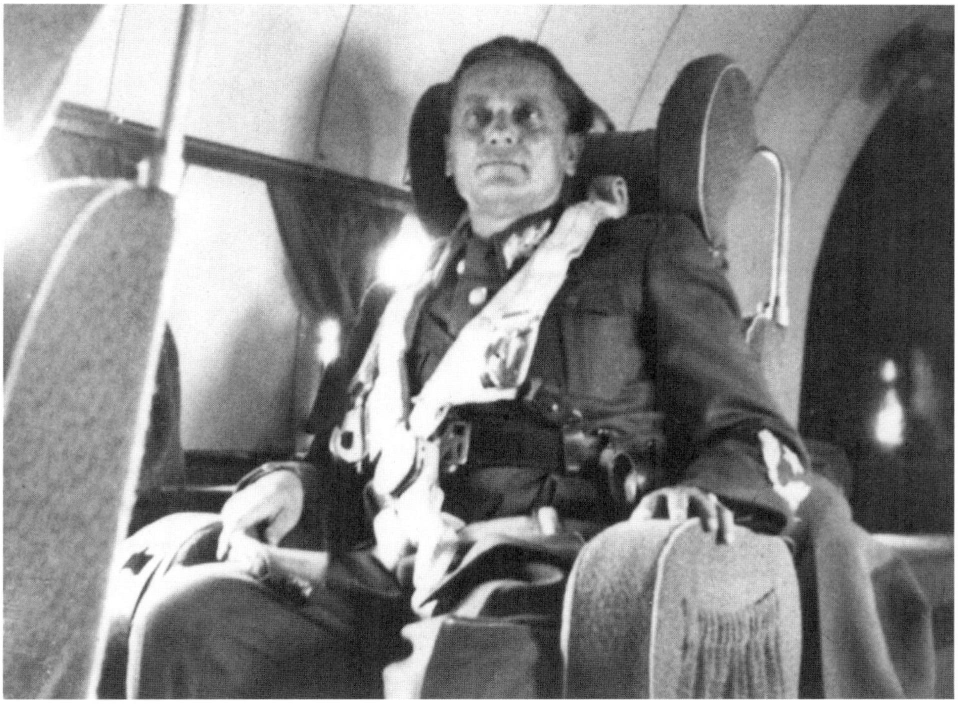

Josip Broz Tito on a plane to Rome, 8 August 1944.
Military Museum Belgrade, 19627 282.

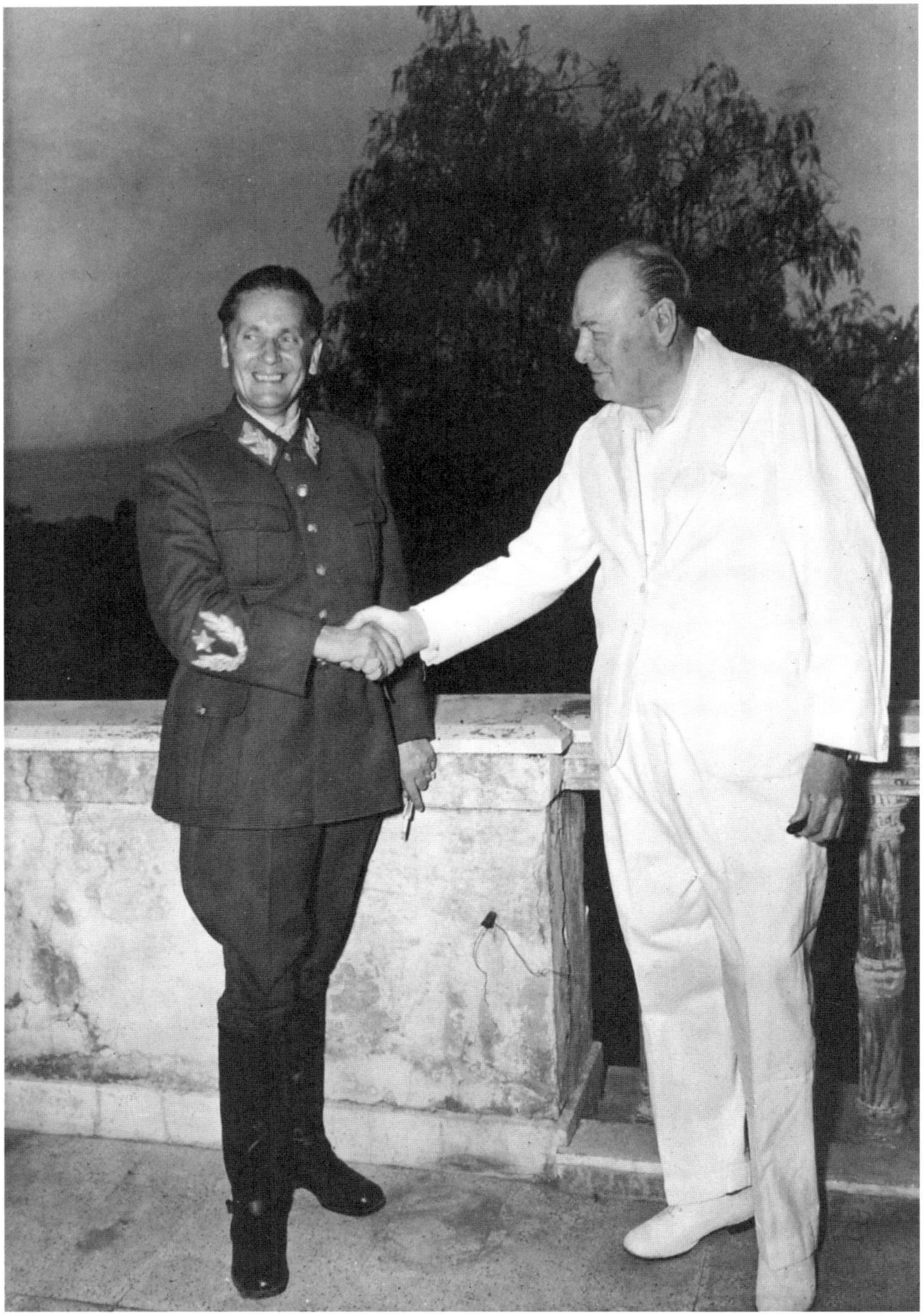

Josip Broz Tito and Winston Churchill. Photographer unknown.

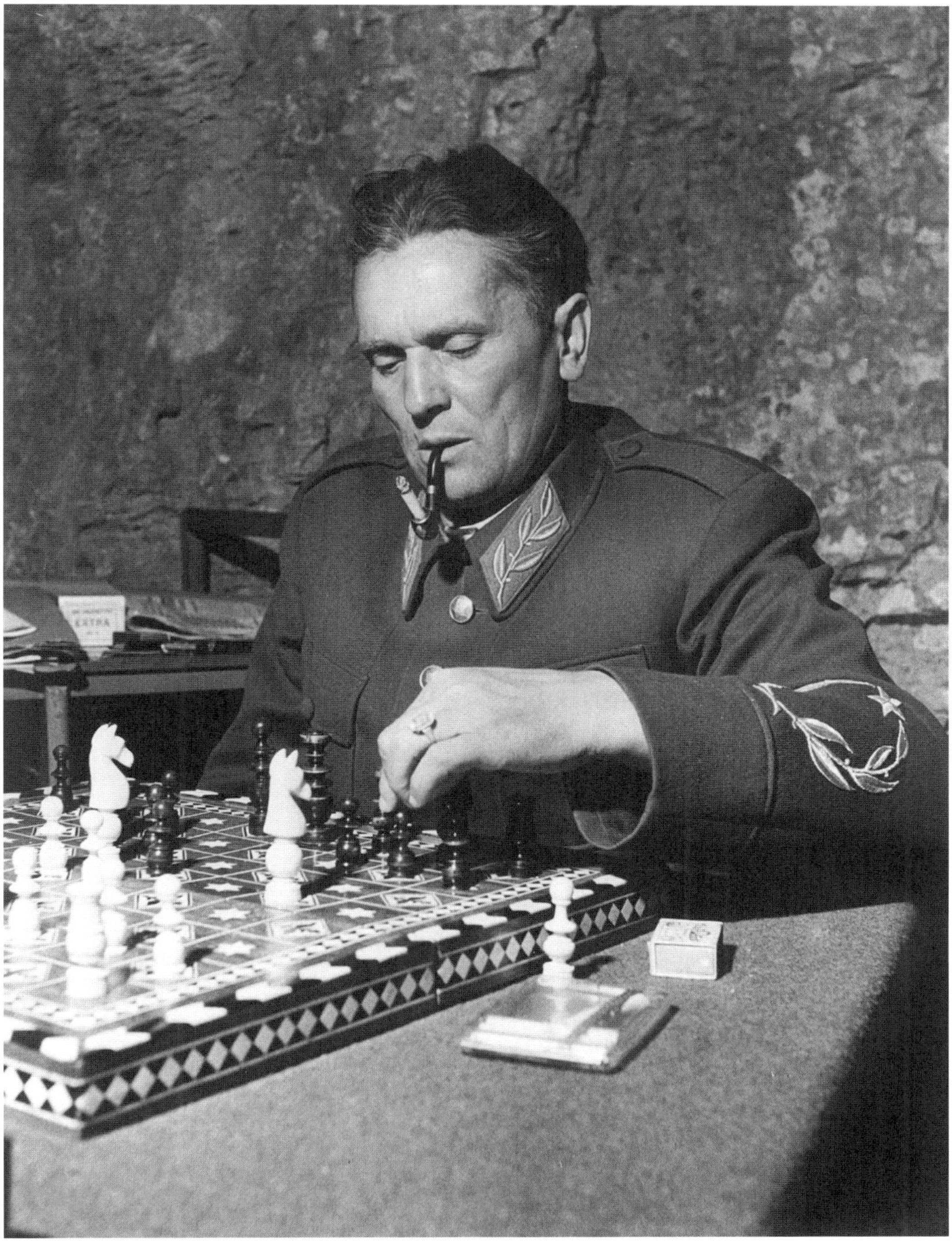

Marshal Tito on Vis, 1944. Photo: John Phillips. Museum of Yugoslavia, MIJ-1993-005.

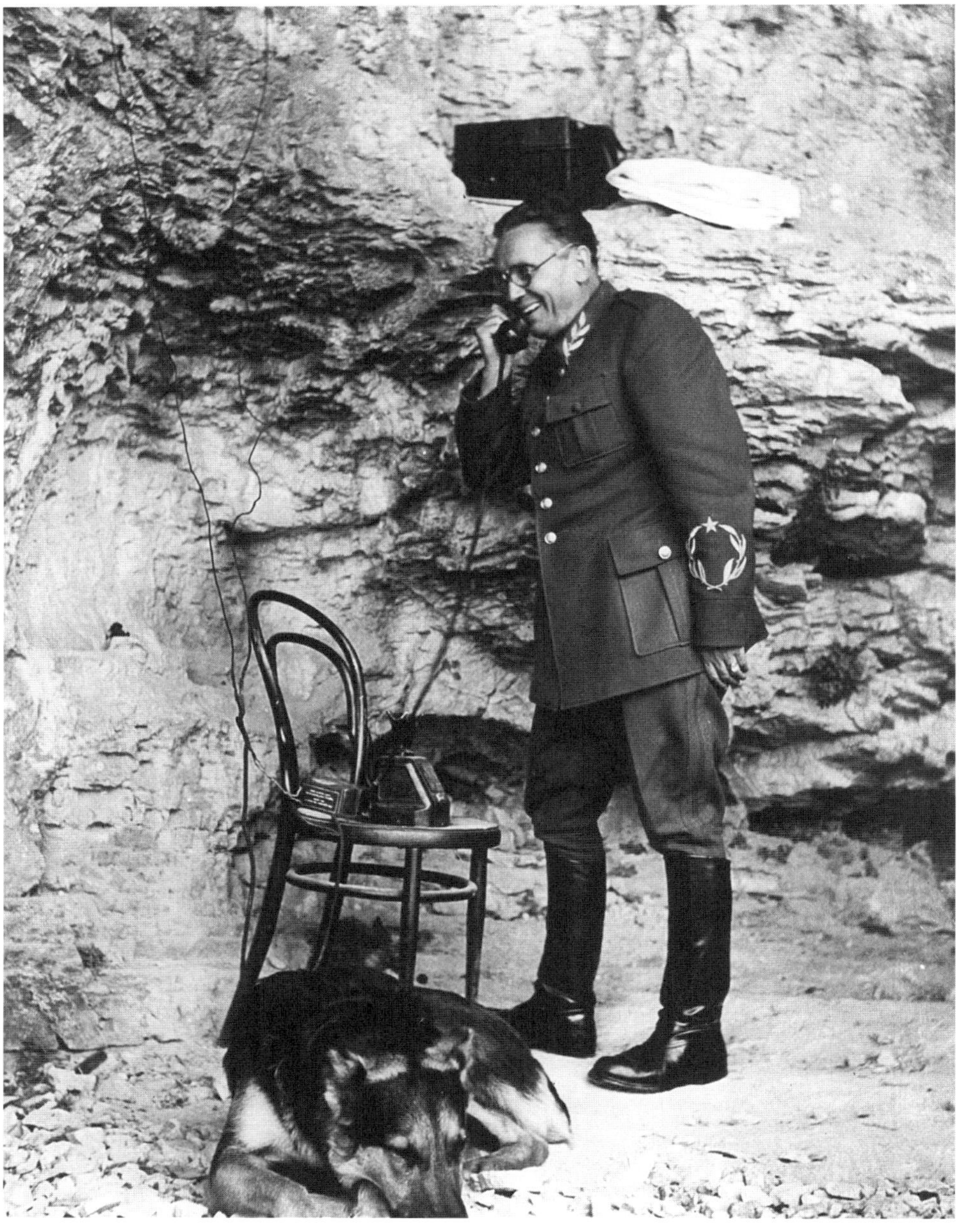

Marshal Tito on Vis, 1944. Photo: John Phillips.
Museum of Yugoslavia, MIJ-1993-001.

Photographs of Partisan Women

Representations of women in the movement, along with gender equality and the activities of the Anti-Fascist Women's Front, comprise a distinct thematic strand within Partisan photography. Women communists played a big role in the pre-war feminist movement that was outlawed in the mid-1930s, while the pre-war struggle for gender equality served as the foundation for the move to greater inclusion of women in the Partisan movement during wartime. From the very beginning of the People's Liberation War, women were allowed to stand as candidates and participate in elections, as confirmed by the Foča regulations of 1942. Women received the right to vote on 11 November 1945.[1] According to various estimates, around 100,000 women were active in the Partisan movement. Photographs of Partisan women were frequently published, often emphasising their heroism and role in the Partisan struggle. Furthermore, the photographer Milan Štok stressed the following in his instructions to Partisan photographers:

A special characteristic of our army is our Partisan women. Slovenian women and girls have never participated in combat alongside their husbands and brothers before, firstly because we never had a Slovenian army up to now, and secondly because every woman is now conscious of her place in the sacred struggle. With this mind, what needs to be captured and immortalised on film is the bravery of these women in positions as female fighters, as hospital nurses, and as invaluable support to the military behind the scenes, as administrators, cooks, laundresses or activists. Pictures showing this are severely lacking and we need to hurry so as not to fall behind too much, i.e., so that the events themselves do not overtake us.[2]

It is clear from this that women were allocated typically feminine roles. Despite the fact that a large number of Partisan women fought in the Partisan movement, and given the communist leadership's intention to assert gender equality, there was a genuine difference between proclaimed attitudes and the reality on the ground, and inadequate progress in changing engrained patriarchal patterns of behaviour, so that gender equality was always at best a secondary concern.[3] On the other hand, according to accounts of Partisan women, which Jelena Batinić has considered in detail in her book on female Partisans, their participation in the movement also carried with it an important emancipatory potential.

1 Marko Miletić and Mirjana Radovanović, 'Početak sistematizacije', in: *Lekcije o odbrani, Prilozi za analizu kulturne delatnosti NOP-a.*, ed. idem, Belgrade 2016 (KURS and Rosa Luxemburg Stiftung Southeast Europe), p. 105.

2 Štok, Milan. Fotografski priručnik. Propagandni odsjek Sedmog korpusa. 1944.

3 Jelena Batinić, *Women and Yugoslav Partisans: A History of World War II Resistance*, New York 2015, p. 166.

Consequently, Partisan women came to be perceived for the first time ever as political subjects with a role to play in constructing the new society.[4] In contrast to men, who were often depicted as warriors, women were often allocated the role of caregiver. Men were often represented in ways that highlighted a masculine warrior role, while women were depicted in ways that emphasised their femininity. Relations between the sexes were being newly forged, which brought certain contradictions with it:

Women in the units of the First Brigade were genuinely loved. Care was taken to offer them the nicest items of clothing seized from the enemy, to give them the most beautiful and comfortable shoes, leather bags, headscarves or silk neckscarves. [...] Although there was equality in everything, Partisan women were nonetheless still women; and in the photos you can see that they were dressed up, often with clothes that matched, and were always neat in appearance. Party leadership came to the conclusion that in the First Brigade, as in the entire Sixth Division, 'the relationship between male and female comrades was generally good', but this did not pass without some criticism, as it was said that – without mentioning names – there were 'many instances of individuals [men] who considered their female comrades to be inferior to them, which is to say they believed their female comrades were not in a position to carry out a soldier's tasks like a man', however, with 'political instruction one was able to dispel this general misconception'.[5]

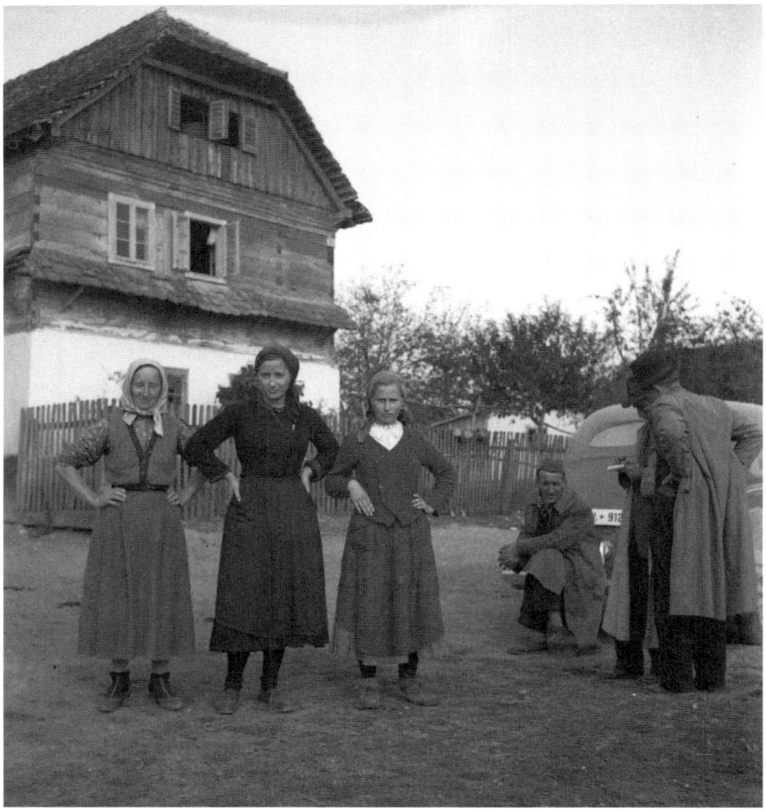

Three women on their way to leave Zagreb illegally to join the Partisans. Photo: Emil Vičić. Croatian History Museum, HPM/MRNH-N-4042.

4 Ibid., p. 167.

5 Jovo Popović, *Prva lička proleterska NOI brigada Marko Orešković*, Belgrade 1988, p. 306.

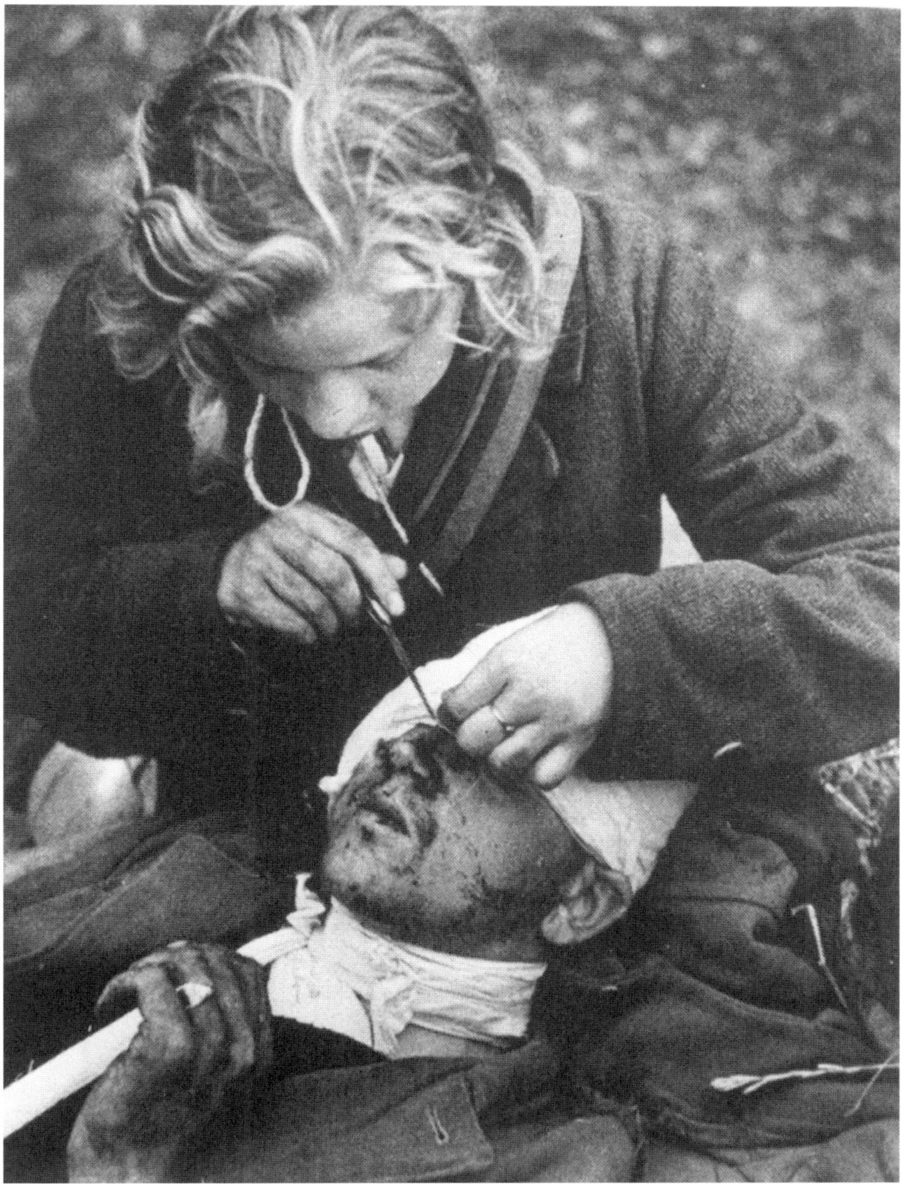

Hospital nurse tending to the wound of a fighter in Gubec Brigade after an attack on Pogornik Bridge near Litija, central Slovenia, September 1944. Photo: John Philips. National Museum of Contemporary History of Slovenia, TN5124/8.

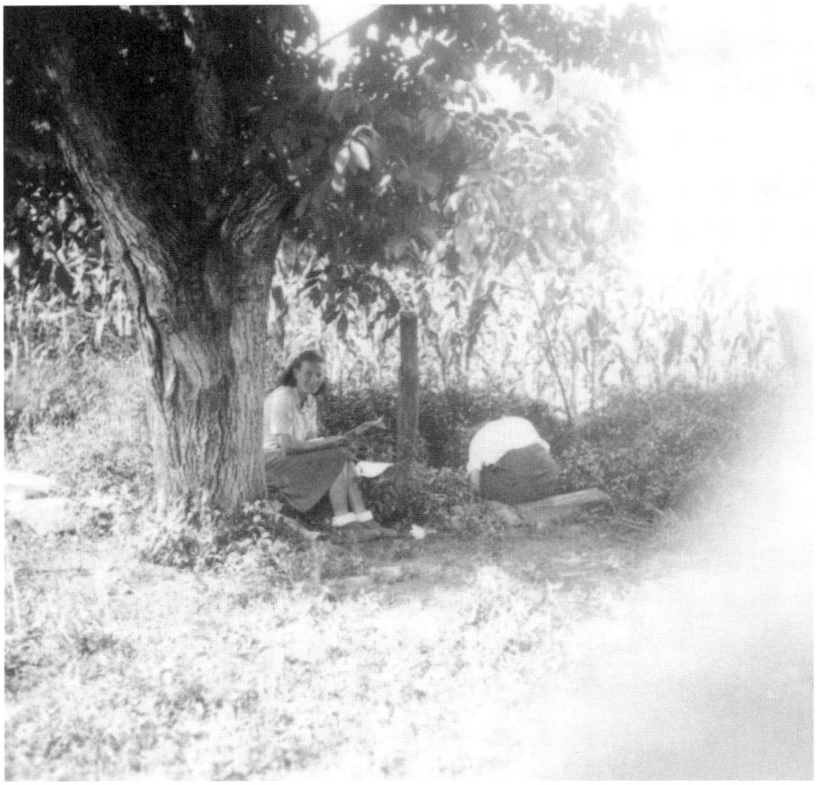

Olga Kreačić-Žoga and Bosiljka Krajačić-Beba, editors of the magazine *Žene u borbi* (Women in the Fight), Topusko, Croatia, 1944. Croatian History Museum, HPM-MRNH-F-4644.

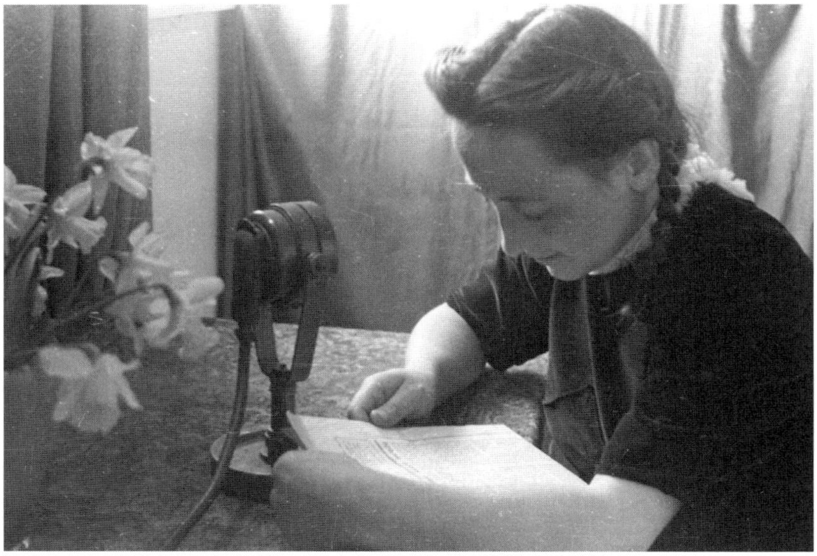

Cilka Maležič of the Liberation Front radio team making a broadcast, Črnomelj, Slovenia, April 1944. Photo: Jože Petek. National Museum of Contemporary History of Slovenia, TN700/

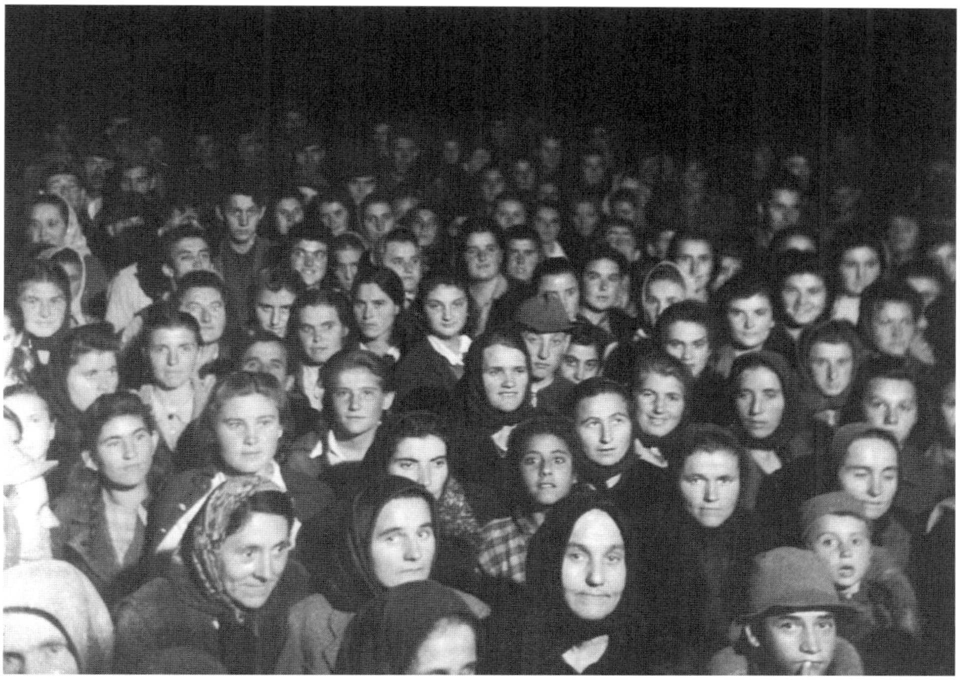

Some of the 650 delegates at the four-day First Regional Conference of the Vojvodina Anti-Fascist Women's Front, which included elections for the Regional Committee, Novi Sad, 1–4 May 1945. Photographer unknown. Museum of Yugoslavia, III-8596.

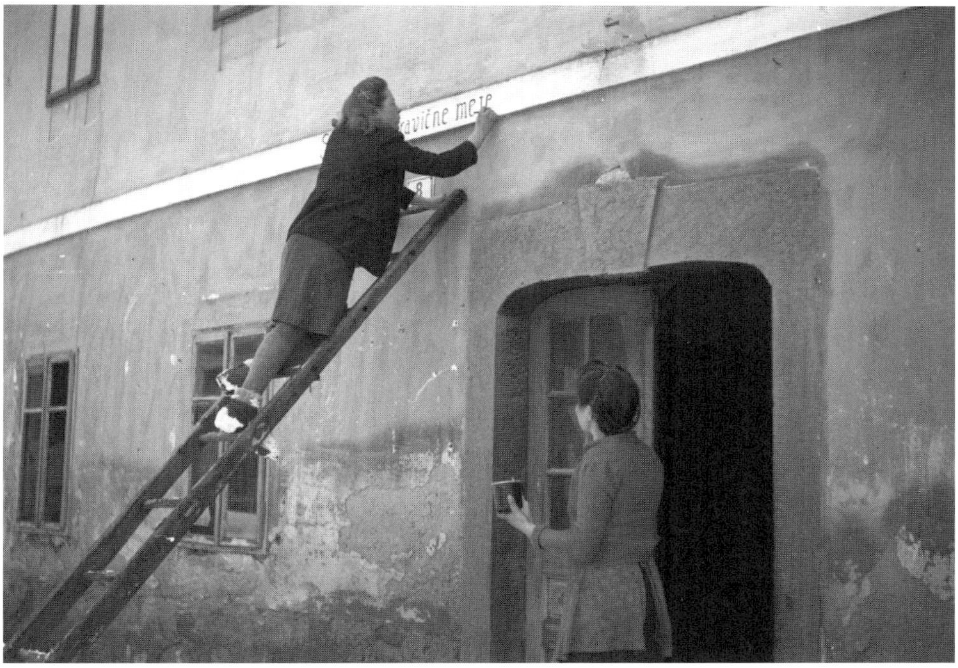

Members of the Youth League of Slovenia drumming up support for a second pre-congress competition, Osilnica, 1945. Photo: Edi Šelhaus. National Museum of Contemporary History of Slovenia, TN1663/4.

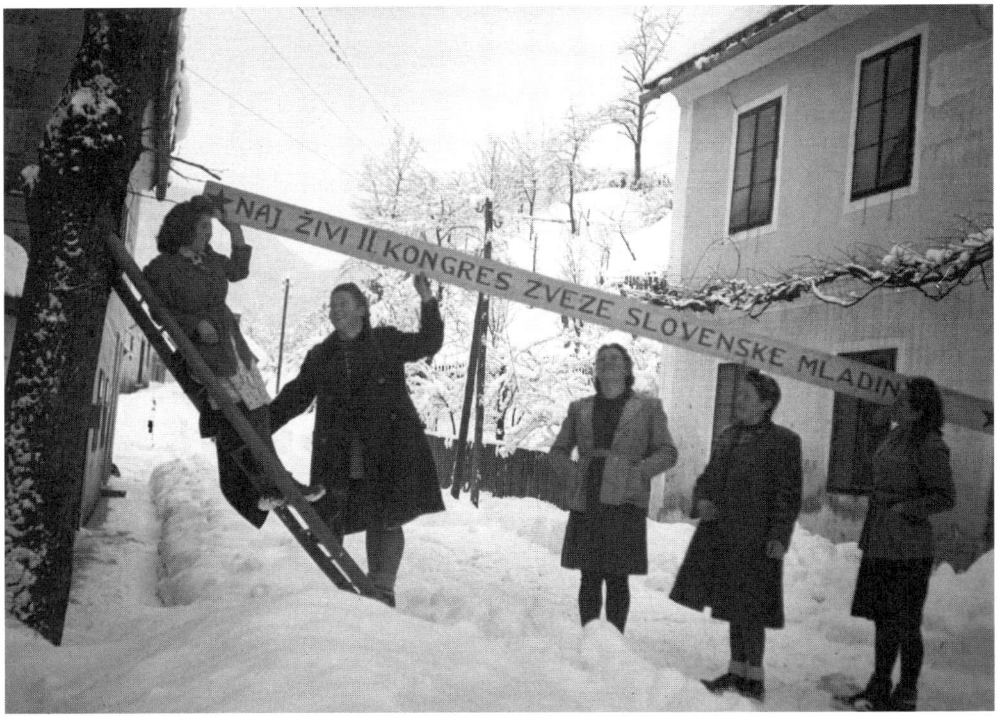

Members of the Youth League of Slovenia drumming up support for a second pre-congress competition, Osilnica, 1945. Photo: Edi Šelhaus. National Museum of Contemporary History of Slovenia, TN1663/5.

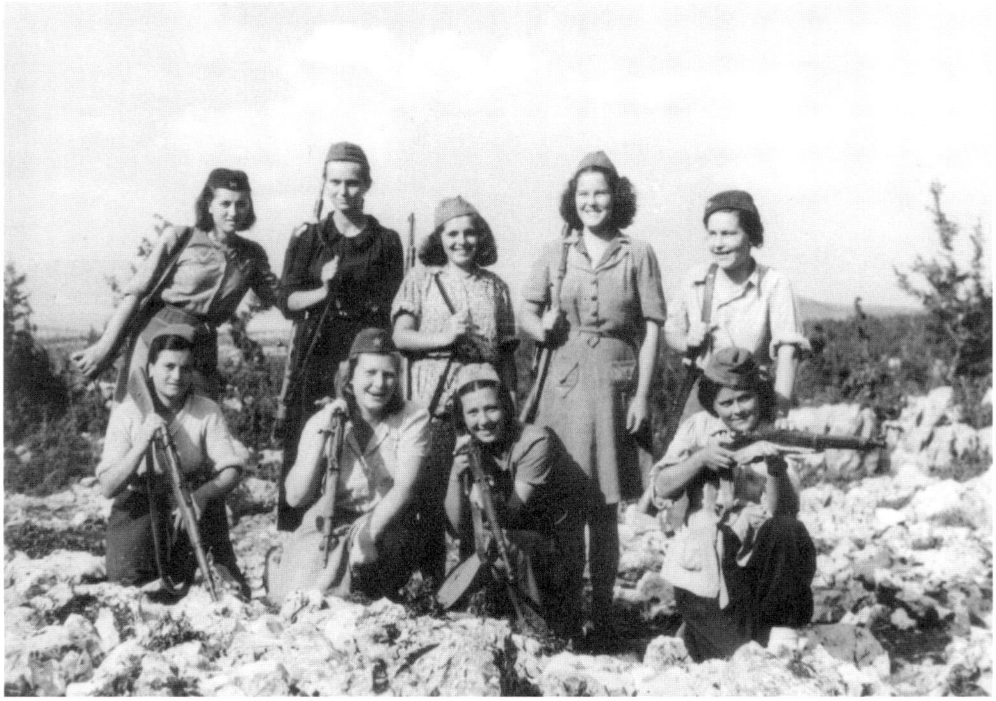

Youth fighters from the Mosor Battalion taking a short break, Ugljane near Mount Mosor, east of Split, Croatia, August 1943. Reproduced with kind permission from Marko Strpić.

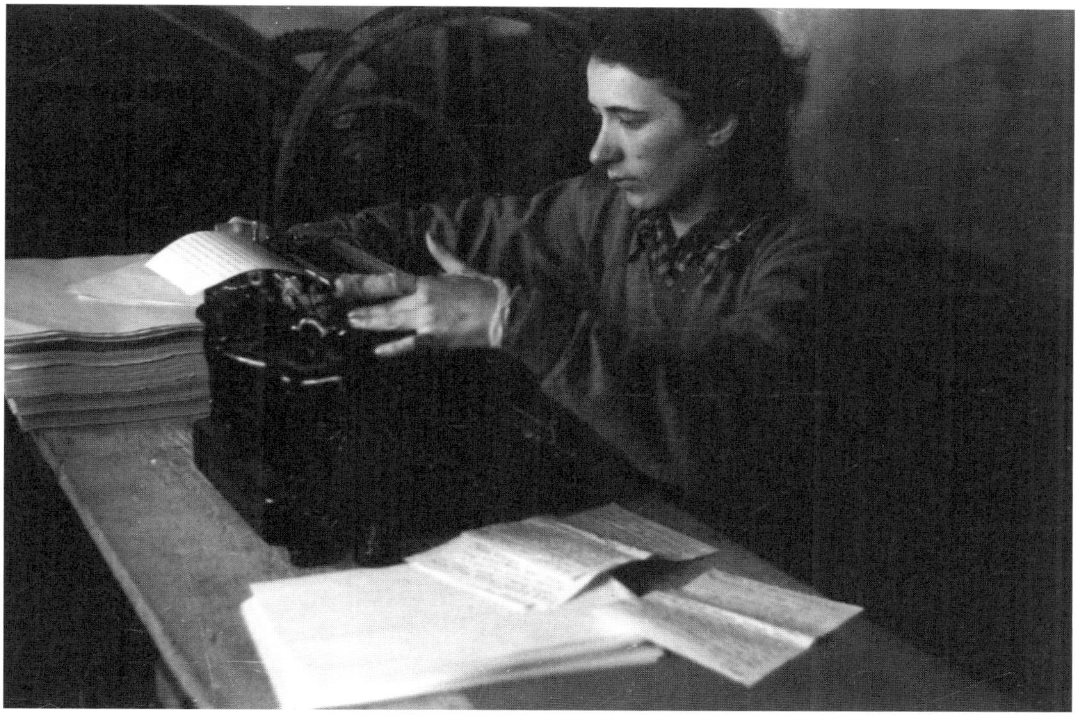

In the editorial office of Vjesnik, the underground newspaper of the Communist Party of Croatia, Lika, Turjanski, Croatia, winter 1943. Croatian History Museum, HPM/MRNH-A-2601-f83-14.

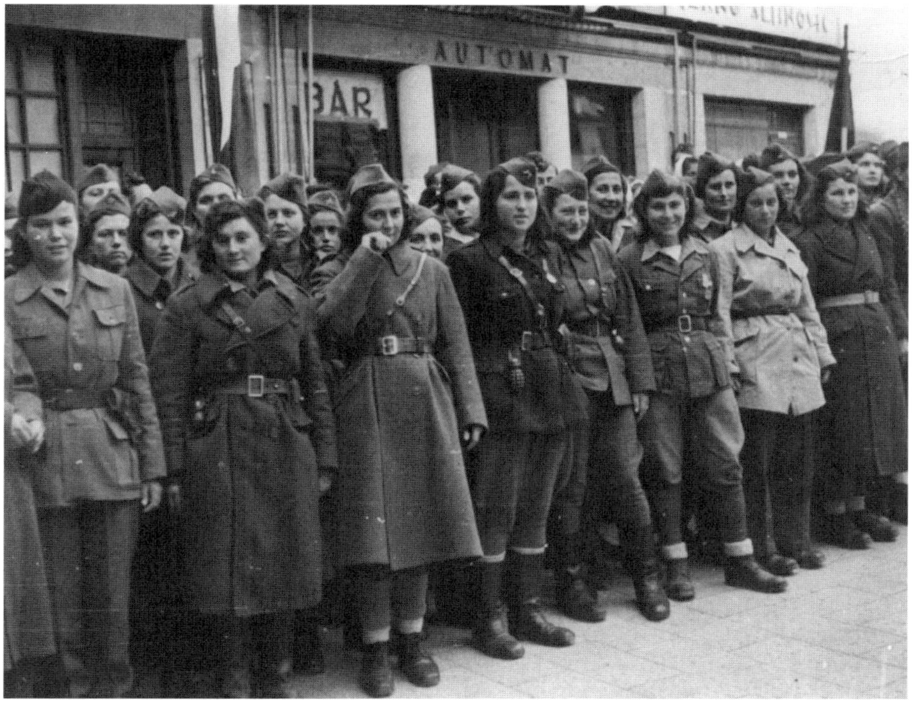

Dalmatian Partisans in liberated Split, Croatia, 1944. Central Committee of League of Communists of Yugoslavia Collection (CK SKJ), 7174.

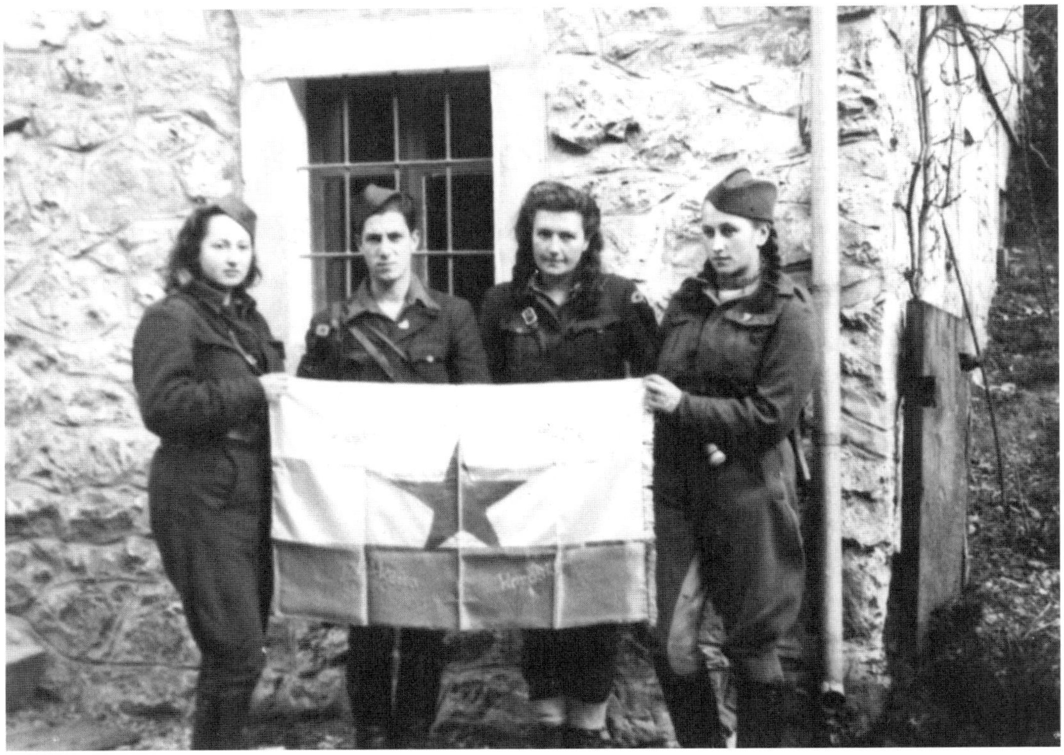

Making flags for the Koroška Detachment, Solčava, Slovenia, 12 November 1944.
Photographer unknown. Museum of Recent History, Celje, FZ25583.

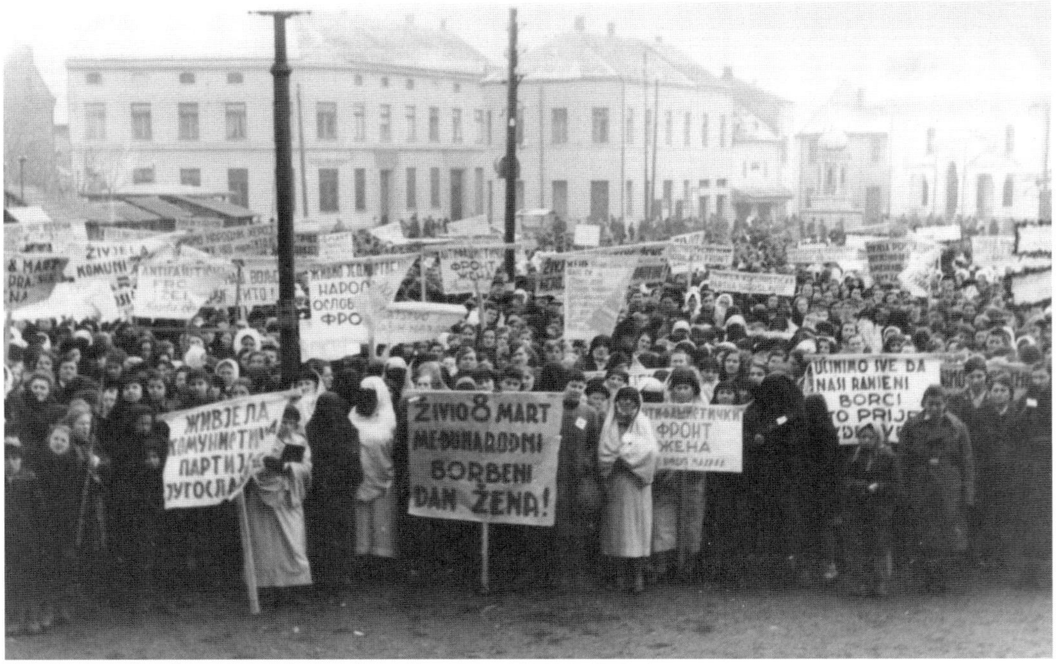

Meeting of the Anti-Fascist Women's Front in Tuzla, Bosnia and Herzegovina, 8 March 1945.
Photo: Drago Mažar. Archives of the Republic of Srpska, Banja Luka.

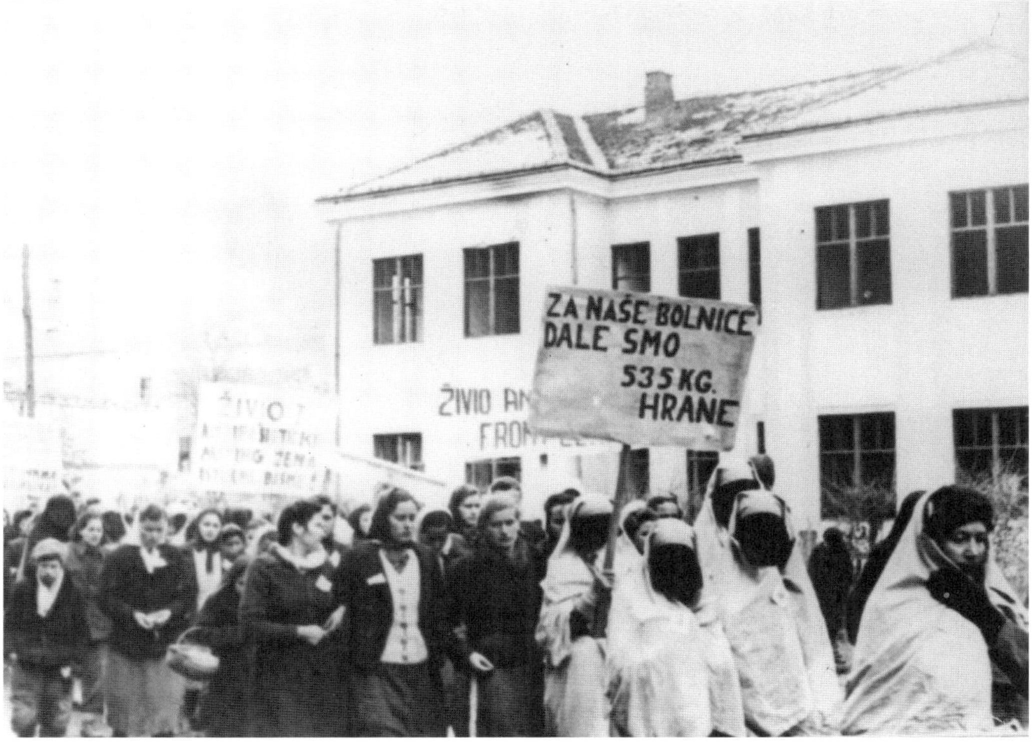

Meeting of the Anti-Fascist Women's Front in Tuzla, Bosnia and Herzegovina, 8 March 1945. Photographer unknown. History Museum of Bosnia and Herzegovina, FNOB 1683.

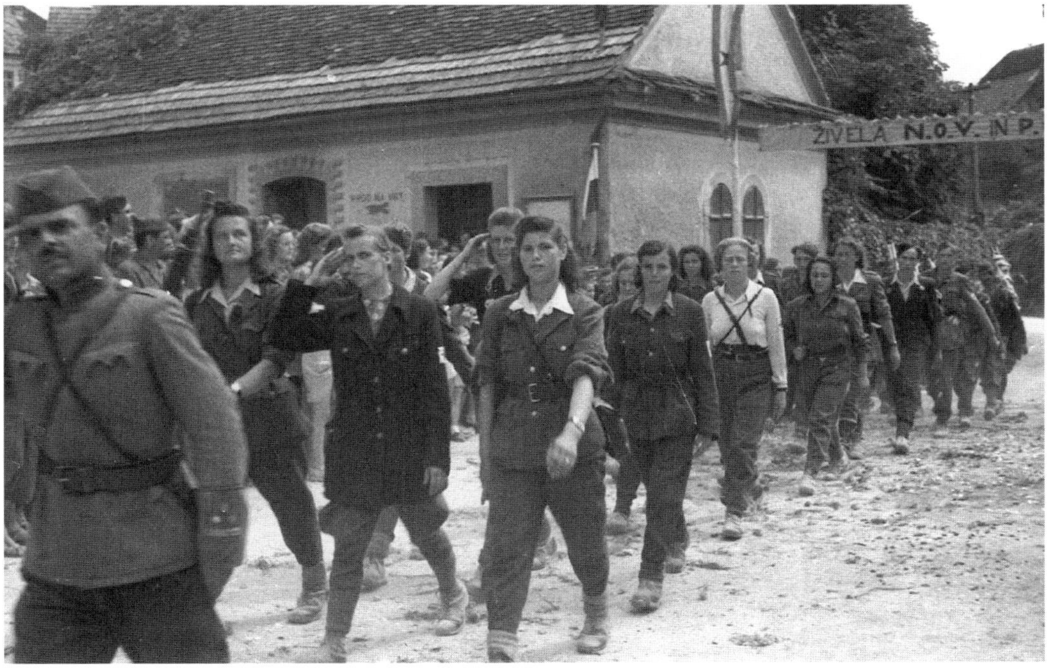

Slovenian and Croatian units parade in front of stands with guests of honour in Metlika, Slovenia, 9 July 1944. Photo: Mirko Trobec. National Museum of Contemporary History of Slovenia, TN184/0.

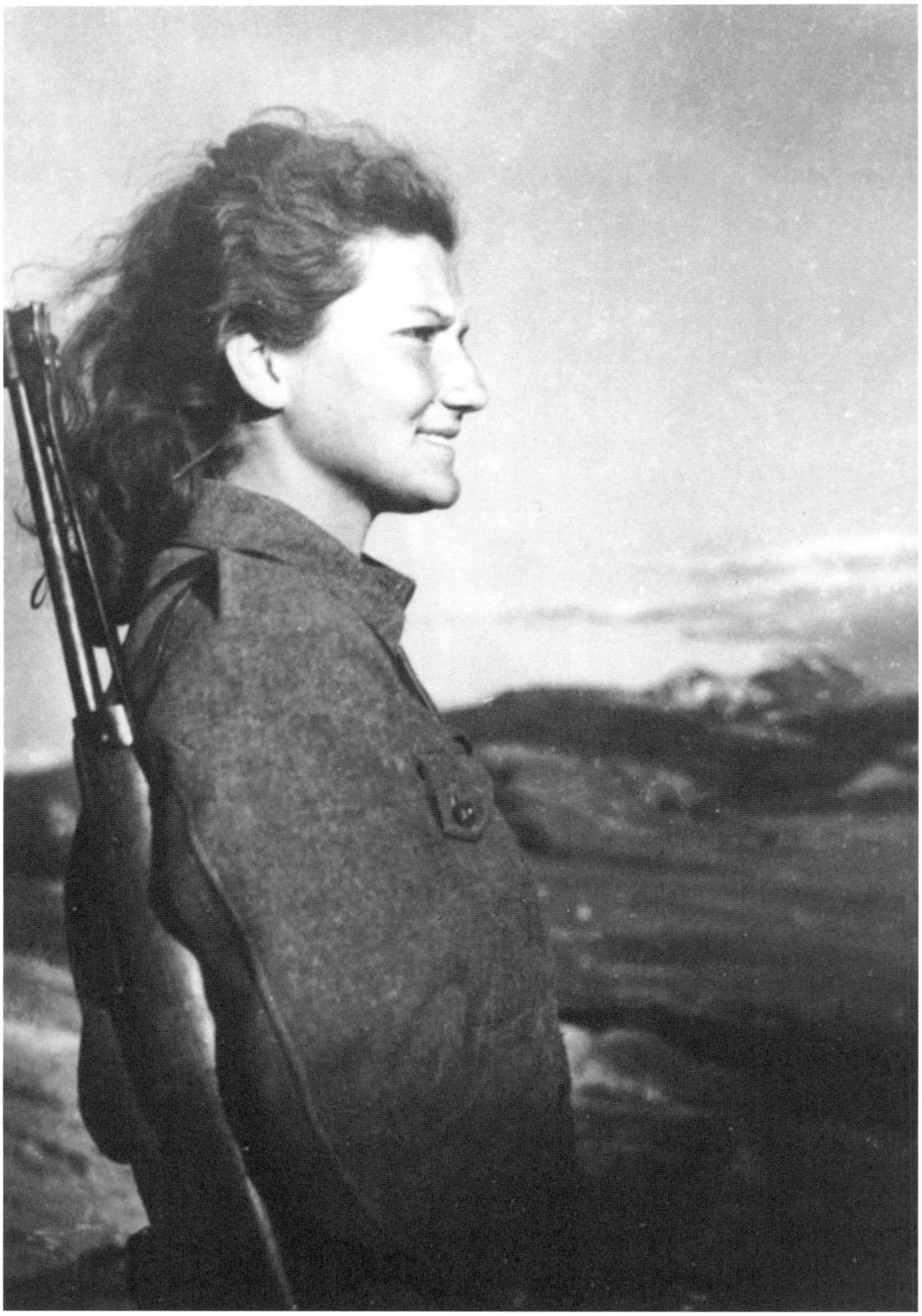

The Partisan Mira Pejić on Mount Šator, Bosnia, 1944. Photo: Žorž Skrigin.

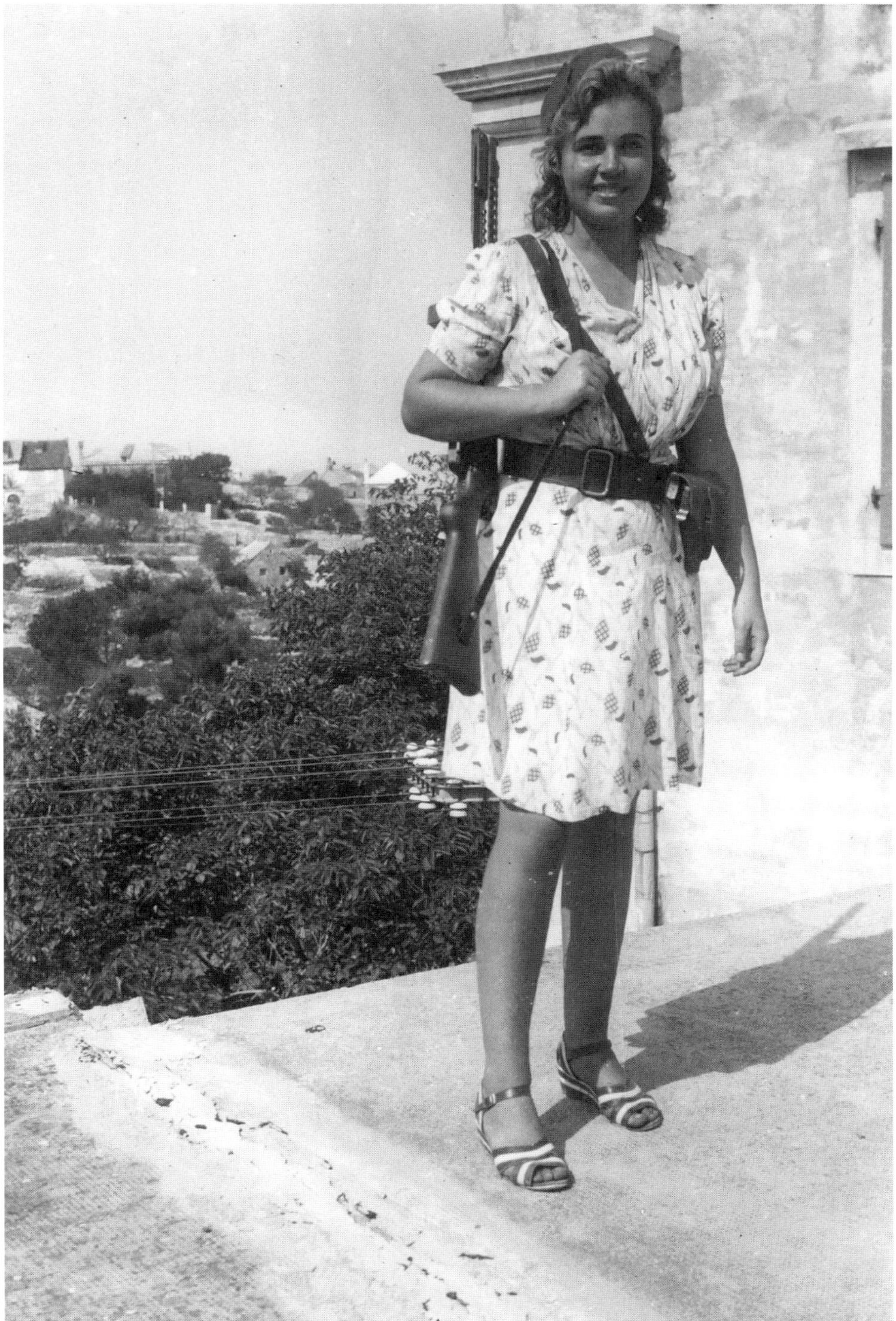

Partisan *in Supetar, 1943. Photographer unknown. Purchased from Mikelija Ćoćij*

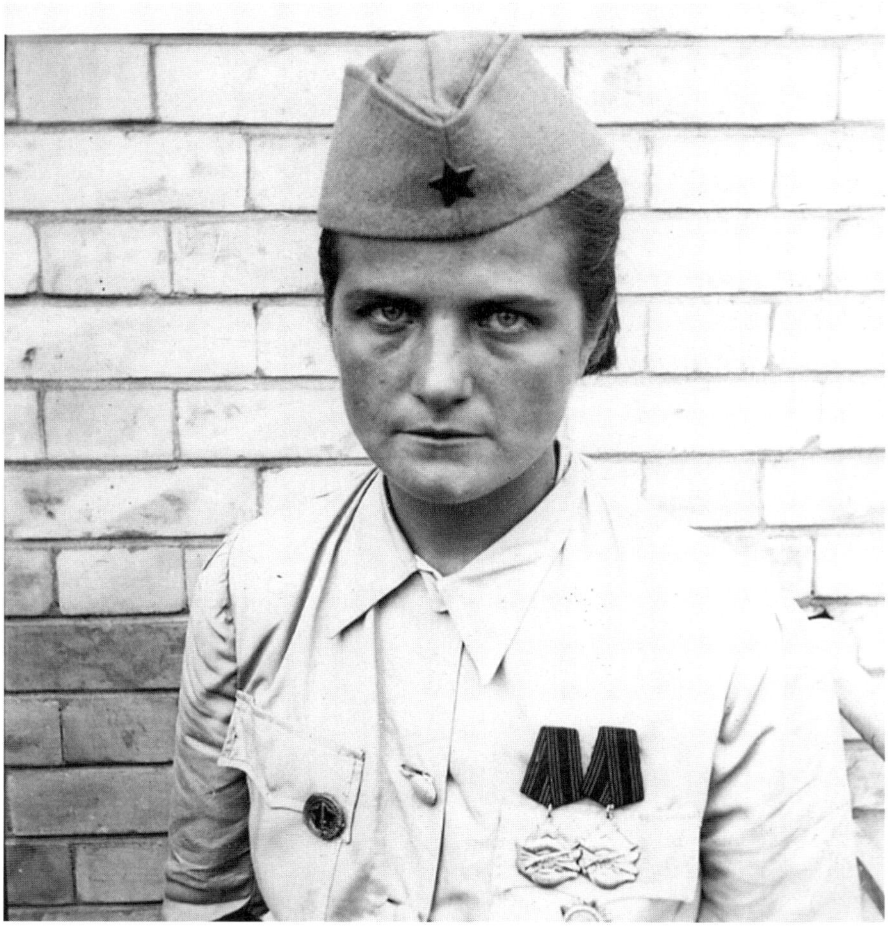

Dragica Mađarec, Partisan from 1941, machine gunner famed for walking barefoot through the snow to fulfil her duties. Photo: Vilko Hajduković. Zagreb City Museum.

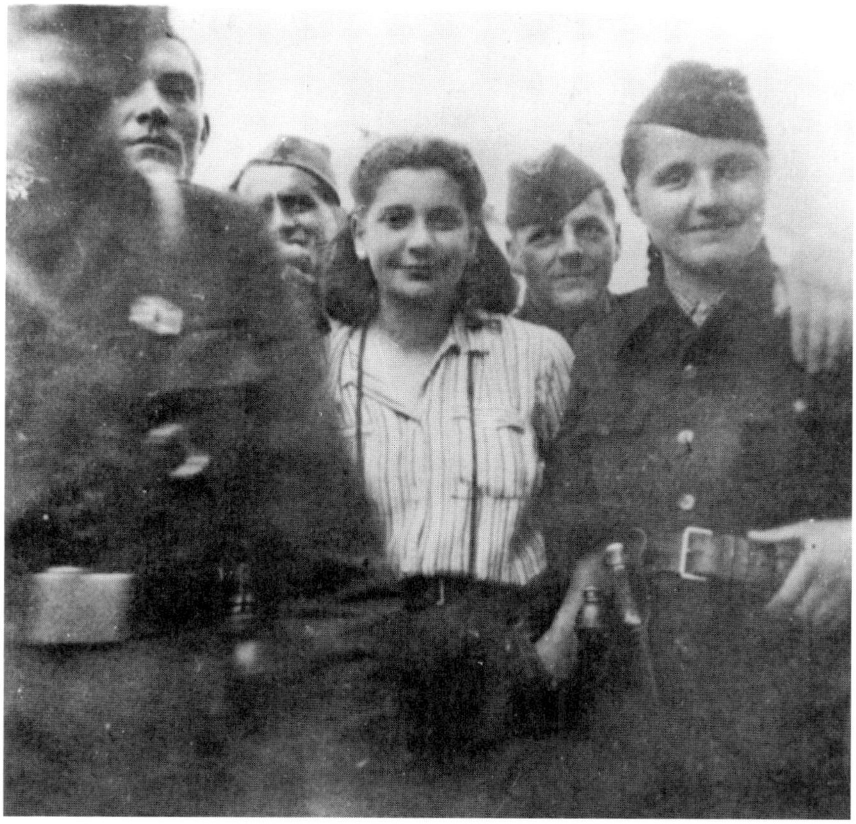

Fighters of the First Krajina Brigade at Bugojno, Bosnia and Herzegovina, 1943.
Photographer unknown. History Museum of Bosnia and Herzegovina, FNOB 18811.

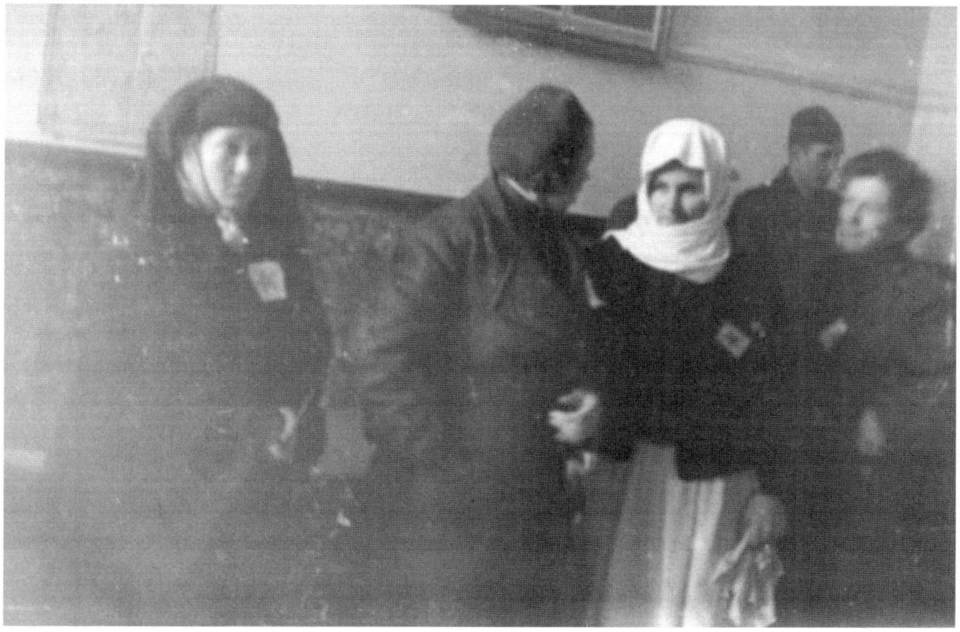

Uncaptioned. Photo: Drago Mažar. Archives of the Republic of Srpska, Banja Luka.

In Combat

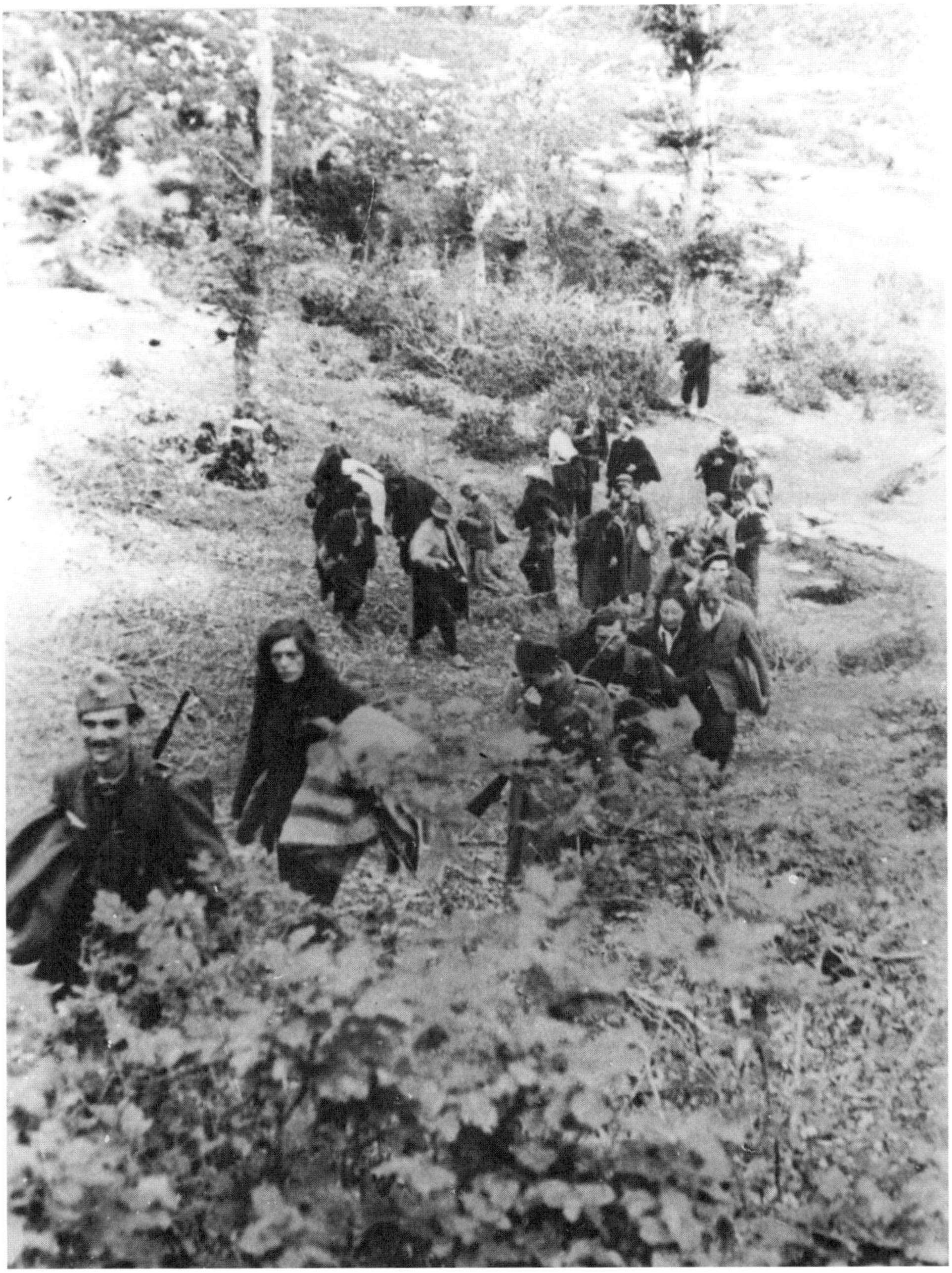

The Dinaric Partisan Detachment returning from a campaign to drive Chetniks out of Crni Lug, Livanjsko polje, Bosnia and Herzegovina, May 1942. Photographer unknown. History Museum of Bosnia and Herzegovina, FNOB 17797.

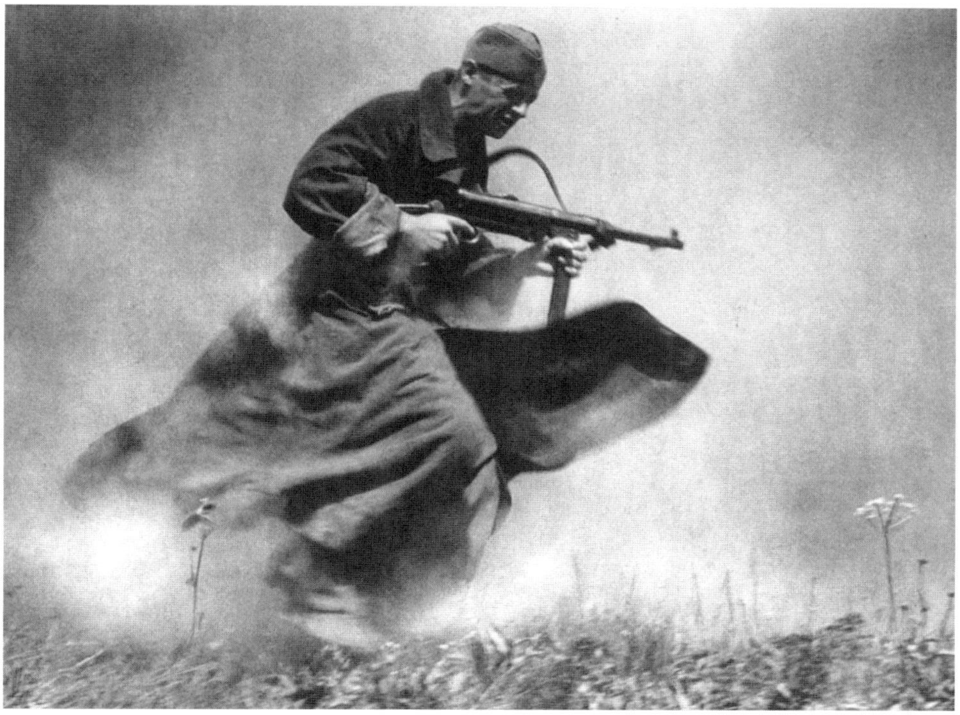

Charging, 1945. Photo: Marjan Pfeifer. Ljubljana Museum of Modern Art, MG 750 F.

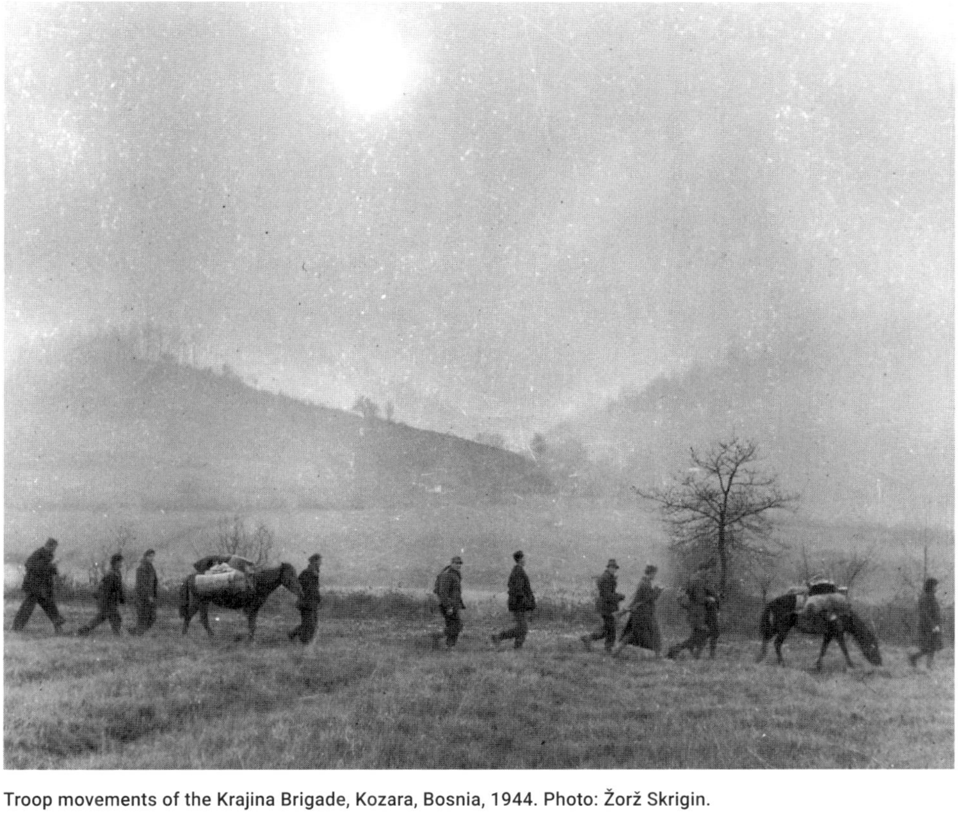

Troop movements of the Krajina Brigade, Kozara, Bosnia, 1944. Photo: Žorž Skrigin.

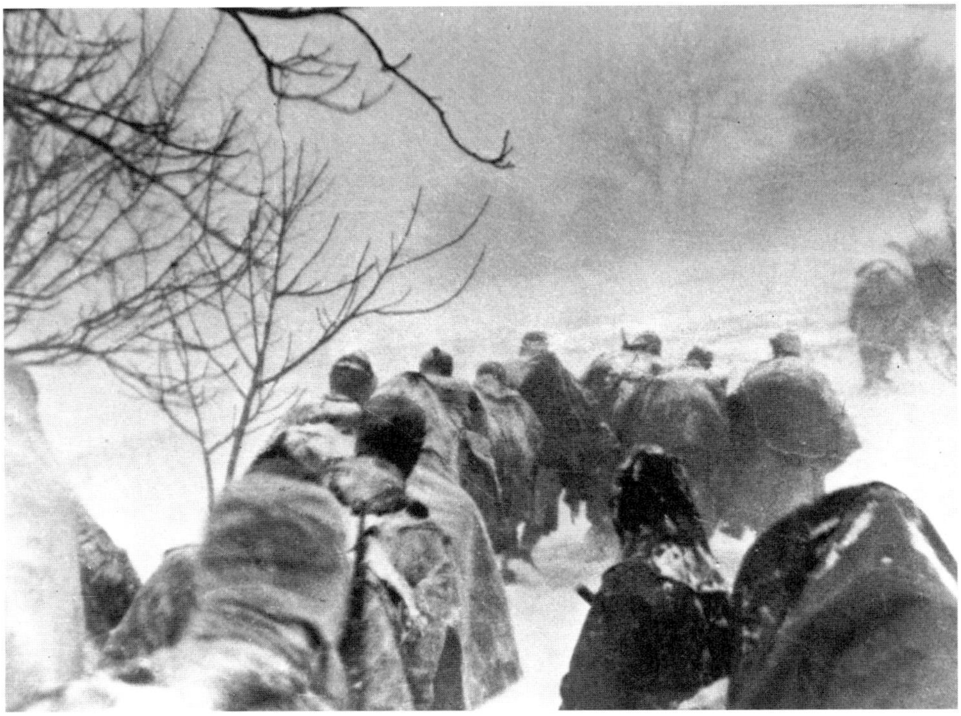

March of the Fourteenth Division in winter. Photo: Jože Petek.
National Museum of Contemporary History of Slovenia, 1325.

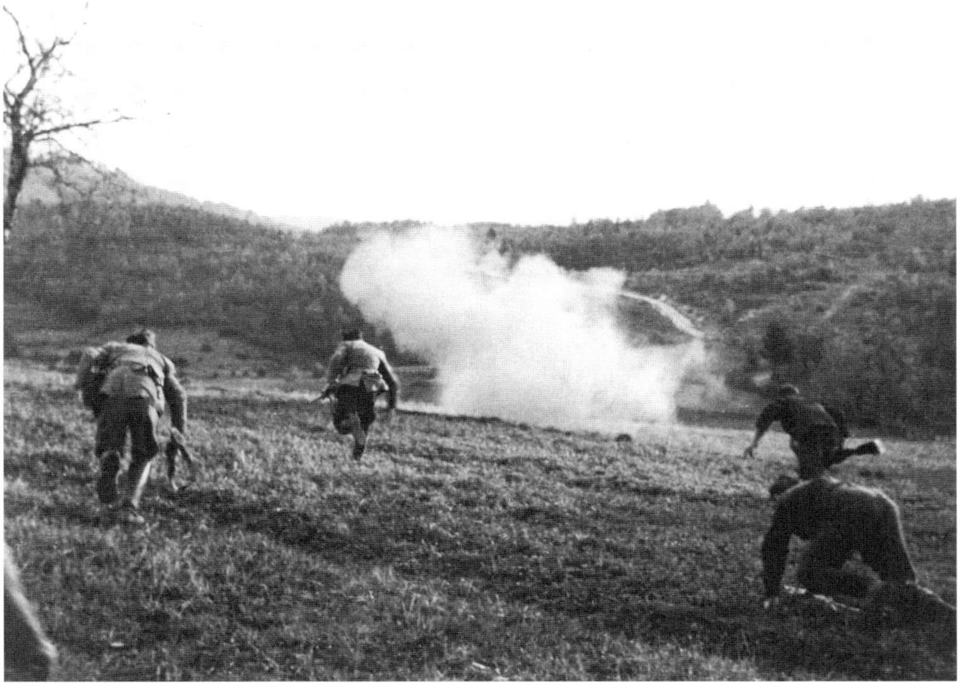

Fighters of the Twelfth Slovenian Brigade in combat, Sveti Križ, 5 August 1944
(after which the Slovene Home Guard were forced into retreat). Photographer unknown.
Museum of Yugoslavia III-1620.

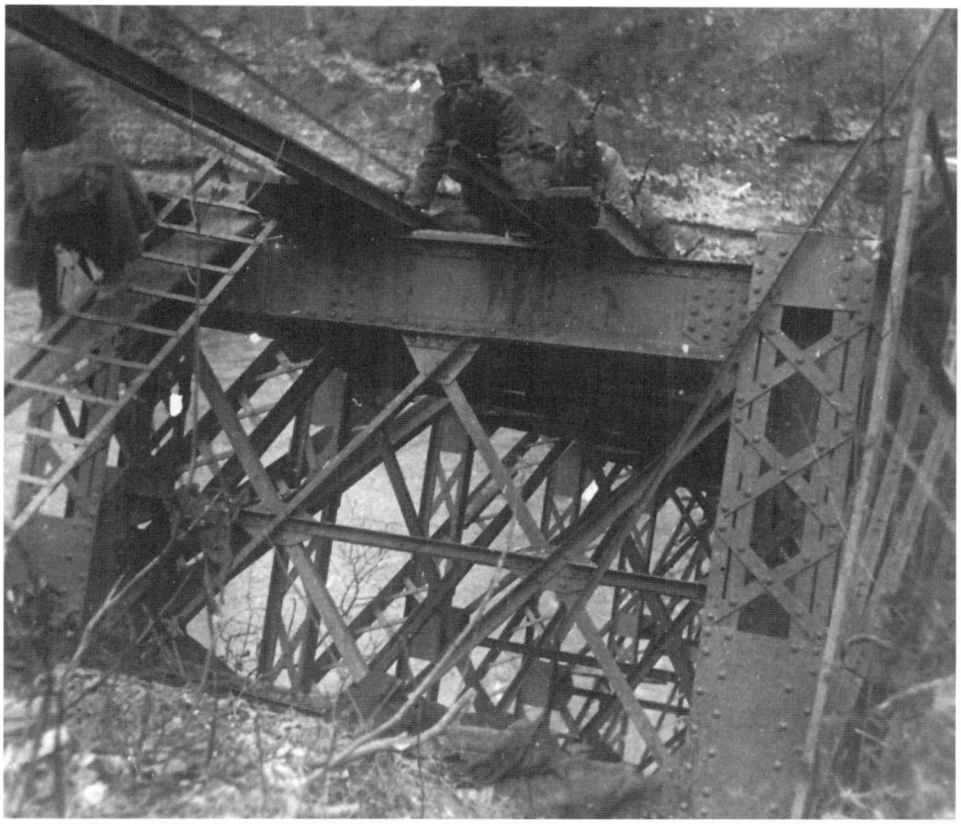

Mijalko Todorović, political commissar of the First Proletarian Brigade, crossing a destroyed bridge at Neretva near Jablanica during the Fourth Offensive, March 1943. Photographer unknown. Military Museum Belgrade, 4428.

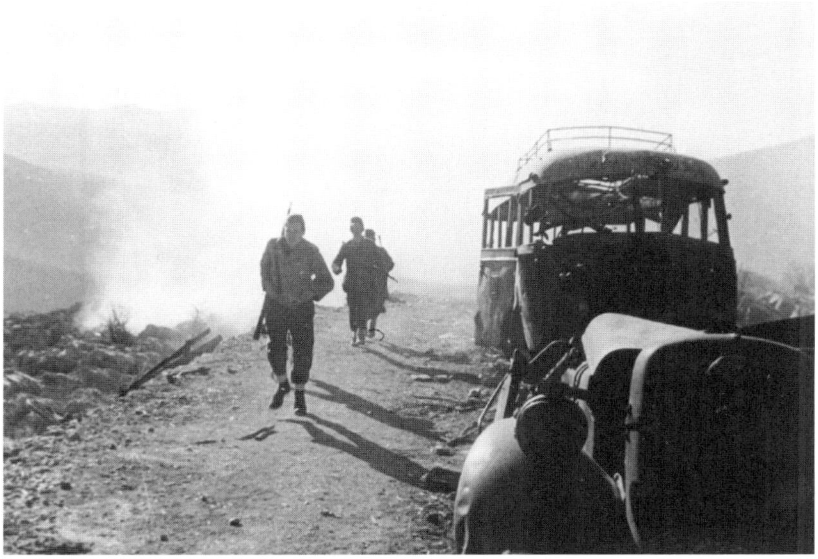

On the road between Podgorica and Kolašin, Montenegro, burnt-out vehicles that had been carrying supplies and food, evidence of the Germans' scorched-earth policy in the face of the advancing Third Division, 1944. Photographer unknown. Military Museum Belgrade, 12337.

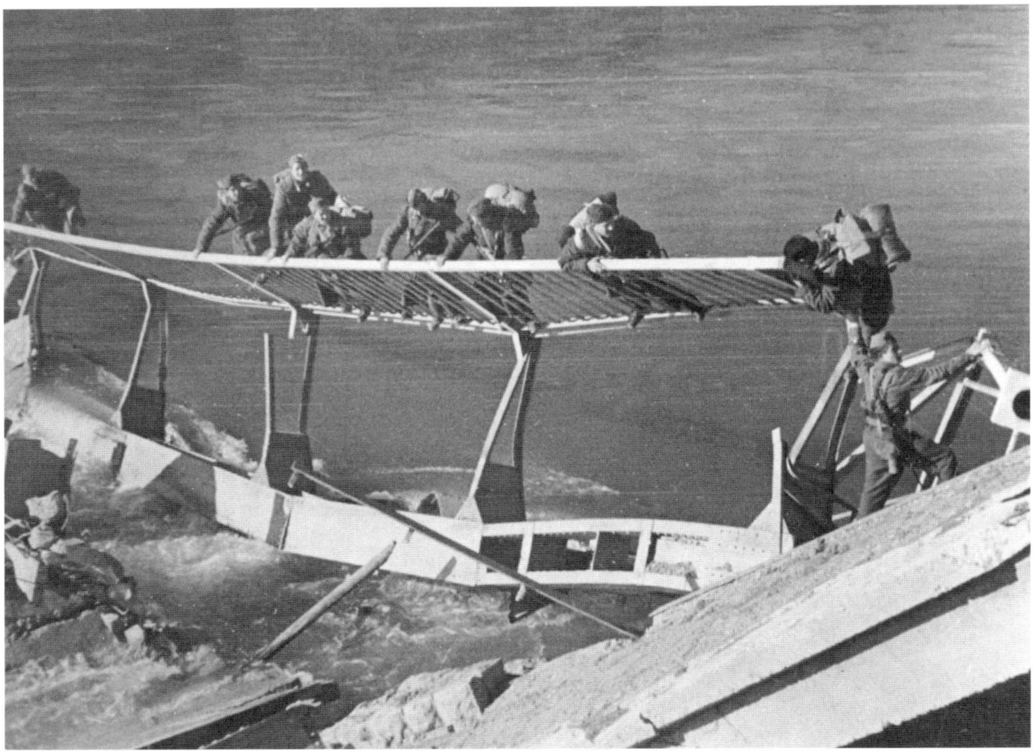

The Second Division crossing the river Morača at Podgorica, Montenegro, 1944.
Photographer unknown. Military Museum Belgrade, 12350.

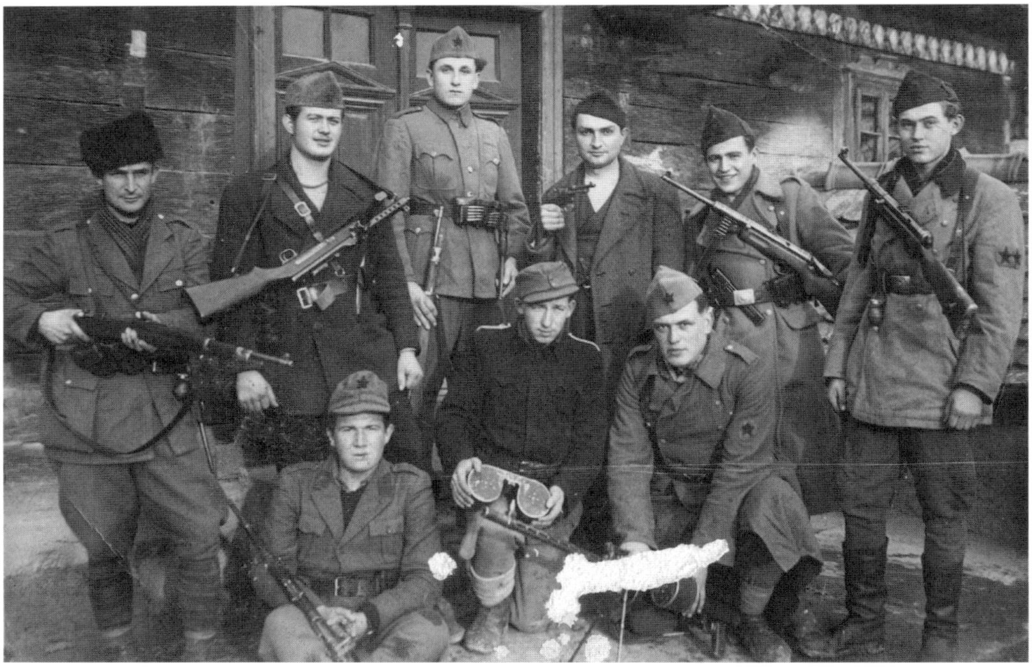

This photograph is especially interesting because of the different uniforms shown in it. The picture was most likely shot in the autumn of 1942 in west Slavonia. One of the Partisans standing up is clearly wearing a uniform of the Slovene Home Guard, identified by its lighter grey-and-olive colour; the Partisan sitting with legs crossed is wearing a German uniform, while the Partisan kneeling in the middle is wearing a fire-fighter's uniform.
Photographer unknown. From the private archive of Robert Čopec.

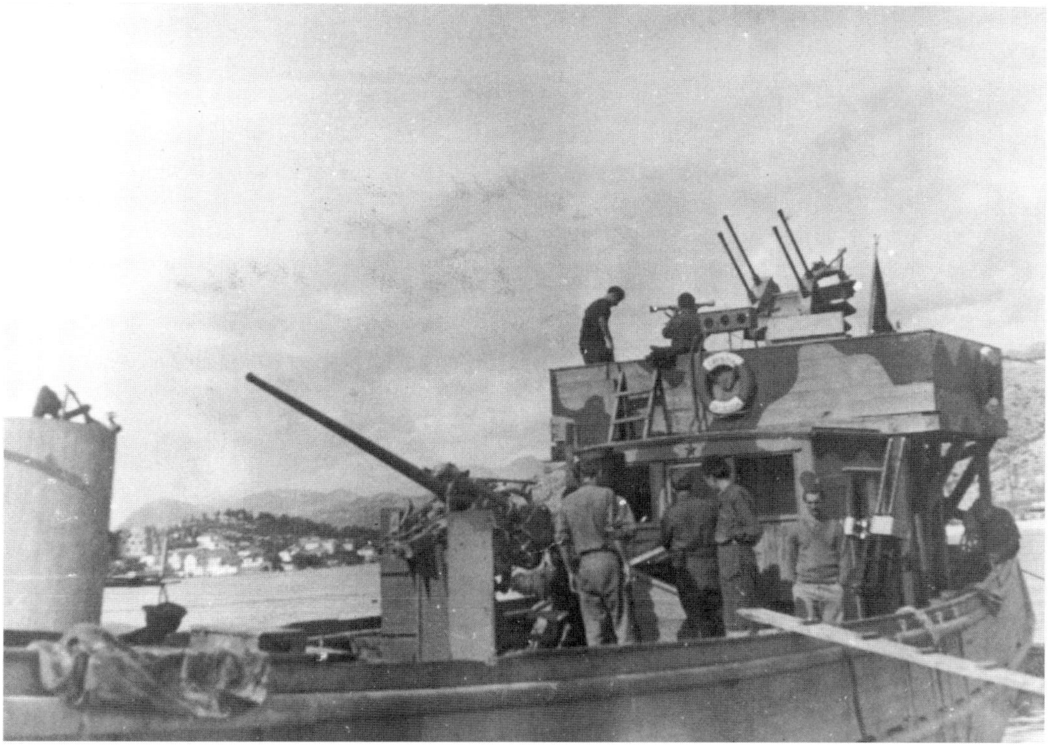

A boat in the Dubrovnik quay, Croatia, October 1944. Photographer unknown.
History Museum of Bosnia and Herzegovina, FNOB 19473.

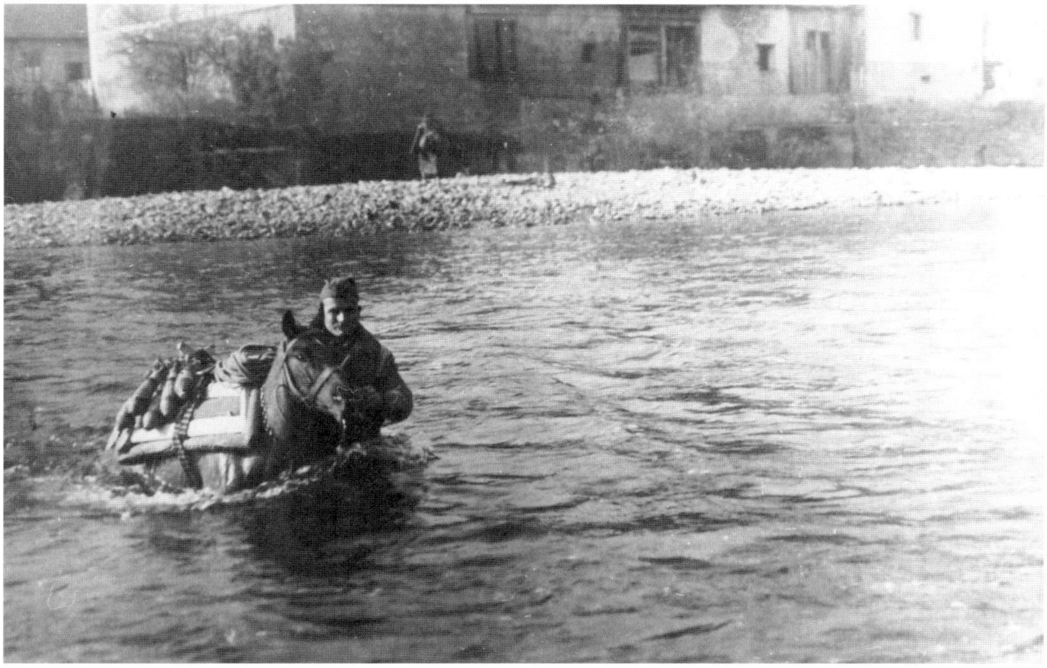

Photograph from the Battle of Istria – a Partisan with a horse in water. Photographer unknown.

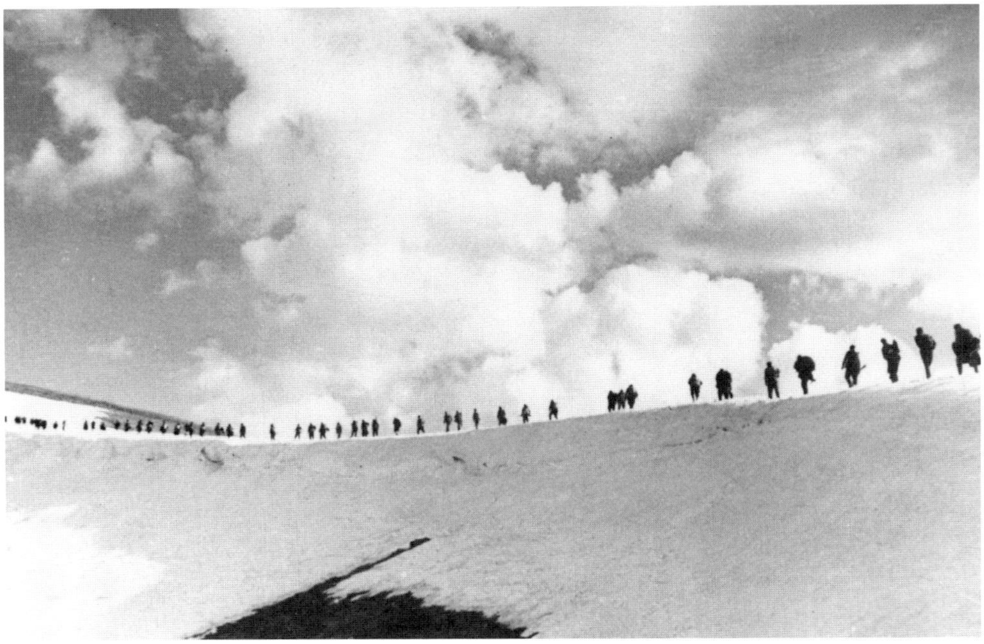

Column of fighters from the Sixth Lika Division walking through the snow at Kupres, Bosnia and Herzegovina, 1943. Photographer unknown. Central Committee of League of Communists of Yugoslavia Collection (CK SKJ), 3898.

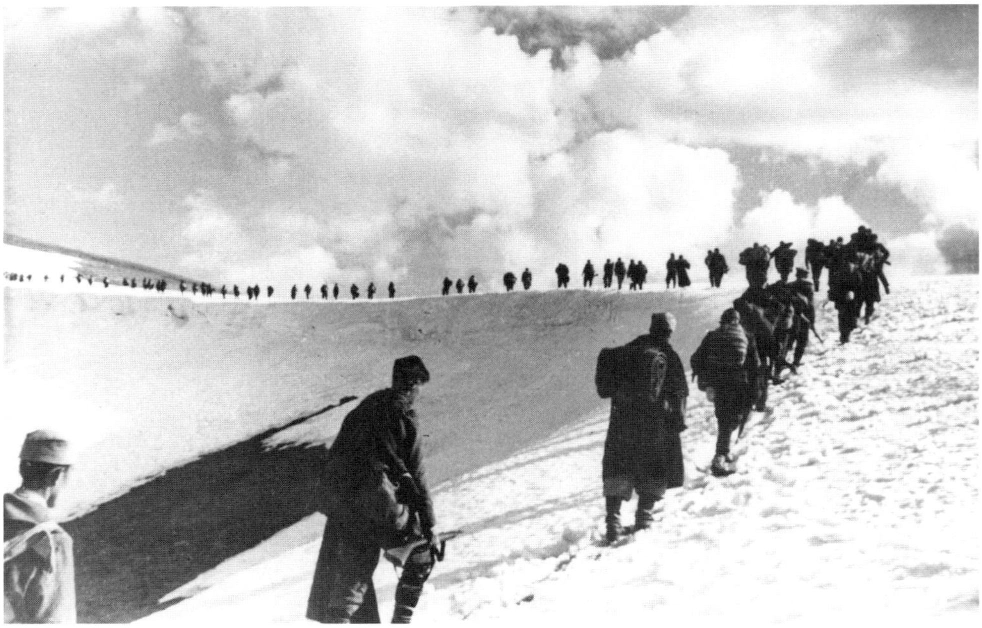

Column of fighters from the Sixth Lika Division walking through the snow at Kupres, Bosnia and Herzegovina, 1943. Photographer unknown. Central Committee of League of Communists of Yugoslavia Collection (CK SKJ), 3899.

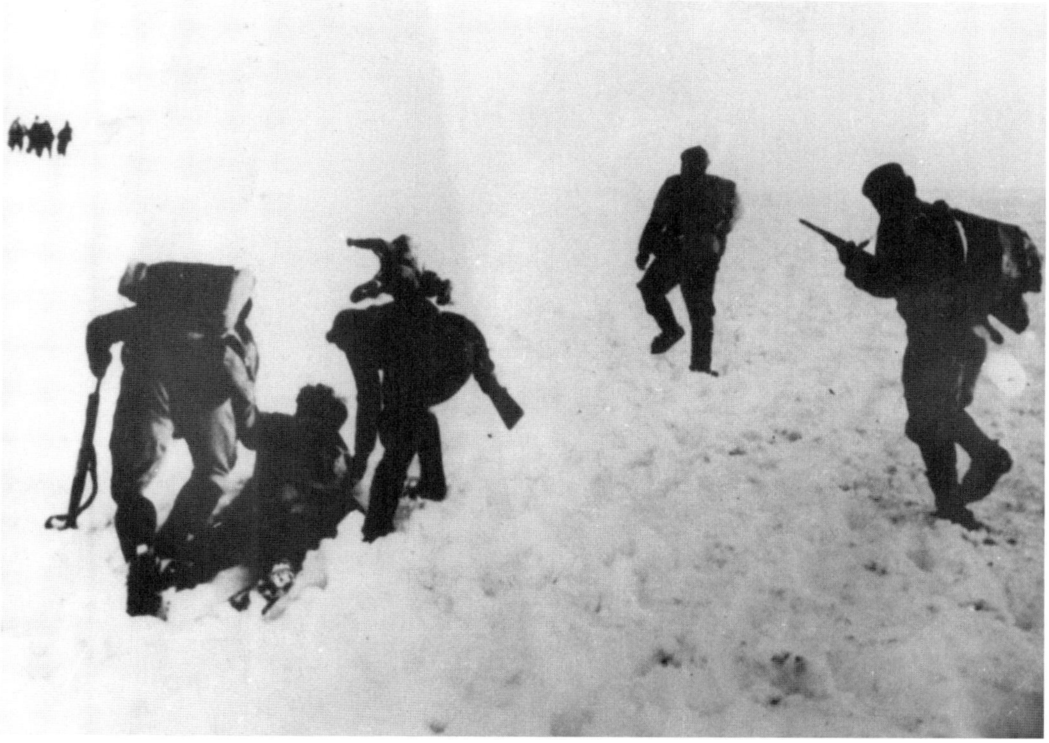

The February march of 1944 – an offensive launched by Macedonian Partisans in east, central, and west Macedonia, after which they were able to liberate part of Macedonia and emerged as an important grouping and force on the Yugoslav front. Photographer unknown.

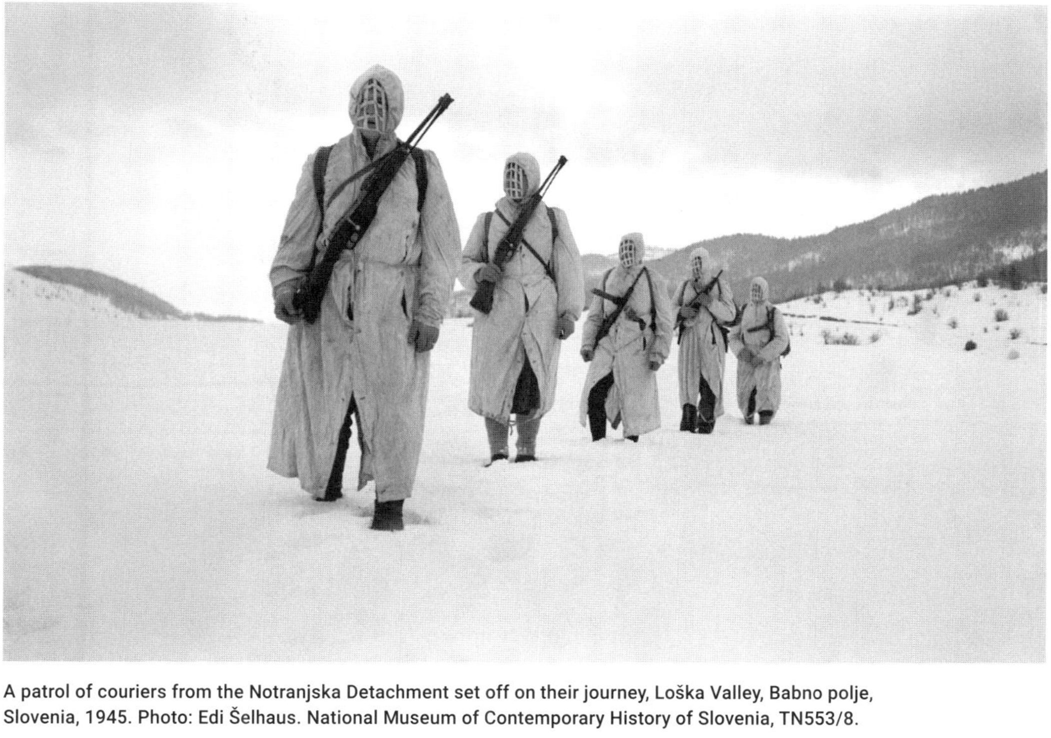

A patrol of couriers from the Notranjska Detachment set off on their journey, Loška Valley, Babno polje, Slovenia, 1945. Photo: Edi Šelhaus. National Museum of Contemporary History of Slovenia, TN553/8.

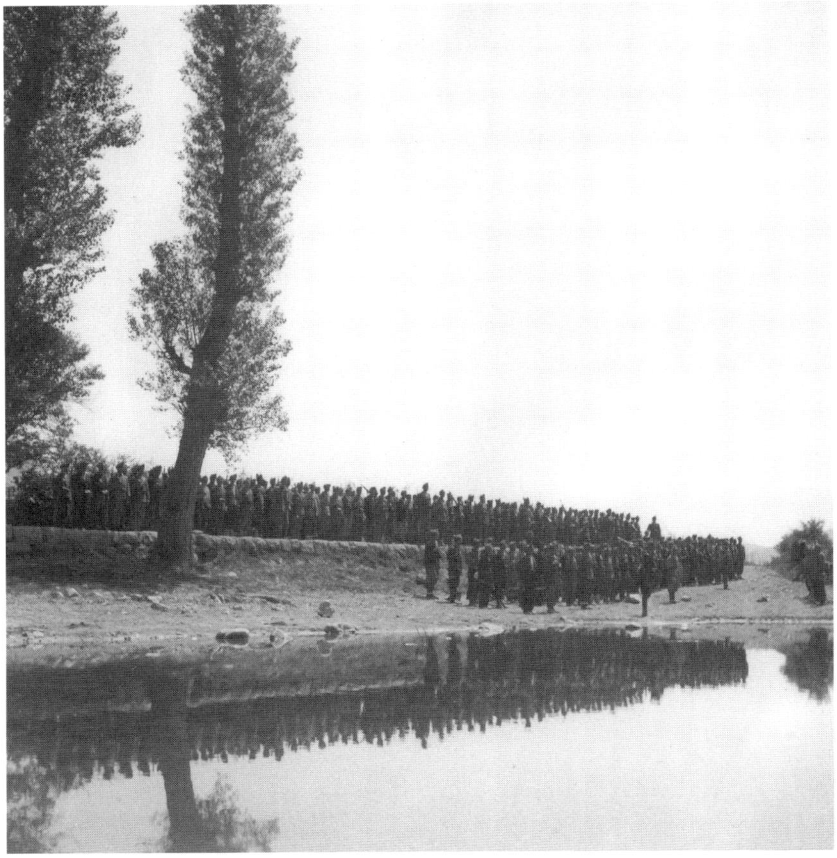

Parade of the Croatian Proletarian Battalion at Brlog, near Otačac, Croatia, immediately after their founding in 1942. Photo: Žorž Skrigin.

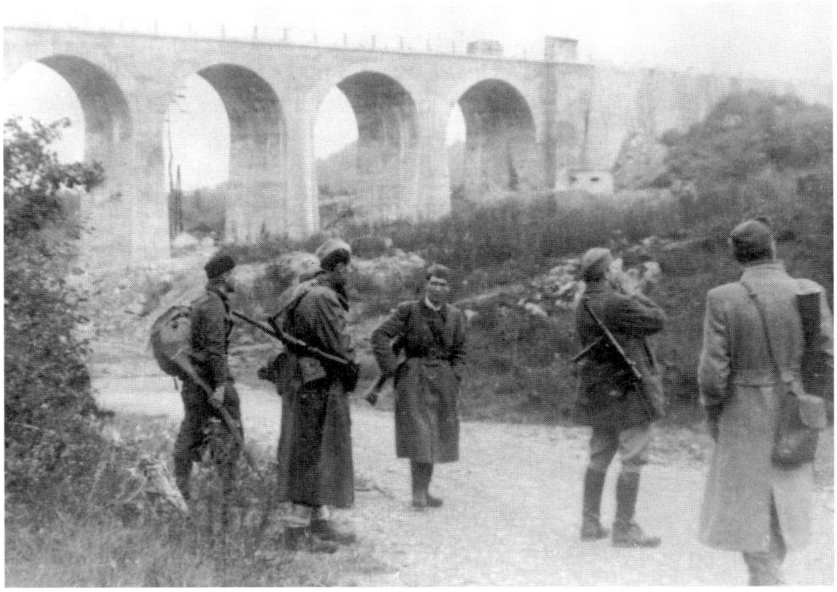

Members of the staff of the First Slovenian Brigade, among them Tone Tomšič, with Stampetta Bridge in the background before it was destroyed in a sabotage attack to disrupt German supply lines, 14 October 1943. Photo: Jože Petek. National Museum of Contemporary History of Slovenia, 2317.

Photographs of Solidarity and Partisan Hospitals

Solidarity is a concept with a special place in Partisan photography. And solidarity was most often conveyed in sequences of photographs depicting Partisan hospitals. In helping and caring for the injured, the humanism of the revolution came to the fore. The Partisans' Medical Service was an impressive feat of organisation, tasked with building hospitals, running pharmaceutical and dental services, medical courses and even veterinary services. From the beginning of the armed uprising in 1941, the Medical Service operated within the various Partisan detachments, with the first fixed-site hospitals established on liberated territory. One of the first hospitals was set up in Užice in 1941, as was the hospital at Petrova Gora – the first Partisan hospital in the territory of Croatia and one that was thereafter successfully maintained all the way through the war. In Slovenia, the best-known hospital was at Kočevski Rog. In 1942, all Partisan military field hospitals were linked together in a medical network, and in September 1942 Statute of the Medical Service of the People's Liberation Army and the Partisan Detachments of Yugoslavia was passed. This order provided for the founding of mobile hospitals in every division. One of the biggest mobile hospitals was the Supreme Command's Central Hospital. The first surgical team went into service in September 1942. Across Yugoslavia, 3,081 doctors worked for the Medical Service, 319 of whom women. Some 213 doctors lost their lives while in service to the Partisans.[1] The Slovenian doctor Janez Milčinski took a series of exceptionally important photographs of Partisan hospitals.

1 Unknown author, 'Briga za ranjenike i partizanske bolnice', URL: http://izlozba.sabh.hr/briga-za-ranjenike-i-partizanske-bolnice/ (accessed 11 February 2017).

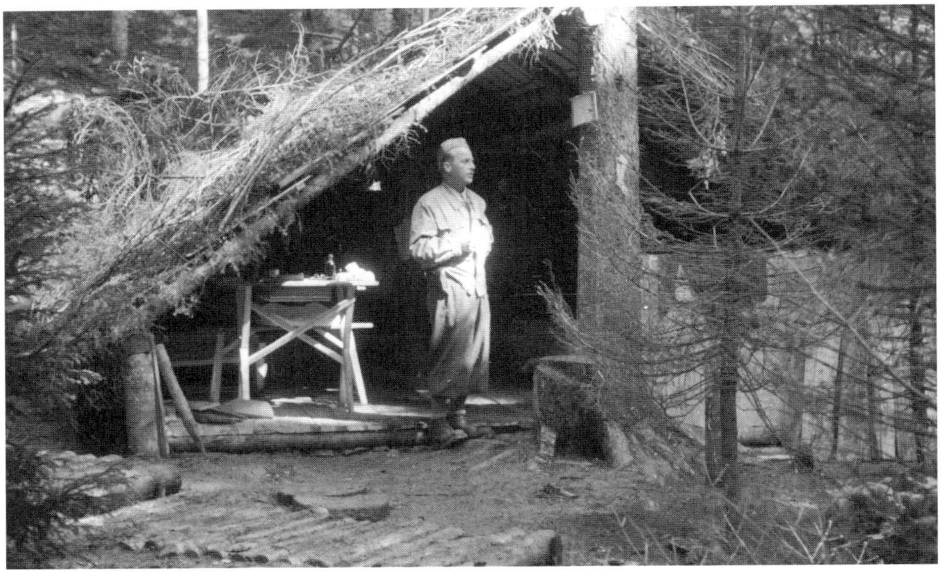

Dr Bogdan Brecelj in the makeshift Partisan field hospital Drveni kamen, Kočevski Rog, September 1943. Photographer unknown. National Museum of Contemporary History of Slovenia, TN33/27.

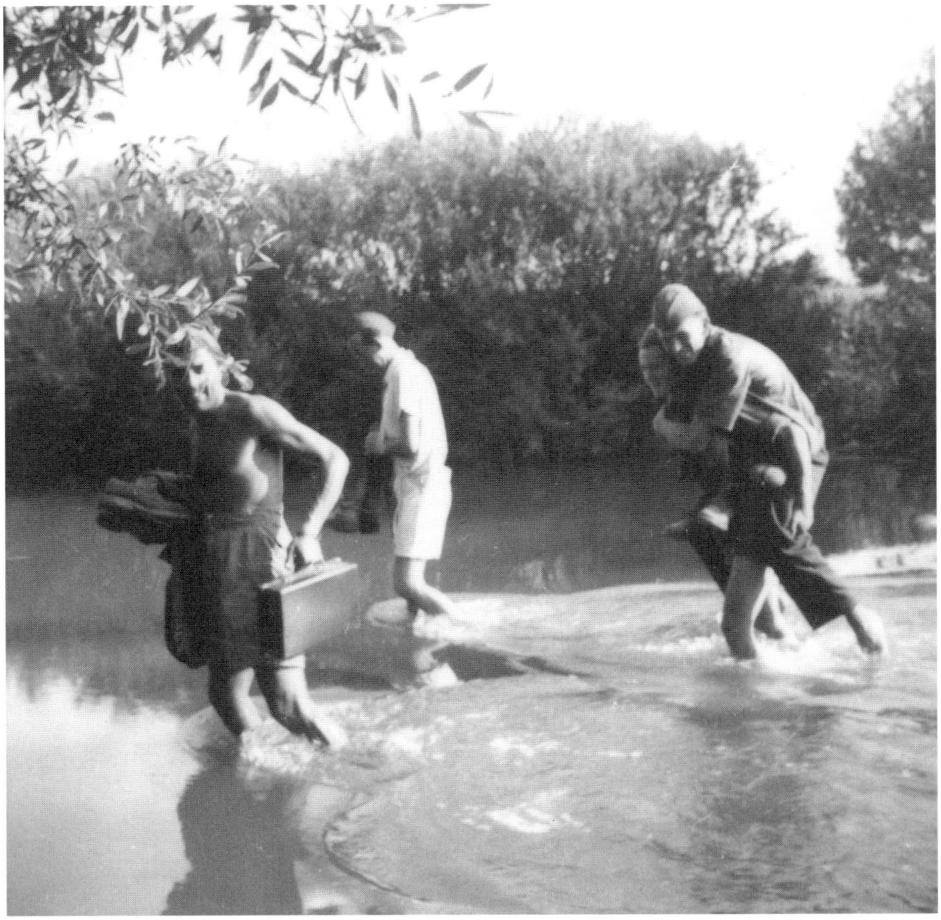

Crossing the river in the final push for victory, May 1945. Photographer unknown. Croatian History Museum, HPM-MRNH-A-11700 7.

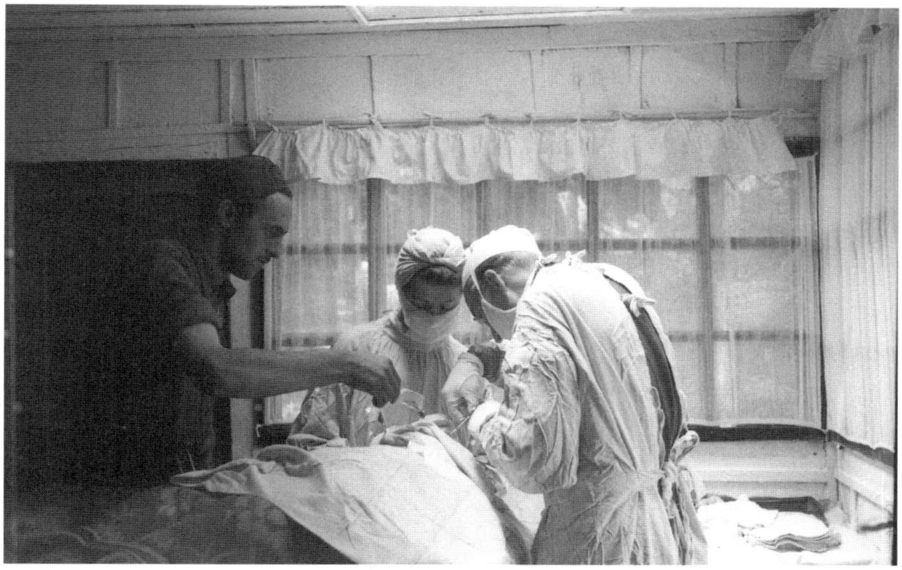

Aseptic surgical procedure at the Zgornji Hrastnik hospital, with Polde Košorok assisting on left, Marija Jeras centre and Dr Janez Milčinski operating on the right, 1944/45, Slovenia. Photographer unknown. National Museum of Contemporary History of Slovenia, 1232/8.

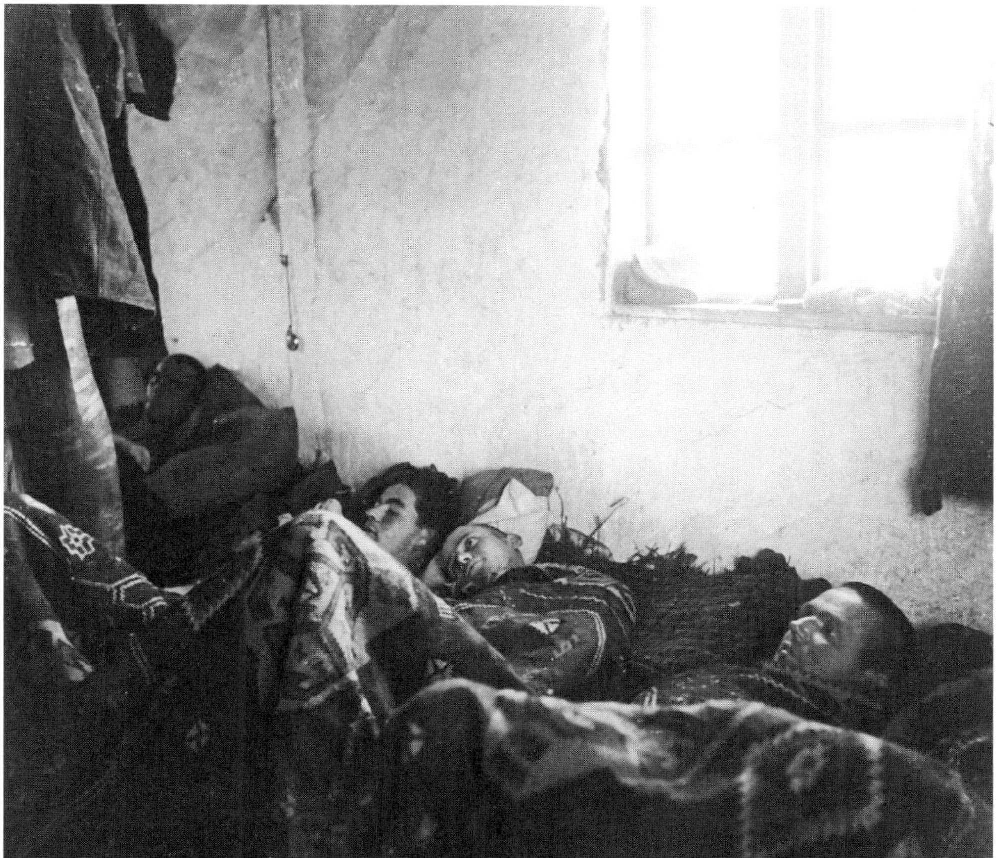

Partisan casualties in the hospital at Bosanski Petrovac, Bosnia and Herzegovina, 1942. Photo: Žorž Skrigin. Museum of Yugoslavia, III-3456.

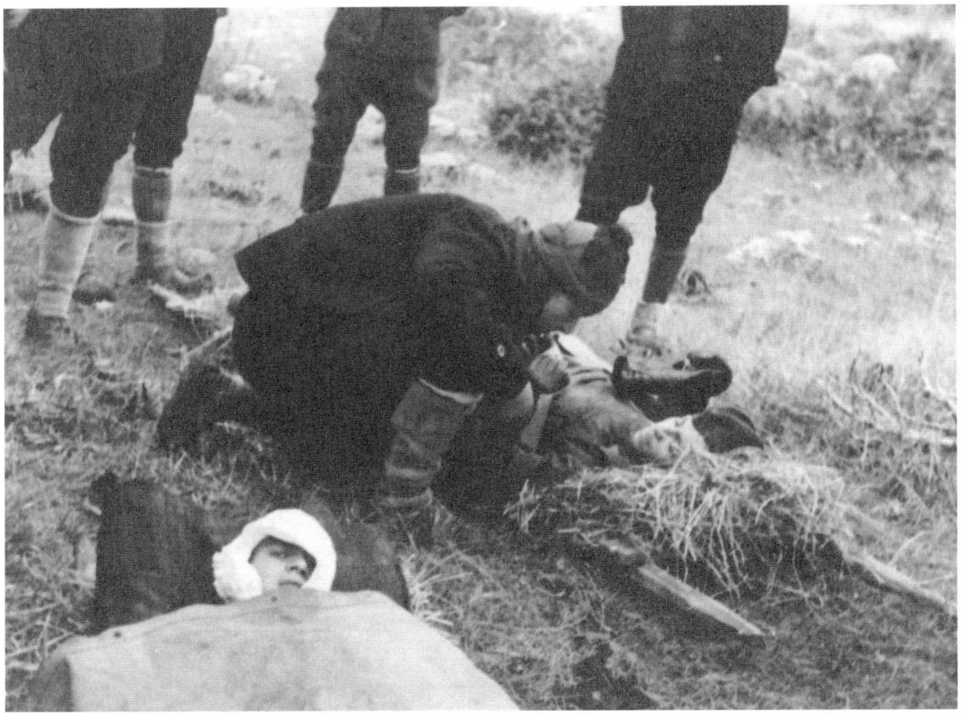

Uncaptioned. Photo: Drago Mažar. Archives of the Republic of Srpska, Banja Luka.

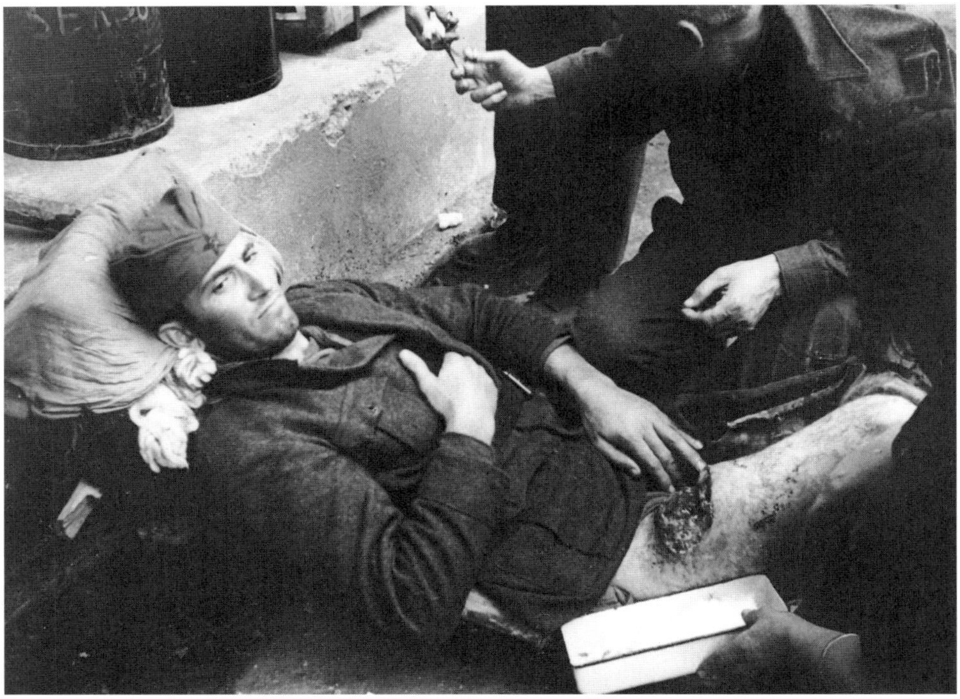

An Italian-made bomb was dropped on this fighter from the Sixth Montenegrin Brigade as it engaged in combat against Chetnik units. The incendiary exploded just above the photographed soldier's knee, creating a massive wound. Impressively, he kept his cool and helped dress the wound himself. Morača Monastery, mid-February 1944, Montenegro. Photographer unknown. Museum of Yugoslavia, III-4516.

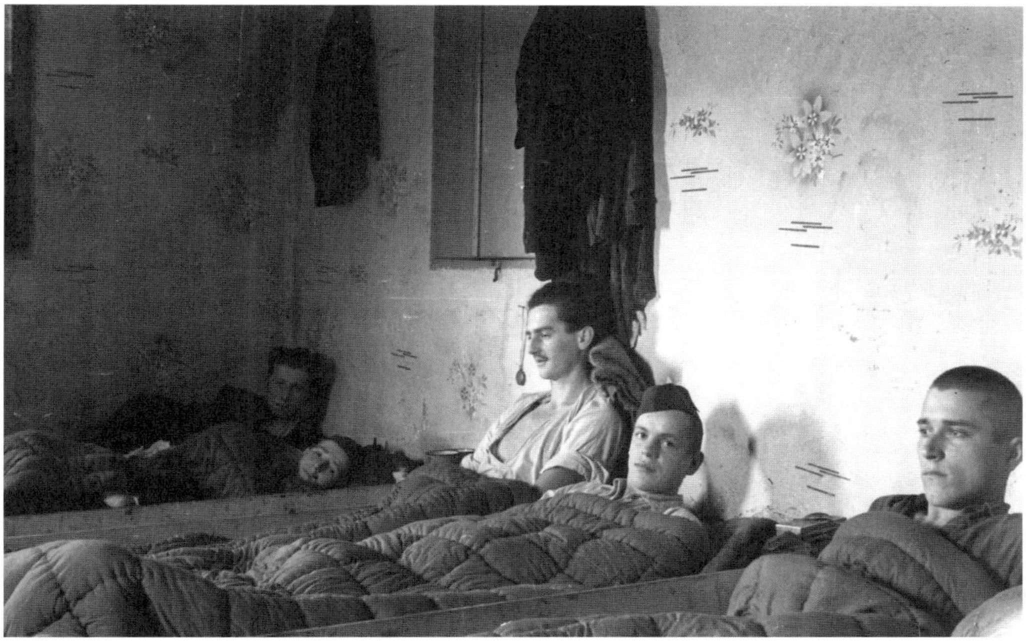

The Žumberak Slovenian Central Military Hospital and Medical School of the Seventh Corps (from November 1944 to January 1945), Slovenia. Photo: Dr Janez Milčinski. National Museum of Contemporary History of Slovenia, TN1223/34.

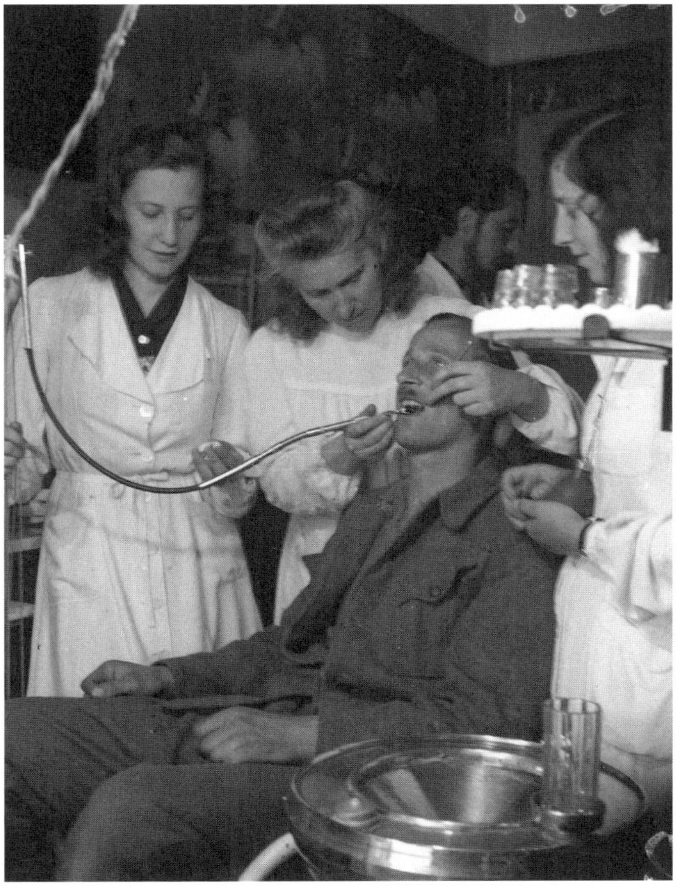

Partisan dental clinic, Črnomelj, Slovenia, 1944/45. Photographer unknown. National Museum of Contemporary History of Slovenia, TN193/2.

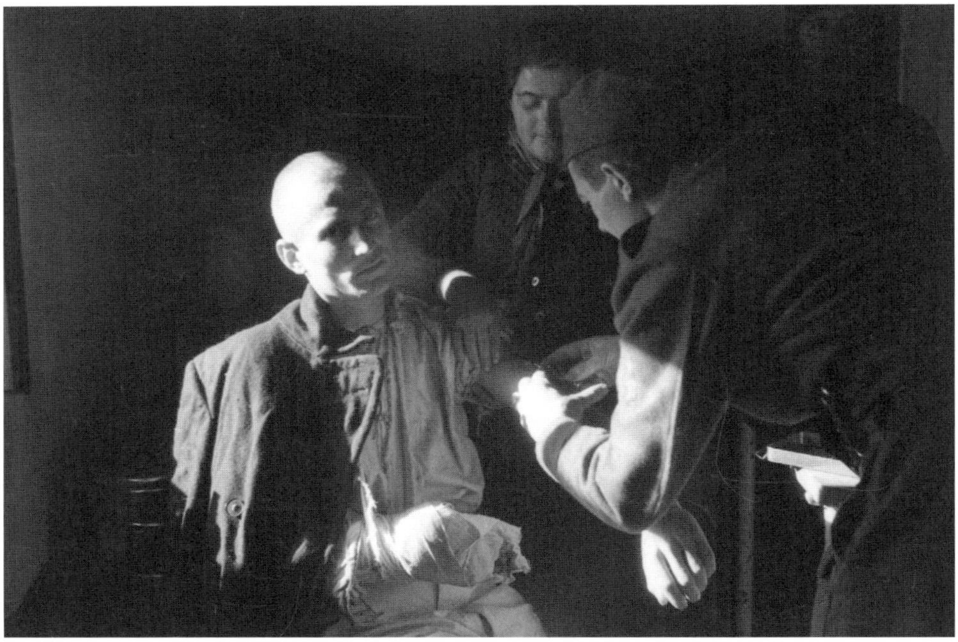

Bandaging the injured in the clinic at the Partisan hospital in Turjanski, Lika, Croatia, winter 1943.
Photographer unknown. Croatian History Museum, HPM-MRNH-A-2601-f83 035.

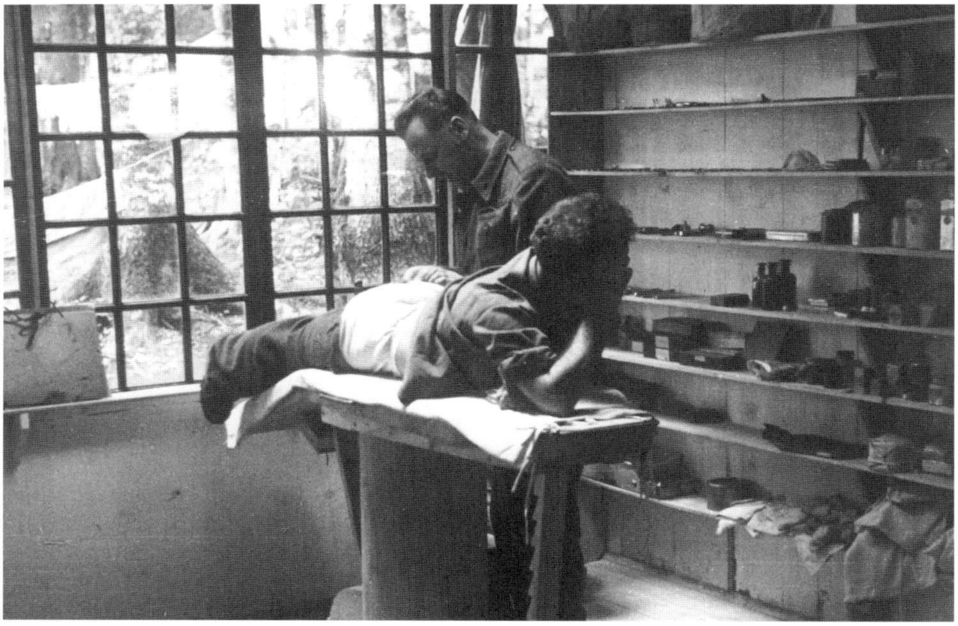

Light surgery performed by uniformed doctor, Slovenia. Photographer unknown.
National Museum of Contemporary History of Slovenia, accession no. unknown.

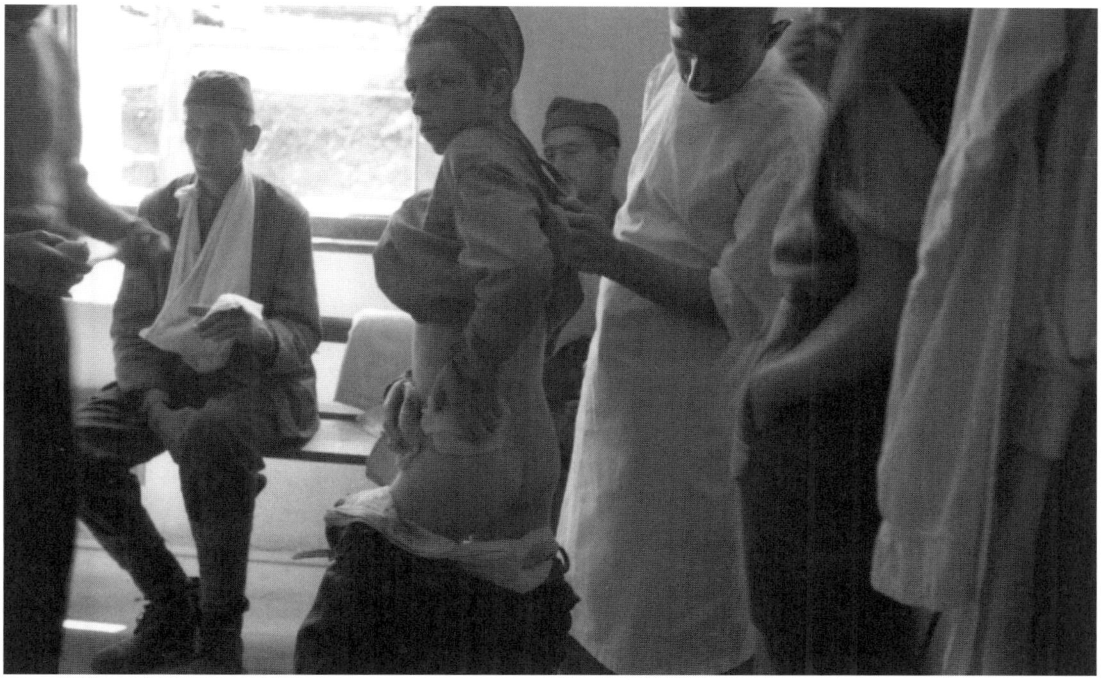

Clinic of the Thirteenth Primorje-Gorenje Division, Gorski kotar, Croatia, 1944.
Photographer unknown. Croatian History Museum, HPM-MRNH-A-2603-f18 035.

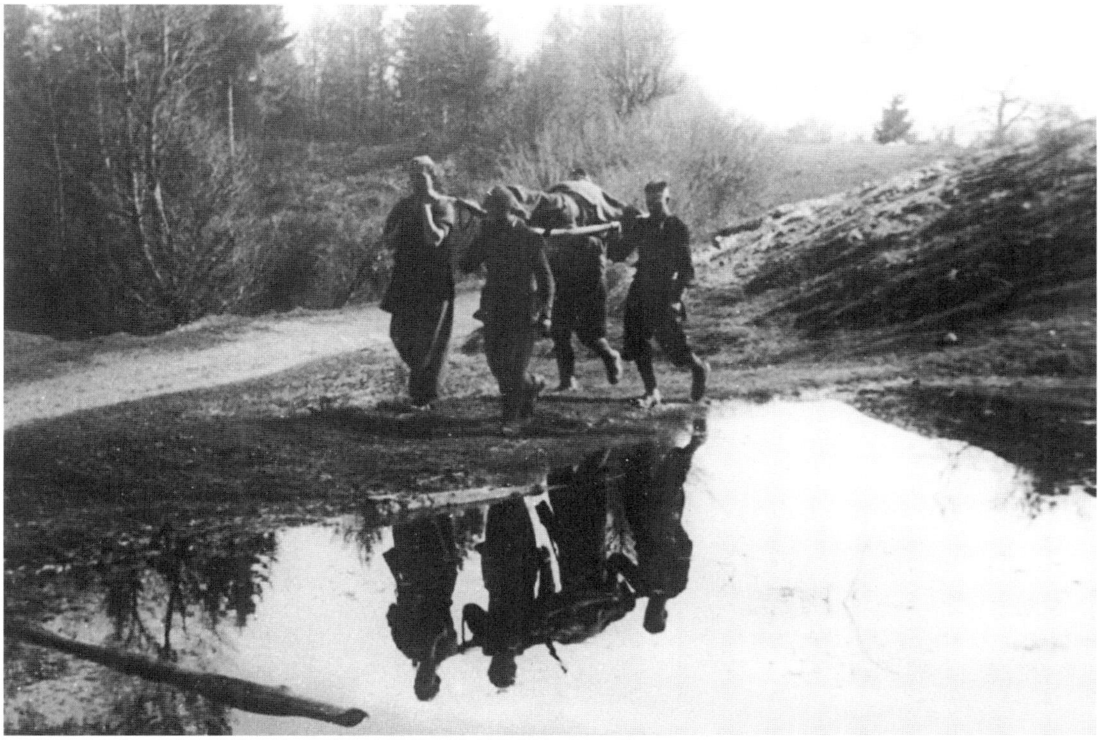

Transporting the injured to hospital, Hrastnik, Slovenia, 1944. Photographer unknown.
Museum of Yugoslavia, III-3370.

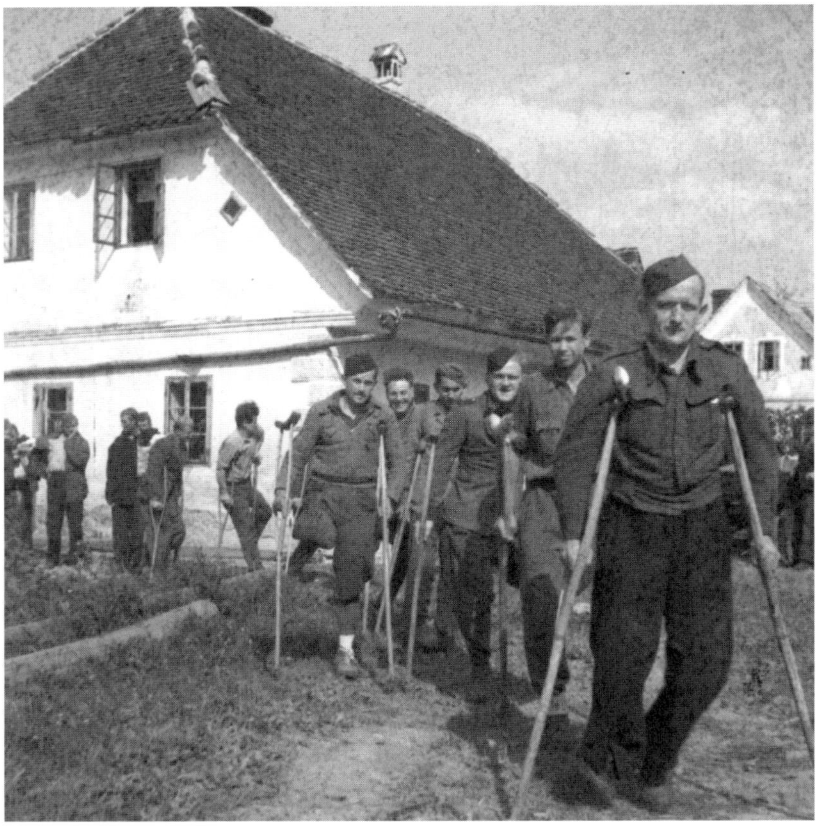

A group of severely injured Partisan soldiers and a unit in the Ninth Corps, Notranjska, Slovenia, September 1944. Photographer unknown. National Museum of Contemporary History of Slovenia, TN314/4.

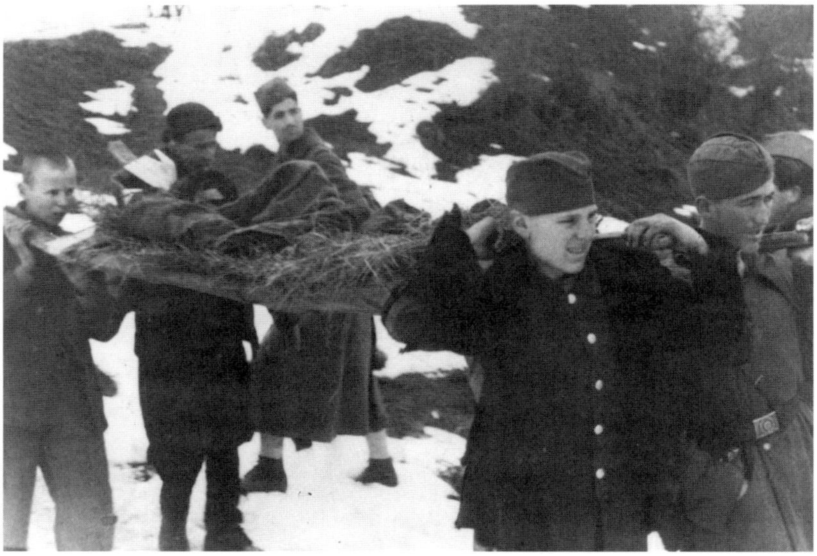

Injured members of the Seventeenth Majevica Brigade being transferred to the wound-dressing station at Redžići in Bosnia and Herzegovina, late January 1945. Military Museum Belgrade, 6767.

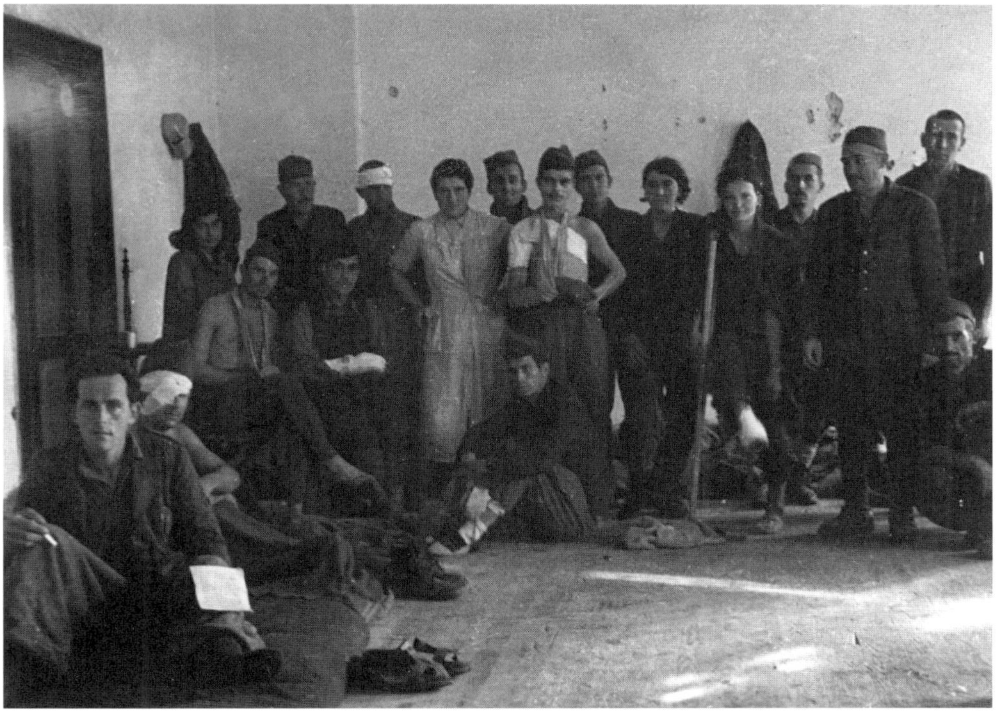

Staff and patients at the hospital in Livno, Bosnia and Herzegovina, 1943. Museum of Yugoslavia, III-1793.

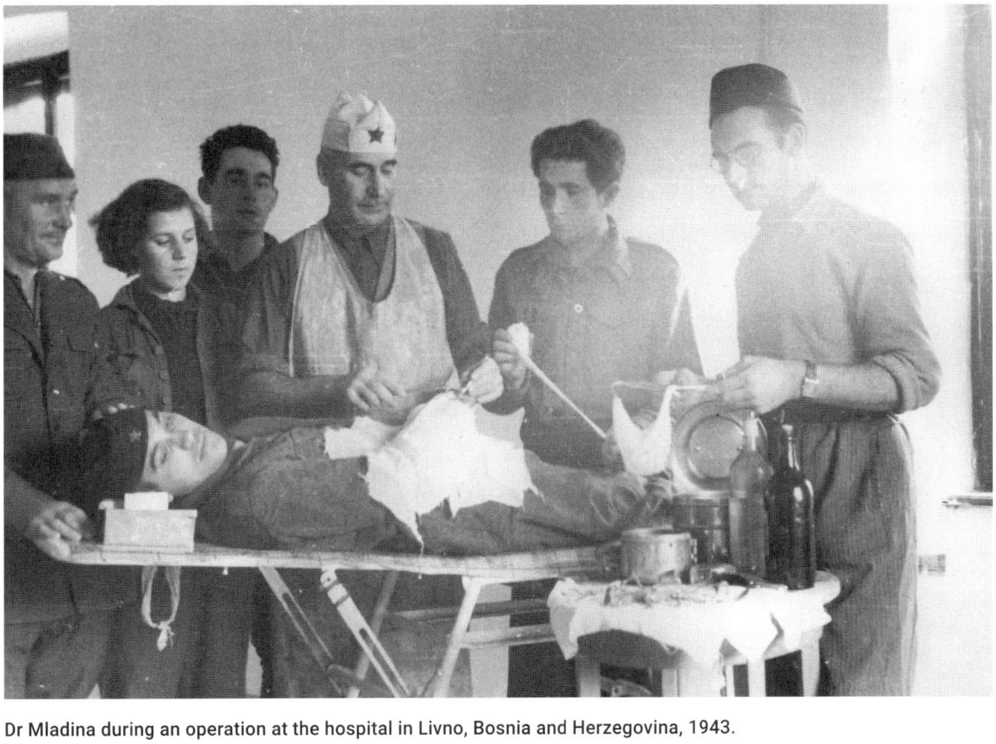

Dr Mladina during an operation at the hospital in Livno, Bosnia and Herzegovina, 1943. Photographer unknown.

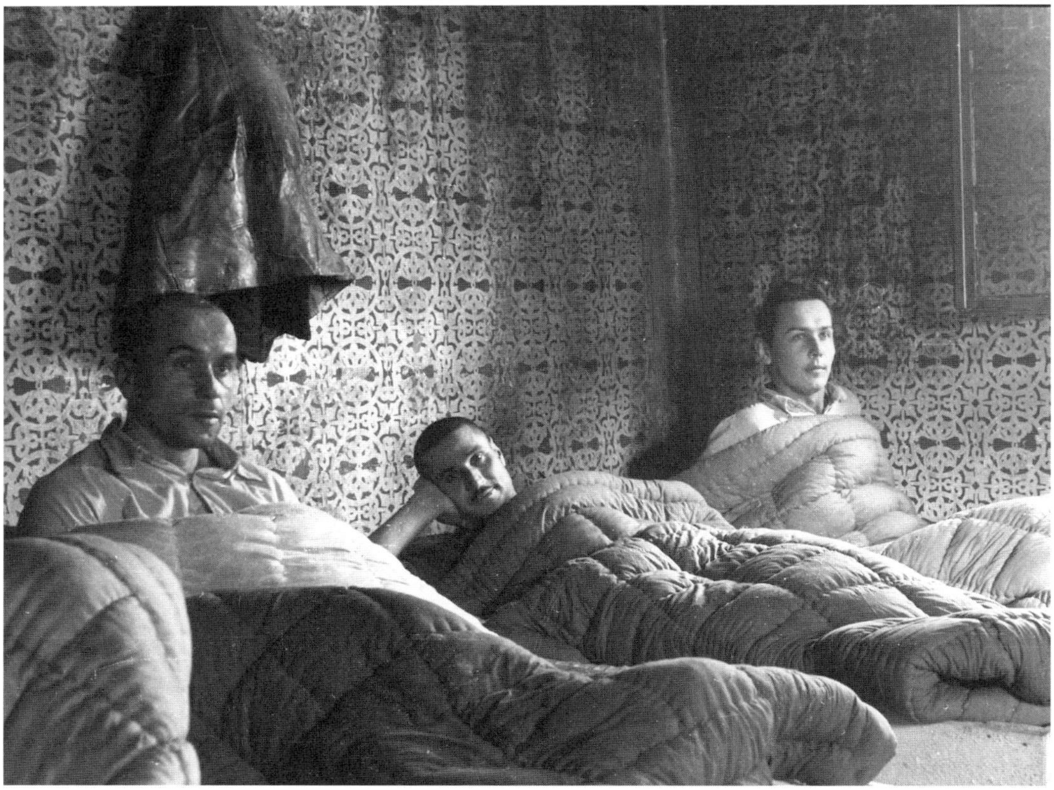

Scene from the hospital in Gorjanci, Slovenia. Photo: Dr Janez Milčinski.
National Museum of Contemporary History of Slovenia, TN1223/979.

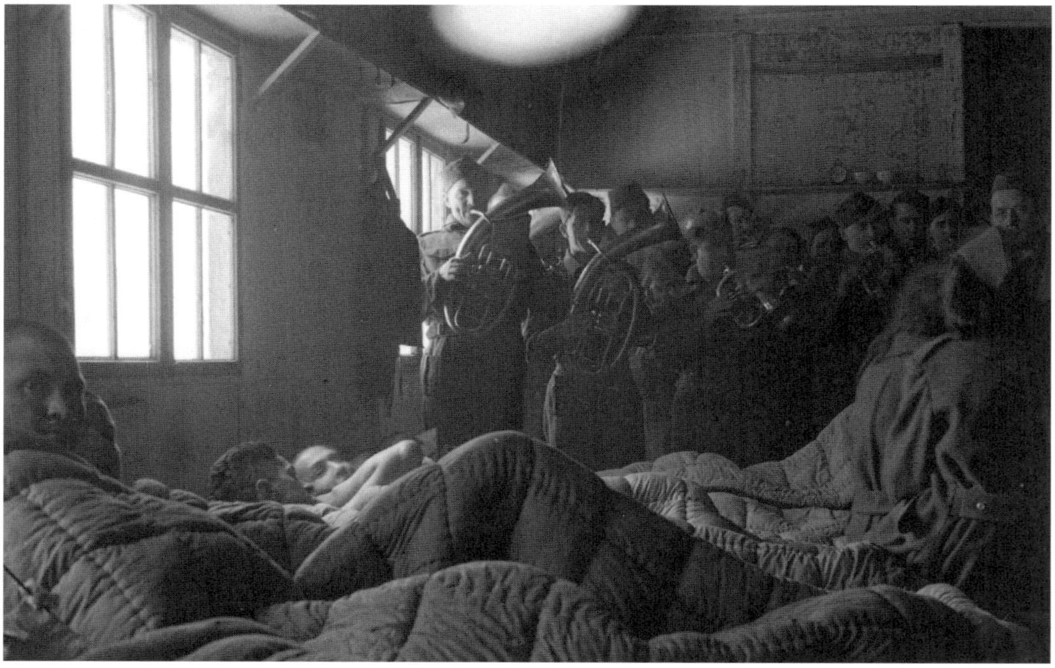

Music to lift the patients' spirits, hospital in Gorjanci. Photo: Dr Janez Milčinski.
National Museum of Contemporary History of Slovenia, TN1223/981.

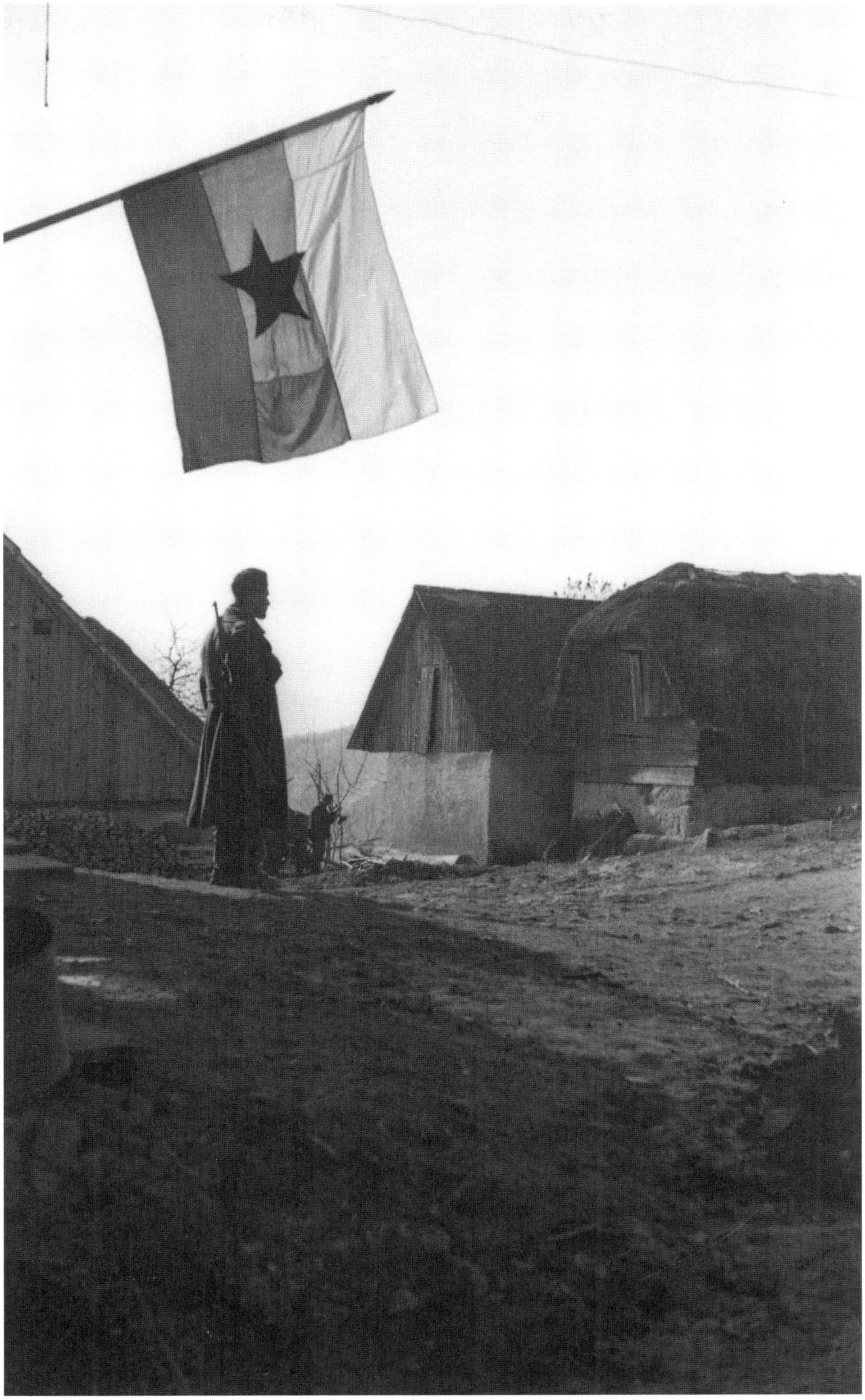

Scene from the hospital in Gorjanci, Slovenia. Photo: Dr Janez Milčinski.
National Museum of Contemporary History of Slovenia, TN1224/21.

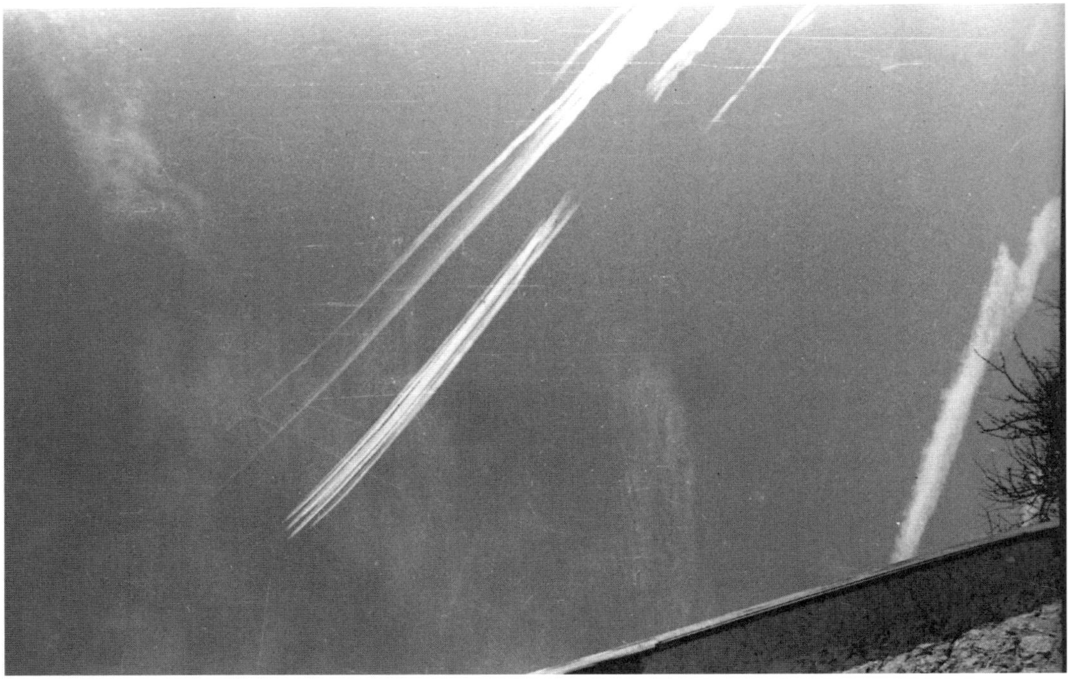

Scene from the hospital in Gorjanci, Slovenia. Photo: Dr Janez Milčinski. National Museum of Contemporary History of Slovenia, TN1224/31.

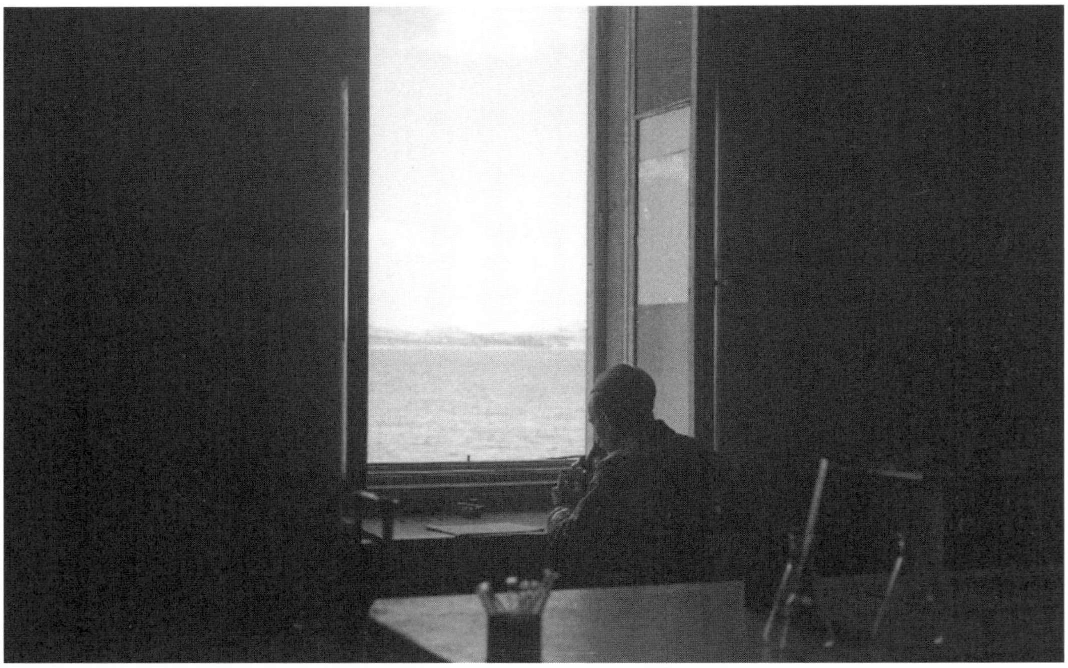

View from the hospital window, Zadar, Croatia, April/March 1945. Photo: Dr Janez Milčinski. National Museum of Contemporary History of Slovenia, 1234/17.

Millitary Successes

While often badly shot and with little aesthetic value, photographs of objects seized in combat or through ambushes – weapons, munitions, clothes, food, telegraphs, vehicles and photography supplies – amount to the first images of Partisan victory. These pictures had a powerful and stirring effect on morale in the Partisan units, and form a distinct category of their own.

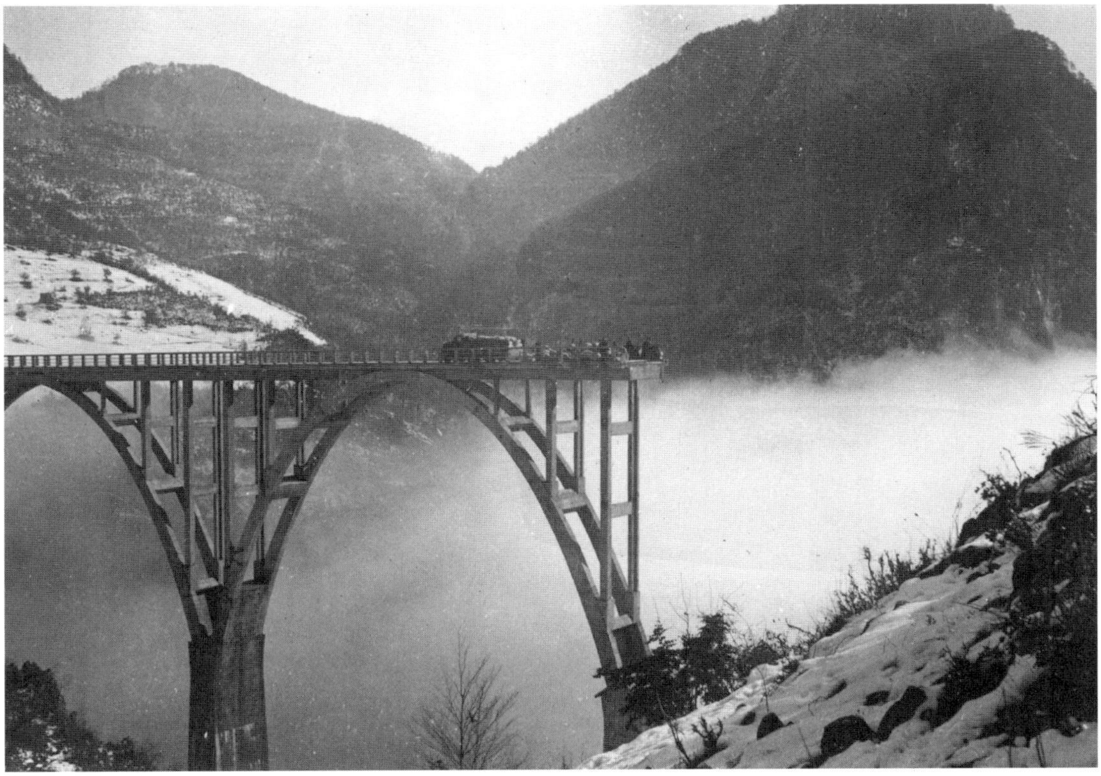

Destroyed bridge on the river Tara, Montenegro, 1943. Croatian History Museum, HPM-MRNH-F-1043.

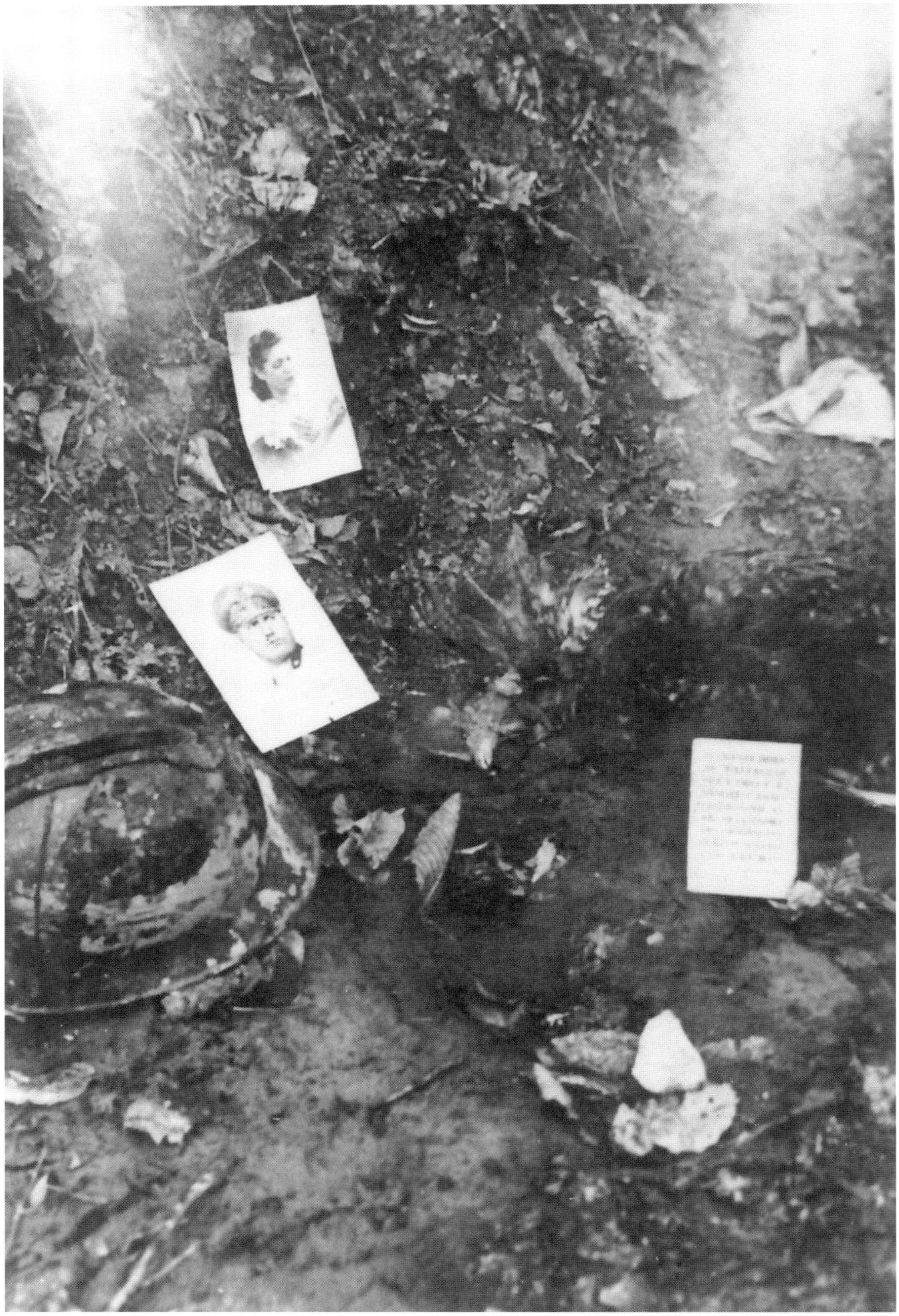

Personal items belonging to an Italian soldier killed in the Rama valley during the Fourth Offensive, 1943. Military Museum Belgrade, 4469.

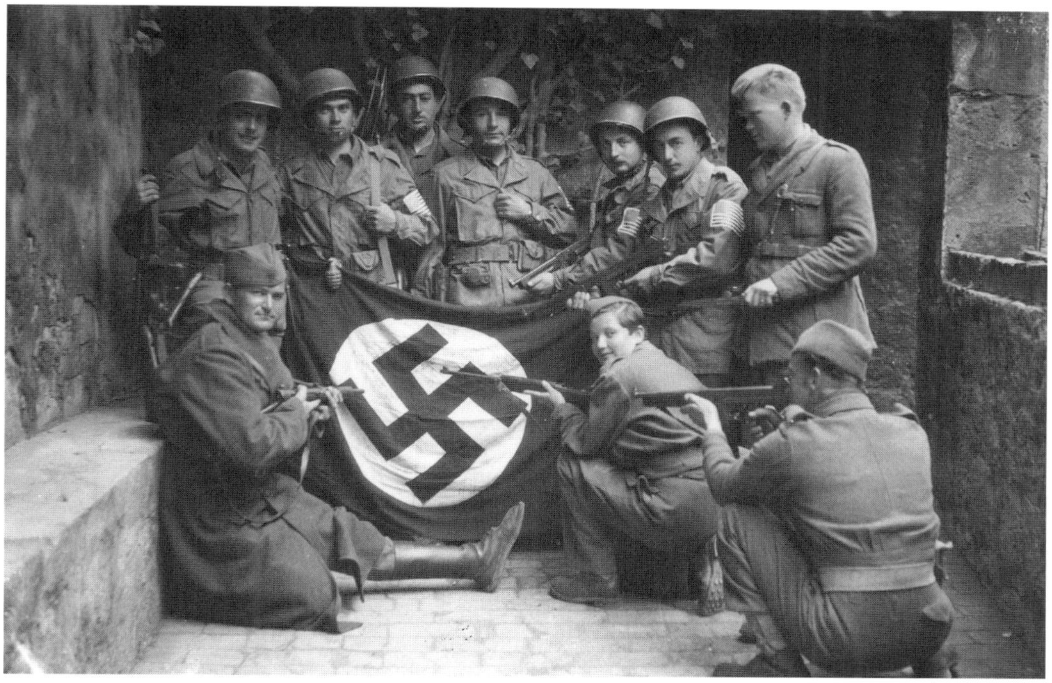

American GIs (helmeted) and Yugoslav soldiers of the NOV i POJ, posing around a captured Nazi flag, Vis, 1944. Photo: Andrija Božanić. Croatian History Museum, HPM/MRNH-F-10355.

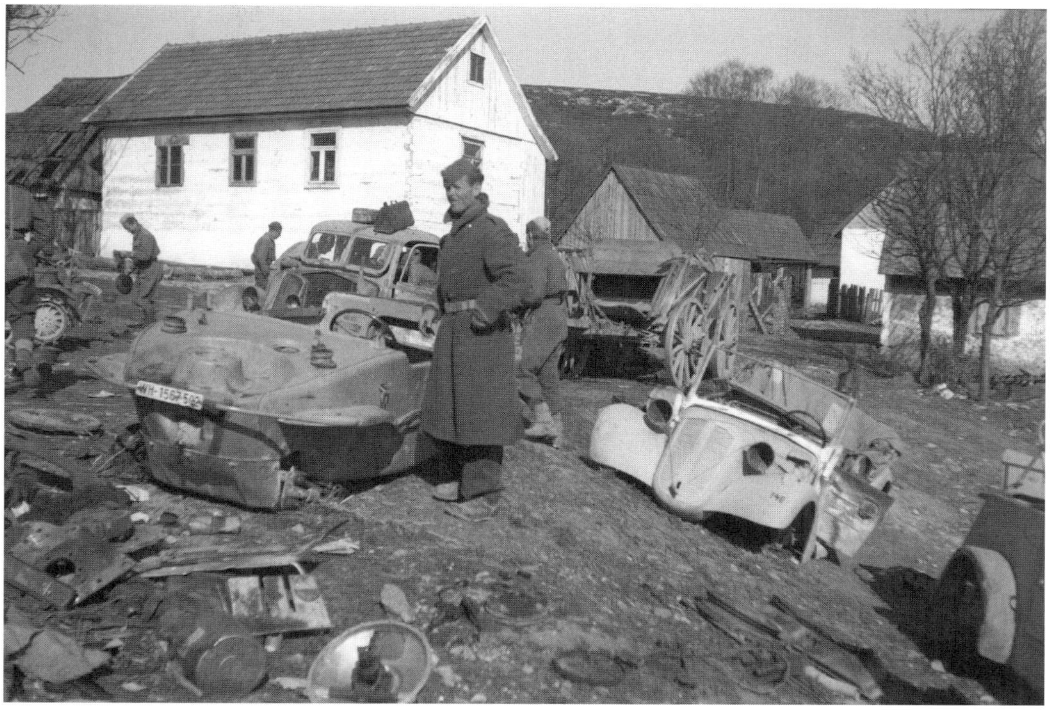

The remains of a car destroyed by Germans in retreat. Photo: Mlekuž. National Museum of Contemporary History of Slovenia, TN786/5.

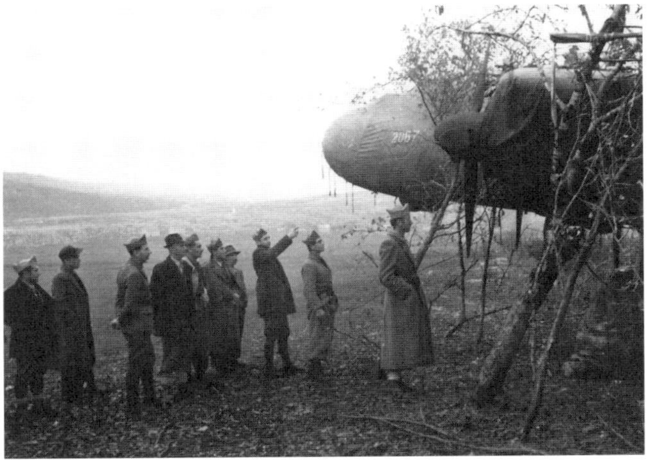

Delegates at the Second Session of the AVNOJ, inspecting a plane. Photographer unknown. Museum of Yugoslavia, III-252.

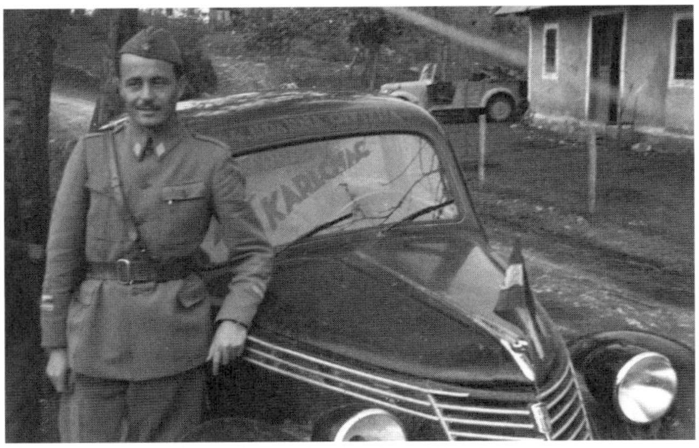

A car belonging to the Thirty-Fourth Assault Division, Otočac, Croatia, 24 April 1945. Photo: Ivo Pelicon. National Museum of Contemporary History of Slovenia, TN707/23.

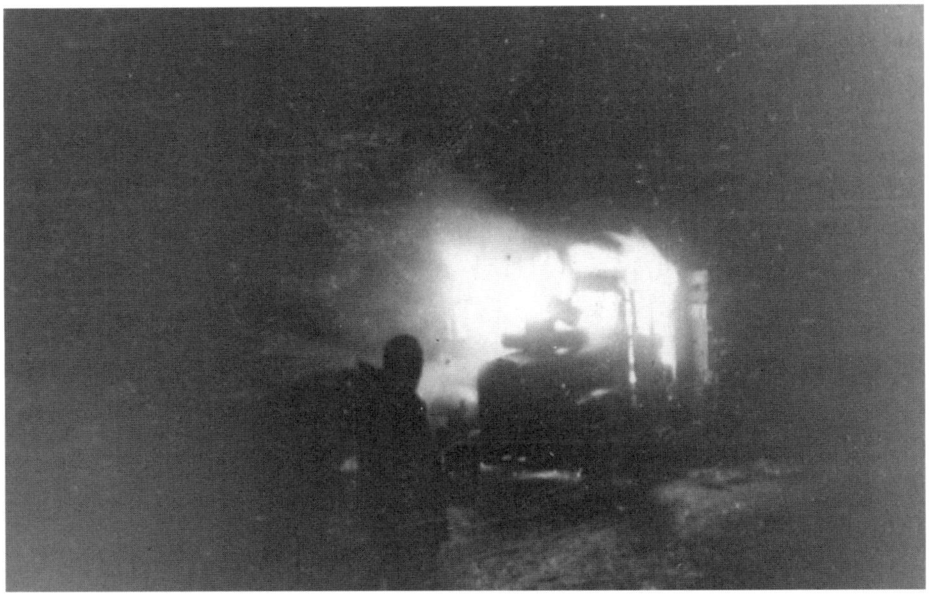

Enemy supply vehicle ablaze, intercepted by Tenth Zagreb Corps, one of many such vehicles targeted by Partisan ambushes in Šumećani (near Zagreb), 1944. Zagreb City Museum, accession no. unknown.

Photographs of Defeated Enemy Forces

As mentioned earlier, Partisan photography evolved in a context in which the German occupiers and quisling authorities denied the legitimacy of the Partisan movement and its very right to exist.[1] The only route out of occupation was through armed resistance to preserve and maintain the civilizational and emancipatory standards achieved thus far.[2] Partisans were oriented towards the future – towards life and progress. Death was an admission of defeat, and not an ideal in and of itself. As hinted at earlier, this was an important practical difference between Partisan imagery and that of the Axis forces. The Yugoslav peoples did not unite because of an 'ethnic bond' or Yugoslav traditions and a unique sense of belonging. They instead banded together in a common struggle against fascism that created an emancipatory community rather than an identity-based one.

The Partisans seldom photographed fallen comrades because taking such photographs was strictly forbidden for propaganda reasons. The fascists exploited their dead for propaganda purposes, and death was an integral part of fascist ideology and culture, with a death cult visible in the various insignia, such as the skull-and-crossbones. We rarely find trophy photographs of enemy soldiers among the Partisan photographers. One of the few recorded photographs of the Partisan execution of German soldiers dates from the battle of Rijeka, in the Drenova neighbourhood. This photograph was taken by Hugo Fischer Ribarić, but to this day his motives remain unexplained. His choice of photographic subject could in that case be interpreted as a form of conscientious protest or a response to a command.

As for wartime violence, the focus is mainly on photographs that depict war crimes against civilians and the consequences of devastation in war. Yet in most cases, the underlying themes are affirmative and serve to gain wider support among the people in building a new, more just society. Decades later in the Vietnam War (1955–75), North Vietnamese photographers operated in conditions like those of the Partisans. In a similarly asymmetrical conflict, the conditions of production were identical, as was the choice of themes: the depiction of the heroic efforts of fighters and the civilian population in resisting the

1 Krunoslav Stojaković, 'Revolucionarno nasilje u narodnooslobodilačkom ratu', in: *Kazna i zločin: Snage kolaboracije u Srbiji*, Milan Radanović (ed.), Belgrade 2014 (Rosa Luxemburg-Stiftung), p. 21.
2 Ibid., p. 24.

foreign occupier, and the difficult challenge of how to develop a good relationship between photographic aesthetics and the ideology that they were trying to represent through photography.[3]

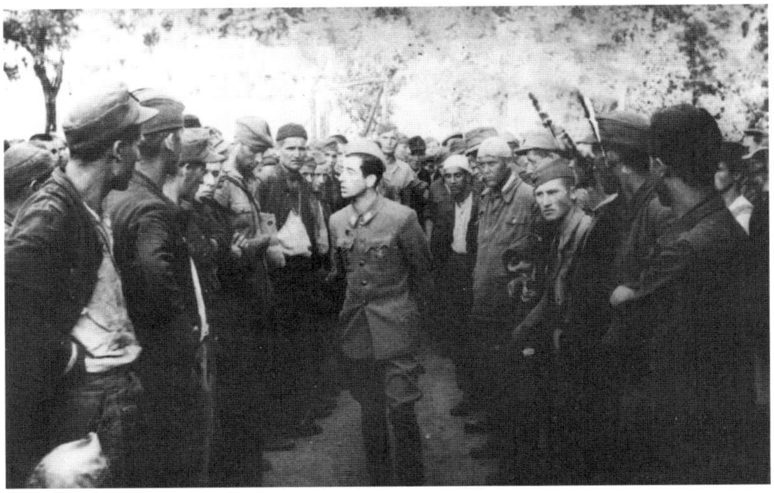

Nisim Albahari speaking to troops after leaving a house of captured Slovene Home Guards, early May 1945. Photographer unknown. History Museum of Bosnia and Herzegovina, FNOB 3651.

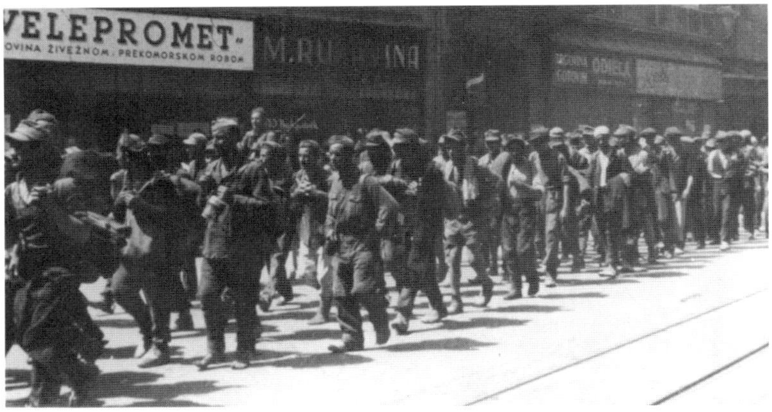

Captured German Wehrmacht soldiers, Zagreb, May 1945. Photo: Jan Beran. History Museum of Bosnia and Herzegovina, FNOB 6614.

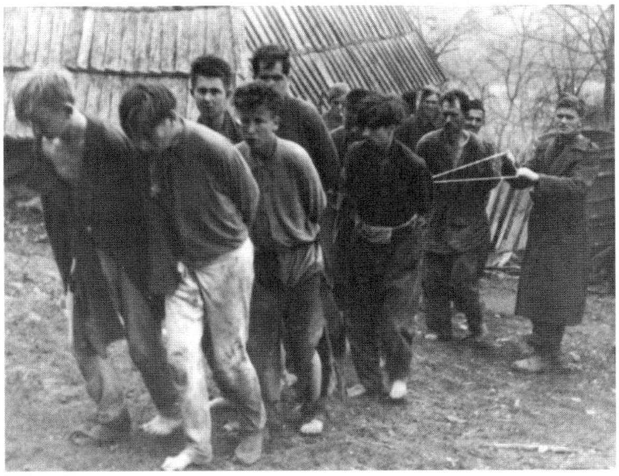

Captured German SS. Photographer unknown. History Museum of Bosnia and Herzegovina, FNOB 19422.

3 Thy Phu, 'Vietnamese Photography and the Look of Revolution', in: Photography and Optical Unconscious, Shawn Michelle Smith and Sharon Sliwinski (eds.). Durham, North Carolina 2017, p. 306.

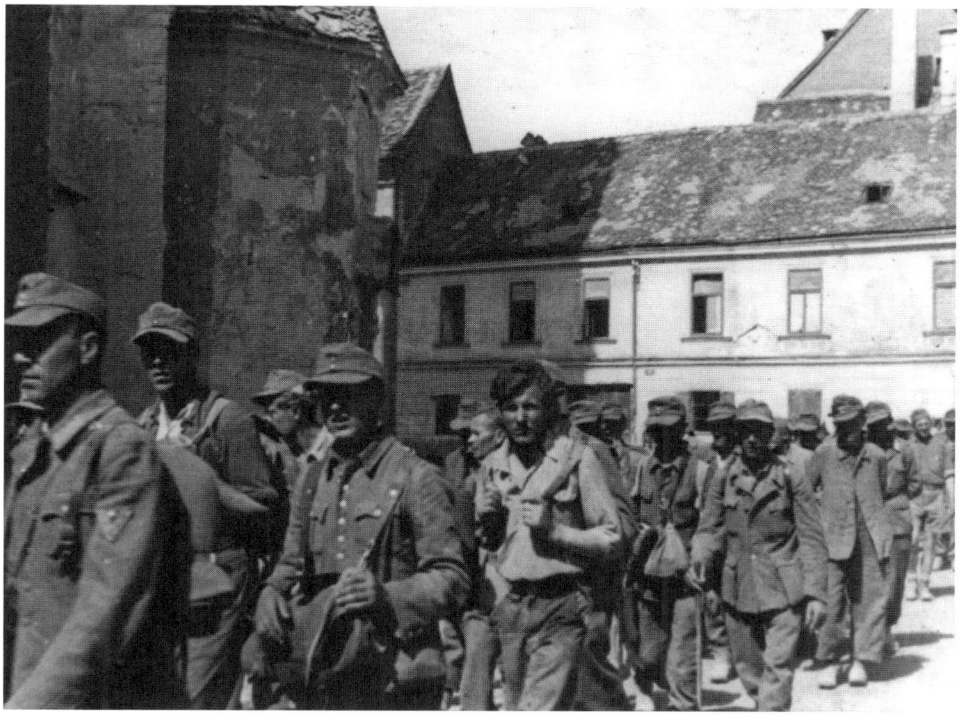

Captured Wehrmacht soldiers, Celje, Slovenia, May 1945.
History Museum of Bosnia and Herzegovina, FNOB 6663.

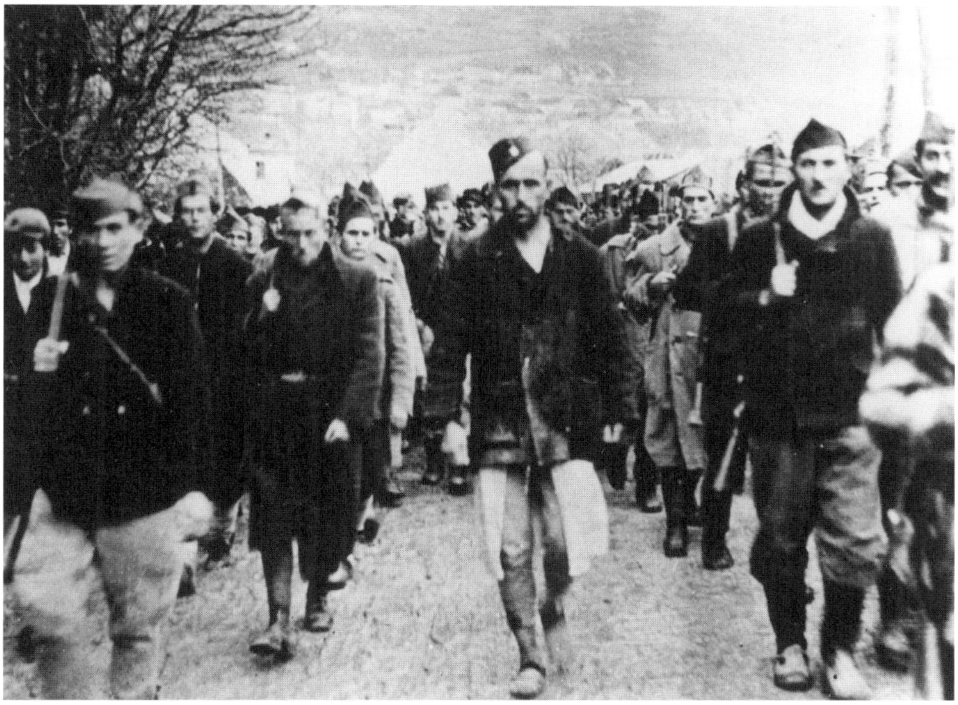

The embittered people accompany the notorious Ustashe First Lieutenant Mirko Perajica to his execution after sentencing him to death, Livno, Bosnia and Herzegovina, 1942.
History Museum of Bosnia and Herzegovina, FNOB 11972.

Exhibitions and News Board Displays

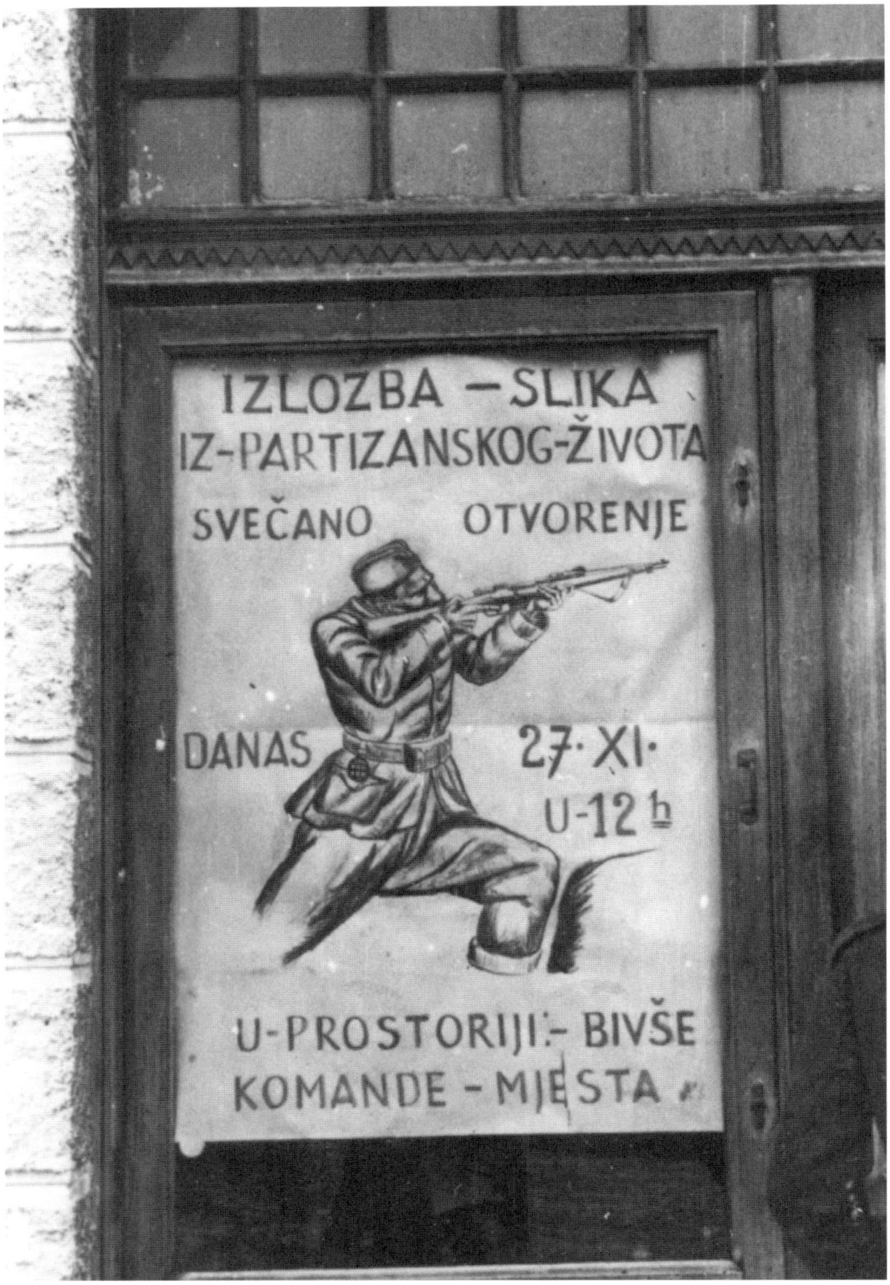

Second Session of the AVNOJ, Jajce, Bosnia and Herzegovina, 29 November 1943.
Photographer unknown. Croatian History Museum, HPM/MRNH-F-5377.

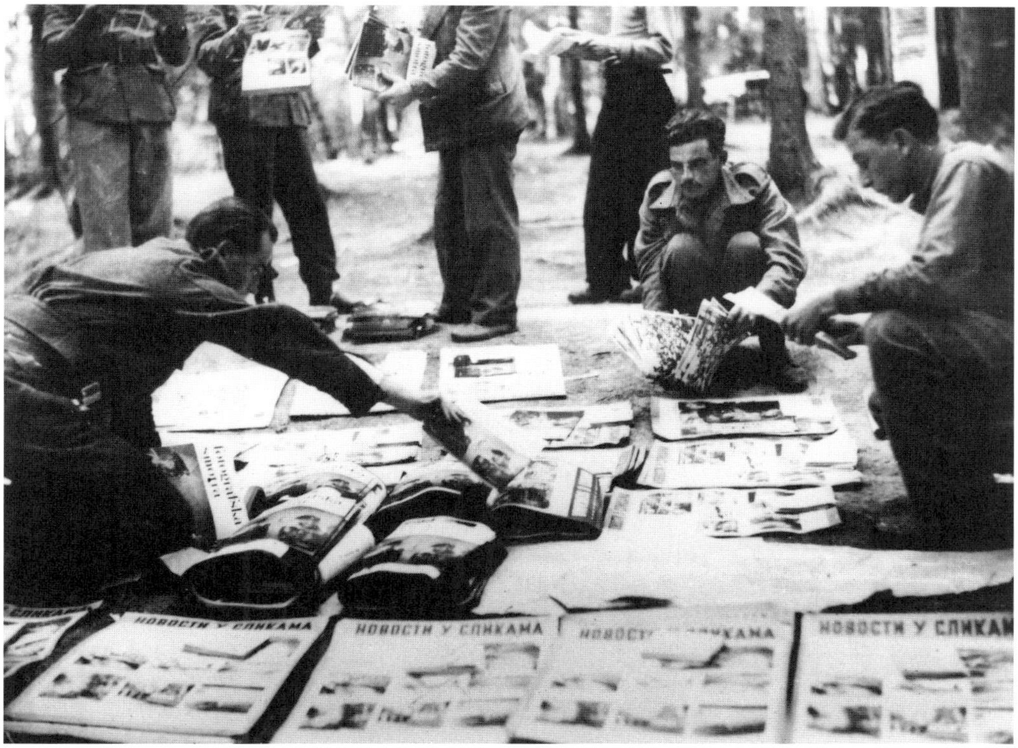

Sorting propaganda material in the agitprop department at Zvečevo, Croatia, autumn 1944. Photographer unknown. Museum of Yugoslavia, III-1370.

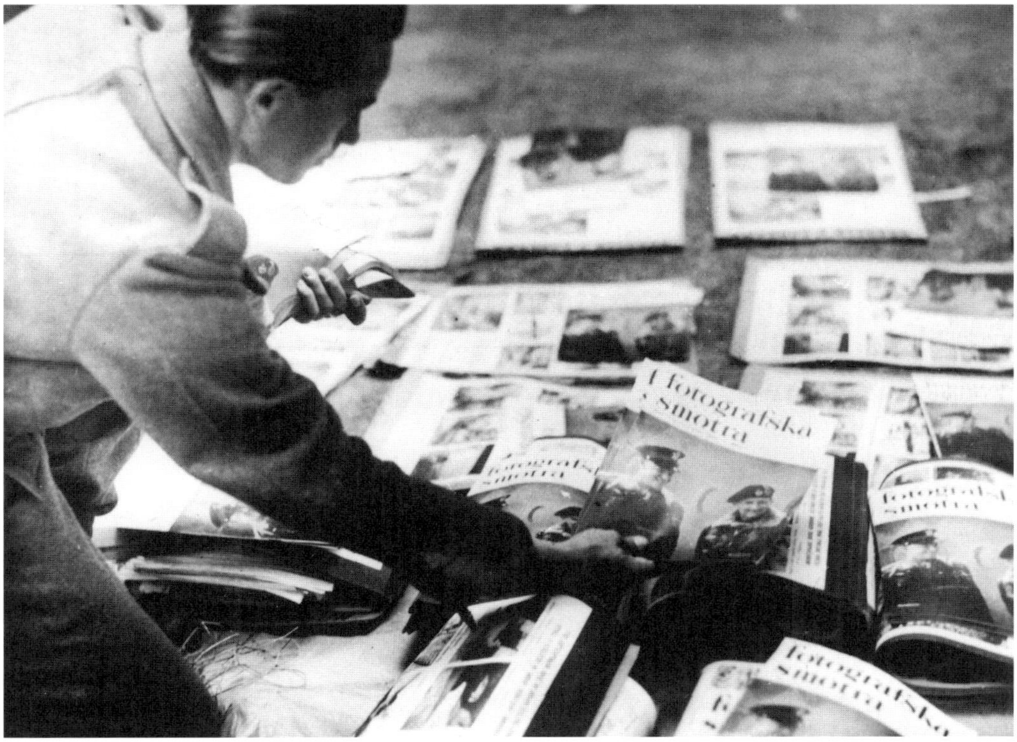

Sorting propaganda material in the agitprop department at Zvečevo, Croatia, autumn 1944. Photographer unknown. Museum of Yugoslavia, III-1373.

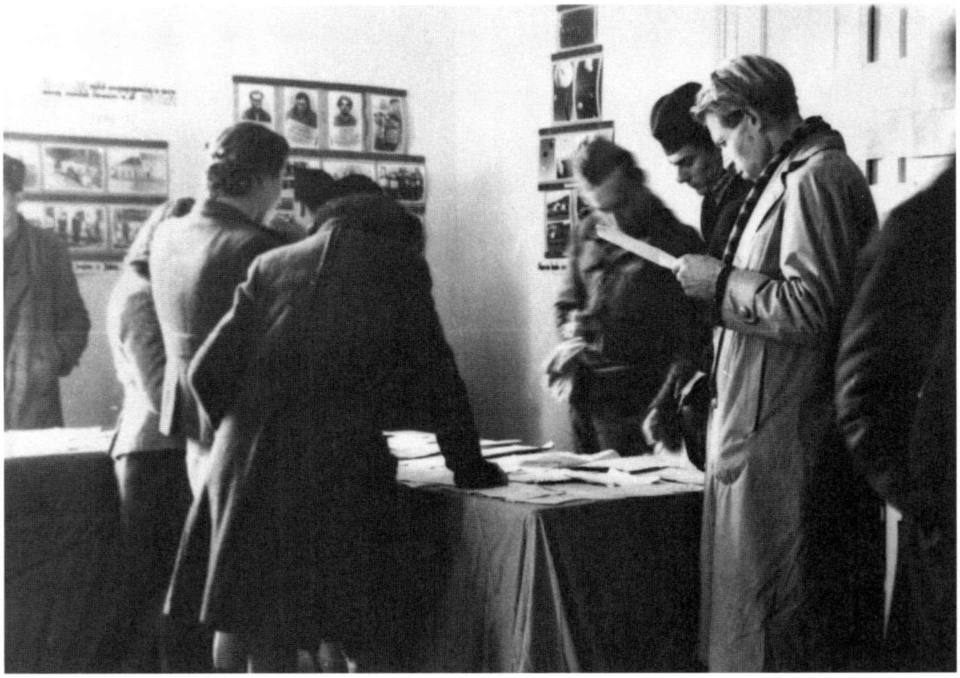

Photography exhibition in Gornji Grad, Slovenia, 20 November 1944. Photo: Marjan Mlekuž.
National Museum of Contemporary History of Slovenia, TN454/2.

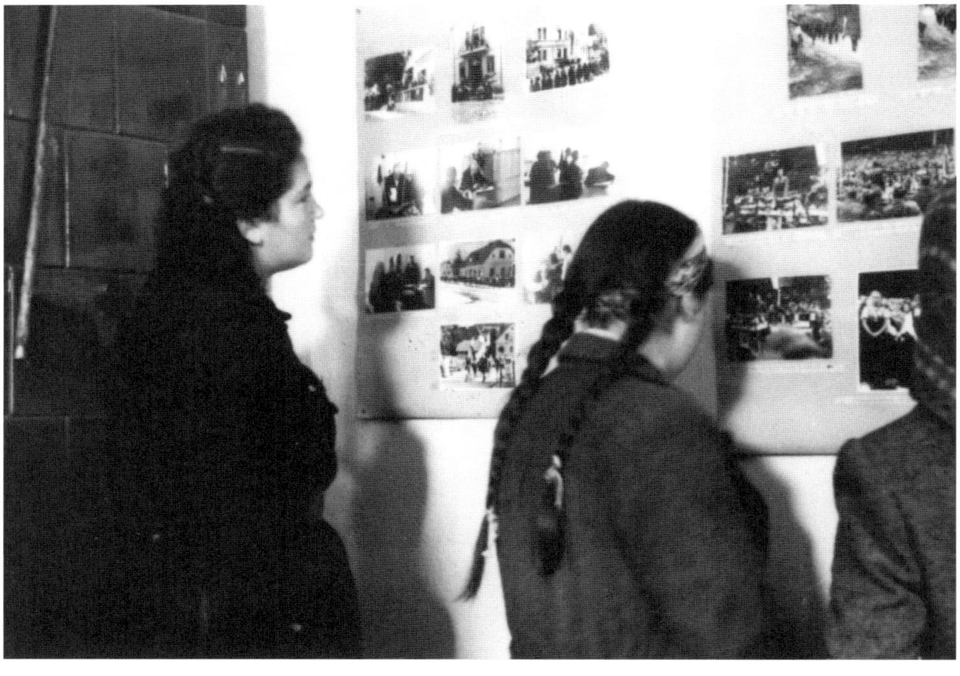

Exhibition of Jože Petek's war reportage and photographs, Gornji Grad, Slovenia,
20 November 1944. Photographer unknown. Museum of Recent History, Celje FZ21635.

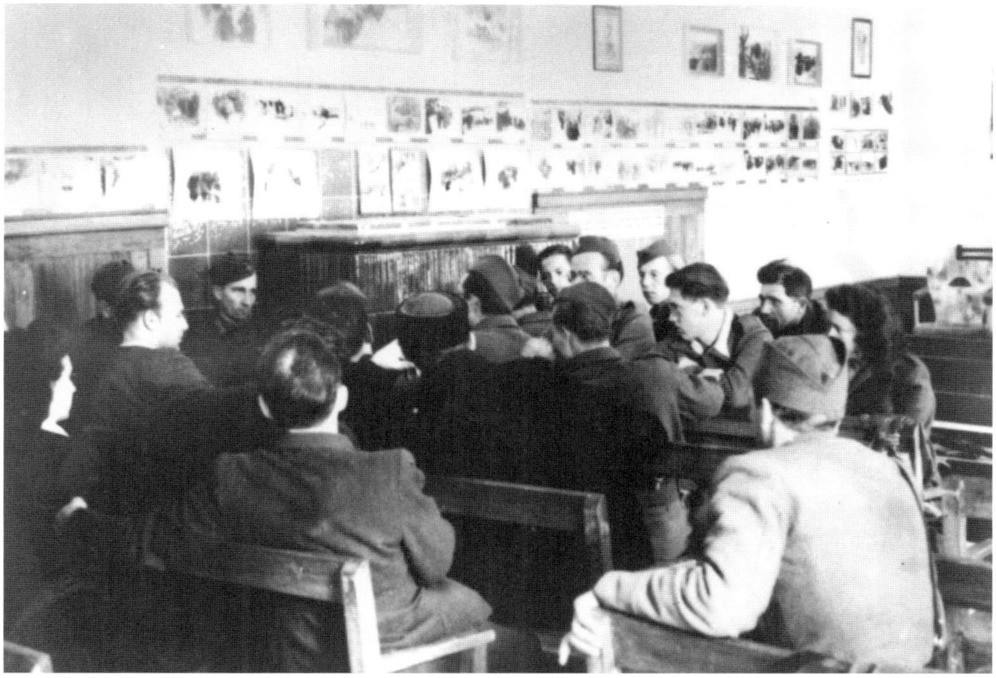

Exhibition of Jože Petek's war reportage and photographs, Gornji Grad, Slovenia,
20 November 1944. Photographer unknown. Museum of Recent History, Celje FZ21636.

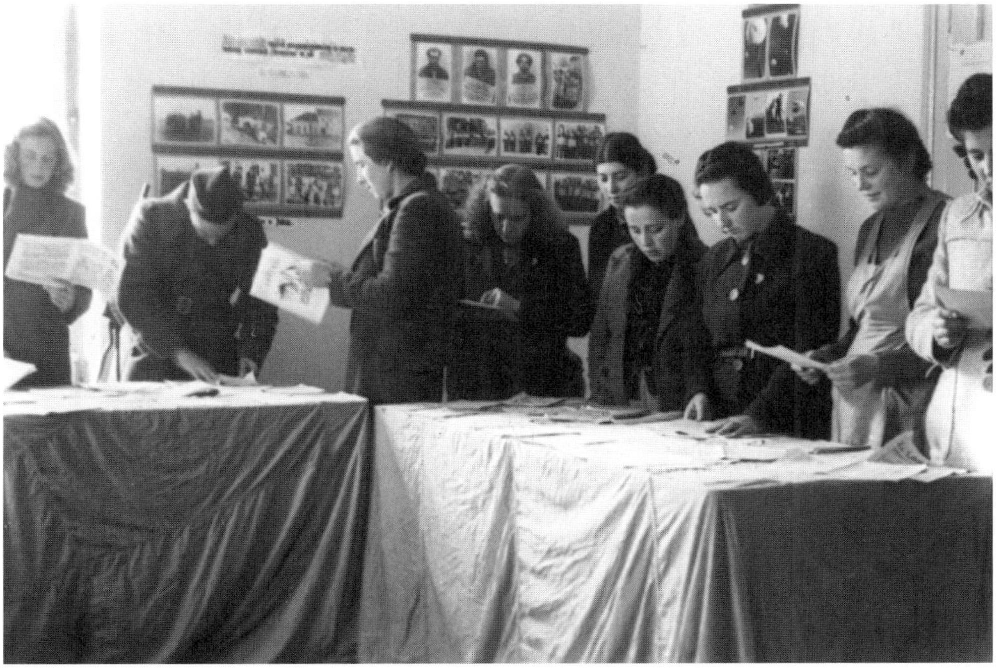

Exhibition of Jože Petek's war reportage and photographs, Gornji Grad, Slovenia,
20 November 1944. Photographer unknown. Museum of Recent History, Celje FZ21771.

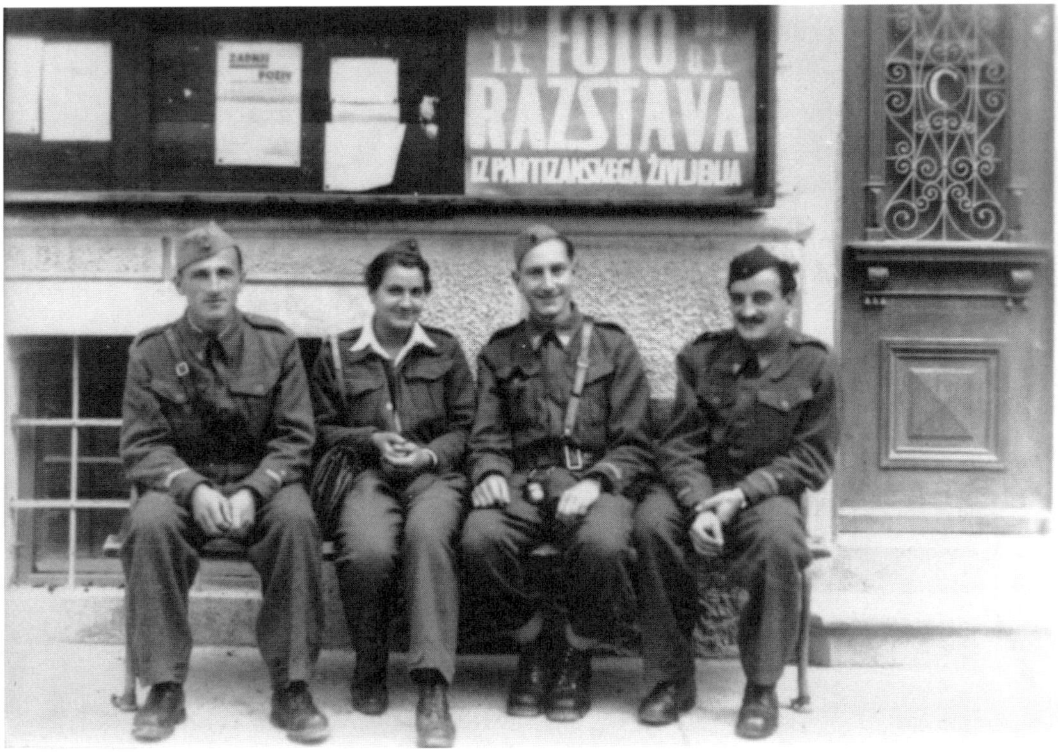

Stane Zabovnik (left), Vera Hreščak-Bebler, Radovan Gobec and Jože Škrinjar (right), Gornji Grad, Slovenia, November 1944. Photographer unknown. Museum of Recent History, Celje FZ25550.

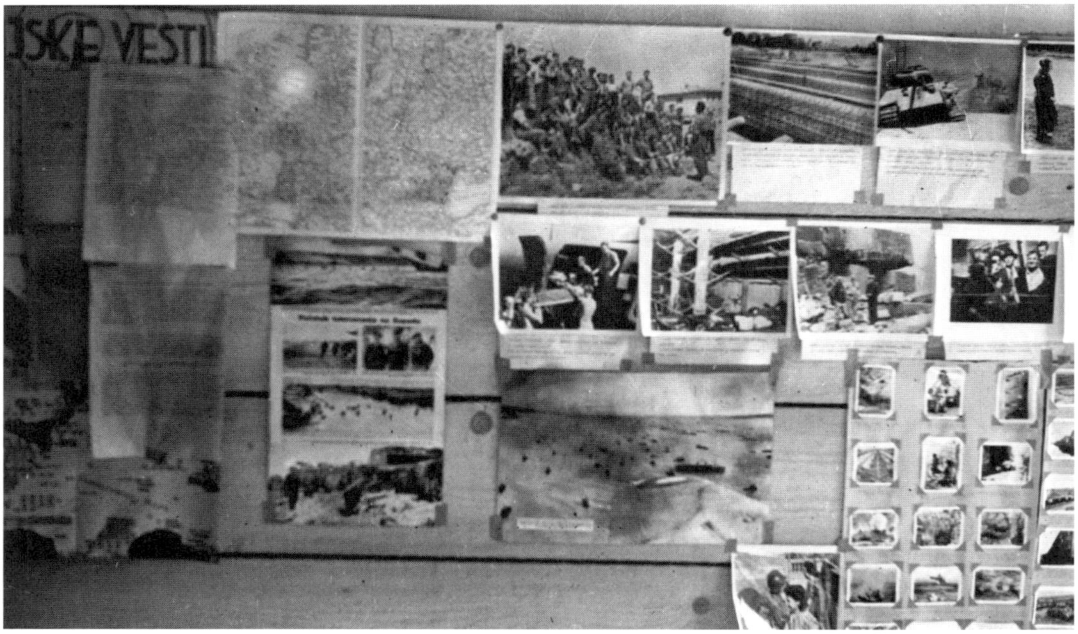

Photographs on wall of Črnomelj reading room, Črnomelj, 10 April 1945. Photo: Viršek Stane and Franc Cerar. National Museum of Contemporary History of Slovenia, TN129/11.

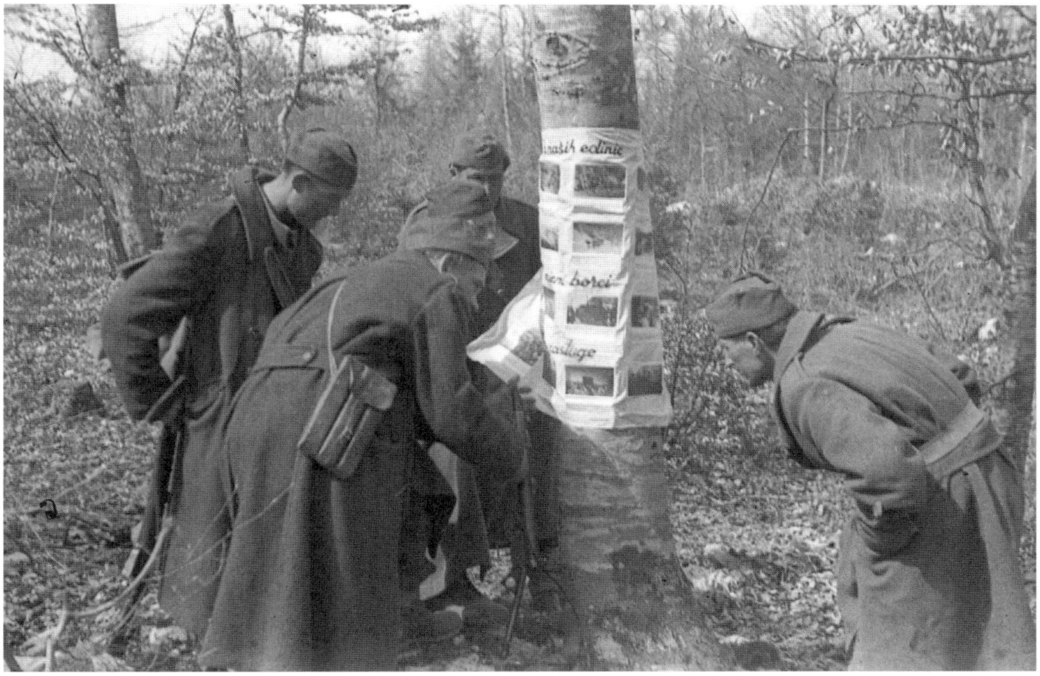

Fighters of the First Battalion of the Tenth Brigade looking at photographs from a travelling exhibition, in this case a makeshift display on tree trunks, Suha krajina, Slovenia, 25 March 1945. Photo: Milan Štok. National Museum of Contemporary History of Slovenia, TN904/24.

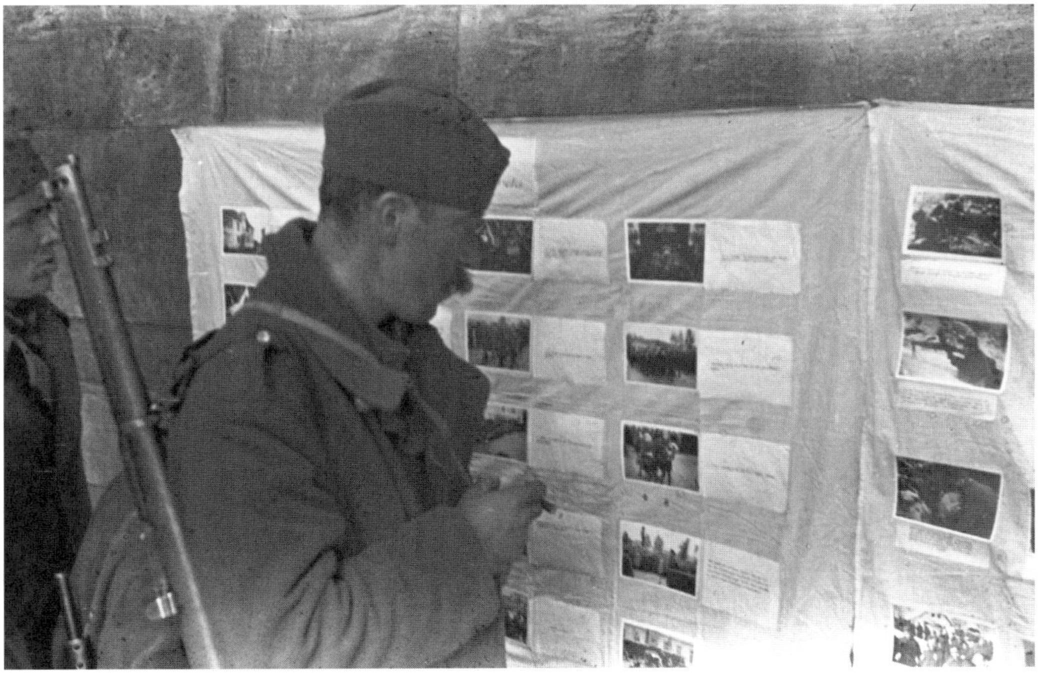

Soldiers visiting a photography exhibition, Suha Krajina, Slovenia, 25 March 1945. Photo: Milan Štok. National Museum of Contemporary History of Slovenia, TN904/5.

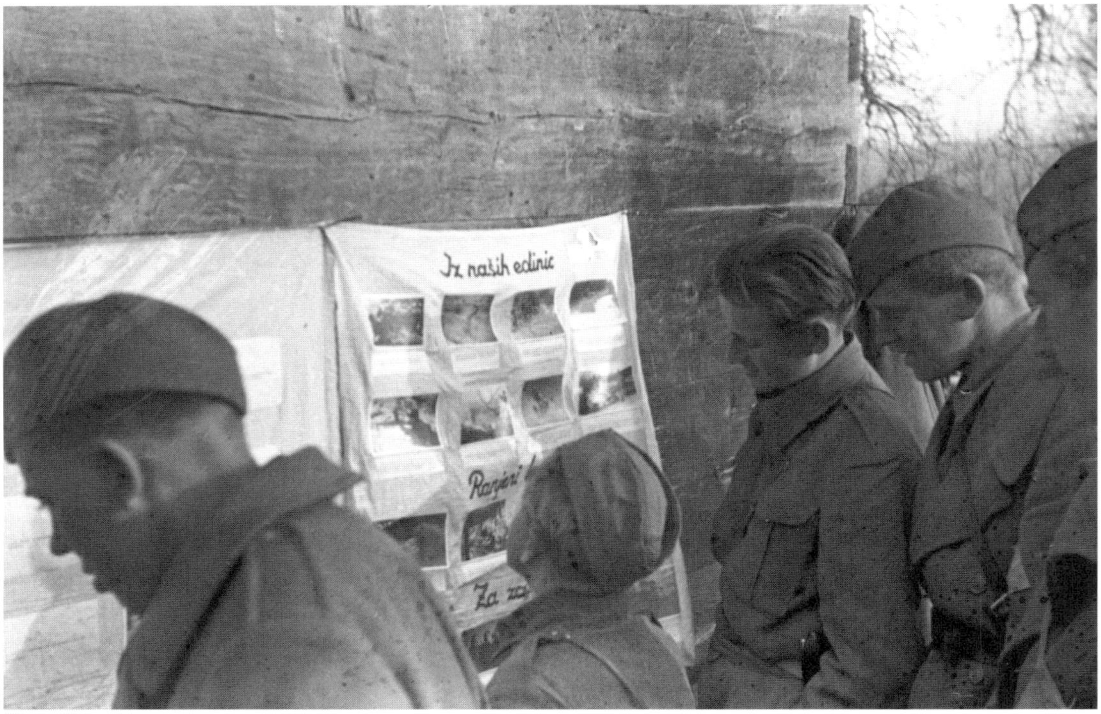

Soldiers at a makeshift photography exhibition, Suha Krajina, Slovenia, 25 March 1945.
Photo: Milan Štok. National Museum of Contemporary History of Slovenia, TN904/6.

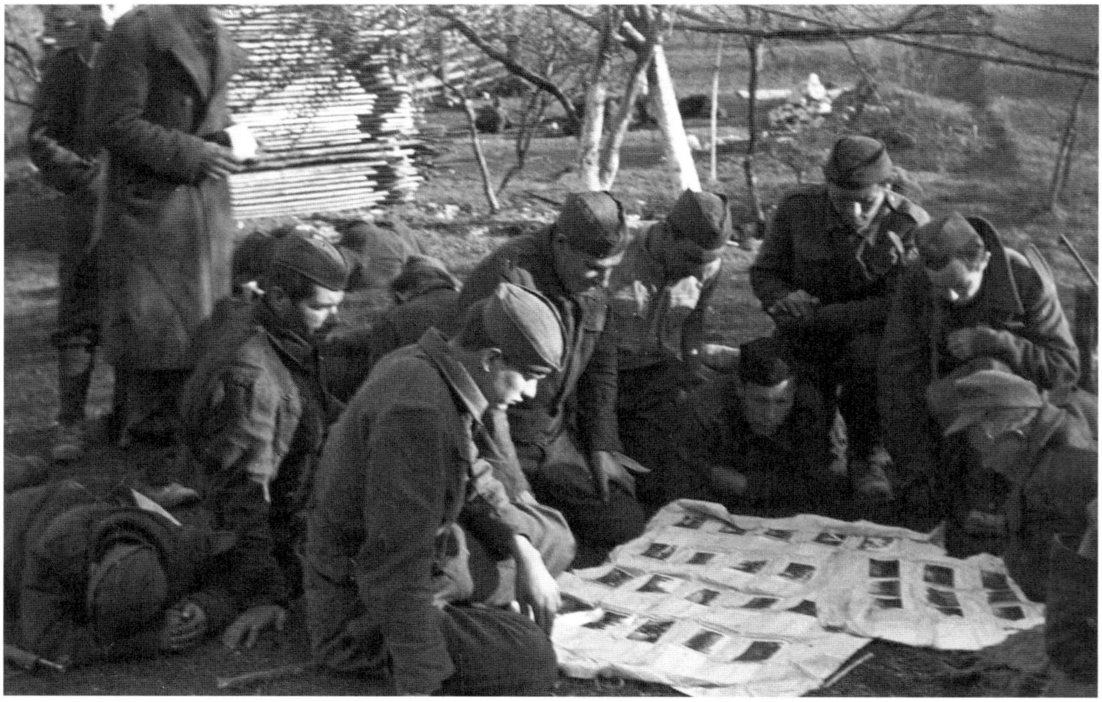

Fighters of the Second Battalion of the Fourteenth Brigade looking at photographs, presented during a politics class, documenting the Fontanot Brigade and funeral of Franc Rožman-Stane, 24 March 1945.
Photo: Milan Štok. National Museum of Contemporary History of Slovenia, TN934/19.

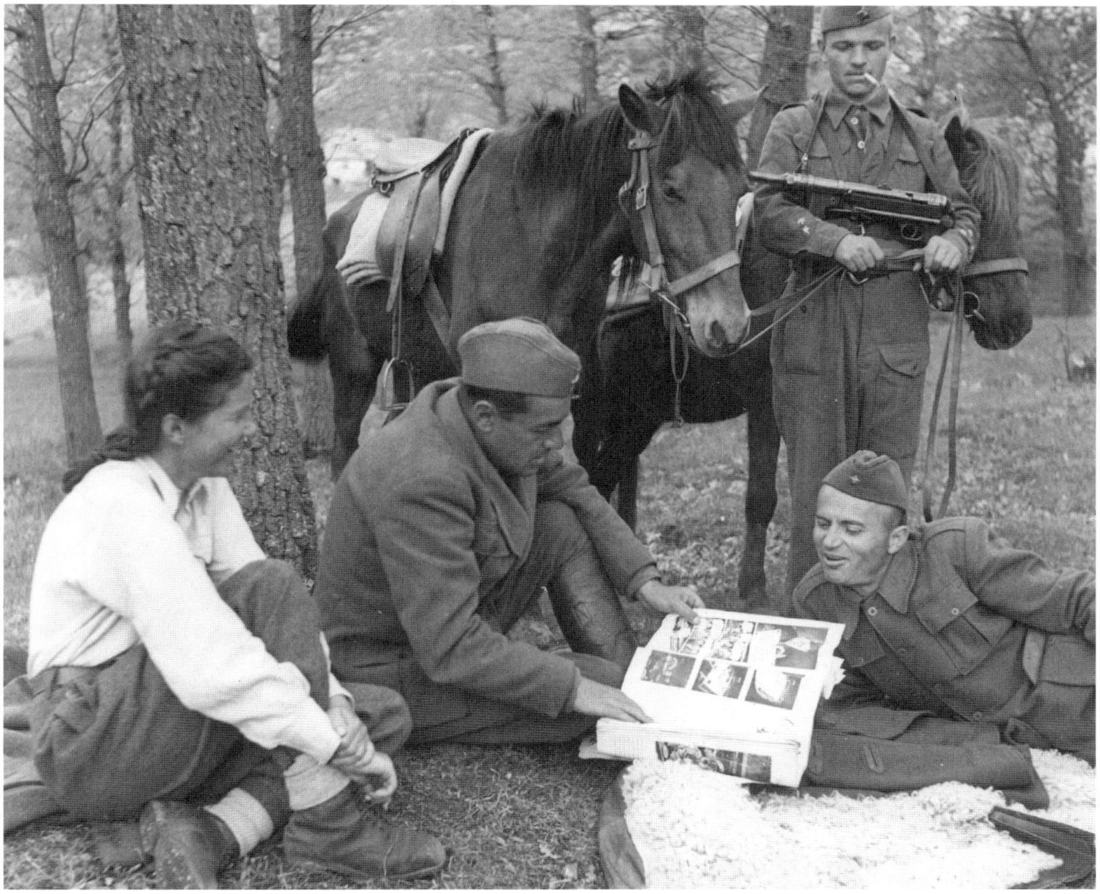

An unknown Partisan woman, Vladislav Ribnikar, poet Radovan Zogović and Radovan Bulatović (standing), leafing through an album of photographic prints. Photographer unknown. Military Museum Belgrade, 4637.

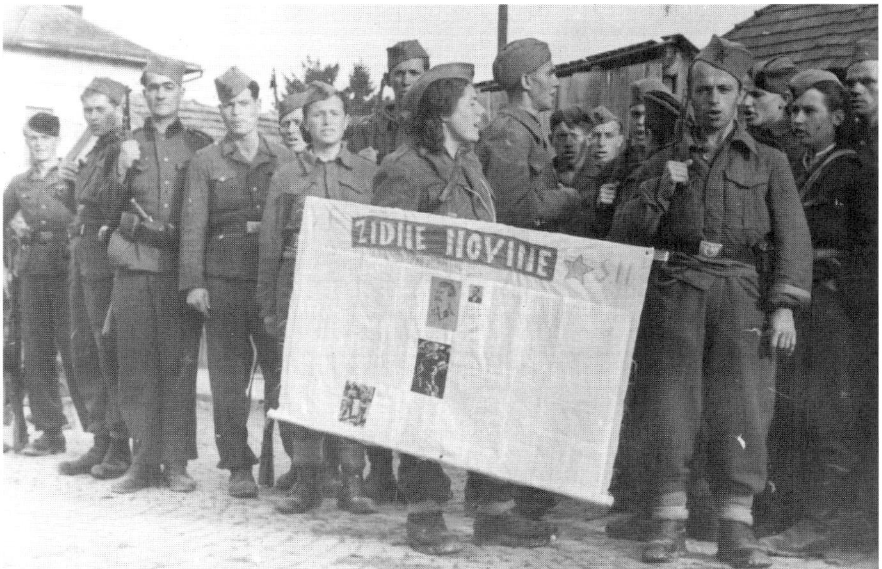

News posters to place on walls. Photo: Drago Mažar. Archives of the Republic of Srpska, Banja Luka.

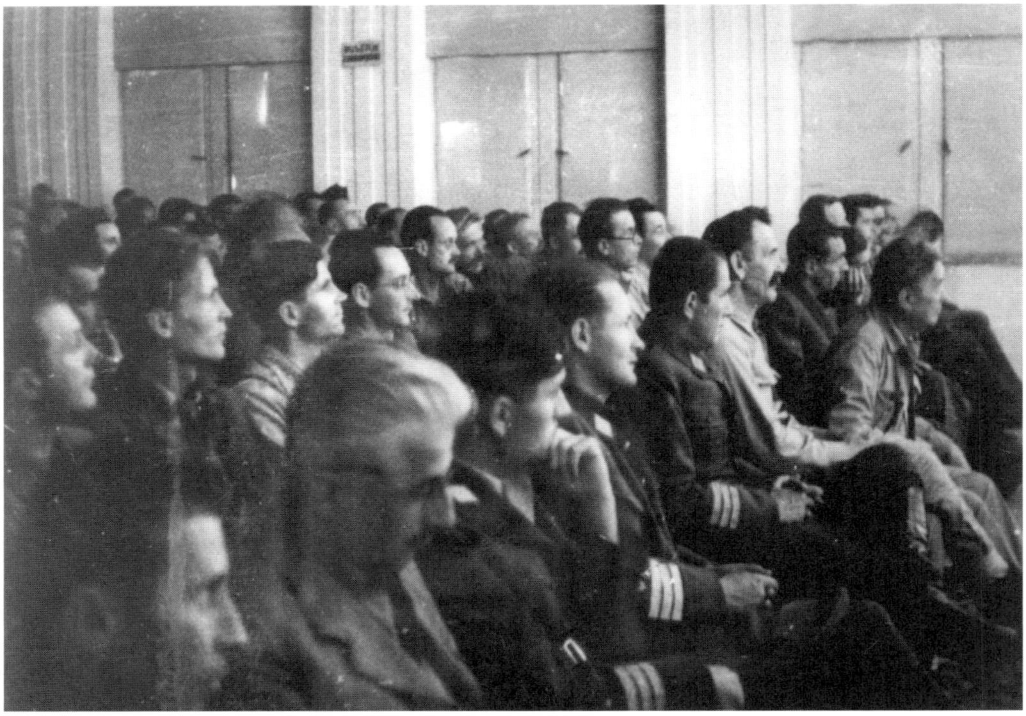

An exhibition celebrating the formation of the First Dalmatian Brigade on the island of Vis, Croatia.
September 1944. Croatian History Museum, HPM-MRNH-R-5634.

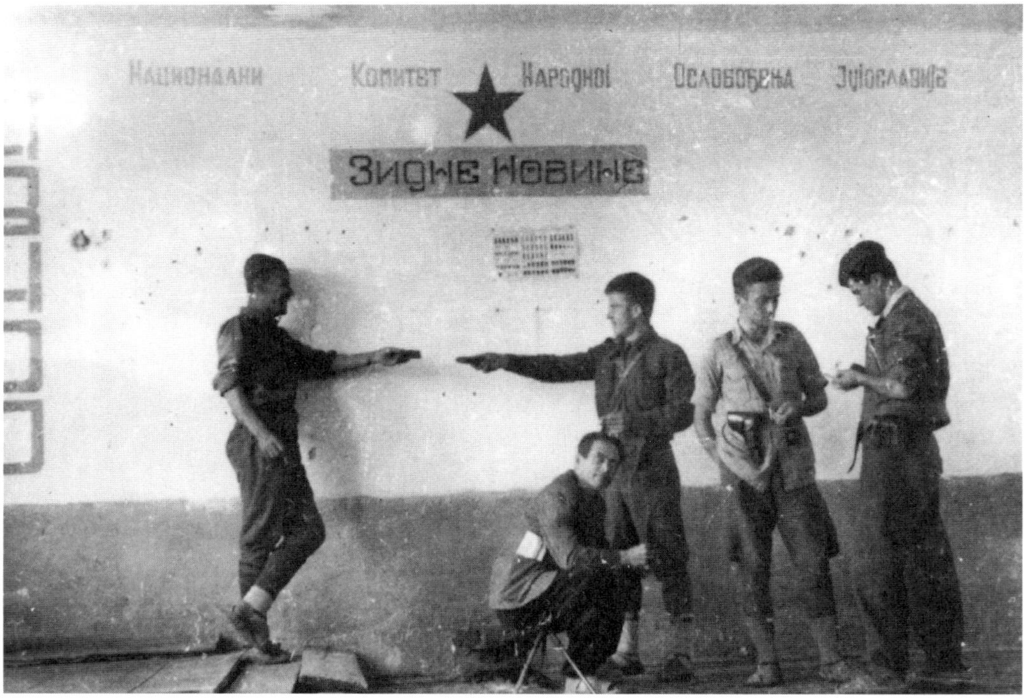

Todo Kurtović with comrades in a hall for special functions, Hrasno, 1943.
Photographer unknown. History Museum of Bosnia and Herzegovina, FNOB 3146.

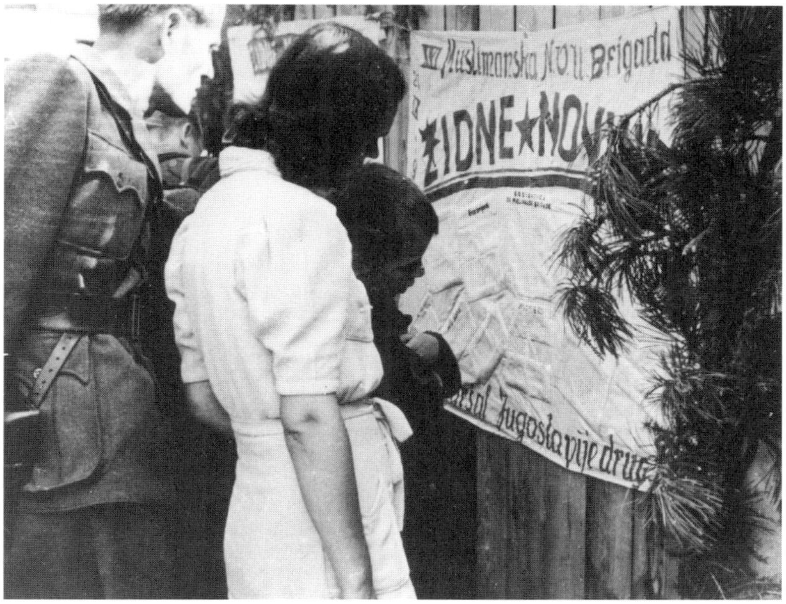

News posters written by the Sixteenth Muslim Brigade in Tuzla, 21 September 1944. Photographer unknown. History Museum of Bosnia and Herzegovina, FNOB 14248.

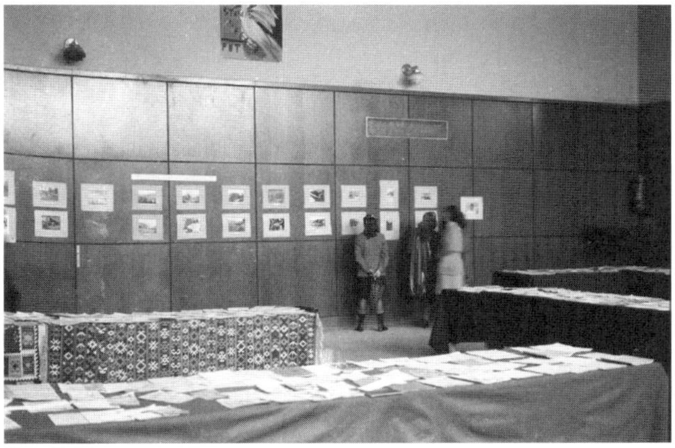

View of hall hosting an exhibition of photographs, pictures, caricatures and prints from the People's Liberation War, Crikvenica, Croatia, September/October 1943. Croatian History Museum, HPM/ MRNH-A- 2601-f69-001.

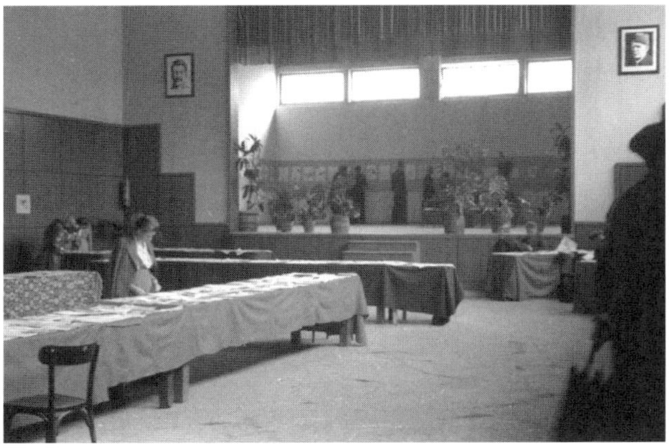

View of hall hosting an exhibition of photographs, pictures, caricatures and prints from the People's Liberation War, Crikvenica, Croatia, September/October 1943. Croatian History Museum, HPM/ MRNH-A-2601-f69-003.

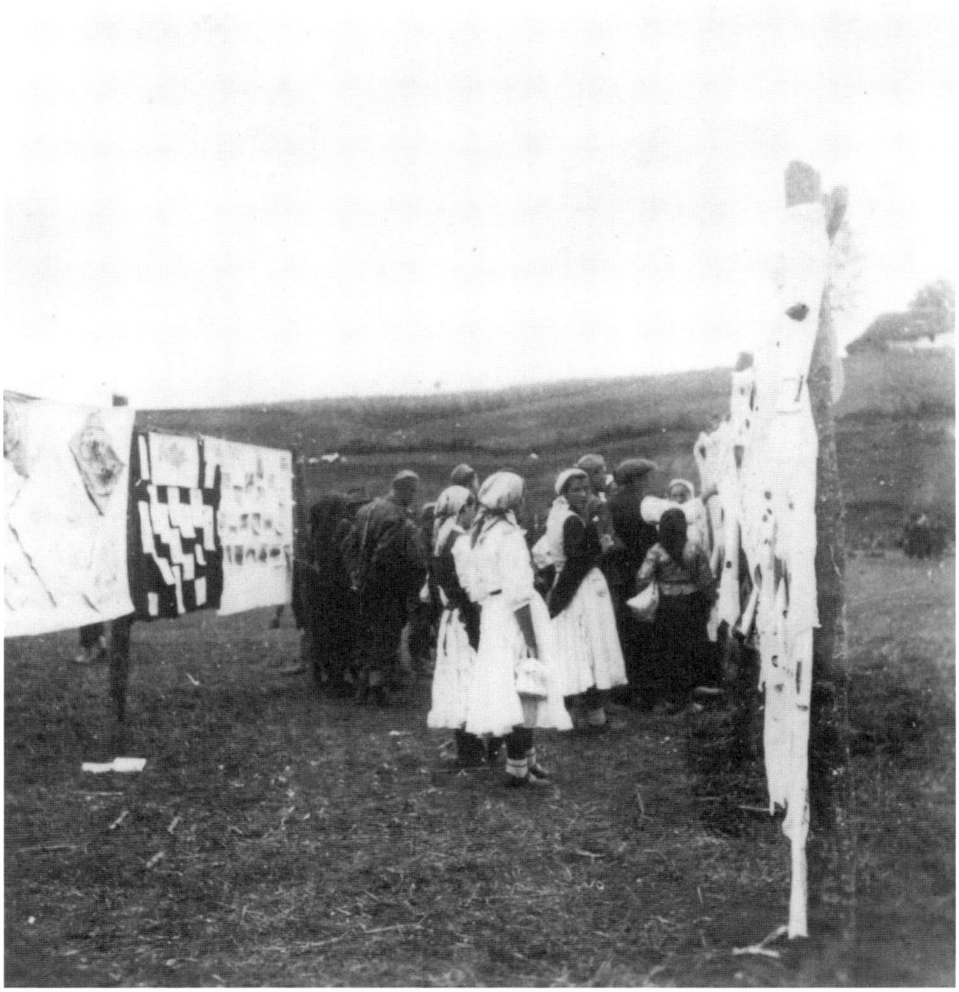

Exhibition of craftwork, photographs and newspaper issues held as part of a youth festival in celebration of the third anniversary of the uprising in Kordun, summer 1944. Photographer unknown. Croatian History Museum, HPM/MRNH-F-4744.

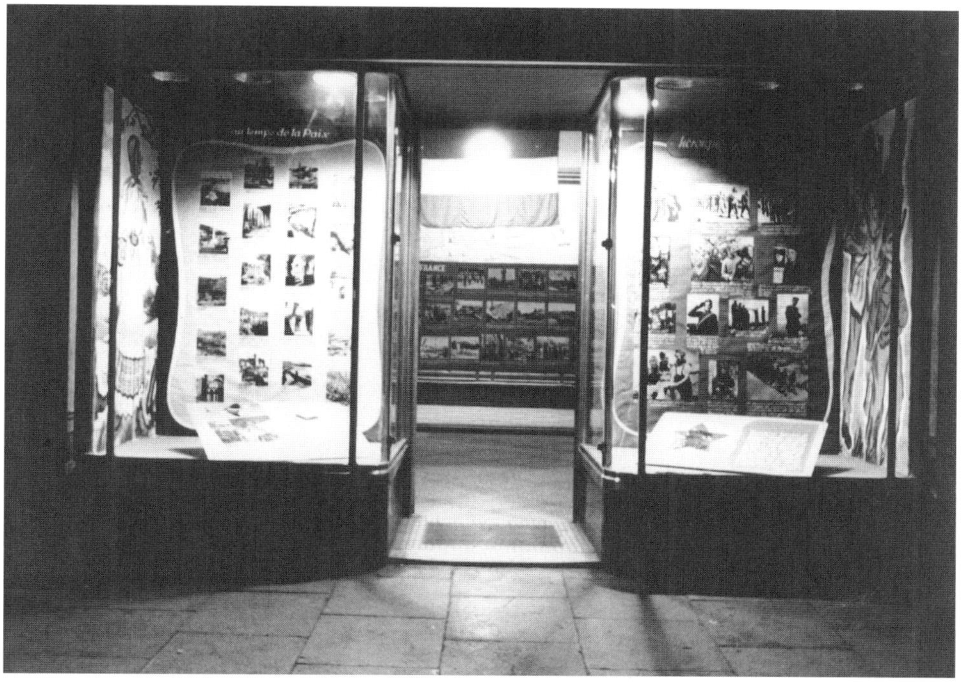

We have Vanja Žanko's family to thank for preserving a photographic record of the particularly interesting exhibition *L'exposition sur la Yugoslavie nouvelle*, held in Algiers in 1944. The photographs represent the Partisan struggle and promote Yugoslavia as a country of art.

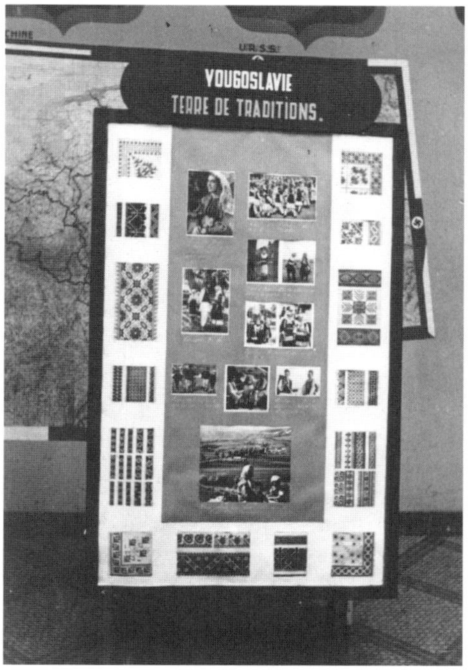

Outside display of L'exposition sur la Yugoslavie nouvelle, Algiers 1944. Photographer unknown. Photograph reproduced with the kind permission of Dunja Žanko Darrot.

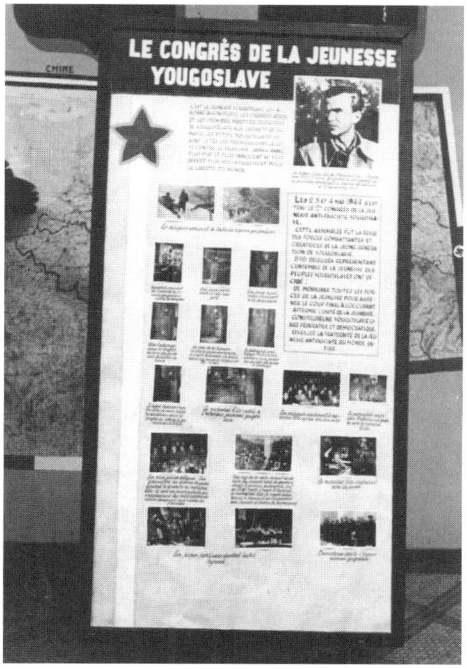

Display detail from *L'exposition sur la Yugoslavie nouvelle,* Algiers 1944. Photographer unknown. Photograph reproduced with the kind permission of Dunja Žanko Darrot.

Liberation

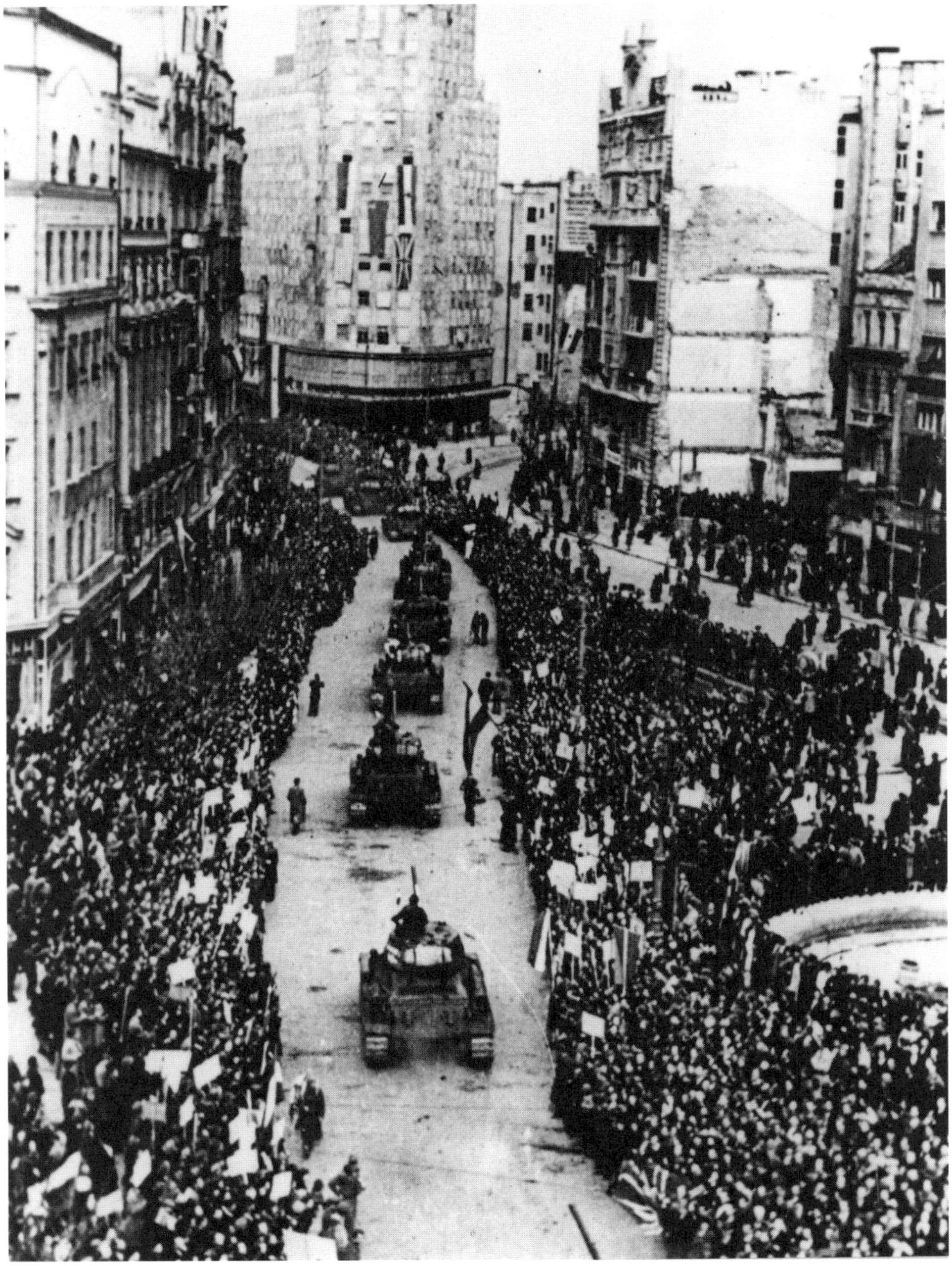

The liberation of Yugoslav capital Belgrade, October 1944. Photographer unknown. History Museum of Bosnia and Herzegovina, FNOB 19439.

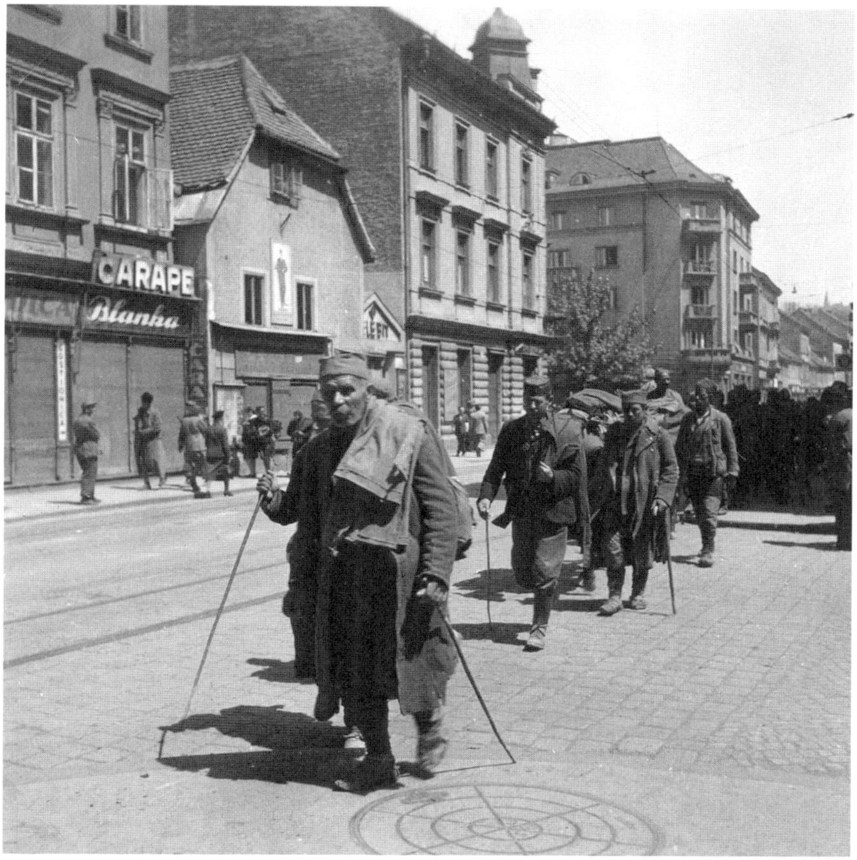

Montenegrin Chetniks retreating west, Zagreb, Croatia, May 1945.
Photo: Milan Pavić. Croatian History Museum, HPM-MRNH-A-11697 94.

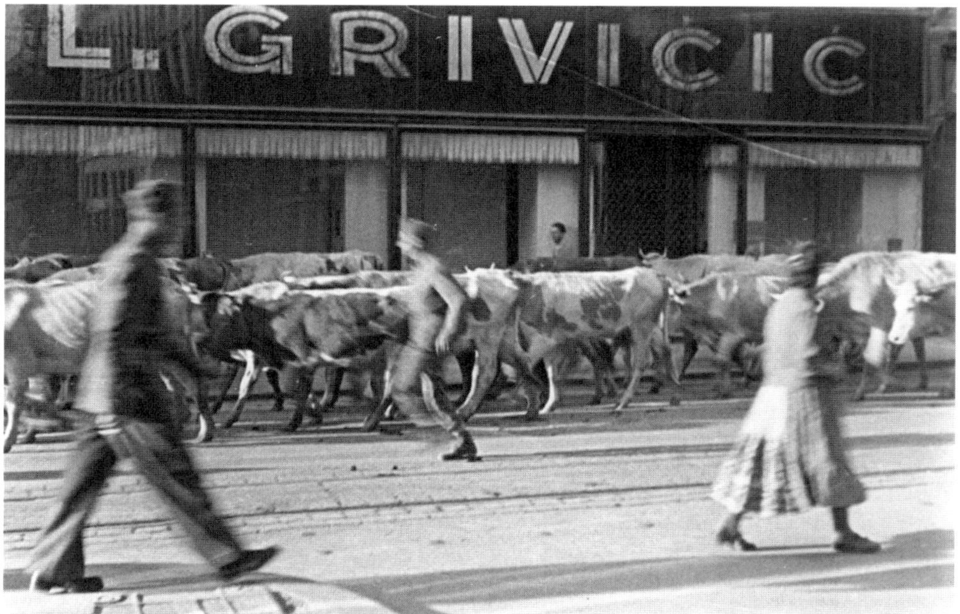

Zagreb during the liberation, May 1945. Photographer unknown.
Croatian History Museum, HPM-MRNH-N-2501.

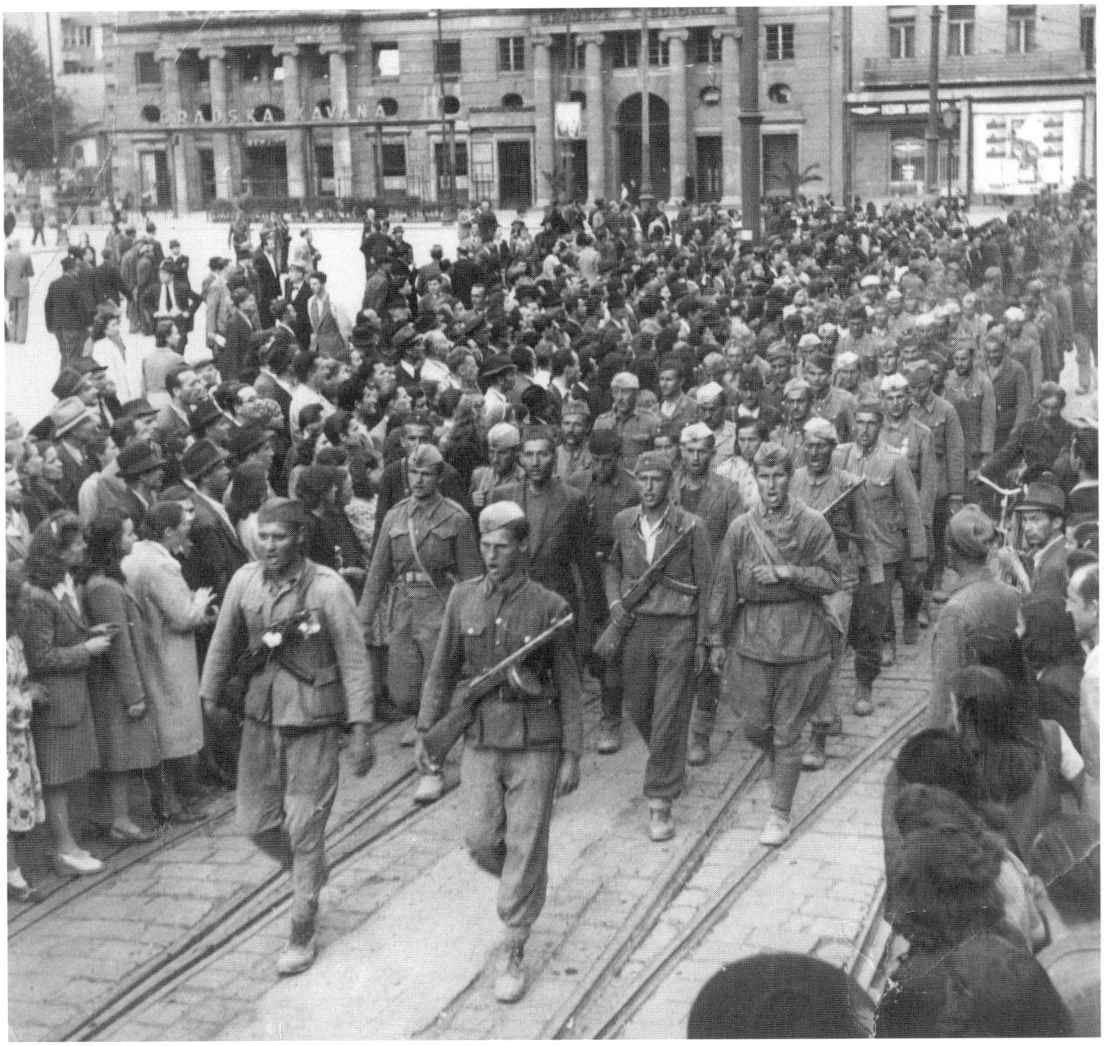

The Partisans enter Zagreb, 8 May 1945. Photo: Milan Pavić.
Croatian History Museum, HPM-MRNH-F-11201.

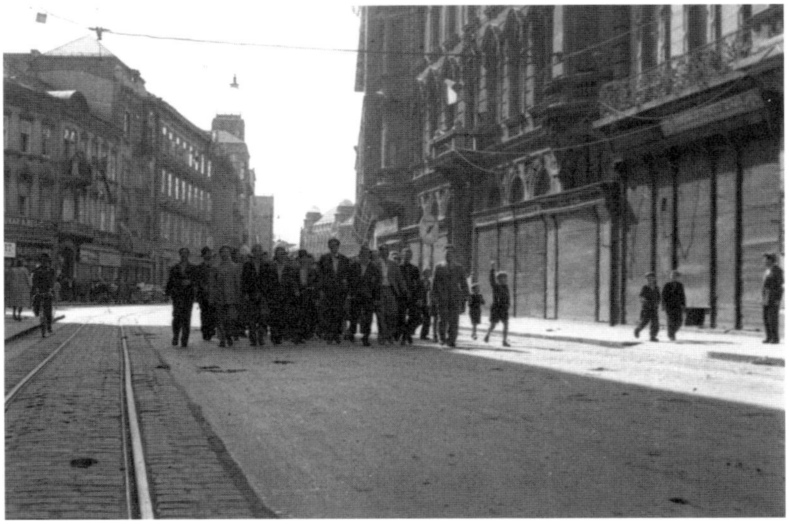

Zagreb during the liberation, May 1945. Photographer unknown. Croatian History Museum, HPM-MRNH-F-2560.

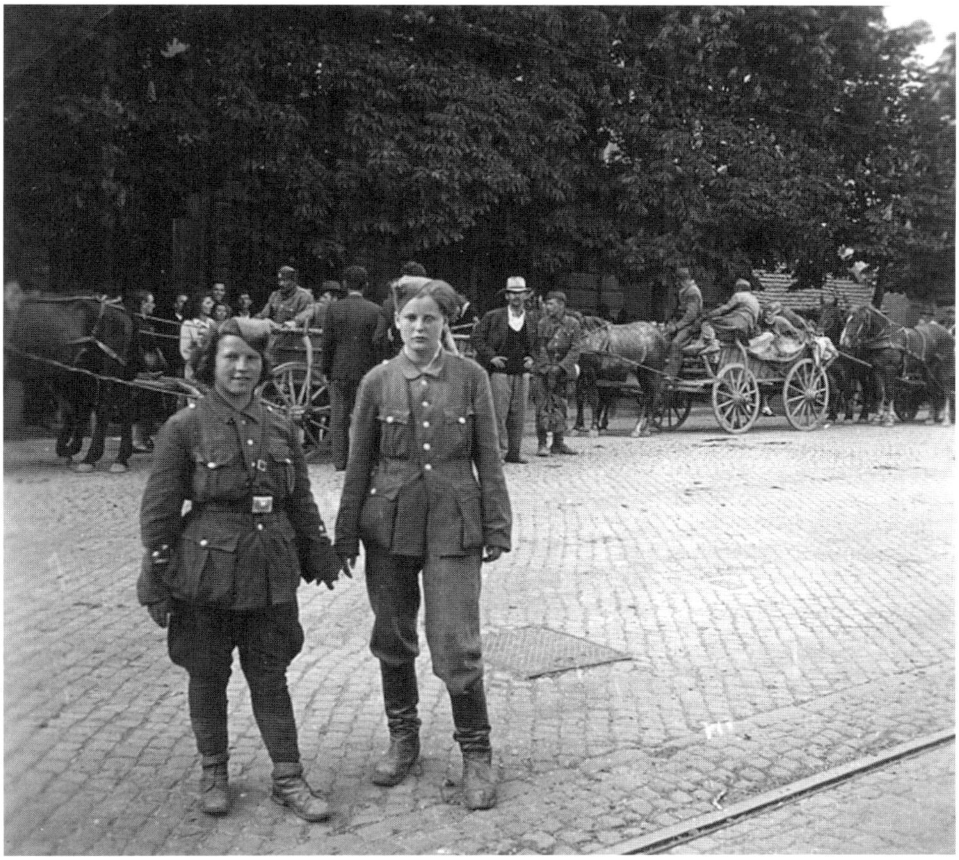

The Yugoslav Army entering Zagreb, Maksimirska St., May 1945.
Photo: 'Zaza'. Zagreb City Museum.

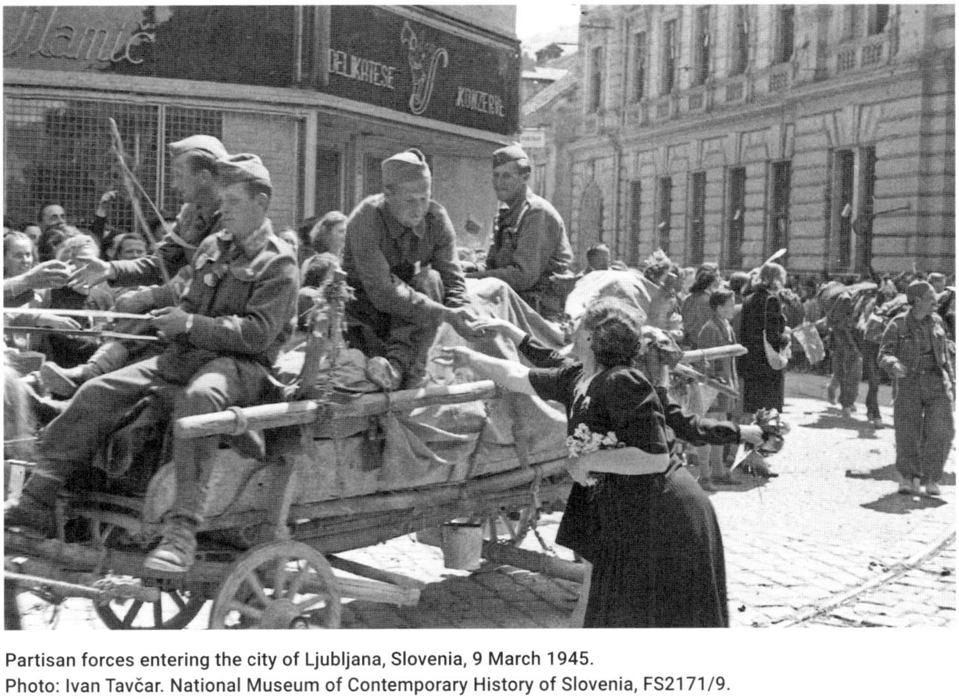

Partisan forces entering the city of Ljubljana, Slovenia, 9 March 1945.
Photo: Ivan Tavčar. National Museum of Contemporary History of Slovenia, FS2171/9.

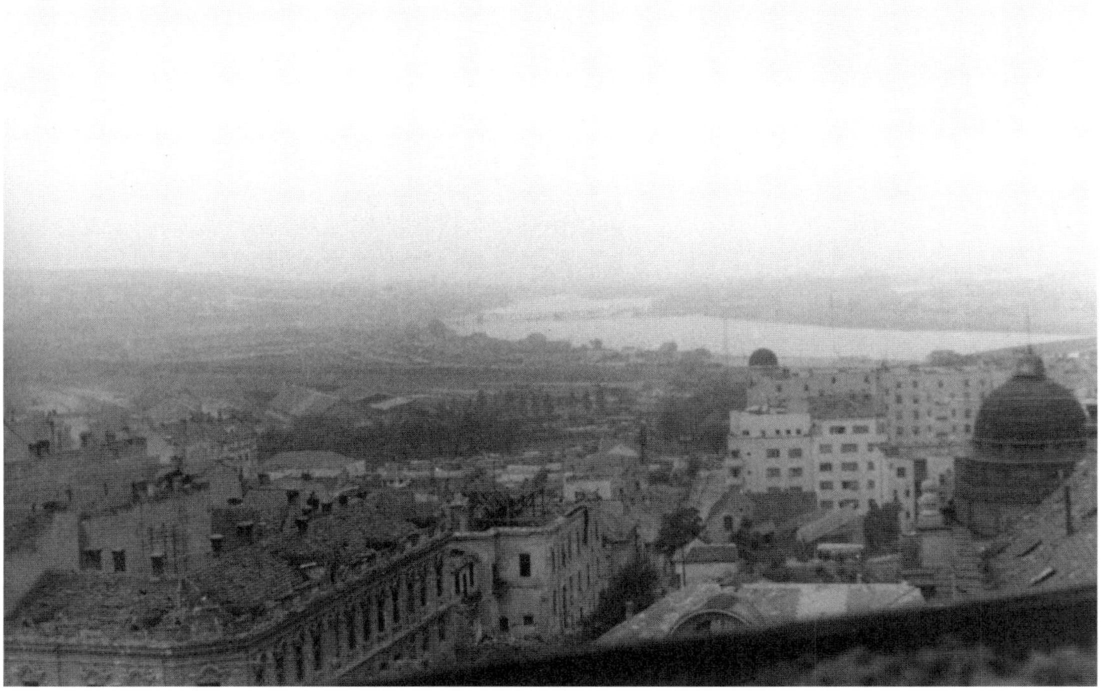

View of liberated Belgrade, 20 October 1944. Photographer unknown.
Military Museum Belgrade, 2264.

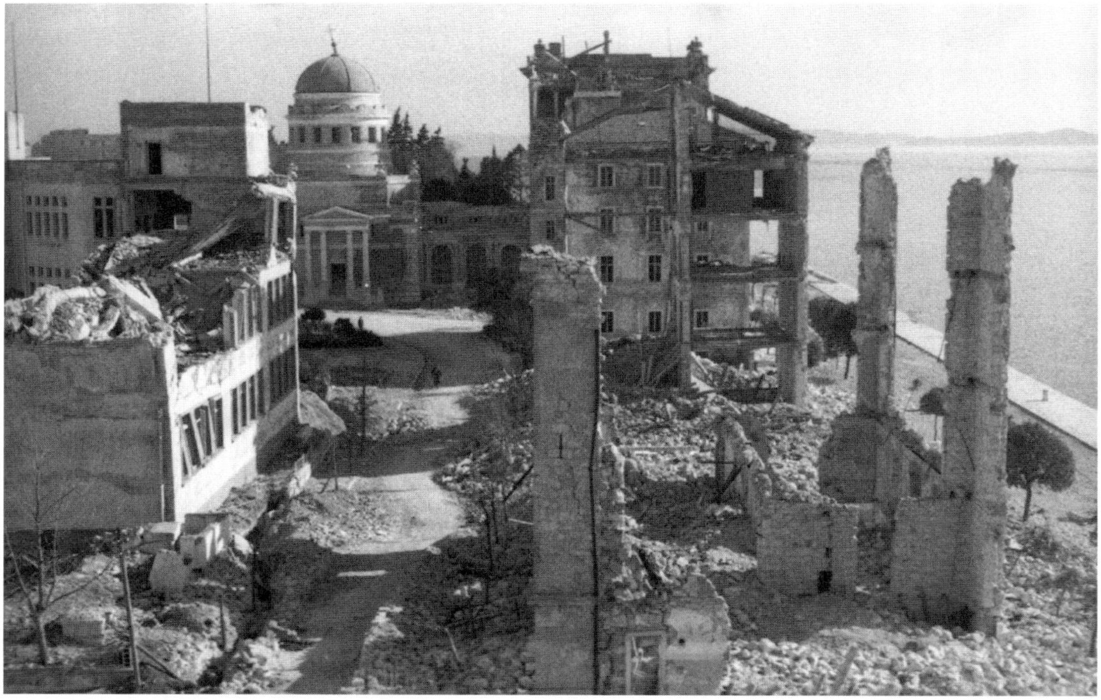

View from hospital of the ruins of Zadar, Croatia, after Allied bombardment. March 1945.
Photo: Dr Janez Milčinski. National Museum of Contemporary History of Slovenia, 1238/7.

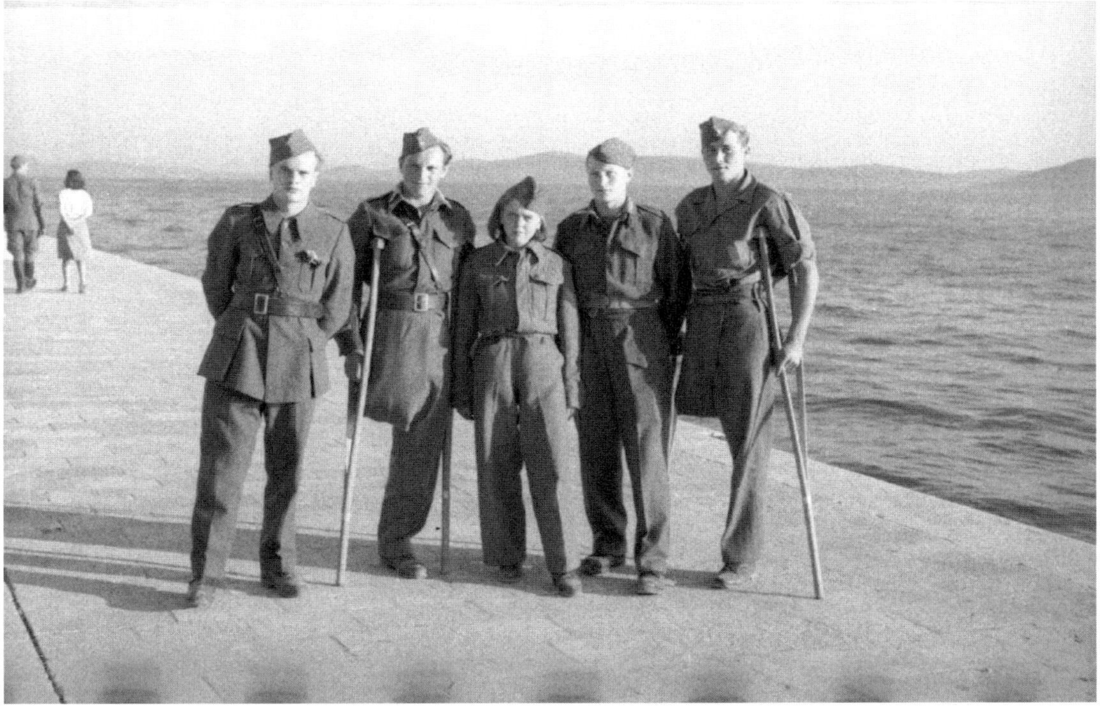

Wounded partisan fighters in Zadar, Croatia, 1944. Photo: Dr Janez Milčinski. National Museum of Contemporary History of Slovenia, 1241/11.

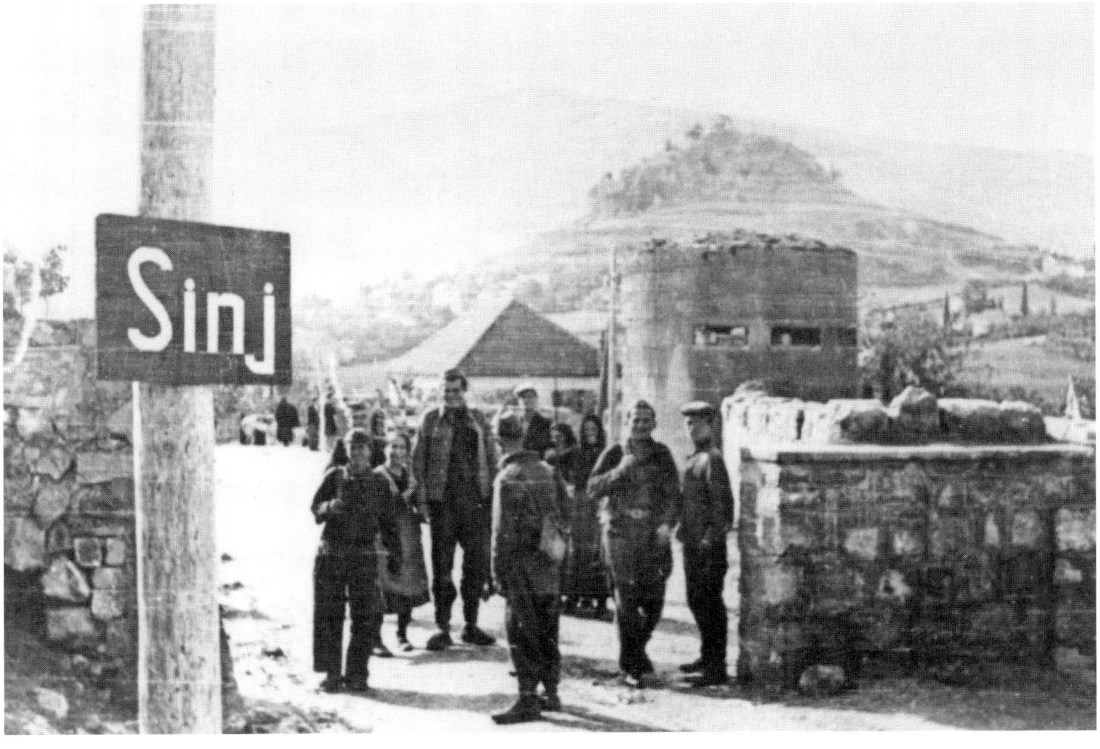

A group of fighters from the Eighth Dalmatian Brigade of the Twentieth Dalmatian Division in liberated Sinj, 25 October 1944. Photographer unknown. Military Museum Belgrade, 8453.

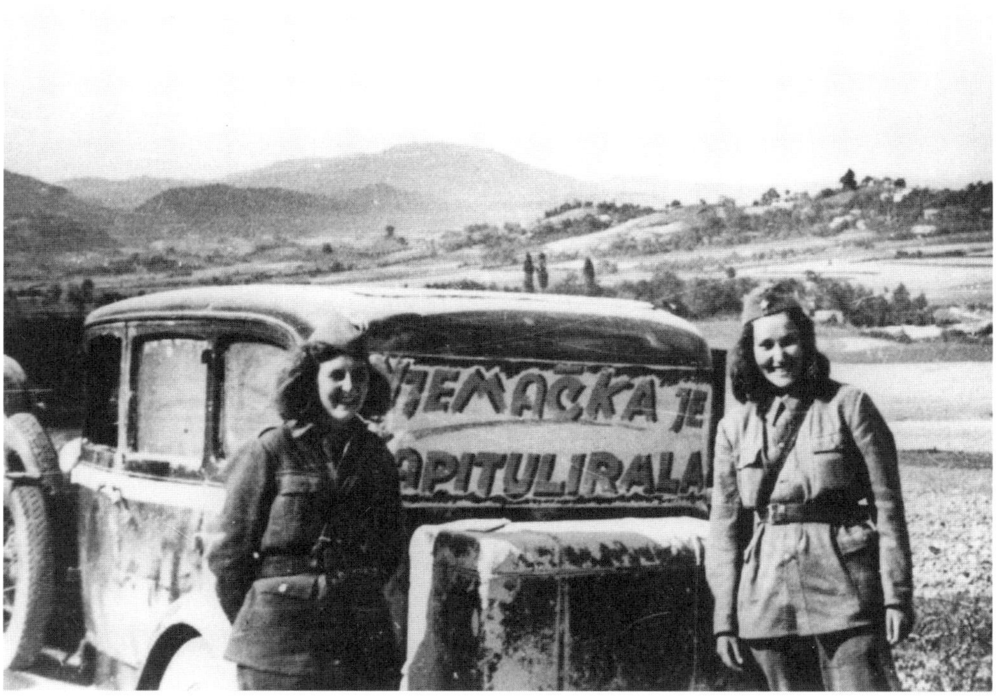

Fighters from the Tenth Krajina Brigade in Krašić, Croatia, on the way from Karlovac to Zidani Most, May 1945. Photographer unknown. History Museum of Bosnia and Herzegovina, FNOB 6144.

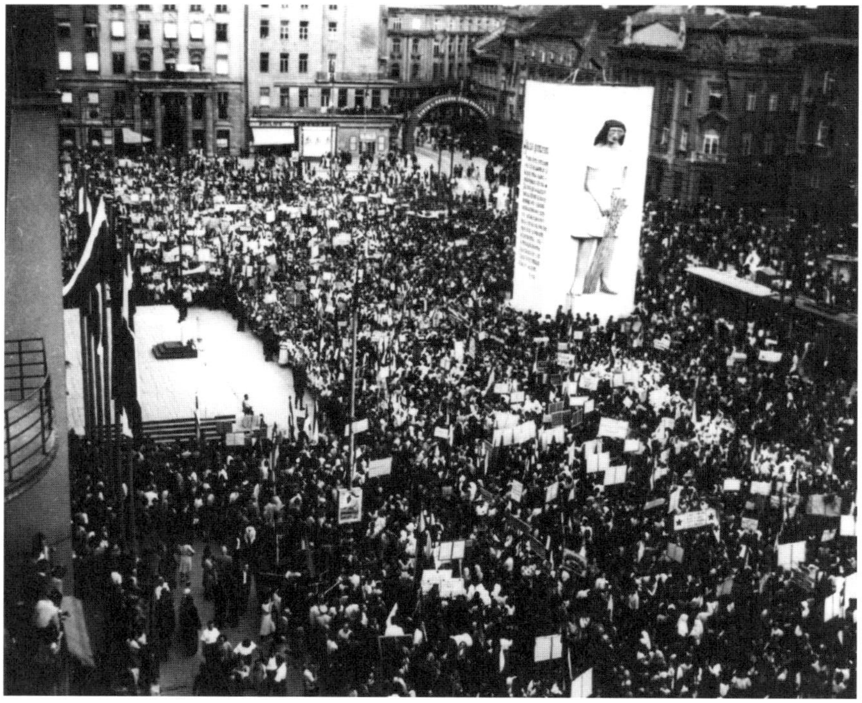

Rally in Zagreb on Trg Republike Hrvatske (Republic of Croatia Square) during the First Congress of the Anti-Fascist Women's Front in 1945. Photographer unknown. History Museum of Bosnia and Herzegovina, FNOB 10700.

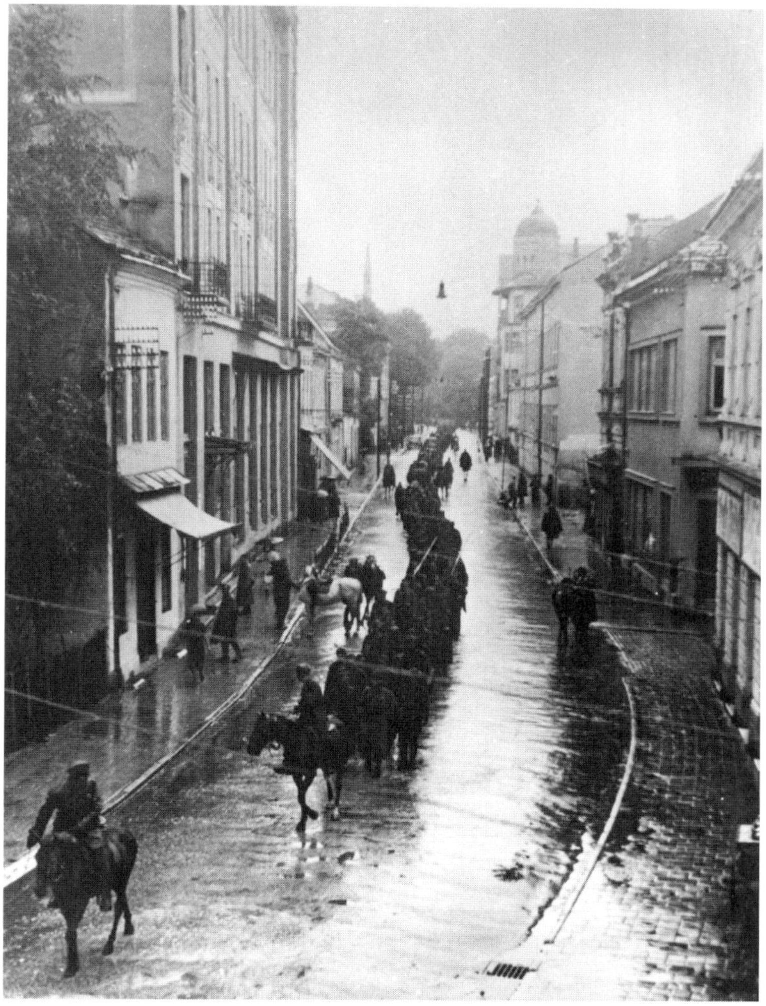

People's Liberation Army entering Tuzla, 17 September 1944. Photographer unknown. History Museum of Bosnia and Herzegovina, FNOB 19424.

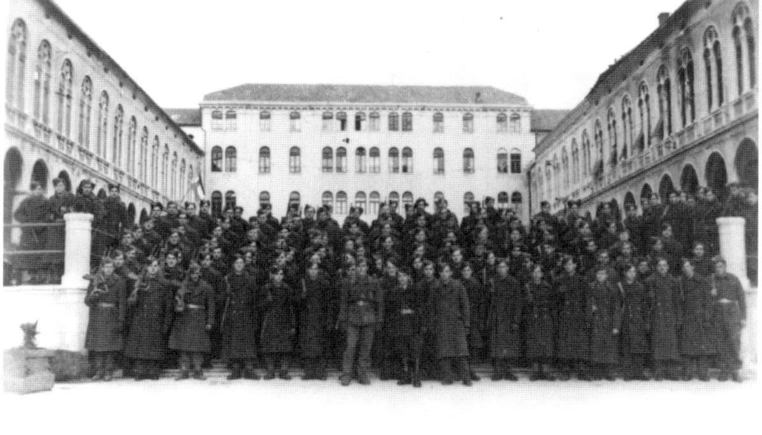

The First Company of the Third Battalion of the Fifth Overseas Brigade, Split, Croatia, January 1945. Photographer unknown. Museum of Recent History, Celje FZ2960.

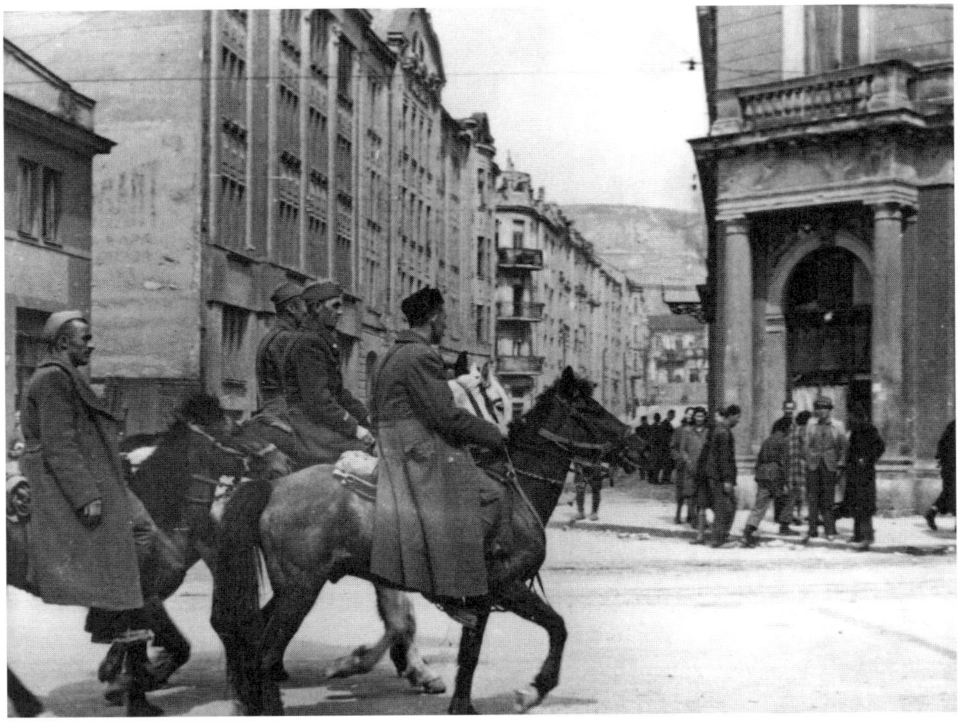

Rally during the liberation of Sarajevo in the neighbourhood of Marijin dvor.
Photo: Ivica Lisac. History Museum of Bosnia and Herzegovina, FNOB 10831.

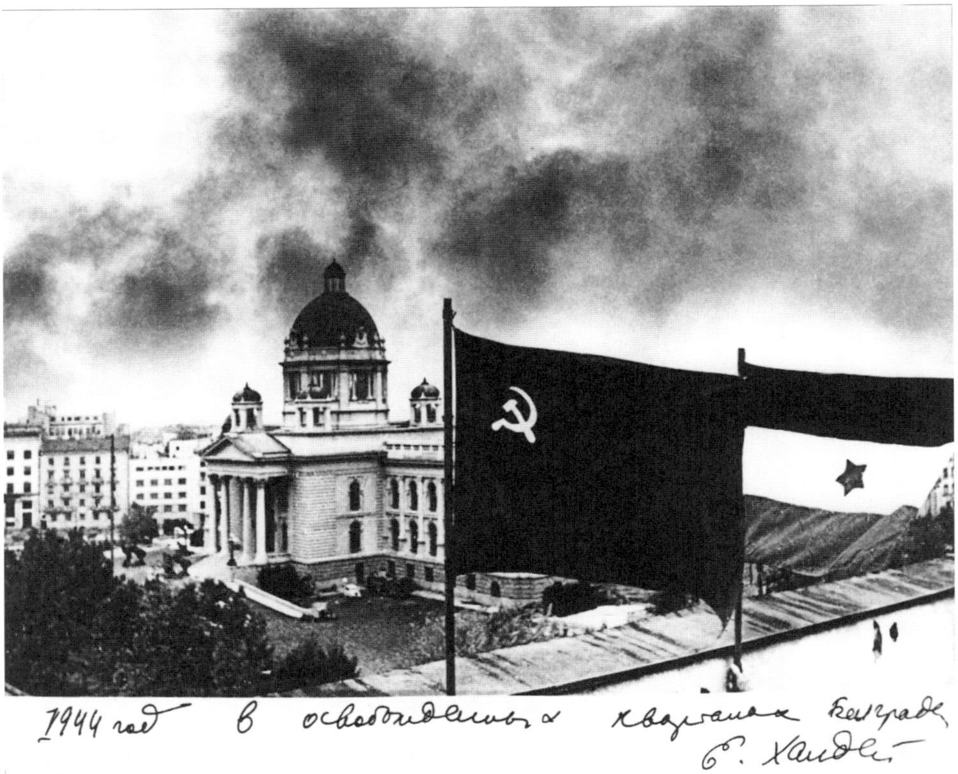

In liberated Belgrade, 1944. Photographer unknown. Museum of Yugoslavia, III-7466.

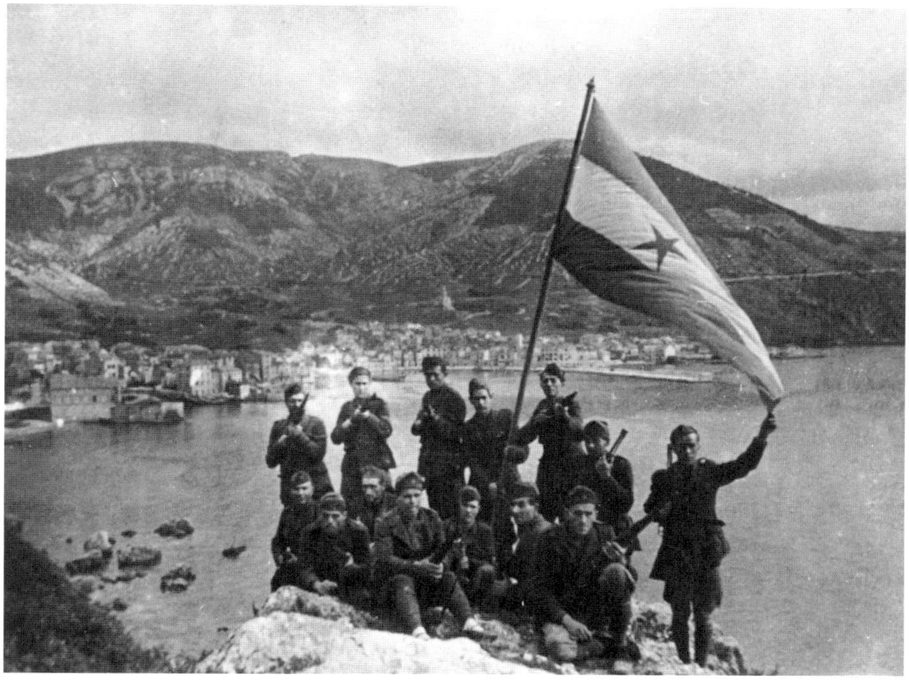

A group of fighters from the People's Liberation Army after the surrender of Italy in liberated Komiža on the island of Vis. Photographer unknown. Central Committee of League of Communists of Yugoslavia Collection (CK SKJ).

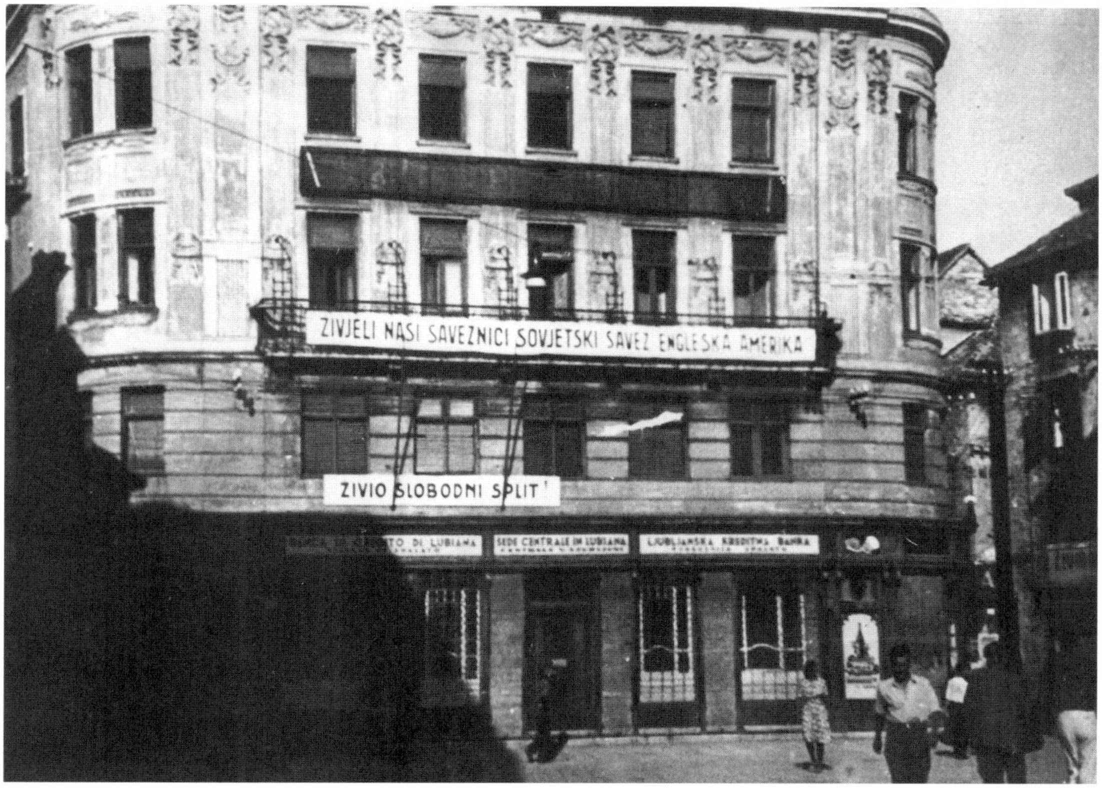

Slogans on the People's Square in liberated Split. Photographer unknown.

Working with the Allies

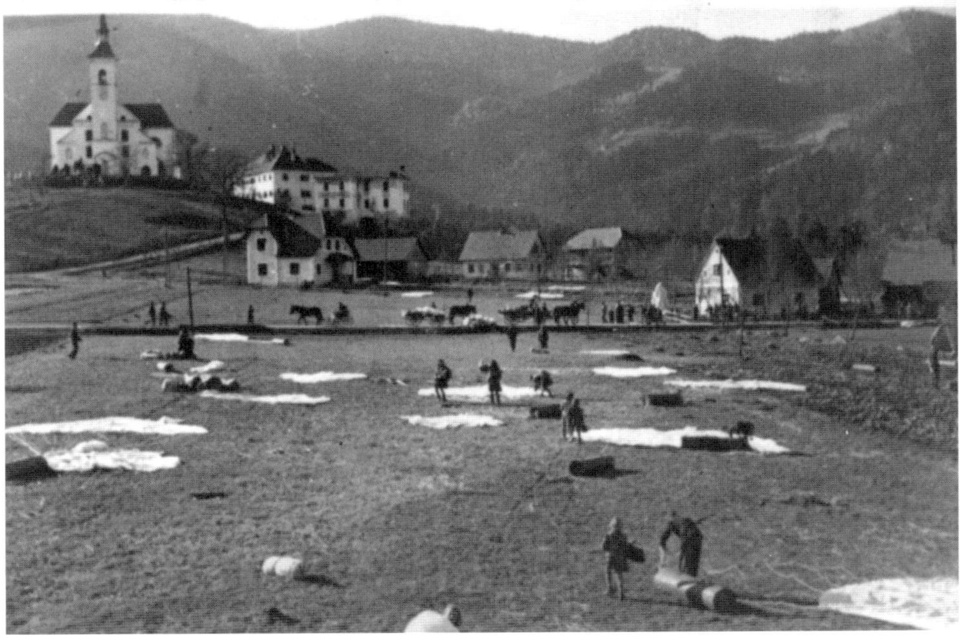

Allied help touching down on liberated territory, Radmirje, Slovenia. Photographer unknown. Museum of Recent History, Celje, FZ2 1580.

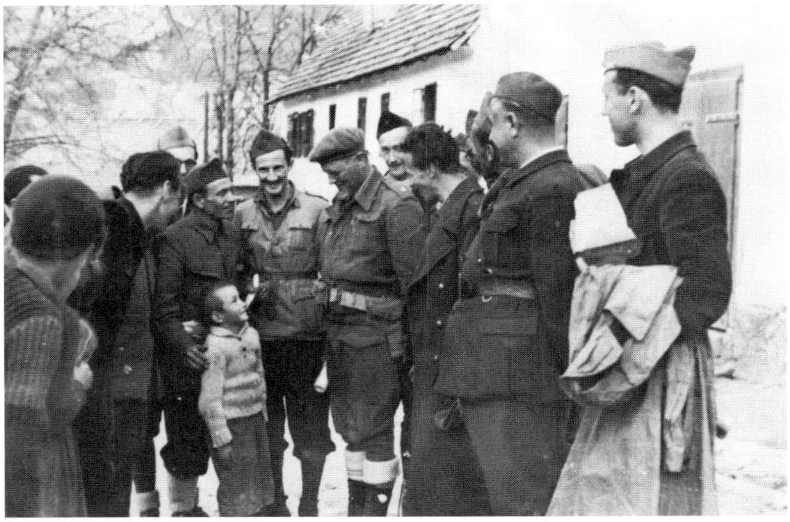

Randolph Churchill (centre) of the British military mission with Partisan military and political leaders, including Joža Horvat, Andrija Hebrang, Leo Mates, Dr Mladen Iveković and Vicko Maslov, Slunj, Croatia, spring 1944. Photo: Photography Service of ZAVNOH. Croatian History Museum, HPM-MRNH-A-2601 f23 32a s.

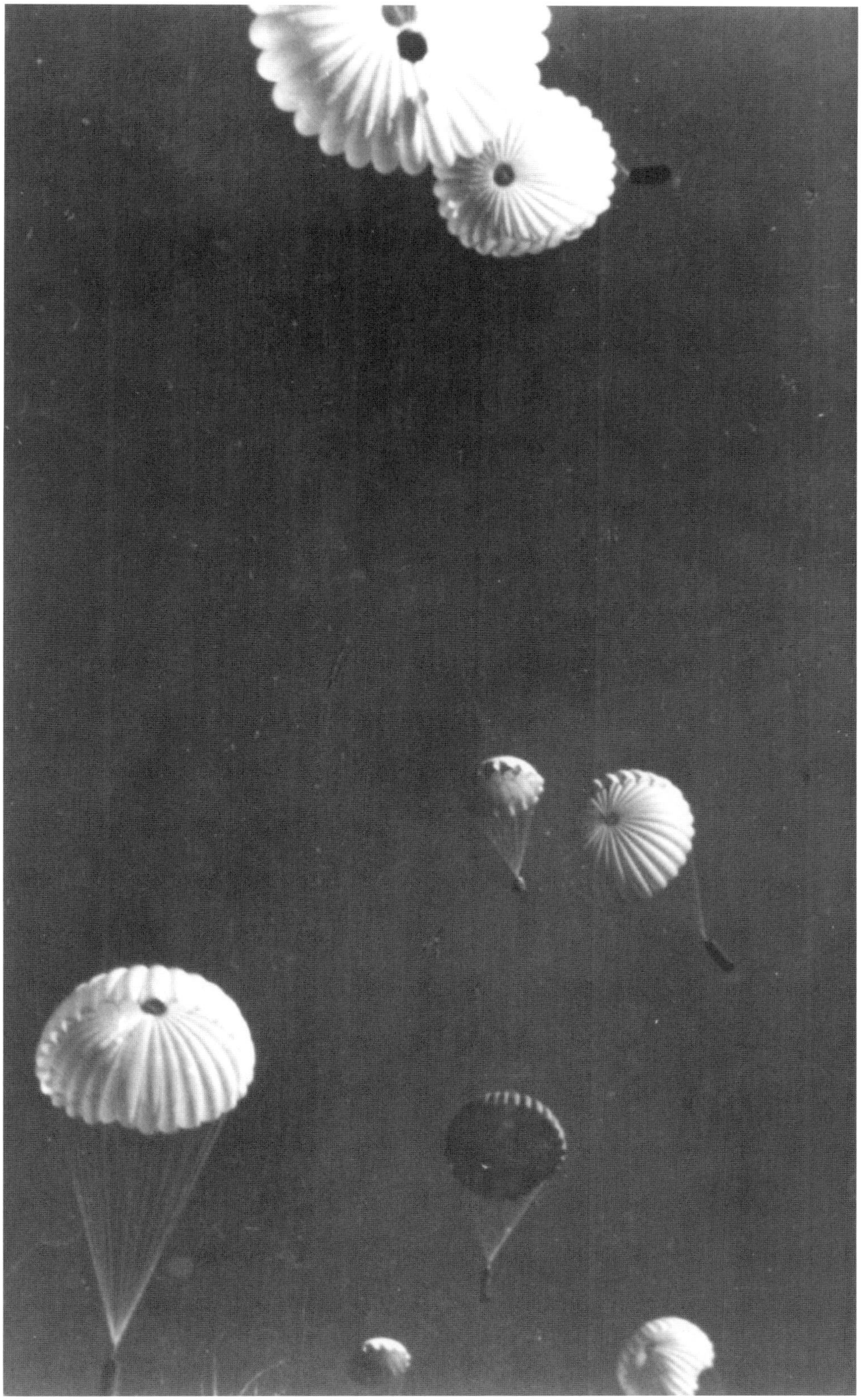

Allied help landing on liberated territory. Photographer unknown. Museum of Recent History, Celje, FZ2 1585.

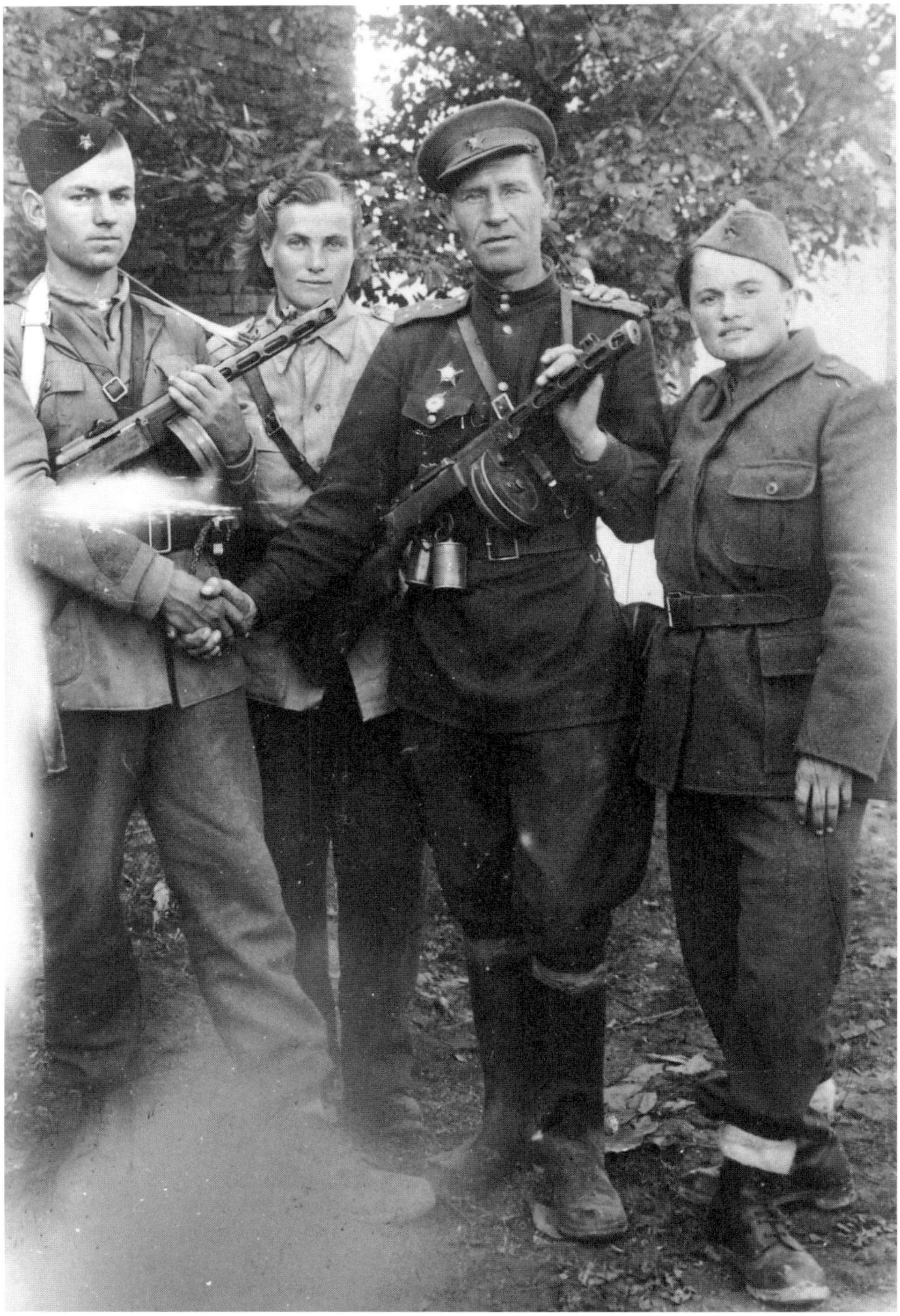

A meeting of fighters from the Eighth Montenegrin Brigade with soldiers from the Red Army, Kosmaj, Serbia, 1944. Photographer unknown. (Reproduced for the Museum of the Revolution of Yugoslav Peoples in March 1962), Museum of Yugoslavia.

Studio Photography after Partisan Victory

Towards the end of the war, when victory was in sight, a special kind of photography emerged outside the official production channels of Partisan photography but nevertheless inextricably intertwined with it. This was now the photography of victors and anyone else who felt the need to immortalise their personal participation in the historic events by visiting a photo studio. In this way, they recorded the historical moment with their co-fighters for posterity. Most of these photographs were taken in photo studios belonging to local photographers. After the liberation of Belgrade, Zagreb and all other cities, photo stores were often filled to the brim with soldiers eager to be photographed.[1] This was the case, for example, in Koprivnica, Croatia, where soldiers stood in long lines to get their photograph taken. What is especially interesting about these photographs is that they show ordinary soldiers whose likenesses are captured in the artificial environment of the photographic studio. The aesthetics of these stylised images are now determined by professional portrait photographers practicing their craft on their own terms.

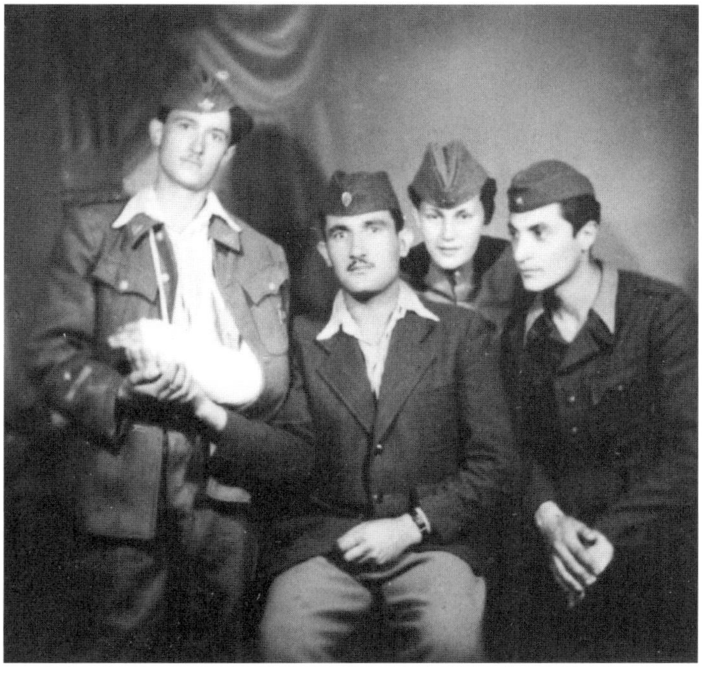

Recuperating casualties from the Seventh Krajina Brigade, near Gornji Vakuf, central Bosnia. Photographer unknown. History Museum of Bosnia and Herzegovina, FNOB 1360.

1 Bogdan S Bosiočić, 21. *slavonska udarna brigade*, Belgrade 1981, p. 95.

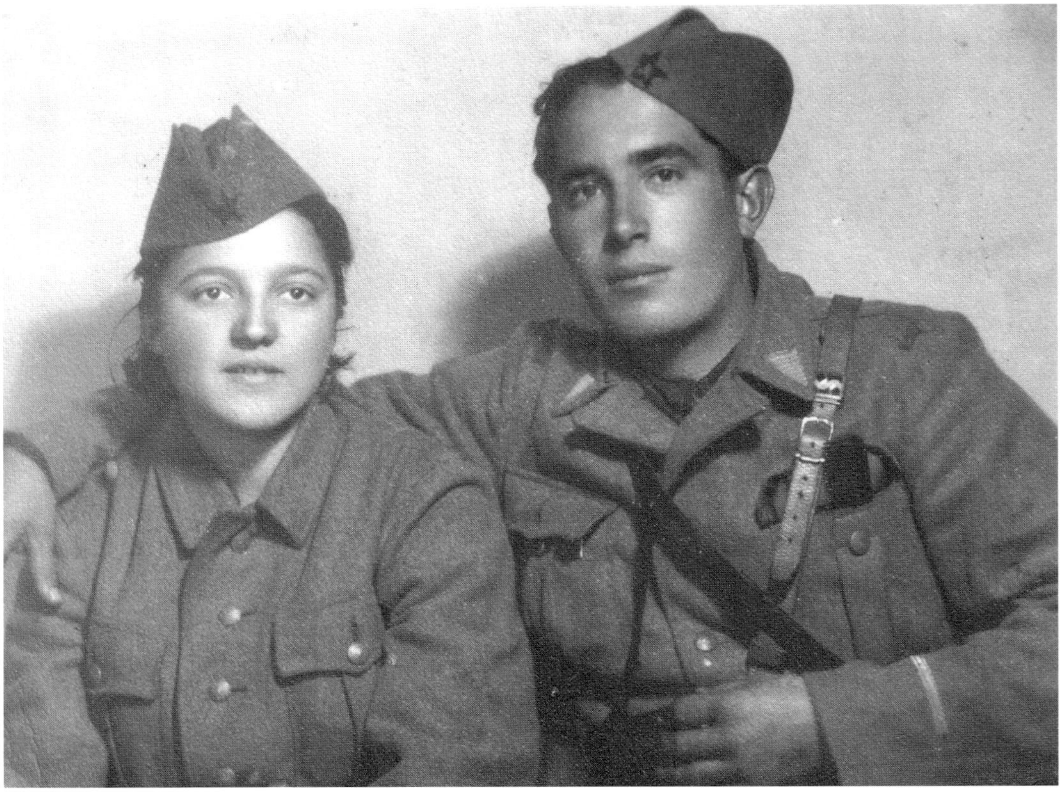

Photo taken after the liberation of Belgrade, 26 October 1944. Reproduced with the kind permission of Marko Strpić.

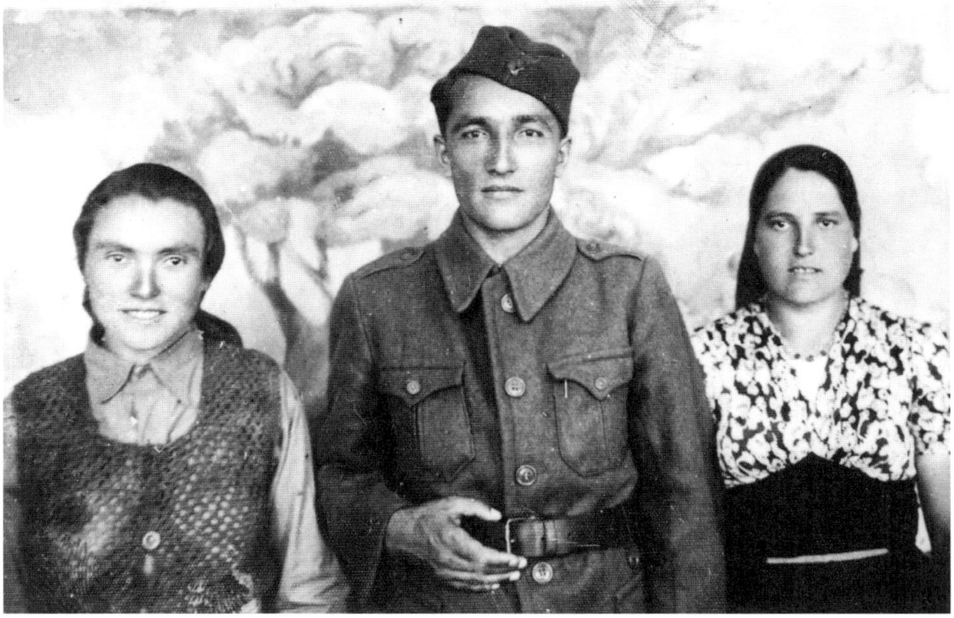

Kosa Pilipović (left), born 1919, homemaker in Donji Jelovac until she was captured in the Kozara Offensive and taken to a concentration camp in Croatia, where she was incarcerated for two to three months. After her release and return to Donji Jelovac she was elected councillor for the popular government and committee member of the Anti-Fascist Women's Front in late 1942. Pilipović joined the Communist Party of Yugoslavia on 15 February 1943 and became a company commander for Donji Jelovac in the Zoja Brigade. Photographer unknown. History Museum of Bosnia and Herzegovina, FNOB 1509.

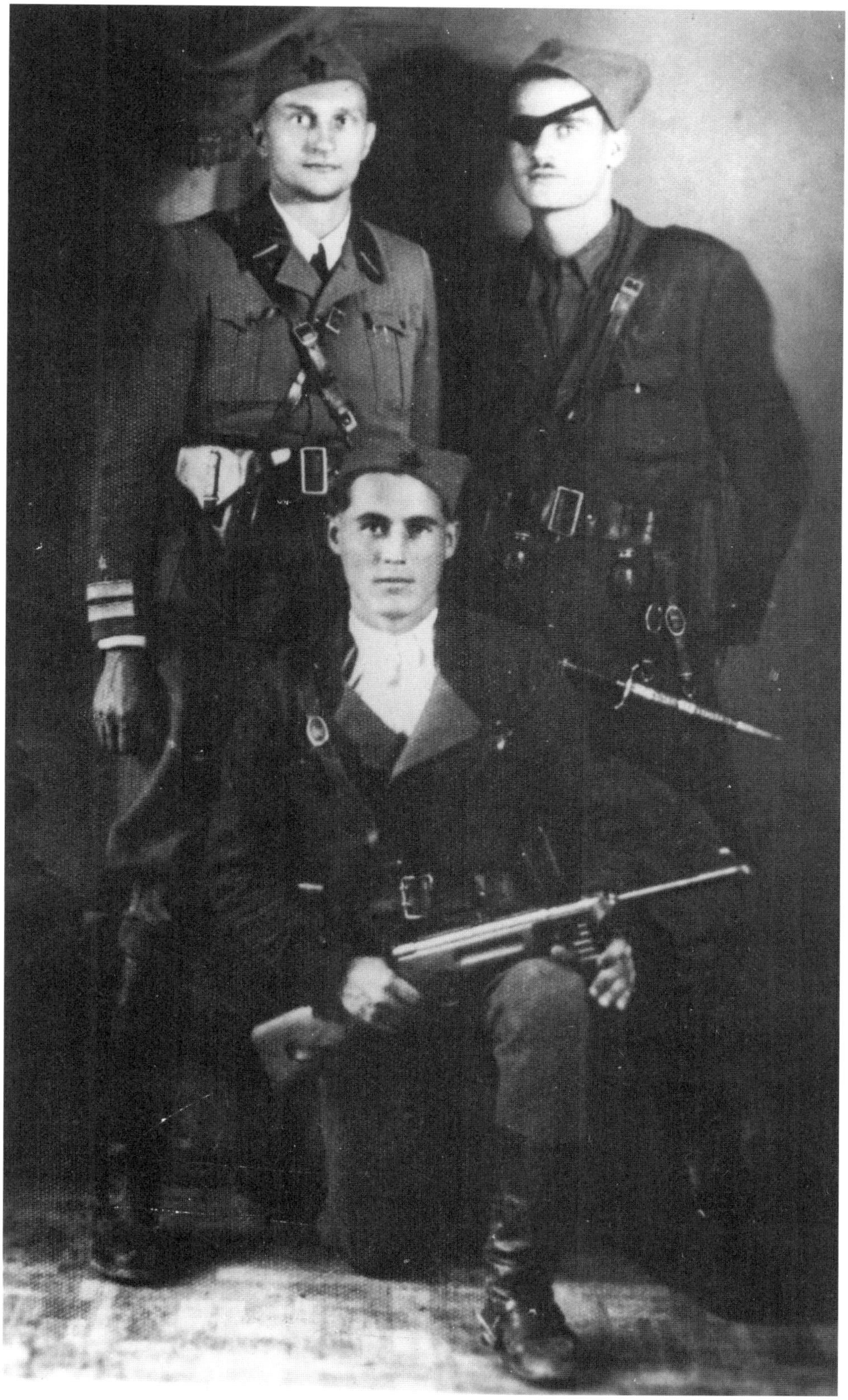

Todor Vujasinović-Tošo (left) with two comrades. Photographer unknown.
Historical Museum of Bosnia and Herzegovina, FNOB 4602.

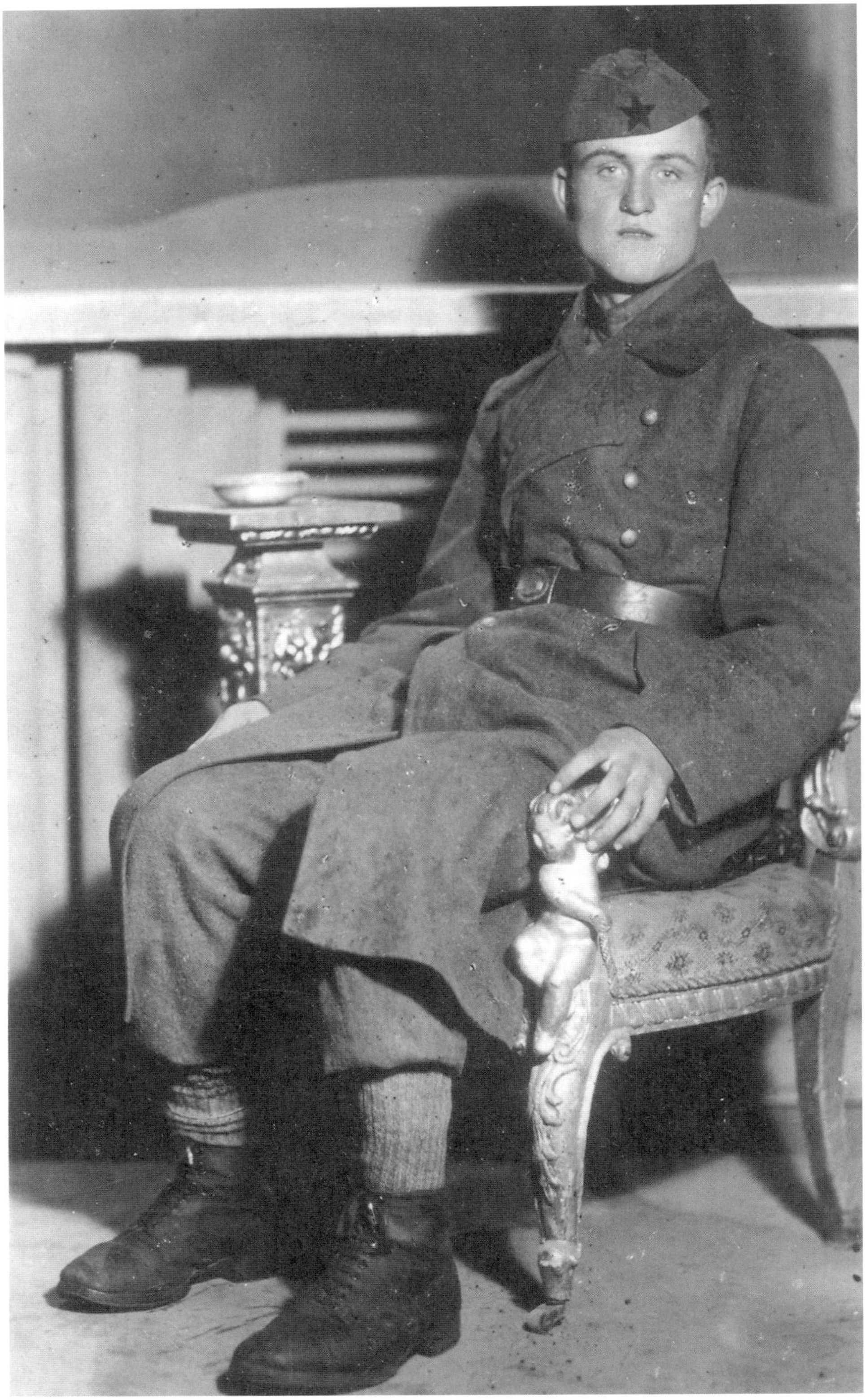

'A memento and long-lasting memory of comrade Dragan Anđelić Anti', 19 October 1944.
Photographer unknown. Reproduced with the kind permission of Marko Strpić.

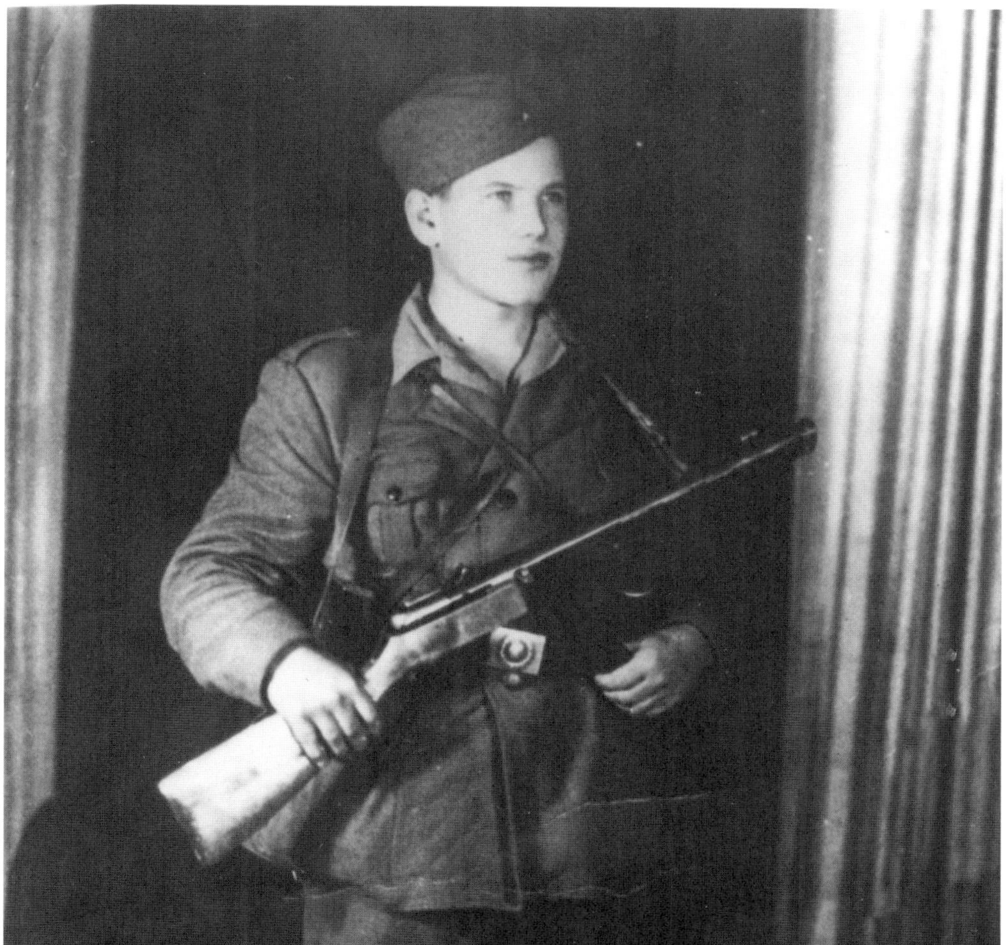

A courier for the Third Kragujevac Battalion of the First Proletarian Brigade, 1944. Photographer unknown. History Museum of Bosnia and Herzegovina, FNOB 4707.

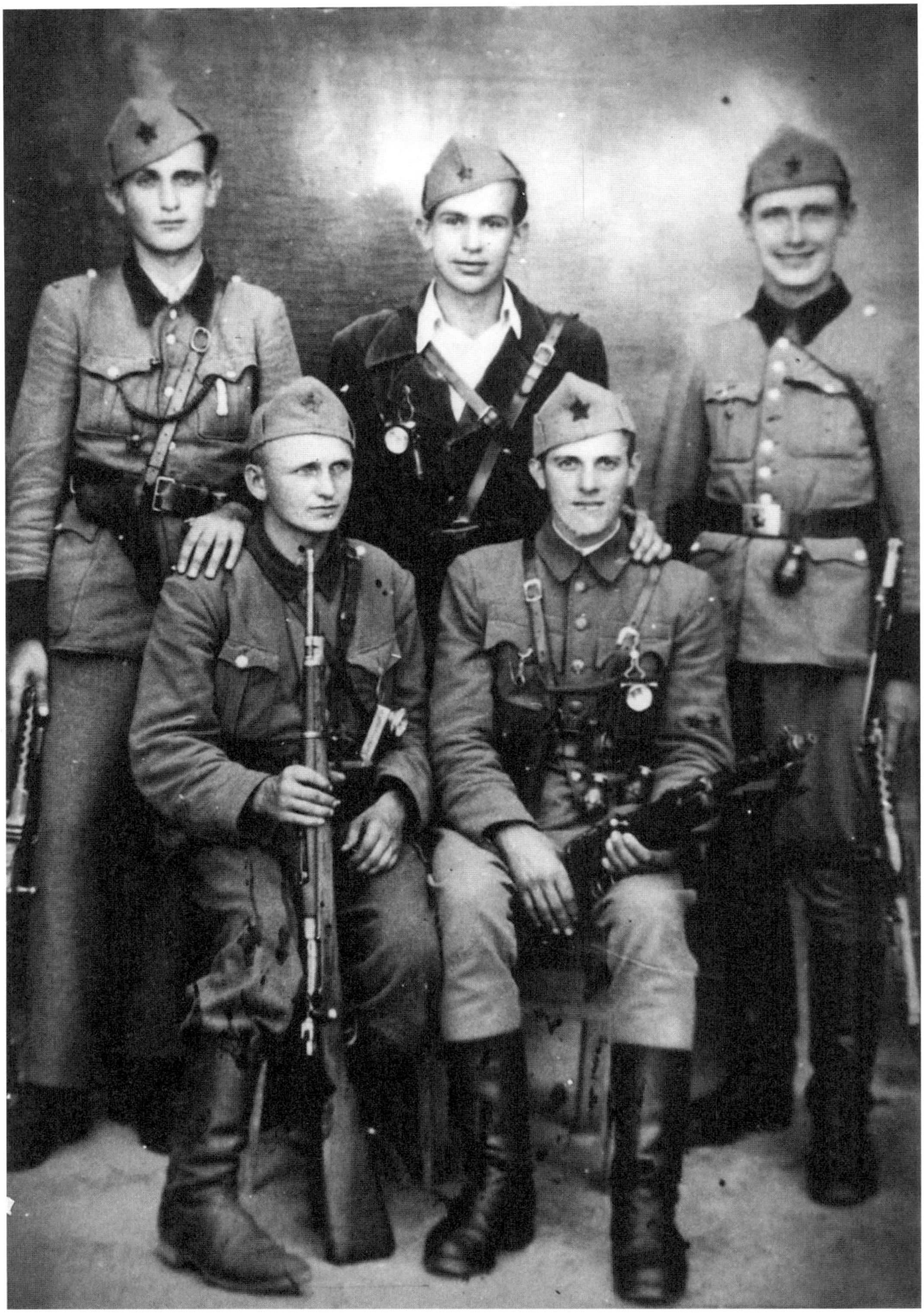

Mirko Vorkapić, information officer of the Osijek Detachment with his group from the Sixth Slavonian Corps, autumn 1943. Photographer unknown. Zagreb City Museum.

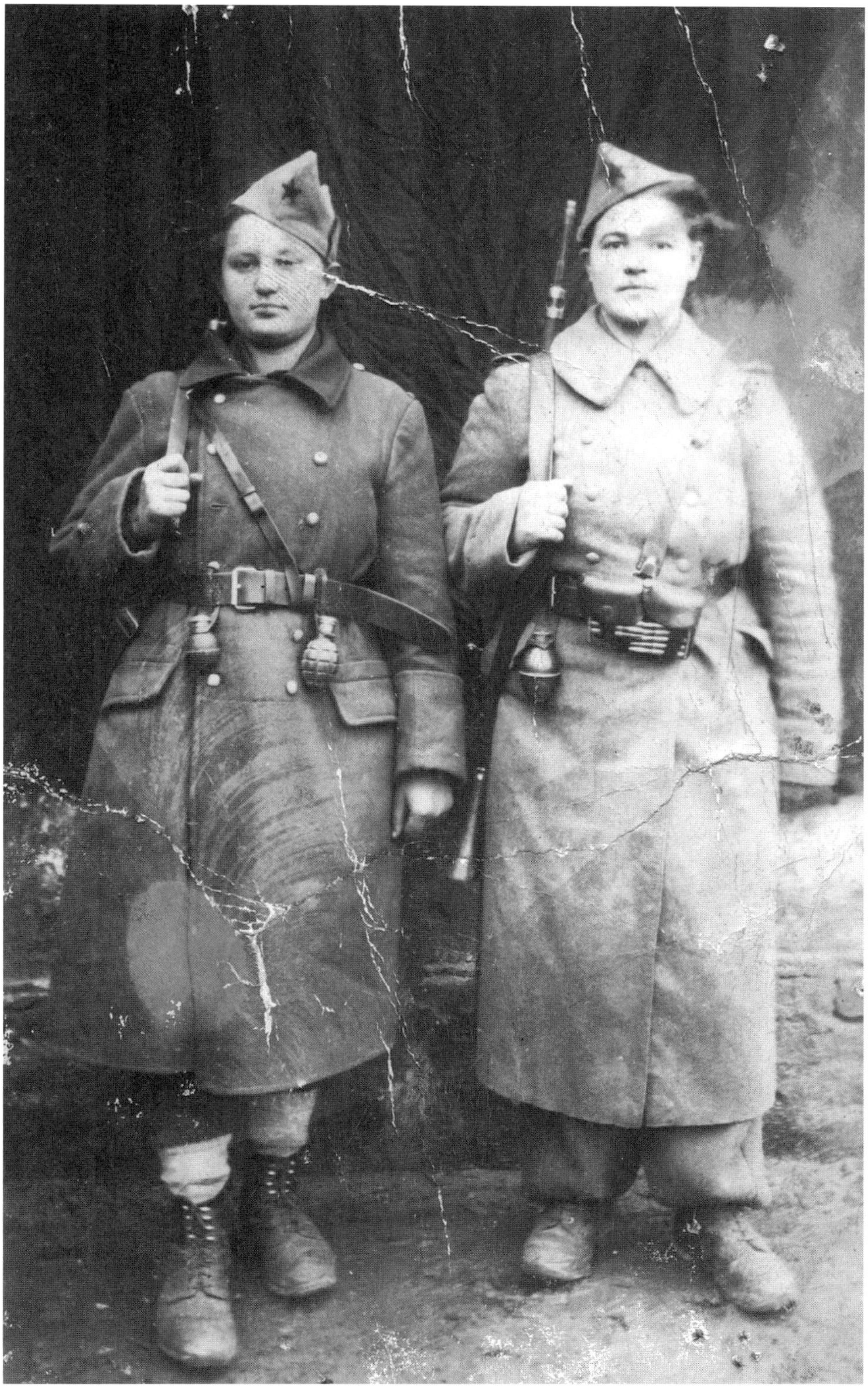

Two hospital nurses of the First Battalion, Second Moslavina Brigade: Vlahović Milka from the village of Rogoža and Katica Baloch, killed in 1944 during the bombardment of Dubrava, the same year this photograph was taken. Photographer unknown. Zagreb City Museum.

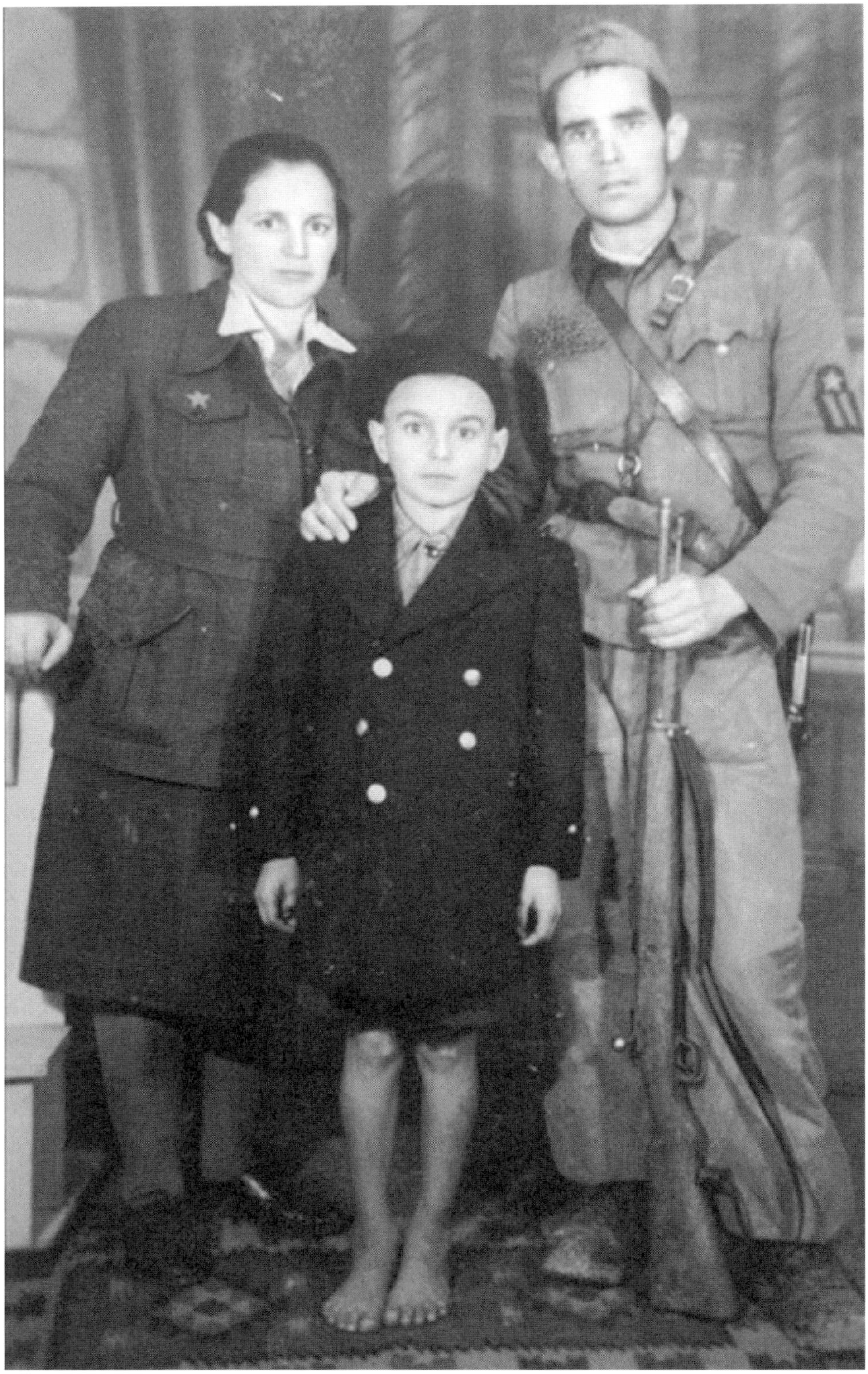

Unknown sitters in liberated Tuzla, October 1943. Photographer unknown.

Private Photographs

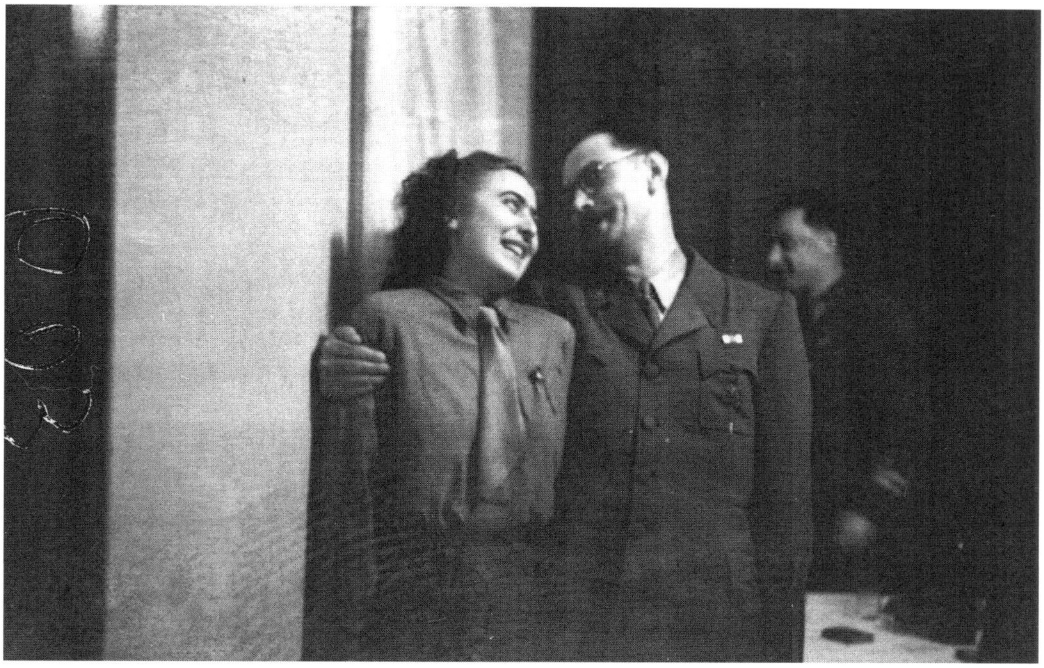

Alenka Gerlovič and Franc Leskovšek-Luka in high spirits, Črnomelj, Slovenia, 3 April 1945. Photo: Stane Lenardič. National Museum of Contemporary History of Slovenia, TN603/6.

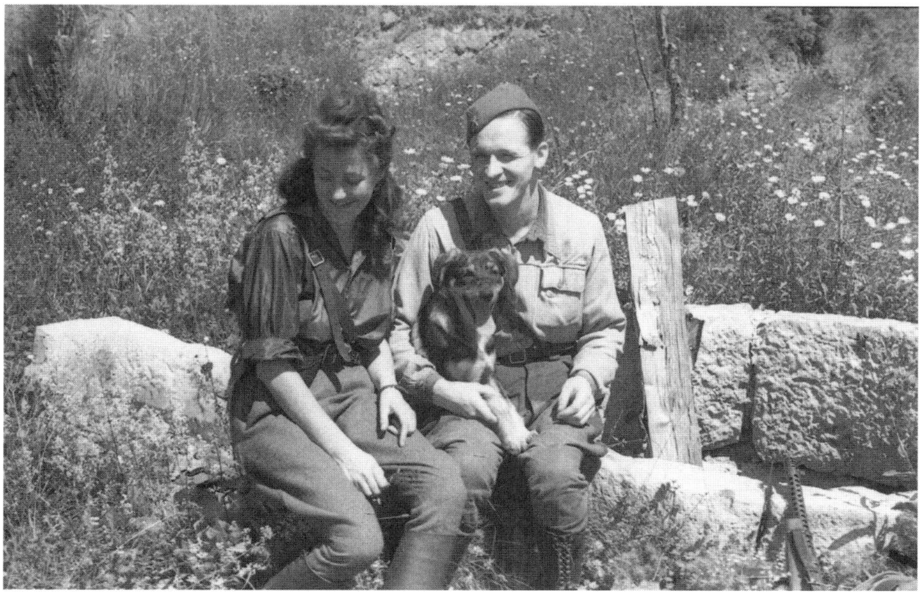

Dr Marija Jeras and an unknown Partisan woman. Photo: Dr Janez Milčinski. National Museum of Contemporary History of Slovenia, 1232/32.

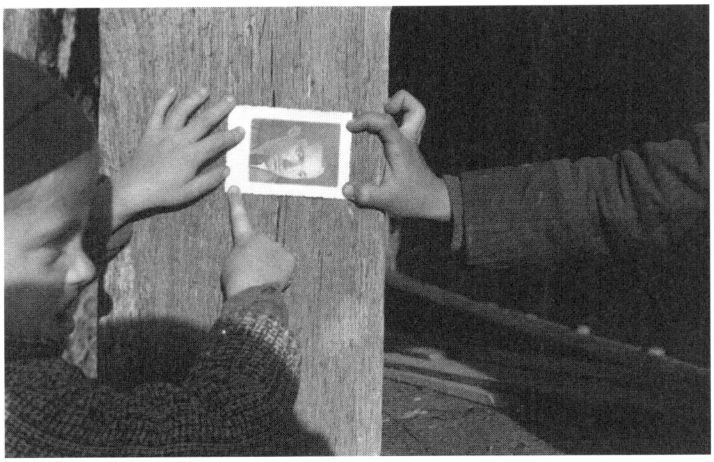

The private mementos of Partisans from Ribnica, Slovenia, October 1943. Photo: Vinko Bavec. National Museum of Contemporary History Slovenia, TN52/17.

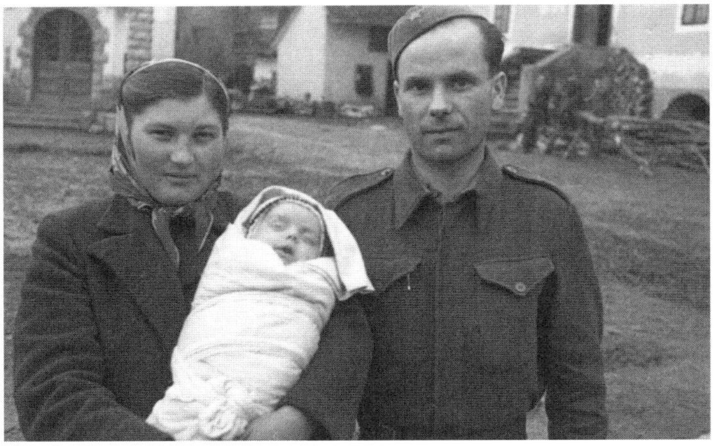

A father and mother with their newborn child. Photographer unknown. National Museum of Contemporary History Slovenia, TN691a/35.

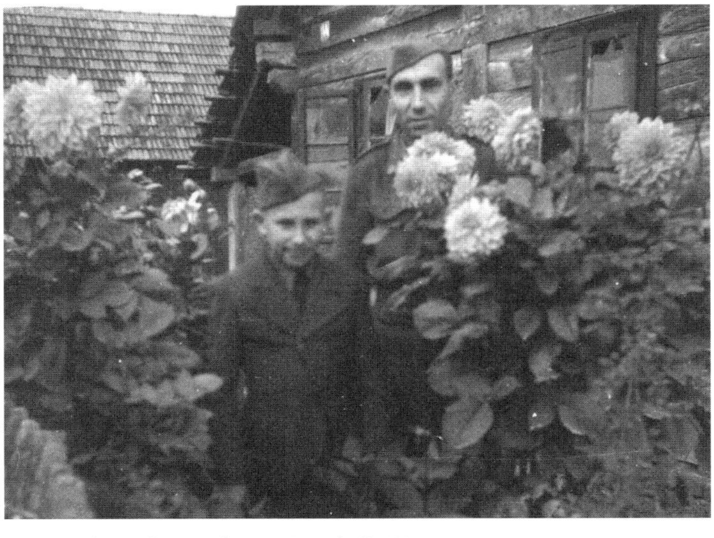

Photographer and year unknown. Zagreb City Museum.

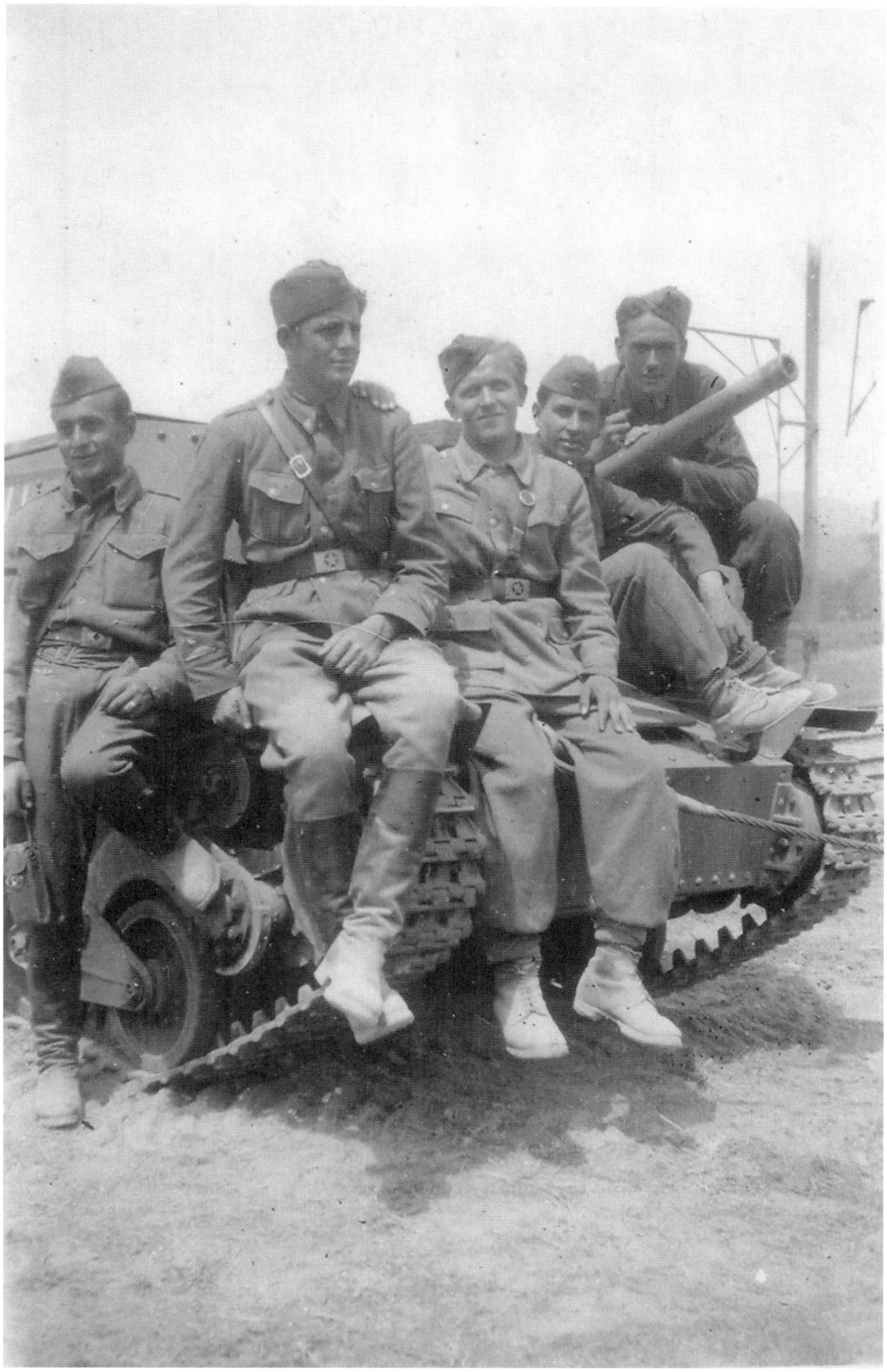

Ante Alerić (centre right). Reproduced with the kind permission of Marko Strpić.

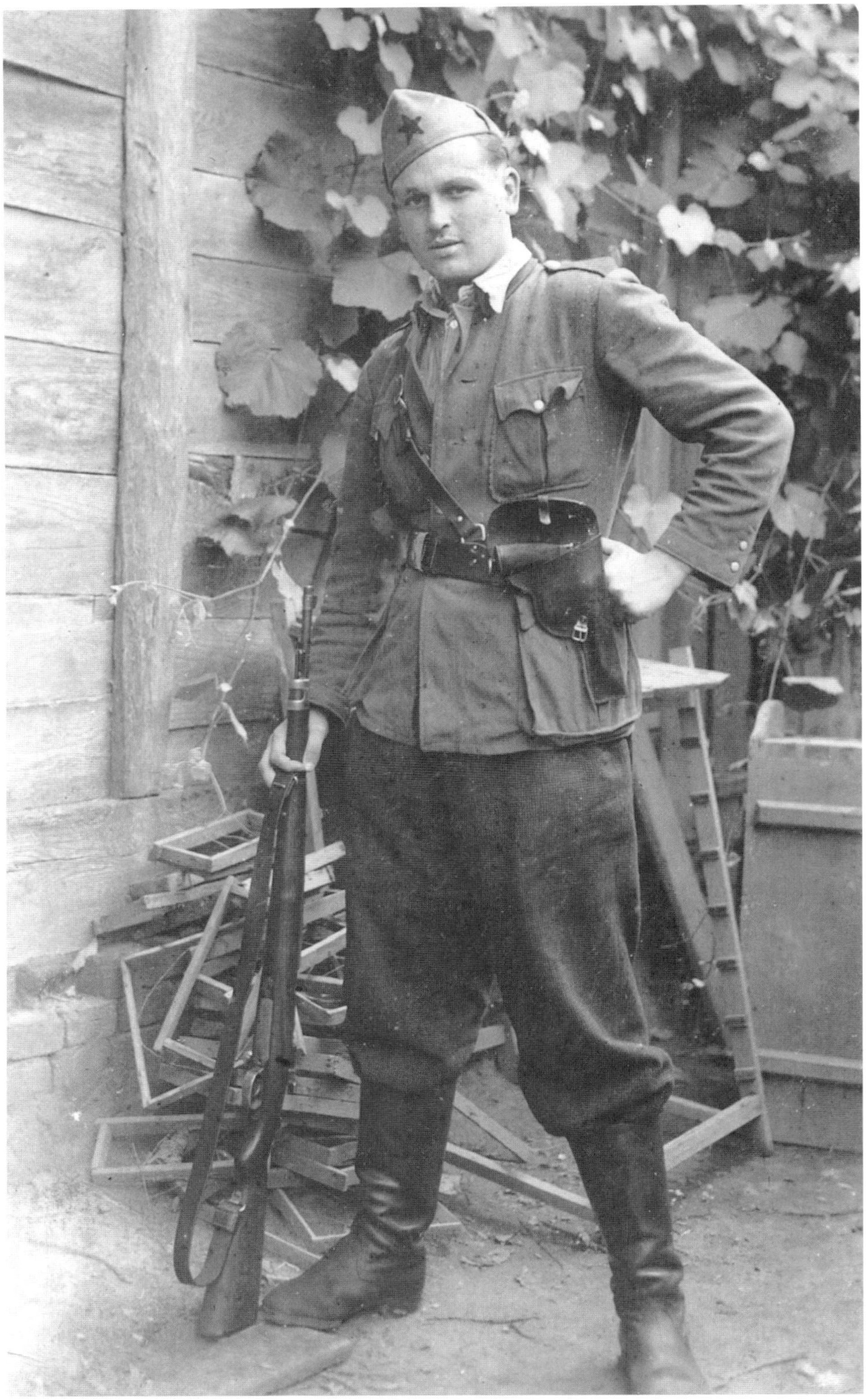

Zvonko Ivanković-Vonta, an instructor for the First Party Course for Moslavina, Ninth Zagreb Corps. Photographer unknown. Zagreb City Museum.

Conclusion

Tomorrow they will be called.
How will they get there, how will they reply to Tjentište?
Tell me, girl, how will they reply?
In photography's wondrous landscapes there are no human voices.
No call.
No reply.[1]

This book has researched the historical framework in which Partisan photography arose: its organisation, contents and functions. From a present-day perspective, we have also set Partisan photography against the wider backdrop of activist struggles that have occurred since the Second World War, and which continue to this day. Partisan photographic production was in effect the manifestation of Walter Benjamin's belief in the 'democratic potential of the photographic medium and its instrumentalising role in the radical critique of bourgeois society, in photographs that appeared simultaneously alongside the phenomenon of socialism because of their inherent reproducibility and accessibility to a wider audience.'[2] This is because, besides professional photographers, amateur photographers also matured into the profession in the Partisan movement, with many becoming fully fledged professional photographers later on. Caught at the interstices of culture, propaganda and documentation, photographs served all these purposes, and photography's function cannot be viewed unambiguously from one of these positions alone. The idea of liberation is only possible when interpreted through the ideal of building a completely free society in which the camera is understood as materially embodied ideology. Photography transforms art into a revolutionary force. In other words, because of photography's realist quality, it is exceptionally close to realism in literature. However, Marx opposed the idea that art should only be an educational instrument for socialist propaganda.[3] Only later did Benjamin's camera and writing affirm a different meaning, whereby photography is perceived as a true form of revolutionary art. From this angle, Benjamin's camera is interpreted as materially embodied ideology and also 'as a symbol of a "historical life process" that could stop ideology'.[4]

1 Čedomir Minderović, 'Fotografija', in: *Zbornik radova Sutjeska*, vol. 5, Belgrade 1961, p. 576.
2 Antigoni Memou, *Photography and Social Movements: From the Globalisation of the Movement (1968) to the Movement Against Globalisation (2001)*, Manchester 2013, p. 163.
3 W. J. Thomas Mitchell, *The Rhetoric of Iconoclasm*, Chicago 1967, p. 179.
4 W. J. Thomas Mitchell, *Iconology: Image, Text, Ideology*, Chicago 1986, p. 181.

It is important to mention that many of the photographs in this book are not attributed to a single individual photographer, and this should not be viewed as a shortcoming. In the wartime struggle against fascism, most photographers were guided by a common idea and motivation, and created collective work with a clear goal. Theirs was a collective body acting together. Such collectivism can be traced back to the artistic conflicts of the 1920s and 1930s, with an elite individualism present at one pole and collective action at the other.

The Partisan archive emerged during wartime, as the wartime emergence of academic institutions also attests. One of the first motions passed in December 1942 in Bihać by the Executive Committee of the Anti-Fascist Council for the People's Liberation of Yugoslavia was on the founding statutes of the 'People's University', which 'became a unified type of vocational college aimed at the entire population and the site of the highest level of tertiary education available'.[5]

In Slovenia, for example, today's National Museum of Contemporary History is a direct successor of the Museum of the People's Revolution, which was itself perhaps a successor of the Academic Institute established by the Executive Committee of the Liberation Front on 12 January 1944. Its aim was to gather archival, artistic and other historical materials on liberated territory. The Slovenian Partisans had an unusual position in the Partisan movement in that they were not directly supervised by the Supreme Command of the People's Liberation Army before 1944. This archive is one of the best-preserved and best-organised Partisan photography archives today. In Croatia, the State Anti-Fascist Council for the People's Liberation of Croatia (ZAVNOH) decided to found the Museum of the People's Liberation. On 3 September 1944, Mladen Iveković issued reports from ZAVNOH's information department to the district people's committees regarding the museum. They stated that they should gather printed matter, orders, objects, drawings, photographs and all possible remaining documentation for the purpose of building a museum archive.[6]

Indeed, the creation of a small photographic archive is one product that arose from writing and researching this book. The contextualisation I have provided will help future researchers, and it poses new questions about the role of photography in social movements – about its identity, value and social function. In the present-day environment on post-Yugoslav territory, and across Europe more widely, publishing such a book and archive is especially important in the struggle against the rehabilitation of fascist movements and the strengthening of right-wing parties across Europe. Marx correctly assumed that the photography industry would be an industry of the future. Now as never before, digital photography has replaced text, and the millions of photographs exchanged every day are an elementary means of communication. The language of photography is becoming the language of the current age, and it is assuming one of the central roles in the ideological struggle: 'Language is not a passive reflection of the real world; it is a path through which we represent and see it as "reality."'[7]

5 Dušan Nedeljković, 'Prosvetna reforma oslobodilačkog rata i revolucije u Bihaću u 1942.–1943.' in: *Bihaćka republika*, vol. 1, Nataša Todorović (ed.), Bihać 1965, p. 498.

6 ZAVNOH, *Zbornik dokumenata 1944*. Institut za historiju radničkog pokreta Hrvatske.

7 David Bate, *Photography: The Key Concepts*, Oxford 2009, p. 33.

How is the diverse meaning of these photographs encoded at present? Their meaning is locked in a struggle against revisionist narratives – a semiotic struggle for the figure of the freedom fighter, which others have attempted to depict as a terrorist. Nowadays a real political struggle is being waged over visual signifiers and representations of the world. It is my hope that this book will occupy a meaningful position in these struggles, because ideologies are represented through photography, as well as through other media. In the global world of capitalist exchange, photography archives have become commodities. Leading global photography archives, such as Getty Images, aim to establish control over imagery on a global scale via intellectual property relations. Such archives are unlikely to contain photographs that disseminate powerful political messages or record social struggles. In the Croatian context of the destruction of archives, especially during the 1990s, such systematic neglect and the incessant fabrication of bogus facts are hampered by the 'inconvenient' material presented in this book. The political ramifications of such an archive and its clear and unambiguous framing within the context of political struggle are urgently needed, indeed now more than ever. As Boris Buden writes: 'The vision with which and for which communists fought became our reality' and the present moment is defined by 'the disintegration of sovereign national states and the establishment of new forms of global sovereignty'[8]. The moment has arrived to use material such as presented here to question such a vision and grasp its former and present-day function. Memory and archives, as Gal Kirn has noted, are emptying out as the whole drama of events is being reduced to caricature: a heroic epic spectacle built into a state narrative or an existentialist psychological drama that calls for reconciliation with the collaborators.[9]

In her essay *The Heroism of Vision*, the well-known American thinker Susan Sontag expresses scepticism towards photography and its revolutionary use: 'The best writing on photography has been by moralists – Marxists or would-be Marxists – hooked on photographs but troubled by the way photography inexorably beautifies.'[10] In dealing with the medium of photography, we cannot, of course, escape aesthetics. In our case, aesthetics does not assume the most important position in the discussion, because in conditions of war there was little time to debate aesthetics.[11]

If we view Partisan photography as activist photography, one interesting example for comparison is the Israeli collective ActiveStills, which has been active since 2005. In following the Palestinian struggle against the Israeli occupation, they attempt to act by expressing solidarity with the struggle at the level of representation. They consider their act of photographing an intervention, an act of protest, and not just a form of witness record. They wish for representations of 'others who suffer' to be translated into the right to freedom of movement, protection from violence, and human dignity – and they call their work 'visual activism'.

8 Boris Buden, 'Još o komunističkim krvolocima ili zašto smo se ono bili rastali?', in: *Prelom – Journal for Images and Politics*, 3, 2003, pp. 51–57.
9 Gal Kirn, 'On the Specific (In)existence of the Partisan Film in Yugoslavia's People's Liberation Struggle', in: *Partisans in Yugoslavia: Literature, Film and Visual Culture*, Miranda Jakiša and Nikica Gilić (eds.), Bielefeld 2015, p. 222.
10 Susan Sontag, *On Photography*, New York 1977, p. 105.
11 Branko Petranović, *Istorija Jugoslavije 1918-1988.: treća knjiga Socijalistička Jugoslavija 1945–1988.*, Belgrade 1988, p. 375.

According to Vered Maimon, art historian and writer in the theory of photography at the University of Tel Aviv, what is nowadays called visual activism includes 'activist' photography and photographs of the 'resistance'. This wording is a response to Martha Rosler and Allan Sekula's radical critique of photojournalism and documentary photographs.[12] Their critique posited that in the discourse of documentary photography, there is a focus on the 'brave photographer' or on the feelings of the viewer, but never on the photograph's subject. This dichotomy results in the production of a passive viewer and affirms existing power relations, in which information on those without power is passed on to those in power. Consequently, documentary photography does not address the economic, social and political conditions responsible for inequality in the first place.

ActiveStills thus aims to engage with the domain of representation in another way. By essentially placing themselves in the service of the Palestinian collective resistance, they help to produce visual material, generate evidence and advocate for future legal campaigns. Transmission, circulation and distribution are integral components of struggle in their work. A good example of this are the photographs of the Palestinian peace activist Bassem Ibrahim Abu Rahma, who was killed in 2009 by an Israeli soldier in the West-Bank village of Bil'in. A photograph of him flying a kite by the Israeli wall was printed on a poster commemorating his death, and, sometime later, reproduced on a monument marking the place of his death. As a placard, the photograph was thus transformed into a shield that demonstrators used to protect themselves from teargas canisters – the same kind of projectile that killed Bassem. The community has appropriated his photograph and today it has a powerful mobilising potential. In this way, as with Partisan photography, the picture becomes an agent of transformation and political change, and not a fixed representation that depicts the resistance of an object for passive contemplation. Its exposure in public space helps individuals both identify with it and recognise themselves as political subjects. The work of this Israeli photography collective hints at the possibilities of regeneration, imagined through creative strategies for visualising the political sphere.

Although Partisan photography speaks of collectivism, we should not forget the individual fates of the people in the photographs, nor their tragic destiny. We find one such tale in the memories of Čedomir Minderović, who twenty years after the war stumbled across a photograph of his younger brother – a twenty-year-old who died at the Battle of Sutjeska – in an archive completely by chance. His brother had been a young man, whom Minderović said knew more of the Mississippi than the cold waters of the Sutjeska. Appalled by the photograph, by his brother's frozen state and mortality, Minderović wrote:

Sometimes we travel into the landscape of these photographs, we pull them through the light of everyday life, often by chance, and linger with the photographs still in our hands, without even realising it, and grow tired and flustered – as if we have a departure before us that has yet to happen and never will. Distant dead platforms and harbours beckon but our limbs are made of lead; while they are tensed, bloodless lips have already frozen over. I received his photograph

12 Vered Maimon and Shiraz Grinbaum, introduction to *ActiveStills: Photography as Protest in Palestine/Israel*, ed. idem, London 2016, p. 33.

yesterday. It was noon. Immediately afterwards on Terazija Square, I passed through the lunchtime crowds – no one could imagine what I was carrying in my breast pocket, for people at noon passing over sun-baked pavements do not feel the horror of photography.[13]

This was what Jacques Derrida, founder of the theory of the contemporary archive, described after his friend Roland Barthes died, also linking death and photography: 'I have become Total-Image, which is to say, Death in person.'[14]

This book has shown that photography has a pivotal role to play in historic political struggles, including within the Partisan movement. We need to rethink and jettison the assumption of photography's innocence, because, now more than ever before, photography is displacing the political struggle to the level of representation. This book speaks of a movement that managed to create, in impossible conditions, a system that managed to represent all its struggles and all its contradictions. Photography's pivotal role in contemporary social and political struggles also raises the question of its potential to change public opinion, open a space for public discussion and evoke solidarity across the globe. This is what Partisan photography should be to us today.

13 Minderović 1961 (see note 1).
14 Jacques Derrida, *The Work of Mourning*, Chicago 2001, p. 54.

List of Partisan Photographers

While the names of many Partisan photographers will never be known, I wish to take the opportunity here to publish a list of names of all photographers I came across while researching this book. This list demonstrates once again the scale of photographic production in the Partisan movement, and it lays the foundations for further study by future researchers.

Abramović, (Miloš) Slavka
Born in 1925 in Beli Manastir. Member of the First Proletarian Brigade from October 1944 and of the headquarters' support unit of the First Battalion.

Afrić, Vjekoslav (1906–1980)
Actor at the Croatian National Theatre in Zagreb. He joined the Partisans in 1942 and became a member of the Theatre of People's Liberation. He also photographed for the Partisans.

Aković, (Velije) Ismet (1920–1945)
Photographer from Gračanica, Bosnia and Herzegovina. He joined the People's Liberation Army on 18 February 1945. Died in Romania on 15 April 1945.

Anđelić, Ljubo
He took photographs throughout the Fifth Offensive, during which all of his film was destroyed. On 9 June 1943 he took photographs of the injured Josip Broz Tito and, on an earlier occasion, of Vladimir Nazor at Vučevo. He died in Ljubin Grob near Tjentište in 1943.

Baić, Dušan
Photographer of the Fourth Corps of the Yugoslav People's Liberation Army (the First Corps of the Croatian People's Liberation Army).

Bajić, Krsto (1919–1944)
Photographer, declared People's Hero. Political commissar of the First Battalion of First Proletarian Brigade. Died on 23 August 1944 in combat with Chetnik units on Zlatibor.

Bakarić, Vladimir (1912–1983)
He was the pre-war secretary of the League of Communist Youth at the University of Zagreb. Sentenced to six months' imprisonment in Belgrade because of his actions. During the war, after being active in the underground resistance, he joined the Partisans as the political commissar of the General Staff of Croatia. He was one of the founders of the ZAVNOH (the Croatian Anti-Fascist Council), and from 1944 took over from Andrija Hebrang as secretary of the Central Committee of the Communist Party of Croatia. After the war he became the first prime minister in the republic government and one of the most powerful politicians. He photographed for the Partisans alongside his main duties.

Baruh, Jakov
Born on 11 September 1908 in Banja Luka, where he worked as a photographer. He fled to Split after his photography shop, Foto Rekord, was closed down after the founding of the Independent State of Croatia. The Italian occupying authorities sent him from there to Vela Luka on Korčula. He left for the People's Liberation Army in 1942, first as a fighter in the Korčula Partisan Detachment, before later fighting in other Dalmatian units.

Baruh, Moric
Born in Sarajevo in 1911, he worked as a photographer in Banja Luka. He fled to Split after the Independent State of Croatia was founded. From Split, he left for the People's Liberation Army in 1943. He was a fighter in the Dalmatian Partisan units.

Batinić, Anđelko
Photographer of the Fourth Battalion of the First Dalmatian Brigade and member of the photography unit of the District People's Liberation Committee for Dalmatia.

Bavec, Marija (née Lovšin) (1904–1985)
The only female Slovenian Partisan photographer, wife of photographer Vinko Bavec. Her photographs of female Partisan fighters and her own family during the war are of particular interest. They are now preserved in the Museum of Contemporary History in Ljubljana.

Bavec, Vinko (1899–1969)
A trader and husband of photographer Marija Bavec. Fought in WWI. He was one of the most successful publishers of postcards. During WWII he worked as a Partisan photographer.

Benčić, Stevan
A pre-war Belgrade photographer for the daily newspaper *Politika*. He moved to Hvar and managed an important photography business in the 1930s.

Beran, Jan (1927–1993)
Photographer and well-known post-war cameraman, director, playwright, scriptwriter and translator.

Bervar, Ciril
Photographer.

Berzoli, Lauro
Photographer of the Third Battalion of the Sixth Proletarian Division.

Bibić, Nikola (1923–2001)
Photographer and fighter in the Thirteenth Proletarian Brigade. Photographed the First Croatian Proletarian Battalion and organised courses for amateur photographers in the Partisan movement. After the war he had an enviable photography career as a photographer for the newspaper *Borba*.

Bitenc, Jože (b. 1893)
A railway worker who joined the Kranj Company in 1941 and took his first photographs in the Partisan movement

Bojčević, Pavle
Member of the Second Dalmatian Proletarian Brigade, a Partisan photographer and radio-telegraphist.

Borovčanin, Grujo
In eastern Serbia he was nicknamed 'doctor activist' and the 'village photographer'.

Bračič, Mirko (1915–1943)
Also known by his Partisan name **Miran Bradač**, he was a Partisan commander, political commissar and commander of the Loško Detachment, Alpine Operative Zone, and the Fourteenth Slovenian Division. Photographed Partisan life. Accidentally died during the liberation of Kočevje from a stray bullet shot by Franc Bobnar-Gedžo and was later declared a People's Hero.

Brelih, Miloš (1916–2002)
Partisan photographer and post-war engineer. One of the founders of Kričača, an illegal radio station that operated in occupied Ljubljana from November 1941 to April 1942. Later head of the radio communication department in the General Staff of the Slovenian Partisans. In 1945 after the war, became the director of a former German factory for airplane parts in Maribor, converting it into the first Slovenian car factory, TAM.

Brenk, France (b. 1912)
Worked in the Partisans as part of the agitprop group of the Slovene People's Liberation Committee, organising photography courses and leading the photography unit.

Brvar, Ciril (b. 1920)
Member of the photography unit of the Fourth Operative Zone that was then led by Jože Petek, with whom he collaborated closely.

Bulatović, Raca
Born in 1923 in Đakovica. Involved in the People's Liberation Struggle from 1941. After time in the Montenegrin units, moved to the Second Proletarian Brigade in 1944. Was a political commissar for a hospital and reconnaissance company, and photographed throughout the war.

Cerar, Frane (b. 1912)
He was imprisoned in the Italian concentration camp on the island of Rab. After Italy's surrender, became the commissar for the Artillery Brigade of the Fourteenth Division. Injured, he photographed the Partisan hospital at Kočevski Rog. Active in the photography unit of both the Slovenian National Liberation Council and the General Staff of Slovenia.

Cerjan, Stjepan-Puba
An underground Partisan agent in Zagreb from the Trnje neighbourhood, member of the League of Communist Youth, a Partisan and photographer, injured at Mraclin in 1945.

Ciglič, Marjan
Born in 1924 in Kranj. He helped the Liberation Front by recording German war crimes. Later became a fighter and commissar in the First Battalion of Prešeren Brigade, a machine gunner and photographer. Responsible for political agitation and propaganda in the brigade.

Crnelić, Milan
Member of the photo service of the District People's Liberation Committee of Slavonia.

Cvrtila, Franjo (b. 1927)
Joined the Partisans as a sixteen-year-old child. Member of the Sixteenth Joža Vlahović Youth Brigade. Lives in Zagreb today.

Čaldarević, Mladen (1916–2010)
Born in Bijeljina. He studied teaching, philosophy, English and psychology in Zagreb, and graduated in Belgrade after the war. A prominent left-wing intellectual, he avoided Ustashe persecution by joining the Partisans on 10 April 1941 in Jabukovac near Petrinja. After specialising in sociology, he lectured at universities in Zagreb, Belgrade and Sarajevo, as well as at the American universities of Columbia, Stanford and Berkeley. He took photographs of the combat at Sutjeska. His collection of photographs can be found in the Croatian State Archive.

Čanak, Ratko
Photographer.

Čarkić, Mišo
Photographer and member of the League of Communist Youth of Yugoslavia.

Čitaković, Sreten (b. 1917)
Member of the Kolubara Company, shot portraits of Soje Stanišić, one of the first women Partisan fighters, and of Ivo Lola Ribar and Aleksandar Ranković at the beginning of the war.

Ćurćić, Milica
Photographer.

Damnjanović, Živorad
Photographer and member of the League of Communist Youth. He was killed in 1943.

Deković, Ivan (1921–1944)
Photographer from Rogoznica and collaborator in the People's Liberation Movement. He was executed at Stupin.

Dolački, Josip
Head of the photography unit in Pokupski. Photographs from Zagreb arrived through connections first in Pokuplje and Moslavina, from where they were distributed further.

Dragila, Pero
Member of the photo service of the District People's Liberation Committee of Slavonia. Photographed the liberation of Zagreb. After WWII and the Informbiro's resolution, emigrated to Prague.

Elijas, (Rudolf) Tauber
Photographer from Sarajevo born in 1920. After the Independent State of Croatia was established, fled to the Italian occupation zone. He was interned in Dalmatia in the concentration camp on the island of Rab, from where he joined the Partisan movement on 9 September 1943. He died in late 1944 at Banijska Jabukovac.

Ercegović, (Ivan) Josip
Born in 1907, a photographer by occupation. In 1943 he joined the Mosor Partisan Detachment. After that, he left for the First Montenegrin Battalion of the First Proletarian People's Liberation Assault Brigade. After this deployment, he left for the headquarters of the First Proletarian Division, bringing his two cameras with him, and serving as head of the courier service. He trained as a carpenter in Zagreb, and also participated in the trade-union movement. Active as an underground resistance agent from the start of WWII. Was arrested several times but always managed to destroy confidential material in time.

Faneli, Mauricije Mario
Photographed the liberation of Belgrade and Zagreb. Developed all shot film upon his arrival in Zagreb.

Fischer Ribarić, Hugo
Born in 1908; he lived in Crikvenica and joined the Partisans from there, carrying his photography equipment with him from the shop that he had managed. He later became one of the founders of the photography unit of the ZAVNOH.

Fischer, Hari
Born in 1918 in Vienna. He worked as a photographer in Dubrovnik. Under the Italian occupation, like most Jews, he fled from the Ustashe; he was first interned in the Kupari concentration camp near Dubrovnik, and later in the concentration camp on Rab. From there he joined the Partisan movement in 1943 as a fighter in the Seventh Banija Division, and later became a photographer in the photography unit of the Seventh Corps.

Gattin, Živko (1923–2018)
He was the only photographer who shot in colour during WWII in Croatia. One of the founders of the newspaper *Slobodna Dalmacija*. After the war he briefly served as head of photo documentation in the press department for the Parliament of the Republic of Croatia, before focusing on his career in agronomy.

Gavrić, Tiosav
Born in 1920 in the village of Degurić near Valjevo, a trader by profession. During the war he was the photographer for the Third Company of the First Battalion.

Goldstein, Emil
Born in 1920 in Sarajevo, a photographer by occupation. He was injured during the Sixth Enemy Offensive, and afterwards worked divided his

time between the agitprop groups of the Ninth Dalmatian Division and the Eighth Corps.

Grbin, Ljubomir
Took photographs in El Shatt.

Gregorić, Pavle (1892–1989)
Pre-war communist and member of the Central Committee of the Communist Party of Croatia, a ZAVNOH organiser and councillor at the First and Second Session of the AVNOJ. One set of his photographs is in Pavle Gregorić's holdings in the Croatian State Archive and is partly available to the public.

Grgić, Ernest
Born in 1913 in Sarajevo. He was a pre-war photographer in Croatia, a member of the Communist Party of Yugoslavia from 1934. During the Spanish Civil War he fought in the Divizionario unit in the Forty-Fifth Division, close to Blagoje Parović. He returned from Spain with the rank of sergeant in 1938. In the People's Liberation Struggle he worked on radiotelegraph devices at the headquarters of the First Proletarian Division. He was injured in the Battle of Zvornik. In TANJUG he invited Vili Šimunov-Barba to work with him on compiling a photography portfolio that Ivo 'Lola' Ribar would have then taken to Cairo. He was married to Dina Zlata Grgić.

Gvozdenović, Jovica
Photographer and member of the Thirty-First Serbian People's Liberation Assault Brigade.

Hreljanović, Viktor (1923 –1997)
Photographer from Rijeka who photographed the city's liberation.

Ilić, Milenko
Photographer from Kosjerić.

Ingolič, Anton (1907–1992)
He photographed his time spent in exile in Serbia, where he was banished to at the start of the war. He photographed life in the concentration camps in Paraćin and Zaječar, as he managed to smuggle a camera in. He took around 200 pictures in Serbia. In Ćuprija he took pictures of the hanging of resistance members in the town centre. He was a well-known Slovenian writer.

Ivančić, Stane
Born in 1911 in Bovec. He joined the People's Liberation Army on 2 February 1943.

Ivanovski, Ivan
Photo lab technician and sergeant in the Forty-Second Air Division.

Iveković, Mladen (1903–1970)
A lawyer by occupation, he gained his doctorate in 1928. He was a pre-war member of the Communist Party of Yugoslavia, imprisoned in 1936 and 1938. Also a leading member of AGITPROP and the Communist Party of Croatia. He was an editor on many newspapers and set up the journal *Pregled*. Together with Andrija Hebrang, he left Jasenovac in a prisoner exchange. He was a member of the Executive Committee of AVNOJ, chief-editor of *Vjesnik*, head of the ZAVNOH's propaganda department and one of the most important actors at the First Congress of Cultural Workers of Croatia in Topusko (25 June 1944). He photographed through out the war. His estate is now in the Croatian State Archive, and his photographs are in the Croatian History Museum.

Jakac, Božidar (1899–1989)
Born in Novo Mesto, he was a Slovenian painter and photographer, a school counsellor on teaching practices and a documentary filmmaker. He joined the Partisans in 1943 and made many paintings and photographs. He was one of the founding members of the Academy of Art and Design in Ljubljana.

Jakovljević, Vladeta
Photo lab technician and a young sergeant in the Forty-Second Air Division.

Janać, (Jožef) Petar (b. 1927)
Photographer from Bačka Palanka. Member of the Youth Company.

Jančić, (Radoslav) Angelina (b. 1926)
Photo technician.

Janković, (Krsta) Aleksandar
Born in 1909 in Drenovac, near Kragujevac. Worked as a photographer in the Third Krajina Brigade from October 1944.

Janković, Simon
Member of the Tenth Herzegovinian Brigade. He possessed a camera and photographed throughout the war.

Jelič, Peter
Photographer.

Jeraj, Jožica (b. 1925)
Apprentice in the same photography studio where photographer Miloš Trobec worked. They worked together on photographs for undercover agents. From 1944 he worked in the photography unit of the General Staff of Slovenia.

Jesenovec, Sandi
Born in 1926 in Škofja Loka, he worked at the Šelhaus photography studio. At the beginning of the war, together with Edi Šelhaus, he shot photographs for the resistance movement. Afterwards, on 3 August 1943, he left for the Partisans where he initially worked as a courier, and from 9 June 1944 in the geodetic section of the staff of the Ninth Corps and was responsible for setting up their photo lab. He shot photographs in a large format (9 x 12 cm). The National Museum of Contemporary History of Slovenia has preserved 2,506 of his negatives. He photographed many Partisans and the liberation of Trieste and Gorica.

Jokić, (Jovan) Rade (1907–1992)
Born in Valjevo to a family of artisan producers, he was a member of the workers' movement and the Communist Party of Yugoslavia from 1937 onwards. His sister-in-law was married to the painter Đorđe Andrejević-Kun. During the war he was a member of the Valjevo Detachment, captured in 1942. In June 1944 he joined the Partisans once again after his return from captivity.

Jovanović, (Jovo) Drago (1900–1943)
Born in Priboj at Lopar; after finishing primary school he completed his training as a photographer and opened the Foto Drago photography shop. During the war he collaborated with the underground movement and also developed Partisan film that arrived from Majevica. His studio served as the site of undercover meetings, held under the pretext of photography events. In November 1943 he left Tuzla with units of the People's Liberation Army. He died in 1943 near Kalesija.

Jovanović, Jovan
Head of the photo service, aide to the head of the intelligence service and lieutenant-colonel of the Forty-Second Air Division.

Kabić, Danilo
Photojournalist for TANJUG, later one of the better-known photojournalists.

Kalajdžić, Mustafa
Photographer of the photography team of the Thirteenth Herzegovinian People's Liberation Assault Brigade, working in the propaganda department of the brigade staff.

Kapor, Čedo (1914–2004)
Born in Trebinje, a fighter in the Spanish Civil War, he was a commissar in the Tenth Herzegovinian Brigade and photographer in the First Herzegovinian–Montenegrin Assault Battalion. Besides these roles, he was also a secretary for Herzegovina for the Total People's Defence and an instructor for the Operational Headquarters of Herzegovina.

Kenelić, (Stevana) Dušan
Born in 1926 in Bokšić Lug, near Našice. Photographer for the staff of the Third Krajina Proletarian Brigade.

Klaus, Vladimir-Klis
Slovenian Partisan photographer who took pictures of the consequences of air strikes on Zadar in 1945, and the liberation of Ljubljana on 9 May 1945.

Klemenčič, Dore (1911–1988)
Painter, member of Šercer's Brigade. Head of printing, literature and photography in the Ninth Corps. Worked in the education department of the Slovene People's Liberation Committee at Črnomelj.

Knežić, Luka (1912–1943)
Pre-war member of the workers' movement, member of the Communist Party of Yugoslavia from 1941 and a photographer. In the Mostar Battalion from September 1941. He died in Šćit near Prozor in Bosnia and Herzegovina.

Kohn, Elvira (1914–2003)
Born in Rijeka. Worked as a photographer in Dubrovnik before the war. She took pictures throughout her imprisonment in the concentration camp on Rab, into which she managed to smuggle her Leica camera. After Italy's surrender and the camp's liberation, she and her mother joined the People's Liberation Movement. She worked for the photography unit of the propaganda department of the ZAVNOH.

Kolobratar, Đuro
Photographer from Bor. Member of the Tenth Brigade of the Twenty-Third Division of the People's Liberation Army of Yugoslavia.

Konjhodžić, Mahmud (1905 –1979)
Born in Ljubuški, Bosnia and Herzegovina. Studied law in Belgrade and Zagreb, graduating in 1931. He worked as a correspondent for the newspaper *Politika*. At the beginning of the war he worked undercover in Zagreb, later as a journalist and photographer in the propaganda department of ZAVNOH, was a staffer at *Vjesnik* and founding member of TANJUG. Authored many reports and articles during many years of service.

Kopinič, Dare
Photographer for the Slovene People's Liberation Committee in Črnomelj. Started a Slovene Partisan photo archive there.

Koprivec, Ignac (1907–1980)
Head of the photography unit of the General Staff of Slovenia and editor of the magazine *Slovenski partizan*.

Korčagin, Mića
Born in 1922 in Smederevska Palanka, photographer.

Koren, Đurđa
Photographer from Velika Gorica. Married name *Šipušić* .

Korsun, N.
Photographer.

Kos, Alfred
Member of the photography unit of the Council of Slovenian National Liberation.

Kostić, (Matija) Vlado
Born in 1922 in Ličje, near Gadžin Han in Serbia. Member of the First Proletarian Brigade from November 1944, serving in the First Battalion.

Kotnik, Jože (b. 1914)
Took photographs on liberated territory in Kočevje.

Kovač, Voja
Head of the propaganda department of the Second Brigade of the Twenty-Fifth Serbian Division.

Krajačić, Ivan-Stevo (1906–1986)
One of the most important informants to make photographic records throughout the war. All his photographs and camera were lost when a plane

crashed at Čemernica. Randolph Churchill, son of Winston Churchill, was injured in the crash, too.

Krnjajić, Petar
He photographed a district Party conference at Banija in Ljeskovac in May of 1942. Repeatedly passed on sensitive photographic material to enemy forces. Later sentenced and executed for the destruction of the village of Prekopa.

Krajina, Rudi
Photographer.

Kramar, Viktor
A Slovenian photographer and underground Partisan agent.

Križan, Janko
Born in 1918 in the village of Boljevci, near Zemun, Serbia, where he worked as a photographer. He was a platoon commander in the People's Liberation Army.

Kržišnik, Zdravko (b. 1921)
Developed film and organised the photography archive in the photography unit of the General Staff. Was immortalised in a picture by France Cerar in a photo lab in Črnomelj in March 1943.

Latinović, Milan
Photographer of the headquarters' support unit of the First Proletarian Brigade.

Lekić, (Aksentija) Radisav (1921–1942)
Born in Mrčajevci. As a fighter in the Ljubićki Battalion, was captured by Bulgarian forces and executed on 8 December 1942.

Lenardič, Stane-Žan (1918–2008)
Started taking photographs at age fourteen. Worked as a military correspondent and photographer for the Partisans. He bravely photographed the attacks on Šlander Brigade, embedded with the troops. Later active in filmmaking. He was a TANJUG correspondent for the Slovenian littoral.

Lilik, Miroslav
Photographer. Photographed prisoners of war at Bleiburg.

Lipar, Ivan-Iztok
Photographer.

Lisac, Ivica
Sarajevo photographer, Partisan undercover agent in enemy territory.

Lukateli, Anton (b. 1916)
Painter and photographer during the Battle of Sutjeska. Involved in the People's Liberation Struggle from 1941.

Magajna, Mario (1916–2007)
Born in Trieste, was a member of the Liberation Front. Shot photographs on x-ray plates in Trieste's hospital and photographed the battle to liberate Trieste.

Manjiček, Franjo
Farmer. Exempted from military service due to disability. This gave him a degree of freedom of movement. Involved in photographic documentation. Captured by the Ustashe and taken to the Jasenovac concentration camp, where he was killed in 1944.

Marenčić, Janez (1914–2007)
A lawyer by occupation. During the war he was a member of the Slovenian Ninth Corps; mostly active as a photographer, most likely for the Primorje Brigade.

Marinček, Ivan
Born in Nova Vasa near Ptuj. During the war worked as a radio technician for the Slovenian General Staff. He was a master of black-and-white photography and one of the pioneers of Slovenian film. Photographed the congress of the Anti-Fascist Women's Front in Ljubljana.

Marjanović, Risto (1885–1969)
Already worked as a wartime photojournalist in WWI. Now considered the founding father of Serbian photo-journalism. Refused to work for the Serbian quisling government; during WWII took photographs in secret. He documented the liberation of Belgrade in 1945.

Masterl, Marjan (b. 1917)
He photographed the occupation of Škofja Loka and then joined the Gorenje Detachment where he became an intelligence officer and photographer. He took exceptionally interesting photographs at the First Partisan Skiing Competition held on 21 January 1945.

Mate, Jelič
Head of the photography unit of the Ninth Corps.

Matašin, Miro
Pre-war member of the League of Communist Youth, head of the photography unit of the Nineteenth Assault Division and head of the photography unit of the District People's Liberation Committee of Slavonija.

Mažar, Drago (1918–1991)
People's Hero. Was head of a sabotage group before leaving to join the Partisans, subsequently becoming the commander of the First Company for Bosanska Krajina, and later commander of the Sixth Partisan Detachment and an intelligence officer for Operations in Bosanska Krajina. He lost three brothers and his mother in the war.

Mehobej, Stevo
Photographed the Partisans as they entered and liberated Zagreb.

Mešterović, Đura
Photographer.

Milčinski, Janez (1913–1993)
Lawyer and doctor. During the war he worked as a doctor and shot many photographs of artistic value. He was one of the founders of the Partisan Medical Service. Worked in a Partisan hospital and birth clinic, Spodnji Hrastnik in Kočevski Rog. He is behind many photographs well preserved to this day.

Milković, Simo
A Partisan underground agent and photographer from Rijeka.

Mičić, Milorad
Born in 1911 in Belgrade. Died in Lovas as a member of the Fourth Serbian Assault Brigade.

Mihić, Mate
Commissar and photographer.

Mitrović, Mitar
Photographer.

Mlekuž, Riko (b. 1910)
Worked at the Purač photography studio, in Murska Sobota before WWII, and later at Studio Kramarič in Ljubljana. A co-organiser of Mussolini's assassination, he was arrested and sent to Rome, but managed to escape from the train. In Celje he worked at Studio Pelikan for a short time before leaving to join the Partisan units, where he became a photographer for the Fourteenth Division.

Mosinger, Franjo (1899–1956)
One of the most important Croatian photographers of the interwar period. He studied architecture in Vienna but returned to Zagreb in 1918 and took over his father's studio in Ilica – the first Croatian art photography institute. He later moved his studio to Dolac in Zagreb, and in 1935 opened a studio on Belgrade's Knez Mihajlova. He recorded his departure for the Partisans in a photo diary, started 11 May 1943, under the name of Slobodan Antunović. He worked in the agitprop group of the Central Committee of the Communist Party of Croatia and founded a photography unit in Otočac. One year later he was severely injured

and transferred via Vis to the hospital in Bari. He made political caricatures the whole time. 'Bolesnici sobe br. 22' and 'Medicinari u Grumu'.

Munjas, Petar (1922–1978)
Born in the village of Gojak, which he left for Belgrade in 1933 to train as a photographer. He lived in difficult conditions as an apprentice, running away from his photography master to Smederevska Palanka where he finished his photography training and joined the trade-union movement.

Nedeljković, Konstantin
Trained photographer from Leskovac and supporter of the Communist Party of Yugoslavia. He was arrested in 1941 and executed in the Banjica concentration camp.

Nešković, Bora
Photographer.

Nikolić, Dragan
Photographer.

Nikolić, (Save) Zdravko (b. 1920)
Born in Ljubinić, near Obrenovac, Serbia. A trader by occupation, he worked in the People Liberation's Struggle as a photographer from 1944. Photographer for the First Battalion, Sixth Proletarian Division.

Nikoliš, Branko
Photographed Allied pilots in the Croatian settlement of Rađenovac, not far from Novska, and the fleeing of civilians in Vrginmost. A pre-war merchant from Sjeničak by trade.

Nisim, Baruh (1915–1943)
Born in Banja Luka, worked as a photographer in Belgrade. Member of the Communist Party of Yugoslavia from July 1943. As a fighter in the Sixth Belgrade Battalion, First Proletarian Brigade, he died in November 1943 during the struggle to liberate Travnik.

Oblak, Matej
Photographer in the Vipava photography workshop.

Orlić, Zvonimir (1910–1942)
Born in Pula, a photographer by occupation. A member of the Mostar Battalion from April 1942. He was killed in Ostrožac, not far from Konjice, in July the same year.

Orović, Savo (1888–1974)
Participated in WWI as an officer in the Montenegrin Army, and later in the Kingdom of Serbs, Croats, and Slovenes. He later gained the rank of colonel. After the April War, he helped organise the 13 July Uprising. Member of the Communist Party of Yugoslavia from 1943. In the Partisans he gained the rank of lieutenant general. Took photographs throughout the war and managed to preserve negatives from many significant battles such as Sutjeska and Drvar. Member of AVNOJ.

Pantelić, Radovan
Photographer.

Parać, (Ivan) Jakov
Born in 1922 in Moseć near Drniš. Photographer and worker, member of the League of Communist Youth from 1943. Member of the headquarters' support unit of the First Proletarian Brigade and a political delegate.

Pašić, Emir
Political delegate for the First Company of the Second Battalion, a high school student and photographer for the Thirteenth Herzegovinian People's Liberation Assault Brigade.

Pavlić, Drago
Photographer.

Pavletić, Ivica
Photographer.

Pavlin, Miran-Miro (b. 1921)
At the start of WWII, shot photographs in occupied Ljubljana and set up an undercover studio in Gregorič St., becoming one of the most important chroniclers of life in occupied Ljubljana.

Pavlović, Živan
Born in 1945 in Kikinda in Serbia.
Died at Pleternica where he was also buried.

Perajica, (Ivan) Antonio (1915–1992)
Born in Čvrljevo near Drniš. A pre-war photographer who founded his own studio in 1934. His work for Cinecittá led him to Italy because of the war, and after Italy's surrender he arrived in Dalmatia along with members of the Garibaldi Brigade. He was in the First Proletarian Brigade, Third Battalion from September 1943 with the rank of sergeant. He worked as a photographer and cinematographer. Member of the Communist Party of Yugoslavia from 1944.

Petek, Jože (1912–1945)
One of the most talented Slovenian photographers. After joining the Partisans in 1943, he photographed the march of the Fourteenth Division across Croatia and Štajerska, taking photographs of exceptional documentary value. He was betrayed and killed in an ambush on 3 January 1945.

Peter, Fajfar
Photographer in the Ninth Corps.

Petrović, (Jakša) Batrić (b. 1915)
Originally from Klopot near Podgorica. Member of the First Proletarian Brigade from September 1944. Member of the First Battalion and brigade photographer.

Pfeifer, Marijan (1910–1992)
Born in Ljubljana. Trained as a graphic artist in Vienna, learnt the craft of photography in Graz. Worked as a photographer in the Partisan movement. He photographed the liberation of Maribor. Before the war, he worked in a Yugoslav printing office in Ljubljana. His photograph *Na juriš* (Charging) is considered by many to be one of the best Partisan war photographs.

Pipenbacher, Gojko (b. 1902)
Polyglot and pre-war president of the Ljubljana photography club. Joined the Partisan movement in 1943. Set up the photography service of the Eighteenth Division, before transferring to agitprop in the Seventh Corps.

Pirnat, Ivan (b. 1901)
Amateur photographer who later became editor of the magazine *Polet* and member of the section of the Slovene People's Liberation Committee in Črnomelj.

Plavšić, Nikola
Head of the photography unit of the General Staff of the People's Liberation Army and the Partisan Detachment of Vojvodina, a position he was allocated in an order dated 26 December 1944.

Pocajt, Marjan
Member of the photography and film section of the Seventh Corps.

Popov, Petar (b. 1895)
Arrested by the Ustashe on 5 May 1941 and taken to an unknown destination.

Popović, Nikola
Photographer of the Thirty-Second Division.

Popović, Slobodan-Bakula (1923–1941)
Photographer who was active during the Republic of Užice. During the same period, he was the secretary of the Regional Committee of the League of Communist Youth. As a fighter in the First Požega Company, he died in 1941 in an enemy aerial attack on Požega in Serbia.

Potočnjak, Vlado (1924–1997)
Painter and member of the photo service of the District People's Liberation Committee of Slavonia.

Povh, Dušan (1921–2000)
Photographed the consequences of the Italian Occupation on his home town of Novo Mesto. Worked in the studio of the central logistics team of the Communist Party of Slovenia.

Poznjak, (Jakov) Ivan
Born in 1926. From 21 October 1944 served in the Second Dalmatian Brigade.

Prešern, Jakob (1888–1975)
Born in Begunje na Gorenjskem. Fought in WWI. During WWII documented the Italian occupation of Ljubljana and the city's liberation.

Radivojević, Dragić
Photographer in the Fourth Serbian Assault Brigade. Died in Lovas, Croatia.

Rakić, Milivoje
Photographer.

Rebić, Marijan
Photographer from Knin.

Ritopečki, Jovan (1923–1989)
Photographer from Pančevo. Radio technician, war reporter and photographer of the First Vojvodina Brigade.

Roca, Ante (1905–1989)
Born in Vodice. Active as a photographer from 1921. Communist Party member from 1924.
He participated in the People's Liberation Struggle from 1943, first in the headquarters' support unit of the Nineteenth North Dalmatian Division, and later as a ZAVNOH photographer in the department for technical work.

Romac, Paško (1913–1982)
Born in Vukšić by Benkovac. A pre-war communist who was sentenced to long-term imprisonment because of his political convictions.
He escaped from the prison camp in Sremska Mitrovica through a tunnel dug there in August 1941. Afterwards, he helped found the Fruška Gora Partisan Detachment, becoming the political commissar of the First Proletarian Brigade.
As a member of the political department, he was assigned Party work in September 1942. Afterwards he became the political commissar of the First Vojvodina Brigade. During the war he took photographs with his own camera.

Romanič, Peter
Member of the photography unit of the Slovene People's Liberation Committee, responsible for recording photos of political life.

Ruljančić, Jure (1913–1998)
Member of the photography unit of the Dalmatia District People's Committee.

Savić, Branko (1915–2009)
Born in Bjelovar. He completed a photography course in Berlin and returned to Belgrade after the National Socialists came to power. Photographed for TANJUG just before the end of the war.

Sege, Nikola
Born in 1909 in Vrbas, Vojvodina. Worked as a photographer in Osijek, Croatia. Involved in the People's Liberation Army from 1943.

Skrigin, Žorž (1910–1997)
Born in Odessa. One of the most active Partisan photographers. He worked as a ballet dancer at the Croatian National Theatre in Zagreb and was a pre-war member of the Zagreb Fotoklub. He died in Belgrade, leaving behind an envious photographic legacy.

Sladić, Vjekoslav
Born in Laslavić, a photographer by occupation and a member of the Kotar Committee of the Communist Party of Croatia, Karlovac.

Smolej, Slavko (1909–1961)
Born in Jesenice. Arrested on 20 January 1942 because of his participation in the Liberation Front. He joined the People's Liberation Army

on 6 May 1945. Photographed and developed images for the Jesenice–Bohinj Detachment in Slovenia.

Sočan, Jule
Born in 1909. Photographer and underground Partisan agent in Ljubljana from early 1941, later taking photographs for Tomšič Brigade.

Solkan, Gorica
Photographer in the People's Liberation Struggle from 23 October 1944. Died on 17 January 1945 in the village of Sotin, Croatia.

Spasić, Levča
Photographer.

Spasić, Stojan
Photographer of the First Battalion and a news correspondent.

Stajer, Jože
Photographer and underground Partisan agent.

Starčević, (Nikola) Blagoje (1927–1943)
Worked in a photo store called Foto Drago, owned by the Tuzla photographer Draga Jovanović. In 1943, at age seventeen, he voluntarily joined the newly formed Eighteenth Croatian Brigade. Died in combat fighting German units.

Stevanović, (Milutin) Milivoj
Born in 1903 in Ivoševci by Knin, Croatia. A participant in the People's Liberation Struggle from 1 December 1944 and a photographer in a school for non-commissioned officers (NCO) in the air force.

Šaković, Ismet (1920–1945)
Photographer from Gračanica who mastered his trade in Doboj. At the age of fifteen he opened a photography shop, but died in combat fighting German forces on 13 March 1945 on Romanija, a mountain in Bosnia and Herzegovina.

Šelhaus, Edi (1919–2011)
After fascist persecution, the Šelhaus family moved to Zagreb where the father opened a photography studio, while the mother continued working in Škofja Loka. Edi *Šelhaus* was called up for the German units in 1943, but left for the Partisans and joined the Škofja Loka Detachment.
In the summer of 1944, he was severely injured. While awaiting transport to Bari at the Partisan airport Podzemelj, the agitprop worker Fran Brenk noticed him, after having set up the Slovenian Partisan photo service along with Franjo Veselko.

Ševkan, (Ibrahim) Revro (1914–1944)
Born in Mostar, Bosnia and Herzegovina. Worker and photographer who joined the People's Liberation Struggle in 1942. Died at Gornji Vakuf in Bosnia and Herzegovina in 1944.

Šibelja, Anton (1914–1945)
Shipyard worker, member of the TIGR movement [full name: Revolutionary Organisation of the Julian March, TIGR] and of the Communist Party of Italy from 1936. Helped organise the first military actions around Trieste in 1942 before leaving to join the Partisans, working in a technical workshop. He also operated as an underground Partisan agent often travelling to enemy territory.
At the end of the war he headed the workshop of the Ninth Slovenian Corps. He was one of the inventors of the 'Partisan cannon', made from Italian mortar tubes with a diameter of 81 cm. He also invented various other munitions parts and vehicles. He took photographs all through the war.

Šimunov, Vili-Barba
One of the first photographers of the Supreme Command and TANJUG. Killed in Drvar in 1944.

Škodlar, Čoro (1902–1966)
Painter, photographer and writer. He joined the Partisan movement in 1943 and was responsible for procuring photography supplies. One of the few photographers who also shot in colour.

Štajer, Božidar
Photographer.

Štok, Milan
Head of the photography unit of the Seventh Corps and author of the Partisan Photography Handbook (*Fotografski priručnik*).

Šubek, Stjepan
Photographer.

Tačković, Mate
Photographed the entry of the People's Liberation Army and the Partisan Detachments of Yugoslavia into Stara Gradiška in April 1945. Photographer in the Twenty-Eighth Slavonian Assault Division and photo service of the District People's Liberation Committee of Slavonia.

Tadić, Nedeljko
Head of the photography unit of the Thirteenth Herzegovinian People's Liberation Assault Brigade.

Tavčar, Ivan (1889–1966)
Photographer and mountaineer.

Trobec, Ivan
Photographer.

Trobec, Mirko
Photographer.

Vajner, Slaviša known as Čiča (1903–1942)
Born in Novi Vinodolski on the Croatian coast. Graduated in Koprivnica, studied in Zagreb. On Mount Romanija in Bosnia and Herzegovina, organised the First Partisan company. Member of the General Staff of the People's Liberation Partisan Detachment for Bosnia and Herzegovina. Died at Han Pijesak in the Republic of Srpska, where he committed suicide so as not to fall into the hands of German units. He carried his camera with him the whole time.

Vavpotič, Rudi
Born in 1919 in Maribor, member of the photography unit of the General Staff of Slovenia in Vojna Vas, near Črnomelj.

Veselko, Franjo (b. 1905)
Member of the photography unit of the General Staff of Slovenia, and later head of the photography unit of the Slovene People's Liberation Committee. He was responsible for uncovering several thousand German photographs in the editorial office of the newspaper *Piccolo*, including photographs of the German landings at Drvar.

Vičić, Emil
Photographer, designer and architect. Post-war curator of the art exhibition at the Technical Museum in Zagreb.

Vidin, (Vlatko) Vlatko
Born in 1923. Photographer and fighter.

Vidmar, Drago (1901–1982)
Painter. Studied in Zagreb, later lived in Paris. He took photographs during WWII and in 1944 became the organisational secretary of the Slovenian National Theatre.

Vidmar, Nande (1899–1981)
Brother of Drago Vidmar. He was also a painter who photographed during WWII. Member of the Liberation Front from 1941, the following year he became a member of the Communist Party of Yugoslavia. He recorded troop movements of Partisan units and the funeral of the Partisan commander Franc Rožman-Stane. He became a member of the photography unit of the Slovene People's Liberation Committee and also made watercolours.

Viršek, Stane (b. 1915)
Took his first photographs with Mirko Bračič's camera in the Fourteenth Division, before joining the Ljubljana Brigade and suffering severe inju-

ries. Member of the photography unit of the Council of Slovenian National Liberation.

Vivoda, Joakim
Photographer.

Vujnić, (Mile) Stevo (b. 1924)
Photographer from the village of Kričke near Drniš in Croatia. Member of the First Dalmatian Brigade from July 1942 and the Second Dalmatian Brigade from June 1943. Was the battalion's deputy political commissar.

Vujošević, Jovan
Photographer.

Zafron, Frane
Dalmatian photographer born in Vodice in 1916. Arrested by Italians on 10 March 1943. After a month in jail, he left for the Partisans and was active in the North Dalmatian Detachment.

Zagoričnik, Valerija
Born in 1926 in Celje. Photographer of the General Staff of the People's Liberation Army and the Partisan Detachment of Vojvodina.

Zalar, Slavko (1921–1987)
Photographer of the Second Battalion of First Dalmatian Brigade, taking pictures on Vis. Later the photographer of the Fourth Battalion of the First Dalmatian Brigade and member of the photography unit of the District People's Liberation Committee for Dalmatia.

Zupančić, Maksimilijan-Milijan (1911–1968)
Joined the Partisans in 1943. A professional photographer who set up a journalist service, first in Novo Mesto, Slovenia, before later working with other photographers in setting up the Slovenian Partisan Photo Service in Črnomelj. Noteworthy for his services in procuring photographic supplies and in improving the quality of Partisan photography.

Živković, Borislav
Photography laboratory technician and a young sergeant in the Forty-Second Air Division.

Živković, (Milutin) Đorđe (1923–1944)
Amateur photographer and agricultural worker, member of the League of Communist Youth from 1943. Member of the First Battalion of the People's Liberation Army of Serbia and, later, of Šumadija Brigade. Severely injured and captured on 4 December 1943 in Prijepolje in southwest Serbia, killed on 3 April 1944 in the Belgrade concentration camp of Sajmište.

Žorž, Bogomir
Photographer of the Fourth Zone.

Bibliography

Archives

Banja Luka, Arhiv Republike Srpske | Archives of the Republic of Srpska.

Belgrade, Muzej Jugoslavije | Museum of Yugoslavia, Photo Archive.

Belgrade, Vojni Arhiv | Military Archive, NOVJ, NDH, NOB collections.

Belgrade, Vojni Muzej | Military Museum.

Celje, Muzej novejše zgodovine | Museum of Recent History, Photo Archive.

https://www.znaci.net [accessed 11.02.2021].

Jasenovac, Javna ustanova Spomen-područje Jasenovac (JUSP) | Jasenovac Memorial Museum.

Jerusalem, Yad Vashem – The World Holocaust Remembrance Center.

Ljubljana, Arhiv Republike Slovenije | Archives of the Republic of Slovenia, *Zbirka narodnoosvobodilnega tiska 1941.–1945.* and *Zbirka NOB tiska–brošure 1062–1065* collections.

Ljubljana, Inštitut za novejšo zgodovino | Institute of Contemporary History, Photo Archive.

Ljubljana, Moderna galerija | Modern Gallery, Photo Archive.
Ljubljana, Muzej novejše zgodovine Slovenije | National Museum of Contemporary History of Slovenia, Photo Archive.
Maribor, Umetnostna galerija | Art Gallery.

Private archives of Robert Čopec, Dunja Žanko Darrot, Ingrid Gattin Pogutz, Marko Strpić.

Sarajevo, Arhiv Bosne i Hercegovine | Archive of Bosnia and Herzegovina, NDH collection.

Sarajevo, Historijski muzej Bosne i Hercegovine | History Museum of Bosnia-Herzegovina, NOB collection.

Tuzla, Arhiv tuzlanskog kantona, KPBiH Gračanica | Archive of the Canton of Tuzla, District Committee Archive.

Zagreb, Hrvatski državni arhiv | Croatian State Archives, ZAVNOH Archive, collection 216 (MNP NDH).

Zagreb, Hrvatski povijesni muzej | Croatian History Museum, Photo Archive.

Zagreb, Muzej grada Zagreba | Zagreb City Museum, Photo Archive.

Published Archive Material

Građa za historiju NOP u Slavoniji. Vol.5: 1.4.–31.5.1943. Slavonski Brod: Historijski institut Slavonije 1966.

Građa za povijest narodnooslobodilačke borbe u sjeverozapadnoj Hrvatskoj 1941.–1945. Vols. I–II. Zagreb 1981.

Sabor u Topuskom. Treće zasjedanje Zemaljskog antifašističkog vijeća narodnog oslobođenja Hrvatske. Zagreb 1975.

Trials of War Criminals before the Nuremberg Military Tribunals under Control Council Law. Vol.XI/10. United States Government Printing Office. Washington 1950.

Zbornik dokumenata i podataka o narodno-oslobodilačkom ratu jugoslovenskih naroda. Vol.I/20: Borbe u Srbiji 1941–1944. Belgrade 1965.

Zbornik dokumenata i podataka o narodno-oslobodilačkom ratu jugoslovenskih naroda. Vol.II/6: Dokumenti vrhovnog štaba Narodnooslobodilačke vojske Jugoslavije 1942. Belgrade 1957.

Zbornik dokumenata i podataka o narodno-oslobodilačkom ratu jugoslovenskih naroda. Vol.II/7: Dokumenta vrhovnog štaba Narodnooslobodilačke vojske Jugoslavije 1942–1943. Belgrade 1959.

Zbornik dokumenata i podataka o narodno-oslobodilačkom ratu jugoslovenskih naroda. Vol.II/10: Dokumenta vrhovnog štaba Narodnooslobodilačke vojske Jugoslavije 1943. Belgrade 1962.

Zbornik dokumentata i podata o narodno-oslobodilačkom ratu jugoslovenskih naroda. Vol.II/12. Belgrade 1971.

Zbornik dokumenata i podataka o narodno-oslobodilačkom ratu jugoslovenskih naroda. Vol.II/15. Belgrade 1982.

Zbornik dokumenata i podataka o narodnooslobodilačkom ratu jugoslovenskih naroda. Vol.V/4: Borbe u Hrvatskoj 1944. godine. Belgrade 1961.

Zbornik dokumenata i podataka o narodno-oslobodilačkom ratu jugoslovenskih naroda. Vol.V/26: Borbe u Hrvatskoj 1944. godine. Belgrade 1961.

Zbornik dokumenata i podataka o narodno-oslobodilačkom ratu jugoslovenskih naroda. Vol.V/30: Borbe u Hrvatskoj 1941.-1942. godine. Belgrade 1963.

Zbornik dokumenata i podataka o narodnooslobodilačkom ratu jugoslovenskih naroda. Vol.V/34: Borbe u Hrvatskoj 1944. godine. Belgrade 1966.

Zbornik dokumenata i podataka o narodno-oslobodilačkom ratu jugoslovenskih naroda. Vol.IX/3: Partijsko-politička dokumenta 1943. godine. Belgrade 1967.

Zbornik dokumenata i podataka o narodno-oslobodilačkom ratu jugoslovenskih naroda. Vol.IX/6: Partijsko-politička dokumenta 1943. godine. Belgrade 1967.

Zbornik dokumenata i podataka o narodno-oslobodilačkom ratu jugoslovenskih naroda. Vol.V/26: Borbe u Hrvatskoj 1944. godine. Belgrade 1961.

Zemaljsko antifašističko vijeće narodnog oslobođenja Hrvatske, zbornik dokumenata 1944. Zagreb 1975.

Monographs, Edited Volumes, Exhibition Catalogues

Antić, Vinko. *Vinodoska Selca u borbi.* Selca: Udruženje boraca narodnooslobodilačkog rata 1975.

Azoulay, Ariella. *The Civil Contract of Photography.* New York: Zone Books 2008.

Barthes, Roland. *Camera Lucida.* New York: Hill and Wang 1981.

Bate, David. *Photography: The Key Concepts.* Oxford and New York: Berg 2009.

Batinić, Jelena. *Women and Yugoslav Partisans: A History of World War II Resistance.* Cambridge: Cambridge University Press 2015.

Begović, Sima. *Logor Banjica 1941–1944.* Vol.2. Belgrade: Institut za savremenu istoriju 1989.

Benjamin, Walter. *Illuminations: Essays and Reflections.* Arendt, Hannah (ed.). Zohn, Harry (trans.). New York: Schocken Books, 1968.

Benjamin, Walter. *Eseji.* Belgrade: Nolit 1974.

Benjamin, Walter. *The Work of Art in the Age of Its Technological Reproducibility, and Other Writings on Media.* Ed. Michael W. Jennings, Brigid Doherty and Thomas Y. Levin. Cambridge, Massachusetts and London: Belknap Press of Harvard University Press 2008.

Bokan, Branko J. *Srez Sanski Most u NOB 1941–1945. godine.* Sanski Most: Skupština opštine Sanski Most 1980.

Borojević, Ljubomir, Samardžija Dušan and Bašić, Rade. *Peta kozaračka brigada.* Belgrade: Narodna knjiga 1973.

Bosiočić, Bogdan S. *21. slavonska udarna brigada.* Belgrade: Vojnoizdavački zavod 1981.

Butorović, Radule. *Sušak i Rijeka u NOB.* Rijeka: Centar za historiju radničkog pokreta i NOR Istre, Hrvatskog primorja i Gorskog Kotara 1975.

Ćemalović, Enver. *Mostarski bataljon.* Mostar: Skupština opštine Mostar i Odbor za istoriju revolucionarnog radićkog pokreta i NOB-a Mostara 1986.

Čobanski, Mila, Golubović, Zvonimir and Kumanov, Živan. *Novi Sad u ratu i revoluciji 1941–1945.* Novi Sad: Institut za izučavanje Vojvodine 1976.

Čukić, Milorad and Lagator, Špiro. *Partizanke prve proleterske.* Belgrade: NIP 1978.

Davidović, Radivoje and Belić-Koročkin-Davidović, Mirjana: *Stevan Filipović, istina o istorijskoj fotografiji.* Belgrade Čigoja 2012.

Dedijer, Vladimir. *Dnevnik III 1941–1944.* Rijeka: GRO Liburnija, Zagreb: Mladost 1981.

Derrida, Jacques. *The Work of Mourning.* Chicago and London: The University of Chicago Press 2001.

Dugandžić, Andreja and Okić, Tijana. *The Lost Revolution. Women's Antifascist Front between Myth and Forgetting.* Sarajevo: Crvena 2018.

Fabec, Franc and Vončina, Dejan. *Slovenska odporniška fotografija 1941.–1945.* Ljubljana: Modrijan 2005.

Faber, Sebastiaan. *Memory Battles of The Spanish Civil War.* Nashville: Vanderbilt University Press 2018.

Glišić, Venceslav. *Užička republika.* Belgrade: Nolit 1986.

Goldberg, Vicki. *The Power of Photography: How Photographs Changed Our Lives.* New York: Abbeville Press 1991.

Gončin, Milorad. *U rovovima Srema.* Belgrade: NIRO Eksport-pres 1981.

Hariman, Robert and Louis Lucaites, John. *No Caption Needed: Iconic Photographs, Public Culture, and Liberal Democracy.* Chicago: University of Chicago Press 2007.

Hlevnjak, Branka and Ivanuš, Rhea. *Hrvatska antiratna fotografija: Prvi svjetski, Drugi svjetski i Domovinski rat.* Zagreb: Udruga za promicanje oblikovanja i umjetnosti, Design Art d. o. o., Centar za kulturu i obrazovanje 2008.

Huljić, Veseljko. *Vis 1941–1945*. Split: Institut za historiju radničkog pokreta Dalmacije 1979.

Huljić, Veseljko and Dželebdžić, Milovan. *Veze u Narodnooslobodilačkoj borbi 1943.-1945.* Vol.II. Belgrade: Vojnoizdavački zavod 1984.

Israeli, Raphael. *The Death Camps of Croatia. Visions and Revisions, 1941–1945*. New Brunswick and London: Transaction Publishers 2013.

Ivanuš, Rhea. *Fotografski albumi u zbirci fotografija, filmova i negativa Hrvatskoga povijesnog muzeja*. Zagreb: Hrvatski povijesni muzej 2006.

Jakšić, Pavle. *Nad uspomenama*. Vol.I. Belgrade: Izdavačko preduzeće Rad 1990.

Kallis, Aristotle. *Nazi Propaganda and the Second World War*. New York: Palgrave MacMillan 2006.

Kladnik, Tomaž, Jurjavčič, Katarina and Dežman, Jože. *Vojne fotografije 1941.-1945. Partizanske jedinice*. Ljubljana: Defensor 2010.

Kemp, Martin. *Christ to Coke: How Image Becomes Icon*. New York: Oxford University Press 2012.

Kocković, Braco. *I tamo smo samo ljudi bili (tragovima partizanskih ranjenika)*. Zagreb: Spektar 1982.

Konjikušić, Davor. *Fotografija i moć*. Zagreb: Akademie of Dramatic Arts (thesis) 2014.
Koščević, Želimir. *U fokusu: ogledi o hrvatskoj fotografiji*. Zagreb: Školska knjiga 2006.

Kracauer, Siegfried. *Das Ornament der Masse. Essays*. Frankfurt/Main: Suhrkamp Verlag 1977.

Krstulović, Vicko. *Memoari jugoslavenskog revolucionara I*. Sarajevo: Buybook 2012.

Kurtović, Nikolina. *Communist Stardom in the Cold War: Josip Broz Tito in Western and Yugoslav Photography, 1943-1980*. Toronto: University of Toronto (diss.) 2010.

Lozić, Vladko. *Fotoklub Zagreb 1892.-1992. Prilozi za povjesnicu*. Zagreb 2000.

Lukač, Dušan. *Ustanak u Bosanskoj krajini*. Belgrade: VIZ Belgrade 1967.

Maclean, Fitzroy. *The Life and Times of Josip Broz-Tito*, New York: Harper 6c Brothers 1957.

Manošek, Valter. Holokaust u Srbiji. Vojna okupaciona politika i uništavanje Jevreja 1941-1942. Belgrade: Službeni list SRJ 2007.

Marx, Karl. *Das Kapital*. Vol.I. Frankfurt/Main, Berlin and Vienna: Ullstein Verlag 1973.

Matašin, Miro. *Ratne fotografije: Salon Becić*. Exh. cat. Slavonski Brod: Muzej radničkog i narodnooslobodilačkog pokreta 1981.

Mataušić, Nataša. *Koncentracioni logor Jasenovac*. Zagreb: Spomen područje Jasenovac 2008.

Matić, Branko. *Valjevski partizani 1941-1942 na fotografijama Rada Jokića*. Valjevo: self-published 2015.

Mažar, Drago. *Partizanski album*. With a preface by Jovo Popović. Banja Luka: Glas 1981.

Memou, Antigoni. *Photography and Social Movements: From the Globalisation of the Movement (1968) to the Movement against Globalisation (2001)*. Manchester and New York: Manchester University Press 2013.

Mihovilović, Djordje. *Jasenovac 1945.–1947. Fotomonografija*. Jasenovac: Javna ustanova Spomen-područje Jasenovac 2016.

Miletić, Miloš and Radovanović, Mirjana (eds.). *Lekcije o odbrani: Prilozi za analizu kulturne delatnosti NOP-a*. Belgrade: KURS and Rosa Luxemburg Stiftung Southeast Europe 2016.

Miletić, Miloš and Radovanović, Mirjana (eds.). *Lekcije o odbrani II: Da li je moguće stvarati umetnost revolucionarno?* Belgrade: KURS and Rosa Luxemburg Stiftung Southeast Europe 2017.

Milosavljević, Olivera. *Potisnuta istina. Kolaboracija u Srbiji 1941-1944* (= Ogledi 7). Belgrade: Helsinški odbor za ljudska prava u Srbiji 2006.

Mitchell, W. J. Thomas. *The Rhetoric of Iconoclasm*. The University of Chicago Press 1967.

Mitchell, W. J. Thomas. *Iconology: Image, Text, Ideology*. Chicago: The University of Chicago Press 1986.

Orović, Savo. *Fotografije iz Narodnooslobodilačkog rata 1941.-1945*. Belgrade: Vojnoistorijski institut Jugoslovenske armije 1951.

Orović, Savo. *Ratni dnevnik 1941.-1945*. Belgrade: Hronometar 1972.

Pavlin, Mile. *Jeseniško-bohinjski odred*. Ljubljana: Knjižnica NOV in POS 1970.

Petranović, Branko. *Istorija Jugoslavije 1918-1988*. Vol.1: Kraljevina Jugoslavija 1914–1941. Belgrade: Nolit 1988.

Petranović, Branko. *Istorija Jugoslavije 1918-1988*. Vol.3: Socijalistička Jugoslavija 1945-1988. Belgrade: Nolit 1988.

Phillips, John. *Jugoslovenska priča*. Belgrade: Jugoslovenska revija 1983.

Popović, Jovo. *Prva lička proleterska NOI brigada Marko Orešković*. Belgrade: Vojnoizdavački i novinski centar 1988.

Popović, Koča. *Beleške uz ratovanje*. Belgrade: BIGZ 1988.

Prosoli, Iva. *Monografska obrada umjetničkog opusa Toše Dabca*. Vol.2. Zagreb: Institut za savremenu istoriju 2018.

Radanović, Milan. *Oslobođenje. Beograd, oktobar 1944.* Belgrade: Rosa Luxemburg Stiftung Southeast Europe 2014.

Roberts, Walter E. *Tito, Mihailović and the Allies*, 1941-1945. Durham: Duke University Press 1987.

Rosler, Martha. *Decoys and Disruptions: Selected Writings, 1975–2001*. Cambridge and London: MIT Press 2004.

Samardžija, Stevo. *Četrnaesta srednjebosanska NOU brigada*. Banja Luka: Skupština opštine Prnjavor 1983.

Skrigin, Žorž. *Rat i pozornica*. Belgrade: Turistička štampa 1968.

Sontag, Susan. *On Photography*. New York: RosettaBooks 2005.

Stephan, Halina. *"Lef" and the Left Front of the Arts*. Munich: Sagner 1981.

Štok, Milan. *Fotografski priručnik. Propagandni odsjek Sedmog korpusa. sine loco* 1944.

Todić, Milanka. *Istorija srpske fotografije (1839-1940)*. Belgrade: Prosveta, Muzej primenjene umetnosti 1993.

Todić, Milanka. *Nemoguće, umetnost nadrealizma*. Belgrade: Muzej primenjene umetnosti 2002.

Tomasevich, Jozo. *Rat i revolucija u Jugoslaviji 1941.-1945. Okupacija i kolaboracija*. Zagreb: EPH, Novi Liber 2010.

Tonković, Marija. *Fotograf Franjo Mosinger u kontekstu Nove objektivnosti i Bauhausa*. Zagreb: Filozofski fakultet (diss.) 2011.

Uziel, Daniel. *The Propaganda Warriors: The Wehrmacht and the Consolidation of the German Home Front*. Oxford et al.: Peter Lang 2008.

Vitaljić, Sandra. *Rat slikama. Suvremena ratna fotografija*. Zagreb and Mostar: Algoritam 2013.

Vojinović, Aleksandar. *Ante Pavelić*. Zagreb: Centar za informacije i publicitet 1988.

Yeomans, Rory. *Visions of Annihilation: The Ustasha Regime and the Cultural Politics of Fascism, 1941–1945*. Pittsburgh: University of Pittsburgh Press 2013.

Zrinščak, Irina. *Zlatno doba hrvatske fotografije*. Zagreb: Grafički fakultet Sveučilišta u Zagrebu (diss.) 2013.

Articles in Edited Volumes and Monographs

Afrić, Vjeko. Lika i teatar bez kulisa. In: Šnajder, Djuro. *Šesta proleterska divizija*. Zagreb: EPOHA 1964, pp. 538–544.

Afrić, Vjeko. Sa Kazalištem narodnog oslobođenja u Bihaću. In: Todorović, Nataša (ed.). *Bihaćka republika*. Vol.I. Bihać: Muzej AVNOJ-a i Pounja 1965, pp. 500–517.
Afrić, Vjeko. Umjetnici u redovima boraca. In: Malić, Josip (ed.). *Zbornik sjećanja: Zagreb 1941-1945*. Vol.III. Zagreb: Gradska konferencija SSRNH, Institut za historiju radničkog pokreta Hrvatske and Školska knjiga 1984.

Barthes, Roland. The Photographic Message. In: Sontag, Susan (ed.). *A Barthes Reader*. New York: Hill and Wang 1982, pp. 194–210.

Borcić, Mane. Kulturno-prosvjetna i propagandna djelatnost u kotarevima Slunj i Veljun tokom NOR-a. In: Zatezalo, Djuro (ed.). *Kotar Slunj i kotar Veljun u NOR-u i socijalističkoj izgradnji*. Vol.II. Karlovac: Historijski arhiv u Karlovcu 1988.

Breton, André, Rivera, Diego [and Trotsky, Leo]. Manifesto for an Independent Revolutionary Art. In: Caws, Mary Ann (ed.). *Manifesto: A Century of Isms*. Lincoln: University of Nebraska Press 2001, pp. 472–477.

Cerjan, Stjepan. Ustaj, evo ustaša! In: Tihić, Esad (ed.). *Revolucionarni omladinski pokret u Zagrebu 1941–45*. Vol.II. Zagreb: Gradska konferencija SSRNH, Gradski odbor Saveza udruženja boraca NOR-a, Sveučilišna naklada Liber 1984.

Čitaković, Sreten. Fotografije iz partizanskog života. In: Tripković, Zoran (ed.). *Slikarstvo arhitektura fotografija skulptura. Izbor tekstova emitovanih u emisijama Radio Valjeva Valjeva*. Valjevo: Novinska i radio ustanova Napred. OOUR Radio Valjevo 1979.

Dozet, Perica. Moj dolazak u Zagreb. In: Malić, Josip (ed.). *Zbornik sjećanja Zagreb 1941–1945*. Vol.4. Zagreb: Gradska konferencija SSRNH, Institut za historiju radničkog pokreta Hrvatske i Školska knjiga 1984.

Dragosavljević, Mirjana. Od politizacije umetničkog polja do revolucionarne umetnosti. In: Miletić, Miloš and Radovanović, Mirjana (eds.). *Lekcije o odbrani. Prilozi za analizu kulturne delatnosti NOP-a*. Belgrade: KURS and Rosa Luxemburg Stiftung Southeast Europe 2016, pp. 11–45.

Egić, Obrad. Treći bataljon Pete dalmatinske brigade. In: Savković, Svetislav (ed.). *Neretva, zbornik radova*. Vol.3. Belgrade: Vojnoizdavački zavod 1965.

Fabec, Franc. Photography during the Slovene National Liberation Struggle. In: Pirjevec, Jože and Repe, Bože (eds.). *Resistance, Suffering, Hope: The Slovene Partisan Movement 1941-1945*. Ljubljana: National Committee of Combatants' Societies of the Slovene National Liberation Struggle Ljubljana, Trieste: Založništvo tržaškega tiska Trieste in cooperation with Slovenska kulturno gospodarska zveza 2008, pp. 94–101.

Graovac, Dušan. Organizacija i djelatnost NOO-a u Lici između Drugog i Trećeg zasjedanja ZAVNOH-a. In: Zatezalo, Djuro (ed.). *Treća godina Narodnooslobodilačkog rata na području Karlovca, Korduna, Like, Pokuplja i Žumberka*. Karlovac: Historijski arhiv u Karlovcu 1977.

Grbac, Zvonko. O vojnoobavještajnom radu za NOP u neprijateljskim vojnim i drugim institucijama. In: Albahari,

Nisim et al. (eds.). *Sarajevo u revoluciji. U borbi do punog oslobođenja (novembar 1943.-april 1945).* Sarajevo: Istorijski arhiv Sarajevo 1976.

Hanaček, Ivana, Kutleša, Ana and Vuković, Vesna. Problem umjetnosti kolektiva: Slučaj udruženja umjetnika Zemlja. In: Miletić, Miloš and Radovanović, Mirjana (eds.). *Lekcije o odbrani: Da li je moguće stvarati umetnost revolucionarno?* Belgrade: KURS and Rosa Luxemburg Stiftung Southeast Europe 2017.

Horvatinčić, Sanja. Ballad of the Hanged: The Representation of Second World War Atrocities in Yugoslav Memorial Sculpture. In: Unetič, Ines et al. (eds.). *Art and Its Responses to Changes in Society.* Cambridge: Cambridge Scholar Publishing 2016, pp. 186–208.

Hrvačić, Fabijan. Listovi, brošure i leci – ubojito oružje protiv neprijatelja u Pokuplju i Žumberku. In: Zatezalo, Djuro (ed.). *Četvrta godina narodnooslobodilačkog rata na području Karlovca, Korduna, Like, Pokuplja i Žumberka.* Karlovac: Historijski arhiv u Karlovcu 1981.

Ivanuš, Rhea. Ratni ciklus Ante Roce *Svjetlo na pepelu* i Zadar 1944. In: Cukrov, Tončika (ed.). *Ante Roca fotograf stvarnosti.* Zagreb: Hrvatski fotosavez 2013.

Izveštaj Propagandnog odsjeka 5. brigade od 15. ožujka 1945. godine o radu kulturno-prosvjetne sekcije od 15. veljače do 15. ožujka 1945. godine. In: Jovanović, Stanimir and Mirčetić, Dragoljub. *Peta srpska NOU brigada.* Belgrade: Vojnoizdavački i novinski centar 1989.

Kirn, Gal. On the Specific (In)existence of the Partisan Film in Yugoslavia's People's Liberation Struggle. In: Jakiša, Miranda and Gilić, Nikica (eds.). *Partisans in Yugoslavia: Literature, Film and Visual Culture.* Bielefeld: transcript Verlag 2015, pp. 197–226.

Komelj, Miklavž. Partizanska umetnost iskosa. In: Vasiljević, Marija (ed.). *Umetnost kao otpor fašizmu.* Belgrade: Muzej istorije Jugoslavije 2015.

Konjhodžić, Mahmud. Različite veze. In: Tihić, Esad and Kalem, Momčilo (eds.). *Veze u NOB: Ratna sećanja 1941-1945.* Vol.4. Belgrade: Vojnoizdavački zavod 1981.

Lukić, Dragoje. Zločini okupatora i njegovih saradnika nad decom kozarskog područja 1941.-1945. godine. In: Antonić, Zdravko and Marjanović, Joco (eds.). *Kozara u Narodnooslobodilačkoj borbi i socijalističkoj revoluciji: radovi za naučnog skupa održanog na Kozari (Mrakovica) 27. i 28. oktobra 1977. godine.* Prijedor: Nationalpark Kozara 1980.

Ljubič-Bogo, Mirko. Oris dejavnosti in služb. In: Lah-Boris, Borivoj (ed.). *Artilerija 9. korpusa.* Ljubljana: Partizanska knjiga 1985.

Maimon, Vered and Grinbaum, Shiraz. Introduction. In: idem (eds.). *ActiveStills. Photography as Protest in Palestine/Israel.* London: Pluto Press 2016, pp. 28–39.

Marić, Mihajlo. Fragmenti iz okupiranog Beograda. In: Tihić, Esad and Kalem Momčilo (eds.). *Veze u NOB-u 1941 –1945. Ratna sećanja.* Vol.V. Belgrade: Vojnoizdavački zavod 1981.

Mikulić, Mario. Plakati i Titove slike širom okupiranog Sarajeva. In: Malić, Hrvoje (ed.). *Sarajevo u revoluciji. U borbi do punog oslobođenja (novembar 1943–april 1945.).* Sarajevo: Oslobođenje 1981.

Miletić, Miloš and Radovanović, Mirjana. Lekcije o odbrani: Prilozi za analizu kulturne delatnosti NOP-a. In: idem (eds.). *Lekcije o odbrani, Prilozi za analizu kulturne delatnosti NOP-a.* Belgrade: KURS and Rosa Luxemburg Stiftung Southeast Europe 2016, pp. 49–146.

Miletić, Miloš and Radovanović, Mirjana. Početak sistematizacije. In: idem (eds.). *Lekcije o odbrani, Prilozi za analizu kulturne delatnosti NOP-a.* Belgrade: KURS and Rosa Luxemburg Stiftung Southeast Europe 2016, pp. 103–107.

Minderović, Čedomir. Fotografija. In: *Zbornik radova Sutjeska.* Vol.5. Belgrade: Vojnoizdavački zavod JNA Vojno delo 1961.

Mutnjaković, Andrija. Ante Roce. In: Cukrov, Tončika (ed.). *Ante Roca fotograf stvarnosti.* Zagreb: Hrvatski fotosavez 2013.

Nedeljković, Dušan. Prosvetna reforma oslobodilačkog rata i revolucije u Bihaću u 1942.-1943. In: Todorović, Nataša (ed.). *Bihaćka republika.* Vol.I. Bihać: Muzej AVNOJ-a i Pounja 1965.

Passariello, Phyllis. Desperately Seeking Something: Che Guevara as Secular Saint. In: Hopgood, James F. (ed.). *The Making of Saints: Contesting Sacred Ground.* Tuscaloosa: The University of Alabama Press 2005, pp. 75–89.

Pavić, Milan. Kamera je zabilježila posljednje događaje u Zagrebu. In: Malić, Josip (ed.). *Zbornik sjećanja Zagreb.* Zagreb: Gradska konferencija SSRNH Zagreb, Institut za historiju radničkog pokreta Hrvatske 1984.

Pavičić, Sofija-Maša and Fak-Horvatić, Zorka. Borbena Prva ženska gimnazija. In: Tihić, Esad (ed.). *Revolucionarni omladinski pokret u Zagrebu 1941.–1945.* Vol.II. Zagreb: Gradska konferencija SSRNH, Gradski odbor Saveza udruženja boraca NOR-a, Sveučilišna naklada Liber 1984.

Perović, Lepa. Ilegalni partijski rad u Zagrebu. In: Malić, Josip (ed.). *Zbornik sjećanja Zagreb 1941–1945.* Vol.4. Zagreb: Gradska konferencija SSRNH, Institut za historiju radničkog pokreta Hrvatske i Školska knjiga 1984, pp. 8–17.

Phu, Thy. Vietnamese Photography and the Look of Revolution. In: Smith, Shawn Michelle and Sliwinski, Sharon (eds.). *Photography and the Optical Unconscious.* Durham and London: Duke University Press 2017, pp. 268–320.

Radanović, Milan. Antimasonska izložba. In: Pisarri, Milovan and Rädle Rena (eds.). *Mesta stradanja i antifašističke borbe u Beogradu 1941-44. Priručnik za čitanje grada.* Belgrade: Rosa Luxemburg Stiftung Southeast Europe 2016, pp. 74–76.

Radanović, Milan. Ilegalna štamparija Pokrajinskog komiteta KPJ za Srbiju Daničareva 24. In: Pisarri, Milovan and Rädle, Rena (eds.). *Mesta stradanja i antifašističke borbe u Beogradu 1941–1944. Priručnik za čitanje grada*. Belgrade: Rosa Luxemburg Stiftung Southeast Europe 2016, pp. 109–113.

Radić, Josif. Borba omladine železničke zanatske škole. In: Malić, Hrvoje (ed.). *Sarajevo u revoluciji. U borbi do punog oslobođenja (novembar 1943–april 1945.)*. Sarajevo: Oslobođenje 1981.

Renyi, Andras. Time to Gaze. In: idem (ed.). *Col Tempo. The W. Project, Peter Forgac's Installation*. Budapest: Muscarnok Non-profit Ltd. 2009.

Roksandić, Drago. Prvi kongres kulturnih radnika Hrvatske (Topusko, 25.-27. lipnja 1944.): Iskustvo i aproprijacije. In: idem and Cvijović Javorina, Ivana (eds.). *Intelektualci i rat 1939.–1947. Zbornik radova s Desničinih susreta 2011*. Zagreb: Plejada d. o. o. 2012, pp. 97–118.

Ruchatz, Jens. The Photograph as Externalization and Trace. In: Astrid Erll and Ansgar Nünning (eds.). *Cultural Memory Studies: An International and Interdisciplinary Handbook*. Berlin: Walter de Gruyter 2008, pp. 367–378.

Škrinjar, Sonja. Djevojke iz treće ženske. In: Tihić, Esad (ed.). *Revolucionarni omladinski pokret u Zagrebu 1941.-1945.* Vol.II. Zagreb: Gradska konferencija SSRNH, Gradski odbor Saveza udruženja boraca NOR-a, Sveučilišna naklada Liber 1984.

Stojaković, Krunoslav. Revolucionarno nasilje u narodnooslobodilačkom ratu. In: Radanović, Milan (ed.). *Kazna i zločin: Snage kolaboracije u Srbiji*. Belgrade: Rosa Luxemburg Stiftung 2014, pp. 11–26.

Susović, Dragutin. U partijskoj tehnici. In: Malić, Josip (ed.). *Zbornik sjećanja Zagreb 1941–1945*. Vol.3. Zagreb: Gradska konferencija SSRNH, Institut za historiju radničkog pokreta Hrvatske i Školska knjiga 1984.

Tom Lasić, Vida. Slovenačke partizanske radio-stanice. In: Tihić, Esad and Kalem, Momčilo (eds.). *Veze u NOB: Ratna sećanja 1941.-1945.* Vol.4. Belgrade: Vojnoizdavački zavod 1981.

Tonković, Marija. Fotografija tridesetih godina. In: Kolešnik, Ljiljana and Prelog, Petar (eds.). *Moderna umjetnost u Hrvatskoj 1898.-1975.* Zagreb: Institut za povijest umjetnosti 2012, pp. 186–219.

Trnjaković, Mile. Sjećanja na rad omladinske organizacije na području Bosanskog Petrovca do kraja 1942. godine. In: Čerkez, Vladimir (ed.). *Bosanski Petrovac u NOB. Zbornik sjećanja*. Vol.IV. Bosanski Petrovac: Opštinski odbor SUBNORA Bosanski Petrovac 1974.

Ugarković, Stipe. Partijska tehnika u okupiranom Zagrebu. In: *Ustanak naroda Jugoslavije 1941*. Belgrade: Vojnoizdavački zavod JNA Vojno delo 1964.

Veber, Norbert. Delatnost u okupiranom Zagrebu. In: Tihić, Esad and Kalem, Momčilo (eds.). *Veze u NOB: Ratna sećanja 1941.–1945.* Vol.4. Belgrade: Vojnoizdavački zavod 1981.

Newspaper and Magazine Articles, Catalogue Entries

Bernstein, Walter. Interview with Tito of Yugoslavia. In: *Yank, The Army Weekly*, 16.06.1944, pp. 8–9.

Bernstein, Walter. Walk through Yugoslavia. In: *Yank, The Army Weekly*, 28.07.1944, pp. 8–9.

Briski Uzelac, Sonja. Mit o nevinom oku i moć reprezentacije pogleda u kulturi. In: *Ars Adriatica*, issue 5, 2015, pp. 203–210.

Broz, Josip Tito. Komunisti i katolici. In: *Proleter*, 1936.

Buden, Boris. Još o komunističkim krvolocima ili zašto smo se ono bili rastali? In: *Prelom – Journal for Images and Politics*, issue 3, 2003, pp. 51–57.

Hrvatski narod, Njihov prijašnji rad bila je politika – sadašnja naša politika jest rad, 09.11.1942, issue 524.

Kirn, Gal. Towards the Partisan Counter-Archive: Poetry, Sculpture and Film on/of the People's Liberation Struggle. In: *Slavica Tergestina (The Yugoslav Partisan Art Issue)*, issue 17, 2016, pp. 100–125.

Komelj, Miklavž. Dva predavanja o partizanskoj umjetnosti. In: *Jat: časopis studenata kroatistike*, Vol.1, issue 1, June 2013, pp. 80–130.

Labus, Alan. Upravljanje medijima, cenzura, te položaj i uloga novinara u Nezavisnoj Državi Hrvatskoj. In: *Studia lexicographica*, year 3, issue 1–2 (3–4), 2009, pp. 99–126.

Magaš, Lovorka. Izložba Deutscher Werkbunda *Film und Foto* na zagrebačkoj *Međunarodnoj fotografskoj izložbi* i hrvatska fotografija početkom 1930-ih. In: *Radovi Instituta za povijest umjetnosti*, issue 34, 2010, pp. 189–200.

Močnik, Rastko. The Partisan Symbolic Politics. In: *Slavica Tergestina (The Yugoslav Partisan Art Issue)*, issue 17, 2016, pp. 18–38.

Phillips, John. Marshal Tito. In: *Life*, 16, issue 17, 1944, pp. 35–38.

Prvi kongres kulturnih radnika Hrvatske. Topusko, 25.– 27.VI.1944. In: *ČSP*, 8, issue 2/3, 1976, pp. 16–17.

Przyblyski, Jeannene M. Revolution at a Standstill: Photography and the Paris Commune of 1871. In: *Yale French Studies*, issue 101, 2001, pp. 54–78.

Putrić, Mato. Kako se odlazilo u partizane. In: *Večernji list*, 26/27.04.1975.

Tretyakov, Sergei. From the Photo-Series to Extended Photo-Observation. In: *October*, issue 118, 2006, pp. 159–178.

Online Sources

Antifašistički Split, ratna kronika 1941.–1945: Listopad 1944.–svibanj 1945. Od oslobođenja grada do kraja rata. Odricanja i muke okrunjeni pobjedom. URL: https://www.ratnakronikasplita.com/kronika/1944-2. [accessed: 30.01.2021].

Associated Press. Eyes of Victims in 1941 Massacre Haunt German. In: *Deseret News*, 07.03.1997. URL: https://www.deseret.com/1997/3/7/19299147/eyes-of-victims-in-41-massacre-haunt-german [accessed: 07.02.2021].

Berner, Margit. *The Nazi Period Collections of Physical Anthropology in the Museum of Natural History.* Vienna 2009. URL: https://coltempo.hu/catalog/margit_berner.html [accessed: 22.01.2021].

Davidović, Radivoje. S „lajkom" na zadatak. In: *Yugopapier* 1983. URL: https://www.yugopapir.com/2016/01/slobodanka-vasic-autor-istorijske.html [accessed: 07.02.2021].

Dirik, Dilar. *The Representation of Kurdish Women Fighters in the Media.* URL: https://kurdishquestion.com/oldarticle.php?aid=the-representation-of-kurdish-women-fighters-in-the-media [accessed: 04.11.2017].

Field, Peter. History in the Making. In: *Journal*, issue 18, 2010. URL: https://worker01.e-flux.com/pdf/article_161.pdf. [accessed: 22.01.2021].

Fotografija partizanke Milje Marin: Simbol svega pozitivnog. In: *Buka*, 09.05.2014. URL: https://www.6yka.com/novost/55806/fotografija-partizanke-milje-marin-simbol-svega-pozitivnog [accessed: 07.02.2021].

Gligorijević, Jovana. Što čekate? Što trpite? In: *Reme*, 08.11.2012. URL: https://www.vreme.com/cms/view.php?id=1081728 2012 [accessed: 07.02.2021].

https://izlozba.sabh.hr/briga-za-ranjenike-i-partizanske-bolnice/ [accessed: 11.02.2017].

https://www.jusp-jasenovac.hr/Default.aspx?sid=6248 [accessed: 07.02.2021].

Konjikušić, Davor. *Nacistički zločini celjski.* In: *Novosti*, issue 746, 07.04. 2014. URL: https://arhiva.portalnovosti.com/2014/04/nacisticki-zlocini-celjski/ [accessed: 07.02.2021].

Konjikušić, Davor and Miklavž, Komelj. *Partizanska umjetnost je proboj kroz nemoguće.* Novost 2016. URL: https://www.portalnovosti.com/miklav-komelj-partizanska-umjetnost-je-proboj-kroz-nemoguce [accessed: 02.01.2017].

Lukić, Dragoje. Lepa Radić 1943. nije imala ni 18 godina: Kako su otkriveni potresni snimci vešanja mlade partizanke. In: *Yugopapir*, March 1968. URL: https://www.yugopapir.com/2017/10/lepa-radic-43-nije-imala-ni-18-godina.html [accessed: 07.02.2021].

Mihaljević, Nikica. Krvavi ustaški Disneyland: Srbi su lijeni, Židovi drski. In: *Express*, 02.07.2016. URL: https://www.express.hr/life/krvavi-ustaski-disneyland-srbi-su-lijeni-zidovi-drski-5978# [accessed: 02.02.2021].

Radanović, Milan. *Stjepan Filipović: heroj radničke i antifašističke borbe: 70 godina od smrti.* 21.05.2012. URL: https://www.starosajmiste.info/blog/stjepan-filipovic-heroj-radnicke-i-antifasisticke-borbe-70-godina-od-smrti/ [accessed: 07.02.2021].

Radišić, Nebojša and Pejić, Milana. Priča o Stjepanu Stevi Filipoviću. In: *Blic*, 22.05.2017. URL: https://www.blic.rs/vesti/drustvo/herojska-lekcija-koju-ne-smemo-da-zaboravimo-hrvat-koji-je-zeleo-da-umre-sa-srbima/7enh5k3 [accessed: 07.02.2021].

Rovčanin, Snežana. Kvadrati filma spojili i most. In: *Večernje novosti*, 07.05.2007. URL: https://www.novosti.rs/vesti/naslovna/reportaze/aktuelno.293.html:197712-Kvadrati-filma-spojili-i-most [accessed: 02.02.2021].

Šarac, Damir. Dr. Živko Gattin: Za čitanje "Slobodne" se strijeljalo! In: *Slobodna Dalmacija*, Juni 2013. URL: https://www.slobodnadalmacija.hr/scena/kultura/clanak/id/204129/dr-zivko-gatin-za-citanje-slobodne-se-strijeljalo [accessed: 30.01.2021].

Šiljak, Lea. Elvira Kohn. In: *Centro*, May 2003. URL: https://www.centropa.org/biography/elvira-kohn#During%20the%20War. [accessed: 30.01.2021].

Steyerl, Hito. In Defense of the Poor Image. In: *e-flux Journal*, issue 10, 2009. URL: https://www.e-flux.com/journal/10/61362/in-defense-of-the-poor-image/ [accessed: 11.02.2021].